Isn't It Time You GOT WIRED with Prentice Hall?

Whether you're looking for information for a research paper, a chance to test your knowledge and study for a big exam, or an easy way to stay in touch with your instructor, you'll find it all online at ***www.prenhall.com/giannetti***. With a click of the keyboard you can:

QUIZ YOURSELF.

Practice makes perfect. At ***www.prenhall.com/giannetti*** you'll find a full range of quizzes that you can take right on your computer screen. Whether you opt for multiple-choice or short answer, there's no need to wait until next week's class for results—you'll get instant scoring and feedback about how you've done, immediately!

CHAT WITH YOUR INSTRUCTOR.

A quick "send" option gets your essays and quizzes right to your instructor, along with any questions or concerns you didn't express in class. And you'll get answers back when you need them most.

FIND AN AUTHOR.

From ***www.prenhall.com/giannetti*** you can link directly to many dynamic film websites. Appreciate the opportunity to turn right to the source for the information on Hollywood, cinematography, film editing, film festivals, and more.

With more insight, more resources, and more exercises to keep you on your toes, what are you waiting for? Step out of the classroom and into a new world of discovery with Prentice Hall and ***www.prenhall.com/giannetti***.

Learning doesn't stop in your classroom anymore!
www.prenhall.com/giannetti
ANTICIPATED LIVE JANUARY 1, 2002

9th edition

Understanding Movies

LOUIS GIANNETTI

Case Western Reserve University

Prentice Hall

Upper Saddle River, New Jersey 07458

Library of Congress Cataloging-in-Publication Data

Giannetti, Louis D.

    Understanding movies / Louis Giannetti.—9th ed.

      p. cm.

    Includes bibliographical references and index.

    ISBN 0-13-040813-1 (pbk.)

    1. Motion pictures. I. Title.

  PN1994.G47 2002

791.43—dc21

                          2001021511

Editor in chief: Leah Jewell

Senior acquisitions editor: Carrie Brandon

Editorial production/supervision
  and interior design: Mary Araneo

Manufacturing buyer: Sherry Lewis

Cover designer: Robert Farrar-Wagner

Cover photo: *Gladiator* (U.S.A., 2000), with Russell Crowe,
  directed by Ridley Scott.   *(Dreamworks Pictures)*

This book was set in 10.5/12.5 New Baskerville by A & A Publishing Services, Inc.
and printed and bound by R. R. Donnelly, Inc. The cover was printed by
Phoenix Color Corp.

For permission to use copyrighted material, see "Acknowledgments" page xii.

© 2002, 1999, 1996, 1993, 1990, 1987, 1982, 1976, 1972 by Pearson Education, Inc.
Upper Saddle River, New Jersey 07458

Printed in the United States of America

10 9 8 7 6 5 4 3 2

ISBN 0-13-040813-1

PRENTICE-HALL INTERNATIONAL (UK) LIMITED, *London*
PRENTICE-HALL OF AUSTRALIA PTY. LIMITED, *Sydney*
PRENTICE-HALL CANADA INC., *Toronto*
PRENTICE-HALL HISPANOAMERICANA, S.A., *Mexico*
PRENTICE HALL OF INDIA PRIVATE LIMITED, *New Delhi*
PRENTICE-HALL OF JAPAN, INC., *Tokyo*
PEARSON EDUCATION ASIA PTE. LTD., *Singapore*
EDITORA PRENTICE-HALL DO BRASIL, LTDA., *Rio de Janeiro*

In Memoriam
Lynn R. Jones
1939–1970

Take him and cut him out in little stars,
And he will make the face of heav'n so fine
That all the world will be in love with Night
And pay no worship to the garish Sun.
—WILLIAM SHAKESPEARE

Contents

Preface

*The real voyage of discovery consists not in seeking new
landscapes, but in having new eyes.*

—MARCEL PROUST, NOVELIST AND ART CRITIC

Cineliteracy is long overdue in American education, and not just at the college
level. According to *The Television and Video Almanac,* the average American family watches about seven hours of television per day. That's a lot of time watching
moving images. Yet, for the most part, we watch them uncritically, passively,
allowing them to wash over us, rarely analyzing how they work on us, how they
can shape our values. The following chapters may be of use in understanding
how television and movies communicate, and the complex network of language systems they use. My purpose is not to teach viewers how to respond to
moving images, but to suggest some of the reasons people respond as they do.

In this ninth edition, I have retained the same principle of organization
as the earlier editions, structuring the chapters around the realism–formalism
dichotomy. Each chapter isolates the various language systems and spectrum of
techniques used by filmmakers in conveying meaning. Naturally, the chapters
don't pretend to be exhaustive: They're essentially starting points. They
progress from the most narrow and specific aspects of cinema (photography
and movement) to the most abstract and comprehensive (ideology and theory). The chapters are not tightly interdependent: They can be read out of
sequence. Inevitably, such a looseness of organization involves a certain
amount of overlapping, but I have tried to keep this to a minimum. Technical
terms are **boldfaced** the first time they appear in each chapter, which means
that they are defined in the Glossary.

Each chapter has been updated to reflect recent developments in the
field. I have also included many new photos and captions, most of them from
recently released movies.

The final chapter, "Synthesis: *Citizen Kane*," is a recapitulation of the main ideas of the previous chapters, applied to a single movie. The chapter can also serve as a rough model for a term paper. VCR and DVD have allowed film analysis to be much more systematic, because a movie in cassette or disk form can be repeated many times. In my own courses, I require my students to select a scene—preferably under three minutes—and analyze all its components according to the chapters of this book. Of course, a term paper is not likely to be as detailed as the *Citizen Kane* analysis, but the same methodology can be applied. If the chapters are read in a different sequence, the term paper can be organized in a corresponding manner. For example, many people would prefer to begin an analysis with story or theme, and then proceed to matters of style and technique. *Citizen Kane* is an ideal choice because it includes virtually every technique the medium is capable of, in addition to being one of the most critically admired films in history and a popular favorite among students.

A word about the photos in this book. Most of the illustrations are publicity photos, taken with a 35-mm still camera. They are not frame enlargements from the movie itself, for such enlargements reproduce poorly. They are generally too harshly contrasting and lacking in detail compared to the moving image on a large screen. When exactitude was necessary, as in the series from *The Seven Samurai* (9–14) or the edited sequence from *Potemkin* (4–18), I included actual blowups from the movies themselves. Most of the time, however, I preferred to use publicity photos because of their superior technical resolution.

Acknowledgments

I would like to thank the following friends and organizations for their help, advice, and criticism: Mary Araneo, Scott Eyman, Jon Forman, Dave Wittkowsky, the staff of *The Observer*, the Case Western Reserve University Film Society, and my students at C.W.R.U. I'm grateful to Ingmar Bergman, who was kind enough to allow me to use the frame enlargements from *Persona;* and Akira Kurosawa, who graciously consented to my using enlargements from *The Seven Samurai.*

I would also like to acknowledge and thank the following individuals and institutions for their assistance in allowing me to use materials under their copyright: Andrew Sarris, for permission to quote from "The Fall and Rise of the Film Director," in *Interviews with Film Directors* (New York: Avon Books, 1967); Kurosawa Productions, Toho International Co., Ltd., and Audio Brandon Films for permission to use the frame enlargements from *The Seven Samurai;* from *North by Northwest,* The MGM Library of Film Scripts, written by Earnest Lehman (Copyright © 1959 by Loews Incorporated. Reprinted by permission of the Viking Press, Inc.); Albert J. LaValley, *Focus on Hitchcock* (© 1972. Reprinted by permission of Prentice-Hall, Inc., Englewood Cliffs, New Jersey); Albert Maysles, in *Documentary Explorations,* edited by G. Roy Levin (Garden City, N.Y.: Doubleday & Company, Inc., 1971); Vladimir Nilsen, *The Cinema as a Graphic Art* (New York: Hill and Wang, a Division of Farrar, Straus and Giroux); Maya Deren, "Cinematography: The Creative Use of Reality," in *The Visual Arts Today,* edited by Gyorgy Kepes (Middletown, Conn: Wesleyan University Press, 1960); Marcel Carné, from *The French Cinema,* by Roy Armes (San Diego, Cal.: A. S. Barnes & Co., 1966); Richard Dyer MacCann, "Introduction," *Film: A Montage of Theories* (New York: E. P. Dutton & Co., Inc.), copyright © 1966 by Richard Dyer Mac-Cann, reprinted with permission; V. I. Pudovkin, *Film Technique* (London: Vision, 1954); André Bazin, *What Is Cinema?* (Berkeley: University of California Press, 1967); Michelangelo Antonioni, "Two Statements," in *Film Makers on Film Making,* edited by Harry M. Geduld (Bloomington: University of Indiana Press, 1969); Alexandre Astruc, from *The New Wave,* edited by Peter Graham (London: Secker & Warburg, 1968, and New York: Doubleday & Co.); Akira Kurosawa, from The Movies As Medium, edited by Lewis Jacobs (New York: Farrar, Straus and Giroux, 1970); Pauline Kael, *I Lost It at the Movies* (New York: Bantam Books, 1966).

LOUIS GIANNETTI
Cleveland, Ohio

Photography

Paramount Pictures and Touchstone Pictures

*People inscribe their histories, beliefs, attitudes, desires
and dreams in the images they make.*
—ROBERT HUGHES, ART CRITIC

Overview

The three styles of film: realism, classicism, and formalism. Three broad types of cinema: documentaries, fiction films, and avant-garde movies. The signified and the signifier: how form shapes content in movies. Subject matter plus treatment equal content. The shots: apparent distance of the camera from the subject. The angles: looking up, down, or at eye level. Lighting styles: high key, low key, high contrast. The symbolism of light and darkness. Color symbolism. How lenses distort the subject matter: telephotos, wide-angle, and standard lenses. Filtered reality: more distortions. Special effects and the optical printer. The cinematographer: the film director's main visual collaborator.

Realism and Formalism

Even before the turn of the last century, movies began to develop in two major directions: the **realistic** and the **formalistic**. In the mid-1890s in France, the Lumière brothers delighted audiences with their short movies dealing with everyday occurrences. Such films as *The Arrival of a Train* (**4–3**) fascinated viewers precisely because they seemed to capture the flux and spontaneity of events as they were viewed in real life. At about the same time, Georges Méliès was creating a number of fantasy films that emphasized purely imagined events. Such movies as *A Trip to the Moon* (**4–4**) were typical mixtures of whimsical narrative and trick photography. In many respects, the Lumières can be regarded as the founders of the realist tradition of cinema, and Méliès of the formalist tradition.

Realism and formalism are general rather than absolute terms. When used to suggest a tendency toward either polarity, such labels can be helpful, but in the end they're just labels. Few films are exclusively formalist in style, and fewer yet are completely realist. There is also an important difference between realism and reality, although this distinction is often forgotten. Realism is a particular *style*, whereas physical reality is the source of all the raw materials of film, both realistic and formalistic. Virtually all movie directors go to the photographable world for their subject matter, but what they do with this material—how they shape and manipulate it—is what determines their stylistic emphasis.

Generally speaking, realistic films attempt to reproduce the surface of reality with a minimum of distortion. In photographing objects and events, the filmmaker tries to suggest the copiousness of life itself. Both realist and formalist film directors must select (and hence, emphasize) certain details from the chaotic sprawl of reality. But the element of selectivity in realistic films is less obvious. Realists, in short, try to preserve the illusion that their film world is unmanipulated, an objective mirror of the actual world. Formalists, on the other hand, make no such pretense. They deliberately stylize and distort their raw materials so that only the very naive would mistake a manipulated image of an object or event for the real thing. Style is part of the show.

1–1a. *The Perfect Storm* (U.S.A., 2000), *with George Clooney, directed by Wolfgang Petersen.* (Warner Bros.)

Realism and Formalism. Critics and theorists have championed film as the most realistic of all the arts in capturing how an experience actually looks and sounds, like this thrilling recreation of a ferocious storm at sea. A stage director would have to suggest the storm symbolically, with stylized lighting and off-stage sound effects. A novelist would have to recreate the event with words, a painter with pigments brushstroked onto a flat canvas. But a film director can create the event with much greater credibility by plunging the camera (a proxy for us) in the middle of the most terrifying ordeals without actually putting us in harm's way. In short, film realism is more like "being there" than any other artistic medium or any other style of presentation. Audiences can experience the thrills without facing any of the dangers.

Dames presents us with another type of experience entirely. The choreographies of Busby Berkeley are triumphs of artifice, far removed from the real world. Depression-weary audiences flocked to movies like this precisely to get away from everyday reality. They wanted magic and enchantment, not reminders of their real-life problems. Berkeley's style was the most formalized of all choreographers. He liberated the camera from the narrow confines of the proscenium arch, soaring overhead, even swirling amongst the dancers, and juxtaposing shots from a variety of vantage points throughout the musical numbers. He often photographed his dancers from unusual angles, like this **bird's-eye shot.** Sometimes he didn't even bother using dancers at all, preferring a uniform contingent of good-looking young women who are used primarily as semi-abstract visual units, like bits of glass in a shifting kaleidoscope of formal patterns. Audiences were enchanted.

1–1b. *Dames* (U.S.A., 1934), *choreographed by Busby Berkeley, directed by Ray Enright.* (Warner Bros.)

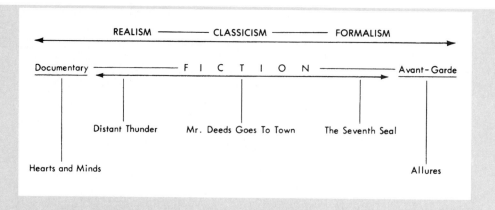

1-2. Classification chart of styles and types of film.
Critics and scholars categorize movies according to a variety of criteria. Two of the most common methods of classification are by style and by type. The three principal styles—realism, classicism, and formalism—might be regarded as a continuous spectrum of possibilities, rather than airtight categories. Similarly, the three types of movies—documentaries, fiction, and **avant-garde** films—are also terms of convenience, for they often overlap. Realistic films like *Distant Thunder* **(1-4)** can shade into the documentary. Formalist movies like *The Seventh Seal* **(1-6)** have a personal quality suggesting the traditional domain of the avant-garde. Most fiction films, especially those produced in America, tend to conform to the **classical paradigm.** Classical cinema can be viewed as an intermediate style that avoids the extremes of realism and formalism—though most movies in the classical form lean toward one or the other style.

We rarely notice the style in a realistic movie; the artist tends to be self-effacing, invisible. Such filmmakers are more concerned with *what's* being shown rather than how it's manipulated. The camera is used conservatively. It's essentially a recording mechanism that reproduces the surface of tangible objects with as little commentary as possible. Some realists aim for a rough look in their images, one that doesn't prettify the materials with a self-conscious beauty of form. "If it's too pretty, it's false," is an implicit assumption. A high premium is placed on simplicity, spontaneity, and directness. This is not to suggest that these movies lack artistry, however, for at its best, the realistic cinema specializes in art that conceals art.

Formalist movies are stylistically flamboyant. Their directors are concerned with expressing their unabashedly subjective experience of reality, not how other people might see it. Formalists are often referred to as **expressionists,** because their self-expression is at least as important as the subject matter itself. Expressionists are often concerned with spiritual and psychological truths, which they feel can be conveyed best by distorting the surface of the material world. The camera is used as a method of commenting on the subject matter, a way of emphasizing its essential rather than its objective nature. Formalist movies have a high degree of manipulation, a stylization of reality.

Most realists would claim that their major concern is with *content* rather than *form* or technique. The subject matter is always supreme, and anything that distracts from the content is viewed with suspicion. In its most extreme form, the realistic cinema tends toward documentary, with its emphasis on photographing actual events and people **(1–3)**. The formalist cinema, on the other hand, tends to emphasize technique and expressiveness. The most extreme example of this style of filmmaking is found in the avant-garde cinema **(1–7)**.

1–3.   *Hearts and Minds* (U.S.A., 1975), *directed by Peter Davis.*
The emotional impact of a documentary image usually derives from its truth rather than its beauty. Davis's indictment of America's devastation of Vietnam consists primarily of TV newsreel footage. This photo shows some Vietnamese children running from an accidental bombing raid on their community, their clothes literally burned off their bodies by napalm. "First they bomb as much as they please," a Vietnamese observes, "then they film it." It was images such as these that eventually turned the majority of Americans against the war. Fernando Solanas and Octavio Gettino, Third World filmmakers, have pointed out, "Every image that documents, bears witness to, refutes or deepens the truth of a situation is something more than a film image or purely artistic fact; it becomes something which the System finds indigestible." Paradoxically, in no country except the United States would such self-damning footage be allowed on the public airwaves—which are controlled, or at least regulated, by governments. No other country has a First Amendment, guaranteeing freedom of expression. *(Warner Bros.)*

Some of these movies are totally abstract; pure forms (that is, nonrepresentational colors, lines, and shapes) constitute the only content. Most fiction films fall somewhere between these two extremes, in a mode critics refer to as **classical cinema (1–5).**

Even the terms *form* and *content* aren't as clear-cut as they may sometimes seem. As the filmmaker and author Vladimir Nilsen pointed out: "A photograph is by no means a complete and whole reflection of reality: the photographic picture represents only one or another selection from the sum of physical attributes of the object photographed." The form of a shot—the way in which a subject is photographed—is its true content, not necessarily what the subject is perceived to be in reality. The communications theorist Marshall

1–4.   *Distant Thunder* (India, 1973), *directed by Satyajit Ray*.
In most realistic films, there is a close correspondence of the images to everyday reality. This criterion of value necessarily involves a comparison between the internal world of the movie with the external milieu that the filmmaker has chosen to explore. The realistic cinema tends to deal with people from the lower social echelons and often explores moral issues. The artist rarely intrudes on the materials, however, preferring to let them speak for themselves. Rather than focusing on extraordinary events, realism tends to emphasize the basic experiences of life. It is a style that excels in making us feel the humanity of others. Beauty of form is often sacrificed to capture the texture of reality as it's ordinarily perceived. Realistic images often seem unmanipulated, haphazard in their design. They frequently convey an intimate snapshot quality—people caught unawares. Generally, the story materials are loosely organized and include many details that don't necessarily forward the plot but are offered for their own sake, to heighten the sense of authenticity.   *(Cinema 5)*

McLuhan pointed out that the content of one medium is actually another medium. For example, a photograph (visual image) depicting a man eating an apple (taste) involves two different mediums: Each communicates information—content—in a different way. A verbal description of the photograph of the man eating the apple would involve yet another medium (language), which communicates information in yet another manner. In each case, the precise information is determined by the medium, although superficially all three have the same content.

In literature, the naive separation of form and content is called "the heresy of paraphrase." For example, the content of *Hamlet* can be found in a college outline, yet no one would seriously suggest that the play and outline are the same "except in form." To paraphrase artistic information is inevitably to change its content as well as its form. Artistry can never be gauged by subject

1–5. *Mr. Deeds Goes to Town* **(U.S.A., 1936),** *with Gary Cooper (with tuba), directed by Frank Capra.*

Classical cinema avoids the extremes of realism and formalism in favor of a slightly stylized presentation that has at least a surface plausibility. Movies in this form are often handsomely mounted, but the style rarely calls attention to itself. The images are determined by their relevance to the story and characters, rather than a desire for authenticity or formal beauty alone. The implicit ideal is a functional, invisible style: The pictorial elements are subordinated to the presentation of characters in action. Classical cinema is story oriented. The narrative line is seldom allowed to wander, nor is it broken up by authorial intrusions. A high premium is placed on the entertainment value of the story, which is often shaped to conform to the conventions of a popular genre. Often the characters are played by stars rather than unknown players, and their roles are sometimes tailored to showcase their personal charms. The human materials are paramount in the classical cinema. The characters are generally appealing and slightly romanticized. The audience is encouraged to identify with their values and goals. *(Columbia Pictures)*

matter alone. The manner of its presentation—its forms—is the true content of paintings, literature, and plays. The same applies to movies.

The great French critic André Bazin noted, "One way of understanding better what a film is trying to say is to know how it is saying it." The American critic Herman G. Weinberg expressed the matter succinctly: "The way a story is told is part of that story. You can tell the same story badly or well; you can also tell it well enough or magnificently. It depends on who is telling the story."

Realism and *realistic* are much overtaxed terms, both in life and in movies. We use these terms to express so many different ideas. For example, people often praise the "realism" of the boxing matches in *Raging Bull.* What they really mean is that these scenes are powerful, intense, and vivid. These traits owe very little to realism as a style. In fact, the boxing matches are extremely stylized. The images are often photographed in dreamy slow motion,

1–6. *The Seventh Seal* **(Sweden, 1957),** *with Bengt Ekerot and Max von Sydow, cinematography by Gunnar Fischer, directed by Ingmar Bergman.*
The formalist cinema is largely a director's cinema: We're often aware of the personality of the filmmaker. There is a high degree of manipulation in the narrative materials, and the visual presentation is stylized. The story is exploited as a vehicle for the filmmaker's personal obsessions. Formalists are not much concerned with how realistic their images are, but with their beauty or power.. The most artificial genres—musicals, sci-fi, fantasy films—are generally classified as formalist. Most movies of this sort deal with extraordinary characters and events—such as this mortal game of chess between a medieval knight and the figure of Death. This style of cinema excels in dealing with ideas—political, religious, philosophical— and is often the chosen medium of propagandistic artists. Its texture is densely symbolic: Feelings are expressed through forms, like the dramatic high-contrast lighting of this shot. Most of the great stylists of the cinema are formalists. *(Janus Films)*

1–7. *Allures* (U.S.A., 1961), *directed by Jordan Belson.*
In the avant-garde cinema, subject matter is often suppressed in favor of abstraction and an emphasis on formal beauty for its own sake. Like many artists in this idiom, Belson began as a painter and was attracted to film because of its temporal and kinetic dimensions. He was strongly influenced by such European avant-garde artists as Hans Richter, who championed the "absolute film"—a graphic cinema of pure forms divorced from a recognizable subject matter. Belson's works are inspired by philosophical concepts derived primarily from Oriental religions, but these are essentially private sources and are rarely presented explicitly in films themselves. Form is the true content of Belson's movies. His animated images are mostly geometrical shapes, dissolving and contracting circles of light, and kinetic swirls. His patterns expand, congeal, flicker, and split off into other shapes, only to re-form and explode again. It is a cinema of uncompromising self-expression—personal, often inaccessible, and iconoclastic.   *(Pyramid Films)*

with lyrical crane shots, weird accompanying sound effects (like hissing sounds and jungle screams), staccato editing in both the images and the sound. True, the subject matter is based on actual life—the brief boxing career of the American middleweight champion of the 1940s, Jake La Motta. But the stylistic treatment of these biographical materials is extravagantly subjective **(1–8a)**.

At the opposite extreme, the special effects in *Total Recall* are so uncannily realistic that we would swear they were real if we didn't know better. In the scene pictured **(1–8b)**, for example, we see a plump bald character magically transformed into Arnold Schwarzenegger after he removes his lifelike headpiece. Such fantasy materials can be presented with astonishing "realism" thanks to the brilliance of Dream Quest, one of the most prestigious special effects organizations in America.

9

1–8a. *Raging Bull* (U.S.A., 1980), *with Robert De Niro, directed by Martin Scorsese.*
(United Artists)

1–8b. *Total Recall* (U.S.A., 1990), *with Arnold Schwarzenegger, directed by Paul Verhoeven.* (Tri-Star Pictures)

Realism and formalism are best used as *stylistic* terms rather than terms to describe the nature of the subject matter. For example, although the story of *Raging Bull* is based on actual events, the boxing matches in the film are stylized. In this photo, the badly bruised Jake La Motta resembles an agonized warrior, crucified against the ropes of the ring. The camera floats toward him in lyrical slow motion while the soft focus obliterates his consciousness of the arena.

In *Total Recall,* on the other hand, the special effects are so realistic they almost convince us that the impossible is possible. If special effects look fake, our pleasure is diminished. In short, it's quite possible to present fantasy materials in a realistic style. It's equally possible to present reality-based materials in an expressionistic style.

Form and content are best used as relative terms. They are useful concepts for temporarily isolating specific aspects of a movie for the purposes of closer examination. Such a separation is artificial, of course, yet this technique can yield more detailed insights into the work of art as a whole. By beginning with an understanding of the basic components of the film medium—its various language systems, as it were—we will see how form and content in the cinema, as in the other arts, are ultimately the same.

The Shots

The **shots** are defined by the amount of subject matter that's included within the **frame** of the screen. In actual practice, however, shot designations vary considerably. A **medium shot** for one director might be considered a **close-up** by another. Furthermore, the longer the shot, the less precise are the designations. In general, shots are determined on the basis of how much of the human figure is in view. The shot is not necessarily defined by the distance between the camera and the object photographed, for in some instances certain lenses distort distances. For example, a **telephoto lens** can produce a close-up on the screen, yet the camera in such shots is generally quite distant from the subject matter.

Although there are many different kinds of shots in the cinema, most of them are subsumed under the six basic categories: **(1)** the **extreme long shot, (2)** the **long shot, (3)** the **full shot, (4)** the medium shot, **(5)** the close-up, and **(6)** the **extreme close-up.** The **deep-focus shot** is usually a variation of the long or extreme long shot **(1–9).**

The *extreme long shot* is taken from a great distance, sometimes as far as a quarter of a mile away. It's almost always an exterior shot and shows much of the locale. Extreme long shots also serve as spatial frames of reference for the closer shots and for this reason are sometimes called **establish-**

1–9. *Okaeri* (Japan, 1995), *directed by Makoto Shinozaki.* The setting dominates most extreme long shots. Humans are dwarfed into visual insignificance, making them appear unimportant and vulnerable. Shinozaki's desperate lovers seem oppressed even by Nature—vast, stark, merciless. *(Dimension Films)*

1-10. *Mary Shelley's Frankenstein* (U.S.A., 1994), *with Robert De Niro (under wraps) and Kenneth Branagh, directed by Branagh.*
At its most distant range, the long shot encompasses roughly the same amount of space as the staging area of a large theater. Setting can dominate characters unless they're located near the foreground. Lighting a long shot is usually costly, time consuming, and labor intensive, especially if it's in deep focus, like this shot. The laboratory had to be moody and scary, yet still sufficiently clear to enable us to see back into the "depth" of the set. Note how the lighting is layered, punctuated with patches of gloom and accusatory shafts of light from above. To complicate matters, whenever a director cuts to closer shots, the lighting has to be adjusted accordingly so that the transitions between cuts appear smooth and unobtrusive. Anyone who has ever visited a movie set knows that people are waiting most of the time—usually for the director of photography (D.P.) to announce that the lighting is finally ready and the scene can now be photographed. *(TriStar Pictures)*

ing shots. If people are included in extreme long shots, they usually appear as mere specks on the screen **(1–9).** The most effective use of these shots is often found in **epic** films, where locale plays an important role: westerns, war films, samurai films, and historical movies.

The *long shot* **(1–10)** is perhaps the most complex in the cinema, and the term itself one of the most imprecise. Usually, long-shot ranges correspond approximately to the distance between the audience and the stage in the live theater. The closest range within this category is the *full shot,* which just barely includes the human body in full, with the head near the top of the frame and the feet near the bottom.

The *medium shot* contains a figure from the knees or waist up. A functional shot, it's useful for shooting exposition scenes, for carrying movement, and for dialogue. There are several variations of the medium shot. The *two-shot* contains two figures from the waist up **(1–11).** The *three-shot* contains three figures; beyond three, the shot tends to become a full shot, unless the other figures are in the background. The **over-the-shoulder shot** usually contains two figures, one with part of his or her back to the camera, the other facing the camera.

1–11. *As Good As It Gets* **(U.S.A., 1997),** *with Jack Nicholson and Helen Hunt, directed by James L. Brooks.*
Above all, the medium shot is the shot of the couple, romantic or otherwise. Generally, two-shots have a split focus rather than a single dominant: The bifurcated composition usually emphasizes equality, two people sharing the same intimate space. The medium two-shot reigns supreme in such genres as romantic comedies, love stories, and buddy films. *(TriStar Pictures)*

The *close-up* shows very little if any locale and concentrates on a relatively small object—the human face, for example. Because the close-up magnifies the size of an object, it tends to elevate the importance of things, often suggesting a symbolic significance. The *extreme close-up* is a variation of this shot. Thus, instead of a face, the extreme close-up might show only a person's eyes or mouth.

The *deep-focus shot* is usually a long shot consisting of a number of focal distances and photographed in depth **(1–10).** Sometimes called a *wide-angle shot* because it requires a **wide-angle lens** to photograph, this type of shot captures objects at close, medium, and long ranges simultaneously, all of them in sharp focus. The objects in a deep-focus shot are carefully arranged in a succession of planes. By using this layering technique, the director can guide the viewer's eye from one distance to another. Generally, the eye travels from a close range to a medium to a long.

The Angles

The **angle** from which an object is photographed can often serve as an authorial commentary on the subject matter. If the angle is slight, it can serve as a subtle form of emotional coloration. If the angle is extreme, it can represent the major meaning of an image. The angle is determined by where the *camera* is placed, not the subject photographed. A picture of a person photographed from a high angle actually suggests an opposite interpretation from an image of the same person photographed from a low angle. The subject matter can be identical in the two images, yet the information we derive from both clearly shows that the form is the content, the content the form.

Filmmakers in the realistic tradition tend to avoid extreme angles. Most of their scenes are photographed from eye level, roughly five to six feet off the ground—approximately the way an actual observer might view a scene. Usually these directors attempt to capture the clearest view of an object. **Eye-level shots** are seldom intrinsically dramatic, because they tend to be the norm. Virtually all directors use some eye-level shots, especially in routine exposition scenes.

Formalist directors are not always concerned with the clearest image of an object, but with the image that best captures an object's expressive essence. Extreme angles involve distortions. Yet many filmmakers feel that by distorting the surface realism of an object, a greater truth is achieved—a symbolic truth. Both realist and formalist directors know that the viewer tends to identify with the camera's lens. The realist wishes to make the audience forget that there's a camera at all. The formalist is constantly calling attention to it.

1–12. *Bonnie and Clyde* **(U.S.A., 1967),** *with Faye Dunaway and Warren Beatty, directed by Arthur Penn.*
High angles tend to make people look powerless, trapped. The higher the angle, the more it tends to imply fatality. The camera's angle can be inferred by the background of a shot: High angles usually show the ground or floor; low angles the sky or ceiling. Because we tend to associate light with safety, high-key lighting is generally nonthreatening and reassuring. But not always. We have been socially conditioned to believe that danger lurks in darkness, so when a traumatic assault takes place in broad daylight, as in this scene, the effect is doubly scary because it's so unexpected.   *(Warner Bros.)*

1–13. *Halloween: The Curse of Michael Myers (U.S.A.,* 1995), *with George Wilbur, directed by Joe Chappelle.*
Extreme low angles can make characters seem threatening and powerful, for they loom above the camera—and us—like towering giants. We are collapsed in a position of maximum vulnerability—pinned to the ground, dominated. *(Dimension Films)*

There are five basic angles in the cinema: **(1)** the bird's-eye view, **(2)** the high angle, **(3)** the eye-level shot, **(4)** the low angle, and **(5)** the oblique angle. As in the case of shot designations, there are many intermediate kinds of angles. For example, there can be a considerable difference between a low and extreme low angle—although usually, of course, such differences tend to be matters of degree. Generally speaking, the more extreme the angle, the more distracting and conspicuous it is in terms of the subject matter being photographed.

The *bird's-eye view* is perhaps the most disorienting angle of all, for it involves photographing a scene from directly overhead **(1–1b)**. Because we seldom view events from this perspective, the subject matter of such shots might initially seem unrecognizable and abstract. For this reason, filmmakers tend to avoid this type of camera **setup.** In certain contexts, however, this angle can be highly expressive. In effect, bird's-eye shots permit us to hover above a scene like all-powerful gods. The people photographed seem antlike and insignificant.

Ordinary *high-angle shots* are not so extreme, and therefore not so disorienting. The camera is placed on a **crane,** or some natural high promontory, but the sense of audience omnipotence is not overwhelming. High angles give a viewer a sense of a general overview, but not necessarily one implying destiny or fate. High angles reduce the height of the objects photographed and usually include the ground or floor as background. Movement is slowed down: This angle tends to be ineffective for conveying a sense of speed, useful for suggesting tediousness. The importance of setting or environment is increased: The locale often seems to swallow people. High angles reduce the importance of a subject. A person seems harmless and insignificant photographed from above. This angle is also effective for conveying a character's self-contempt.

Some filmmakers avoid angles because they're too manipulative and judgmental. In the movies of the Japanese master Yasujiro Ozu, the camera is usually placed four feet from the floor—as if an observer were viewing the events seated Japanese style. Ozu treated his characters as equals; his approach discourages us from viewing them either condescendingly or sentimentally. For the most part, they are ordinary people, decent and conscientious. But Ozu lets them reveal themselves. He believed that value judgments are implied through the use of angles, and he kept his camera neutral and dispassionate. Eye-level

1–14. *How Green Was My Valley* (U.S.A., 1941), *cinematography by Arthur Miller, directed by John Ford.*

Lyricism is a vague but indispensable critical term suggesting subjective emotions and a sensuous richness of expression. Derived from the word *lyre,* a harplike stringed instrument, lyricism is most often associated with music and poetry. Lyricism in movies also suggests a rhapsodic exuberance. Though lyrical qualities can be independent of subject matter, at its best, lyricism is a stylistic externalization of a film's basic concept. John Ford was one of the supreme masters of the big studio era, a visual lyricist of the first rank. He disliked overt emotions in his movies. He preferred conveying feelings through forms. Stylized lighting effects and formal compositions such as this invariably embody intense emotions. "Pictures, not words, should tell the story," Ford insisted.   *(Twentieth Century-Fox)*

shots permit us to make up our own minds about what kind of people are being presented.

Low angles have the opposite effect of high. They increase height and thus are useful for suggesting verticality. More practically, they increase a short actor's height. Motion is speeded up, and in scenes of violence especially, low angles capture a sense of confusion. Environment is usually minimized in low angles, and often the sky or a ceiling is the only background. Psychologically, low angles heighten the importance of a subject. The figure looms threateningly over the spectator, who is made to feel insecure and dominated. A person photographed from below inspires fear and awe (1–13). For this reason, low angles are often used in propaganda films or in scenes depicting heroism.

An *oblique angle* involves a lateral tilt of the camera. When the image is projected, the horizon is skewed (1–15). People photographed at an oblique angle will look as though they're about to fall to one side. This angle is sometimes used for **point-of-view shots**—to suggest the imbalance of a drunk, for example. Psychologically, oblique angles suggest tension, transition, and impending movement. The natural horizontal and vertical lines of a scene are converted into unstable diagonals. Oblique angles are not used often, for they can disorient a viewer. In scenes depicting violence, however, they can be effective in capturing precisely this sense of visual anxiety.

1–15. *Shallow Grave* **(Great Britain, 1994),** *with Kerry Fox, Ewan McGregor, and Christopher Eccleston; directed by Danny Boyle.*
Oblique angles, sometimes known as "Dutch tilt" shots, produce a sense of irresolution, of visual anxiety. The scene's normal horizontal and vertical lines are tilted into tense, unresolved diagonals. Such shots are generally employed in thrillers, especially in scenes such as this that are meant to throw the spectator off balance with a shocking revelation.   *(Gramercy Pictures)*

Light and Dark

Generally speaking, the **cinematographer** (who is also known as the director of photography, or D.P.) is responsible for arranging and controlling the lighting of a film and the quality of the photography. Usually the cinematographer executes the specific or general instructions of the director. The illumination of most movies is seldom a casual matter, for lights can be used with pinpoint accuracy. Through the use of spotlights, which are highly selective in their focus and intensity, a director can guide the viewer's eyes to any area of the photographed image. Motion picture lighting is seldom static, for even the slightest movement of the camera or the subject can cause the lighting to shift. Movies take so long to complete, primarily because of the enormous complexities involved in lighting each new shot. The cinematographer must make allowances for every movement within a continuous **take.** Each different color, shape, and texture reflects or absorbs differing amounts of light. If an image is photographed in depth, an even greater complication is involved, for the lighting must also be in depth. Furthermore, cinematographers don't have at their disposal most of the darkroom techniques of a still photographer: variable paper, dodging, airbrushing, choice of development, enlarger filters, etc. In a color film, the subtle effects of lights and darks are often obscured, for color tends to obliterate shadings and flatten images: Depth is negated.

There are a number of different styles of lighting. Usually designated as a lighting *key,* the style is geared to the theme and mood of a film, as well as its **genre.** Comedies and musicals, for example, tend to be lit in **high key,** with bright, even illumination and few conspicuous shadows. Tragedies and melodramas are usually lit in **high contrast,** with harsh shafts of lights and dramatic streaks of blackness. Mysteries, thrillers, and gangster films are generally in **low key,** with diffused shadows and atmospheric pools of light **(1–16).** Each lighting key is only an approximation, and some images consist of a combination of lighting styles—a low-key background with a few high-contrast elements in the foreground, for example. Movies shot in studios are generally more stylized and theatrical, whereas location photography tends to use available illumination, with a more natural style of lighting.

Lights and darks have had symbolic connotations since the dawn of humanity. The Bible is filled with light–dark symbolism. Rembrandt and Caravaggio used light–dark contrasts for psychological purposes as well. In general, artists have used darkness to suggest fear, evil, the unknown. Light usually suggests security, virtue, truth, joy. Because of these conventional symbolic associations, some filmmakers deliberately reverse light–dark expectations **(1–12).** Hitchcock's movies attempt to jolt viewers by exposing their shallow sense of security. He staged many of his most violent scenes in the glaring light.

Lighting can also be used to subvert subject matter. Paul Brickman's *Risky Business* is a coming-of-age comedy, and like most examples of its genre, the adolescent hero (Tom Cruise) triumphs over the System and its hypocritical morality. But in this movie, the naive hero learns to play the game and becomes a winner by being even more hypocritical than the upholders of the System.

▶ Color Plate 1. **Edward Scissorhands** (U.S.A., 1990), *with Johnny Depp, directed by Tim Burton.*

Color, like virtually every other film technique, can be used realistically or formalistically. Burton is one of the foremost expressionists of the contemporary cinema, a conjuror of magical worlds of color and light and myth and imagination. His worlds are created in the sealed-off confines of the studio, far removed from the contaminations of prosaic reality.

(Twentieth Century–Fox)

▶ Color Plate 2. **Aliens** (U.S.A., 1986), *with Sigourney Weaver and Carrie Henn, directed by James Cameron.*

Although the futuristic setting of this sci-fi film contains some supernatural elements, it uses color in a rigorously realistic manner. *Aliens* is a testosterone world of cold, hard surfaces, heavy-metal technology, and blue-gray fluorescence. This is not a place for children and other gentle creatures. The colors are radically muted, mostly military tans and drab earth colors. Only the red filter adds a note of alarm and urgency.

(Twentieth Century–Fox)

▶ Color Plate 3. ***American Beauty*** **(U.S.A., 1999),** *with Kevin Spacey and Mena Suvari, directed by Sam Mendes.*
Red is a color that's often linked with sex, but the dramatic context determines whether the red (and the sex) is seductive or repellent. In this film, the unhappily married protagonist (Spacey) escapes the banality of his suburban hell by fantasizing about a flirtatious teenager (Suvari), a friend of his daughter. He often imagines her nude, covered with red rose petals— a symbol of his fiercely aroused sexuality, his reawakening manhood.   *(DreamWorks Pictures)*

▶ Color Plate 4. ***Savage Nights*** **(France, 1993),** *with Cyril Collard and Romane Bohringer, directed by Collard.*
But red is also the color of danger. Of violence. Of blood. Blood is a major transmitter of HIV, a precursor of AIDS. This movie explores the sadomasochistic behavior of an HIV-positive bisexual (Collard) who has unprotected sex with two lovers, including Bohringer. Maybe she's color blind.   *(Gramercy Pictures)*

▶ Color Plate 5. ***The Age of Innocence* (U.S.A., 1993),** *with Michelle
Pfeiffer and Daniel Day-Lewis, directed
by Martin Scorsese.*
Bright colors tend to be cheerful, so
directors often desaturate them, especially if the subject matter is sober or
grim. Based on the great American
novel by Edith Wharton, this movie
explores a forbidden love among New
York's upper crust in the 1870s. The
film's images seem almost washed in
sepia, like faded photos. The colors are
tastefully subdued, correct, almost
repressed, reflecting the conservative
values of the society itself. *(Columbia
Pictures)*

▶ Color Plate 6. ***Life Is Beautiful* (Italy, 1998),** *with Roberto Benigni, directed by Benigni.*
This movie begins as a slapstick comedy, and the colors are warm and sunny, typical of
Mediterranean settings. But as the Nazi Holocaust spreads southward, our hero, an Italian
Jew (Benigni), is arrested and shipped to a German concentration camp by rail (pictured). The
colors begin to pale. Once inside the death camp, virtually all the color is drained from the
images. Only a few faded flickers of skin tones occasionally punctuate the ashen pallor of the
camp and its prisoners. *(Miramax Films)*

▶ Color Plate 7. **_Married to the Mob_** (U.S.A., 1988), *with Michelle Pfeiffer and Matthew Modine, directed by Jonathan Demme.*
Gangster variations. Both of these movies (C.P.7 and C.P.8) explore the world of organized crime. The tone of each is radically different, determined in part by the color palette of each. Demme's likable Mafia comedy is a cartoon version. Like most cartoons, the colors are gaudy and deliciously trashy. Who would ever guess that Modine (an F.B.I. agent) is an outsider? *(Orion Pictures)*

▶ Color Plate 8. **_The Godfather_** (U.S.A., 1972), *with Marlon Brando (red rose), directed by Francis Ford Coppola.*
The Godfather is a far more realistic treatment, photographed by the great Gordon Willis, who is famous for his low-key lighting magic. The colors are not only subdued, they're suffocating in airless dark rooms. In this shadowy world, only an occasional wisp of color is allowed to escape—a vibrant red rose, pale yellow light filtering discreetly through the blinds, a few splotches of mottled flesh tones. The rest is darkness. *(Paramount Pictures)*

▶ Color Plate 9. *johns* **(U.S.A., 1996),** *with David Arquette and Lukas Haas, directed by Scott Silver.*

Color clichés. In order to avoid being predictable, imaginative filmmakers often torpedo popular stereotypes by using color antiromantically. Movies set in Hollywood usually emphasize its lush glamour, but *johns* explores the world of two street prostitutes (pictured) as they crisscross the dusty side streets of an unfamiliar Hollywood, bleached under the scorching sun. This is not the Tinseltown of tourist brochures but the real-life boulevard of broken dreams. In this photo, the predominant color is white—hot, glaring, pitiless. Note the almost total absence of green vegetation. *(First Look Pictures)*

▶ Color Plate 10. *Four Weddings and a Funeral* **(Great Britain, 1994),** *with Andie MacDowell and Hugh Grant, directed by Mike Newell.*

This romantic comedy goes to extreme lengths to avoid being sappy and sentimental. Hence this weird concluding scene of love triumphant at last, which takes place in a cold London downpour, blue with shivers and shudders and chill. *(Gramercy Pictures)*

▶ Color Plate 11. ***The Little Mermaid*** **(U.S.A., 1989),** *directed by John Musker and Ron Clements.*
We live in a golden age of animation, encompassing many styles and an extraordinarily broad range of colors. From the very beginning in the 1930s, the Disney organization was in the forefront in developing color as an expressive emotional language in animation. Disney is still in the vanguard. Note the subtle violets in this photo, the sinister yet slightly campy blacks, and the playful squiggle of pink to the left—a pure abstract expressionist whimsy. *(Walt Disney Pictures)*

▶ Color Plate 12. ***Chicken Run*** **(Great Britain, 2000),** *directed by Peter Lord and Nick Park.*
There's hardly a primary color in all of *Chicken Run*, a clay-animation fable of infinite subtlety, not only in its color spectrum, but its sophisticated script and witty dialogue as well. Note the elongated shadows and sculptural side-lighting: The image looks as though it was photographed in the "magic hour." Of course, in a studio, any time can be the magic hour. *(DreamWorks Pictures)*

▶ Color Plate 13. ***Saving Private Ryan*** **(U.S.A., 1998),** *with Tom Hanks, directed by Steven Spielberg.*
Different wars, different colors. Location has much to do with what colors are permissible in a movie. These two war films (C.P.13 and C.P.14) have totally different looks, each determined by its setting. *Saving Private Ryan* deals with the World War II era and is set in battle-torn Europe. The documentarylike images are dominated by grays and have a dusty, worn look, as though even nature has exhausted itself after too many years of death and destruction. *(DreamWorks Pictures)*

▶ Color Plate 14. ***Platoon*** **(U.S.A., 1986),** *with Tom Berenger, directed by Oliver Stone.*
The war in Vietnam was fought in part in the jungles of that bomb-pocked tropical land. The lush, colorful foliage often conceals unspeakable horrors, and the atrocities are committed by both sides. During battle, nature is violently defiled, exploding into a blazing inferno of heat and flames, radiating red, yellow, and scorching white. *(Orion Pictures)*

▶ Color Plate 15. ***Shakespeare in Love*** **(Great Britain, 1998),** *with Gwyneth Paltrow and Joseph Fiennes, directed by John Madden.*
The richly textured costumes of this period picture are rendered in all their luxurious opulence by the movie's Renaissance-style colors and lighting effects. The British are unsurpassed masters of period films, thanks to their magnificent heritage in live theater, most notably producing the plays of Shakespeare. *(Miramax Films)*

▶ Color Plate 16. *The Road Warrior* (Australia, 1982), *with Vernon Welles, directed by George Miller.*
Some costumes are pastiches of various styles, as in this sci-fi picture, which is set in a desolate, post-apocalyptic desert landscape. This bleak setting is strewn with debris and the discarded artifacts of a former civilization. Black is often the color of villainy, but in this movie, the villainy is wittily undercut by such campy touches as the off-the-shoulder feathers and a red-tinged Mohawk mane. Scary. And weirdly funny.   *(Warner Bros.)*

▶ Color Plate 17. *Titanic* (U.S.A., 1997), *with Kate Winslet and Leonardo Di Caprio, written and directed by James Cameron.*
As the "unsinkable" ocean liner slowly surrenders to the frigid waters of the Atlantic, the scenes get darker, colder, and more desperate. The colors, so richly luxurious in the earlier scenes, begin to fade with the light as they're swallowed by the enveloping waters. But the young lovers, radiating humanity with their warm fleshtones and halo lighting, cling to each other like a beacon of hope in the final stages of the wounded ship's watery descent. They're like doomed tragic lovers of a nineteenth-century romantic novel.
(Twentieth Century-Fox/Paramount Pictures)

▶ Color Plate 18. *Dark Victory* (U.S.A., 1939), *with Bette Davis and George Brent, directed by Edmund Goulding, "colorized" by Turner Entertainment.*
"Tell me the truth now. Do you think this suit is *too* blue?"   *(Warner Bros./Turner Entertainment)*

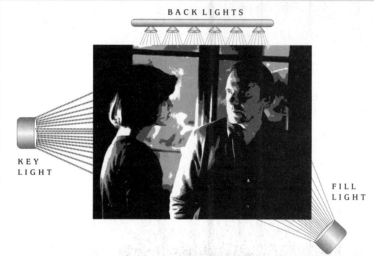

BACK LIGHTS

KEY LIGHT

FILL LIGHT

1–16. *Red* **(France/Poland/Switzerland, 1994),** *with Irene Jacob and Jean-Louis Trintignant, cinematography by Piotr Sobocinski, directed by Krzysztof Kieslowski.*
During the Hollywood big studio era, cinematographers developed the technique of **three-point lighting,** which is still widely practiced throughout the world. With three-point lighting, the **key light** is the primary source of illumination. This light creates the **dominant** of an image—that area that first attracts our eye because it contains the most compelling contrast, usually of light and shadow. Generally, the dominant is also the area of greatest dramatic interest, the shot's focal point of action, either physical or psychological. **Fill lights,** which are less intense than the key, soften the harshness of the main light source, revealing subsidiary details that would otherwise be hidden by shadow. The **backlights** separate the foreground figures from their setting, heightening the illusion of three-dimensional depth in the image. Three-point methods tend to be most expressive with low-key lighting such as this. When a shot is bathed with high-key illumination, the three sources of light are more equally distributed over the surface of the image, and hence are more bland photographically.   *(Miramax Films)*

1–17. *Double Indemnity (U.S.A., 1944), with Barbara Stanwyck and Fred MacMurray, directed by Billy Wilder.*

Film noir (literally, black cinema) is a style defined primarily in terms of light—or the lack of it. This style typified a variety of American genres in the 1940s and early 1950s. Noir is a world of night and shadows. Its milieu is almost exclusively urban. The style is profuse in images of dark streets, cigarette smoke swirling in dimly lit cocktail lounges, and symbols of fragility, such as windowpanes, sheer clothing, glasses, and mirrors. Motifs of entrapment abound: alleys, tunnels, subways, elevators, and train cars. Often the settings are locations of transience, like cheap rented rooms, piers, bus terminals, and railroad yards. The images are rich in sensuous textures, like neon-lit streets, windshields streaked with mud, and shafts of light streaming through windows of lonely rooms. Characters are imprisoned behind ornate lattices, grillwork, drifting fog and smoke. Visual designs emphasize harsh lighting contrasts, jagged shapes, and violated surfaces. The tone of film noir is fatalistic and paranoid. It's suffused with pessimism, emphasizing the darker aspects of the human condition. Its themes characteristically revolve around violence, lust, greed, betrayal, and depravity. *(Paramount Pictures)*

Most of the film is shot in low-key lighting—unusual for any comedy—which darkens the tone of the comic scenes. By the conclusion of the film, we're not entirely sure if the hero's "success" is ironic or straight. The movie would probably have been funnier if it had been shot in the usual high key, but the low-key photography makes it a more serious comedy—ironic and paradoxical.

Lighting can be used realistically or expressionistically. The realist tends to favor available lighting, at least in exterior scenes. Even out of doors, however, most filmmakers use some lamps and reflectors, either to augment the natural light or, on bright days, to soften the harsh contrasts produced by the sun. With the aid of special **lenses** and more light-sensitive film stocks, some directors have managed to dispense with artificial lighting completely. Available lighting tends to produce a documentary look in the film image, a hard-edged quality and an absence of smooth modeling. For interior shots, realists tend to prefer images with an obvious light source—a window or a lamp. Or they often use a diffused kind of lighting with no artificial, strong contrasts. In short, the realist doesn't use conspicuous lighting unless its source is dictated by the context.

1–18. *The Empire Strikes Back Special Edition* (U.S.A., 1997), *directed by Irvin Kershner.* High-contrast lighting is aggressively theatrical, infusing the photographed materials with a sense of tension and visual anguish. This dueling sequence is rendered more dynamic by the jagged knife blades of light that pierce the pervasive darkness. In the background, a desperate cosmic search is tearing up the sky. High-contrast lighting is typical of such genres as crime films, melodramas, thrillers, and mysteries. The lack of light in such movies symbolizes the unknown, deceptive surfaces, evil itself. *(Twentieth Century Fox)*

Formalists use light less literally. They are guided by its symbolic implications and will often stress these qualities by deliberately distorting natural light patterns. A face lighted from below almost always appears sinister, even if the actor assumes a totally neutral expression. Similarly, an obstruction placed in front of a light source can assume frightening implications, for it tends to threaten our sense of safety. On the other hand, in some contexts, especially in exterior shots, a silhouette effect can be soft and romantic **(1–34c)**.

When a face is obviously lighted from above, a certain angelic quality, known as the halo effect, is the result. "Spiritual" lighting of this type tends to border on the cliché, however. **Backlighting,** which is a kind of semisilhouetting, is soft and ethereal. Love scenes are often photographed with a halo effect around the heads of the lovers to give them a romantic aura. Backlighting is especially evocative when used to highlight blonde hair **(1–20a).**

Through the use of spotlights, an image can be composed of violent contrasts of lights and darks. The surface of such images seems disfigured, torn up. The formalist director uses such severe contrasts for psychological and thematic purposes **(1–18).**

By deliberately permitting too much light to enter the aperture of the camera, a filmmaker can overexpose an image—producing a blanching flood of

a   b

1–19. *Leatherface: The Texas Chainsaw Massacre III* (U.S.A., 1990), *with R. A. Mihailoff, directed by Jeff Burr.*
Many people would argue that the backlit low-key lighting of **(a)** is more frightening than frontal lighting of **(b)**. Horrific as Leatherface's features are, at least we know what we have to deal with, whereas the faceless killer **(a)** conjures unspeakable unseen terrors.   *(New Line Cinema)*

light over the entire surface of the picture. **Overexposure** has been most effectively used in nightmare and fantasy sequences. Sometimes this technique can suggest a kind of horrible glaring publicity, a sense of emotional exaggeration.

Color

Color in film didn't become commercially widespread until the 1940s. There were many experiments in color before this period, however. Some of Méliès's movies, for example, were painted by hand in assembly line fashion, with each painter responsible for coloring a minute area of the filmstrip. The original version of *The Birth of a Nation* (1915) was printed on various tinted stocks to suggest different moods: The burning of Atlanta was tinted red, the night scenes blue, the exterior love scenes pale yellow. Many silent filmmakers used this tinting technique to suggest different moods.

Sophisticated film color was developed in the 1930s, but for many years a major problem was its tendency to prettify everything. If color enhanced a sense of beauty—in a musical or a historical extravaganza—the effects were often appropriate. Thus, the best feature films of the early years of color were usually those with artificial or exotic settings. Realistic dramas were thought to be unsuitable vehicles for color. The earliest color processes tended also to emphasize garishness, and often special consultants had to be called in to harmonize the color schemes of costumes, makeup, and decor.

1–20a. *Braveheart* **(U.S.A., 1995),** *with Sophie Marceau and Mel Gibson, directed by Gibson.* *(Paramount Pictures)*

Art historians often distinguish between a "painterly" and a "linear" style, a distinction that's also useful in the photographic arts. A **painterly** style is soft-edged, sensuous, and romantic, best typified by the Impressionist landscapes of Claude Monet and the voluptuous figure paintings of Pierre Auguste Renoir. Line is deemphasized: Colors and textures shimmer in a hazily defined, radiantly illuminated environment. On the other hand, a **linear** style emphasizes drawing, sharply defined edges, and the supremacy of line over color and texture. In the field of painting, a linear style typifies such artists as Leonardo Da Vinci and the French classicist Jean-Auguste-Dominique Ingres.

Movies can also be photographed in a painterly or linear style, depending on the lighting, the lenses, and filters. The shot from *Braveheart* might almost have been painted by Renoir. Cinematographer John Toll used soft focus lenses and warm "natural" backlighting (creating a halo effect around the characters' heads) to produce an intensely romantic lyricism. Wyler's post-World War II masterpiece, *The Best Years of Our Lives,* was photographed by the great Gregg Toland. Its linear style is austere, deglamourized, shot in razor-sharp deep-focus. It was a style suited to the times. The postwar era was a period of disillusionment, sober reevaluations, and very few sentimental illusions. The high-key cinematography is polished, to be sure, but it's also simple, matter-of-fact, the invisible servant of a serious subject matter.

1–20b. *The Best Years of Our Lives* **(U.S.A., 1946),** *with Harold Russell, Teresa Wright, Dana Andrews, Myrna Loy, Hoagy Carmichael (standing), and Fredric March; directed by William Wyler.* *(RKO).*

Furthermore, each color process tended to specialize in a certain base hue—red, blue, or yellow, usually—whereas other colors of the spectrum were somewhat distorted. It was well into the 1950s before these problems were resolved. Compared with the subtle color perceptions of the human eye, however, and despite the apparent precision of most present-day color processing, cinematic color is still a relatively crude approximation.

The most famous color films tend to be expressionistic. Michelangelo Antonioni's attitude was fairly typical: "It is necessary to intervene in a color film, to take away the usual reality and replace it with the reality of the moment." In *Red Desert* (photographed by Carlo Di Palma), Antonioni spray-painted natural locales to emphasize internal psychological states. Industrial wastes, river pollution, marshes, and large stretches of terrain were painted gray to suggest the ugliness of contemporary industrial society and the heroine's drab, wasted existence. Whenever red appears in the movie, it suggests sexual passion. Yet the red—like the loveless sexuality—is an ineffective coverup of the pervasive gray.

1-21. *This Is Elvis* (U.S.A., 1981), *with Elvis Presley, directed by Malcolm Leo and others.* Documentaries are often photographed on the run. Cinematographers don't usually have a chance to augment the lighting, but have to capture the images as best they can under conditions that are almost totally uncontrolled. Many documentaries are photographed with hand-held cameras for maximum portability and with fast film stocks, which can register images using only ambient light. The images are valued not for their formal beauty, which is usually negligible (or nonexistent), but for their authenticity and spontaneity. Such images offer us privileged moments of intimacy that are all the more powerful because they're not simulated. They're the real thing. *(Warner Bros.)*

1–22. *From Here to Eternity* (U.S.A., 1953), *with Montgomery Clift and Burt Lancaster, directed by Fred Zinnemann.*

The expert cinematographers of the big-studio era were adept in revealing a surprising amount of detail even in scenes that take place at night, as in this photo. The preponderance of shadow in this shot clearly establishes the nighttime milieu, but note how an offscreen street lamp conveniently manages to illuminate the characters' facial expressions and body language. (They're both very drunk, sitting in the middle of a dirt road.) Sometimes studio-era D.P.s preferred to use the day-for-night filter, which gives the illusion of an evening setting even though the scene was originally photographed in daylight. To many present-day audiences, however, day-for-night shots look artificial, too bright and crisp to be convincing. *(Columbia Pictures)*

Color tends to be a subconscious element in film. It's strongly emotional in its appeal, expressive and atmospheric rather than intellectual. Psychologists have discovered that most people actively attempt to interpret the lines of a composition, but they tend to accept color passively, permitting it to suggest moods rather than objects. Lines are associated with nouns; color with adjectives. Line is sometimes thought to be masculine; color feminine. Both lines and colors suggest meanings, then, but in somewhat different ways.

Since earliest times, visual artists have used color for symbolic purposes. Color symbolism is probably culturally acquired, though its implications are surprisingly similar in otherwise differing societies. In general, cool colors (blue, green, violet) tend to suggest tranquility, aloofness, and serenity. Cool colors also have a tendency to recede in an image. Warm colors (red, yellow, orange) suggest aggressiveness, violence, and stimulation. They tend to come forward in most images.

1–23. *Crime and Punishment* (U.S.A., 1935), *with Peter Lorre (center), cinematography by Lucien Ballard, directed by Josef von Sternberg.*
Sternberg was a master of atmospheric lighting effects and closely supervised the photography of his films. His stories are unfolded primarily in terms of light and shade, rather than conventional dramatic means. "Every light has a point where it is brightest, and a point toward which it wanders to lose itself completely," he explained. "The journey of rays from that central core to the outposts of blackness is the adventure and drama of light." Note how the closed form of the **mise en scène** and the light encircling the protagonist (Lorre) produce an accusatory effect, a sense of entrapment. *(Paramount Pictures)*

Some filmmakers deliberately exploit color's natural tendency to garishness. Fellini's *Juliet of the Spirits* features many bizarre costumes and settings to suggest the tawdry but fascinating glamour of the world of show business. Bob Fosse's *Cabaret* is set in Germany and shows the early rise of the Nazi party. The colors are somewhat neurotic, with emphasis on such 1930s favorites as plum, acid green, purple, and florid combinations, like gold, black, and pink.

Black-and-white photography in a color film is sometimes used for symbolic purposes. Some filmmakers alternate whole episodes in black and white with entire sequences in color. The problem with this technique is its facile symbolism. The jolting black-and-white sequences are too obviously "significant" in the most arty sense. A more effective variation is simply not to use too much color, to let black and white predominate. In De Sica's *The Garden of the Finzi-Continis*, which is set in Fascist Italy, the early portions of the movie are

1–24. *Starman* **(U.S.A., 1984),** *with Karen Allen and Jeff Bridges, directed by John Carpenter.* Not every shot in a movie is photographed in the same style. Many of the earlier portions of this sci-fi film are photographed in a plain, functional style. After the earthling protagonist (Allen) falls in love with an appealing and hunky alien (Bridges), the photographic style becomes more romantic. The city's lights are etherealized by the shimmering soft-focus photography. The halo effect around the lovers' heads reinforces the air of enchantment. The gently falling snowflakes conspire to enhance the magical moment. These aren't just lovers, these are soul mates. *(Columbia Pictures)*

richly resplendent in shimmering golds, reds, and almost every shade of green. As political repression becomes more brutal, these colors almost imperceptibly begin to wash out, until near the end of the film the images are dominated by whites, blacks, and blue-grays (see also **Color Plate 6**).

In the 1980s, a new computer technology was developed, allowing black-and-white movies to be "colorized"—a process that provoked a howl of protest from most film artists and critics. The colorized versions of some genres, like period films, musicals, and other forms of light entertainment, are not damaged too seriously by this process, but the technique is a disaster in carefully photographed black-and-white films, like *Citizen Kane,* with its **film noir** lighting style and brilliant deep-focus photography (see Chapter 12, "Synthesis: *Citizen Kane"*).

Colorization also throws off the compositional balance of some shots, creating new **dominants.** In the shot from *Dark Victory* **(C.P. 18),** for example, the dominant is Brent's blue suit, which is irrelevant to the dramatic context. In the original black-and-white version, Davis is the dominant, her dark outfit contrasting with the white fireplace that frames her figure. Distracting visual dominants undercut the dramatic impact of such scenes. We keep thinking Brent's suit *must* be important. It is, but only to the computer.

Lenses, Filters, Stocks, Opticals, and Gauges

Because the camera's lens is a crude mechanism compared to the human eye, some of the most striking effects in a movie image can be achieved through the distortions of the photographic process itself. Particularly with regard to size and distance, the camera lens doesn't make mental adjustments but records things literally. For example, whatever is placed closest to the camera's lens will appear larger than an object at a greater distance. Hence, a coffee cup can totally obliterate a human being if the cup is in front of the lens and the human is standing at long-shot range.

Realist filmmakers tend to use normal, or standard, lenses to produce a minimum of distortion. These lenses photograph subjects more or less as they are perceived by the human eye. Formalist filmmakers often prefer lenses and **filters** that intensify given qualities and suppress others. Cloud formations, for example, can be exaggerated threateningly or softly diffused, depending on what kind of lens or filter is used. Different shapes, colors, and lighting intensities can be radically altered through the use of specific optical modifiers. There are literally dozens of different lenses, but most of them are subsumed under three major categories: those in the standard (nondistorted) range, the telephoto lenses, and the wide angles.

The *telephoto lens* is often used to get close-ups of objects from extreme distances. For example, no cinematographer is likely to want to get close enough to a lion to photograph a close-up with a standard lens. In cases such as these, the telephoto is used, thus guaranteeing the safety of the cinematographer while still producing the necessary close-up. Telephotos also allow cinematographers to work discreetly. In crowded city locations, for example, passersby are likely to stare at a movie camera. The telephoto permits the cinematographer to remain hidden—in a truck, for example—while he or she shoots close shots through a windshield or window. In effect, the lens works like a telescope, and because of its long focal length, it is sometimes called a *long lens.*

Telephoto lenses produce a number of side effects that are sometimes exploited by directors for symbolic use. Most long lenses are in sharp focus on one distance plane only. Objects placed before or beyond that distance blur, go out of focus—an expressive technique, especially to the formalist filmmaker **(1–25).** The longer the lens, the more sensitive it is to distances; in the case of extremely long lenses, objects placed a mere few inches away from the selected focal plane can be out of focus. This deliberate blurring of planes in the background, foreground, or both can produce some striking photographic and atmospheric effects.

The focal distance of long lenses can usually be adjusted while shooting, and thus, the director is able to neutralize planes and guide the viewer's eye to various distances in a sequence—a technique called **rack focusing,** or selective focusing. In *The Graduate,* director Mike Nichols used a slight focus shift instead of a cut when he wanted the viewer to look first at the young heroine, who then blurs out of focus, then at her mother, who is standing a few feet

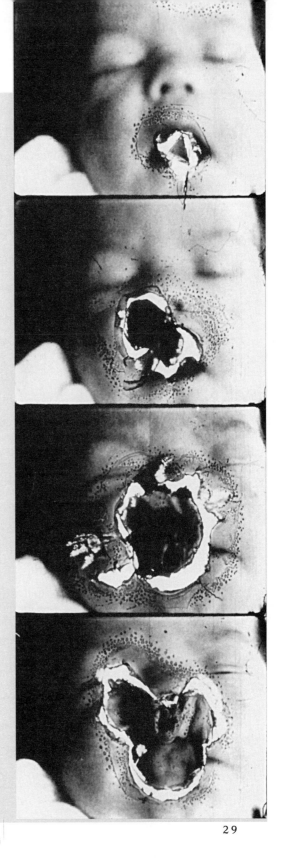

1-25. *Dog Star Man* (U.S.A., 1959–1964), *directed by Stan Brakhage.*

Avant-garde filmmakers are often anti-illusionist—they attempt to break down the realism of an image by calling attention to its artificiality and its material properties. A movie image is printed on a strip of celluloid, which can be manipulated, even violated. In this sequence, a baby emerges from the mouth of another baby. Brakhage is playing with the idea of what's "behind" a film image. *(Anthology Film Archives)*

1–26.   Six Degrees of Exaggeration.

The lens of each of these six shots provides a commentary on the relationship of the characters to their surroundings.

1–26a. *Scream* **(U.S.A., 1996),** *with Courteney Cox, directed by Wes Craven.*

Some telephoto lenses are so precise they can focus on a thin slice of action that's only a few inches deep. Note how the gun and Cox's hands are radically blurred. So is the background behind her. Our eyes are forced to concentrate on the face of the character during a decisive moment of her life.   *(Dimension Films)*

1–26b.   *Too Beautiful for You* **(France, 1989),** *with Carole Bouquet and Gerard Depardieu, directed by Bertrand Blier.*

Moderate telephoto lenses are often used to enhance the lyrical potential of an image. Although not so extreme a telephoto as **(a)**, Blier's lens converts the reflections on the autos' rooftops into rhapsodic brushstrokes of light, heightening the erotic ecstasy of the characters.   *(Orion Pictures)*

1–26c.   *King of the Hill* **(U.S.A., 1993),** *with Jesse Bradford (left) and Jeroen Krabbe, directed by Steven Soderbergh.*

A ne'er-do-well father (Krabbe) has just told his young son that he'll have to stay home alone for several weeks while the father tries to hustle a living on the road. The boy's anxiety and fear are intensified by his sharp focus, the father's remoteness by his somewhat blurred presentation. If Soderbergh wanted to emphasize the father's feelings, the boy would be in soft focus and the father in sharp. If the director wanted to stress the equality of their emotions, he would have used a wide-angle lens, which would render both characters in sharp focus. *(Gramercy Pictures)*

continued   ▶

1–26d. *Schindler's List* (U.S.A., 1993), *with Liam Neeson (outstretched arms), directed by Steven Spielberg.*

Wide-angle lenses are used whenever deep-focus photography is called for. Objects a few feet from the lens as well as those in the "depth" of the background are in equal focus, reinforcing the interconnectedness of the visual planes. This movie deals with a German industrialist (Neeson) who saved the lives of hundreds of Jews during the Nazi Holocaust. Because deep focus allows for the repetition of visual motifs into infinity, Spielberg is able to suggest that Jews all over Europe were being herded in a similar manner, but their fate was not so lucky as Schindler's Jews.   *(Universal Pictures)*

1–26e. Publicity photo of *Rumble in the Bronx* (U.S.A., 1996), *with Jackie Chan, directed by Stanley Tong.*

Extreme wide-angle lenses exaggerate distances between depth planes, a useful symbolic technique. As distorted by the wide-angle lens, Chan's fist is nearly as large as his head and his feet seem to be standing in another county.   *(New Line Cinema)*

1–26f. *Runaway Bride* (U.S.A., 1999), *with Julia Roberts and Richard Gere, directed by Garry Marshall.*

Check out the lights in the background. A shrewdly chosen filter makes them look blurry, floating dreamily like woozy fireflies. Do we need to hear the dialogue to know that these two are falling for each other? Do we need to be told that the movie is a romantic comedy? The filtered photography says it all.

(Paramount Pictures and Touchstone Pictures)

off in a doorway. The focus-shifting technique suggests a cause–effect relationship and parallels the heroine's sudden realization that her boyfriend's secret mistress is her own mother. In *The French Connection,* William Friedkin used selective focus in a sequence showing a criminal under surveillance. He remains in sharp focus while the city crowds of his environment are an undifferentiated blur. At strategic moments in the sequence, Friedkin shifted the focus plane from the criminal to the dogged detective who is tailing him in the crowd.

Long lenses also flatten images, decreasing the sense of distance between depth planes. Two people standing yards apart might look inches away when photographed with a telephoto lens. With very long lenses, distance planes are so compressed that the image can resemble a flat surface of abstract patterns. When anything moves toward or away from the camera in such shots, the mobile object doesn't seem to be moving at all. In *Marathon Man,* the hero (Dustin Hoffman) runs desperately toward the camera, but because of the flattening of the long lens, he seems almost to be running in place rather than moving toward his destination.

The *wide-angle lenses,* also called "short lenses," have short focal lengths and wide angles of view. These are the lenses used in deep-focus shots, for they preserve a sharpness of focus on virtually all distance planes. The distortions involved in short lenses are both linear and spatial. The wider the angle, the more lines and shapes tend to warp, especially at the edges of the image. Distances between various depth planes are also exaggerated with these lenses: Two people standing a foot away from each other can appear yards apart in a wide-angle image.

1–27.   Filmstrips of the four principal gauges used in movies, expressed in millimeters wide.

Photographic quality depends in part on the gauge of the film used to photograph and project the images. **(1)** Suitable for projecting in an average-sized room, 8 mm and Super 8 mm are primarily for home use. **(2)** The gauge ordinarily used in schools and museums is 16 mm; if projected in extremely large halls, 16-mm images tend to grow fuzzy and the color tends to fade. **(3)** The standard gauge for the vast majority of movie theaters is 35 mm. **(4)** For epic subjects requiring a huge screen, 70 mm is generally used; the images retain their linear sharpness and color saturation even in enormous theaters.

(1)   (2)   (3)   (4)

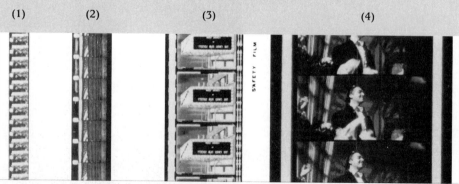

Movement toward or away from the camera is exaggerated when photographed with a short lens. Two or three ordinary steps can seem like unhumanly lengthy strides—an effective technique when a director wants to emphasize a character's strength, dominance, or ruthlessness. The fish-eye lens is the most extreme wide-angle modifier; it creates such severe distortions that the lateral portions of the screen seem reflected in a sphere, as though we were looking through a crystal ball.

Lenses and filters can be used for purely cosmetic purposes—to make an actor or actress taller, slimmer, younger, or older. Josef von Sternberg sometimes covered his lens with a translucent silk stocking to give his images a gauzy, romantic aura. A few glamour actresses beyond a certain age even had clauses in their contracts stipulating that only beautifying soft-focus lenses could be used for their close-ups. These optical modifiers eliminate small facial wrinkles and skin blemishes.

There are even more filters than there are lenses. Some trap light and refract it in such a way as to produce a diamondlike sparkle in the image. Many filters are used to suppress or heighten certain colors. Color filters can be espe-

1–28. *Kids* **(U.S.A., 1995),** *with Yakira Peguero and Leo Fitzpatrick, directed by Larry Clark.*
Fast film stocks are highly sensitive to light and can record images with no additional illumination except what's available on a set or location—even at night. These stocks tend to produce harsh light–dark contrasts, an absence of details, and images so grainy that they can appear more painterly than linear. Fast stocks are especially effective in fiction films that purport to be realistic and documentarylike, such as this controversial depiction of some urban teenagers and their high-risk sexual practices. *(Excalibur Films)*

1–29. *Pas De Deux* (Canada, 1968), *directed by Norman McLaren.* The optical printer is an invaluable piece of equipment, particularly to the formalist filmmaker, because, among other things, it allows the superimposition of two or more realities within a unified space. This film uses a technique called chronophotography, in which the movements of two dancers are staggered and overlayed by the optical printer to produce a stroboscopic effect: As the dancers move, they leave a ghostly imprint on the screen. *(National Film Board of Canada)*

cially striking in exterior scenes. Robert Altman's *McCabe and Mrs. Miller* (photographed by Vilmos Zsigmond) uses green and blue filters for many of the exterior scenes, yellow and orange for interiors. These filters emphasize the bitter cold of the winter setting and the communal warmth of the rooms inside the primitive buildings.

Though there are a number of different kinds of film stocks, most of them fall within the two basic categories: fast and slow. **Fast stock** is highly sensitive to light and in some cases can register images with no illumination except what's available on location, even in nighttime sequences **(1–28)**. **Slow stock** is relatively insensitive to light and requires as much as ten times more illumination than fast stocks. Traditionally, slow stocks are capable of capturing colors precisely, without washing them out.

Fast stocks are commonly associated with documentary movies, for with their great sensitivity to light, these stocks can reproduce images of events while they're actually occurring. The documentarist is able to photograph people and places without having to set up cumbersome lights. Because of this light sensitivity, fast stocks produce a grainy image in which lines tend to be fuzzy and colors tend to wash out. In a black-and-white film, lights and darks contrast sharply and many variations of gray can be lost.

Ordinarily, technical considerations such as these would have no place in a book of this sort, but the choice of stock can produce considerable psychological and aesthetic differences in a movie. Since the early 1960s, many fiction filmmakers have switched to fast stocks to give their images a documentary sense of urgency.

The **optical printer** is an elaborate machine that produces many special effects in the cinema. It includes a camera and projector precisely aligned, and

1–30. *Multiplicity* (U.S.A., 1996), *with (from left to right) Michael Keaton, Michael Keaton, Michael Keaton, and Michael Keaton; directed by Harold Ramis.*
The American cinema has always been on the cutting edge of film technology, especially in the area of special effects. Computer-generated images have allowed filmmakers to create fantasy worlds of the utmost realism. In this movie, for example, Keaton plays a man who has lost his wife and his job, and must clone himself in order to function effectively. Computer artist Dan Madsen created a film reality that obviously has no counterpart in the outside physical world. Critic Stephen Prince has observed that such technological advancements as computer-generated images have radically undermined the traditional distinctions between realism and formalism in film theory. See Stephen Prince, "True Lies: Perceptual Realism, Digital Images, and Film Theory," in *Film Quarterly* (Spring, 1996). *(Columbia Pictures)*

it permits the operator to rephotograph all or a portion of an existing frame of a film. **Double exposure,** or the superimposition of two images, is one of the most important of these effects, for it permits the director to portray two levels of reality simultaneously. For this reason, the technique is often used in fantasy and dream sequences, as well as in scenes dealing with the supernatural. The optical printer can also produce **multiple exposures,** or the superimposition of many images simultaneously. Multiple exposures are useful for suggesting mood, time lapses, and any sense of mixture—of time, places, objects, events. The optical printer can combine one actor with moving images of others in a different time and place.

1-31. Twentieth Century–Fox publicity photo of Marilyn Monroe (1953). Cinematographers often comment that the camera "likes" certain individuals and "doesn't like" others, even though these others might be good-looking people in real life. Highly photogenic performers like Marilyn Monroe are rarely uncomfortable in front of the camera. Indeed, they often play to it, ensnaring our attention. Photographer Richard Avedon said of Marilyn, "She understood photography, and she also understood what makes a great photograph—not the technique, but the content. She was more comfortable in front of the camera than away from it." Philippe Halsman went even further, pointing out that her open mouth and frequently open décolletage were frankly invitational: "She would try to seduce the camera as if it were a human being. . . . She knew that the camera lens was not just a glass eye but a symbol of the eyes of millions of men, so the camera stimulated her strongly." *(Twentieth Century–Fox)*

The Cinematographer

The cinema is a collaborative enterprise, the result of the combined efforts of many artists, technicians, and businesspeople. Because the contributions of these individuals vary from film to film, it's hard to determine who's responsible for what in a movie. Most sophisticated viewers agree that the director is generally the dominant artist in the best movies. The principal collaborators—actors, writers, cinematographers—perform according to the director's unifying sensibility. But directorial dominance is an act of faith. Many films are stamped by the personalities of others—a prestigious **star,** for example, or a skillful editor who manages to make sense out of a director's botched **footage.**

Cinematographers sometimes chuckle sardonically when a director's visual style is praised by critics. Some directors don't even bother looking through the viewfinder and leave such matters as composition, angles, and lenses up to the cinematographer. When directors ignore these important formal elements, they throw away some of their most expressive pictorial opportunities and function more like stage directors, who are concerned with dramatic

1-32. *The Emigrants* **(Sweden, 1972),** *with Liv Ullmann and Max von Sydow, photographed and directed by Jan Troell.*
If we were to view a scene similar to this in real life, we would probably concentrate most of our attention on the people in the wagon. But there are considerable differences between reality and cinematic realism. Realism is an artistic style. In selecting materials from the chaotic sprawl of reality, the realist filmmaker necessarily eliminates some details and emphasizes others into a structured hierarchy of visual significance. For example, the stone wall in the foreground of this shot occupies more space than the humans. Visually, this dominance suggests that the rocks are more important than the people. The unyielding stone wall symbolizes divisiveness and exclusion—ideas that are appropriate to the dramatic context. If the wall were irrelevant to the theme, Troell would have eliminated it and selected other details from the copiousness of reality—details that would be more pertinent to the dramatic context. *(Warner Bros.)*

rather than visual values—that is, with the script and the acting rather than the photographic quality of the image itself.

On the other hand, a few cinematographers have been praised for their artistry when in fact the effectiveness of a film's images is largely due to the director's pictorial skills. Hitchcock provided individual frame drawings for most of the shots in his films, a technique called **storyboarding.** His cinematographers framed up according to Hitchcock's precise sketches. Hence, when Hitchcock claimed that he never looked through the viewfinder, he meant that he assumed his cinematographer had followed instructions.

Sweeping statements about the role of the cinematographer are impossible to make, for it varies widely from film to film and from director to director. In actual practice, virtually all cinematographers agree that the style of the photography should be geared to the story, theme, and mood of the film. William Daniels had a prestigious reputation as a glamour photographer at MGM and for many years was known as "Greta Garbo's cameraman." Yet Daniels also shot Erich von Stroheim's harshly realistic *Greed,* and the cinematographer won an Academy Award for his work in Jules Dassin's *Naked City,* which is virtually a semidocumentary.

During the big-studio era, most cinematographers believed that the aesthetic elements of a film should be maximized—beautiful pictures with beautiful people was the goal. Today such views are considered rigid and doctrinaire. Sometimes images are even coarsened if such a technique is considered appropriate to the dramatic materials. For example, Vilmos Zsigmond, who photographed *Deliverance,* didn't want the rugged forest setting to appear too pretty

1–33. *Women on the Verge of a Nervous Breakdown* **(Spain, 1988),** *with Carmen Maura, directed by Pedro Almodóvar.*
What's wrong with this photo? For one thing, the character is not centered in the composition. The image is asymmetrical, apparently off balance because the "empty" space on the right takes up over half the viewing area. Visual artists often use "negative space" such as this to create a vacuum in the image, a sense of something missing, something left unsaid. In this case, the pregnant protagonist (Maura) has just been dumped by her lover. He is an unworthy swine, but inexplicably, perversely, she still loves him. His abandonment has left a painful empty place in her life. *(Orion Pictures)*

because beautiful visuals would contradict the Darwinian theme of the film. He wanted to capture what Tennyson described as "nature red in tooth and claw." Accordingly, Zsigmond shot on overcast days as much as possible to eliminate the bright blue skies. He also avoided reflections in the water because they tend to make nature look cheerful and inviting. "You don't make beautiful compositions just for the sake of making compositions," cinematographer Laszlo Kovacs has insisted. Content always determines form; form should be the embodiment of content.

"Many times, what you don't see is much more effective than what you do see," Gordon Willis has noted. Willis is arguably the most respected of all American cinematographers, a specialist in low-key lighting styles. He photographed all three of Francis Ford Coppola's *Godfather* films—which many traditionalists consider too dark. But Willis was aiming for poetry, not realism. Most of the interior scenes were very dark to suggest an atmosphere of evil and secrecy **(C.P.8)**.

Willis's preference for low levels of light has been enormously influential in the contemporary cinema. Unfortunately, many filmmakers today regard low-key lighting as intrinsically more "serious" and "artistic," whatever the subject matter. These needlessly dark movies are often impenetrably obscure when shown on the television screen in VCR or DVD formats. Conscientious filmmakers often supervise the transfer from film to video because each medium requires different lighting intensities. Generally, low-key images must be lightened for video and DVD.

Some film directors are totally ignorant of the technology of the camera and leave such matters entirely to the cinematographer. Other filmmakers are very sophisticated in the art of the camera. For example, Sidney Lumet, who is best known for directing such realistic New York City dramas as *The Pawnbroker, Dog Day Afternoon,* and *Serpico,* always makes what he calls a "lens chart" or a "lens plot." In Lumet's *Prince of the City,* for instance, the story centers on a Serpicolike undercover cop who is gathering information on police corruption. Lumet used no "normal" lenses in the movie, only extreme telephotos and wide-angle lenses, because he wanted to create an atmosphere of distrust and paranoia. He wanted the space to be distorted, untrustworthy. "The lens tells the story," Lumet explained, even though superficially the film's style is gritty and realistic.

There are some great movies that are photographed competently, but without distinction. Realist directors are especially likely to prefer an unobtrusive style. Many of the works of Luis Buñuel, for example, can only be described as "professional" in their cinematography. Buñuel was rarely interested in formal beauty—except occasionally to mock it. Rollie Totheroh, who photographed most of Chaplin's works, merely set up his camera and let Chaplin the actor take over. Photographically speaking, there are few memorable shots in his films. What makes the images compelling is the genius of Chaplin's acting. This photographic austerity—some would consider it poverty—is especially apparent in those rare scenes when Chaplin is off camera.

1–34a. *Muriel's Wedding* (Australia, 1995), *with Toni Collette (with flowers), directed by P. J. Hogan.* (Miramax Films)

1–34b. *Kafka* (U.S.A., 1991), *with Jeremy Irons (left), directed by Steven Soderbergh.* (Miramax Films)

Cinematography is very important, but it usually can't make or break a movie—only make it better or worse. For example, the low-budget *Muriel's Wedding* was shot mostly on location using available lighting. The photography is adequate, but nothing more. In this shot, for instance, the protagonist (Collette) has the key light on her, but the background is too busy and the depth layers of the image are compressed into an undifferentiated messy blur. Nonetheless, the movie was an international hit and was widely praised by critics, thanks mostly to Collette's endearing performance, a funny script, and Hogan's exuberant direction. No one complained about the lackluster photography.

On the other hand, the cinematography of *Kafka* is ravishing—bold, theatrical, richly textured. This shot alone must have taken many hours to set up. But the movie was a failure, both with the public and with most critics. In short, not all beautifully photographed movies

continued ▶

1–34c. *Days of Heaven* **(U.S.A., 1978),** *written and directed by Terrence Malick.* (*A Paramount Picture*)

are great. And not all great movies are beautifully photographed. Many of them—especially realistic films—are plain and straightforward. Realists often don't *want* you to notice the photography. They want you to concentrate on *what's* being photographed, not on how it's being photographed.

Perhaps an ideal synthesis is found in a movie like *Days of Heaven*. Malick's powerful allegory of human frailty and corruption is written in a spare, poetic idiom. The actors are also first-rate, needy, and touching in their doomed vulnerability. The film was photographed by Nestor Almendros, who won a well-deserved Oscar for his cinematography. The story is set in the early twentieth century in a lonely wheat-growing region of the American midwest. Malick wanted the setting to suggest a lush Garden of Eden, a lost paradise. Almendros suggested that virtually the entire movie could be shot during the "magic hour." This is a term used by photographers to denote dusk, roughly the last hour of the day before the sun yields to night. During this fleeting interlude, shadows are soft and elongated, figures are lit from the side rather than from above, rimmed with a golden halo, and the entire landscape is bathed in a luminous glow. Naturally, shooting one hour a day was expensive and time-consuming. But they got what they wanted: Whether focusing on a close-up of a locust munching on a stalk of wheat, or an extreme long shot of a rural sunset, the images are rapturous in their lyricism. We feel a sense of poignant loss when the characters must leave this land of milk and honey.

But there are far more films in which the *only* interesting or artistic quality is the cinematography. For every great work like Fritz Lang's *You Only Live Once*, Leon Shamroy had to photograph four or five bombs of the ilk of *Snow White and the Three Stooges*. Lee Garmes photographed several of von Sternberg's visually opulent films, but he also was required to shoot *My Friend Irma Goes West*, a piece of garbage.

In this chapter, we've been concerned with visual images largely as they relate to the art and technology of cinematography. But the camera must have materials to photograph—objects, people, settings. Through the manipulation of these materials, the director is able to convey a multitude of ideas and emotions spatially. This arrangement of objects in space is referred to as a director's *mise en scène*—the subject of the following chapter.

FURTHER READING

ALTON, JOHN, *Painting with Light* (Berkeley: University of California Press, 1995). Reprint of a classic work.

COE, BRIAN, *The History of Movie Photography* (London: Ash & Grant, 1981).

COPJEC, JOAN, ed. *Shades of Noir* (London and New York: Routledge, 1994). Essays on the origins and persistence of film noir.

EYMAN, SCOTT, *Five American Cinematographers* (Metuchen, N.J., and London: Scarecrow Press, 1987). Interviews with Karl Struss, Joseph Ruttenberg, James Wong Howe, Linwood Dunn, and William Clothier.

FIELDING, RAYMOND, *The Techniques of Special Effects Cinematography* (New York: Hastings House, 1965). Somewhat dated, but still valuable.

FINCH, CHRISTOPHER, *Special Effects: Creating Movie Magic* (New York: Abbeville, 1984). Lavishly illustrated.

MASCELLI, JOSEPH, *The Five C's of Cinematography* (Hollywood: Cine/Graphics, 1965). A practical manual.

SCHAEFER, DENNIS, and LARRY SALVATO, eds., *Masters of Light* (Berkeley: University of California Press, 1984). Excellent collection of interviews with contemporary cinematographers.

SCHECHTER, HAROLD, AND DAVID EVERITT, *Film Tricks: Special Effects in Movies* (New York: Dial, 1980).

YOUNG, FREDDIE, *The Work of the Motion Picture Cameraman* (New York: Hastings House, 1972). Technical emphasis.

Mise en Scène

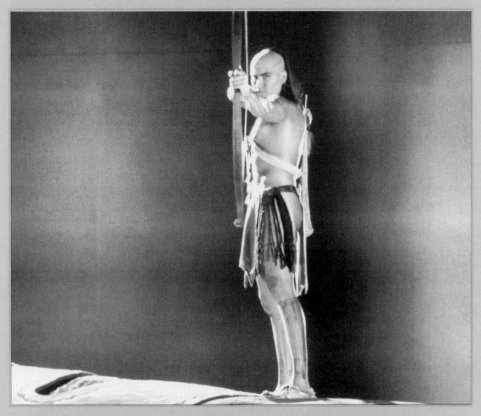

Paramount Pictures/Columbia Pictures

One must compose images as the old masters did their canvases, with the same preoccupation with effect and expression.

—MARCEL CARNÉ, FILMMAKER

Overview

Mise en scène: How the visual materials are staged, framed, and photographed. The frame's aspect ratio: dimensions of the screen's height and width. Film, TV, video. Functions of the frame: excluding the irrelevant, pinpointing the particular, symbolizing other enclosures. The symbolic implications of the geography of the frame: top, bottom, center, and edges. What's off-frame and why. How images are structured: composition and design. Where we look first: the dominant. The territorial imperative: How space can be used to communicate ideas about power. Staging positions vis-à-vis the camera and what they suggest. How much room for movement: tight and loose framing. Proxemic patterns and how they define the relationships between people. Camera proxemics and the shots. Open and closed forms: windows or proscenium-framed images? The fifteen elements of a mise en scène analysis.

Mise en scène (pronounced meez on sen, with the second syllable nasalized) was originally a French theatrical term meaning "placing on stage." The phrase refers to the arrangement of all the visual elements of a theatrical production within a given playing area—the stage. This area can be defined by the proscenium arch, which encloses the stage in a kind of picture frame; or the acting area can be more fluid, extending even into the auditorium. No matter what the confines of the stage may be, its mise en scène is always in three dimensions. Objects and people are arranged in actual space, which has depth as well as height and width. This space is also a continuation of the same space that the audience occupies, no matter how much a theater director tries to suggest a separate "world" on the stage.

In movies, mise en scène is somewhat more complicated, a blend of the visual conventions of the live theater with those of painting. Like the stage director, the filmmaker arranges objects and people within a given three-dimensional space. But once this arrangement is photographed, it's converted into a two-dimensional *image* of the real thing. The space in the "world" of the movie is not the same as that occupied by the audience. Only the image exists in the same physical area, like a picture in an art gallery. Mise en scène in the movies resembles the art of painting in that an image of formal patterns and shapes is presented on a flat surface and is enclosed within a **frame.** But cinematic mise en scène is also a fluid choreographing of visual elements that are constantly in flux.

The Frame

Each movie image is enclosed by the frame of the screen, which defines the world of the film, separating it from the actual world of the darkened auditorium. Unlike the painter or still photographer, the filmmaker doesn't conceive of the framed compositions as self-sufficient statements. Like drama, film is a tem-

2–1. *Manhattan* (U.S.A., 1979), *with Woody Allen and Diane Keaton, directed by Allen.*
Mise en scène is a complex analytical term, encompassing four distinct formal elements:
(1) the staging of the action, **(2)** the physical setting and decor, **(3)** the manner in which
these materials are framed, and **(4)** the manner in which they are photographed. The art of
mise en scène is indissolubly linked with the art of cinematography. In this shot, for example, the story content is simple: The characters are conversing, getting to know each other,
becoming attracted. Gordon Willis's tender, low-key lighting, combined with the beauty of
the setting—the sculpture garden of New York's Museum of Modern Art—provides the
scene with an intensely romantic atmosphere. *(United Artists)*

poral as well as spatial art, and consequently the visuals are constantly in flux. The
compositions are broken down, redefined, and reassembled before our eyes. A
single-frame image from a movie, then, is necessarily an artificially frozen
moment that was never intended to be yanked from its context in time and
motion. For critical purposes, it's sometimes necessary to analyze a still frame in
isolation, but the viewer ought to make due allowances for the dramatic context.

The frame functions as the basis of composition in a movie image.
Unlike the painter or still photographer, however, the filmmaker doesn't fit the
frame to the composition, but the compositions to a single-sized frame. The ratio
of the frame's horizontal and vertical dimensions—known as the **aspect ratio**—
remains constant throughout the movie. Screens come in a variety of aspect
ratios, especially since the introduction of **widescreen** in the early 1950s. Prior to
that time, most movies were shot in a 1.33:1 aspect ratio, though even in the
silent era filmmakers were constantly experimenting with different-sized screens
(2–6).

45

2–2. *Notorious* (U.S.A., 1946), *with Leopoldine Konstantine, Ingrid Bergman, and Claude Rains; directed by Alfred Hitchcock.*
Hitchcock always regarded himself as a formalist, calculating his effects with an extraordinary degree of precision. He believed that an unmanipulated reality is filled with irrelevancies: "I do not follow the geography of a set, I follow the geography of the screen," he said. The space around actors must be orchestrated from shot to shot. "I think only of that white screen that has to be filled up the way you fill up a canvas. That's why I draw rough setups for the camera-man." Here, the mise en scène is a perfect analogue of the heroine's sense of entrapment, with-out violating the civilized veneer demanded by the dramatic context. The dialogue in such instances can be perfectly neutral, for the psychological tensions are conveyed by the place-ment of the camera and the way the characters are arranged in space. *(RKO)*

Today, most movies are projected in one of two aspect ratios: the 1.85:1 (standard) and the 2.35:1 (widescreen). Some films originally photographed in widescreen are cropped down to a conventional aspect ratio after their initial commercial release. This appalling practice is commonplace in movies that are reduced from 35 mm to 16 mm, the standard gauge used in most noncommer-cial exhibitions like those at colleges and museums. The more imaginatively the widescreen is used, the more a movie is likely to suffer when its aspect ratio is violated in this manner. Generally, at least a third of the image is hacked away by lopping off the edges of the frame. This kind of cropping can result in many visual absurdities: A speaker at the edge of the frame might be totally absent in the "revised" composition, or an actor might react in horror at something that never even comes into view. When shown on television—which has an aspect ratio of approximately 1.33:1—some of the greatest widescreen films can actu-ally seem clumsy and poorly composed.

In the traditional visual arts, frame dimensions are governed by the nature of the subject matter. Thus, a painting of a skyscraper is likely to be verti-cal in shape and would be framed accordingly. A vast panoramic scene would probably be more horizontal in its dimensions. But in movies, the frame ratio is standardized and isn't necessarily governed by the nature of the materials being photographed. This is not to say that all film images are therefore inorganic, however, for in this regard the filmmaker can be likened to a sonneteer, who chooses a rigid form precisely because of the technical challenges it presents. Much of the enjoyment we derive in reading a sonnet results from the tension between the subject matter and the form, which consists of fourteen intricately rhymed lines. When technique and subject matter are fused in this way, aesthetic pleasure is heightened. The same principle can be applied to framing in film.

The constant size of the movie frame is especially hard to overcome in vertical compositions. A sense of height must be conveyed in spite of the dominantly horizontal shape of the screen. One method of overcoming the problem is through **masking.** In his 1916 drama, *Intolerance,* D. W. Griffith blocked out portions of his images through the use of black masks. These in effect connected the darkened portions of the screen with the darkness of the auditorium. To emphasize the steep fall of a soldier from a wall, the sides of the image were masked out. To stress the vast horizon of a location, Griffith masked out the lower third of the image—thus creating a widescreen effect. Many kinds of masks are used in this movie, including diagonal, circular, and oval shapes. Some years later, the Soviet director Eisenstein urged the adoption of a square screen, on which masked images could be projected in whatever shape was appropriate to the subject matter. No one picked up on the idea.

2–3. *Air Force One* **(U.S.A., 1997),** *with Gary Oldman and Harrison Ford, directed by Wolfgang Petersen.*
The movie frame temporarily defines the acting area for the duration of the shot. Whoever controls the space within the frame's limits controls the action. Notice how the villain (Oldman, always in top form when he's bad) dominates the President of the United States (Ford, of course), forcing him into the lower right corner of the mise en scène, seemingly on the brink of being pushed totally off screen. In instances such as these, the darkness off frame symbolizes the oblivion of death. *(Columbia Pictures)*

2–4. *Lawrence of Arabia* (Great Britain, 1962), *with Omar Sharif and Peter O'Toole, directed by David Lean.*
The widescreen aspect ratio provides some big problems when transferred to a video format. There are several solutions, but all of them have drawbacks. The crudest solution is simply to slice off the edges of the film image and concentrate on the middle, the assumption being that the center is where the dominant focus is likely to be. This shot would just barely contain the faces of the two characters and nothing past the center of their heads—an uncomfortably tight squeeze. A second solution is called "pan and scan" in which a TV camera scans the scene, panning to one or the other character as each speaks—like watching a tennis match on rough seas. A similar approach is to reedit the scene by cutting to each character, thus isolating them into their own separate space cubicles. But the essence of the shot demands that we see both characters at the same time. The drama lies in the subtle interactions of the characters, and this interaction would be lost by editing. A fourth solution is called "letter-boxing"—simply to include the entire movie image and block out the top and bottom of the TV screen. Many people object to this method, complaining that nearly half the screen is thus left empty, making an already small screen smaller. *(Columbia Pictures)*

In the silent movie era, the **iris** (a circular or oval mask that can open up or close in on a subject) was rather overused. In the hands of a master, however, the iris can be a powerful dramatic statement. In *The Wild Child,* François Truffaut used an iris to suggest the intense concentration of a young boy: The surrounding blackness is a metaphor of how the youngster "blocks out" his social environment while focusing on an object immediately in front of him.

As an aesthetic device, the frame performs in several ways. The sensitive director is just as concerned with what's left out of the frame as with what's included. The frame selects and delimits the subject, editing out all irrelevancies and presenting us with only a "piece" of reality. The materials included within a shot are unified by the frame, which in effect imposes an order on them. The frame is thus essentially an isolating device, a technique that permits the director to confer special attention on what might be overlooked in a wider context.

The movie frame can function as a metaphor for other types of enclosures. Some directors use the frame voyeuristically. In many of the films of Hitchcock, for example, the frame is likened to a window through which the audience may satisfy its impulse to pry into the intimate details of the characters' lives. In fact, *Psycho* and *Rear Window* use this peeping technique literally.

Certain areas within the frame can suggest symbolic ideas. By placing

2–5. *The Honeymooners* **(1955),** *with Jackie Gleason and Art Carney, produced by CBS television.*

Video and television are actually different mediums. Video is a method of transmission from another medium, usually a movie or a live theater production. In other words, video is a secondhand recording that inevitably diminishes the original artistic form. However, seeing a movie or play on video is better than not seeing it at all. Broadcast television, on the other hand, is an art that has evolved its own set of rules, including an aspect ratio that resembles the pre-1950 movie screen. Note how tightly framed this comic sketch is: The TV camera stays pretty much in the medium-shot range, and the performers confine their movements to just a few square feet of space. Blown up to fit a big movie screen, these images would probably look cramped and visually crude, notwithstanding the brilliance of the actors. *(CBS)*

an object or actor within a particular section of the frame, the filmmaker can radically alter his or her comment on that object or character. Placement within the frame is another instance of how form is actually content. Each of the major sections of the frame—center, top, bottom, and sides—can be exploited for such symbolic purposes.

The central portions of the screen are generally reserved for the most important visual elements. This area is instinctively regarded by most people as the intrinsic center of interest. When we take a snapshot of a friend, we generally center his or her figure within the confines of the viewfinder. Since childhood, we have been taught that a drawing must be balanced, with the middle serving as the focal point. The center, then, is a kind of norm: We *expect* dominant visual elements to be placed there. Precisely because of this expectation, objects in the center tend to be visually undramatic. Central dominance is generally favored when the subject matter is intrinsically compelling. Realist filmmakers prefer central dominance because formally it's the most unobtrusive kind of framing.

49

2–6. *Napoleon (France, 1927), directed by Abel Gance.*

Napoleon is the most famous widescreen experiment of the silent era. Its triptych sequences—such as the French army's march into Italy (pictured)—were shot in what Gance called "Polyvision." The process involved the coordination of three cameras so as to photograph a 160° panorama—three times wider than the conventional aspect ratio. *(Universal Pictures)*

a

2–7. *2001: A Space Odyssey* b
(U.S.A./ Great Britain, 1968),
directed by Stanley Kubrick.
The widescreen is particularly suited
to capturing the vastness of a locale.
If this image were cropped to a conventional aspect ratio **(b)** much of
the feel of the infinity of space would
be sacrificed. We tend to scan an
image from left to right, and therefore, in Kubrick's composition **(a)**,
the astronaut seems to be in danger
of slipping off into the endlessness of
space. If the composition is turned
upside down, however **(c)**, the astronaut seems to be coming home into
the safety of the spacecraft.   *(MGM)*

c

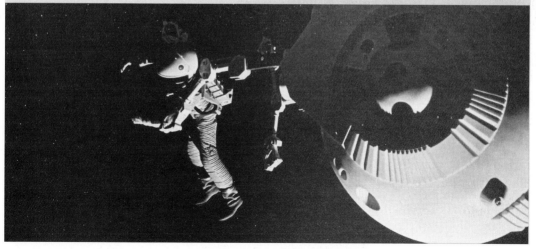

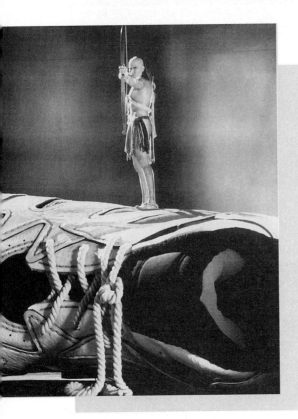

2–8. The *Indian in the Cupboard* (U.S.A., 1995), *with Litefoot, directed by Frank Oz.*
The mise en scène of the live theater is usually scaled in proportion to the human figure. Cinematic mise en scène can be microscopic or cosmic **(2–7)** with equal ease, thanks to the magic of special effects. In this photo, for example, the mise en scène represents only a few inches of space. Its scale is defined not by the human figure but by the tennis shoe that the three-inch-tall character is standing on.
(Paramount Pictures/Columbia Pictures)

The viewer is allowed to concentrate on the subject matter without being distracted by visual elements that seem off center. However, even **formalists** use the middle of the screen for dominance in routine expository shots.

The area near the top of the frame can suggest ideas dealing with power, authority, and aspiration. A person placed here seems to control all the visual elements below, and for this reason, authority figures are often photographed in this manner. This dominance can also apply to objects—a palace, the top of a mountain. If an unattractive character is placed near the top of the screen, he or she can seem threatening and dangerous, superior to the other figures within the frame **(2–3)**. However, these generalizations are true only when the other figures are approximately the same size or smaller than the dominating figure.

The top of the frame is not always used in this symbolic manner. In some instances, this is simply the most sensible area to place an object. In a medium shot of a figure, for example, the person's head is logically going to be near the top of the screen, but obviously this kind of framing isn't meant to be symbolic. It's merely reasonable, since that's where we'd *expect* the head to appear in medium shots. Mise en scène is essentially an art of the long and extreme long shot, for when the subject matter is detailed in a closer shot, the director has fewer choices concerning the distribution of visual elements.

The areas near the bottom of the frame tend to suggest meanings opposite from the top: subservience, vulnerability, and powerlessness. Objects and figures placed in these positions seem to be in danger of slipping out of

2-9. *Tokyo Story* **(Japan, 1953),** *directed by Yasujiro Ozu.*
Ozu's mise en scène is usually formal, its compositional weights balanced with exquisite delicacy. Note how the diagonal thrust of the tree branches (in an image otherwise composed of stately verticals and horizontals) counteracts the weight of the three figures on the right. The scene is staged within a prosceniumlike enclosure—a frame within a frame—reinforcing its ceremonial dignity. Ozu exploits these formal compositions as ironic foils to the human materials: The intense emotions of the characters are often at odds with the decorum prescribed by such social rituals. "The Ozu scene is balanced, asymmetrical, pleasing to the eye; it is at the same time rigid and uncompromising, as all empty compositions are," Donald Richie has pointed out. "When the actor enters and behaves in a way contrary to the expectations created by such a formal decor, the result is an often touching spontaneity. This composition, then, exists but to be broken." *(New Yorker Films)*

the frame entirely. For this reason, these areas are often exploited symbolically to suggest danger. When there are two or more figures in the frame and they are approximately the same size, the figure nearer the bottom of the screen tends to be dominated by those above.

The left and right edges of the frame tend to suggest insignificance, because these are the areas farthest removed from the center of the screen. Objects and figures placed near the edges are literally close to the darkness outside the frame. Many directors use this darkness to suggest those symbolic ideas traditionally associated with the lack of light—the unknown, the unseen, and the fearful. In some instances, the blackness outside the frame can symbolize oblivion or even death. In movies about people who want to remain anonymous and unnoticed, the director sometimes deliberately places them off center, near the "insignificant" edges of the screen.

2–10. *Greed* **(U.S.A., 1924),** *with Gibson Gowland and Jean Hersholt, directed by Erich von Stroheim.*
Highly symmetrical designs are generally used when a director wishes to stress stability and harmony. In this photo, for example, the carefully balanced weights of the design reinforce these (temporary) qualities. The visual elements are neatly juxtaposed in units of twos, with the two beer-filled glasses forming the focal point. The main figures balance each other, as do the two converging brick walls, the two pairs of curtains, the two windows, the two people in each window, the shape of the picture above the men, and the shape of the resting dog below them. *(MGM)*

Finally, there are some instances when a director places the most important visual elements completely off frame. Especially when a character is associated with darkness, mystery, or death, this technique can be highly effective, for the audience is most fearful of what it can't see. In the early portions of Fritz Lang's *M*, for example, the psychotic child-killer is never seen directly. We can only sense his presence, for he lurks in the darkness outside the light of the frame. Occasionally, we catch a glimpse of his shadow streaking across the set, and we're aware of his presence by the eerie tune he whistles when he's emotionally excited or upset.

There are two other off-frame areas that can be exploited for symbolic purposes: the space behind the set and the space in front of the camera. By not showing us what is happening behind a closed door, the filmmaker can provoke the viewer's curiosity, creating an unsettling effect, for we tend to fill in

2–11. *Midnight Express* (U.S.A., 1978), *with Brad Davis (hands raised), directed by Alan Parker.*

All the compositional elements of this shot contribute to a sense of entrapment. The protagonist is totally surrounded, not only by the ring of soldiers who have their guns poised for a kill, but also by an outer ring of compositional weights—the airplane above, the stairs and railing to the left, the bench and huddled bystanders at the lower portions of the frame, and the three gunmen sealing off the right. The high angle and the gridlike lines of the concrete runway reinforce the sense of entrapment. The image might almost be entitled NO EXIT. *(Columbia Pictures)*

such vacuums with vivid imaginings. The final shot from Hitchcock's *Notorious* is a good example. The hero helps the drugged heroine past a group of Nazi agents to a waiting auto. The rather sympathetic villain (Claude Rains) escorts the two, hoping his colleagues won't become suspicious. In a **deep-focus long shot,** we see the three principals in the foreground while the Nazi agents remain near the open door of the house in the upper background—watching, wondering. The hero maliciously locks the villain out of the car, then drives out of frame, leaving the villain stranded without an explanation. His colleagues call out his name, and he is forced to return to the house, dreading the worst. He climbs the stairs and reenters the house with the suspicious agents, who then close the door behind them. Hitchcock never does show us what happens behind the door.

The area in front of the camera can also create unsettling effects of this sort. In John Huston's *The Maltese Falcon,* for example, we witness a murder

2–12. *Indiana Jones and the Last Crusade* (U.S.A., 1989), *with Alison Doody, Harrison Ford, and Sean Connery; directed by Steven Spielberg.*
Why is this shot funny? For one thing, the mise en scène is absurdly symmetrical. The Jones boys, father and son, have been reduced to the ignominy of parallel placement. Even their ropes are fastidiously parallel. They are imprisoned by the closed form: sealed off on the left by the fireplace and the standing woman, on the right by the table and chair. Their hats and ties are miraculously intact, even though they have been taken prisoners. The prissy neatness and balance of the mise en scène are symbolic of their total subjugation. But of course, you can't hold a good man down for long—not to speak of two good men. *(Paramount Pictures)*

without ever seeing the killer. The victim is photographed in a **medium shot** as a gun enters the frame just in front of the camera. Not until the end of the movie do we discover the identity of the off-frame killer.

Composition and Design

Although the photographable materials of movies exist in three dimensions, one of the primary problems facing the filmmaker is much like that confronting the painter: the arrangement of shapes, colors, lines, and textures on a flat rectangular surface. In the classical cinema, this arrangement is generally held in some kind of balance or harmonious equilibrium. The desire for balance is analogous to people balancing on their feet, and indeed to most manufactured structures, which are balanced on the surface of the earth. Instinctively, we assume that balance is the norm in most human enterprises.

In movies, however, there are some important exceptions to this rule. When a visual artist wishes to stress a *lack* of equilibrium, many of the standard conventions of **classical** composition are deliberately violated. In movies, the

2-13a. ***Once Were Warriors*** **(New Zealand, 1994),** *with Temuera Morrison and Rena Owen, directed by Lee Tamahori.* *(Fine Line Features)*

The movie frame is not an ornamental mounting for a self-contained image, as it is with a painting or a drawing. The cinematic frame segments and isolates the photographic fragment from its larger context, providing a subtle commentary on the subject matter. *Once Were Warriors* is a harrowing account of a wife batterer, and the frame in this shot suggests a symbolic prison, with the wife trapped in the same confined space with her volatile husband. Note how he dominates most of the playing space, while she is crowded to the right, literally up against the wall in fear. Similarly, the shot from *The End of August at the Hotel Ozone* is taken from behind an adult character as he nearly obliterates our view of a scared youngster. Compositions such as this would not be found in the fields of painting or live theater because the frame in those mediums is essentially a neutral surround of the subject matter. In movies, the frame (temporarily) presents us with a frozen moment of truth which will soon dissolve into another composition.

2-13b. ***The End of August at the Hotel Ozone*** **(Czechoslovakia, 1969),** *directed by Jan Schmidt.* *(New Line Cinema)*

dramatic context is usually the determining factor in composition. What is superficially a bad composition might actually be highly effective, depending on its psychological context. Many films are concerned with neurotic characters or events that are out of joint. In such cases, the director might well ignore the conventions of classical composition. Instead of centering a character in the image, his or her spiritual maladjustment can be conveyed symbolically by photographing the subject at the edge of the frame. In this manner, the filmmaker throws off the visual balance and presents us with an image that's psychologically more appropriate to the dramatic context **(1–33).**

There are no set rules about these matters. A classical filmmaker like Buster Keaton used mostly balanced compositions. Filmmakers outside the classical tradition tend to favor compositions that are asymmetrical or off center. In movies a variety of techniques can be used to convey the same ideas and emotions. Some filmmakers favor visual methods, others favor dialogue, still others editing or acting. Ultimately, whatever works is right **(2–14).**

The human eye automatically attempts to harmonize the formal elements of a composition into a unified whole. The eye can detect as many as seven or eight major elements of a composition simultaneously. In most cases, however, the eye doesn't wander promiscuously over the surface of an image but is guided to specific areas in sequence. The director accomplishes this through the use of a **dominant contrast,** also known as the **dominant.** The dominant is that area of an image that immediately attracts our attention because of a conspicuous and compelling contrast. It stands out in some kind of isolation from the other elements within the image. In black-and-white movies, the dominant contrast is generally achieved through a juxtaposition of lights and darks. For example, if the director wishes the viewer to look first at an actor's hand rather than his face, the lighting of the hand would be harsher than that of the face, which would be lit in a more subdued manner. In color films, the dominant is often achieved by having one color stand out from the others.

After we take in the dominant, our eye then scans the **subsidiary contrasts** that the artist has arranged to act as counterbalancing devices. Our eyes are seldom at rest with visual compositions, then, even with paintings or still photographs. We look somewhere first, then we look at those areas of diminishing interest. None of this is accidental, for visual artists deliberately structure their images so a specific sequence is followed. In short, movement in film isn't confined only to objects and people that are literally in motion.

In most cases, the visual interest of the dominant corresponds with the dramatic interest of the image. Because films have temporal and dramatic contexts, however, the dominant is often movement itself, and what some aestheticians call **intrinsic interest.** Intrinsic interest simply means that the audience, through the context of a story, knows that an object is more important dramatically than it appears to be visually. Thus, even though a gun might occupy only a small portion of the surface of an image, if we know that the gun is *dramatically* important, it will assume dominance in the picture despite its visual insignificance.

2–14a. *Macbeth* (U.S.A./Great Britain, 1971), *with Francesca Annis and Jon Finch, directed by Roman Polanski.*

Movie images are generally scanned in a structured sequence of eye-stops. The eye is first attracted to a dominant contrast that compels our most immediate attention by virtue of its conspicuousness, and then travels to the subsidiary areas of interest within the frame. In this photo, for example, the eye is initially attracted to the face of Lady Macbeth, which is lit in high contrast and is surrounded by darkness. We then scan the brightly lit "empty" space between her and her husband. The third area of interest is Macbeth's thoughtful face, which is lit in a more subdued manner. The visual interest of this photo corresponds to the dramatic context of the film, for Lady Macbeth is slowly descending into madness and feels spiritually alienated and isolated from her husband. *(Columbia Pictures)*

2–14b. *Macbeth* (U.S.A., 1948), *with Peggy Webber, directed by Orson Welles.*

Realists and formalists solve problems in different ways, with different visual techniques. Polanski's presentation of Lady Macbeth's madness is conveyed in a relatively realistic manner, with emphasis on acting and subtle lighting effects. Welles took a more formalistic approach, using physical correlatives to convey interior states, such as the iron fence's knifelike blades, which almost seem to pierce Webber's body. The fence is not particularly realistic or even functional: Welles exploited it primarily as a symbolic analogue of her inner torment. Neither approach is better or worse. It all depends on how well it's done. *(Republic Pictures)*

2–15. *The Decline of the American Empire* (Canada, 1986), *with (clockwise from upper left) Louise Portal, Dominique Michel, Dorothée Berryman, Geneviève Rioux; directed by Denys Arcand.*

A group of women work out, talk, and laugh in a health club while the men in their lives prepare a gourmet meal in an apartment. The circular design in this shot reinforces the air of camaraderie among the women. The shot's design embodies their shared experiences and interconnectedness: literally, a relaxed circle of friends. *(Cineplex Odeon Films)*

Movement is almost always an automatic dominant contrast, provided that the other elements in the image are stationary. Even a third-rate director can guide the viewer's eyes through the use of motion. For this reason, lazy filmmakers ignore the potential richness of their images and rely solely on movement as a means of capturing the viewer's attention. On the other hand, most directors will vary their dominants, sometimes emphasizing motion, other times using movement as a subsidiary contrast only. The importance of motion varies with the kind of shot used. Movement tends to be less distracting in the longer shots but highly conspicuous in the closer ranges.

Unless the viewer has time to explore the surface of an image at leisure, visual confusion can result when there are more than eight or nine major compositional elements. If visual confusion is the deliberate intention of an image—as in a battle scene, for example—the director will sometimes overload the composition to produce this effect **(2–22).** In general, the eye struggles to

2–16a. ***She's the One*** **(U.S.A., 1996),** *with Mike McGlone and Jennifer Aniston, directed by Edward Burns.* (Twentieth Century–Fox)

Parallelism is a common principle of design, implying similarity, unity, and mutual reinforcement. The composition of the shot from *She's the One* links the characters romantically. They're placed in parallel positions with similar gestures. Both are seated at a bar, with their chins resting against their left hands, both with slightly embarrassed, bemused expressions. The shot might almost be titled: Made for Each Other. Symmetrical parallelism is rarely found in nature: Usually the parallel elements betray a human hand, sometimes with deliberate comical effect, as in many of the shots of *Men in Black*.

2–16b. ***Men in Black*** **(U.S.A., 1996),** *with Tommy Lee Jones and Will Smith, directed by Barry Sonnenfeld.* (Columbia Pictures)

2–17. *Superman* (U.S.A./Great Britain, 1978), *with Glenn Ford, directed by Richard Donner.*

Because the top half of the frame tends to be intrinsically heavier than the bottom, directors usually keep their horizon well above the middle of the composition. They also place most of the visual weights in the lower portions of the screen. When a filmmaker wishes to emphasize the vulnerability of the characters, however, the horizon is often lowered, and sometimes the heaviest visual elements are placed above the characters. In this witty shot, for example, the parents of little Clark Kent are astonished—and visually imperiled—by the superhuman strength of their adopted son.

(Warner Bros.)

unify various elements into an ordered pattern. For example, even in a complex design, the eye will connect similar shapes, colors, textures, etc. The very repetition of a formal element can suggest the repetition of an experience. These connections form a visual rhythm, forcing the eye to leap over the surface of the design to perceive the overall balance. Visual artists often refer to compositional elements as *weights*. In most cases, especially in classical cinema, the artist distributes these weights harmoniously over the surface of the image. In a totally symmetrical design—almost never found in fiction movies—the visual weights are distributed evenly, with the center of the composition as the axis point. Because most compositions are asymmetrical, however, the weight of one element is counterpoised with another. A shape, for example, counteracts the weight of a color. Psychologists and art theorists have discovered that certain portions of a composition are intrinsically weighted. The German art historian Heinrich Wölfflin, for instance, pointed out that we tend to scan pictures from left to right, all other compositional elements being equal. Especially in classical compositions, the image is often more heavily weighted on the left to counteract the intrinsic heaviness of the right.

The upper part of the composition is heavier than the lower. For this reason, skyscrapers, columns, and obelisks taper upward or they would appear top-heavy. Images seem more balanced when the center of gravity is kept low, with most of the weights in the lower portions of the screen. A landscape is seldom divided horizontally at the midpoint of a composition, or the sky would

2–18. *Jules and Jim* (France, 1961), *with Henri Serre, Jeanne Moreau, and Oskar Werner; directed by François Truffaut.*

Compositions grouped into units of three, five, and seven tend to suggest dynamic, unstable relationships. Those organized in units of two, four, or six, on the other hand, tend to imply fixed, harmonious relationships. This triangular composition is organically related to the theme of the movie, which deals with the shifting love relationships between the three characters. The woman is almost invariably at the apex of the triangle: She likes it that way. *(Janus Films)*

appear to oppress the earth. Epic filmmakers like Eisenstein and Ford created some of their most disquieting effects with precisely this technique: They let the sky dominate through its intrinsic heaviness. The terrain and its inhabitants seem overwhelmed from above (see **1–9**).

Isolated figures and objects tend to be heavier than those in a cluster. Sometimes one object—merely by virtue of its isolation—can balance a whole group of otherwise equal objects. In many movies, the protagonist is shown apart from a hostile group, yet the two seem evenly matched despite the arithmetical differences. This effect is conveyed through the visual weight of the hero in isolation (**3–13**).

Psychological experiments have revealed that certain lines suggest directional movements. Although vertical and horizontal lines seem to be visually at rest, if movement *is* perceived, horizontal lines tend to move from left to right,

2–19. *The Graduate (U.S.A., 1967), with Anne Bancroft and Dustin Hoffman, directed by Mike Nichols.*

Viewers can be made to feel insecure or isolated when a hostile foreground element (Bancroft) comes between us and a figure we identify with. In this scene, our hero, Benjamin Braddock, college graduate, feels threatened. An older woman, a friend of his parents, tries to seduce him—he thinks. He's not sure. His feelings of entrapment and imminent violation are conveyed not by his words, which are stammering and embarrassed, but by the mise en scène. Blocked off in front by her seminude body, he is also virtually confined at his rear by the window frame—an enclosure within an enclosure (the room) within the enclosure of the movie frame. *(Avco Embassy Pictures)*

vertical lines, from bottom to top. Diagonal or oblique lines are more dynamic—that is, in transition. They tend to sweep upward. These psychological phenomena are important to the visual artist, especially the filmmaker, for the dramatic context is not always conducive to an overt expression of emotion. For example, if a director wishes to show a character's inward agitation within a calm context, this quality can be conveyed through the dynamic use of line: An image composed of tense diagonals can suggest the character's inner turmoil, despite the apparent lack of drama in the action. Some of the most expressive cinematic effects can be achieved precisely through this tension between the compositional elements of an image and its dramatic context **(2–21)**.

A skeletal structure underlies most visual compositions. Throughout the ages, artists have especially favored S and X shapes, triangular designs, and circles. These designs are often used simply because they are thought to be inherently beautiful. Visual artists also use certain compositional forms to

2-20. *The Grifters* (U.S.A., 1990), *with John Cusack and Anjelica Huston, directed by Stephen Frears.*

Every shot can be looked at as an ideological cell, its mise en scène a graphic illustration of the power relationships between the characters. Where the characters are placed within the frame is more than an aesthetic choice—it's profoundly territorial. In this film, the protagonist (Cusack) has an unresolved Oedipal conflict with his mother (Huston). They are in an almost constant struggle for dominance. The mise en scène reveals who's the stronger. In a predominantly light field, the darker figure dominates. The right side of the frame is heavier—more dominant—than the left. The standing figure towers over the seated figure. The top of the frame (Huston's realm) dominates the center and bottom. She's a killer. *(Miramax Films)*

emphasize symbolic concepts. For example, binary structures emphasize parallelism—virtually any two-shot will suggest the couple, doubles, shared space **(2–31).** Triadic compositions stress the dynamic interplay among three main elements. Circular compositions can suggest security, enclosure, the female principle **(2–15).**

Design is generally fused with a thematic idea, at least in the best movies. In *Jules and Jim,* for example, Truffaut consistently used triangular designs, for the film deals with a trio of characters whose relationships are constantly shifting yet always interrelated. The form of the images in this case is a symbolic representation of the romantic triangle of the dramatic content. These triangular designs dynamize the visuals, keeping them off balance, subject to change **(2–18).** Generally, designs consisting of units of three, five, and seven tend to produce these effects. Designs composed of two, four, or six units seem more stable and balanced **(2–10).**

2-21a. *The 400 Blows* (France, 1959), *with Jean-Pierre Léaud, directed by François Truffaut.*
The space between the main characters and the camera is usually kept clear so we can view the characters without impediment. But sometimes filmmakers deliberately obscure our view to make a dramatic or psychological point. The reckless young protagonist of *The 400 Blows* tries to act tough most of the time, and that usually means: Stay cool, and don't let them see you cry. When the dramatic context or the character's nature doesn't permit the film artist to express emotions openly, they can sometimes be conveyed through purely visual means. Here, the youth's anxiety and tenseness are expressed through a variety of formal techniques. His inward agitation is conveyed by the diagonal lines of the fence. His sense of entrapment is suggested by the tight framing (sides, top, bottom), the shallow focus (rear), and the obstruction of the fence itself (foreground). *(Janus Films)*

2-21b. *Gattaca* (U.S.A., 1997), *with Uma Thurman and Ethan Hawke, directed by Andrew Niccol.*
Similar techniques can be used even in less obviously dramatic scenes. For example, why do these two look scared and trapped? There are at least three reasons: 1) the dramatic context of the story, which leads us to believe they have good reason to feel paranoid; 2) the acting, which de-emphasizes the beauty of the performers in favor of expressing a deepening anxiety and increasing terror; and 3) the mise en scène, which confines them in a tight frame, pins them down in a high angle shot, and corners them in a dark alcove, with the shadow of an imprisoning cage superimposed over their pale features.
(Columbia Pictures)

Territorial Space

So far we've been concerned with the art of mise en scène primarily as it relates to the structuring of patterns on a two-dimensional surface. But since most movie images deal with the illusion of volume and depth, the film director must keep these spatial considerations in mind while composing the visuals.

2–22. *Big* (U.S.A., 1988), *with Jared Rushton and Tom Hanks, directed by Penny Marshall.* In shots emphasizing disorder or confusion, the film director sometimes deliberately over-loads the composition to produce a sense of visual chaos. In this photo, for example, the lines, shapes, and compositional weights form no discernible design. *(Twentieth Century–Fox)*

It's one thing to construct a pleasing arrangement of shapes, lines, colors, and textures; but movie images must also tell a story in time, a story that generally involves human beings and their problems. Unlike notes of music, then, forms in film are not usually pure—they refer specifically to objects in reality.

Directors generally emphasize volume in their images precisely because they wish to avoid an abstract, flat look in their compositions. In most cases, filmmakers compose on three visual planes: the foreground, the midground, and the background. Not only does this technique suggest a sense of depth, it can also radically alter the dominant contrast of an image, serving as a kind of qualifying characteristic, either subtle or conspicuous. For example, a figure is often placed in the midground of a composition. Whatever is placed in the foreground will comment on the figure in some way **(2–21).** Some foliage, for instance, is likely to suggest a naturalness and blending with nature. A gauzy curtain in the foreground can suggest mystery, eroticism, and femininity. The crosshatching of a window frame can suggest self-division. And so on, with as many foreground qualifiers as the director and cinematographer can think of. These same principles apply to backgrounds, although objects placed in these areas tend to yield in dominance to mid- and foreground ranges.

One of the most elementary, yet crucial, decisions the film director makes is what shot to use vis-à-vis the materials photographed. That is, how much detail should be included within the frame? How close should the camera get to the subject—which is another way of saying how close should *we* get to the subject, since the viewer's eye tends to identify with the camera's lens. These are not minor problems, for the amount of space included within the frame can radically affect our response to the photographed materials. With any given subject, the filmmaker can use a variety of shots, each of which includes or excludes a given amount of surrounding space. But how much space is just right in a shot? What's too much or too little?

Space is a medium of communication, and the way we respond to objects and people within a given area is a constant source of information in life as well as in the movies. In virtually any social situation, we receive and give off signals relating to our use of space and those people who share it. Most of us aren't particularly conscious of this medium, but we instinctively become alerted whenever we feel that certain social conventions about space are being violated. For example, when people enter a movie theater, they tend to seat themselves at appropriate intervals from each other. But what's appropriate? And who or what defines it? Why do we feel threatened when someone takes a seat next to us in a nearly empty theater? After all, the seat isn't ours, and the other person has paid for the privilege of sitting wherever he or she wishes. Is it paranoid to feel anxiety in such a situation, or is it a normal instinctive response?

2–23.   *The Godfather Part II* (U.S.A., 1974), *with Troy Donahue, Al Pacino, and Talia Shire; directed by Francis Ford Coppola.*
Backgrounds are rarely neutral territory, especially in shots that are in deep focus and in movies that are photographed on location. In this scene, a ne'er-do-well spoiled sister defies her authoritarian brother (Pacino) by insisting on marrying a sleazy lounge lizard, whom the brother scarcely deigns to acknowledge. The image is split in half, with the brother dominating his sister from the top right, even though he's in the background. The sleazoid is isolated on the left by the imprisoning curved fireplace from above and a correspondingly curved chair that keeps him distanced from his precious prey. Their touching hands is a brave gesture of solidarity, though far too feeble to withstand the brother's wrath. He will prevail, as usual.   *(Paramount Pictures)*

2–24a. *The Blue Angel* **(Germany, 1930),** *with Marlene Dietrich (left foreground), directed by Josef von Sternberg.* (Janus Films)

Density of texture refers to the amount of visual detail in a picture. How much information does the filmmaker pack into the image and why? Most movies are moderately textured, depending on the amount of light thrown on the subject matter. Some images are stark, whereas others are densely textured. The degree of density is often a symbolic analogue of the quality of life in the world of the film. The cheap cabaret setting of *The Blue Angel* is chaotic and packed, swirling in smoke and cluttered with tawdry ornaments. The atmosphere seems almost suffocating. The stark futuristic world of *THX 1138* is sterile, empty.

2–24b. *THX 1138* **(U.S.A., 1971),** *with Robert Duvall and Donald Pleasence, directed by George Lucas.* (Warner Bros.)

A number of psychologists and anthropologists—including Konrad Lorenz, Robert Sommers, and Edward T. Hall—have explored these and related questions. Their findings are especially revealing in terms of how space is used in cinema. In his study *On Aggression,* for example, Lorenz discusses how most animals—including humans—are territorial. That is, they lay claim to a given area and defend it from outsiders. This territory is a kind of personal haven of safety and is regarded by the organism as an extension of itself. When living creatures are too tightly packed into a given space, the result can be stress, tension, and anxiety. In many cases, when this territorial imperative is violated, the intrusion can provoke aggressive and violent behavior, and sometimes a battle for dominance ensues over control of the territory.

Territories have a spatial hierarchy of power. That is, the most dominant organism of a community is literally given more space, whereas the less dominant are crowded together. The amount of space an organism occupies is generally proportioned to the degree of control it enjoys within a given territory. These spatial principles can be seen in many human communities as well. A classroom, for example, is usually divided into a teaching area and a student seating area, but the proportion of space allotted to the authority figure is greater than that allotted to each of those being instructed. The spatial structure of virtually any kind of territory used by humans betrays a discernible concept of authority. No matter how egalitarian we like to think ourselves, most of us conform to these spatial conventions. When a distinguished person enters a crowded room, for example, most people instinctively make room for him or her. In fact, they're giving that person far more room than they themselves occupy.

But what has all this got to do with movies? A great deal, for space is one of the principal mediums of communication in film. The way that people are arranged in space can tell us a lot about their social and psychological relationships. In film, dominant characters are almost always given more space to occupy than others—unless the film deals with the loss of power or the social insignificance of a character. The amount of space taken up by a character in a movie doesn't necessarily relate to that person's actual social dominance, but to his or her dramatic importance. Authoritarian figures like kings generally occupy a larger amount of space than peasants; but if a film is primarily about peasants, they will dominate spatially. In short, dominance is defined contextually in film—not necessarily the way it's perceived in real life.

The movie frame is also a kind of territory, though a temporary one, existing only for the duration of the shot. The way space is shared within the frame is one of the major tools of the **metteur en scène,** who can define, adjust, and redefine human relationships by exploiting spatial conventions. Furthermore, once a relationship has been established, the director can go on to other matters simply by changing the camera **setup.** The film director, in other words, is not confined to a spatial area that's permanent throughout the scene. A master of mise en scène can express shifting psychological and social nuances with a single shot—by exploiting the space between characters, the

2-25a. *Grand Illusion* **(France, 1937),** *with (center to right) Erich von Stroheim, Pierre Fresnay, and Jean Gabin; directed by Jean Renoir.*
Tight and loose framing derive their symbolic significance from the dramatic context: They're not intrinsically meaningful. In Renoir's World War I masterpiece, for example, the tight frame, in effect, becomes a symbolic prison, a useful technique in films dealing with entrapment, confinement, or literal imprisonment. *(Janus Films)*

2-25b. *What's Love Got to Do With It* **(U.S.A., 1993),** *with Laurence Fishburne and Angela Bassett, directed by Brian Gibson.*
In this scene, the Fishburne character has just suffered a traumatic shock, and Bassett tries to comfort him by holding him close. The tightly framed shot provides nurturing intimacy: Moving the camera so close to the characters suggests a protective buffer against the hostile outside world. The tight framing doesn't confine, it cocoons the characters.
(©Touchstone Pictures. All Rights Reserved.)

2-26a, b, c.
The full front position is the most intimate type of staging; the most accessible, direct, and clear; and often the most aggressive, especially if the actors are moving toward the camera.

2-26a. *Sons of the Desert* **(U.S.A., 1933),** *with Stan Laurel and Oliver Hardy, directed by William Seiter.*
Actors almost never look at the camera, but there have been a few exceptions, especially among comic performers. Like Eddie Murphy in our own time, Oliver Hardy was a supreme master of this technique. Whenever Stan does something really dumb (which usually results in a loss of dignity for his partner), Ollie turns to the camera—to us—trying to restrain his exasperation, appealing to our sympathy as fellow superior beings. Only we can truly appreciate the profound depths of his patience. The dimwitted Stanley, totally puzzled as usual, is standing in a quarter-turn position, absorbed by other matters entirely, wondering how he'll defend himself against Ollie's inevitable another-fine-mess accusation. *(MGM)*

2-26b. *Leaving Las Vegas* **(U.S.A., 1996),** *with Nicolas Cage and Elizabeth Shue, directed by Mike Figgis.*
The full front position offers us an intimate view of the characters, especially in close-up: we can explore their faces as spiritual landscapes. In complex shots such as this, we are privy to more information than the characters themselves. The Cage character is too ashamed to look directly at his companion, and he recounts his sad story with his back turned to her. We are allowed an intimate view of his melancholy face as well as her compassionate expression as she listens. *(United Artists)*

2-26c. *Armageddon* **(U.S.A., 1999),** *with Bruce Willis (front and center), directed by Michael Bay.*
The full front position can also be confrontational, for the characters appear to face us straight on, without flinching. What could be more appropriate for a group of space warriors who are preparing to save the planet as we know it?

(Touchstone Pictures and Jerry Bruckheimer, Inc.)

2–27. *U-Turn (U.S.A., 1997), with Sean Penn and Jennifer Lopez, directed by Oliver Stone.*
The profile position catches characters unaware as they face each other or look off frame left or right. We're allowed unimpeded freedom to stare, to analyze. Less intimate than the full-front or quarter-turn position, the profile view is also less emotionally involving. We view the characters from a detached, neutral perspective. *(TriStar Pictures)*

depth planes within the images, the intrinsically weighted areas of the frame, and the direction the characters are facing vis-à-vis the camera.

An actor can be photographed in any of five basic positions, each conveying different psychological undertones: (1) *full front*—facing the camera; (2) the *quarter turn;* (3) *profile*—looking off frame left or right; (4) the *three-quarter turn;* and (5) *back to camera.* Because the viewer identifies with the camera's lens, the positioning of the actor vis-à-vis the camera will determine many of our reactions. The more we see of the actor's face, the greater our sense of privileged intimacy; the less we see, the more mysterious and inaccessible the actor will seem.

The full-front position is the most intimate—the character is looking in our direction, inviting our complicity. In most cases, of course, actors ignore the camera—ignore us—yet our privileged position allows us to observe them with their defenses down, their vulnerabilities exposed. On those rare occasions when a character acknowledges our presence by addressing the camera, the sense of intimacy is vastly increased, for in effect we agree to become his or her chosen confidants. One of the greatest masters of this technique was Oliver Hardy, whose famous slow burn was a direct plea for sympathy and understanding (**2–26a**).

The quarter turn is the favored position of most filmmakers, for it provides a high degree of intimacy but with less emotional involvement than the full-front position. The profile position is more remote. The character seems

73

unaware of being observed, lost in his or her own thoughts **(2–27).** The three-quarter turn is more anonymous. This position is useful for conveying a character's unfriendly or antisocial feelings, for in effect, the character is partially turning his or her back on us, rejecting our interest **(2–28).** When a character has his or her back to the camera, we can only guess what's taking place internally. This position is often used to suggest a character's alienation from the world. It is useful in conveying a sense of concealment, mystery. We want to see more **(2–29).**

The amount of open space within the territory of the frame can be exploited for symbolic purposes. Generally speaking, the closer the shot, the more confined the photographed figures appear to be. Such shots are usually referred to as **tightly framed.** Conversely, the longer, **loosely framed** shots tend

2–28.   *Night Moves* (U.S.A., 1975), *with Gene Hackman (extreme right, in three-quarter-turn position), directed by Arthur Penn.*
The three-quarter-turn position is a virtual rejection of the camera, a refusal to cooperate with our desire to see more. This type of staging tends to make us feel like voyeurs prying into the private affairs of the character, who seems to wish we'd go away. In this shot, Penn's mise en scène embodies a sense of alienation: Each character is imprisoned in his or her own space cubicle. They look buried alive.   *(Warner Bros.)*

2–29. *Red Desert* (Italy, 1964), *with Carlo Chionetti, Monica Vitti, and Richard Harris (back to camera); directed by Michelangelo Antonioni.*

When characters turn their backs to the camera, they seem to reject us outright or to be totally unaware of our existence. We long to see and analyze their facial expressions, but we're not permitted this privilege. The character remains an enigma. Antonioni is one of the supreme masters of mise en scène, expressing complex interrelationships with a minimum of dialogue. The protagonist in this film (Vitti) is just recovering from an emotional break-down. She is still anxious and fearful, even of her husband (Chionetti). In this shot, she seems trapped, like a wounded and exhausted animal, between her husband and his business associate. Note how the violent splashes of red paint on the walls suggest a hemorrhaging effect. *(Rizzoli Film)*

to suggest freedom. Prison films often use tightly framed **close-ups** and medium shots because the frame functions as a kind of symbolic prison. In *A Condemned Man Escapes,* for example, Robert Bresson begins the movie with a close-up of the hero's hands, which are bound by a pair of handcuffs. Throughout the film, the prisoner makes elaborate preparations to escape, and Bresson preserves the tight framing to emphasize the sense of claustrophobia that the hero finds unendurable. This spatial tension is not released until the end of the movie when the protagonist disappears into the freedom of the darkness outside the prison walls. His triumphant escape is photographed in a loosely framed long shot—the only one in the film—which also symbolizes his sense of spiritual release. Framing and spatial metaphors of this kind are common in films dealing with the theme of confinement—either literal, as in Renoir's *Grand Illusion* (**2–25a**), or psychological, as in *The Graduate* (**2–19**).

2–30. Publicity photo for *Much Ado About Nothing* (Great Britain, 1993), *with Michael Keaton, Keanu Reeves, Robert Sean Leonard, Kate Beckinsale, Emma Thompson, Kenneth Branagh, and Denzel Washington; directed by Branagh.*
Publicity photos often feature performers who look directly into the camera, inviting us to join their world, seducing us with their friendly smiles. Of course, during the movie itself, actors almost never look into the camera. We are merely allowed to be voyeurs while they studiously ignore our existence. *(The Samuel Goldwyn Company)*

Often a director can suggest ideas of entrapment by exploiting perfectly neutral objects and lines on the set. In such cases, the formal characteristics of these literal objects tend to close in on a figure, at least when viewed on the flat screen **(2–28).** Michelangelo Antonioni is a master of this technique. In *Red Desert,* for example, the heroine (Monica Vitti) describes a mental breakdown suffered by a friend she once knew. The audience suspects she's speaking of her own breakdown, however, for the surface of the image implies constriction: While she talks, she's riveted to one position, her figure framed by the lines of a doorway behind her, suggesting a coffinlike enclosure. When figures are framed within a frame in this manner, a sense of confinement is usually emphasized (see also **2–29).**

Territorial space within a frame can be manipulated with considerable psychological complexity. When a figure leaves the frame, for example, the camera can adjust to this sudden vacuum in the composition by **panning** slightly to make allowances for a new balance of weights. Or the camera can remain stationary, thus suggesting a sense of loss symbolized by the empty space that the character formerly occupied. Hostility and suspicion between two characters can be conveyed by keeping them at the edges of the composition, with a maximum of space between them **(2–31d)** or by having an intrusive character force his or her physical presence into the other character's territory, which is temporarily defined by the confines of the frame.

Proxemic Patterns

Spatial conventions vary from culture to culture, as anthropologist Edward T. Hall demonstrated in such studies as *The Hidden Dimension* and *The Silent Language*. Hall discovered that **proxemic patterns**—the relationships of organisms within a given space—can be influenced by external considerations. Climate, noise level, and the degree of light all tend to alter the space between individuals. People in Anglo-Saxon and Northern European cultures tend to use more space than those in warmer climates. Noise, danger, and lack of light tend to make people move closer together. Taking these cultural and contextual considerations into account, Hall subdivided the way people use space into four major proxemic patterns: **(1)** the *intimate,* **(2)** the *personal,* **(3)** the *social,* **(4)** the *public* distances.

Intimate distances range from skin contact to about eighteen inches away. This is the distance of physical involvement—of love, comfort, and tenderness between individuals. With strangers, such distances would be regarded as intrusive. Most people would react with suspicion and hostility if their space were invaded by someone they didn't know very well. In many cultures, maintaining an intimate distance in public is considered bad taste.

The personal distance ranges roughly from eighteen inches away to about four feet away. Individuals can touch if necessary, since they are literally an arm's-length apart. These distances tend to be reserved for friends and acquaintances rather than lovers or members of a family. Personal distances preserve the privacy between individuals, yet these ranges don't necessarily suggest exclusion, as intimate distances almost always do.

Social distances range from four feet to about twelve feet. These are the distances usually reserved for impersonal business and casual social gatherings. It's a friendly range in most cases, yet somewhat more formal than the personal distance. Ordinarily, social distances are necessary when there are more than three members of a group. In some cases, it would be considered rude for two individuals to preserve an intimate or personal distance within a social situation. Such behavior might be interpreted as standoffish.

2–31a. *Like Water for Chocolate* **(Mexico, 1992),** *with Lumi Cavazos and Marco Leonardi,* *directed by Alfonso Arau.* *(Miramax Films)*

2–31a, b, c, d.
Although each of these photos portrays a conversation between a man and a woman, each is staged at a different proxemic range, suggesting totally different undertones. The intimate proxemics of *Like Water for Chocolate* are charged with erotic energy: The characters are liter-ally flesh to flesh. In *Return to Paradise*, the characters are strongly attracted to each other,

2–31b. *Return to Paradise* **(U.S.A., 1998),** *with Vince Vaughn and Anne Heche, directed by* *Joseph Ruben.* *(Polygram Films)*

continued ▶

2–31c. *Your Friends & Neighbors* **(U.S.A., 1998),** *with Ben Stiller and Catherine Keener, directed by Neil LaBute.* *(Gramercy Pictures)*

2–31 continued

but they remain at a more discreet personal proxemic range, with each respecting the other's space. The characters in *Your Friends & Neighbors* are more wary, especially the woman, who seems to find her blowhard date extremely resistible. The characters in *Zabriskie Point* are barely on speaking terms. The social proxemic range between them implies a lot of suspicion and reserve. Psychologically, they're miles apart. Each of these shots contains similar subject matter, but the real content of each is defined by its form—in this case, the proxemic ranges between the actors.

2–31d. *Zabriskie Point* **(U.S.A., 1970),** *with Rod Taylor and Daria Halprin, directed by Michelangelo Antonioni.* *(MGM)*

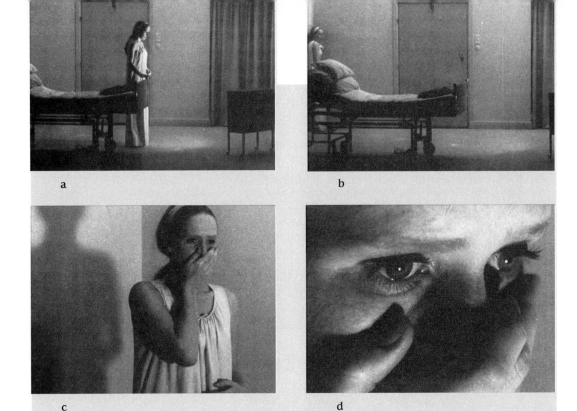

a

b

c

d

2–32. *Persona* **(Sweden, 1966),** *with Liv Ullmann, directed by Ingmar Bergman.*
Throughout this scene, which contains no dialogue, Bergman uses space to communicate his
ideas—space within the frame and the space implied between the camera (us) and the subject. The character is in a hospital room watching the news on television **(a).** Suddenly, she
sees a horrifying scene of a Buddhist monk setting himself on fire to protest the war in Vietnam. She retreats to the corner of the room, to the very edge of the frame **(b).** Bergman then
cuts to a closer shot **(c),** intensifying our emotional involvement. The full horror of her reaction is conveyed by the extreme close-up **(d),** bringing us into an intimate proximity with her.
(United Artists)

Public distances extend from twelve feet to twenty-five feet and more.
This range tends to be formal and rather detached. Displays of emotion are
considered bad form at these distances. Important public figures are generally
seen in the public range, and because a considerable amount of space is
involved, people generally must exaggerate their gestures and raise their voices
to be understood clearly.

Most people adjust to proxemic patterns instinctively. We don't usually
say to ourselves, "This person is invading my intimate space" when a stranger
happens to stand eighteen inches away from us. However, unless we're in a
combative mood, we involuntarily tend to step away in such circumstances.
Obviously, social context is also a determining factor in proxemic patterns. In a
crowded subway car, for example, virtually everyone is in an intimate range, yet
we generally preserve a public attitude by not speaking to the person whose
body is literally pressed against our own.

Proxemic patterns are perfectly obvious to anyone who has bothered to observe the way people obey certain spatial conventions in actual life. But in movies, these patterns are also related to the **shots** and their distance ranges. Although shots are not always defined by the literal space between the camera and the object photographed, in terms of psychological effect, shots tend to suggest physical distances.

Usually, filmmakers have a number of options concerning what kind of shot to use to convey the action of a scene. What determines their choice—though usually instinctively rather than consciously—is the emotional impact of the different proxemic ranges. Each proxemic pattern has an approximate camera equivalent. The intimate distances, for example, can be likened to the close and **extreme close shot** ranges. The personal distance is approximately a medium close range. The social distances correspond to the medium and **full shot** ranges. And the public distances are roughly within the long and **extreme long shot** ranges. Because our eyes identify with the camera's lens, in effect we are placed within these ranges vis-à-vis the subject matter. When we are offered a close-up of a character, for example, in a sense we feel that we're in an intimate relationship with that character. In some instances, this technique can bind us to the character, forcing us to care about him or her and to identify with his or her problems. If the character is a villain, the close-up can produce an emotional revulsion in us; in effect, a threatening character seems to be invading our space.

In general, the greater the distance between the camera and the subject, the more emotionally neutral we remain. Public proxemic ranges tend to encourage a certain detachment. Conversely, the closer we are to a character, the more we feel that we're in proximity with him or her and hence the greater our emotional involvement. "Long shot for comedy, close-up for tragedy" was one of Chaplin's most famous pronouncements. The proxemic principles are sound, for when we are close to an action—a person slipping on a banana peel, for example—it's seldom funny, because we are concerned for the person's safety. If we see the same event from a greater distance, however, it often strikes us as comical. Chaplin used close-ups sparingly for this very reason. As long as Charlie remains in long shots, we tend to be amused by his antics and absurd predicaments. In scenes of greater emotional impact, however, Chaplin resorted to closer shots, and their effect is often devastating on the audience. We suddenly realize that the situation we've been laughing at is no longer funny.

Perhaps the most famous instance of the power of Chaplin's close-ups is found at the conclusion of *City Lights*. Charlie has fallen in love with an impoverished flower vendor who is blind. She believes him to be an eccentric millionaire, and out of vanity he allows her to continue in this delusion. By engaging in a series of monumental labors—love has reduced him to work—he manages to scrape together enough money for her to receive an operation that will restore her sight. But he is dragged off to jail before she can scarcely thank him for the money. The final scene takes place several months later. The young woman can now see and owns her own modest flower shop. Charlie is released

2-33a. *The Gold Rush* (U.S.A., 1925), *with Charles Chaplin and Georgia Hale, directed by Chaplin.*

Both these scenes involve a fear of rejection by a woman Charlie holds in awe. The scene from *The Gold Rush* is predominantly comical. The tramp has belted his baggy pants with a piece of rope, but he doesn't realize it is also a dog's leash, and while dancing with the saloon girl, Charlie is yanked to the floor by the jittery dog at the other end of the rope. Because the camera remains relatively distant from the action, we tend to be more objective and detached and we laugh at his futile attempts to preserve his dignity. On the other hand, the famous final shot from *City Lights* isn't funny at all and produces a powerful emotional effect. Because the camera is in close, *we* get close to the situation. The proxemic distance between the camera and the subject forces us to identify more with his feelings, which we can't ignore at this range. *(rbc Films)*

2-33b. *City Lights* (U.S.A., 1931), *with Charles Chaplin, directed by Chaplin.*

from prison, and disheveled and dispirited, he meanders past her shop window. She sees him gazing at her wistfully and jokes to an assistant that she's apparently made a new conquest. Out of pity she goes out to the street and offers him a flower and a small coin. Instantly, she recognizes his touch. Hardly able to believe her eyes, she can only stammer, "You?" In a series of alternating close-ups, their embarrassment is unbearably prolonged **(2–33b).** Clearly, he is not the idol of her romantic fantasies, and he is painfully aware of her disappointment. Finally, he stares at her with an expression of shocking emotional nakedness. The film ends on this image of sublime vulnerability.

The choice of a shot is generally determined by practical considerations. Usually, the director selects the shot that most clearly conveys the dramatic action of a scene. If there is a conflict between the effect of certain proxemic ranges and the clarity needed to convey what's going on, most filmmakers will opt for clarity and gain their emotional impact through some other means. But there are many times when shot choice isn't necessarily determined by functional considerations.

Open and Closed Forms

The concepts of **open** and **closed forms** are generally used by art historians and critics, but these terms can also be useful in film analysis. Like most theoretical constructs, they are best used in a relative rather than absolute sense. There are no movies that are completely open or closed in form, only those that tend toward these polarities. Like other critical terms, these should be applied only when they are relevant and helpful in understanding what actually exists in a movie.

Open and closed forms are two distinct attitudes about reality. Each has its own stylistic and technical characteristics. The two terms are loosely related to the concepts of realism and formalism as they have been defined in these chapters. In general, realist filmmakers tend to use open forms, whereas formalists lean toward closed. Open forms tend to be stylistically recessive, whereas closed forms are generally self-conscious and conspicuous.

In terms of visual design, open form emphasizes informal, unobtrusive compositions. Often, such images seem to have no discernible structure and suggest a random form of organization. Objects and figures seem to have been found rather than deliberately arranged **(2–35).** Closed form emphasizes a more stylized design. Although such images can suggest a superficial realism, seldom do they have that accidental, discovered look that typifies open forms. Objects and figures are more precisely placed within the frame, and the balance of weights is elaborately worked out.

Open forms stress apparently simple techniques, because with these unself-conscious methods the filmmaker is able to emphasize the immediate, the familiar, the intimate aspects of reality. Sometimes such images are photographed in only partially controlled situations, and these **aleatory** conditions

2–34. *Mrs. Soffel* **(U.S.A., 1984),** *with Diane Keaton (center), directed by Gillian Armstrong.* Period films have a tendency to look stagey and researched, especially when the historical details are too neatly presented and the characters are posed in a tightly controlled setting. Armstrong avoided this pitfall by staging many of her scenes in open form, almost like a documentary caught on the run. Note how the main character (Keaton) and her children are almost obscured by the unimportant extra at the left. A more formal image would have eliminated such "distractions" as well as the cluttered right side of the frame and brought the principal characters toward the foreground. Armstrong achieves a more realistic and spontaneous effect by deliberately avoiding an "arranged" look in her mise en scène. *(MGM/United Artists)*

can produce a sense of spontaneity and directness that would be difficult to capture in a rigidly controlled context **(2–36).**

Closed forms are more likely to emphasize the unfamiliar. The images are rich in textural contrasts and compelling visual effects. Because the mise en scène is more precisely controlled and stylized, there is often a deliberate artificiality in these images—a sense of visual improbability, of being one remove from reality. Closed forms also tend to be more densely saturated with visual information; richness of form takes precedence over considerations of surface realism. If a conflict should arise, formal beauty is sacrificed for truth in open forms; in closed forms, on the other hand, literal truth is sacrificed for beauty.

Compositions in open and closed forms exploit the frame differently. In open-form images, the frame tends to be deemphasized. It suggests a window, a temporary masking, and implies that more important information lies outside the edges of the composition. Space is continuous in these shots, and to emphasize its continuity outside the frame, directors often favor panning their camera across the locale. The shot seems inadequate, too narrow in its confines to contain the copiousness of the subject matter. Like many of the paintings of Edgar Degas (who usually favored open forms), objects and even

2–35. *The Garden of the Finzi-Continis* (Italy, 1970), *with Dominique Sanda (center), directed by Vittorio De Sica.*
Realist directors are more likely to prefer open forms, which tend to suggest fragments of a larger external reality. Design and composition are generally informal. Influenced by the aesthetic of the documentary, open-form images seem to have been discovered rather than arranged. Excessive balance and calculated symmetry are avoided in favor of an intimate and spontaneous effect. Still photos in open form are seldom picturesque or obviously artful. Instead, they suggest a frozen instant of truth—a snapshot wrested from the fluctuations of time. This scene deals with the exportation of Italian Jews to Nazi Germany. Their lives are suddenly thrown into chaos.. *(Cinema 5)*

figures are arbitrarily cut off by the frame to reinforce the continuity of the subject matter beyond the formal edges of the composition.

In closed forms, the shot represents a miniature proscenium arch, with all the necessary information carefully structured within the confines of the frame. Space seems enclosed and self-contained rather than continuous. Elements outside the frame are irrelevant, at least in terms of the formal properties of the individual shot, which is isolated from its context in space and time **(2–37).**

For these reasons, still photos taken from movies that are predominantly in open form are not usually very pretty. There is nothing intrinsically striking or eye-catching about them. Books about movies tend to favor photos in closed form because they are usually more obviously beautiful, more "composed." The beauty of an open-form image, on the other hand, is more elusive. It can be likened to a snapshot that miraculously preserves some candid rare expression, a kind of haphazard instant of truth, a certain visual ambiguity.

In open-form movies, the dramatic action generally leads the camera. In such movies as *Faces* and *Husbands,* for example, John Cassavetes emphasized the fluidity of the camera as it dutifully follows the actors wherever they wish to

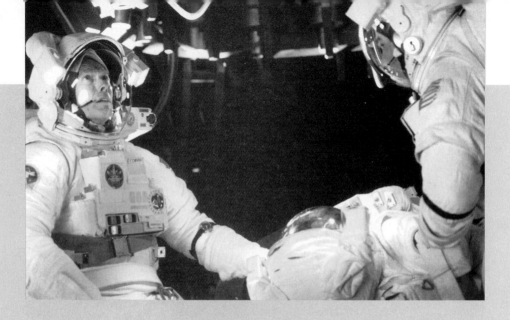

2-36. *Space Cowboys* **(U.S.A., 2000),** *with Clint Eastwood and Tommy Lee Jones; directed by Eastwood.*
This photo is in open form, but it's also tightly framed, allowing the characters very little room for movement. Open form always suggests an incomplete visual idea, with important information missing or cut off by the unaccommodating frame. Of course, *all* images have to be cut off somewhere, but in open-form images, the outer edges of the picture often seem inappropriately arbitrary, producing an unbalanced composition, as though the tumultuous sprawl of the subject matter was too uncontrolled to be packaged tidily. Often, such scenes are photographed with a **hand-held camera** to suggest a haphazard, impromptu recording.   *(Warner Bros.)*

go, seemingly placed at their disposal. Such films suggest that chance plays an important role in determining visual effects. Needless to say, it's not what actually happens on a set that's important, but what *seems* to be happening on the screen. In fact, many of the simplest effects in an open-form movie are achieved after much painstaking labor and manipulation.

In closed-form films, on the other hand, the camera often anticipates the dramatic action. Objects and actors are visually blocked out within the confines of a predetermined camera setup. **Anticipatory setups** tend to imply fatality or determinism, for in effect, the camera seems to know what will happen even before it occurs. In the films of Fritz Lang, for example, the camera often seems to be waiting in an empty room: The door opens, the characters enter, and the action then begins. In some of Hitchcock's movies, a character is seen at the edge of the composition, and the camera seems to be placed in a disadvantageous position, too far removed from where the action is apparently going to occur. But then the character decides to return to that area where the camera has been waiting. When such setups are used, the audience also tends to anticipate actions. Instinctively, we expect something or someone to fill in the visual vacuum of the shot. Philosophically, open forms tend to suggest freedom of choice, a multiplicity of options open to the characters. Closed forms, con-

2-37. *Another Country* **(Great Britain, 1984),** *with Rupert Everett (center doorway), directed by Marek Kanievska.*
In closed form, the frame is a self-sufficient miniature universe with all the formal elements held in careful balance. Though there may be more information outside the frame, for the duration of any given shot this information is visually irrelevant. Closed forms are often used in scenes dealing with entrapment or confinement, such as this shot in which the protagonist is about to be disciplined by his boarding school superiors. *(Orion Classics)*

versely, tend to imply destiny and the futility of the will: The characters don't seem to make the important decisions; the camera does—and in advance.

Open and closed forms are most effective in movies where these techniques are appropriate to the subject matter. A prison film using mostly open forms is not likely to be emotionally convincing. Most movies use both open and closed forms, depending on the specific dramatic context. Renoir's *Grand Illusion,* for example, uses closed forms for the prison camp scenes and open forms after two of the prisoners escape.

Like most cinematic techniques, open and closed forms have certain limitations as well as advantages. When used to excess, open forms can seem sloppy and naive, like an artless home movie. Too often, open forms can seem uncontrolled, unfocused, and even visually ugly. Occasionally, these techniques are so blandly unobtrusive that the visuals are boring. On the other hand, closed forms can seem arty and pretentious. The images are so unspontaneous that their visual elements look computer-programmed. Many viewers are turned off by the stiff formality of some closed-form films. At their worst, these movies can seem decadently overwrought—all icing and no cake.

A systematic mise en scène analysis of any given shot includes the following fifteen elements:

a

2–38. *Full Metal Jacket* **(Great Britain/U.S.A., 1987),** *directed by Stanley Kubrick.*
Even within a single scene, filmmakers will switch from open to closed forms, depending on
the feelings or ideas that are being stressed in each individual shot. For example, both of
these shots take place during a battle scene in the Vietnamese city of Hue. In **(a)**, the characters are under fire, and the wounded soldier's head is not even in the frame. The form is
appropriately open. The frame functions as a temporary masking device that's too narrow in
its scope to include all the relevant information. Often, the frame seems to cut figures off in
an arbitrary manner in open form, suggesting that the action is continued off screen, like
newsreel footage that was fortuitously photographed by a camera operator who was unable
to superimpose an artistic form on the runaway materials. In **(b)**, the form is closed, as four
soldiers rush to their wounded comrade, providing a protective buffer from the outside
world. Open and closed forms aren't intrinsically meaningful, then, but derive their significance from the dramatic context. In some cases, closed forms can suggest entrapment
(2–37); in other cases, such as **(b)**, closed form implies security, camaraderie.   *(Warner Bros.)*

b

1. *Dominant.* Where is our eye attracted first? Why?

2. *Lighting key.* High key? Low key? High contrast? Some combination of these?

3. *Shot and camera proxemics.* What type of shot? How far away is the camera from the action?

4. *Angle.* Are we (and the camera) looking up or down on the subject? Or is the camera neutral (eye level)?

5. *Color values.* What is the dominant color? Are there contrasting foils? Is there color symbolism?

6. *Lens/filter/stock.* How do these distort or comment on the photographed materials?

7. *Subsidiary contrasts.* What are the main eye-stops after taking in the dominant?

8. *Density.* How much visual information is packed into the image? Is the texture stark, moderate, or highly detailed?

9. *Composition.* How is the two-dimensional space segmented and organized? What is the underlying design?

10. *Form.* Open or closed? Does the image suggest a window that arbitrarily isolates a fragment of the scene? Or a proscenium arch, in which the visual elements are carefully arranged and held in balance?

11. *Framing.* Tight or loose? Do the characters have no room to move around, or can they move freely without impediments?

12. *Depth.* On how many planes is the image composed? Does the background or foreground comment in any way on the midground?

13. *Character placement.* What part of the framed space do the characters occupy? Center? Top? Bottom? Edges? Why?

14. *Staging positions.* Which way do the characters look vis-à-vis the camera?

15. *Character proxemics.* How much space is there between the characters?

These visual principles, with appropriate modifications, can be applied to any image analysis. Of course, while we're actually watching a movie, most of us don't have the time or inclination to explore all fifteen elements of mise en scène in each shot. Nonetheless, by applying these principles to a still photo, we can train our eyes to "read" a movie image with more critical sophistication.

For example, the image from *M* (**2–40**) is a good instance of how form (mise en scène) is actually content. The shot takes place near the end of the movie. A psychotic child-killer (Lorre) has been hunted down by the members of the underworld. These "normal" criminals have taken him to an abandoned warehouse where they intend to prosecute and execute the psychopath for his heinous crimes and in doing so take the police heat off themselves. In this scene, the killer is confronted by a witness (center) who holds an incriminating piece of evidence—a balloon. The components of the shot include the following:

2-39. Production photo from *Booty Call* (U.S.A., 1997), *with (front to rear) director Jeff Pollack and actor Jamie Foxx, co-producers John M. Eckert and John Morrissey, and (standing) actor Tommy Davidson.*

Many filmmakers insist on using a video assist monitor on their sets as a quick-check device before actually shooting a scene on film stock. Stock is more expensive and not nearly so immediate in terms of feedback. By photographing a scene with a video camera, the director can correct any problems in the staging and mise en scène. The actors can check to see if their performances are too subdued or too broad or too whatever. The cinematographer can preview the lighting and camerawork. And the producers can see if their money is going down the drain. When everyone is satisfied, they can then proceed to shoot the scene on movie stock. The video run-through is like a preliminary sketch for a finished painting or a dress rehearsal for a stage play. *(Columbia Pictures)*

1. *Dominant.* The balloon, the brightest object in the frame. When the photo is turned upside down and converted to a pattern of abstract shapes, its dominance is more readily discernible.

2. *Lighting key.* Murky low key, with high-contrast spotlights on the balloon and the four main figures.

3. *Shot and camera proxemics.* The shot is slightly more distant than a full shot. The camera proxemic range is social, perhaps about ten feet from the dominant.

4. *Angle.* Slightly high, suggesting an air of fatality.

5. *Color values.* The movie is in black and white.

6. *Lens/filter/stock.* A standard lens is used, with no apparent filter. Standard slow stock.

7. *Subsidiary contrasts.* The figures of the killer, the witness, and the two criminals in the upper left.

8. *Density.* The shot has a high degree of density, especially considering the shadowy lighting. Such details as the texture of the brick walls, the creases in the clothing, and the expressive faces of the actors are highlighted.

9. *Composition.* The image is divided into three general areas—left, center, and right—suggesting instability and tension.

10. *Form.* Definitely closed: The frame suggests a constricting cell, with no exit for the prisoner.

11. *Framing.* Tight: The killer is trapped in the same territory with his threatening accusors.

12. *Depth.* The image is composed on three depth planes: the two figures in the foreground, the two figures on the stairs in the midground, and the brick wall of the background.

13. *Character placement.* The accusers and balloon tower above the killer, sealing off any avenue of escape, while he cowers below at the extreme right edge, almost falling into the symbolic blackness outside the frame.

14. *Staging positions.* The accusers stand in a quarter-turn position, implying a greater intimacy with us than the main character, who is in the profile position, totally unaware of anything but his own terror.

15. *Character proxemics.* Proxemics are personal between the foreground characters, the killer's immediate problem, and intimate between the men on the stairs, who function as a double threat. The range between the two pairs is social.

Actually, a complete mise en scène analysis of a given shot is even more complex. Ordinarily, any **iconographical** elements, in addition to a costume and set analysis, are considered part of the mise en scène. But since these elements are discussed in Chapters 6 and 7, respectively, we confine ourselves only to these fifteen formal characteristics.

In these first two chapters, we've been concerned with the most important source of meaning in the movies—the visual image. But of course movies exist in time and have many other ways of communicating information. Photography and mise en scène are merely two language systems of many. For this rea-

2–40. *M* **(Germany, 1931),** *with Peter Lorre (extreme right), directed by Fritz Lang.* (Janus Films)

son, a film image must sometimes be restrained or less saturated with meanings than a painting or still photo, in which all the necessary information is contained within a single image. The principles of variation and restraint exist in all temporal arts. In movies, these principles can be seen in those images that seem rather uninteresting, usually because the dominant is found elsewhere—in the music, for example, or the **editing.** In a sense, these images are visual rest areas.

A filmmaker has literally hundreds of different ways to convey meanings. Like the painter or still photographer, the movie director can emphasize visual dominants. In a scene portraying violence, for example, he or she can use diagonal and zigzagging lines, aggressive colors, close-ups, extreme angles, harsh lighting contrasts, unbalanced compositions, large shapes, and so on. Unlike most other visual artists, the filmmaker can also suggest violence through movement, either of the subject itself, the camera, or both. The film artist can suggest violence through editing, by having one shot collide with another in a kaleidoscopic explosion of different perspectives. Furthermore, through the use of the soundtrack, violence can be conveyed by loud or rapid dialogue, harsh sound effects, or strident music. Precisely because there are so many ways to convey a given effect, the filmmaker will vary the emphasis, sometimes stressing image, sometimes movement, other times sound. Occasionally, especially in climactic scenes, all three are used at the same time.

FURTHER READING

ARNHEIM, RUDOLF, *Art and Visual Perception: A Psychology of the Creative Eye* (Berkeley: University of California Press, 1954). Primarily about paintings and drawings.

BORDWELL, DAVID, JANET STAIGER, and KRISTIN THOMPSON, *The Classical Hollywood Cinema: Film Style and Mode of Production to 1960* (New York: Columbia University Press, 1985). A fine scholarly study.

BRAUDY, LEO, *The World in a Frame* (Garden City, N.Y.: Doubleday, 1976). Filled with intelligent insights.

DONDIS, DONIS A., *A Primer of Visual Literacy* (Cambridge, Mass., and London, England: The M.I.T. Press, 1974). Primarily on design and composition.

DYER, RICHARD. *The Matter of Images* (London and New York: Routledge, 1993). The ideological implications of images.

FREEBURG, VICTOR O., *Pictorial Beauty on the Screen* (New York: Macmillan, 1923). A discussion of the conventions of classical composition.

HALL, EDWARD T., *The Hidden Dimension* (Garden City, N.Y.: Doubleday, 1969). How humans and other animals use space.

NILSEN, VLADIMIR, *The Cinema As a Graphic Art* (New York: Hill and Wang, 1959). How reality is shaped by form, with major emphasis on classical composition.

RUESCH, JURGEN, and WELDON KEES, *Nonverbal Communication* (Berkeley: University of California Press, 1966).

SOMMERS, ROBERT, *Personal Space* (Englewood Cliffs, N.J.: Prentice-Hall, 1969). How individuals use and abuse space.

Movement

Warner Bros.

The opening of a door, a hand, or an eye can bring about a climax as thrilling as a crash of locomotives on the screen.
—RICHARD DYER MACCANN

Overview

How movement can "mean." Different types of movement: realistic, pantomime, mime. Dance and choreography: the art of motion. The psychology of movement: lateral motions, left or right, up or down, toward or away from the camera? Movement in relation to the shots and angles. Movement and film genres: slapstick comedies, action films, dance movies, animation, and musicals. Movement as metaphor: kinetic symbolism. The moving camera: kineticizing space. Dolly shots versus editing: the implications of each. Stasis versus dynamism: tripods or tracks? The mercurial instability of the hand-held camera. Lyricism: cranes and other flying forms. Faux movement: zoom shots. Mechanical distortions of motion: animation, fast motion, slow motion, reverse motion, and freeze frames.

"Movies," "motion pictures," "moving pictures"—all these phrases suggest the central importance of motion in the art of film. Cinema derives from the Greek word for "movement," as do the words *kinetic, kinesthesia,* and *choreography*—terms usually associated with the art of dance. Yet oddly enough, filmgoers and critics give surprisingly little consideration to movement per se as a medium of communication, as a language system. Like the image itself, motion is usually

3–1.   Publicity photo of cinematographer Billy Bitzer, *perched in front of a moving railroad engine with his famous "Biograph camera," circa 1908.*
Almost from the inception of movies, innovative film artists like D. W. Griffith attempted to kineticize their images by moving the camera into the action or alongside it by mounting these bulky recording machines on various moving vehicles. Billy Bitzer, Griffith's gifted D.P., is regarded as the cinema's first great cinematographer.   *(Kino on Video)*

thought of in terms of gross subject matter. We tend to remember "what happens" only in a general sense. If we were to describe a sequence from a ballet in such vague terms, our discussion would certainly strike the sophisticated dance enthusiast as naive. Yet cinematic sequences—which can be choreographed with just as much or even greater complexity—are seldom appreciated for their kinetic richness and beauty.

Kinetics

Like images, motion can be literal and concrete or highly stylized and **lyrical.** In the kinetic arts—pantomime, ballet, modern dance—we find a wide variety of movements, ranging from the realistic to the formally abstract. This stylistic spectrum can also be seen in movies. For example, a naturalistic actor like Spencer Tracy used only realistic movements, the same sort that could be observed in actual life. Tracy moves so simply in his films that he hardly seems to be acting. Pantomimists are more stylized in their movements. Chaplin, for example, tended to use motion more balletically, more symbolically. A swaggering gait and a twirling cane symbolized Charlie's (usually fleeting) arrogance and conceit.

Even more stylized are the movements of performers in a musical. In this **genre,** characters express their most intense emotions through song and dance. A dance number is seldom meant to be taken literally: It's a stylized **convention** that we accept as a symbolic expression of certain feelings and ideas. In *Singin' in the Rain,* for example, Gene Kelly does an elaborate dance routine in a downpour. He twirls around lampposts, splashes through puddles like a happy idiot, and leaps ecstatically through a pelting rain—literally nothing can dampen the exhilaration of his love. A wide gamut of emotions is expressed in this sequence, with each kinetic variation symbolizing the character's feelings about his girl. She can make him feel dreamy, childlike, erotically stimulated, brave and forthright, dopey and moonstruck, and finally wild with joy. In some kinds of action genres, physical contests are stylized in a similar manner. Samurai and kung-fu films, for example, often feature elaborately choreographed sequences **(3–4).**

Ballet and mime are even more abstract and stylized. A great mime like Marcel Marceau was not so much concerned with expressing literal ideas (which is more properly the province of pantomime) as the *essence* of an idea, stripped of superfluities. A twisted torso can suggest an ancient tree, bent elbows its crooked branches, fluttering fingers the rippling of its leaves. In ballet, movements can be so stylized that we can't always assign a discernible content to them, though the narrative context generally provides us with at least a vague sense of what the movements are supposed to represent. On this level of abstraction, however, movements acquire self-justifying characteristics. They are **lyrical**: That is, we respond to them more for their own beauty than for their function as symbolic expressions of ideas.

3–2a. *Temptress Moon* (China/Hong Kong, 1997), *with Gong Li (white dress), directed by Chen Kaige.* *(Miramax Films)*

Stasis and motion—two different worldviews. The image from *Temptress Moon* portrays a static world of frozen possibilities, where women are expected to be subservient, silent, and still. The world of professional football portrayed in *Any Given Sunday* is a breathless blur of motion, where the whirling camera is hardly able to keep the (mostly male) characters in focus.

3–2b. *Any Given Sunday* (U.S.A., 1999), *with Al Pacino, directed by Oliver Stone.* *(Warner Bros.)*

The function of the choreographer is to translate feelings and ideas into movement, sometimes dreamlike and surreal, sometimes exquisitely lyrical, other times vibrantly energetic.

3–3a. *Oklahoma!* **(U.S.A., 1955),** *choreography by Agnes de Mille, directed by Fred Zinnemann.*
Though primarily a stage choreographer, Agnes de Mille revolutionized the American musical by introducing lengthy ballet sequences. Often these ballets developed the story and deepened the characterization. This famous "dream ballet," a faithful translation of her choreography for the landmark 1943 stage musical by Rodgers and Hammerstein, is a projection of the heroine's anxieties. Like many dreams, it combines concrete realistic details with symbolic stylizations into a surrealistic space that's both familiar and strange. Agnes de Mille exerted an enormous influence on film choreography, especially the work of Gene Kelly. *(Miramax Films)*

3–3b. *An American in Paris* **(U.S.A., 1951),** *with Gene Kelly and Leslie Caron, choreography by Kelly, score by George Gershwin, directed by Vincente Minnelli.*
Kelly worked in a broad range of dancing styles—tap, ballroom, modern, and ballet. He was usually at his best in muscular, gymnastic styles, with an emphasis on virile trajectories and bravura leaps. But he was also charming in nonchalant styles, to which he usually added a characteristic swagger. He often incorporated lengthy ballet sequences in his movies, generally a dream sequence or a fantasy. Kelly's dancing is sexy, with an emphasis on pelvic movements, tensed loins, twisting torsos, and close-to-the-floor gyrations. He usually wore close-fitting clothes to emphasize his well-muscled body. He also allowed his personality to shine through, breaking the formality of the choreography with a cocky grin or an ecstatic smile that's as hammy as it is irresistible. *(MGM)*

3–3c. *Seven Brides for Seven Brothers* **(U.S.A., 1954),** *with Jacques D'Amboise (flying aloft), choreography by Michael Kidd, directed by Stanley Donen.*
Unlike such important film choreographers as Busby Berkeley, Gene Kelly, and Bob Fosse, the versatile Michael Kidd had no signature style. He could work his magic in a variety of idioms. For example, his choreography in this classic musical is athletic and pumped up with testosterone. Kidd also choreographed the romantically ethereal "Dancing in the

Dark" number from *The Band Wagon*, with Fred Astaire and Cyd Charisse gliding lyrically through New York's Central Park like enraptured apparitions. It is one of the all-time great dance numbers in the history of movies. In 1997, Michael Kidd was given an honorary Academy Award for lifetime achievement in film choreography. *(MGM)*

a   b

c   d

3–4. *Enter the Dragon* (Hong Kong, 1973), *with Bruce Lee (dark trousers), directed by Robert Clouse.*

Physical contests such as brawls, sword fights, and Oriental self-defense methods can be choreographed with considerable kinetic grace. The kung-fu sequences staged by the legendary Bruce Lee are particularly stylized, almost like an acrobatic dance. *(Warner Bros.)*

    This concern with kinetic beauty for its own sake can be seen in certain schools of modern dance. Many of the choreographies of Merce Cunningham and Erick Hawkins, for example, aren't meant to symbolize anything of a narrative nature. Abstract motion is presented for its own sake, somewhat in the same manner that pure colors, shapes, and lines are offered for their own sakes in abstract painting. In movies, nonrepresentational movements are most often found in **avant-garde** films, which seldom tell stories.

    In dance, movements are defined by the space that encloses the choreography—a three-dimensional stage. In film, the **frame** performs a similar function. However, with each **setup** change, the cinematic "stage" is redefined. The intrinsic meanings associated with various portions of the frame are closely related to the significance of certain kinds of movements. For example, with vertical movements, an upward motion seems soaring and free because it conforms to the eye's natural tendency to move upward over a composition. Movements in this direction often suggest aspiration, joy, power, and authority—those ideas associated with the superior portions of the frame. Downward movements suggest opposite ideas: grief, death, insignificance, depression, weakness, and so on.

Because the eye tends to read a picture from left to right, physical movement in this direction seems psychologically natural, whereas movement from the right to left often seems inexplicably tense and uncomfortable. The sensitive filmmaker exploits these psychological phenomena to reinforce the dramatic ideas. Frequently the protagonists of a movie travel toward the right of the screen, whereas the villains move toward the left. In John Huston's *The Red Badge of Courage,* the hero moves from right to left when he runs away from a battle in fear. Later, when he courageously joins an infantry charge, his movements are from left to right.

Movement can be directed toward or away from the camera. Because we identify with the camera's lens, the effect of such movements is somewhat like a character moving toward or away from us. If the character is a villain, walking toward the camera can seem aggressive, hostile, and threatening, for in effect, he or she is invading our space. If the character is attractive, movement toward the camera seems friendly, inviting, sometimes seductive. In either case, movement toward the audience is generally strong and assertive, suggesting confidence on the part of the moving character (**3–31**).

Movement away from the camera tends to imply opposite meanings. Intensity is decreased and the character seems to grow remote as he or she withdraws from us. Audiences feel safer when villains move away in this man-

3-5. ***Shall We Dance?*** **(Japan, 1997),** *with Koji Yakusyo, directed by Masayuki Suo.* Dance as metaphor. This charming social comedy centers on a 42-year-old "sarariman" (salaryman) who secretly takes up ballroom dancing—a totally foreign concept in Japan where such a hobby would be considered weird. In a society that makes a fetish of social conformity, any act of individualism is likely to be viewed as ridiculous and laughable. "The nail that sticks out gets hammered down" is a proverb that virtually all Japanese schoolchildren learn when they're very young. Even as adults, they are intensely afraid of appearing different. Nonetheless, our accountant hero decides to take dancing lessons. He's so ashamed that he doesn't even tell his wife. Besides, they hardly speak anymore, though they're unfailingly polite. He feels that there's something pretentious about imitating "Western" oddities, something unmanly about wanting to be graceful. Most Japanese would agree that it's eccentric and showoffy to perform strange steps in front of other people. Yet his daily grind lacks excitement and romance. He is virtually a stranger to his family. And maybe—just once—he would like to stand out in a crowd. This shot embodies his double life: Above the desk, he's a conscientious accountant, but down below, he's practicing his dance steps. *(Miramax Films)*

3-6. *Godzilla* (U.S.A./Japan, 1998), *directed by Roland Emmerich.*
Movement in film is closely related to mise en scène. The top of the image is often associated with power and control, the bottom with vulnerability. In this special effects shot, a newsreel cameraman and city traffic are about to be flattened as Godzilla puts his foot down. People are totally impotent before the monster's overwhelming force. *(Toho Co. Ltd./TriStar Pictures)*

ner, for they thereby increase the protective distance between us and them. In some contexts, such movements can seem weak, fearful, and suspicious. Most movies end with a withdrawal of some sort, either of the camera from the locale or of the characters from the camera.

There are considerable psychological differences between lateral movements on the screen and depth movements—that is, movements toward or away from the camera. A script might simply call for a character to move from one place to another, but *how* the director chooses to photograph this movement will determine much of its psychological implications. Generally speaking, if the character moves from right to left (or vice versa), he or she will seem determined and efficient, a person of action. Unless the camera is at **extreme long shot** range, these movements are necessarily photographed in brief **takes**—shots lasting only a few seconds. Lateral movements tend to emphasize speed and efficiency, so they are often used in action movies.

On the other hand, when a character moves in or out of the depth of a scene, the effect is often one of slowness. Unless the camera is at close range or an extreme **wide-angle lens** is used, movements toward or away from the camera take longer to photograph than lateral movements. With a **telephoto lens,** such movements can seem hopelessly dragged out. Furthermore, when depth movement is photographed in an uninterrupted lengthy take, the audience tends to anticipate the conclusion of the movement, thus intensifying the sense of tedium while we wait for the character to arrive at his or her destination. Especially when a character's physical goal is apparent—the length of a long corridor, for example—audiences generally grow restless if they are forced to view the entire movement **(3–7)**.

Most classical filmmakers would photograph the action in several different setups, thus compressing the time and space from the inception of the movement to its conclusion. Classical filmmakers also tend to stage movement diagonally, to create a more dynamic trajectory of motion.

The distance and **angle** from which movement is photographed determine much of its meaning. In general, the longer and higher the shot, the slower the movement tends to appear. If movement is recorded from close and low angles, it seems more intense, speeded up. A director can photograph the same subject—a running man, for example—in two different setups and produce opposite meanings. If the man is photographed in an extreme long shot from a high angle, he will seem ineffectual and impotent. If he's photographed from a low angle in a **medium shot,** he will seem a dynamo of energy. Although the subject matter in each setup is absolutely identical, the true content of each shot is its form.

Even film critics (who should know better) are often ignorant of these perceptual differences, thinking of movement only in terms of story and gross physical action. The result has been a good deal of naive theorizing on what is "intrinsically cinematic." The more movement is perceived as extravagant in real life, they argue, the more "filmic" it becomes. **Epic** events and exterior locations are presumed to be fundamentally more suited to the medium than intimate, restricted, or interior subjects. Such views are based on a misunderstanding of movement in film. True, one can use the terms *epic* and *psychological* in describing the general emphasis of a movie. Even on this general level, however, arguments about intrinsically cinematic subjects are usually crude. No sensible person would claim that Tolstoy's *War and Peace* is intrinsically more novelistic than Dostoyevsky's *Crime and Punishment,* although we may refer to one as an epic and the other as a psychological novel. In a similar vein, only a naive viewer would claim that Michelangelo's *Sistine Ceiling* is intrinsically more visual than a Vermeer painting of a domestic scene. It is different, yes, but not necessarily better or worse, and certainly not through any intrinsic quality. In short, there are some good and bad epic works of art, and some good and bad psychological works. It's the treatment that counts, not the material per se.

Movement in film is a subtle issue, for it's necessarily dependent on the kind of shot used. The cinematic close-up can convey as much movement as the most sweeping vistas in an extreme long shot. In fact, in terms of the area covered on the screen's surface, there is actually more movement in a close-up showing tears running down a person's face than there is in an extreme long shot of a parachutist drifting fifty feet **(3–8)**.

Epic and psychological movies use movement in different ways, with emphasis on different shots. Epic movies usually depend on the longer shots

3-7 a & b. *L'Avventura* **(Italy, 1960),** *with Monica Vitti, directed by Michelangelo Antonioni.*

Psychological films often use movements in and out of the depth of an image, especially to create a sense of tediousness and exhaustion. Shots of this sort require **anticipatory setups** that reinforce these qualities, for we see the destination of a character's movement long before it's completed. Here, the heroine's search for her lover in the corridors of a hotel suggests the futility of her love affair. The endless succession of doors, fixtures, and hallways implies, among other things, the repetition of the frustration she is now experiencing. Much of the meaning of shots such as these lies in their duration: Space is used to suggest time. Needless to say, Antonioni's movies are among the slowest paced of the contemporary cinema: Long after the viewer has had time to absorb the visual information of a shot, it continues on the screen. When this film was originally shown at the Cannes Film Festival, an audience of hostile critics kept shouting "Cut! Cut!" at the screen. The shots were so lengthy and the pace so slow that viewers assumed the director was inept at editing. But like many of Antonioni's works, *L'Avventura* is about spiritual erosion, and the movie's slow rhythm is organically related to this theme. *(Janus Films)*

3–8a. *The Stunt Man* (U.S.A., 1980), *directed by Richard Rush.* (Twentieth Century-Fox)

3–8b. *The Wild Child* (France, 1969), *with Jean-Pierre Cargol, directed by François Truffaut.* (United Artists)

Unlike movement in dance or the live theater, cinematic movement is always relative. Only gross movements are likely to be perceived in an extreme long shot, whereas the flicker of an eye can rivet our attention in a close-up. In these photos, for example, the path of the boy's tear covers more screen space than the pilot's fall from the sky.

for their effects, whereas psychological films tend to use the closer shots. Epics are concerned with a sense of sweep and breadth, psychological movies with depth and detail. Epics often emphasize events, psychological films the implications of events. One stresses action, the other reaction.

Two filmmakers can approach the same story and produce totally different results. *Hamlet* is a good example. Laurence Olivier's film version of this play is essentially an epic, with emphasis on the longer shots. Franco Zeffirelli's version is primarily a psychological study, dominated by close and medium shots. Olivier's movie emphasizes setting. There are many **long shots,** especially of the brooding castle of Elsinore. Much is made of Hamlet's interaction with this moody locale. We are informed at the beginning of the film that the story is about "a man who could not make up his mind." The long shots are used to emphasize this interpretation visually. Most of them are **loosely framed,** suggesting that Hamlet (played by Olivier) has considerable freedom of movement, freedom to act. But he refuses to use this freedom, preferring to sulk in dark corners, paralyzed with indecision. When he does move, the motion is generally recorded from long distances, thus reinforcing the impotence of the protagonist in relationship to his environment.

Zeffirelli's *Hamlet* (with Mel Gibson) is usually photographed in **tightly framed** close and medium shots. Unlike Olivier's indecisive Hamlet, Gibson's is impulsive and rash, a man who often acts before he thinks. Imprisoned by the confining close shots, the tortured hero virtually spills off the edges of the frame into oblivion. The unstable hand-held camera can barely keep up with him as he lunges hyperkinetically from place to place. If the same movements were photographed from a long-shot range, of course, the character would seem to move more normally.

In the live theater, these two interpretations would have to be achieved through other means. Although the drama is in part a visual medium, the "frame" size (the confines of the set or the proscenium arch) remains the same for the duration of the play. The live theater, in short, is restricted to "long shots," where such distortions of movement are virtually impossible.

If there is a great deal of movement in the closer shots, its effect on the screen will be exaggerated. For this reason, filmmakers tend to use these ranges for relatively static scenes. The animation of two people talking and gesturing, for example, has enough movement to prevent most medium shots from appearing static.

Close-ups are even more subtle in their recording of movement. Robert Bresson and Carl Dreyer often highlighted subtle movements by photographing an expressive face in close-up. In fact, these two filmmakers referred to the human face as a spiritual "landscape." In Dreyer's *Passion of Joan of Arc,* for instance, one of the most powerful scenes is a close shot of Joan as a tear slowly trickles down her face. Expanded thousands of times by the close-up, the path of the tear represents a cataclysmic movement on the screen, far more powerful than the inane cavalry charges and clashing armies of routine epic films.

Hackneyed techniques are almost invariably the sign of a second-rate filmmaker. Certain emotions and ideas—like joy, love, hatred—are so prevalent in the cinema that serious artists are constantly searching for new methods of presentation, methods that transform the familiar into something fresh and unexpected. For example, death scenes are common in movies. But because of their frequency, they are often presented tritely. Of course, death remains a universal concern, one that can still move audiences if handled with any degree of originality and imagination.

3–9. *Hamlet* **(U.S.A./Great Britain/Italy, 1990),** *with Glenn Close and Mel Gibson, directed by Franco Zeffirelli.*
When the camera is close to the action, as in this photo, even small gestures seem magnified and highly kinetic. Gibson's portrayal of Shakespeare's tragic hero is volatile, exploding with energy—a far cry from the contemplative and indecisive Hamlet made famous in Laurence Olivier's 1948 film version of the play. *(Icon Distribution, Inc.)*

One method of avoiding staleness is to convey emotions through kinetic symbolism. Like the choreographer, the filmmaker can exploit the meanings inherent in certain types of movements. Even so-called abstract motions tend to suggest ideas and feelings. Some movements strike us as soft and yielding, for example, whereas others seem harsh and aggressive. Curved and swaying motions are generally graceful and feminine. Those that are straight and direct strike us as intense, stimulating, and powerful. Further-more, unlike the choreographer, the filmmaker can exploit these symbolic movements even without having people perform them.

If a dancer were to convey a sense of grief at the loss of a loved one, his or her movements would probably be implosive, withdrawn, with an emphasis on slow, solemn, downward movements. A film director might use this same kinetic principle but in a totally different physical context. For instance, in Wal-ter Lang's *The King and I,* we realize that the seriously ailing king (Yul Brynner) has died when we see a close-up of his hand slowly slipping toward the bottom of the frame, disappearing finally off the lower edge into darkness.

In Eisenstein's *Old and New* (also known as *The General Line*), a valuable stud bull dies, and its death has disastrous consequences for the agricultural commune that has purchased the animal. These consequences are expressed through two parallel shots emphasizing the same kinetic symbolism. First, Eisenstein shows us an **extreme close-up** of the dying bull's eye as it slowly

3–10. *Top Hat* **(U.S.A., 1935),** *with Ginger Rogers and Fred Astaire, choreography by Astaire and Hermes Pan, directed by Mark Sandrich.*

Astaire's dancing style is the epitome of cool—elegant, debonair, effortless. He influenced such classical choreographers as Jerome Robbins and George Balanchine, and such dancers as Rudolf Nureyev, who described Astaire as "the greatest dancer in American history." His range was extraordinarily broad, encompassing the wit and speed of tap, the airy romanticism of ballroom styles, and later in his career, the ethereal lyricism of modern dance. He insisted on artistic control over his dance numbers. A perfectionist, he also insisted on a six-week rehearsal period before production began. In his nine RKO musicals, he and Hermes Pan worked out the choreography, then taught the steps to Ginger Rogers, who usually came in shortly before production. The camera is essentially functional: It records the movements of the dancers in lengthy takes, at full-shot range, panning and tilting after them as unobtrusively as possible. Their dance numbers are actually love scenes: He woos his lady kinetically. In fact, they rarely even kiss on screen. She is usually reluctant, cool to his verbal advances, but once the music begins, their bodies undulate and sway in rhythmic syncopation, and soon she's a lost creature, yielding completely to her kinesthetic destiny. *(RKO)*

3–11. *Two Tars* (U.S.A., 1928), *with Oliver Hardy and Stan Laurel (in sailor suits), directed by James Parrott.*
The comedy of Laurel and Hardy—like that of most slapstick comedians—is quintessentially kinetic. They were unrivaled in their ability to swell a tiny gesture into an apocalyptic orgy of destruction. Their comedies are filled with rituals of revenge and slow escalations of hostility, snowballing finally into total mass demolition—a story formula they used many times with brilliant results. *(MGM)*

closes. The mournful lowering of the eyelid is magnified many times by the closeness of the shot. Eisenstein then cuts to a shot of the sun lowering on the horizon, its streaming shafts of light slowly retracting as the sun sinks below the earth's rim. Trivial as a bull's death might seem, to the hardworking members of the commune it suggests an almost cosmic significance. Their hopes for a better future die with the animal.

Of course, context is everything in movies. The kind of symbolism in *Old and New* would probably seem pretentious and arty in a more realistic movie. However, the same kinetic *principle* can be used in almost any kind of context. In Mel Gibson's *Braveheart*, for example, the beheading of the rebel hero (played by Gibson) exploits downward movements in several ways. As the executioner's ax sweeps down toward the hero's neck, we see a close-up of Princess Isabelle, a tear slowly rolling down her face. Just as the ax strikes the hero's neck, we see a handkerchief (a memento of his dead wife's love) fall from his hand to the ground in slow motion—a poetic symbol of his release from life.

In Charles Vidor's *Ladies in Retirement*, these same kinetic principles are used in a totally different context. An impoverished housekeeper (Ida Lupino) has asked her aging employer for financial assistance to prevent the housekeeper's two retarded sisters from being put away in an asylum. The employer, a vain, selfish woman who acquired her wealth as the mistress of a rich man, refuses to help her employee. As a last resort, the desperate housekeeper decides to kill the old woman and use her isolated cottage as a refuge for the good-naturedly dotty sisters. The murder scene itself is conveyed through

3–12. *Frantic (U.S.A., 1988), with Harrison Ford, directed by Roman Polanski.*
Filmmakers often exploit "negative space" to anticipate action that has not yet occurred. In this photo, for example, the anticipatory camera seems to be waiting for something to fill in the empty space on the right. The unsuspecting protagonist does not know that he will soon be threatened by a careening auto that will almost run him down. But we have already been forewarned of the impending action by Polanski's framing. Anticipatory setups like these are especially common in thrillers. They are a kind of warning to the viewer to be prepared: Art as well as nature abhors a vacuum. *(Warner Bros.)*

kinetic symbolism. We see the overdressed dowager playing a ditty at her piano. The housekeeper, who plans to strangle the woman from behind, slowly creeps up while she is singing. But instead of showing us the actual strangulation, Vidor cuts to a medium close shot of the floor, where, one by one, the dowager's pearls drop to the floor. Suddenly, a whole clump of pearls splatters near the old lady's now motionless feet. The symbolism of the dropping pearls is appropriate to the context, for they embody not only the woman's superfluous wealth, but her vanity and selfishness as well. Each falling pearl suggests an elegantly encrusted drop of blood: Drop by drop, her life ebbs away, until the remaining strands of pearls crash to the floor and the wretched creature is dead. By conveying the murder through this kinetic symbolism, Vidor prevents us from witnessing the brutal event, which probably would have lost the audience's sympathy for the housekeeper.

In each of these instances, the filmmakers—Lang, Eisenstein, Gibson, and Vidor—were faced with a similar problem: how to present a death scene with freshness and originality. Each director solved the problem by exploiting similar movements: a slow, contracting, downward motion—the same kind of movement that a dancer would use literally on a stage.

Kinetic symbolism can be used to suggest other ideas and emotions as well. For example, ecstasy and joy are often expressed by expansive motions,

3–13. *Yojimbo* (Japan, 1961), *directed by Akira Kurosawa.*

Kurosawa's movies are rich in symbolic kinetic techniques. He often creates dramatic tensions by juxtaposing static visual elements with a small but dynamic whirlpool of motion. In this scene, for example, the greatly outnumbered protagonist (Toshiro Mifune) prepares to do battle with a group of vicious hoodlums. In static visual terms, the samurai hero seems trapped by the enclosing walls and the human wall of thugs that blocks off his space. But surrounding the protagonist is a furiously whipping wind (the dominant contrast of the shot), which symbolizes his rage and physical power. *(Janus Films)*

3-14. *The French Connection* (U.S.A., 1971), *directed by William Friedkin.*

Expansive outward movements and sunburst effects are generally associated with explosive emotions, like joy or terror. In this shot, however, the symbolism is more complex. The scene occurs at the climax of a furious chase sequence in which the protagonist (Gene Hackman, with gun) finally triumphs over a vicious killer by shooting him—just as he seems on the verge of eluding the dogged police officer once again. This kinetic outburst on the screen symbolizes not only the bullet exploding in the victim's body, but a joyous climax for the protagonist after his humiliating and dangerous pursuit. The kinetic "ecstasy of death" also releases the dramatic tension that has built up in the audience during the chase sequence: In effect, we are seduced into sharing the protagonist's joy in the kill. *(Twentieth Century-Fox)*

fear by a variety of tentative or trembling movements. Eroticism can be conveyed through the use of undulating motions. In Kurosawa's *Rashomon,* for example, the provocative sexuality of a woman is suggested by the sinuous motions of her silk veil—a movement so graceful and tantalizing that the protagonist (Toshiro Mifune) is unable to resist her erotic allure. Since most Japanese viewers regard overt sexuality in the cinema as tasteless—even kissing is rare in their movies—sexual ideas are often expressed through these symbolic methods.

Every art form has its rebels, and cinema is no exception. Because movement is almost universally regarded as basic to film art, a number of directors have experimented with the idea of stasis. In effect, these filmmakers are

3–15a & b.   *Highlander III: The Sourcerer* (U.S.A., 1995), *with Mario Van Peebles and Christopher Lambert, directed by Andy Morahan.*

The closer and tighter the shot, the more motion dominates. In longer, more loosely framed shots, movement tends to recede in importance, usually in direct proportion to the distance of the kinetic action from the camera. Even the slightest alterations in framing can affect our reactions. The two shots portrayed here imply subtle differences. In the more loosely framed long shot **(a),** the protagonist (Lambert) is dominated by his enemy, who controls the left, top, and right sides of the mise en scène. The protagonist, who can barely move, is squeezed into the lower right corner of the screen—the most vulnerable position. The villain's control over his adversary is reinforced by the amount of space allowed for his movements. By allowing more space and distance, the director is able to present the fight with a greater degree of stylization and objectivity. The control of the visual elements within the frame becomes a spatial metaphor for the villain's (temporary) control over the hero. In the more desperate, tightly framed medium shot **(b),** the protagonist is regaining control. He dominates nearly two-thirds of the space within the frame, and the villain has his back against the wall. We know who's winning in each of these shots by seeing how much movement the characters can command within the confines of the frame. *(Dimension Films)*

a

b

deliberately working against the nature of their medium, stripping it of all but the most essential motions. Such filmmakers as Bresson, Ozu, and Dreyer have been described as **minimalists** because their kinetic techniques are so austere and restrained. When virtually nothing seems to be moving in an image, even the slightest motion can take on enormous significance. In many cases, this stasis is exploited for symbolic purposes: Lack of motion can suggest spiritual or psychological paralysis, as in the movies of Antonioni, for example.

The Moving Camera

Before the 1920s, filmmakers tended to confine movements to the subject photographed. There were relatively few who moved their cameras during a shot, and then usually to keep a moving figure within the frame. In the 1920s, such German filmmakers as F. W. Murnau and E. A. Dupont moved the camera within the shot not only for physical reasons but for psychological and thematic reasons as well. The German experiments permitted subsequent filmmakers to use the mobile camera to communicate subtleties previously considered impossible. True, **editing**—that is, moving the camera *between* shots—is faster, cheaper, and less distracting. But cutting is also abrupt, disconnected, and unpredictable compared to the fluid lyricism of a moving camera.

A major problem of the moving camera involves time. Films that use this technique extensively tend to seem slow-moving, since moving in or out of

3–16.   *Circle of Friends* (Ireland, 1994), *with Minnie Driver and Chris O'Donnell, directed by Pat O'Connor.*
Movement is not always an automatic dominant. In this scene, for example, unimportant characters dance in and out of the frame, occasionally obscuring our view of the two central characters, who are not moving much as they dance and talk. Note how O'Connor shoots the scene with a telephoto lens, with the romantic couple in focus and the other dancers blurred into an undulating sea of irrelevance. What matters for these two is here and now in each other's arms. The rest of the world seems very far away.   *(Savoy Pictures)*

3–17. *Forrest Gump* (U.S.A., 1994), *with Tom Hanks, directed by Robert Zemeckis.*
Reverse dolly shots such as this are more unsettling than conventional traveling shots. When we dolly *into* a scene, we can usually see where we're headed, to a geographical goal of some sort. But when the camera moves in reverse, sweeping backwards as it keeps the running protagonist in frame, we have no sense of a final destination, just the urgent, desperate need to flee. *(Paramount Pictures)*

a scene is more time-consuming than a straight cut. A director must decide whether moving the camera is worth the film time involved and whether the movement warrants the additional technical and budgetary complications. If a filmmaker decides to move the camera, he or she must then decide how. Should it be mounted on a vehicle or simply moved around the axis of a stationary tripod? Each major type of camera movement implies different meanings, some obvious, others subtle. There are seven basic moving camera shots: **(1) pans, (2) tilts, (3) crane shots, (4) dolly shots, (5) zoom shots, (6) hand-held shots,** and **(7) aerial shots.**

Panning shots—those movements of the camera that scan a scene horizontally—are taken from a stationary axis point, with the camera mounted on a tripod. Such shots are time-consuming because the camera's movement must ordinarily be smooth and slow to permit the images to be recorded clearly. Pans are also unnatural in a sense, for when the human eye pans a scene, it jumps from one point to another, skipping over the intervals between points. The most common use of a pan is to keep the subject within frame. If a person moves from one position to another, the camera moves horizontally to keep the person in the center of the composition. Pans in extreme long shots are especially effective in epic films where an audience can experience the vastness of a locale. But pans can be just as effective at medium and close ranges. The so-called **reaction shot,** for instance, is a movement of the camera away from the central attraction—usually a speaker—to capture the reaction of an onlooker or listener. In such cases, the pan is an effective way of preserving the cause–effect relationship between the two subjects and of emphasizing the solidarity and connectedness of people.

The **swish pan** (also known as a flash pan and a zip pan) is a variation of this technique and is often used for transitions between shots—as a substitute cut. The swish pan involves a whirling of the camera at a speed so rapid that only blurred images are recorded (**3–2b**). Although they actually take more time than cuts, swish pans connect one scene to another with a greater sense of simultaneity than cuts can suggest. For this reason, flash pans are often used to connect events at different locales that might otherwise appear remote from each other.

Pan shots tend to emphasize the unity of space and the connectedness of people and objects within that space. Precisely because we expect a panning shot to emphasize the literal contiguity of people sharing the same space, these shots can surprise us when their realistic integrity is violated. In Robert Benton's *Places in the Heart,* for example, the final shot of the movie connects the

3–18.   *Cabaret* (U.S.A., 1972), *with Joel Grey, choreographed and directed by Bob Fosse.*
A former dancer, Fosse was the foremost stage choreographer–director of his generation, winning many Tony Awards for his Broadway musicals. He also directed a half dozen or so movies, including this classic musical, his greatest work on film. Fosse's dancers are rarely elegant or lyrical. Rather, they are more likely to scrunch their shoulders, hunch up their back, or thrust out their pelvis. Fosse also loved glitzy/tacky costumes—usually accompanied by hats, which were integrated into his dance numbers. He is also the most witty of choreographers, with his dancers snapping their fingers in unison, mincing to a percussive beat like cartoon characters, or locking their knees and pointing their toes inwardly. Above all, Fosse's dance numbers are sexy—not the wholesome athletic sex appeal of a Gene Kelly choreography, but something funkier, more raffish, and down-and-dirty. His mature style is uniquely cinematic, not merely an objective recording of a stage choreography. In *Cabaret,* for example, he intercuts shots from the musical numbers with shots of the dramatic action and vice versa. In some numbers, he cuts to an avalanche of colliding shots to create a choreography that could not exist in the literal space of a theatrical stage.   *(Allied Artists)*

world of the living with the dead. The film is a celebration of the simple Christian values that bind a small Texas community together during the troubled times of the 1930s depression. The final shot takes place in church. The camera begins to pan the congregation in a long sweeping motion down each row of pews. Interspersed among the surviving characters are several that we know to be dead, including a murderer and his victim, worshipping side by side. Though the rest of the movie is realistically presented, this final shot leaps to a symbolic level, suggesting that the unified spirit of the community includes all its members, deceased as well as living.

Tilt shots are vertical movements of the camera around a stationary horizontal axis. Many of the same principles that apply to pans apply to tilts: They can be used to keep subjects within frame, to emphasize spatial and psychological interrelationships, to suggest simultaneity, and to emphasize cause–effect relationships. Tilts, like pans, can also be used subjectively in **point-of-view shots:** The camera can simulate a character's looking up or down a scene, for instance. Since a tilt is a change in angle, it is often used to suggest a psychological shift within a character. When an eye-level camera tilts downward, for example, the person photographed suddenly appears more vulnerable.

Dolly shots, sometimes called trucking or tracking shots, are taken from a moving vehicle (dolly). The vehicle literally moves in, out, or alongside a moving figure or object while the action is being photographed. Tracks are

3–19.   Production photo from the set of *Broken Arrow* **(U.S.A., 1996),** *with Christian Slater, director John Woo (in white shirt), and John Travolta.*
Action and adventure films are among the most kinetic of genres, stressing physical movement above all other qualities. Action films also tend to be violent, fast-paced, and steeped in machismo values. The genre is dominated by Americans, though it has attracted such international talent as Hong Kong's John Woo. Asian films in general tend to be slow-paced, but action films made in the East (and especially Hong Kong) are often frenzied, with one brawl spilling over into the next, driving toward an orgiastic explosion of violence at the climax. Woo's American movies have been somewhat less frantic, though still energetically and stylishly directed.   *(Twentieth Century-Fox)*

3-20. *Singin' in the Rain* (U.S.A., 1952), *with Gene Kelly and Cyd Charisse, choreographed by Kelly, directed by Kelly and Stanley Donen.*
Cyd Charisse, tall, elegant, and gorgeous, was the foremost female dancer during MGM's golden age of musicals, the 1950s. Trained in ballet rather than tap, she was usually at her best in classy numbers such as this balletic dream sequence. However, she could also convey a sizzling eroticism in such torrid dance numbers as those from *It's Always Fair Weather* and *The Band Wagon*. Stage choreography is always viewed from a stationary position. Film choreography can be more complex. In movies, the camera can be choreographed as well as the dancers. Kelly's choreographies often feature lyrical crane shots in which the camera's swirling motions are dreamily counterpointed by the motions of the dancers, a virtual *pas de trois.* *(MGM)*

sometimes laid on the set to permit the vehicle to move smoothly—hence the term *tracking shot*. If these shots involve long distances, the tracks have to be laid or withdrawn while the camera is moving in or out. Today, any vehicular movement of the camera can be referred to as a dolly shot. The camera can be mounted on a car, a train, even a bicycle.

Tracking is a useful technique in point-of-view shots to capture a sense of movement in or out of a scene. If a filmmaker wants to emphasize the *destination* of a character's movement, the director is more likely to use a straight cut between the initiation of the movement and its conclusion. If the experience of the movement itself is important, the director is more likely to dolly. Thus, if a character is searching for something, the time-consuming point-of-view dolly helps to elongate the suspense of the search. Similarly, the reverse dolly and the **pull-back dolly** are effective techniques for surprising the audience with a revelation **(3–17, 3–21).** By moving back, the camera reveals something startling, something previously off frame.

A common function of traveling shots is to provide an ironic contrast with dialogue. In Jack Clayton's *The Pumpkin Eater,* a distraught wife (Anne Bancroft) returns to an ex-husband's house, where she has an adulterous liaison

3–21. *Gone With the Wind* (U.S.A., 1939), *with Vivien Leigh (left, in front of boiling cauldron), directed by Victor Fleming.*
The pull-back dolly or crane shot begins with a close view of a subject, then withdraws to reveal the larger context. The contrast between the close and distant views can be funny, shocking, or sadly ironic. In this famous scene, the camera begins with a close shot of the heroine (Leigh), then slowly pulls back, revealing the wounded bodies of hundreds of soldiers, and stopping finally at a distant long-shot range, in front of a high flagpole, the tattered Confederate flag blowing in the wind like a shredded remnant. *(MGM)*

with him. As the two lie in bed, she asks him if he had been upset over their divorce and whether or not he missed her. He assures her that he wasn't upset, but while their voices continue on the soundtrack, the camera belies his words by slowly dollying through his living room, revealing pictures and mementos of the ex-wife. The shot is a kind of direct communication between the director and audience, bypassing the characters. These techniques are deliberate authorial intrusions. They are favored by filmmakers who view their characters with skepticism or irony—Lubitsch and Hitchcock, for example.

One of the most common uses of dolly shots is to emphasize psychological rather than literal revelations. By slowly tracking in on a character, the filmmaker is getting close to something crucial. The movement acts as a signal to the audience, suggesting, in effect, that we are about to witness something important. A cut to a close-up would tend to emphasize the rapidity of the discovery, but slow dolly shots suggest a more gradual revelation. For example, in Clive Donner's *The Caretaker* (also known as *The Guest*), this technique is used several times. Based on Harold Pinter's play, the movie concerns two brothers and an old tramp who tries to set one brother against the other. The dialogue, as is often the case in a Pinter script, is evasive and not very helpful in providing

3-22a. *Strictly Ballroom* (Australia, 1992), *with Tara Morice and Paul Mercurio, directed by Baz Lurhmann.* (Miramax Films)

3-22b. *Dance with Me* (U.S.A., 1998), *with Chayanne and Jane Krakowski, directed by Randa Haines.* (Mandalay Entertainment)

"Dance is the activity where the sexual connection is most explicit," Michael Malone has pointed out, "which is why movies use it to symbolize sex and why skillful dancing is an invariable movie clue to erotic sophistication, a prerequisite for the lover." Eroticism underlies virtually all dances centered on the couple, whether the style is a sizzling flamenco with bodies literally pressed together as in *Strictly Ballroom*; or an edgy, pulsating Latin-American number as in *Dance with Me*; or even a stately, formalized eighteenth century English gavotte as in the Jane Austen adaptation, *Mansfield Park*. In each, the male courts his partner with sinuously seductive urgency. See Michael Malone, *Heroes of Eros: Male Sexuality in the Movies* (New York: E.P. Dutton, 1979).

3-22c. *Mansfield Park* (Great Britain, 1999), *with Frances O'Connor and Alessandro Nivola, directed by Patricia Rozema.* (Miramax Films)

an understanding of the characters. The brothers are different in most respects. Mick (Alan Bates) is materialistic and aggressive. Aston (Robert Shaw) is gentle and withdrawn. Each brother has a crucial speech in which the camera slowly tracks from a long range to a close-up. Neither of the speeches is really very informative, at least not on a literal level. However, the juxtaposition of the dialogue with the implications of the dolly shot helps the audience to feel that it has finally "arrived" at an understanding of each character.

A stationary camera tends to convey a sense of stability and order, unless there is a great deal of movement within the frame. The moving camera—by its very instability—can create ideas of vitality, flux, and sometimes disorder. Orson Welles exploited the mobile camera to suggest the title character's dynamic energy in *Othello*. Early in the movie, the confident Moor is often photographed in traveling shots. In the ramparts scene, he and Iago walk with military briskness as the camera moves with them at an equally energetic pace. When Iago tells him of his suspicions, the camera slows down, then comes to a halt. Once Othello's mind has been poisoned, he is photographed mostly from stationary setups. Not only has his confident energy drained away, but a spiritual paralysis invades his soul. In the final shots of the movie, he barely moves, even within the still frame. This paralysis motif is completed when Othello kills himself.

When the camera literally follows a character, the audience assumes that it will discover something along the way. A journey, after all, usually has a destination. But traveling shots are often symbolic rather than literal. In Federico Fellini's *8½*, for example, the moving camera is used to suggest a variety of thematic ideas. The protagonist, Guido (Marcello Mastroianni), is a film director who's trying to put together a movie near a bizarre health spa. Everywhere he turns, he's confronted by memories, fantasies, and realities more fantastic than anything he can imagine. But he is paralyzed by indecision. What, if anything, from all this copious flux will he select for his movie? He can't use it all, for it won't fit together—the materials are too sprawling. Throughout the film, the camera wanders restlessly, prowling over the fantastic locale, compulsively hoarding images of faces, textures, and shapes. All are absorbed by Guido, but he is unable to detach them from their contexts to form a meaningful artistic structure.

A number of film theorists have discussed the unique capacity of cinema to convert space into time and time into space. The amount of time it takes to photograph a concrete object can be the main purpose of a shot, especially a traveling shot. The acknowledged master of these types of dolly shots was Max Ophüls. In movies such as *Letter From an Unknown Woman* and *The Earrings of Madame De . . . ,* the heroines throw themselves into imprudent but glorious love affairs. The camera tracks relentlessly as the women become more irrevocably involved with their lovers. As critic Andrew Sarris pointed out, Ophüls uses his dolly shots as metaphors of time's cruel prodigality. His world is one of tragic flux and instability in which love is destined to run its eventually bitter course. These lengthy tracking shots preserve the continuity of time by preserving the continuity of space. There is no time for pause and reflection "between shots" in these films. This symbolic technique can be overlooked by the casual viewer because the dolly shots are to some degree functional: They follow characters in their daily round of activities. But a stationary camera would be just as functional (not to mention less expensive), for the characters could move toward or away from a fixed setup.

Hand-held shots are generally less lyrical, more noticeable than vehicular shots. Hand-held cameras, which are usually mounted with a harness on the

3-23. ***Born on the Fourth of July*** (U.S.A., 1989), *with Tom Cruise, directed by Oliver Stone.* In film as in the other arts, subject matter usually determines technique. This scene portrays an antiwar protest rally during the Vietnam War era. The scene is deliberately shot in a ragged manner, with shaky hand-held shots, fragmentary editing, and open-form asymmetrical compositions that look like newsreel footage captured in the midst of the chaos. A stable, aesthetically balanced shot would be more beautiful, but such a composition would be completely at odds with the essence of the subject matter. *(Universal City Studios)*

cinematographer's shoulder, were perfected in the 1950s to allow camera operators to move in or out of scenes with greater flexibility and speed. Originally used by documentarists to permit them to shoot in nearly every kind of location, these cameras were quickly adopted by many fiction film directors as well. Hand-held shots are often jumpy and ragged. The camera's rocking is hard to ignore, for the screen exaggerates these movements, especially if the shots are taken from close ranges. For this reason, filmmakers often use the hand-held camera for point-of-view shots. In Mike Nichols's *The Graduate,* for example, a hand-held shot is used to simulate the hero's attempts to maneuver through a crowded room of people.

Crane shots are essentially airborne dolly shots. A crane is a kind of mechanical arm, often more than twenty feet in length. In many respects, it resembles the cranes used by the telephone company to repair lines. It can lift a cinematographer and camera in or out of a scene. It can move in virtually any direction: up, down, diagonally, in, out, or any combination of these. In Hitchcock's *Notorious,* the camera sweeps from an extreme high-angle long shot of a ballroom to an extreme close-up of the hand of the heroine (Ingrid Bergman) clasping a small key.

The Steadicam is a camera stabilizing device that was perfected in the 1970s. It allows cinematographers to move smoothly through a set or location without shaking or bobbing. The Steadicam enables filmmakers to eliminate the need for such expensive devices as cranes and dollies, which can restrict

120

camera movements considerably. The Stedicam also reduced the need for extra crew members to activate the cumbersome old technology of tracks, hand-operated dollies, and many types of cranes. Perhaps the most impressive use of the Steadicam during the 1970s was in Kubrick's horror classic, *The Shining,* where the camera was able to follow a young boy's tricycle as he eerily peddled down empty hotel corridors.

Zoom lenses don't usually involve the actual movement of the camera, but on the screen their effect is very much like an extremely fast tracking or crane shot. The zoom is a combination of lenses, which are continuously variable, permitting the camera to change from close wide-angle distances to extreme telephoto positions (and vice versa) almost simultaneously. The effect of the zoom is a breathtaking sense of being plunged into a scene, or an equally jolting sense of being plucked out of it. Zoom shots are used instead of dolly or crane shots for a number of reasons. They can zip in or out of a scene much faster than any vehicle. From the point of view of economy, they are cheaper than dolly or crane shots since no vehicle is necessary. In crowded locations, zoom lenses can be useful for photographing from long distances, away from the curious eyes of passersby.

3–24. *The Crucible* **(U.S.A., 1996),** *with Winona Ryder (behind smoking cauldron), directed by Nicholas Hytner.*

When adapting a play—especially a famous stage drama like Arthur Miller's *The Crucible*—the film director must decide whether or not to "open it up." That is, whether the confined interiors of most stage sets ought to be transferred to the wide open spaces afforded by natural locations. To do so risks dissipating the spatial tension of the original, which is usually conceived by the playwright as a kind of No Exit situation. Nicholas Hytner, who is one of Britain's most famous stage directors, decided to open up Miller's tale of witch-hunt hysteria in seventeenth-century Puritan Salem. Hytner also decided to use movement as metaphor: "I had a feeling that the whole hysteria should work like an infection, like a virus, which immediately suggested that the thing should be moving around. You should not only see the hysterics, but you should actually feel the hysterics traveling from one place to another, which means traveling people and traveling cameras." This technique resulted in a brilliant movie, which heightened rather than lessened the impact of Miller's stagebound drama. (Miller wrote the screenplay of the movie and was very pleased with Hytner's concept.) *(Twentieth Century–Fox)*

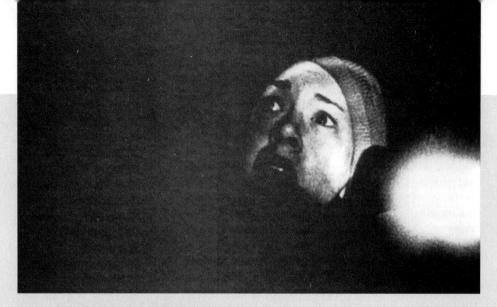

3–25. *The Blair Witch Project* (U.S.A., 1999), *with Heather Donahue, directed by Dan Myrick and Eduardo Sanchez.*
A rocking, turbulently roiling camera can produce a sense of nausea in some people, almost like sea-sickness aboard a violently swaying boat on rough waters. This low-budget thriller had its audiences literally hurling in the aisles—sometimes even before they reached the aisles. Virtually the entire movie was shot with an unstable hand-held camera, to suggest an on-the-spot documentary recording of events while they're actually taking place. The film is a good example of how budgetary liabilities can be converted into aesthetic virtues. The story centers on three college students who go to an isolated forest to explore a local myth about witchcraft. They plan to videotape the entire project. There was no set to build, no lights to set up, no costumes to sew, and no costly special effects to drain the budget. The cast consisted of only three nonprofessional actors. The movie cost a piddling $35,000 and grossed an astonishing $150 million. *(Artisan Entertainment)*

There are certain psychological differences between zoom shots and those involving an actual moving camera. Dolly and crane shots tend to give the viewer a sense of entering into or withdrawing from a set: Furniture and people seem to stream by the sides of the screen as the camera penetrates a three-dimensional space. Zoom lenses foreshorten people and flatten space. The edges of the image simply disappear at all sides. The effect is one of sudden magnification. Instead of feeling as though we are entering a scene, we feel as though a small portion of it has been thrust toward us. In shots of brief duration, these differences are not significant, but in more lengthy shots, the psychological differences can be pronounced.

Aerial shots, usually taken from a helicopter, are really variations of the crane shot. Like a crane, the helicopter can move in virtually any direction. When a crane is impractical—usually on exterior locations—an aerial shot can duplicate the effect. The helicopter shot can be much more extravagant, of course, and for this reason is occasionally used to suggest a swooping sense of freedom. In *Apocalypse Now,* Francis Coppola used aerial shots to produce a godlike sense of inexorability, as swirling American helicopters annihilate a Vietnamese village. The sequence is a kinetic tour de force, suffusing the action with a sense of exhilaration—and horror. Virtually every shot in this brilliantly edited sequence contains a forward rush, a sense of being swept up by events that are out of control.

Mechanical Distortions of Movement

Movement in film is not a literal phenomenon but an optical illusion. Present-day cameras record movement at twenty-four frames per second (fps).

3-26.   *Ballet Mécanique* (France, 1924), *directed by Fernand Léger.*
Best known for his cubist paintings, Léger was also an avant-garde filmmaker. One of the first to explore abstraction in the cinema, he created many striking kinetic effects by animating and choreographing ordinary objects like crockery, dishes, and machine gears.   *(Museum of Modern Art)*

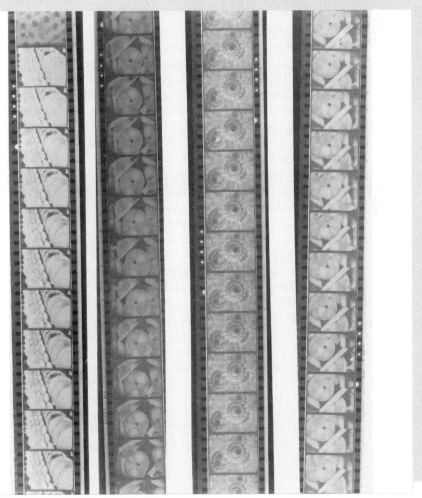

That is, in each second, twenty-four separate still pictures are photographed. When the film is shown in a projector at the same speed, these still photographs are mixed instantaneously by the human eye, giving the illusion of movement. This phenomenon is called the *persistence of vision.* By simply manipulating the timing mechanism of the camera and/or projector, a filmmaker can distort movement on the screen. There are five basic distortions of this kind: **(1) animation, (2) fast motion, (3) slow motion, (4) reverse motion,** and **(5) freeze frames.**

There are two fundamental differences between animation and live-action movies. In animation sequences, each frame is photographed separately, rather than continuously at the rate of twenty-four frames per second. Another difference is that animation, as the word implies, doesn't ordinarily involve the photographing of subjects that move by themselves. The subjects photographed are generally drawings or static objects. Thus, in an animated movie, thousands of frames are separately photographed. Each frame differs from its neighbor only to an infinitesimal degree. When a sequence of these frames is projected at twenty-four fps, the illusion is that the drawings or objects are moving and, hence, are "animated."

A popular misconception about animated movies is that they are intended primarily for the entertainment of children—perhaps because the field was dominated for so many years by Walt Disney. In actuality, the gamut of sophistication in the genre is as broad as in live-action fiction films. The works of Disney and the puppet films of the Czech Jiri Trnka appeal to both children and adults. A few of these films are as sophisticated as the drawings of Paul Klee. There are even some X-rated animated films, most notably Ralph Bakshi's *Fritz the Cat* and *Heavy Traffic.*

Another popular misconception about animated movies is that they are simpler than live-action films. The contrary is more often the case. For every second of screen time, twenty-four separate drawings usually have to be photographed. Thus, in an average ninety-minute feature, over 129,600 drawings are necessary. Furthermore, some animators use transparent plastic sheets (called **cels**), which they layer over each other to give the illusion of depth to their drawings. Some single frames consist of as many as three or four layers of cels. Most animated films are short precisely because of the overwhelming difficulty of producing all the necessary drawings for a longer movie. Feature-length animated movies are usually produced in assembly line fashion, with dozens of artists drawing thousands of separate frames.

Technically, animated films can be as complex as live-action movies. The same techniques can be used in both forms: traveling shots, zooms, angles, various lenses, editing, **dissolves,** etc. The only difference is that animators *draw* these elements into their images. Furthermore, animators also can use most of the techniques of the painter: different kinds of paints, pens, pencils, pastels, washes, acrylics, and so on.

Some filmmakers have even combined the techniques of live action with animation. In *Neighbors,* for example, Norman McLaren used a technique

3–27a.   *Beauty and the Beast* (U.S.A., 1991), *directed by Gary Trousdale and Kirk Wise.*   *(©Walt Disney Productions)*

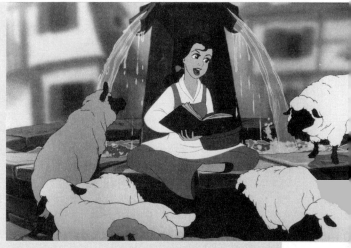

a

Beginning with the "Silly Symphonies" of the early 1930s, the field of animation was dominated for many years by Walt Disney. The Disney organization is still in the forefront, with bold innovations in subject matter, style, and technology. Like many of their movies, *Beauty and the Beast* is adapted from a well-known fairy tale, though the Disney version has a pronounced feminist twist with its feisty, courageous heroine, who is also an avid reader. *Toy Story* is the first animated feature film that was entirely created using computer technology. The movie was a huge commercial and critical success, as was its sequel. *Dinosaur* is startlingly realistic, considering its prehistoric cast of characters. The movie combines computer-generated characters with live-action backgrounds and a wide array of special effects.

3–27b.   *Toy Story* (U.S.A., 1995), *directed by John Lasseter.*   *(© The Disney Company)*

b

c

3–27c.   *Dinosaur* (U.S.A., 2000), *directed by Ralph Zondag and Eric Leighton.*   *(© Disney Enterprises, Inc.)*

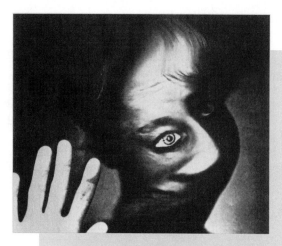

3-28a. *Photocopy Cha Cha* (U.S.A., 1991), *by Chel White,* included in *The 23rd International Tournée of Animation.* *(Expanded Entertainment)*

3-28b. *Can Film* (Bulgaria, 1992), *by Zlaten Radev,* included in *The Fourth Animation Celebration.* *(© Expanded Entertainment)*

3-28c. *Words, Words, Words* (Czech Republic, 1993), *by Michaela Ravlatova,* included in *The 24th International Tournée of Animation.* *(The Samuel Goldwyn Company)*

A number of commentators have referred to the contemporary animation scene as a golden age, encompassing a broad spectrum of styles and techniques from all over the world. *Photocopy Cha Cha* is the first animated movie created on a copy machine, by one of the most innovative of all animation artists. Unconventional artists love to create hybrid works, like *Can Film*, which combines stewed tomato cans with clay animation. *Words, Words, Words,* on the other hand, is rather traditional, using deliberately crude line drawings, but emphasizing a sophisticated literary text.

called *pixillation,* which involves photographing live actors frame by frame, a method sometimes called *stop-motion photography.* When the sequence is projected on the screen, the actors move in abrupt, jerky motions, suggesting a primitive cartoon figure. Other filmmakers have combined animation and theatrical film techniques within the same frame, either through the use of the optical printer or through computer graphic special effects **(3–29).**

One of the most successful instances of combining live action with animation is *Who Framed Roger Rabbit,* directed by Robert Zemeckis. Richard

Williams was the director of animation for the project, which involved over 320 animators. Nearly two million drawings were made for the movie. Some single frames were so complex that they required two dozen drawings. The integration of real details with cartoon characters is startling. A cartoon rabbit drinks from a real coffee cup, which rattles. Cartoon characters throw real shadows on the set. They bump into live people, knocking them down.

Fast motion is achieved by having events photographed at a slower rate than twenty-four fps. Ordinarily, the subject photographed moves at a normal pace. But when the sequence is projected at twenty-four fps, the effect is one of acceleration. This technique is sometimes used to intensify the natural speed of a scene—one showing galloping horses, for example, or cars speeding past the camera. Early silent comedies were photographed before the standardization of cameras and projectors at twenty-four fps, and therefore their sense of speed is exaggerated at present-day projector speeds. Even at sixteen or twenty fps, however, some of these early directors used fast motion for comic effects.

According to the French aesthetician Henri Bergson, when people act mechanically rather than flexibly, comedy is the result. People, unlike machines, can think, feel, and act reasonably. A person's intelligence is measured by his or her ability to be flexible. When behavior becomes machinelike and inflexible, we find it laughable. One aspect of machinelike behavior is speed: When a per-

3-29. *The Mask* **(U.S.A., 1994),** *with Jim Carrey, special effects by Industrial Light & Magic, directed by Chuck Russell.*
There have been several experiments in the past combining live action and animation within the same frame, most notably Disney's *Song of the South* and *Mary Poppins*. Since the invention of computer graphics special effects, however, these two styles can be combined within a single character, as this shot illustrates. Our love-smitten hero is so overcome with passion that he can't restrain his thumping heart from throbbing out of his chest—a cartoon heart for a human(ish) character. *(New Line Cinema)*

son's movements are speeded up on film, he or she seems unhuman, ridiculous. Dignity is difficult in fast motion, for acceleration robs us of our humanity. The Upton Inn mixup in Richardson's *Tom Jones* is funny precisely because the fast motion captures the machinelike predictability of all the characters: Tom flies from Mrs. Waters's bed, Mr. Fitzpatrick flies off the handle, Squire Western screams for his daughter, and the servants scream for their lives (**3–30**).

   Slow-motion sequences are achieved by photographing events at a faster rate than twenty-four fps and projecting the filmstrip at the standard speed. Slow motion tends to ritualize and solemnize movement. Even the most commonplace actions take on a choreographic gracefulness in slow motion. Where speed tends to be the natural rhythm of comedy, slow, dignified movements tend to be associated with tragedy. In *The Pawnbroker*, Sidney Lumet used slow motion in a **flashback** sequence, showing the protagonist as a young man on an idyllic country outing with his family. The scenes are lyrical and otherworldly—too perfect to last.

   When violent scenes are photographed in slow motion, the effect is paradoxically beautiful. In *The Wild Bunch*, Sam Peckinpah used slow motion to photograph the grisliest scenes of horror—flesh tearing, blood spattering,

3–30.   *Tom Jones* (Great Britain, 1963), *with George Cooper, Albert Finney, and Joyce Redman; directed by Tony Richardson.*
Richardson uses fast motion in this movie when he wishes to emphasize the machinelike behavior of the characters—especially of the randy hero (Finney) whose sex drive often overpowers his judgment. In the famous Upton Inn mixup (pictured), Tom is rudely interrupted in his nocturnal amours by the hot-tempered Mr. Fitzpatrick. The sequence is shot in fast motion to heighten the comedy: The drunken Fitzpatrick flails at our besieged hero as his terrified paramour screams for her life, thus waking all the inhabitants of the inn, including Sophie Western, the only woman Tom truly loves.   *(The Samuel Goldwyn Company)*

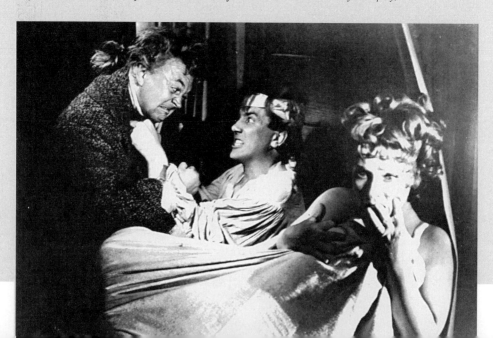

3–31a. *Without Limits* (U.S.A., 1998), *with Billy Crudup, directed by Robert Towne.*

Slow motion is often used in movies about athletic events. The technique can prolong the balletic grace of an athlete's movements. In other cases, such as this, the slow motion heightens the agonized strain in every muscle of an athlete's body as he hurtles himself against the finish wire. *(Warner Bros.)*

3–31b. *The Last of the Mohicans* (U.S.A., 1992), *with Daniel Day-Lewis, directed by Michael Mann.*

Slow motion, of course, prolongs time—sometimes unbearably, as in this shot. The hero is racing to the rescue of the woman he loves, who is under attack during a sudden Indian ambush. A weapon in each hand, photographed at the aggressive full-front position, with the foreground and background an irrelevant blur, Hawkeye (Day-Lewis) is totally focused on his enemy, but the slow-motion photography seems to hold him back—as an agonizing eternity transpires. *(Twentieth Century–Fox)*

3–31c. *Glory* (U.S.A., 1989), *with Matthew Broderick (left), directed by Edward Zwick.*

The great Japanese master, Akira Kurosawa, sometimes used slow motion to convey violence, especially in scenes of battle. Zwick also uses this technique, paradoxically converting a scene of brutality and bloodshed during a famous Civil War battle into a mesmerizing ballet of blasted limbs and flying trajectories of debris. *(Tri-Star Pictures)*

horses toppling, an almost endless variety. By aestheticizing these scenes of ugliness, Peckinpah demonstrates why the men are so addicted to a life of violence when it seems so profitless. Violence becomes almost an aesthetic credo, somewhat as it's portrayed in the fiction of Hemingway. Slow-motion violence became virtually a trademark in the works of Peckinpah.

Reverse motion simply involves photographing an action with the film running reversed. When projected on the screen, the events run backward. Since Méliès's time, reverse motion has not progressed much beyond the gag stage. In *The Knack,* Richard Lester used reverse motion as a comic choreographic retake for a quick laugh when an egg "returns" to its shell. One of the most expressive uses of reverse motion—combined with slow motion—is in Jean Cocteau's *Orpheus.* The protagonist has taken a journey into Hell to regain his lost wife. He makes a serious blunder while there and expresses a wish to return to his original point of decision to correct his mistake. Magically, he is whisked into the past before our eyes, as the previous sequence unfurls backwards in slow motion—to the physical setting where the fateful decision was made. The reverse motion in this sequence is a good instance of how space can be temporalized and time spatialized in the cinema.

A *freeze frame* suspends all movement on the screen. A single image is selected and reprinted for as many frames as is necessary to suggest the halting of motion. By interrupting a sequence with a freeze shot, the director calls

3–32.   *Hair* (U.S.A., 1979), *choreography by Twyla Tharp, directed by Milos Forman.*
Slow motion etherealizes movement, lending it a dreamy, otherworldly grace. Throughout this musical, slow motion is used in the dance numbers to emphasize the individuality rather than the uniformity of the dancers. Twyla Tharp's choreography is organic to the story, which deals with the freewheeling lifestyle of some 1960s hippies. The dance numbers are loose and spontaneous, with each dancer doing his or her own thing—like jiggling links in a chain. *(United Artists)*

attention to an image—offering it, as it were, for our delectation. Sometimes, the image is a fleeting moment of poignance that is over in a fraction of a second, as in the final shot of Truffaut's *The 400 Blows*. Directors also use freeze frames for comic purposes. In *Tom Jones,* Richardson freezes the shot of Tom dangling on a noose while the off-screen narrator urbanely explains to the audience why Tom should not hang until his tale is finished.

In other instances, the freeze frame can be used for thematic purposes. The final image of Richardson's *The Loneliness of the Long Distance Runner* is frozen to emphasize the permanence of the protagonist's status at the end of the picture. Freeze frames are ideal metaphors for dealing with time, for in effect, the frozen image permits no change. Near the end of *True Grit,* for example, Henry Hathaway froze a shot of the protagonist (John Wayne) and his horse leaping over a fence. By halting the shot at the crest of the leap, Hathaway creates a metaphor of timeless grandeur: The image suggests a heroic equestrian statue, immune from the ravages of time and decay. Of course, the total absence of movement is often associated with death, and Hathaway's freeze frame also implies this idea. Perhaps a more explicit metaphor of death can be seen in the conclusion of the western *Butch Cassidy and the Sundance Kid,* where the two heroes (Paul Newman and Robert Redford) are "frozen" just before they are shot to death. The freeze frame suggests an ultimate triumph over death.

Most of these mechanical distortions were discovered by Méliès. For many years after, they were largely ignored by the majority of commercial film-

3-33.   *Viridiana* (Mexico/Spain, 1961), *directed by Luis Buñuel.*
This notorious freeze-frame parody of Leonardo's *Last Supper* is only one example of Buñuel's savage assault on the Church, sentimental liberalism, and middle-class morality. His sardonic wit is often shocking, blasphemous. For example, the context of this freeze frame is a drunken orgy of beggars who pose for a group photo to the accompaniment of Handel's *Messiah.* A woman reeling in boozy stupor "snaps" the picture not with a camera but her genitals. This raucous gesture throws the "disciples" into paroxysms of laughter. Though a nonbeliever, Buñuel was able to infuse a sense of scandal in these sacrilegious jokes. "Thank God I am still an atheist," he once sighed.   *(Audio-Brandon Films)*

makers until the late 1950s, when the French New Wave directors revived them. Since then, many of these techniques have been used promiscuously. Zooms, freeze frames, and slow-motion sequences have become almost de rigueur. In many cases, they have degenerated into clichés—modish flourishes that are tacked on to the materials, regardless of whether the techniques are organic to the spirit of the subject.

In watching a movie, we ought to ask ourselves why a director is moving the camera during a scene. Or why the camera *doesn't* move. Does the director keep the camera close in to the action, thus emphasizing motion? Or does he or she deemphasize movement through the use of longer shots, high angles, and slow-paced action? Are the movements in a scene naturalistic or stylized? Literal or symbolic? Are the camera's movements smooth or choppy? Lyrical or disorienting? What are the symbolic implications of such mechanical distortions as fast and slow motion, freeze frames, and animation?

Movement in film is not simply a matter of "what happens." The director has dozens of ways to convey motion, and what differentiates a great director from a merely competent one is not so much a matter of what happens, but *how* things happen—how suggestive and resonant are the movements in a given dramatic context? Or, how effectively does the form of the movement embody its content?

FURTHER READING

BACHER, LUTZ, *The Mobile Mise en Scène* (New York: Arno Press, 1978). Primarily on lengthy takes and camera movements.

DEREN, MAYA, "Cinematography: The Creative Use of Reality," in *The Visual Arts Today*, Gyorgy Kepes, ed. (Middletown, Conn.: Wesleyan University Press, 1960). A discussion of dance and documentary in film.

GEUENS, JEAN-PIERRE, "Visuality and Power: The Work of the Steadicam," *Film Quarterly* (Winter 1994–1995).

GIANNETTI, LOUIS D., "The Aesthetic of the Mobile Camera," in *Godard and Others: Essays in Film Form* (Cranbury, N.J.: Fairleigh Dickinson University Press, 1975). Symbolism and the moving camera.

HALAS, JOHN, and ROGER MANVELL, *Design in Motion* (New York: Focal Press, 1962). Movement and mise en scène.

HOLMAN, BRUCE L., *Puppet Animation in the Cinema* (San Diego, Cal.: A. S. Barnes, 1975). Emphasis on Czech and Canadian animators.

JACOBS, LEWIS, et al., "Movement" in *The Movies as Medium*, Lewis Jacobs, ed. (New York: Farrar, Straus & Giroux, 1970). A collection of essays.

KNIGHT, ARTHUR, "The Street Films: Murnau and the Moving Camera," in *The Liveliest Art*, rev. ed. (New York: Mentor, 1979). The German school of the 1920s.

LINDSAY, VACHEL, *The Art of the Moving Picture* (New York: Liveright, 1970). Reprint of an early classic study.

STEPHENSON, RALPH, *The Animated Film* (San Diego, Cal.: A. S. Barnes, 1973). Historical survey.

Editing

The foundation of film art is editing.
—V. I. PUDOVKIN

Overview

Real time versus reel time: the problem of continuity. Cutting to continuity: condensing unobtrusively. D. W. Griffith and the development of a universal cutting style. The invisible manipulation of classical cutting: editing for emphasis and nuance. The problem of time. Subjective editing: thematic montage and the Soviet school. Pudovkin and Eisenstein: two early masters of thematic cutting. The famous Odessa Steps sequence of *Potemkin*. The countertradition: the realism of André Bazin. How editing lies. When not to cut and why. Real time and space and how to preserve them. The realist arsenal: sound, deep focus, sequence shots, widescreen. Alfred Hitchcock, supreme master of editing: storyboard sequence from *North by Northwest*.

So far, we've been concerned with cinematic communication as it relates to the single shot, the basic unit of construction in movies. Except for traveling shots and **lengthy takes,** however, shots in film tend to acquire meaning when they are juxtaposed with other shots and structured into an **edited** sequence. Physically, editing is simply joining one strip of film (**shot**) with another. Shots are joined into scenes. On the most mechanical level, editing eliminates unnecessary time and space. Through the association of ideas, editing connects one shot with another, one scene with another, and so on. Simple as this may now seem, the convention of editing represents what critic Terry Ramsaye referred to as the "syntax" of cinema, its grammatical language. Like linguistic syntax, the syntax of editing must be learned. We don't possess it innately.

Continuity

In the earliest years of cinema, the late 1890s, movies were brief, consisting of short events photographed in **long shot** in a single **take.** The duration of the shot and the event were equal. Soon, filmmakers began to tell stories— simple ones, it's true, but requiring more than a single shot. Scholars have traced the development of narrative to filmmakers in France, Great Britain, and the United States.

By the early twentieth century, filmmakers had already devised a functional style of editing we now call *cutting to continuity*. This type of cutting is a technique used in most fiction films even today, if only for exposition scenes. Essentially, this style of editing is a kind of shorthand, consisting of time-honored conventions. Continuity cutting tries to preserve the fluidity of an event without literally showing all of it.

For example, a continuous shot of a woman leaving work and going home might take forty-five minutes. Cutting to continuity condenses the action into five brief shots, each of which leads by association to the next: **(1)** She enters a corridor as she closes the door to her office. **(2)** She leaves the office

4–1. ***The Makioka Sisters* (Japan, 1985),** *directed by Kon Ichikawa.*

How a scene is edited can be very subjective, depending on who's doing the cutting and what the editor wants to emphasize. In this domestic family quarrel, for example, the scene is slanted toward the wronged wife (Keiko Kishi, lower right) and her bullying husband (Teinosuke Sachiko, center left). Her sisters and brother-in-law observe from the rear of the room. But another editor could focus on any of the other four characters, giving them more prominence in the sequence by cutting to their reactions more often, thus conveying the scene primarily from that character's perspective. In short, six different stories could be told, depending on how the sequence is cut together. *(R5/S8)*

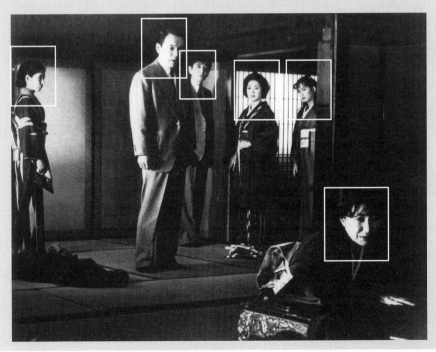

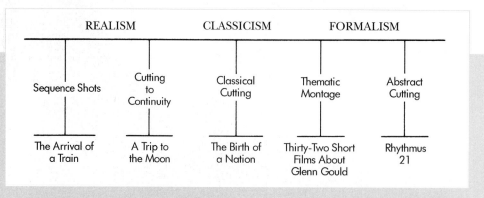

	REALISM		CLASSICISM	FORMALISM	
Sequence Shots	Cutting to Continuity	Classical Cutting	Thematic Montage	Abstract Cutting
The Arrival of a Train	A Trip to the Moon	The Birth of a Nation	Thirty-Two Short Films About Glenn Gould	Rhythmus 21

4–2. Editing styles can be classified according to how intrusive or interpretive the cutting is. The least manipulative style is found in a sequence shot, which contains no editing at all. Cutting to continuity merely condenses the time and space of a completed action. Classical cutting interprets an action by emphasizing certain details over others. Thematic montage argues a thesis—the shots are connected in a relatively subjective manner. Abstract cutting is a purely formalistic style of editing, totally divorced from any recognizable subject matter.

building. **(3)** She enters and starts her car. **(4)** She drives her car along a highway. **(5)** Her car turns into her driveway at home. The entire forty-five-minute action might take ten seconds of screen time, yet nothing essential is left out. It's an unobtrusive condensation.

To keep the action logical and continuous, there must be no confusing breaks in an edited sequence of this sort. Often, all the movement is carried out in the same direction on the screen to avoid confusion. For example, if the woman moves from right to left in one shot and her movements are from left to right in the other shots, we might think that she is returning to her office. Cause–effect relationships must be clearly set forth. If the woman slams on her brakes, the director is generally obliged to offer us a shot of what prompted the driver to stop so suddenly.

The continuity of actual space and time is fragmented as smoothly as possible in this type of editing. Unless the audience has a clear sense of a continuous action, an editing transition can be disorienting. Hence, the term **jump cut,** which means an editing transition that's confusing in terms of space and time. To make their transitions smooth, filmmakers generally use **establishing shots** at the beginning of their stories or at the beginning of any new scene within the narrative.

Once the location is established, filmmakers then can cut to closer shots of the action. If the events require a considerable number of cuts, the filmmaker might cut back to a **reestablishing shot**—a return to the opening long shot. In this way, the viewer is reminded of the spatial context of the closer shots. "Between" these various shots, time and space can be expanded or contracted with considerable subtlety.

4–3.   *The Arrival of a Train* (France, 1895), *directed by Louis and Auguste Lumière.*
The Lumière brothers might be regarded as the godfathers of the documentary movement.
Their brief *actualités* (as they called them) are primitive documentaries shot for the most part
in single takes. These early newsreels often contained several different sequences, but rarely
is there much cutting within a sequence—hence the term *sequence shot* (that is, a complex
action photographed in a continuous take, without cuts). Audiences of this era were so astonished by the novelty of a moving picture that this alone was enough to hold their attention.
See also Bill Nichols, *Representing Reality: Issues and Concepts in Documentary* (Bloomington:
Indiana University Press, 1991).   *(Museum of Modern Art)*

By 1908, when the American genius D. W. Griffith entered the field of
filmmaking, movies had already learned how to tell stories thanks to the technique of cutting to continuity. But the stories were simple and crude compared
to those in more sophisticated narrative mediums like literature and drama.
Nonetheless, movie storytellers already knew that by breaking up an action into
different shots, the event can be contracted or expanded, depending on the
number of shots. In other words, the shot, not the scene, was the basic unit of
film construction.

4-4. *A Trip to the Moon* (France, 1902), *directed by Georges Méliès.*
Around 1900, in America, England, and France, filmmakers began to tell stories. Their narratives were crude, but they required more than just one shot to complete. Méliès was one of the first to devise the style of cutting to continuity. The narrative segments are connected by a fade-out. The next scene then fades in, often in a different location and at a different time, though usually with the same characters. Méliès advertised these films as stories in "arranged scenes." *(Museum of Modern Art)*

Movies before Griffith were usually photographed in stationary long shot—roughly the position of a close observer in the live theater. Because film time doesn't depend on the duration of the literal event, filmmakers of this era introduced a more subjective time, one that's determined by the duration of the shots (and the elapsed time implied between them), not by the actual occurrence.

D. W. Griffith and Classical Cutting

The basic elements of editing syntax were already in place when Griffith entered the field, but it was he more than any other individual who molded these elements into a language of power and subtlety. Film scholars have called this language *classical cutting*. Griffith has been called the Father of Film because he consolidated and expanded many of the techniques invented by his predecessors and was the first to go beyond gimmickry into the realm of art. By 1915, the year of his masterpiece *The Birth of a Nation*, classical cutting was already an editing style of great sophistication and expressiveness. Griffith had seized on the principle of the association of ideas in the concept of editing and expanded it in a variety of ways.

Classical cutting involves editing for dramatic intensity and emotional emphasis rather than for purely physical reasons. Through the use of the

4–5. *The Birth of a Nation* (U.S.A., 1915), *directed by D. W. Griffith.*
Griffith's greatest gift to the cinema was classical cutting—a style of editing that still characterizes most of the fiction films around the world. Classical cutting allows filmmakers to inflect their narratives, to add nuances and emphasis. It also subjectivizes time. For example, in this famous last-minute rescue finale, Griffith cross-cuts to four different groups. Despite the sense of speed suggested by the brevity of the shots, the sequence actually expands time. Griffith used 255 separate shots for about twenty minutes of screen time. *(Museum of Modern Art)*

close-up within the scene, Griffith managed to achieve a dramatic impact that was unprecedented. Close-ups had been used earlier, but Griffith was the first to use them for psychological rather than physical reasons alone. Audiences were now permitted to see the smallest details of an actor's face. No longer were performers required to flail their arms and tear their hair. The slightest arch of an eyebrow could convey a multitude of subtleties.

By splitting the action into a series of fragmentary shots, Griffith achieved not only a greater sense of detail, but a far greater degree of control over his audience's reactions. In carefully selecting and juxtaposing long, **medium,** and close shots, he constantly shifted the spectator's point of view within a scene—expanding here, excluding there, emphasizing, consolidating, connecting, contrasting, paralleling, and so on. The possibilities were far ranging. The space and time continuum of the real scene was radically altered. It

4–6. *Thirty-Two Short Films About Glenn Gould* (Canada, 1994), *with Colm Feore, directed by François Girard.*

This movie combines elements from documentary filmmaking, fiction films, and the avant-garde. Its editing style is radically subjective. The movie features documentary footage of the late Glenn Gould, a controversial and eccentric Canadian pianist considered to be one of the great musicians of the twentieth century. There are also many re-created scenes with the brilliant Colm Feore playing the quirky and obsessive artist. The movie's structure is not a straightforward narrative, but a series of fragments, loosely based on the thirty-two-part *Goldberg Variations* of Johann Sebastian Bach—one of Gould's most celebrated virtuoso performances. The film is structured around ideas rather than a linear story, and for this reason, thematic montage is its style of editing.   *(The Samuel Goldwyn Company)*

was replaced by a subjective continuity—the association of ideas implicit in the connected shots.

In its most refined form, classical cutting presents a series of psychologically connected shots—shots that aren't necessarily separated by real time and space **(4–12).** For example, if four characters are seated in a room, a director might cut from one speaker to a second with a dialogue exchange, then cut to a **reaction shot** of one of the listeners, then to a **two-shot** of the original speakers, and finally to a close-up of the fourth person. The sequence of shots represents a kind of psychological cause–effect pattern. In other words, the breakup of shots is justified on the basis of dramatic rather than literal necessity. The scene

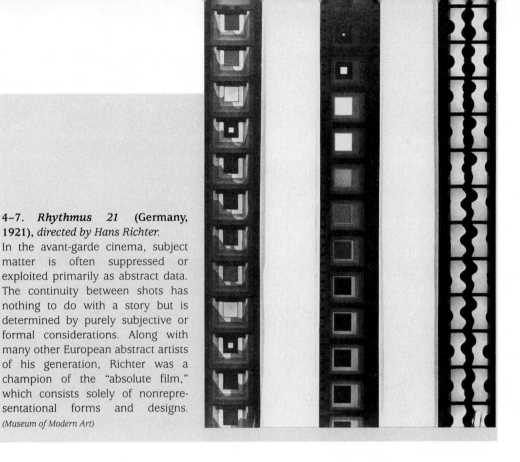

4-7. *Rhythmus 21* (Germany, 1921), *directed by Hans Richter.*
In the avant-garde cinema, subject matter is often suppressed or exploited primarily as abstract data. The continuity between shots has nothing to do with a story but is determined by purely subjective or formal considerations. Along with many other European abstract artists of his generation, Richter was a champion of the "absolute film," which consists solely of nonrepresentational forms and designs. *(Museum of Modern Art)*

could be photographed just as functionally in a single shot, with the camera at long-shot range. This type of setup is known as a **master shot** or a **sequence shot.** Classical cutting is more nuanced and more intrusive. It breaks down the unity of space, analyzes its components, and refocuses our attention to a series of details. The action is mental and emotional rather than literal.

During the golden years of the American studio system—roughly the 1930s and 1940s—directors were often urged (or forced) to adopt the master-shot technique of shooting. This method involved shooting an entire scene in long shot without cuts. This take contained all the dramatic variables and hence served as the basic or "master" shot for the scene. The action was then repeated a number of times, with the camera photographing medium shots and close-ups of the principals in the scene. When all this footage was gathered together, the editor had a number of choices in constructing a story continuity. Often, disagreements arose over the proper sequence of shots. Usually, the studio director was permitted a **first cut**—that is, the sequence of shots representing his or her interpretation of the materials. Under this system, the studios usually had the right to a **final cut.** Many directors disliked master-shot techniques precisely because, with so much footage available, a meddling producer could construct a radically different continuity.

Master shots are still used by many directors. Without a master, editors often complain of inadequate footage—that the available shots won't cut

a

b

c

d

4–8. *Fat City* (U.S.A., 1972), *directed by John Huston.*
Classical cutting involves editing for dramatic emphasis, to highlight details that might otherwise be overlooked. In Huston's fight scene, for example, the entire boxing match could have
been presented in a single setup **(a).** Such a presentation would probably strike us as under-
whelming. Instead, Huston breaks up his shots according to the psychological actions and
reactions within the fighter protagonist (Stacy Keach), his manager (Nicholas Colosanto), and
two friends in the auditorium (Candy Clark and Jeff Bridges).   *(Columbia Pictures)*

smoothly. In complex battle scenes, most directors are likely to shoot many
cover shots—that is, general shots that can be used to reestablish a sequence if
the other shots won't cut. In *The Birth of a Nation,* Griffith used multiple cameras to photograph many of the battle scenes, a technique also used by Akira
Kurosawa in some sequences of *The Seven Samurai.*

Griffith and other classical filmmakers developed a variety of editing
conventions that they thought made the cutting "invisible," or at least didn't
call attention to itself. One of these techniques is the *eyeline match.* We see character A look off frame left. Cut to a shot—from his point of view—of character
B. We assume B is to A's left. Cause–effect.

Another convention of classical cutting is *matching action*. Character A is seated but begins to rise. Cut to another shot of character A concluding the rising action and then moving away. The idea is to keep the action fluid, to mask the cut with a smooth linkage that's not noticed because the motion of the character takes precedence. The continuity of the movement conceals the suture.

The so-called *180° rule* is still observed by filmmakers, though even during the big-studio era there was nothing sacred about it. (For example, John Ford loved violating the 180° rule. He loved violating almost any rule.) This convention involves **mise en scène** as well as editing. The purpose is to stabilize the space of the playing area so the spectator isn't confused or disoriented. An imaginary "axis of action" line is drawn through the middle of a scene, viewed from the **bird's-eye** angle **(4–9).** Character A is on the left; character B is on the right. If the director wanted a two-shot, he or she would use camera 1. If we then go to a close-up of A (camera 2), the camera must stay on the same side of the 180° line to keep the same background—a continuity aid for the spectator. Similarly, a close-up of character B (camera 3) would be shot on the same side of the axis of action.

In shot **reverse angle** exchanges—common for dialogue sequences— the director takes care to fix the placement of the characters from shot to shot.

4–9.   Bird's-eye view of the 180° rule.

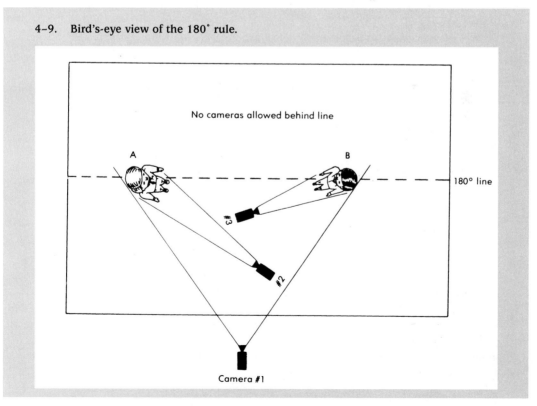

If character A is on the left and character B is on the right in the first shot, they must remain that way in the reverse angle taken from over the shoulder of character B. Usually the reverse angle is not literally 180° opposite, but we agree to accept it as such.

Even today, filmmakers rarely take the camera behind the imaginary axis line, unless their deliberate intention is to confuse the spectator. During fight scenes and other types of chaotic clashes, the filmmaker often wants the spectator to feel threatened, disoriented, anxious. This can be accomplished by deliberately violating the 180° rule.

Griffith also perfected the conventions of the chase—still very much with us. Many of his movies ended with a chase and last-minute rescue sequence. Most of them feature **parallel editing**—the alternation of shots of

4–10.   *It's a Wonderful Life* (**U.S.A., 1946),** *with James Stewart, directed by Frank Capra.* Capra was a master of classical editing. His cutting style was fast, light, seamless. But he never displayed his editing virtuosity for its own sake. Like every other technique, editing is subordinated to the needs of the characters in action—the cardinal commandment of classical cutting. In this and other scenes, Capra included a "reactive character" who guides the viewer's response to the action. This character represents a kind of norm, the way an average person would respond to a given situation. In this scene, for example, Capra's charming fantasy takes a whimsical turn. The forlorn hero (Stewart) listens to his guardian angel (Henry Travers, left) explain why he isn't a very *distinguished* angel (he has yet to earn his wings). A casual bystander (Tom Fadden, center) happens to overhear and is totally spooked by their conversation. Capra is able to punctuate the comedy of the scene by cutting to this character's response whenever the angel says something weird.   *(RKO)*

one scene with another at a different location. By **cross-cutting** back and forth between the two (or three or four) scenes, Griffith conveyed the idea of simultaneous time. For example, near the end of *The Birth of a Nation,* Griffith cross-cuts between four groups. In juxtaposing shots from these separate scenes, he manages to intensify the suspense by reducing the duration of the shots as the sequence reaches its climax. The sequence itself lasts twenty minutes of film time, but the psychological effect of the cross-cutting (the shots average about five seconds each) suggests speed and tension. Generally speaking, the greater the number of cuts within a scene, the greater its sense of speed. To avoid the risk of monotony during this sequence, Griffith changed his **setups** many times. There are **extreme long,** long, medium, and close shots, varied angles, lighting contrasts, even a moving camera (it was mounted on a truck).

If the continuity of a sequence is reasonably logical, the fragmentation of space presents no great difficulties. But the problem of time is more complex. Its treatment in film is more subjective than the treatment of space. Movies can compress years into two hours of projection time. They can also stretch a split second into many minutes. Most films condense time. There are only a handful that attempt to make screen time conform to real time: Agnès Varda's *Cleo From Five to Seven* and Fred Zinnemann's *High Noon* **(4–22)** are perhaps the best-known examples. Both deal with about 90 minutes of time—also the approximate length of the films. Even these movies cheat by compressing time in the expository opening sequences and expanding it in the climactic scenes. In actual practice, time exists in a kind of limbo: As long as the audience is absorbed by the screen action, time is what the film says it is. The problem, then, is to absorb the viewer.

On the most mechanical level, screen time is determined by the physical length of the filmstrip containing the shot. This length is governed generally by the complexity of the image subject matter. Usually, longer shots are more densely saturated with visual information than close-ups and need to be held longer on the screen. Raymond Spottiswoode, an early film theorist, claimed that a cut must be made at the peak of the "content curve"—that is, the point in a shot at which the audience has been able to assimilate most of its information. Cutting after the peak of the content curve produces boredom and a sense of dragging time. Cutting before the peak doesn't give the audience enough time to assimilate the visual action. An image with a complex mise en scène requires more time to assimilate than a simple one. Once an image has been established, however, a return to it during the sequence can be considerably shorter, because it works as a reminder.

But the sensitive treatment of time in editing is largely an instinctive matter that defies mechanical rules. Most great directors have edited their own films, or at least worked in close collaboration with their editors, so crucial is this art to the success of films. The best-edited sequences are determined by mood as well as subject matter. Griffith, for example, generally edited love scenes in long **lyrical** takes, with relatively few setups. His chase

a

b

4-11a & b. *Pulp Fiction* (U.S.A., 1994), *with John Travolta and Uma Thurman, written and directed by Quentin Tarantino.* (Miramax Films)

Why do some movie directors cut while others avoid cutting by including all the variables in a single shot? Still other filmmakers prefer to move their camera along with the action rather than cut between separate shots. The differences may seem unimportant to the average viewer, but serious film artists realize that each of these three techniques suggests different psychological undertones—undertones that even average viewers respond to, though they might not be able to explain their response analytically.

The scene from *Pulp Fiction* takes place in a confined restaurant booth. Logically, Tarantino could have shot the scene with a single set-up, with both characters in profile facing each other. But the dramatic context demands a different strategy. Travolta plays a junkie/hit man whose gangster boss has asked him to take his wife to dinner while the boss is out of town. Wary of her flaky, unpredictable behavior, and fully conscious that a careless slip-up could cost him his life, the Travolta character "keeps his distance" from her—an aloofness that intrigues her. By keeping the two in separate space cubicles with a traditional shot/counter-shot technique, Tarantino stresses their psychological apartness. The editing keeps a distance between them.

continued ▶

4–11c. *Gladiator* **(U.S.A., 2000),** *with Russell Crowe (right), directed by Ridley Scott.* *(DreamWorks Pictures)*

4–11d. *GoodFellas* **(U.S.A., 1990),** *with Lorraine Bracco and Ray Liotta, directed by Martin Scorsese.* *(Warner Bros.)*

The shot from *Gladiator* is more realistic in its presentation, with the sympathetic hero (Crowe) trapped in the same arena with a hungry tiger and a hostile giant who's determined to destroy him. In the movie itself, Ridley Scott cuts to all three of these dramatic variables to stretch out the suspense, but the greatest danger is conveyed in shots like this, where all three must fight to the finish in a relatively confined space.

Scorsese, who is a superlative editor, is also a master of the moving camera, and he often prefers to move with the action rather than break it down into a series of separate shots. Why? Mostly because the moving camera is more fluid, more lyrical. (It's also more expensive and time consuming.) In this wedding dance scene from *GoodFellas*, for example, Scorsese conveys the couple's euphoria by swirling the camera along with the dancers. These spontaneous eruptions destabilize the visual materials, infusing the action with a surge of energy, almost a kinetic high.

and battle scenes were composed of brief shots, jammed together. Paradoxically, the love scenes actually compress real time, whereas the rapidly cut sequences elongate it.

There are no fixed rules concerning rhythm in films. Some editors cut according to musical rhythms (see 5–12). The march of soldiers, for example, could be edited to the beat of a military tune, as can be seen in several marching sequences in King Vidor's *The Big Parade*. This technique is also common with American avant-garde filmmakers, who feature rock music soundtracks or cut according to a mathematical or structural formula. In some cases, a director will cut before the peak of the content curve, especially in highly suspenseful sequences. In a number of movies, Hitchcock teases the audience by not providing enough time to assimilate all the meanings of a shot. Violent scenes are con-

4–12.   *The Last Picture Show* (U.S.A., 1971), *with Cybill Shepherd and Ellen Burstyn, directed by Peter Bogdanovich.*
In its subtlest form, classical cutting can break up even a confined action into smaller units of meaning. François Truffaut once observed that movies in which people tell lies require more shots than those in which they tell the truth. For example, if a young daughter tells her mother that she thinks she is in love with a boy, and the mother responds by warning the girl of some of the emotional dangers involved, there is no reason why the scene shouldn't be photographed in a single setup with both females in the same frame. Essentially, this is how Bogdanovich presents a similar scene **(a)**. However, if the mother were a lying hypocrite, and the daughter suspected that the older woman might be in love with the boy herself, a director would be forced to break the scene down into five or six shots **(b–g)** to give viewers emotional information they wouldn't receive from the characters themselves.   *(Columbia Pictures)*

a

continued ▶

b

c

d

e

f

g

4–13. *The Deer Hunter* **(U.S.A., 1978),** *directed by Michael Cimino.*
Editing is an art as well as a craft. Like all art, it often defies mechanical formulations, taking on a life of its own. For example, when sneak preview audiences were asked for their reactions to this three-hour movie, most viewers responded enthusiastically but felt that the hour-long wedding sequence of the opening could have been cut down. In terms of its plot, nothing much "happens" in this sequence. Its purpose is primarily *lyrical*—a loving celebration of the social rituals that bind the community together. The story content of the sequence could be condensed to a few minutes of screen time—which is exactly what its makers did. When the shortened version was shown to audiences, reactions were negative. Cimino and his editor, Peter Zinner, restored the cut footage. The long wedding sequence is necessary not for its story content so much as for its experiential value. It provides the movie with a sense of balance: The community solidarity of the sequence is what the characters fight *for* in the subsequent battle footage of the film. *(Universal Pictures)*

ventionally cut in a highly fragmented manner. On the other hand, Antonioni usually cuts long after the content curve has peaked. In *La Notte,* for example, the rhythm is languorous and even monotonous: The director attempts to create a sense of weariness in the audience, paralleling that of the characters. Antonioni's characters are usually tired people—in every sense of the term **(see 3–7).**

Tact is another editing principle that's difficult to generalize about, because it too depends on context. No one likes to have the obvious pointed out to us, whether in real life or while watching a movie. Like personal tact, directorial tact is a matter of restraint, taste, and respect for the intelligence of others. Hack directors often present us with emotionally gratuitous shots, falling over themselves to make sure we haven't missed the point.

4–14. *The 4th Man* (Holland, 1984), *with Jeroen Krabbé, directed by Paul Verhoeven.* Editing can shift the action from reality to fantasy in an instant. Often, such shifts are accompanied by a cue—eerie music, for example, or a rippling image that suggests a different level of consciousness. At other times, the shift is undetectable, a deliberate attempt to disorient the viewer. The novelist hero of this movie often intermingles reality with fantasy. In this scene, he is trying to shave while suffering from a colossal hangover. His roommate is practicing his music, making the shaky hero even shakier. In exasperation, he walks over to the roommate and strangles him. A moment later, we see the hero shaving again and the roommate still practicing his music. The strangulation took place only in the hero's vivid imagination. Because it is presented with no transitional cue, we too confuse reality with fantasy—the theme of the film. *(International Spectrafilm Distribution)*

Griffith's most radical experiments in editing are found in his 1916 masterpiece, *Intolerance.* This movie was the first fiction film to explore the idea of **thematic montage.** Both the film and the technique exerted an enormous influence on movie directors of the 1920s, especially in the Soviet Union. Thematic montage stresses the association of *ideas,* irrespective of the continuity of time and space.

Intolerance is unified by the themes of bigotry and persecution. Rather than tell one story, Griffith intercut four. One takes place in ancient Babylon. The second deals with the crucifixion of Jesus. The third concerns the massacre of the Huguenots by the Catholic royalists in sixteenth-century France. The last story takes place in America in 1916 and deals with a battle between labor and management.

The four stories are developed not separately but in parallel fashion. Scenes of one time period are intercut with scenes of another. At the conclusion of the movie, Griffith features suspenseful chase sequences in the first and last stories, a brutal scene of slaughter in the French story, and a slow, tragic climax in the killing of Jesus. The concluding sequence contains literally hundreds of shots, juxtaposing images that are separated by thousands of years and by as many miles. All these different time periods and locations are unified by the central theme of intolerance. The continuity is no longer physical, or even psychological, but conceptual—that is, thematic.

4-15. *Royal Wedding* (U.S.A., 1951), *with Fred Astaire, directed by Stanley Donen.*
Even in the heyday of the Hollywood studio system, when the dominance of classical cutting was virtually unchallenged, there were instances when the realistic continuity of time and space had to be preserved at the expense of editing. For example, in this famous dance sequence, Astaire begins to tap dance on the floor of his hotel room and then—without a cut—he taps up the wall, then onto the ceiling, seemingly defying gravity. How was it done? A revolving set and camera were synchronized so that whenever the hotel room began to turn, Astaire tapped his way onto the new "floor" unobtrusively in one continuous motion. Had director Donen cut to separate shots, the sequence would have lost much of its magical whimsy. *(MGM)*

Intolerance was not a commercial success, but its influence was immense. The filmmakers of the Soviet Union were dazzled by Griffith's movie and based their own theories of montage on his practices in this film. A great many directors have profited from Griffith's experiments in the subjective treatment of time. In *The Pawnbroker*, for example, Sidney Lumet exploits the art of editing to produce a series of parallels that are thematically rather than chronologically related. He uses a kind of subliminal editing, in which some shots are held on the screen for only a fraction of a second. The central character is a middle-aged Jew who survived a Nazi concentration camp twenty-five years earlier; all his loved ones, however, were killed there. He tries to repress the memories of these earlier experiences, but they force their way into his consciousness. Lumet suggests this psychological process by intercutting a few frames of the memory shots during a scene that is occurring in the present. A present-tense event detonates the protagonist's memory of something similar from his past. As past contends with present, the flickering memory shots endure longer, until a **flashback** sequence eventually becomes dominant, and the present is momentarily suspended. With only a few exceptions, however, it was not until the 1960s that such unorthodox editing practices became widespread.

4–16. *Flashdance* (U.S.A., 1983), *with Jennifer Beals, directed by Adrian Lyne.*
Editing is often used to deceive—to conceal rather than reveal. For example, the dance numbers in this film were performed by a double, a professional dancer whose identity is cun-
ningly concealed by the artful lighting and the discreetly distanced camera. The dance shots
were intercut with closer shots of Jennifer Beals, wearing the same costume and moving to
the same music. With the musical number providing the continuity, these intercut shots create the illusion of a continuous movement, with Beals featured throughout. These editing
techniques are also commonly used in such scenes as sword fights, dangerous stunts, and
many other activities requiring specialized skills.   *(Paramount Pictures)*

Filmmakers can interrupt the present with shots not only of the past
but of the future as well. In Sydney Pollack's *They Shoot Horses, Don't They?* short
flash-forwards of a courtroom scene are interspersed throughout the present-
tense story. The flash-forwards suggest predestination: Like the dance contest
of the story proper, the future is rigged, and personal effort is equated with self-
deception. Flash-forwards are also used in Alain Resnais's *La Guerre Est Finie*
and Joseph Losey's *The Go-Between.*

Griffith also restructured time and place through the use of fantasy
inserts. In *Intolerance,* for example, a young woman on the verge of murdering
her unfaithful boyfriend imagines a scene where she is apprehended by the
police. Flashbacks, flash-forwards, and cutaways to fantasies allow filmmakers to
develop ideas thematically rather than chronologically, freeing them to explore
the subjective nature of time. The very flexibility of time in movies makes the
theme of temporality an ideal subject for the medium.

Like Faulkner, Proust, and other novelists, filmmakers have succeeded
in cracking the tyranny of mechanically measured time. One of the most complex instances of the restructuring of time is found in Stanley Donen's *Two for
the Road.* The story deals with the development and gradual disintegration of a
love relationship. It unfolds in a series of mixed flashbacks. That is, the flash-

153

4-17. *West Side Story* (U.S.A., 1961), *directed by Robert Wise and Jerome Robbins.*
Musicals are often edited in a radically formalist style, without having to observe the cutting conventions of ordinary dramatic movies. The editing of *West Side Story* is very abstract. The music, by Leonard Bernstein, and the dance numbers, choreographed by Jerome Robbins, are edited together for maximum aesthetic impact, rather than to forward the story. Nor are the shots linked by some principle of thematic association. Rather, the shots are juxtaposed primarily for their lyrical and kinetic beauty, somewhat like a music video. *(United Artists)*

backs are not in chronological sequence, nor are they completed in any one scene. Rather, they are jumbled and fragmented, somewhat in the manner of a Faulkner novel. To complicate matters, most of the flashbacks take place on the road, during various trips the couple has taken in the past. If each of the time periods of the film were designated with the letters A, B, C, D, and E, its temporal structure might be charted as follows: E (present), A (most distant past), B, C, D, B, A, E, C, D, B . . . ending with E. The audience gradually learns to identify each time period through various continuity clues: the heroine's hair styles, the modes of transportation, the particular crisis during each trip, and so on.

From its crude beginnings, Griffith expanded the art of editing to include a wide variety of functions: locale changes, time lapses, shot variety, emphasis of psychological and physical details, overviews, symbolic inserts, parallels and contrasts, associations, point-of-view shifts, simultaneity, and repetition of **motifs.**

Griffith's method of editing was also more economical. Related shots could be bunched together in the shooting schedule, regardless of their positions (or "time" and "place") in the finished film. Especially in later years, in the era of high-salaried stars, directors could shoot all the star sequences in a brief period and out of cinematic continuity. Less expensive details (extreme long shots, minor actors, close-ups of objects, etc.) could be shot at a more convenient time. Later, the shots would be arranged in their proper sequence on the editor's cutting bench.

Soviet Montage and the Formalist Tradition

Griffith was a practical artist, concerned with communicating ideas and emotions in the most effective manner possible. In the 1920s, the Soviet filmmakers expanded his associational principles and established the theoretical premises for thematic editing, or *montage* as they called it (from the French, *monter,* to assemble). V. I. Pudovkin wrote the first important theoretical treatises on what he called constructive editing. Most of his statements are explanations of Griffith's practices, but he differed with the American (whom he praises lavishly) on several points. Griffith's use of the close-up, Pudovkin claimed, is too limited. It's used simply as a clarification of the long shot, which carries most of the meaning. The close-up, in effect, is merely an interruption, offering no meanings of its own. Pudovkin insisted that each shot should make a new point. Through the juxtaposition of shots, new meanings can be created. The meanings, then, are in the juxtapositions, not in one shot alone.

Filmmakers in the Soviet Union were strongly influenced by the psychological theories of Pavlov, whose experiments in the association of ideas served as a basis for the editing experiments of Lev Kuleshov, Pudovkin's mentor. Kuleshov believed that ideas in cinema are created by linking together fragmentary details to produce a unified action. These details can be totally unrelated in real life. For example, he linked together a shot of Moscow's Red Square with a

4–18. ***Dead Men Don't Wear Plaid*** (U.S.A., 1982), *with Steve Martin and Carl Reiner (bald pate), directed by Reiner.*
Reiner's comic parody of Nazi films and other noir genres of the 1940s is a tour de force of editing. A silly spy plot involving Martin is intercut with footage from such vintage 1940s movies as *Double Indemnity, Suspicion, The Bribe, Out of the Past,* and *Sorry, Wrong Number.* Pudovkin and Kuleshov would have understood perfectly. *(University City Studios)*

shot of the American White House, close-ups of two men climbing stairs with another close-up of two hands shaking. Projected as a continuous scene, the linked shots suggest that the two men are in the same place at the same time.

Kuleshov conducted another famous experiment that provided a theoretical foundation for the use of nonprofessional actors in movies. Kuleshov and many of his colleagues believed that traditional acting skills were quite unnecessary in the cinema. First, he shot a close-up of an actor with a neutral expression. He juxtaposed this with a close-up of a bowl of soup. Then he joined the close-up of the actor with a shot of a coffin containing a female corpse. Finally, he linked the actor's neutral expression with a shot of a little girl playing. When these combinations were shown to audiences, they exclaimed at the actor's expressiveness in portraying hunger, deep sorrow, and paternal pride. In each case, the meaning was conveyed by juxtaposing two shots, not by one alone. Actors can be used as raw material, as objects juxtaposed with other objects. The emotion is produced not by the actor's performance, but by associations brought about by the juxtapositions. In a sense, the *viewer* creates the emotional meanings, once the appropriate objects have been linked together by the filmmaker **(4–20).**

4-19. *Lifeboat* **(U.S.A., 1944),** *with Tullulah Bankhead (center), directed by Alfred Hitchcock.* Hitchcock was one of Pudovkin's most articulate champions. "Cinema is form," Hitchcock insisted. "The screen ought to speak its own language, freshly coined, and it can't do that unless it treats an acted scene as a piece of raw material which must be broken up, taken to bits, before it can be woven into an expressive visual pattern." He referred to the piecing together of fragmentary shots as "pure cinema," like individual notes of music that combine to produce a melody. In this movie, he confined himself entirely to nine characters adrift at sea in a small boat. In other words, this photo contains the raw material for every shot in the film. Formalists insist that the artistry lies not in the materials per se, but in the way they are taken apart and reconstructed expressively. *(Twentieth Century–Fox)*

For Kuleshov and Pudovkin, a sequence was not filmed; it was constructed. Using far more close-ups than Griffith, Pudovkin built a scene from many separate shots, all juxtaposed for a unified effect. The environment of the scene is the source of the images. Long shots are rare. Instead, a barrage of close-ups (often of objects) provides the audience with the necessary associations to link together the meaning. These juxtapositions can suggest emotional and psychological states, even abstract ideas.

The Soviet theorists of this generation were criticized on several counts. This technique detracts from a scene's sense of realism, some critics complained, for the continuity of actual time and place is totally restructured. But Pudovkin and the other Soviet formalists claimed that realism captured in long shot is *too* near reality: It's theatrical rather than cinematic. Movies must capture the essence, not merely the surface, of reality, which is filled with irrelevancies. Only by juxtaposing close-ups of objects, textures, symbols, and other selected details can a filmmaker convey *expressively* the idea underlying the undifferentiated jumble of real life.

Some critics also believe that this manipulative style of editing guides the spectator too much—the choices are already made. The audience must sit back passively and accept the inevitable linking of associations presented on the screen. Political considerations are involved here, for the Soviets tended to link film with propaganda. Propaganda, no matter how artistic, doesn't usually involve free and balanced evaluations.

Like many Soviet formalists, Sergei Eisenstein was interested in exploring general principles that could be applied to a variety of apparently different forms of creative activity. He believed that these artistic principles were organically related to the basic nature of all human activity and, ultimately, to the nature of the universe itself. Like the ancient Greek philosopher Heraclitus, Eisenstein believed that the essence of existence is constant change. He believed that nature's eternal fluctuation is **dialectical**—the result of the conflict and synthesis of opposites. What appears to be stationary or unified in nature is only temporary, for all phenomena are in various states of becoming. Only energy is permanent, and energy is constantly in a state of transition to other forms. Every opposite contains the seed of its own destruction in time, Eisenstein believed, and this conflict of opposites is the mother of motion and change.

The function of all artists is to capture this dynamic collision of opposites, to incorporate dialectical conflicts not only in the subject matter of art but in its techniques and forms as well. Conflict is universal in all the arts, according to Eisenstein, and therefore all art aspires to motion. Potentially, at least, the cinema is the most comprehensive of the arts because it can incorporate the visual conflicts of painting and photography, the kinetic conflicts of dance, the tonal conflicts of music, the verbal conflicts of language, and the character and action conflicts of fiction and drama.

Eisenstein placed special emphasis on the art of editing. Like Kuleshov and Pudovkin, he believed that montage was the foundation of film art. He agreed with them that each shot of a sequence ought to be incomplete, con-

a   b

4–20a, b, c, d.   An "edited sequence" from _Rear Window_ (U.S.A., 1954), _directed by Alfred Hitchcock._

Hitchcock's thriller centers on a photographic journalist (James Stewart) who is confined to his apartment because of a broken leg. Out of boredom, he begins to observe the lives of his neighbors, who live in the apartment building just behind his own. His high-society girlfriend (Grace Kelly, **4–20a**) wants to get married and sees no reason why marriage should interfere with his work. But he puts her off, filling in his idle hours by speculating on the various problems of his neighbors. Each neighbor's window symbolizes a fragment of Stewart's divided sentiments: They are projections of his own anxieties and desires, which center on love, career, and marriage. Each window suggests a different option for the hero. One neighbor is a desperately lonely woman. Another apartment is occupied by lusty newlyweds. A friendless bachelor musician occupies a third apartment. A shallow and promiscuous dancer lives in another. In still another is a childless married couple, who fawn pathetically over their dog

continued   ▶

tributory rather than self-contained. However, Eisenstein criticized the concept of linked shots for being mechanical and inorganic. He believed that editing ought to be dialectical: The conflict of two shots (thesis and antithesis) produces a wholly new idea (synthesis). Thus, in film terms, the conflict between shot A and shot B is not AB (Kuleshov and Pudovkin), but a qualitatively new factor—C (Eisenstein). Transitions between shots should not be smooth, as Pudovkin suggested, but sharp, jolting, even violent. For Eisenstein, editing

c   d

to fill in the vacuum of their lives. In the most sinister apartment is a tormented middle-aged man (Raymond Burr, **4–20c**), who is so harassed by his wife that he eventually murders her. By cutting from shots of the spying hero to shots of the neighbors' windows, Hitchcock dramatizes the thoughts going through Stewart's mind. The audience is moved by the editing style rather than by the material per se or even by the actors' performances. Somewhat like the early experiments of Pudovkin and Kuleshov, who edited together unrelated bits of film to create a new concept, this phony "edited sequence" is composed of totally random publicity photos, and might be viewed as a kind of guilt by associational montage. Such editing techniques represent a form of characterization. Actors sometimes complained that Hitchcock didn't allow them to *act*. But he believed that people don't always express what they're thinking or feeling, and hence the director must communicate these ideas through the editing. The actor, in short, provides only a part of the characterization. The rest is provided by Hitchcock's montage.   *(Paramount Pictures)*

produces harsh collisions, not subtle linkages. A smooth transition, he claimed, was an opportunity lost.

Editing for Eisenstein was an almost mystical process. He likened it to the growth of organic cells. If each shot represents a developing cell, the cinematic cut is like the rupturing of the cell when it splits into two. Editing is done at the point that a shot "bursts"—that is, when its tensions have reached their maximum expansion. The rhythm of editing in a movie should be like the explosions of an internal combustion engine, Eisenstein claimed. A master of dynamic rhythms, his films are almost mesmerizing in this respect: Shots of contrasting volumes, durations, shapes, designs, and lighting intensities collide against each other like objects in a torrential river plunging toward their inevitable destination.

The differences between Pudovkin and Eisenstein may seem academic. In actual practice, however, the two approaches produced sharply contrasting results. Pudovkin's movies are essentially in the classical mold. The shots tend to be additive and are directed toward an overall emotional effect, which is guided by the story. In Eisenstein's movies, the jolting images represent a series of essentially intellectual thrusts and parries, directed toward an ideological argument. The directors' narrative structures also differed. Pudovkin's stories didn't differ much from the kind Griffith used. On the other hand, Eisenstein's stories were much more loosely structured, usually a series of documentarylike episodes used as convenient vehicles for exploring ideas.

When Pudovkin wanted to express an emotion, he conveyed it in terms of physical images—objective correlatives—taken from the actual locale. Thus, the sense of anguished drudgery is conveyed through a series of shots showing details of a cart mired in the mud: close-ups of the wheel, the mud, hands coaxing the wheel, straining faces, the muscles of an arm pulling the wheel, and so on. Eisenstein, on the other hand, wanted film to be totally free of literal continuity and context. Pudovkin's correlatives, he felt, were too restricted by realism.

Eisenstein wanted movies to be as flexible as literature, especially to make figurative comparisons without respect to time and place. Movies should

4–21.   A portion of the Odessa Steps sequence from *Potemkin* (U.S.S.R., 1925), *directed by Sergei Eisenstein.*
Perhaps the most celebrated instance of editing virtuosity in the silent cinema, the Odessa Steps sequence is an illustration of Eisenstein's theory of collision montage in practice. This scene deals with the slaughter of civilians by Cossack troops in Czarist Russia. The director juxtaposed lights with darks, vertical lines with horizontals, lengthy shots with brief ones, close-ups with long shots, static setups with traveling shots, and so on. See also David Mayer, *Eisenstein's Potemkin: A Shot-by-Shot Presentation* (New York: Grossman, 1972).   *(Audio-Brandon Films)*

continued   ▶

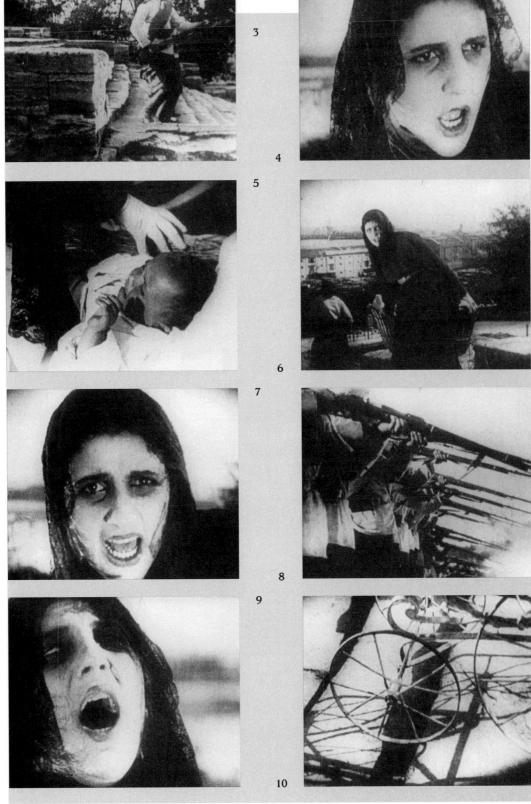

3

4

5

6

7

8

9

10

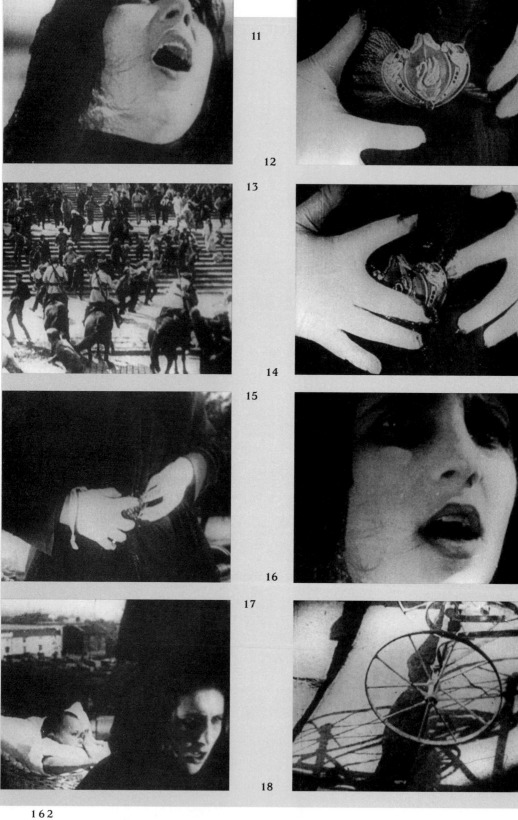

11

12

13

14

15

16

17

18

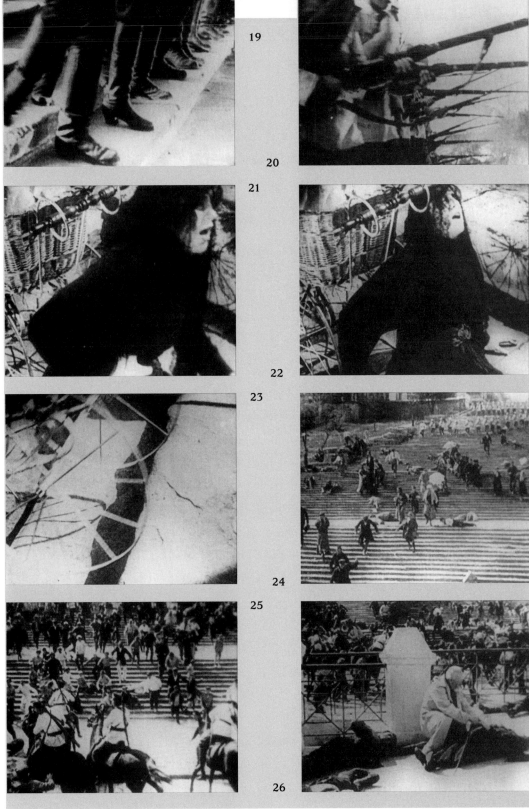

19

20

21

22

23

24

25

26

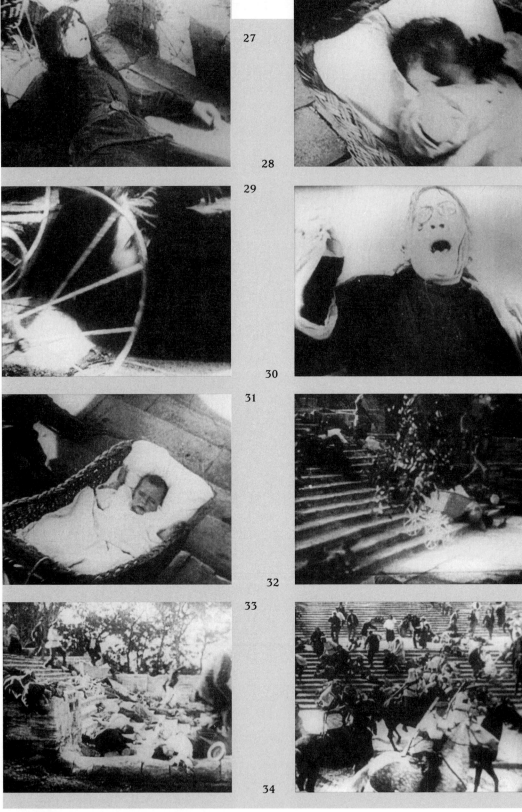

27

28

29

30

31

32

33

34

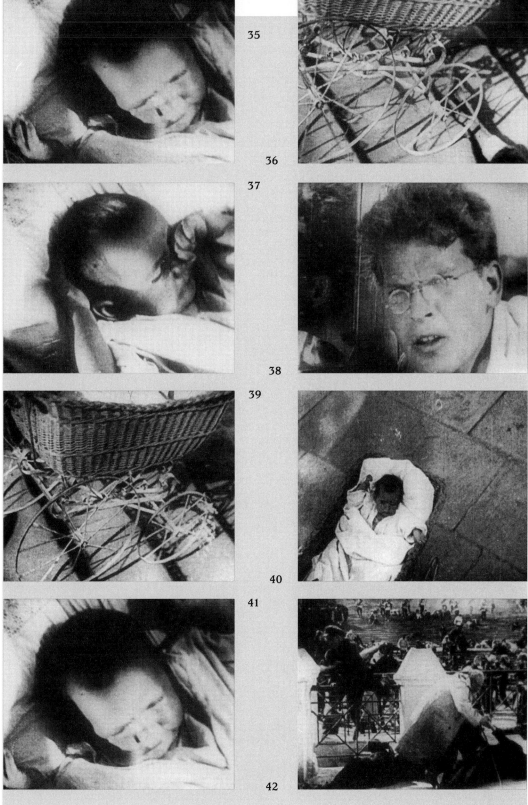

35

36

37

38

39

40

41

42

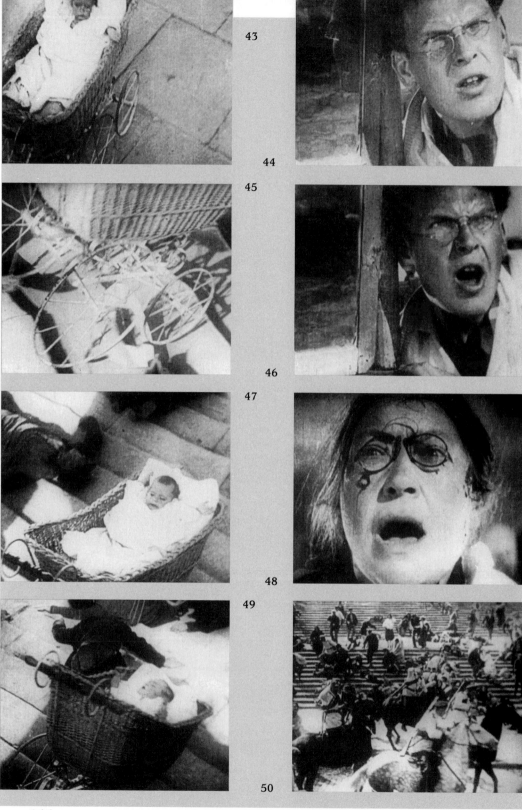

43

44
45

46
47

48
49

50

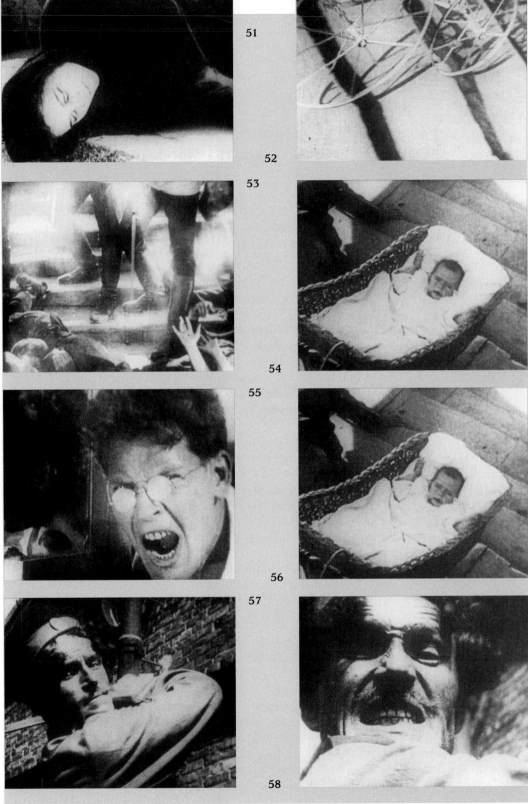

51

52
53

54
55

56
57

58

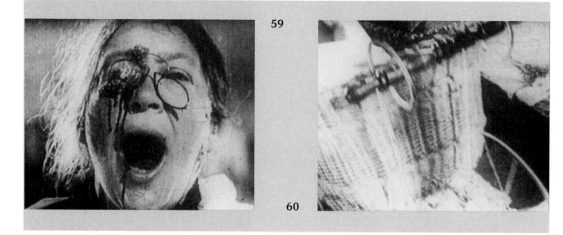

include images that are thematically or metaphorically relevant, Eisenstein claimed, regardless of whether they can be found in the locale or not. Even in his first feature, *Strike* (1925), Eisenstein intercut shots of workmen being machine-gunned with images of oxen being slaughtered. The oxen are not literally on location, but are intercut purely for metaphorical purposes. A famous sequence from *Potemkin* links three shots of stone lions: one asleep, a second aroused and on the verge of rising, and a third on its feet and ready to pounce. Eisenstein considered the sequence an embodiment of a metaphor: "The very stones roar."

Ingenious as these metaphorical comparisons can be, the major problem with this kind of editing is its tendency to be obvious—or impenetrably obscure. Eisenstein saw no difficulty in overcoming the space and time differences between film and literature. But the two mediums use metaphors in different ways. We have no difficulty in understanding what's meant by the comparison "he's timid as a sheep," or even the more abstract metaphor, "whorish time undoes us all." Both statements exist outside of time and place. The simile isn't set in a pasture, nor is the metaphor set in a brothel. Such comparisons are not meant to be understood literally, of course. In movies, figurative devices of this kind are more difficult. Editing can produce a number of figurative comparisons, but they don't work in quite the same way that they do in literature. Eisenstein's theories of collision montage have been explored primarily in the avant-garde cinema, music videos, and TV commercials. Most fiction filmmakers have found them too intrusive and heavy-handed.

André Bazin and the Tradition of Realism

André Bazin was not a filmmaker, but solely a critic and theorist. For a number of years, he was the editor of the influential French journal *Cahiers du Cinéma,* in which he set forth an aesthetic of film that was in sharp opposition to such formalists as Pudovkin and Eisenstein. Bazin was untainted by dogmatism. Although he emphasized the realistic nature of the cinema, he was generous in his praise of movies that exploited editing effectively. Throughout his writings, however, Bazin maintained that montage was merely one of many techniques a director could use in making movies. Furthermore, he believed that in many cases editing could actually destroy the effectiveness of a scene (**4–24** and **4–26**).

Bazin's realist aesthetic was based on his belief that photography, TV, and cinema, unlike the traditional arts, produce images of reality automatically, with a minimum of human interference. This technological objectivity connects the moving image with the observable physical world. A novelist or a painter must represent reality by re-presenting it in another medium—through language and color pigments. The filmmaker's image, on the other hand, is essentially an objective recording of what actually exists. No other art, Bazin felt, can be as comprehensive in the presentation of the physical world. No other art can be as realistic, in the most elementary sense of that word.

Bazin's aesthetic had a moral as well as technological bias. He was influenced by the philosophical movement called Personalism. This school of thought emphasized the individualistic and pluralistic nature of truth. Just as most Personalists agreed that there are many truths, Bazin felt that in the cinema there are many ways of portraying the real. The essence of reality, he believed, lies in its ambiguity. Reality can even be interpreted in opposing, and equally valid, ways, depending on the sensitivities of the artist. To capture this ambiguity, the filmmaker must be modest and self-effacing, a patient observer willing to follow where reality leads. The film artists that Bazin admired most—Flaherty, Renoir, and De Sica, for example—are those whose movies reflect a sense of wonder before the ambiguous mysteries of reality.

4-22. *High Noon* (U.S.A., 1952), *with Gary Cooper and Lloyd Bridges, directed by Fred Zinnemann.*
Almost all movies compress time, condensing many months or even years into a running time of roughly two hours, the average length of most films. Zinnemann's movie is a rare example of a literal adherence to the unities of time, place, and action, for the entire story takes place in a breathless 84 minutes—the film's running time. *(United Artists)*

Bazin believed that the distortions involved in using formalist techniques—especially thematic editing—often violate the complexities of reality. Montage superimposes a simplistic ideology over the infinite variability of actual life. Formalists tend to be too egocentric and manipulative, he felt. They are concerned with imposing their narrow view of reality, rather than allowing reality to exist in its awesome complexity. He was one of the first to point out that such great filmmakers as Chaplin, Mizoguchi, and Murnau preserved the ambiguities of reality by minimizing editing.

Bazin even viewed classical cutting as potentially corrupting. Classical cutting breaks down a unified scene into a certain number of closer shots that correspond implicitly to a mental process. But the technique encourages us to follow the shot sequence without our being conscious of its arbitrariness. "The editor who cuts for us makes in our stead the choice which we would make in real life," Bazin pointed out. "Without thinking, we accept his analysis because it conforms to the laws of attention, but we are deprived of a privilege." He believed that classical cutting subjectivizes an event because each shot represents what the filmmaker thinks is important, not necessarily what we would think.

One of Bazin's favorite directors, the American William Wyler, reduced editing to a minimum in many of his films, substituting the use of **deep-focus** photography and lengthy takes. "His perfect clarity contributes enormously to

4–23. *Dog Day Afternoon* **(U.S.A., 1975), *with Al Pacino, directed by Sidney Lumet.***
Not all realists use an unobtrusive style of editing. Most of Lumet's gritty New York City dramas like *The Pawnbroker, Serpico, Prince of the City,* and *Dog Day Afternoon* are based on actual events and were shot mostly in the streets of the city. All are considered masterpieces of realism, yet all of them are edited in a nervous, jumpy style that connects a wide assortment of characters and explosive events. As early as 1910, the great Russian novelist Leo Tolstoy realized that this fledgling new art form would surpass the magnificent achievements of 19th century literary realism: "This little clinking contraption with the revolving handle will make a revolution in our life—in the life of writers. It is a direct attack on the old methods of literary art. This swift change of scene, this blending of emotion and experience—it is much better than the heavy, long-drawn-out kind of writing to which we are accustomed. It is closer to life." *(Warner Bros.)*

4–24. *Jurassic Park* (U.S.A., 1993), *with Joseph Mazzello, Sam Neill, Ariana Richards, and a friendly brachiosaurus; directed by Steven Spielberg.*

Cheap science-fiction films and low-budget adventure movies often combine realistic elements with the supernatural or the very dangerous, but seldom in the same frame. It's cheaper and easier to keep the terrified people in one shot, then cut to the object of their terror (or fascination) in another shot. Kuleshov would have applauded such a solution. But Bazin claimed that a realistic presentation—that is, *not* cutting, but keeping them both in the same frame—is far more effective, for audiences instinctively sense when a scene of this type is being faked with manipulative editing techniques. The most magical scenes in this movie are those that feature startlingly realistic dinosaurs—never so realistic as when they are combined in the same frame with humans. Bazin would have applauded. *(Universal Pictures/Amblin Entertainment)*

the spectator's reassurance and leaves to him the means to observe, to choose, and form an opinion," Bazin said of Wyler's austere cutting style. In such movies as *The Little Foxes, The Best Years of Our Lives* **(1–20b),** and *The Heiress,* Wyler achieved an unparalleled neutrality and transparency. It would be naive to confuse this neutrality with an absence of art, Bazin insisted, for all of Wyler's effort tends to hide itself.

Unlike some of his followers, Bazin did not advocate a simpleminded theory of realism. He was perfectly aware, for example, that cinema—like all art—involves a certain amount of selectivity, organization, and interpretation. In short, a certain amount of distortion. He also recognized that the values of the filmmaker will inevitably influence the manner in which reality is perceived. These distortions are not only inevitable, but in most cases desirable. For Bazin, the best films were those in which the artist's personal vision is held in delicate balance with the objective nature of the medium. Certain aspects of reality must be sacrificed for the sake of artistic coherence, then, but Bazin felt that abstraction and artifice ought to be kept to a minimum. The materials

4–25a. *The Sorrow and the Pity* (France/ Switzerland/W. Germany, 1970), *directed by Marcel Ophüls.*

Even in the world of documentary films, editing styles can range from ultrarealistic to ultraformalistic. Like most **cinéma-vérité** documentarists, Marcel Ophüls keeps editing to an absolute minimum. Implicit in the art of editing is artifice—that is, the manipulation of formal elements to produce a seductive aesthetic effect. Many documentarists believe that an edited analysis of a scene shapes and aestheticizes it—compromising its authenticity. A selected sequence of shots, however factually based, extrapolates one person's truth from an event and, in so doing, infuses it with an ideology. An unedited presentation, on the other hand, preserves a multiplicity of truths.   *(Cinema 5)*

4–25b. *Looking for Richard* **(U.S.A., 1996),** *with Al Pacino, directed by Pacino.*

The editing style of this documentary is subjective and personal. The movie itself is almost like an intimate diary by a famous actor exploring one of his most celebrated stage roles, Shakespeare's fascinating disciple of evil, Richard III. Pacino's **voice-over** connects many of the shots, which include interviews with other actors, historical artifacts, views of Shakespeare's Old Globe Theatre, and snippets of scenes from the play in rehearsal and performance. The movie is like a dazzling lecture/presentation by someone who is both an artist and an educator.   *(Twentieth Century-Fox)*

Most documentaries fall between these two extremes, as Albert Maysles has pointed out: "We can see two kinds of truth here. One is the raw material, which is the footage, the kind of truth that you get in literature in the diary form—it's immediate, no one has tampered with it. Then there's the other kind of truth that comes in extracting and juxtaposing the raw material into a more meaningful and coherent storytelling form which finally can be said to be more than just raw data. In a way, the interests of the people in shooting and the people in editing (even if it's the same individual) are in conflict with one another, because the raw material doesn't want to be shaped. It wants to maintain its truthfulness. One discipline says that if you begin to put it into another form, you're going to lose some of the veracity. The other discipline says if you don't let me put this into a form, no one is going to see it and the elements of truth in the raw material will never reach the audience with any impact, with any artistry, or whatever. So there are these things which are in conflict with one another and the thing is to put it all together, deriving the best from both. It comes almost to an argument of content and form, and you can't do one without the other."

should be allowed to speak for themselves. Bazinian realism is not mere news-reel objectivity—even if there were such a thing. He believed that reality must be heightened somewhat in the cinema, that the director must reveal the poetic implications of ordinary people, events, and places. By poeticizing the commonplace, the cinema is neither a totally objective recording of the physical world nor a symbolic abstraction of it. Rather, the cinema occupies a unique middle position between the sprawl of raw life and the artificially re-created worlds of the traditional arts.

Bazin wrote many articles overtly or implicitly criticizing the art of editing, or at least pointing out its limitations. If the essence of a scene is based on the idea of division, separation, or isolation, editing can be an effective technique in conveying these ideas. But if the essence of a scene demands the simultaneous presence of two or more related elements, the filmmaker ought to preserve the continuity of real time and space **(4–26).** He or she can do this by including all the dramatic variables within the same mise en scène—that is, by exploiting the resources of the long shot, the lengthy take, deep focus, and **widescreen.** The filmmaker can also preserve actual time and space by **panning, craning, tilting,** or **tracking** rather than cutting to individual shots.

John Huston's *The African Queen* contains a shot illustrating Bazin's principle. In attempting to take their boat down river to a large lake, the two protagonists (Humphrey Bogart and Katharine Hepburn) get sidetracked on a tributary of the main river. The tributary dwindles down to a stream and finally trickles into a tangle of reeds and mud, where the dilapidated boat gets hope-

4-26. *Safety Last* (U.S.A., 1923), *with Harold Lloyd, directed by Fred Newmeyer and Sam Taylor.*

In direct opposition to Pudovkin, Bazin believed that when the essence of a scene lies in the simultaneous presence of two or more elements, editing is ruled out. Such scenes gain their emotional impact through the unity of space, not through the juxtaposition of separate shots. In this famous sequence, for example, Lloyd's comedy of thrills is made more comic and more thrilling by the scene's realistic presentation: The dangling hero and the street below are kept in the same frame. Actually, the distance between the two is exaggerated by the cunning placement of the camera, and there was always at least a platform about three stories below him—"but who wants to fall three stories?" Lloyd asked. *(Museum of Modern Art)*

lessly mired. The exhausted travelers resign themselves to a slow death in the suffocating reeds, and eventually fall asleep on the floor of the boat. The camera then moves upward, over the reeds, where—just a few hundred yards away—is the lake. The bitter irony of the scene is conveyed by the continuous movement of the camera, which preserves the physical proximity of the boat, the intervening reeds, and the lake. If Huston had cut to three separate shots, we wouldn't understand these spatial interrelationships, and therefore the irony would be lost.

Bazin pointed out that in the evolution of movies, virtually every technical innovation pushed the medium closer to a realistic ideal: in the late 1920s, sound; in the 1930s and 1940s, color and deep-focus photography; in the 1950s, widescreen. In short, technology, not critics and theorists, usually alters technique. For example, when *The Jazz Singer* ushered in the talkie revolution in 1927, sound eclipsed virtually every advance made in the art of editing since Griffith's day. With the coming of sound, films *had* to be more realistically edited, whether their directors wished them so or not. Microphones were placed on the set itself, and sound had to be recorded while the scene was being photographed. Usually the microphones were hidden—in a vase of flowers, a wall sconce, etc. Thus, in the earliest sound movies, not only was the camera restricted, but the actors were as well. If they strayed too far from the microphone, the dialogue couldn't be recorded properly.

The effects on editing of these early talkies were disastrous. **Synchronized sound** anchored the images, so whole scenes were played with no cuts—a return to the "primitive" **sequence shot.** Most of the dramatic values were aural.

4-27. *Utamaro and His Five Women* (Japan, 1955), *directed by Kenji Mizoguchi*.
Bazin and his disciples were enthusiastic champions of the films of Mizoguchi. The Japanese master favored the use of lengthy takes rather than editing. He generally cut within a continuous take only when there was a sharp psychological shift within the scene. Used sparingly in this way, the cut acquires a greater dramatic impact than can be found in most conventionally edited movies. *(New Yorker Films)*

Even commonplace sequences held a fascination for audiences. If someone entered a room, the camera recorded the fact, whether it was dramatically important or not, and millions of spectators thrilled to the sound of the door opening and slamming shut. Critics and filmmakers despaired: The days of the recorded stage play had apparently returned. Later these problems were solved by the invention of the **blimp,** a soundproof camera housing that permits the camera to move with relative ease, and by the practice of **dubbing** sound after the shooting is completed (see Chapter 5).

But sound also provided some distinct advantages. In fact, Bazin believed that it represented a giant leap in the evolution toward a totally realistic medium. Spoken dialogue and sound effects heightened the sense of reality. Acting styles became more sophisticated as a result of sound. No longer did performers have to exaggerate visually to compensate for the absence of

4-28.   Clerks (U.S.A., 1994), *with Jeff Anderson and Brian O'Halloran; written, edited, and directed by Kevin Smith.*
Sometimes economics dictates style, as with this witty low-budget feature. Everyone worked for free. Smith shot the movie in the same convenience store he worked at (for $5 an hour) during the day. He also used lengthy takes in a number of scenes. The actors were required to memorize pages of dialogue (often very funny) so that the entire sequence could be shot without a cut. Why? Because Smith didn't need to worry about such costly decisions as where to put the camera with each new cut or how to light each new shot or whether he could afford to rent editing equipment to cut the sequence properly. Lengthy takes require one setup: The lights and camera usually remain stationary for the duration of the scene. The movie's final cost: a piddling $27,575. He charged it. It went on to win awards at the Sundance and Cannes Film Festivals.   *(Miramax Films)*

voices. Talkies also permitted filmmakers to tell their stories more economically, without the intrusive titles that interspersed the visuals of silent movies. Tedious expository scenes could also be dispensed with. A few lines of dialogue easily conveyed what an audience needed to know about the premise of the story.

The use of deep-focus photography also exerted a modifying influence on editing practices. Prior to the 1930s, most cameras photographed interiors on one focal plane at a time. These cameras could capture a sharp image of an object from virtually any distance, but unless an enormous number of extra lights were set up, other elements of the picture that weren't at the same distance from the camera remained blurred, out of focus. One justification for editing, then, was purely technical: clarity of image.

The aesthetic qualities of deep-focus photography permitted composition in depth: Whole scenes could be shot in one setup, with no sacrifice of detail, for every distance appeared with equal clarity on the screen. Deep focus tends to be most effective when it adheres to the real time–space continuum. For this reason, the technique is sometimes thought to be more theatrical than cinematic, for the effects are achieved primarily through a spatially unified mise en scène rather than a fragmented juxtaposition of shots.

Bazin liked the objectivity and tact of deep focus. Details within a shot can be presented more democratically, as it were, without the special attention that a close-up inevitably confers. Thus, realist critics like Bazin felt that audiences would be more creative—less passive—in understanding the relationships between people and things. Unified space also preserves the ambiguity of life. Audiences aren't led to an inevitable conclusion but are forced to evaluate, sort out, and eliminate "irrelevancies" on their own.

In 1945, immediately following World War II, a movement called **neorealism** sprang up in Italy and gradually influenced directors all over the world. Spearheaded by Roberto Rossellini and Vittorio De Sica, two of Bazin's favorite filmmakers, neorealism deemphasized editing. The directors favored deep-focus photography, long shots, lengthy takes, and an austere restraint in the use of close-ups. Rossellini's *Paisan* features a sequence shot that was much admired by realistic critics. An American G.I. talks to a Sicilian young woman about his family, his life, and his dreams. Neither character understands the other's language, but they try to communicate in spite of this considerable obstacle. By refusing to condense time through the use of separate shots, Rossellini emphasizes the awkward pauses and hesitations between the two characters. Through its preservation of real time, the lengthy take forces us to experience the increasing, then relaxing, tensions that exist between them. An abridgement of time through the use of a cut would have dissipated these tensions.

When asked why he deemphasized editing, Rossellini replied: "Things are there, why manipulate them?" This statement might well serve as Bazin's theoretical credo. He deeply admired Rossellini's openness to multiple interpretations, his refusal to diminish reality by making it serve an a priori thesis. "Neorealism by definition rejects analysis, whether political, moral, psychological, logical, or social, of the characters and their actions," Bazin pointed out. "It looks on reality as a whole, not incomprehensible, certainly, but inescapably one."

Sequence shots tend to produce (often unconsciously) a sense of mounting anxiety in the viewer. We expect setups to change during a scene. When they don't, we often grow restless, hardly conscious of what's producing our uneasiness. Jim Jarmusch's bizarre comedy, *Stranger Than Paradise,* uses sequence shots throughout **(4–29).** The camera inexorably waits at a predetermined location. The young characters enter the scene and play out their tawdry, comic lives, complete with boring stretches of silence, glazed expressions of torpor, and random ticks. Finally, they leave. Or they just sit there. The camera sits with them. Fade out. Very weird.

Like many technological innovations, widescreen provoked a wail of protest from many critics and directors. The new screen shape would destroy the

4–29.   *Stranger Than Paradise* (U.S.A., 1984), *directed by Jim Jarmusch.*
Each scene in this movie is a sequence shot—a lengthy take without cuts. Far from being "primitive," the sequence-shot technique produces a sophisticated, wry effect, bizarre and funny. In this scene, the two protagonists (John Lurie and Richard Edson) eat yet another goulash dinner while Lurie berates his stout, outspoken aunt (Cecillia Stark) for still speaking Hungarian after years of living in America. The scene's comic rhythms are accented by the staging: The bickering relatives must bend forward to see each other, while the visitor, caught in the crossfire, tries unsuccessfully to stay neutral.   *(Samuel Goldwyn)*

4-30. *The Straight Story* **(U.S.A., 1999),** *with Richard Farnsworth, directed by David Lynch.*
American movies are usually edited at a fast pace without any slackness or "dead spots" between the shots. *The Straight Story* is a conspicuous exception. Based on true life events, the movie is a road picture, but instead of the usual vroom-vrooming vehicles racing down streets and screeching 'round corners, the vehicle of choice is a '66 John Deere tractor that the elderly hero (Farnsworth) drives from Iowa to Wisconsin where his estranged and ailing brother lives. The movie is cut at a very, very slow pace—to approximate the chugging progress of his antiquated transport.   *(The Straight Story, Inc. and Disney Enterprises, Inc.)*

close-up, many feared, especially of the human face. There simply was too much space to fill, even in long shots, others complained. Audiences would never be able to assimilate all the action, for they wouldn't know where to look. It was suitable only for horizontal compositions, some argued, useful for epic films, but too spacious for interior scenes and small subjects. Editing would be further minimized, the formalists complained, for there would be no need to cut to something if everything was already there, arranged in a long horizontal series.

At first, the most effective widescreen films were, in fact, westerns and historical extravaganzas. But before long, directors began to use the new screen with more sensitivity. Like deep-focus photography, scope meant that they had to be more conscious of their mise en scène. More relevant details had to be included within the frame, even at its edges. Films could be more densely saturated and—potentially, at least—more effective artistically. Filmmakers discovered that the most expressive parts of a person's face were the eyes and mouth, and consequently close-ups that chopped off the tops and bottoms of actors' faces weren't as disastrous as had been predicted.

Not surprisingly, the realist critics were the first to reconsider the advantages of widescreen. Bazin liked its authenticity and objectivity. Here was yet another step away from the distorting effects of editing, he pointed out. As with deep focus, widescreen helped to preserve spatial and temporal continuity. Close shots containing two or more people could now be photographed in one setup without suggesting inequality, as deep focus often did in its variety of depth planes. Nor were the relations between people and things fragmented as they were with edited sequences. Scope was also more realistic because the widescreen enveloped the viewer in a sense of an experience, even with its edges—a cinematic counterpart to the eye's peripheral vision. All the same advantages that had been applied to sound and deep focus were now applied to widescreen: its greater fidelity to real time and space; its detail, complexity, and density; its more objective presentation; its more coherent continuity; its greater ambiguity; and its encouragement of creative audience participation.

Interestingly, several of Bazin's protégés were responsible for a return to more flamboyant editing techniques in the following decades. Throughout the 1950s, Godard, Truffaut, and Chabrol wrote criticism for *Cahiers du Cinéma*. By the end of the decade, they turned to making their own movies. The *nouvelle vague,* or **New Wave** as this movement was called in English, was

4-31.   *The Hidden Fortress* (Japan, 1958), *directed by Akira Kurosawa*.
Most filmmakers bemoaned the advent of widescreen in the 1950s almost as much as they bemoaned sound in the late 1920s. Bazin and other realists embraced the innovation as yet another step away from the distorting effects of montage. Widescreen tends to deemphasize depth in favor of breadth, but Bazin believed that a horizontal presentation of the visual materials could be more democratic—less distorting even than deep focus, which tends to emphasize visual importance in terms of an object's closeness to the camera's lens.   *(Toho Films)*

4–32. *The Innocents* **(Great Britain, 1961),** *with Deborah Kerr, directed by Jack Clayton.*
Throughout most of this psychological thriller (which is based on Henry James's novelette *The Turn of the Screw*), we are not sure if the ghost is "real" or simply the hysterical projection of a repressed governess (Kerr), because we usually see the apparition through her eyes. That is, the camera represents her point of view, which may or may not be reliable. But when an objective camera is used, as in this photo, both the governess and the ghost are included in the same space, with no cutting between separate shots. Hence, we conclude that the spirit figure has an independent existence outside of the governess's imagination. *(Twentieth Century–Fox)*

eclectic in its theory and practice. The members of this group, who were not very tightly knit, were unified by an almost obsessional enthusiasm for film culture, especially American film culture. Unlike that of most previous movements, the range of enthusiasms of these critic/filmmakers was extraordinarily broad: Hitchcock, Renoir, Eisenstein, Hawks, Bergman, Ford, and many more. Although rather dogmatic in their personal tastes, the New Wave critics tended to avoid theoretical dogmatism. They believed that technique was meaningful only in terms of subject matter. In fact, it was the New Wave that popularized the idea that *what* a movie says is inextricably bound up with *how* it's said. They insisted that editing styles ought to be determined not by fashion, the limitations of technology, or dogmatic pronouncements, but by the essence of the subject matter itself.

4–33. *Annie Hall* (U.S.A., 1977), *with Diane Keaton and Woody Allen, edited by Ralph Rosenblum, written and directed by Allen.*

It's very hard to judge a movie's editing. You have to know what was available before the cutting even began—whether the footage was excellent to begin with (which an incompetent editor can still screw up), or whether the editor had a pile of junk to sort through before managing to sculpt at least a moderately respectable movie out of the shards he or she was presented with. "A feature-length film generates anywhere from twenty to forty hours of raw footage," says editor Ralph Rosenblum. "When the shooting stops, that unfinished film becomes the movie's raw material, just as the script had been the raw material before. It now must be selected, tightened, paced, embellished, and in some scenes given artificial respiration." *Annie Hall* was originally conceived by Woody Allen as a story about his own character, Alvy Singer, and his various romantic and professional relationships. The character of Annie Hall (Keaton) was merely one of several plot lines. But both Allen and Rosenblum agreed that the original concept didn't work on the cutting bench. The editor suggested cutting away most of the footage and focusing on a central love story, between Alvy and Annie Hall. The resultant romantic comedy went on to win a number of Oscars, including Best Picture, Best Director, Best Screenplay, and Best Actress for Keaton. Ironically, no award for its editor. See Ralph Rosenblum (and Robert Karen), *When the Shooting Stops . . . The Cutting Begins* (New York: Viking, 1979). *(United Artists)*

Hitchcock's North by Northwest: Storyboard Version

Alfred Hitchcock is widely regarded as the greatest editor in the history of the cinema. His precut scripts were legendary. No other director worked from such precisely detailed plans. He often provided frame drawings of his shots (a technique called **storyboarding**), especially for those sequences involving complex editing. Some of his scripts contained as many as 600 setup sketches. Every shot was calculated for a precise effect. Nothing was superfluous, nothing left to chance. "I would prefer to write all this down, however tiny and however short the pieces of film are—they should be written down in just the same way a composer writes down those little black dots from which we get beautiful sound," he explained.

The following excerpt is not Hitchcock's shooting script of *North by Northwest*, but perhaps the next best thing: a reconstruction of a sequence taken directly from the movie by Albert J. LaValley, which appears in his volume, *Focus on Hitchcock*. Ernest Lehman's "literary" version of this scene is reprinted in Chapter 9.

Each number represents a separate shot; drawings identified with a letter as well represent a continuation of the previous shot, though with enough new action to warrant an additional sketch. The numbers in parentheses indicate the approximate length of the shots in seconds. The following abbrevia-

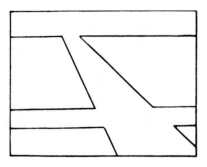

1. E.L.S., aerial. Dissolve to empty road across fields where rendezvous with KAPLAN is to take place. We see and hear bus arriving, door opening.

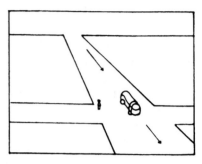

1b. THORNHILL emerges, bus leaves. He is alone. (52)

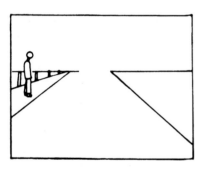

2. L.S., low angle. THORNHILL at roadside, waiting. (5)

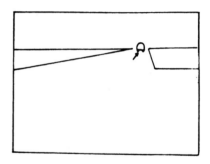

3. E.L.S., P.O.V. Looking down main road: bus going away in distance. (4)

4. M.S. THORNHILL near sign, turns left to right, looking for someone. (3)

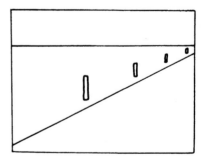

5. L.S., P.O.V. View across road, empty fields with posts. (4)

6. M.S. THORNHILL by sign, turns from right to left, looking. (3)

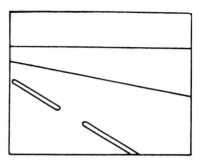

7. L.S., P.O.V. Across fields. (4)

8. M.S. THORNHILL by sign again, waiting, turns head and looks behind him. (3)

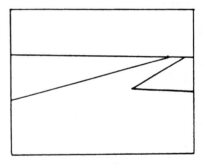

9. E.L.S., P.O.V. The field behind him, road. (4)

10. M.S. THORNHILL by sign, waiting, turning forward—long waiting feeling. (6½)

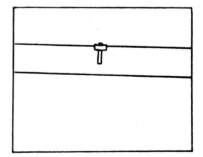

11. E.L.S. Empty landscape across road, signs, post. (3)

12. M.S. THORNHILL by sign. Turns right. (2)

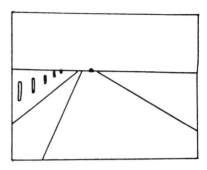

13. E.L.S. Empty main road, car coming in distance. (4)

14. M.S. THORNHILL by sign, looking at car approaching. (¾)

15. L.S. Car goes by fast, whizzing sound, camera pans slightly to right. (1¾)

16. M.S. THORNHILL by sign, moves back to left, follows car with his eyes. (2)

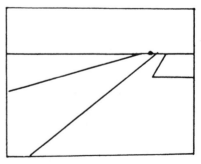

17. E.L.S., P.O.V. Road, car going, sound recedes. (4)

18. M.S. THORNHILL by sign, hands in pockets, turns from left to right. (3)

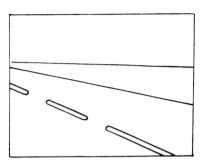

19. L.S., P.O.V. Field across road again. (3)

20. M.S. THORNHILL by sign, same pose, still looking, turns from right to left. (2¾)

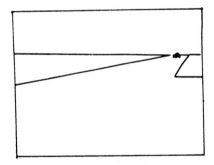

21. E.L.S. Road, car in distance, sounds begin. (3½)

22. M.S. THORNHILL by sign, looking at car, no movement. (2½)

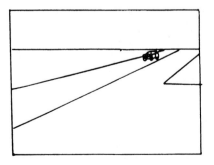

23. E.L.S. Car coming closer, sound increasing. (3¾)

24. M.S. THORNHILL by sign, looking at car coming. (3)

25. L.S. Car closer, rushes past, camera pans a bit to follow it. (3)

26. M.S. THORNHILL by sign, takes hands from pockets, turns left to right to follow car. (3)

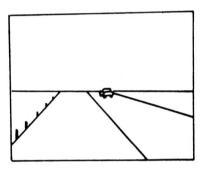

27. E.L.S. View of road, car in distance receding. (3¾)

28. M.S. THORNHILL by sign, waiting again. (2¼)

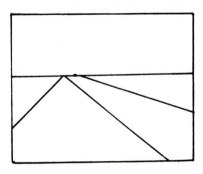

29. E.L.S. Road, truck coming; we hear its sound. (4)

30. M.S. THORNHILL by sign, sound of truck increasing. (3)

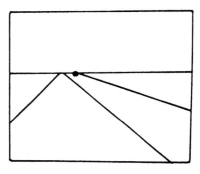

31. E.L.S. Truck coming down road, sound still increasing. (3¾)

32. M.S. THORNHILL by sign. (2¼)

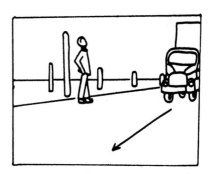

33. L.S. Truck whizzes by.

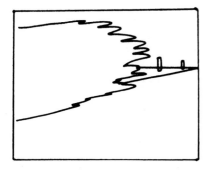

33b. Kicking up dust, obscuring THORNHILL, camera pans slightly left, and he emerges out of the dust gradually. (4)

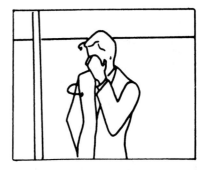

34. M.S. THORNHILL wiping dust from his eyes, turns to right. (7)

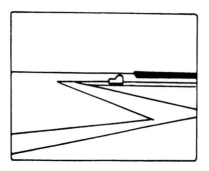

35. E.L.S. Fields across way, car coming out behind corn. (5)

36. M.S. THORNHILL by sign puzzled by car. (5)

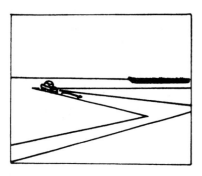

37. E.L.S. Car making turn on dirt road. (4)

38. M.S. THORNHILL awaiting car. (3⅔)

39. L.S. Car nearing main road, camera pans following it to right, a sign there. (4)

40. M.S. THORNHILL waiting to see what will happen. (3⅓)

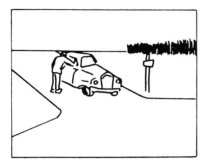

41. L.S. MAN getting out of car, talking to driver, we hear the door of the car slam. (3½)

42. M.S. THORNHILL reacting, wondering, getting ready to meet this man. (2)

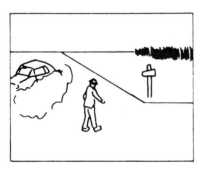

43. L.S. Sound of car turning around, dust raised, car turns around and the MAN walks toward main road opposite THORNHILL, looking back at the car leaving. (1⅘)

44. M.S. THORNHILL, closer than previous shots, eyeing the man. (1½)

45. L.S. Camera pans right slightly; the MAN goes over by the sign and turns his head to look up the road and over at THORNHILL. (4⅓)

46. M.S. Same as 44. THORNHILL's reaction, his head tilts and he looks across the road. (3⅖)

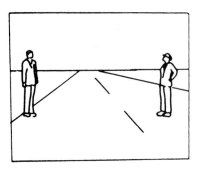

47. L.S., low angle. Road in the middle stretching to infinity, two men oddly stationed on either side of road, the other MAN looking up the road a bit. (7)

48. M.S. THORNHILL's reaction, takes hands out of pockets, opens coat, puts hands on hips, contemplates situation. (6⅓)

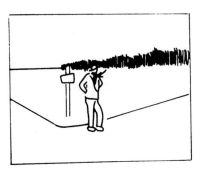

49. L.S. Same as 45, only the MAN turns his head looking the other way. (3½)

50. M.S. Same as 48, but THORNHILL has both hands on hips now, his head looking across. His head turns up road to see if anyone is coming; he looks back, one hand on hip, other at side, at MAN across way.

50b. Starts walking across road part way. (10)

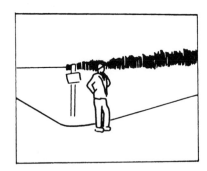

51. L.S., P.O.V. The man on the other side of road, as THORNHILL crosses, camera tracks across road part way, acting as his eyes. (2⅔)

52. M.S. THORNHILL walks across road; synchronous tracking camera continuing movement begun in 50b.

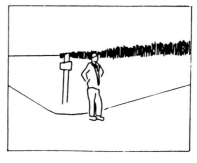

53. L.S., P.O.V. Same as 49, 51 of other MAN across road, but camera tracks in on him, acting as THORNHILL's eyes, continues movement begun in 50b.

54. M.S. THORNHILL on other side of road, but camera tracks to continue movement of 50, 52.

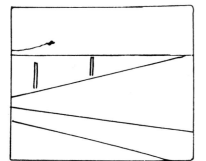

55. E.L.S. Fields with plane at great distance in far left of frame coming right. (2⅔)

54b. Camera continues tracking to other side of road until other man comes in view and THORNHILL begins to talk to him. THORNHILL's hands are a bit nervous in movement; he plays with his little finger; the other man has hands in pockets.

THORNHILL (after a long wait): Hi! (a long pause follows) Hot day. (another pause)

MAN: Seen worse.

THORNHILL (after a long pause): Are you supposed to be meeting someone here?

MAN: Waitin' for the bus. Due any minute.

THORNHILL: Oh. (another pause)

MAN: Some of them crop duster pilots get rich if they live long enough.

THORNHILL: Yeah! (very softly) (21)

56. M.S. Reaction shot of both looking at plane.
THORNHILL: Then . . . a . . . (pause) then your name isn't Kaplan?
MAN: Can't say that it is 'cause it ain't. (pause) Here she comes (as he looks down the road). (11)

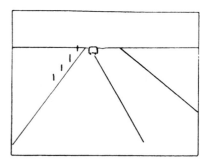

57. E.L.S. Bus coming down the road.
MAN: (voice off) . . . right on time. (2⅔)

58. M.S. Same as 56, two talking then looking again across road at crop duster.
MAN: That's funny.
THORNHILL: What? (very softly)
MAN: That plane's dustin' crops where there ain't no crops.
THORNHILL turns to look. (8)

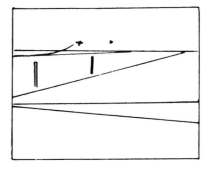

59. E.L.S. Same as 55, field with the plane over it. (4)

60. M.S. Two men off center looking at plane. THORNHILL's hands continue nervous movements; the other's are in his pockets as before. Sound of approaching bus. (3½)

61. L.S. Bus arriving and coming quite close to camera. (1⅝)

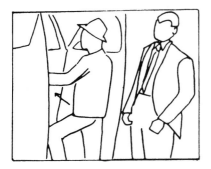

62. M.S. MAN gets on as door of bus opens and seems to shut THORNHILL out. The bus leaves.

62b. THORNHILL puts hands on hips and looks across, then looks at his watch. For a second he is alone in the frame as the bus goes out of sight. (2⅓)

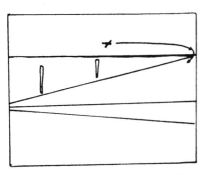

63. E.L.S., P.O.V. Same as 59, what THORNHILL sees across the road; the plane goes to end of frame and turns left, toward him. (5⅙)

64. M.S. THORNHILL in front of road by sign, puzzled and rather innocent looking; sound of plane approaching. (2⅓)

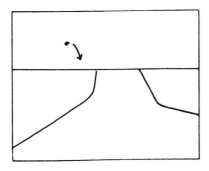

65. E.L.S. Plane coming toward camera, still far, but closer and with sound increasing. (3⅗)

66. M.S. Same as 64. THORNHILL reacting. (2¼)

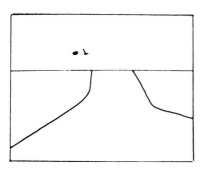

67. E.L.S. Same as 65 but plane closer and louder. (2⅛)

68. M.S. Closer shot of THORNHILL, still puzzled and confused as plane comes at him. (4½)

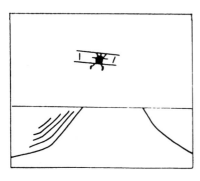

69. L.S. Plane clearly coming at him, filling mid-frame, very loud. (1⅓)

70. THORNHILL drops, a short held shot, he falls out of frame at bottom. (⅔)

71. L.S. THORNHILL falling on ground, both arms on ground, plane behind him, he in a hole. (3½)

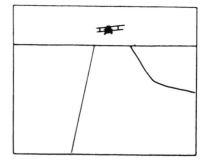

72. L.S. Plane going away from him. (3)

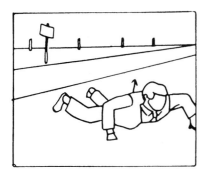

73. L.S. THORNHILL on ground getting up, kneeling on left knee. (3½)

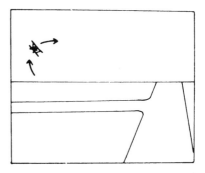

74. E.L.S. Plane going farther away and sound receding. (2⅘)

75. L.S. THORNHILL getting up. (2⅕)

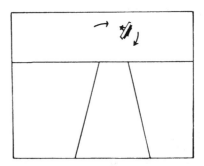

76. E.L.S. Plane in distance banking. (2⅓)

77. M.S. THORNHILL up and about to run. (2⅓)

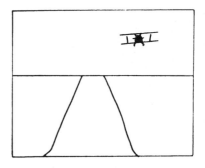

78. L.S. Plane approaching again, sound getting louder. (2)

79. M.S. THORNHILL runs and falls in ditch. (1½)

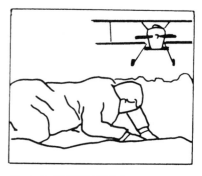

80. L.S. THORNHILL in ditch, sound of plane and bullets sprayed on him, smoke; he turns head to left and faces camera to watch when plane is gone. (5⅓)

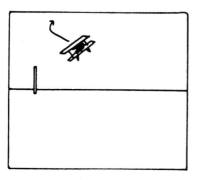

81. L.S. Plane getting ready again, banking. (5⅙)

82. M.S. THORNHILL in ditch coming up, gets up on left arm, sound of receding plane. (2½)

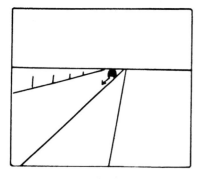

83. E.L.S., P.O.V. The road as THORN-HILL sees it, car in distance. (2½)

84. M.S. Same as 82, THORNHILL rising from ditch, receding plane sound. (1½)

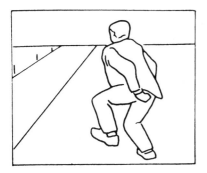

85. L.S., low angle. THORNHILL runs to road to try to stop car.

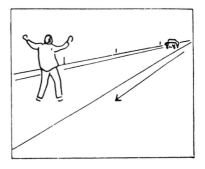

85b. He tries to flag it down. Car sounds approach and it whizzes by. (9½)

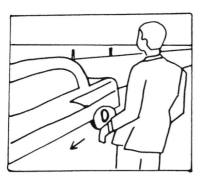

86. M.S. THORNHILL's back after turning left as the car whizzes by. (4⅔)

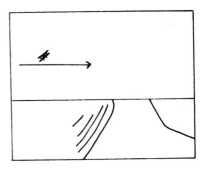

87. E.L.S. Plane in distance, sounds again. (2⅓)

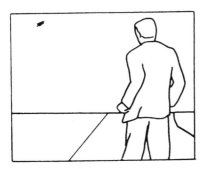

88. L.S. THORNHILL's back with plane in distance at far left coming at him.

88b. L.S. He looks at plane, turns around looking for a place to hide, looks at plane again, turns around and runs toward camera. Camera reverse tracks.

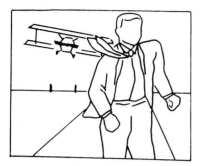

88c. M.S. THORNHILL running toward camera, camera reverse tracking. He turns around twice while running to look at plane; it goes over his head just missing him. (13½)

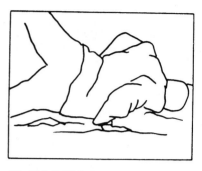

89. M.S. THORNHILL falling, side view, legs up, bullet and plane sounds. (5)

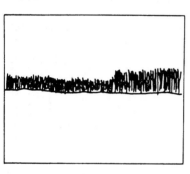

90. L.S., P.O.V. Cornfield, a place to hide. (2½)

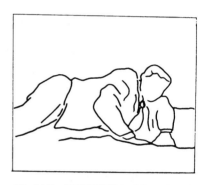

91. M.S. THORNHILL lying flat on ground, looking. (1⅔)

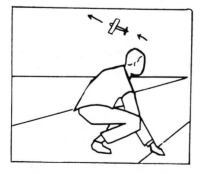

92. L.S. THORNHILL getting up, plane in distance banking again for new attack. (3)

93. M.S. THORNHILL running, turns back to look at plane, camera tracks with him as he runs to cornfield. (4½)

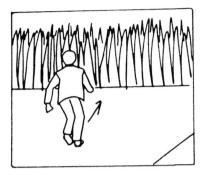

94. L.S., low angle. THORNHILL's back as he runs into cornfield; low camera angle shows lots of ground, stalks. He disappears into corn. (2¾)

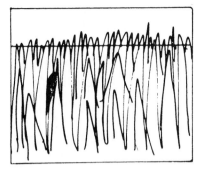

95. L.S. Picture of corn; a patch reveals where THORNHILL is hiding. The corn rustles. (2)

96. M.S. Camera follows THORNHILL down as he falls on ground inside the corn patch. He turns back to look up to see if plane is coming. A cornstalk falls; then he looks down again, up again, down again, up. (7¾)

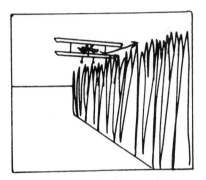

97. L.S. Plane coming along edge of cornfield and over it; it gets very loud. (4½)

98. M.S. Same as 96. Corn rustles, wind from the plane blows over. THORNHILL sees he's out of danger, and smiles a bit, feeling that he's outwitted his pursuers. (15⅖)

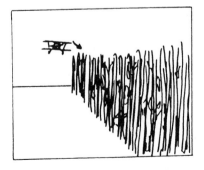

99. L.S. Plane coming in on bend, repeating pattern of 97; it gets louder. (3¼)

100. M.S. Same as 96, 98. THORN-HILL in corn, getting up, looking around, suddenly aware of plane in new way; he's startled that it's coming back. (4⅖)

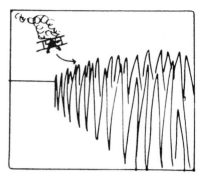

101. L.S. Plane over corn, repeating pattern of 97, only dust coming out of it; plane comes closer to camera. (7)

102. M.S. Same as 96, 98, 100; THORNHILL's reaction to dust, which fills up screen: he coughs, takes out handkerchief, camera follows him as he raises himself up and down; coughing sounds. (12¼)

103. M.S. THORNHILL in corn, new shot; he runs toward camera trying to get out of corn; rustling corn, he looks out of field. (4½)

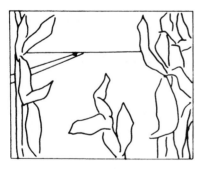

104. E.L.S., P.O.V. Out of cornfield, view of road as framed by corn; tiny speck on road in distance is truck. (2¾)

105. M.S. THORNHILL in corn, but he is standing; he moves forward, looks back up for plane, makes dash for the truck coming down road; he goes out of frame for moment at the end. (3½)

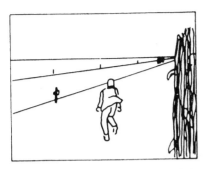

106. L.S. THORNHILL running toward truck, gets to road from corn; truck farther along the road, sounds of truck. (4)

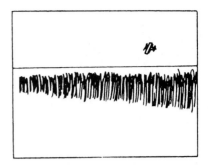

107. E.L.S. Plane banking over corn, getting ready to turn toward him; faint plane sounds; horn of truck. (2)

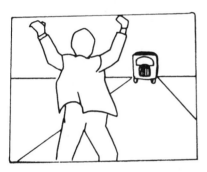

108. L.S., low angle. THORNHILL in road, truck coming, he waves at it. (1⅔)

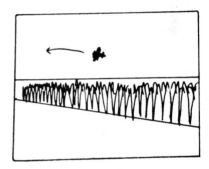

109. E.L.S. Continuation of 107, plane further left. (2)

110. M.S. THORNHILL trying to stop truck, sounds of horns, brakes. (2)

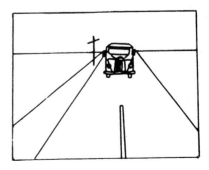

111. L.S. Truck approaching, getting bigger. (2)

112. M.S. Same as 110, but he looks at plane coming in on his left, then puts up both hands instead of one, and bites his tongue. (1½)

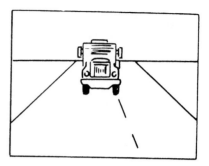

113. L.S. Truck even closer, about fifty feet in front of camera. (1)

114. M.S. Same as 112, 110. THORN-HILL waving frantically now. (1)

115. C.U. Grille of truck as it tries to halt; brake sounds. (1)

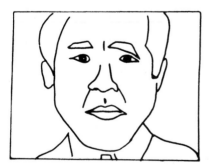

116. C.U. THORNHILL's face in anguish about to be hit.

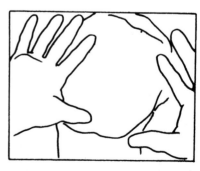

116b. His hands go up and his head goes down. (⅙)

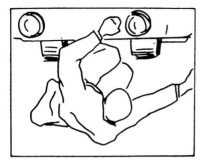

117. L.S. THORNHILL falls under the truck, front view. (1)

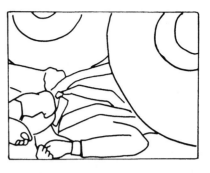

118. M.S. THORNHILL under the truck, side view. (2½)

119. L.S., low angle. Plane comes toward truck (and camera). (1¾)

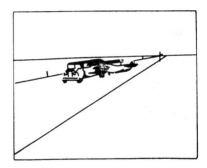

120. L.S. Plane hits truck, view from across road. (1)

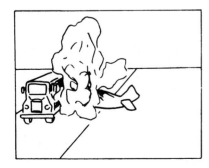

121. L.S. Truck bursts in flames; another angle of truck and plane; music begins and continues to end of scene. (2½)

122. L.S. Shot of truck in flames from in front, two men scramble hurriedly from cab.

DRIVER: Let's get out of here. It's going to explode. (6½)

123. L.S. Backs of men running some-what comically to cornfield. (2)

124. L.S. THORNHILL runs toward camera from explosions of oil truck behind him. Music tends to mute explosion sounds. (2¾)

125. L.S. Reverse angle of THORN-HILL as he now backs away from explosion. A car has just pulled to side of road, followed by a pickup truck with a refrigerator, which pulls to the side in front of it. Doors open and people get out. THORNHILL goes over and talks to them. No sounds are heard (the music continues), but we see his motions of explanation. (9)

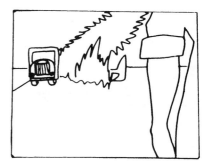

126. L.S. View of explosion in dis-tance with close-up of farmer's arm on right. (2)

127. L.S. THORNHILL and others watch explosion. He backs away from scene to right of frame while they all move closer to the wreck as THORN-HILL retreats unnoticed by them. (11)

128. L.S. Backs of others watching explosion. (6⅓)

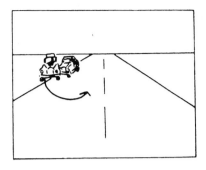

129. L.S. THORNHILL takes the pickup truck with refrigerator in back and pulls out while they are watching the explosion. (3⅗)

130. L.S. Same as 128, but the FARMER turns, seeing his truck being taken, and shouts "Hey." (2½)

131. L.S. Chase by the FARMER, bow-legged and comic; he finally stops as the truck recedes into the distance. "Come back, come back," he is shouting. Dissolve to next sequence. (15)

tions are used: E.L.S., extreme long shot; L.S., long shot; M.S., medium shot; C.U., close-up; P.O.V., a shot taken from Thornhill's point of view.

The premise: Roger Thornhill (Cary Grant) is a fugitive from the law. To prove his innocence, he must talk with a man named Kaplan. Roger is told to come to the scene's location, where he expects to meet Kaplan.

Some questions we ought to ask ourselves about a movie's editing style include: How much cutting is there and why? Are the shots highly fragmented or relatively lengthy? What is the point of the cutting in each scene? To clarify? To stimulate? To lyricize? To create suspense? To explore an idea or emotion in depth? Does the cutting seem manipulative or are we left to interpret the images on our own? What kind of rhythm does the editing establish with each scene? Is the personality of the filmmaker apparent in the cutting or is the presentation of shots relatively objective and functional? Is editing a major language system of the movie or does the film artist relegate cutting to a relatively minor function?

FURTHER READING

BALMUTH, BERNARD, *Introduction to Film Editing* (Boston: Focal Press, 1989). Technical emphasis.

BAZIN, ANDRÉ, *What Is Cinema?* Hugh Gray, ed. and trans. (Berkeley: University of California Press, vol. I, 1967, vol. II, 1971). A collection of essays emphasizing the realistic nature of the film medium.

CHRISTIE, IAN, AND RICHARD TAYLOR, eds. *Eisenstein Rediscovered* (New York and London: Routledge, 1993). A collection of scholarly essays on Eisenstein and his legacy.

DMYTRYK, EDWARD, *On Film Editing* (Boston: Focal Press, 1984). A practical handbook by a former editor turned director.

GRAHAM, PETER, ed., *The New Wave* (London: Secker & Warburg, 1968). A collection of essays by and about Bazin, Truffaut, Godard, and others.

LA VALLEY, ALBERT J., ed., *Focus on Hitchcock* (Englewood Cliffs: N. J.: Prentice-Hall, 1972).

LOBRUTTO, VINCENT, ed., *Selected Takes: Film Editors on Film Editing* (New York: Praeger, 1991).

OLDHAM, GABRIELLA, ed., *First Cut* (Berkeley: University of California Press, 1992). Interviews with twenty-three award-winning film editors.

PUDOVKIN, V. I., *Film Technique and Film Acting.* Ivor Montague, ed. and trans. (New York: Grove Press, 1960). See also *Kuleschov on Film,* Ronald Levaco, ed. and trans. (Berkeley: University of California Press, 1974).

REISZ, KAREL, *The Technique of Film Editing* (New York: Hastings House, 1968). The standard text on the history, practice, and theory of editing.

Sound

Tri-Star Pictures

*Cinematic sound is that which does not simply add to,
but multiplies, two or three times,
the effect of the image.*

—AKIRA KUROSAWA

Overview

The talkie revolution. The late 1920s: early problems with sound recording. Microphones versus cameras. Synchronous and nonsynchronous sounds. A new genre: the musical. What talkies did to editing styles and silent film acting. Sound effects: pitch, volume, tempo, and texture. Off-screen sounds. Sound symbolism. The uses of silence. Functions of music: establish tone, period, ethnicity, and locale. The emotional appeal of music. Music as characterization. Background music. Opera and other musical genres. Spoken language: tone of voice, dialects, vocal emphasis. The ideology of speech. Text versus subtext: What's beneath the language? Monologues, voice-overs, spoken narration: Who's telling this story? Foreign language movies. What to do about translating: dubbing versus subtitles. Rough language: Is it necessary? Why? When?

Historical Background

In 1927, when *The Jazz Singer* ushered in the talkie era, many critics felt that sound would deal a deathblow to the art of movies. But the setbacks were temporary, and today sound is one of the richest sources of meaning in film art. Actually, there never was a silent period. Virtually all movies prior to 1927

5-1.   *The Jazz Singer* **(U.S.A., 1927),** *with Al Jolson, directed by Alan Crosland.*
There had been a number of experiments in synchronous sound prior to this film, but they failed to create much of a stir with the public. Significantly, Warner Brothers managed to break the sound barrier with a new genre, the musical. Actually, even this movie was mostly silent. Only Jolson's musical numbers and a few snatches of dialogue were in synch sound. See John Springer, *All Talking, All Singing, All Dancing!* (New York: Citadel, 1966).   *(Warner Bros.)*

were accompanied by some kind of music. In the large city theaters, full orchestras provided atmospheric background to the visuals. In small towns, a piano was often used for the same purpose. In many theaters, the "Mighty Wurlitzer" organ, with its bellowing pipes, was the standard musical accompaniment. Music was played for practical as well as artistic reasons, for these sounds muffled the noises of the patrons who were occasionally rowdy, particularly when entering the theater.

Most of the early "100 percent talkies" were visually dull. The equipment of the time required the simultaneous (**synchronous**) recording of sound and image: The camera was restricted to one position, the actors couldn't move far from the microphone, and **editing** was restricted to its most minimal function—primarily scene changes. The major source of meaning was the dialogue. The images tended merely to illustrate the soundtrack. Before long, adventurous directors began experimenting. The camera was housed in a soundproof

5–2. *Scarface, Shame of a Nation* (U.S.A., 1932), *with Paul Muni (center), directed by Howard Hawks.*

After the introduction of talkies, American movies—which had always been among the fastest in the world—got even faster. The films of such 1930s masters as Howard Hawks and Frank Capra emphasized speed by having the dialogue delivered 30 to 40% faster than normal. This breathless sense of urgency was especially effective in gangster films, which were immensely popular during the Depression era. In his classic essay, "The Gangster as Tragic Hero," Robert Warshow hit on why the gangster struck such a responsive chord in audiences and why he has held our imagination ever since: "The gangster is the man of the city, with the city's language and knowledge, with its queer and dishonest skills and its terrible daring, carrying his life in his hands like a placard, like a club. . . . It is not the real city, but that dangerous and sad city of the imagination which is so much more important, which is the modern world." *(United Artists)*

5-3. *Monte Carlo* (U.S.A., 1930), *with Claude Allister, directed by Ernst Lubitsch.*
The sophisticated German emigré Ernst Lubitsch was the first great filmmaker to try his hand at the new talkie genre, the musical. Unlike most artists working in this form, Lubitsch tended to avoid elaborate production numbers in favor of simple character-based songs. In this scene, for example, the appalling Prince Otto von Seibenheim has just been jilted by his would-be bride, who, understandably, has fled in terror. As he sings "Give Me a Moment Please," the bridesmaids close in around him, serving as impromptu chorus girls. Lubitsch delighted in these on-camera regroupings, which good-naturedly spoof the artificiality of the genre's conventions. See Scott Eyman, *Ernst Lubitsch: Laughter in Paradise* (New York: Simon & Schuster, 1993). *(Paramount Pictures)*

blimp, thus permitting the camera to move in and out of a scene silently. Soon, several microphones, all on separate channels, were placed on the set. Overhead sound **booms** were devised to follow an actor on a set, so his or her voice was always within range, even when the actor moved around.

Despite these technical advances, **formalist** directors remained hostile to the use of **realistic** (synchronous) sound recording. Eisenstein was especially wary of dialogue. He predicted an onslaught of "highly cultured dramas" that would force the cinema back to its stagey beginnings. Synchronous sound, he believed, would destroy the flexibility of editing and thus kill the very soul of film art. Synchronous sound did, in fact, require a more literal **continuity,** especially in dialogue sequences. Eisenstein's metaphoric cutting, with its leaps in time and space, wouldn't make much sense if realistic sound had to be provided with each image. Indeed, Hitchcock pointed out that the most cinematic sequences are essentially silent. Chase scenes, for example, require only some general sound effects to preserve their continuity.

Most of the talented directors of the early sound era favored **nonsynchronous sound.** The Frenchman René Clair believed that sound should be

5-4. *She Done Him Wrong* (U.S.A., 1933), *with Mae West, directed by Lowell Sherman.*
Tone of voice can be far more communicative than words in revealing a person's thoughts. This is why most sophisticated moviegoers prefer written subtitles to dubbing in foreign language movies. Mae West was an expert in conveying sexual innuendos through tone of voice—so much so, in fact, that censors insisted on monitoring her scenes during production for fear that the apparently neutral dialogue in her screenplays would be delivered in a "salacious" manner. Audiences responded enthusiastically to Mae's insolence and snappy wisecracks. In this film, she's at her outspoken best: cool, lecherous, cynical. In her opening scene, she saucily proclaims herself to be "one of the finest women who ever walked the streets." West preferred playing outcasts, like showgirls and kept women. This afforded her the opportunity of satirizing sexual hypocrisies. Her one-liners are legendary, like the famous "It's not the men in my life that counts, it's the life in my men." Or "Whenever I'm caught between two evils, I take the one I've never tried." Or "I used to be Snow White, but I drifted." Again: "When I'm good, I'm very good; when I'm bad, I'm even better." When asked how tall he is, a handsome young man replies, "Ma'am, I'm six feet seven inches." Naughty Mae smiles and says, "Let's forget about the six feet and talk about the seven inches." Mae's "lewd" comic style—almost exclusively verbal—fueled the wrath of the censors, ushering in the puritanical Production Code in 1934. *(Paramount Pictures)*

used selectively, not indiscriminately. The ear, he believed, is just as selective as the eye, and sound can be edited in the same way images can. Even dialogue sequences needn't be totally synchronous, Clair believed. Conversation can act as a continuity device, freeing the camera to explore contrasting information— a technique especially favored by ironists like Hitchcock and Ernst Lubitsch.

Clair made several musicals illustrating his theories. In *Le Million,* for example, music and song often replace dialogue. Language is juxtaposed ironically with nonsynchronous images. Many of the scenes were photographed without sound and later **dubbed** when the montage sequences were completed. These charming musicals are never immobilized by the stagey confinement that ruined most sound films of this era. The dubbing technique of Clair, though ahead of its time, eventually became a major approach in sound film production.

Several American directors also experimented with sound in these early years. Like Clair, Lubitsch used sound and image nonsynchronously to produce a number of witty and often cynical juxtapositions. The celebrated "Beyond the Blue Horizon" sequence from his musical *Monte Carlo* is a good example of his mastery of the new mixed medium. While the spunky heroine (Jeanette MacDonald) sings cheerily of her optimistic expectations, Lubitsch provides us with a display of technical bravura. Shots of the speeding train that carries the heroine to her destiny are intercut with **close-ups** of the whirring locomotive wheels in rhythmical syncopation with the huffing and the chugging and the tooting of the train. Unable to resist a malicious fillip, Lubitsch even has a chorus of suitably obsequious peasants chime in with the heroine in a triumphant reprise as the train plunges past their fields in the countryside. The sequence is both exhilarating and outrageously funny. Critic Gerald Mast observed, "This visual-aural symphony of music, natural sound, composition, and cutting is as complex and perfect an example of montage-in-sound as Eisenstein's editing devices in *Potemkin* were of montage in silents."

The increased realism brought on by sound inevitably forced acting styles to become more natural. Performers no longer needed to compensate visually for the lack of dialogue. Like stage actors, film players realized that the subtlest nuances of meaning could be conveyed through the voice. Close-ups are another advantage for screen actors. If they are required to mutter under their breath, for example, they can do so naturally. They need not, like the stage actor, mutter in stage whisper—a necessary convention in the live theater.

In the silent cinema, directors had to use titles to communicate nonvi-

5-5. *Wings of Desire* **(Germany, 1988),** *with Bruno Ganz, directed by Wim Wenders.*
Silence can be more powerful than sound in certain cases. In this poetic fantasy about an angel (Ganz) who yearns to become mortal, the protagonist often sits on a statue high above the city of Berlin. The discordant clash of modern life is softened and silenced by the soothing distance. *(Orion Classics)*

sual information: dialogue, exposition, abstract ideas, and so on. In some films, these interruptions nearly ruined the delicate rhythm of the visuals. Other directors avoided titles by dramatizing visually as much as possible. This practice led to many visual clichés. Early in the story, for example, the villain might be identified by showing him kicking a dog, or a heroine could be recognized by the halo-effect lighting around her head, and so forth.

Coming from the world of radio, Orson Welles was an important innovator in the field of sound. In *The Magnificent Ambersons*, he perfected the technique of sound **montage,** in which the dialogue of one character overlaps with that of another, or several others. The effect is almost musical, for the language is exploited not necessarily for the literal information it may convey, but as

5-6. *The Merry Widow* (U.S.A., 1925), *with Mae Murray and John Gilbert, directed by Erich von Stroheim.*

Talkies wiped out the careers of many silent film stars, including that of John Gilbert, the most popular leading man of the late silent era. Gilbert's voice was said to be too high pitched, though in fact it wasn't. The problem was far more complex. Silent film acting was stylized and visually heightened to compensate for the lack of sound. Even by silent standards, Gilbert was known for his emotional intensity—his gestures romantically exaggerated, his ardor raised to a fever pitch. The increased realism brought on by the advent of talkies made such acting techniques seem comically overwrought. Audiences laughed at their former idols. Said critic Scott Eyman, "When a star the stature of Gilbert fell, it was like the fall of an angel, awful and irrevocable." Talkies ushered in a new era, with a new breed of actors. Young leading men like Clark Gable were more relaxed and natural in front of the camera, their style of acting more suited to the new realism of talkies.   *(MGM)*

5–7. *Babe* (Australia, 1995), with James Cromwell and friend, directed by Chris Noonan.

This stylized coming-of-age comedy is narrated by Babe, a young pig (pictured). The fusion of human voices with porcine visuals is surprisingly convincing: The technique persuades most spectators into suspending their disbelief about talking pigs, wise and articulate dogs, and ridiculously oversensitive ducks. Interestingly, when this film was shown in the United States, most of the Australian voice-overs were replaced by American voices to make the story more palatable to U.S. audiences. To almost everyone's surprise, the movie was a big hit, and not just with children. *(Universal Pictures)*

pure sound orchestrated in terms of emotional tonalities. One of the most brilliant episodes using this technique is the leave-taking scene at the final Amberson ball. The scene is shot in **deep focus,** with **expressionistic** lighting contrasts throwing most of the characters into silhouette. The dialogue of one group of characters gently overlaps with that of another, which in turn overlaps with a third group. The effect is hauntingly poetic, despite the relative simplicity of the words themselves. Each person or couple is characterized by a particular sound texture: The young people speak rapidly in a normal to loud volume; a middle-aged couple whispers intimately and slowly. The shouts of various other family members punctuate these dialogue sequences in sudden outbursts. The entire scene seems choreographed, both visually and aurally: Silhouetted figures stream in and out of the **frame** like graceful phantoms, their words floating and undulating in the shadows. The quarrels among the Amberson family are often recorded in a similar manner. Welles's actors don't wait patiently for cues: Accusations and recriminations are hurled simultaneously, as they are in life. The violent words, often irrational and disconnected, spew out in spontaneous eruptions of anger and frustration. Like many family quarrels, everyone shouts, but people only half listen.

Robert Altman used similar sound montage techniques in *M*A*S*H,* *Nashville,* and other movies. Like Welles, Altman often uses language as pure sound, particularly in *McCabe and Mrs. Miller,* in which as many as twenty different soundtracks were mixed. In several scenes, speeches are deliberately thrown away and we're able to catch only a fleeting phrase here and there; however, these phrases are sufficient to give us a sense of what's really going on in a scene. More important, they give us a sense of how language and sounds are actually heard in reality—in ambiguous, elliptical wisps that are often incongruous and funny.

Sound Effects

Although the function of sound effects is primarily atmospheric, they can also be precise sources of meaning in film. The pitch, volume, and tempo of sound effects can strongly affect our responses to any given noise. High-pitched sounds are generally strident and produce a sense of tension in the listener. Especially if these types of noises are prolonged, the shrillness can be totally unnerving. For this reason, high-pitched sounds (including music) are often used in suspense sequences, particularly just before and during the climax. Low-frequency sounds, on the other hand, are heavy, full, and less tense. Often, they are used to emphasize the dignity or solemnity of a scene, like the male humming chorus in *The Seven Samurai*. Low-pitched sounds can also suggest anxiety and mystery: Frequently a suspense sequence begins with such sounds, which then gradually increase in frequency as the scene moves toward its climax.

Sound volume works in much the same way. Loud sounds tend to be forceful, intense, and threatening **(5–8)**. Quiet sounds strike us as delicate, hesitant, and often weak. These same principles apply to tempo. The faster the tempo of sound, the greater the tension produced in the listener **(5–2)**. In the chase sequence of William Friedkin's *The French Connection*, all of these principles are used masterfully. As the chase reaches its climax, the screeching wheels of the pursuing auto and the crashing sound of the runaway train grow louder, faster, and higher pitched.

Off-screen sounds bring off-screen space into play: The sound expands the image beyond the confines of the frame. Sound effects can evoke terror in suspense films and thrillers. We tend to fear what we can't see, so directors will sometimes use off-screen sound effects to strike a note of anxiety. The sound of a creaking door in a darkened room can be more fearful than an image of someone stealing through the door. In Fritz Lang's *M,* the child murderer is identified by a tune he whistles off screen. During the early portions of the movie, we never see him; we recognize him only by his sinister tune.

In several scenes of Hitchcock's *Psycho,* Bernard Herrmann's score—consisting entirely of strings—suggests shrill bird noises. This **motif** is used as a form of characterization. A shy and appealing young man (Anthony Perkins) is associated with birds early in the film. He stuffs birds as a hobby, and his own

5–8. *A Clockwork Orange* **(Great Britain/U.S.A., 1972),** *with Malcolm McDowell, directed by Stanley Kubrick.*
The voice as a weapon. Dialogue that's shouted rather than spoken can be a kind of assault. Throughout this movie, the vicious protagonist (McDowell) barks and snarls at his adversaries like a feral dog on a chain, setting them on edge as they cringe from his aggressive incursions. *(Warner Bros.)*

5–9. *Ran (Chaos,* **Japan, 1985),** *with Mieko Haranda, directed by Akira Kurosawa.*
Kurosawa was a master of sound. In this **loose adaptation** of Shakespeare's *King Lear,* the vengeful character of Lady Kaede (pictured) makes Lady Macbeth look like Mary Poppins. She is characterized by the eerie chafing sound of her silk gowns as she glides across the polished floors like a sinister apparition. *(Orion Classics)*

features are intense and rather hawklike. During a brutal murder sequence, the soundtrack throbs with screeching bird music. The audience assumes the murderer is the boy's mother, but birds have been associated with him, not her. One of Hitchcock's recurrent themes is the transference of guilt. In this film, the transfer is rather complex. The youth has dug up his long-dead mother's body and literally stuffed it. Often, he dresses himself up in her clothing. Although we think we see the mother killing two victims, we have in fact seen the schizophrenic youth as his other self—his mother. The bird music offers an early clue to this psychological transference.

Because images tend to dominate sounds while we're actually experiencing a movie, many sound effects work on a subconscious level. In *Psycho,* the heroine (Janet Leigh) drives her car through a rainstorm. On the soundtrack, we hear her windshield wiper blades slashing furiously against the downpour. Later, when she is taking a shower in a motel, these same sounds are repeated. The source of the water noise is apparent, but the slashing sounds seem to come from nowhere—until a demented killer crashes into the bathroom brandishing a knife.

Sound effects can also serve symbolic functions, which are usually determined by the dramatic context. In Luis Buñuel's *Belle de Jour,* for example, the sounds of jingling bells are associated with the heroine's sexual fantasies. Other symbolic sound effects are more universally understood. In Bergman's *Wild Strawberries,* the protagonist, an elderly professor, has a nightmare. The

5–10. *The Exorcist* (U.S.A., 1973), directed by William Friedkin.
Sound in film is generally geared to space: When a severe discrepancy exists, the effect can be disorienting and even frightening. In this movie, the devil has possessed a young girl (Linda Blair, lying on bed). The sounds emanating from her small body echo loudly, creating a cavernous effect, as if the girl's slight figure had been spiritually expanded thousands of times to accommodate the demons that inhabit it. *(Warner Bros.)*

surrealistic sequence is virtually silent except for the insistent sound of a heartbeat—a *memento mori* for the professor, a reminder that his life will soon end.

In reality, there's a considerable difference between hearing and listening. Our minds automatically filter out irrelevant sounds. While talking in a noisy city location, for example, we listen to the speaker, but we barely hear the sounds of traffic. The microphone is not so selective. Most movie soundtracks are cleaned up of such extraneous noises. A sequence might include selected city noises to suggest the urban locale, but once this context is established, outside sounds are diminished and sometimes even eliminated to permit us to hear the conversation clearly.

After the 1960s, however, a number of directors retained these noisy soundtracks in the name of greater realism. Influenced by the documentary school of **cinéma vérité**—which tends to avoid simulated or re-created sounds—directors like Jean-Luc Godard even allowed important dialogue scenes to be partly washed out by on-location sounds. In *Masculine–Feminine,* Godard's use of sound is especially bold. His insistence on natural noises—all of them as they were recorded on the set—dismayed many critics, who complained of the "cacophonous din." The movie deals with violence and the lack of privacy, peace, and quiet. Simply by exploiting his soundtrack, Godard avoided the need to comment overtly on these themes—they are naggingly persistent in virtually every scene.

The final scene from a movie is often the most important. Because of its privileged position, it can represent the filmmaker's summing up of the significance of the previous scenes. In Ermanno Olmi's *Il Posto* (The Job, also known as *The Sound of Trumpets*), the director undercuts the supposedly "happy ending" with an ironic sound effect. The movie deals with a shy work-

5–11.   *The Rock* (U.S.A., 1995), *with Sean Connery and Nicolas Cage, directed by Michael Bay.*
Moisture and water tend to exaggerate sounds, especially in enclosed spaces. In this suspenseful sequence, for example, the water under Alcatraz Prison makes every clang of metal sound like a reverberating gong. Ancient pipes hiss uncontrollably. Human breathing is gulpy and punctuated with sudden gasps for air. Every tiny gesture seems to detonate a succession of echos that splash, ripple, and finally fade into the watery distance.   *(Hollywood Pictures)*

ing-class youth who struggles diligently to land a lower-level clerking job with a huge, impersonal corporation in Milan. Finally, he is hired. The boy is especially pleased that he has a secure job "for life." Olmi is more ambivalent. The final scene of the film presents a picture of stupifying tedium and entrapment: A close-up of the youth's sensitive face is juxtaposed with the monotonous sound of a mimeograph machine, clacking louder and louder and louder.

Sound effects can also express internal emotions. In Robert Redford's *Ordinary People,* for example, an uptight mother (Mary Tyler Moore) has prepared French toast for her emotionally unstable son. Though it is his favorite breakfast food, the young man is too tense to eat: His ambivalent attitude toward his mother is one of his main problems. Irritated by his "selfish" indifference to her gesture of maternal concern, she swoops up his plate and carries it to the sink, where she stuffs the French toast into the garbage disposal, its grinding roar a symbolic embodiment of her anger and agitation.

Like absolute stasis, absolute silence in a sound film tends to call attention to itself. Any significant stretch of silence creates an eerie vacuum—a sense of something impending, about to burst. Arthur Penn exploited this phenomenon in the conclusion of *Bonnie and Clyde.* The lovers stop on a country road to help a friend (actually an informer) with his truck, which has presumably broken down. Clumsily, he scrambles under the truck. There is a long moment of silence. The two lovers exchange puzzled, then anxious, glances. Suddenly, the

218

soundtrack roars with the noise of machine guns as the lovers are brutally cut down by policemen hiding in the bushes.

Like the **freeze frame,** silence in a sound film can be used to symbolize death, because we tend to associate sound with the presence of ongoing life. Kurosawa used this technique effectively in *Ikiru,* after the elderly protagonist has been informed by a doctor that he is dying of cancer. Stupefied by the specter of death, the old man stumbles out on the street, the soundtrack totally silent. When he's almost run over by a speeding auto, the soundtrack suddenly roars with the noise of city traffic. The protagonist is yanked back into the world of the living.

Music

Music is a highly abstract art, tending toward pure form. It's impossible to speak of the "subject matter" of a musical phrase. When merged with lyrics, music acquires a more concrete content because words, of course, have specific references. Both words and music convey meanings, but each in a different manner. With or without lyrics, music can be more specific when juxtaposed with film images. In fact, many musicians have complained that images tend to rob music of its ambiguity by anchoring musical tones to specific ideas and

5–12. *Saturday Night Fever* **(U.S.A., 1977),** *with Karen Lynn Gorney and John Travolta, directed by John Badham.*
A film's rhythm is often created through its musical score. In this famous dance musical, director Badham used the pulsating Bee Gees disco tune, "Staying Alive," as a basis for both the staging and the editing rhythms. "Every time we shot a shot," Badham explained, "that music would be playing, so that all the movie that is on screen is in exact tempo to that [song]." The film triggered off a disco dance craze that swept the Western world in the late 1970s. *(Paramount Pictures)*

5–13. *Apocalypse Now* **(U.S.A., 1979),** *directed by Francis Ford Coppola.*
The sound mixing in Coppola's surrealistic Vietnam epic is masterful, suffused with grotesque ironies. In this sequence, American helicopters hover and swirl like huge mechanized gods, dropping napalm bombs on a jungle village to the accompaniment of Wagner's inexorable "Ride of the Valkyries," which thunders on the soundtrack. As terrified peasants scurry for shelter, American soldiers prepare to go surfing in the poisonous fumes of battle. *(United Artists)*

emotions. Some music lovers have lamented that Ponchielli's elegant "Dance of the Hours" conjures images of ridiculous dancing hippos, one of Disney's most brilliant sequences in *Fantasia.*

Theories about film music are surprisingly varied. Pudovkin and Eisenstein insisted that music must never serve merely as accompaniment: It ought to retain its own integrity. The film critic Paul Rotha claimed that music must even be allowed to dominate the image on occasion. Some filmmakers insist on purely descriptive music—a practice referred to as **mickeymousing** (so called because of Disney's early experiments with music and **animation**). This type of score uses music as a literal equivalent to the image. If a character stealthily tiptoes from a room, for example, each step has a musical note to emphasize the suspense. Other directors believe that film music shouldn't be too good or it will detract from the images. Most imaginative directors reject this notion. For them, the music of even the greatest composers can be used in movies.

The list of composers who have worked directly in film is a long and impressive one, including Darius Milhaud, Arthur Honegger, Paul Hindemith, Dmitri Shostakovich, Arnold Schoenberg, Sergei Prokofiev, William Walton, Benjamin Britten, Aaron Copland, Quincy Jones, Duke Ellington, The Modern

Jazz Quartet, Virgil Thomson, Kurt Weill, Bob Dylan, George Gershwin, Ralph Vaughan Williams, Richard Rodgers, Cole Porter, Leonard Bernstein, and the Beatles, to mention only a few of the best known.

A filmmaker doesn't need to have technical expertise to use music effectively. As Aaron Copland pointed out, directors must know what they want from music *dramatically:* It's the composer's business to translate these dramatic needs into musical terms. Directors and composers work in a variety of ways. Most composers begin working after they have seen the **rough cut** of a movie— that is, the major footage before the editor has tightened up the slackness between shots. Some composers don't begin until the film has been totally completed except for the music. Directors of musicals, on the other hand, usually work with the composer before shooting begins.

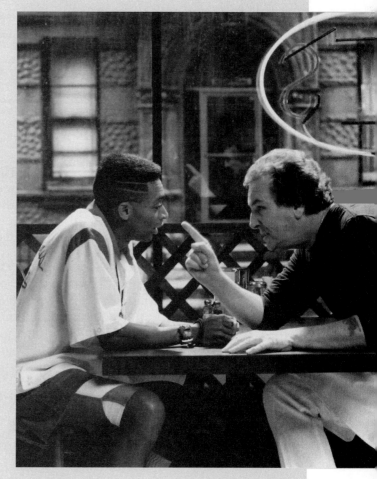

5-14.   *Do the Right Thing* (U.S.A., **1989),** *with Spike Lee and Danny Aiello, written and directed by Lee.* Set in a predominantly African-American section of Brooklyn, this movie explores the tensions between the black community and the Italian-American proprietor (Aiello) of a pizza restaurant. The two cultures are characterized by their music as well as their lifestyles. The African-American characters listen to soul, gospel, and rap music, whereas the ballads of Frank Sinatra are more typical of the Italian-American characters. Coming from a musical family, Spike Lee is painstakingly precise about his musical scores.   *(Universal Pictures)*

5–15. Audiovisual score from *Alexander Nevsky* (U.S.S.R., 1938), *music by Sergei Prokofiev, directed by Sergei Eisenstein.*
The composer need not always subordinate his or her talents to those of the film director. Here, two great Soviet artists aligned their contributions into a totally fused production in which the music corresponds to the movement of the images set in a row. Prokofiev avoided purely "representational" elements (mickeymousing). Instead, the two concentrated sometimes on the images first, other times on the music. The result was what Eisenstein called "vertical montage," where the notes on the staff, moving from left to right, parallel the movements or major lines of the images which, set side by side, also "move" from left to right. Thus, if the lines in a series of images move from lower left to upper right, the notes of music would move in a similar direction on the musical staff. If the lines of a composition were jagged and uneven, the notes of music would also zigzag in a corresponding manner. See Sergei Eisenstein, "Form and Content: Practice," in *Film Sense* (New York: Harvest Books, 1947).

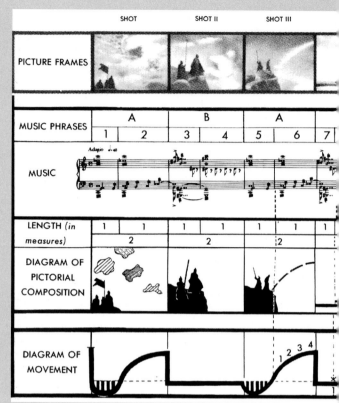

Beginning with the opening credits, music can serve as a kind of overture to suggest the mood or spirit of the film as a whole. John Addison's opening music in *Tom Jones* is a witty, rapidly executed harpsichord piece. The harpsichord itself is associated with the eighteenth century, the period of the film. The occasionally jazzy phrases in the tune suggest a sly twentieth-century overview—a musical equivalent of the blending of centuries found in the movie itself.

Certain kinds of music can suggest locales, classes, or ethnic groups. For example, John Ford's westerns feature simple folk tunes like "Red River Valley" or religious hymns like "Shall We Gather at the River," which are associated with the American frontier of the late nineteenth century. Richly nostalgic, these songs are often played on frontier instruments—a plaintive harmonica or a concertina. Similarly, many Italian movies feature lyrical, highly emotional melodies, reflecting the operatic heritage of that country. The greatest composer of this kind of film music was Nino Rota, who scored virtually all of Fellini's films, as well as such distinguished works as Zeffirelli's *Romeo and Juliet* and Coppola's *Godfather* movies.

Music can be used as foreshadowing, particularly when the dramatic context doesn't permit a director to prepare an audience for an event. Hitch-

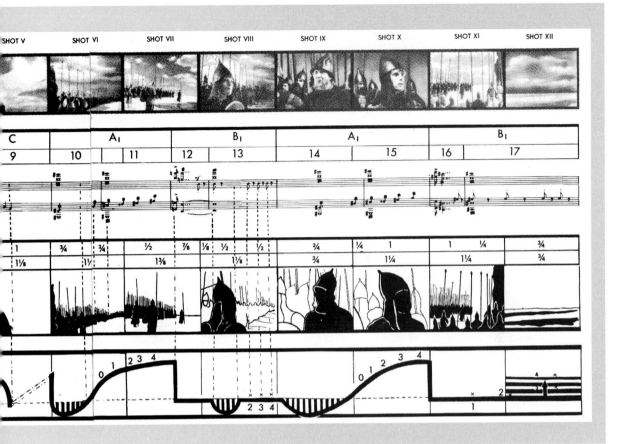

cock, for example, often accompanied an apparently casual sequence with "anxious" music—a warning to the audience to be prepared. Sometimes these musical warnings are false alarms; other times they explode into frightening crescendos. Similarly, when actors are required to assume restrained or neutral expressions, music can suggest their internal—hidden—emotions. Bernard Herrmann's music functions in both ways in *Psycho.*

Modern atonal and dissonant music generally evoke a sense of anxiety in listeners. Often, such music seems to have no melodic line and can even resemble a series of random noises. Giovanni Fusco's music for several of Antonioni's films (*L'Avventura, Red Desert, Eclipse*) produces precisely this sense of neurosis and paranoia. Fusco's music provides a similar function in the movies of Alain Resnais: *Hiroshima Mon Amour* and *La Guerre Est Finie.*

Music can also control emotional shifts within a scene. In John Huston's *The Red Badge of Courage,* for example, the protagonist (Audie Murphy), in an irrational outburst of daring, snatches the Union flag from a dying comrade and charges onto a raging battlefield. To emphasize the youth's surge of patriotism, the scene is accompanied by a spirited rendering of Yankee fighting songs. The charging young soldier stumbles by a wounded Confederate standard-bearer, writhing in pain on the ground, his flag in tatters. The music shifts to an

5–16. *Star Wars* **(U.S.A., 1977),** *with Mark Hamill, Carrie Fisher, and Harrison Ford; directed by George Lucas.*
The enormous popularity of Lucas's *Star Wars* trilogy revived the tradition of large-scale symphonic accompaniments to heighten the dramatic impact of the scenes. John Williams's score is brassy, powerful, and richly orchestrated, very much in the manner of the lushly romantic and full-bodied scores of Hollywood's golden age. Critic Frank Spotnitz noted that "the score is like a second screenplay, commenting on and enriching the first." *(Twentieth Century–Fox)*

agonizing dirge and gradually transforms into a grotesque distortion of "Dixie." The kinetic excitement of the protagonist's charge might easily have overshadowed the poignancy of the wounded Confederate, but with the aid of the music, the audience as well as the protagonist are suddenly brought to a grim halt.

Music can also provide ironic contrast. In many cases, the predominant mood of a scene can be neutralized or even reversed with contrasting music. In *Bonnie and Clyde,* the robbery scenes are often accompanied by spirited banjo music, giving these sequences a jolly sense of fun. In Ermanno Olmi's *The Tree of the Wooden Clogs,* the organ music of Johann Sebastian Bach accompanies many of the scenes, which are virtually documentary re-creations of Italian peasant life around 1900. The music provides these simple episodes with a sense of majesty—celebrating the dignity of labor and the grandeur of the human spirit.

Characterization can be suggested through musical motifs. In Fellini's *La Strada,* the pure, sad simplicity of the heroine (Giulietta Masina) is captured by a melancholy tune she plays on a trumpet. This theme is varied and elabo-

5–17. *Amadeus* (U.S.A., 1984), *with Tom Hulce (right), music by Wolfgang Amadeus Mozart, directed by Milos Forman.*

In addition to being a fairly accurate characterization of the boorish but likable lout who was Wolfgang Amadeus Mozart, this film also explores an interesting religious paradox. Why would God torment a pious servant (Mozart's rival, Antonio Salieri) with a knowledge of his own inescapable mediocrity as a composer, while the irreverent Mozart is blessed with genius? Amadeus means "loved of God." *(New Yorker Films)*

rated on in Nino Rota's delicate score, suggesting that even after her death, her spiritual influence is still felt.

Characterization can be even more precise when lyrics are added to music. In *The Last Picture Show,* for instance, pop tunes of the 1950s are used in association with specific characters. The bitchy Jacy (Cybill Shepherd) is linked to "Cold, Cold Heart." Her deceived boyfriend Duane (Jeff Bridges) is characterized by "A Fool Such As I." *American Graffiti* uses pop tunes in a similar manner. Two young lovers who have just quarreled are shown dancing at a sock hop to the tune of "Smoke Gets in Your Eyes." The lyric "yet today my love has flown away" acquires particular poignancy for the girl because the boy has just told her that he intends to date others when he goes off to college. The lovers are reconciled at the end of the movie when he decides not to leave after all. On the soundtrack, "Only You" is appropriately intuned, its syrupy lyrics emphasizing the destiny of love.

Stanley Kubrick was a bold—and controversial—innovator in the use of film music. In *Dr. Strangelove,* he sardonically juxtaposed Vera Lynn's sentimental World War II tune, "We'll Meet Again," with images of a global nuclear holocaust—a grim reminder that we probably *won't* meet again after World War III. In *2001,* Kubrick juxtaposed images of a twenty-first-century rocket ship gliding through the immense blueness of space with the sounds of Strauss's nineteenth-century "Blue Danube Waltz"—an aural foreshadowing of humanity's obsolete technology in the more advanced technological universe beyond Jupiter. In *A*

225

Clockwork Orange, Kubrick used music as a distancing device, particularly in violent scenes. Musical incongruity undercuts an otherwise vicious gang fight that takes place to the accompaniment of Rossini's urbane and witty overture to *The Thieving Magpie.* A brutal attack and rape scene is accompanied by a grotesque song-and-dance routine set to the tune of "Singin' in the Rain."

A frequent function of film music is to underline speech, especially dialogue. A common assumption about this kind of music is that it merely acts to prop up bad dialogue or poor acting. The hundreds of mediocre love scenes performed to quivering violins have perhaps prejudiced many viewers against this kind of musical accompaniment. However, some of the most gifted actors have benefited from it. In Olivier's *Hamlet,* the composer William Walton worked out his score with painstaking precision. In the "To be or not to be" soliloquy, the music provides a counterpoint to Olivier's subtly modulated delivery, adding yet another dimension to this complex speech.

Musicals and Opera

One of the most enduring and popular film genres is the musical, whose principal raison d'être is song and dance. Like opera and ballet, the narrative elements of a musical are usually pretexts for the production numbers, but some musicals are exceptionally sophisticated dramatically. Musicals can be divided into the realistic and the formalistic. Realistic musicals are generally backstage stories, in which the production numbers are presented as dramatically plausible. Such musicals usually justify a song or dance with a brief bit of dialogue—"Hey kids, let's rehearse the barn number"—and the barn number

5–19. *Footlight Parade* (U.S.A., 1933), *with Ruby Keeler, Joan Blondell, and (standing) James Cagney; directed by Lloyd Bacon.* Musicals were all the rage in the early talkie era, and each of the major Hollywood studios specialized in a house style. The musicals at Warner Brothers, for example, were typically proletarian, with emphasis on "ordinary" people and working-class values. This backstage musical is characteristically fast-paced and down-to-earth, though—weirdly—the film also includes three lavishly-staged Busby Berkeley numbers. *(Warner Bros.)*

is then presented to the audience **(5–19)**. A few realistic musicals are virtually dramas with music. In George Cukor's *A Star Is Born,* for example, the narrative events would hold up without the musical numbers, although audiences would thereby be deprived of some of Judy Garland's best scenes—a documentation, as it were, of her character's talent **(5–20)**. *New York, New York* and *Cabaret* are also dramas interspersed with music.

Formalist musicals make no pretense at realism. Characters burst out in song and dance in the middle of a scene without easing into the number with a plausible pretext. This convention must be accepted as an aesthetic premise, otherwise the entire film will strike the viewer as absurd. Everything is heightened and stylized in such works—sets, costumes, acting, etc. Most of Vincente Minnelli's musicals are of this type: *Meet Me in St. Louis, The Band Wagon* **(5–21)**, *An American in Paris,* and *Gigi.*

Although musicals have been produced in several countries, the **genre** has been dominated by Americans, perhaps because it's so intimately related to the American studio system. In the 1930s, several major studios specialized in a particular type of musical. RKO produced the charming Fred Astaire–Ginger Rogers vehicles such as *Top Hat, Shall We Dance?* and *Carefree,* all directed by Mark Sandrich. Paramount specialized in sophisticated "continental" musicals like Lubitsch's *The Love Parade, One Hour With You,* and *Monte Carlo.* At Warner Brothers, choreographer–director Busby Berkeley delighted audiences with his proletarian show-biz stories like *Gold Diggers of 1933, Dames,* and *Footlight Parade* **(5–19)**. Berkeley's stylistic signature is his fondness for abstract geometrical patterns (created with the **optical printer**) and photography of dancers from unconventional **angles** to suggest a kaleidoscopic effect (see **1–1b**).

5–20.   Publicity photo of Judy Garland in *A Star Is Born* (U.S.A., 1954), *directed by George Cukor.*

To many lovers of musicals, Judy Garland is *the* singer supreme. Even as a little girl, she had a grown woman's voice—deep and powerful, yet capable of surprising poignancy. As a child star at MGM, she was worked like a mule: recording songs, performing on radio, attending publicity events, in addition to acting in two or three films a year and often enduring twelve to fourteen hours of work a day. She was bright, funny, and very high-strung. Soon the workload began to take its toll. While still a teenager, she had five doctors at MGM. One gave her pills for her weight problems. Another gave her pills to help her sleep. Still another gave her pills to wake her up. There were shrinks, psychologists, advisors. The pills she became addicted to triggered wild mood swings. Although she was only four feet nine inches tall, her weight swelled up to 180 pounds. By the age of twenty-eight, she was considered an unemployable drug addict. She had become a monster—demanding, imperious, irresponsible, and unprofessional. There were a series of comebacks, nervous breakdowns, suicide attempts, five husbands, more comebacks, and always more drugs. In between these extremes, she made some of the finest musicals in history, immortalizing many of America's greatest popular songs. Garland was also a gifted dramatic actress, as this film attests—her last great movie performance. In addition, Garland was an appealing comedienne and a respectable dancer. Her one-woman shows in New York and London were the stuff of legends, inspiring legions of cult fans. In the last decade of her life, the 1960s, she was broke most of the time and had wasted away to a frail and haggard ninety pounds. She was found dead in her London apartment in 1969, of a drug overdose. She was only forty-seven years old. Throughout her stormy career, she kept her three children close by her, even while on tour. They all speak of their Mama with affection and smiles. See Gerald Clarke, *Get Happy: The Life of Judy Garland* (New York: Random House, 2000).   *(Warner Bros.)*

In the 1940s and 1950s, the musical was dominated by MGM, which had the finest musical directors under contract: Kelly, Donen, and Minnelli. In fact, this prosperous studio had a virtual monopoly on the musical personalities of the day, including Garland, Kelly, Frank Sinatra, Mickey Rooney, Ann Miller, Vera-Ellen, Leslie Caron, Donald O'Connor, Cyd Charisse, Howard Keel, Mario Lanza, Kathryn Grayson, and many others. MGM also lured away Astaire, Pan, and Berkeley, who, along with Michael Kidd, Bob Fosse, Gower Champion, and the ubiquitous Kelly, created most of the choreographies for the studio. Arthur Freed was the producer of most of MGM's important musicals, including the majority

5-21. *The Band Wagon* (U.S.A., 1953), *with Fred Astaire, Nanette Fabray, and Jack Buchanan; music by Howard Dietz and Arthur Schwartz; directed by Vincente Minnelli.*
The best movie musicals are generally created directly for the screen and are seldom stage adaptations. This charming "Triplets" number would be difficult to pull off in the live theater, for the three performers were required to strap false legs and feet onto their knees, their real legs bent behind them as they execute their song and dance. *(MGM)*

of Minnelli's films, as well as the stylish works of Donen: *On the Town, Singin' in the Rain* (both codirected by Kelly), and the exquisite *Funny Face.*

The combining of music with drama is a practice extending back at least to ancient Greece, but no other medium excels the expressive range of the cinema. The stage has no equivalent to the musical documentary, like *Woodstock* or *Gimme Shelter.* Movie musicals can take the form of animated fantasies, such as the Disney features *Bambi* and *Dumbo.* Musical biographies like *Amadeus* and *The Buddy Holly Story* are commonplace in film. Examples of great musicals created directly for the screen are *Singin' in the Rain* and *The Band*

5-22. *The Yellow Submarine* (Great Britain, 1968), *directed by George Dunning.*
Inspired by the Beatles' revolutionary album, *Sergeant Pepper's Lonely Hearts Club Band,* this animated feature captures the youthful spirit of whimsy and charm that typified British pop culture during the 1960s. *(Apple Films)*

5–23. *New York, New York* (U.S.A., 1977), *with Liza Minnelli and Robert De Niro, music by John Kander and Fred Ebb, directed by Martin Scorsese.*
A number of commentators have pointed out that the most enduring genres tend to evolve toward a revisionist phase—mocking many of the genre's original values by subjecting them to skeptical scrutiny. For example, most musicals of the big-studio era were essentially love stories and are concluded with the obligatory boy-wins-girl finale. Such revisionist musicals as *Cabaret* and *New York, New York,* however, end with the lovers going their separate ways, too absorbed by their own careers to submit to love's rituals of self-sacrifice. *(United Artists)*

Wagon. Others are loose adaptations of stage musicals, like *My Fair Lady, Hair,* and *Little Shop of Horrors.*

The cinema is also an ideal operatic medium, as can be seen in Bergman's *The Magic Flute* and Joseph Losey's *Don Giovanni* (Mozart's two greatest operas). These movies are more flexible spatially than any stage productions could hope to be, without compromising the music. Only a handful of operatic films approach major stature, perhaps because only a handful of first-rate filmmakers have been attracted to the subgenre. One immense advantage is that movie subtitles are far more convenient than theatrical librettos for explaining the action. With subtitles, the spectator can concentrate on the immediacy of the musical moment rather than having to place it within a larger narrative context. Each opera requires a unique approach, some "realistic" **(5–24a),** others more stylized **(5–24b).** One thing is certain: Pictures of singing heads may be accurate recordings of opera performances, but they aren't real movies.

Spoken Language

A common misconception, held even by otherwise sophisticated moviegoers, is that language in film cannot be as complex as it is in literature. The fact that Shakespeare has been successfully brought to the screen—with no significant impoverishment in either language or visual beauty—should stand as

5-24a. *The Magic Flute* (Sweden, 1974), *with Josef Kostlinger, music by Wolfgang Amadeus Mozart, directed by Ingmar Bergman.*

In adapting opera to the screen, the filmmaker must adjust the style of presentation to fit the essence of the materials. For example, Mozart's *The Magic Flute* was originally created for a popular, nonsophisticated audience. Its loony story line is based on fairy tales and the esoteric symbolism of eighteenth-century freemasonry. Bergman decided to stage it "realistically"—that is, as a straightforward presentation in the eighteenth-century manner, complete with all the wires and stage fakery in plain sight, thus creating an air of childlike enchantment. From time to time, Bergman cuts to reaction shots of present-day spectators watching the production from the opera house auditorium. *(Surrogate Release)*

5-24b. *Don Giovanni* (France, 1979), *music by Wolfgang Amadeus Mozart, directed by Joseph Losey.*

The story materials of this opera are more coherent, less supernatural, than those of *The Magic Flute*, and Losey accordingly staged the action in real locations in Italy. Instead of concentrating exclusively on images of the singers, Losey often juxtaposes them with their dramatic environments, allowing the soundtrack to provide the continuity for the fragmentation of the editing. *(New Yorker Films)*

an obvious contradiction to this notion. In fact, a number of great films are not particularly literary. This is not to say that movies are incapable of literary distinction, but only that some filmmakers wish to emphasize other aspects of their art.

In some respects, language in film can be more complex than in literature. In the first place, the words of a movie, like those of the live theater, are spoken, not written, and the human voice is capable of far more nuances than the cold printed page. The written word is a crude approximation of the connotative richness of spoken language. Thus, to take a simple example of no literary merit, the meaning of the words "I will see him tomorrow" seem obvious enough in written form. But an actor can emphasize one word over the others and thus change the meanings of the sentence completely. Here are a few possibilities:

I will see him tomorrow.   (implying, not you or anyone else)
I *will* see him tomorrow.   (implying, and I don't care if you approve)
I will *see* him tomorrow.   (implying, but that's all I'll do)
I will see *him* tomorrow.   (implying, but not anyone else)
I will see him *tomorrow.*   (implying, not today, or any other time)

Of course, a novelist or poet could emphasize specific words by italicizing them. But unlike actors, writers don't generally underline words in every sentence. On the other hand, actors routinely go through their speeches to see which words to stress, which to "throw away," and the ways to best achieve these effects—in each and every sentence. To a gifted actor, the written speech is a mere blueprint, an outline, compared to the complexities of spoken speech. A performer with an excellent voice—a Meryl Streep or a Kenneth Branagh—could wrench ten or twelve meanings from this simple sentence, let alone a Shakespearean soliloquy.

Written punctuation is likewise a simplified approximation of speech rhythms. The pauses, hesitancies, and rapid slurs of speech can only be partially suggested by punctuation:

I will . . . see him—tomorrow.
I will see him—tomorrow!
I . . . will . . . see him—tomorrow?

And so on. But how is one to capture all the meanings that have no punctuation equivalents? Even professional linguists, who have a vast array of diacritical marks to record speech, recognize that these symbols are primitive devices at best, capable of capturing only a fraction of the subtleties of the human voice. An actor like Laurence Olivier built much of his reputation on his genius in capturing little quirks of speech—an irrepressible giggle between words, for example, or a sudden vocal plummeting on one word, a gulp, or a hysterical upsurge in pitch.

By definition, speech patterns deviating radically from the official dialect are generally regarded as substandard—at least by those who take such

5-25. *Xala* **(Senegal, 1975),** *directed by Ousmane Sembene.*
Senegal, a former French colony, has a population of only four million, yet it has produced many of the most important movies of black Africa, most notably those of Sembene, the continent's best-known filmmaker. *Xala* (which roughly translates "the curse of impotence") is spoken in French and Wolof, the native language of Senegal. The movie is an exposé of the nation's servile ruling class, whose members have eagerly embraced the culture of their white colonial predecessors. (At this lavish wedding reception, for example, several Frenchified Beautiful People wonder what the English translation is for "le weekend.") The cultural commentator Hernandez Arregui has observed, "Culture becomes bilingual not due to the use of two languages but because of the conjuncture of two cultural patterns of thinking. One is national, that of the people, and the other is estranging, that of the classes subordinated to outside forces. The admiration that the upper classes express for the United States or Europe is the highest expression of their subjection." Like many Third World artists, Sembene advocates the creation of a truly native culture, somewhat like Emerson's call in the nineteenth century for American artists to stop producing tepid imitations of British models in favor of a truly American idiom. *(New Yorker Films)*

pat distinctions seriously. Dialects can be a rich source of meaning in movies (and in life, too, for that matter). Because dialects are usually spoken by people outside the Establishment, they tend to convey a subversive ideology. The earthiness of cockney and the robust dialects of Britain's midland industrial cities like Liverpool were popularized by such working-class rock groups as the Rolling Stones and the Beatles. A number of continental filmmakers have also exploited the expressive richness of dialects, most notably Lina Wertmüller (**5–28**).

Because language is spoken in movies and plays, these two mediums enjoy an advantage over printed language in that the words of a text can be juxtaposed with the ideas and emotions of a **subtext.** Briefly, a subtext refers to those implicit meanings *behind* the language of a film or play script. For example, the following lines of dialogue might be contained in a script:

5–26. *Bull Durham* **(U.S.A., 1988),** *with Susan Sarandon and Kevin Costner, written and directed by Ron Shelton.*
Southern accents are among the most lyrical dialects of American speech. Perhaps this is why so many of America's finest writers are from the South. This movie, which is narrated by the Sarandon character (a North Carolinian and sometimes English instructor), is punctuated with lyrical flights of fancy that sometimes leave the menfolk speechless with wonderment.   *(Orion Pictures)*

Woman:	May I have a cigarette, please?
Man:	Yes, of course. (lights her cigarette)
Woman:	Thank you. You're very kind.
Man:	Don't mention it.

As written, these four not very exciting lines seem simple enough and rather neutral emotionally. But depending on the dramatic context, they can be exploited to suggest other ideas, totally independent of the apparent meaning of the words. If the woman was flirting with the man, for example, she would deliver the lines very differently than an efficient businesswoman. If they detested one another, the lines would take on another significance. If the man was flirting with a hostile female, the lines would be delivered in yet another way, suggesting other meanings. In short, the meaning of the passage is pro-

5–27. *McCabe & Mrs. Miller* (U.S.A., 1970), *with Julie Christie and Warren Beatty, directed by Robert Altman.*

"What I am after is essentially the subtext," Robert Altman has declared. "I want to get the quality of what's happening between people, not just the words. The words often don't matter, it's what they're really saying to each other without the words. Most of the dialogue, well, I don't even listen to it. As I get confident in what the actors are doing, I don't even listen to it. I find that actors know more about the characters they're playing than I do." *(Warner Bros.)*

vided by the actors, not the language, which is merely camouflage. (For a more detailed discussion of the concept of a subtext, see Chapter 6.)

Any script meant to be spoken has a subtext, even one of great literary distinction. A good example from a classic text can be seen in Zeffirelli's *Romeo and Juliet,* in which Mercutio (John McEnery) is played not as the witty *bon vivant* who's intoxicated with his own talk, but as a neurotic young man with a shaky grasp of reality. This interpretation upset some traditionalists, but in the context of the movie, it reinforces the loving bond between Romeo and his best friend and helps justify Romeo's impulsive (and self-destructive) act of revenge later in the film when Mercutio is killed by Tybalt.

Some contemporary filmmakers deliberately neutralize their language, claiming that the subtext is what they're really after **(5–27)**. Harold Pinter, the dramatist and screenwriter, is perhaps the most famous example of a contemporary writer who stresses the significance of the subtext. In *The Homecoming,* a scene of extraordinary eroticism is conveyed through dialogue involving the request for a glass of water! Pinter claims that language is often a kind of "crosstalk," a way of concealing fears and anxieties. In some respects, this technique can be even more effective in film, where close-ups can convey the meanings behind words more subtly than an actor on a stage. Pinter's movie scripts are

5–28. *All Screwed Up* **(Italy, 1973),** *directed by Lina Wertmüller.*
Wertmüller is acutely sensitive to the ideological implications of dialects. Much of her comedy is mined from the earthy idioms of her working-class southerners in contrast with the standard (Tuscan) dialect spoken in the north of Italy. Her characters frequently swear or express themselves in coarse language, which is often very funny. Much of this comedy is lost in translation. The language is sometimes drained of its vitality, reduced to bland respectability. For example, "Piss off!" becomes "Go away," or worse yet, "Please leave me alone." *(New Line Cinema)*

among the most suggestive subtexts of the contemporary cinema: *The Pumpkin Eater, The Servant, Accident, The Go-Between, The Caretaker, The Homecoming, The French Lieutenant's Woman,* and *Betrayal.*

But these are merely some of the advantages of language that film enjoys over literature—advantages shared, in large part, by the live theater. As an art of juxtapositions, movies can also extend the meanings of language by contrasting spoken words with images. The sentence "I will see him tomorrow" acquires still other meanings when the image shows the speaker smiling, for example, or frowning, or looking determined. All sorts of juxtapositions are possible. The sentence could be delivered with a determined emphasis, but an image of a frightened face (or eye, or a twitching mouth) can modify the verbal determination or even cancel it out. The juxtaposed image could be a **reaction shot**—thus

5–29. *Trainspotting* (Great Britain, 1996), *with Jonny Lee Miller, Ewan McGregor, Kevin McKidd, and Ewen Bremner; directed by Danny Boyle.*
Spoken language is steeped in ideology. It's an instant revealer of class, education, and cultural bias. In most countries, regional dialects are considered substandard—at any rate by those speaking the "official" (that is, ruling-class) dialect. In Great Britain in particular, dialects correlate closely with the class system. People in power speak the same "Establishment" dialect that's taught in the exclusive private schools that still educate most ruling-class Britons. On the other hand, the working-class Scottish dialect of the main characters in this movie clearly places them outside the spheres of power and prestige. They're lowly proles, outsiders, déclassé. Hence, the booze, the drugs, the boredom. *(Miramax Films)*

emphasizing the effect of the statement on the listener. Or the camera could photograph an important object, implying a connection among the speaker, the words, and the object. If the speaker is photographed in long shot, his or her juxtaposition with the environment could also change the meanings of the words. The same line spoken in close-up would emphasize yet different meanings.

This advantage of simultaneity extends to other sounds. Music and sound effects can modify the meanings of words considerably. The same sentence spoken in an echo chamber will have different connotations from the sentence whispered intimately. If a clap of thunder coincided with the utterance of the sentence, the effect would be different from the chirping of birds or the whining of the wind. Because film is also a mechanical medium, the sentence could be modified by a deliberate distortion in the sound recording. In short, depending on the vocal emphasis, the visual emphasis, and the accompa-

5–30. *Sunset Boulevard* **(U.S.A., 1950),** *with Gloria Swanson, directed by Billy Wilder.*
Voice-over monologues are often used to produce ironic contrasts between the past and the present. Almost inevitably, such contrasts suggest a sense of destiny or fate. This film is narrated by a dead character (William Holden). The flashback images show us how he got himself killed: by exploiting the foolishness of a deluded recluse, Norma Desmond (Swanson), who once was a silent film star. Near the end of the movie, she cracks under the strain of his abandonment and shoots him. She now believes that the police and reporters surrounding her are members of a film crew photographing her comeback performance. Holden's final voice-over speech is poetic, uncharacteristically gentle: "So they were turning after all, those cameras. Life, which can be strangely merciful, had taken pity on Norma Desmond. The dream she had clung to so desperately had enfolded her." *(Paramount Pictures)*

nying soundtrack, this simple sentence could have dozens of different meanings in film, some of them impossible to capture in written form.

Movies contain two types of spoken language: the monologue and dialogue. Monologues are often associated with documentaries, in which an off-screen narrator provides the audience with factual information accompanying the visuals. Most documentary theorists are agreed that the cardinal rule in the use of this technique is to avoid duplicating the information given in the image itself. The commentary should provide what's not apparent on the screen. The audience, in short, is provided with two types of information, one concrete (visuals), the other abstract (narration). Cinéma vérité documentarists have extended this technique to include interviews, a practice pioneered by the French filmmaker Jean Rouch. Thus, instead of an anonymous narrator, the soundtrack conveys the actual words of the subjects of the documentary—slum dwellers, perhaps, or students. The camera can focus on the speaker or can roam elsewhere, with the soundtrack providing the continuity.

Monologues have also been used in fiction films. This technique is especially useful in condensing events and time. Narrative monologues can be used omnisciently to provide an ironic contrast with the visuals. In *Tom Jones,* an adaptation of a famous eighteenth-century English novel by Henry Fielding, John Osborne's script features an off-screen narrator who's nearly as witty and urbane as Fielding's, though necessarily less chatty. This narrator sets up the story, provides us with thumbnail sketches of the characters, connects many of the episodes with necessary transitions, and comments philosophically on the escapades of the incorrigible hero.

Off-screen narration tends to give a movie a sense of objectivity and often an air of predestination. Many of the works of Billy Wilder are structured in **flashbacks,** with ironic monologues emphasizing fatality: The main interest is not what happened, but how and why. In *Double Indemnity,* for example, the story is narrated by the fatally wounded hero, who admits his guilt at the opening of the film. As Wilder pointed out, "By identifying the criminals right off the bat—and identifying ourselves with them—we can concentrate on what follows: their efforts to escape, the net closing, closing."

5-31. *The Usual Suspects* **(U.S.A., 1995),** *with Kevin Pollak, Stephen Baldwin, Benicio Del Toro, Gabriel Byrne, and Kevin Spacey; directed by Bryan Singer.*
Voice-overs are especially effective in presenting us with a contrast between what's said socially and what's thought privately. Almost always, the private voice-over contains the truth, the character's real feelings about a situation. *The Usual Suspects,* a quirky psychological crime thriller, is unusual in that the voice-over narrator is a compulsive liar and manipulator. Almost everything he tells us is a crock. And we fall for his story, at least until the final scene when we discover—surprise—we've been duped.   *(Gramercy Pictures.)*

The interior monologue is one of the most valuable tools of filmmakers, for it can convey what a character is thinking. The interior monologue is frequently used in adaptations of plays and novels. Before Olivier, most film soliloquies were delivered as they are on stage: That is, the camera and microphone record a character literally talking to himself. Olivier's *Hamlet* introduced a more cinematic soliloquy. In the "To be or not to be" speech, several of the lines are not spoken but "thought"—via a **voice-over** soundtrack. Suddenly, at a crucial line, Olivier spews out the words in exasperation. Through the use of the soundtrack, private ruminations and public speech can be combined in interesting ways, with new and often more subtle emphases.

A major difference between stage dialogue and screen dialogue is degree of density. One of the necessary conventions of the live theater is articulation: If something is bothering a character, we can usually assume that he or she will *talk* about the problem. The theater is a visual as well as aural medium, but in general, the spoken word is dominant: We tend to hear before we see. If information is conveyed visually in the theater, it must be larger than life, for most of the audience is too far from the stage to perceive visual nuances. The convention of articulation is necessary, therefore, to compensate for this visual loss. Like most artistic conventions, stage dialogue is not usually realistic or natural, even in so-called realistic plays. In real life, people don't articulate their ideas and feelings with such precision. In movies, the convention of articulation can be relaxed. Because the close-up can show the most minute detail, verbal comment is often superfluous. This greater spatial flexibility means that

5–32. *Badlands* (U.S.A., 1973), with Sissy Spacek, written and directed by Terrence Malick.
Not all voice-over narratives are omniscient. This movie is narrated by a bored and dimwitted teenager (Spacek) who talks in *True Romance* clichés and hasn't a glimmer of insight into what wrecked her life. *(Warner Bros.)*

film language doesn't have to carry the heavy burden of stage dialogue. In fact, the image conveys most meanings, so dialogue in film can be as spare and realistic as it is in everyday life, as in such starkly dialogued movies as *The Bridges of Madison County* (**5–33**).

Movie dialogue doesn't have to conform to natural speech. If language is stylized, the director has several options for making it believable. Like Olivier, he or she can emphasize an intimate style of delivery—sometimes even whispering the lines. Welles's Shakespearean films are characterized by a visual flamboyance: The expressionistic stylization of the images in *Othello* complements the artificiality of the language. Generally speaking, if dialogue is nonrealistic, the images must be coexpressive: Sharp contrasts of style between language and visuals can produce jarring and often comic incongruities.

Foreign language movies are shown either in dubbed versions or in their original language, with written subtitles. Both methods of translation have obvious drawbacks. Dubbed movies often have a hollow, tinny sound, and in most cases, the dubbing is performed by less gifted actors than the originals. Sound and image are difficult to match in dubbed films, especially in the closer ranges where the movements of the actors' lips aren't synchronized with the sounds. Even bilingual actors who do their own dubbing are less nuanced when they're not speaking their native language. For example, Sophia Loren's performance in the English language version of *Two Women* is very good, but it lacks the vocal expressiveness of her brilliant line readings in the original Italian. In English, Loren's classy pear-shaped tones are somewhat at odds with her role as an earthy peasant. In a similar vein, actors with highly distinctive voices, like Mae West or John Wayne, sound preposterous when dubbed in German or

5–33. *The Bridges of Madison County* (U.S.A., 1995), *with Meryl Streep and Clint Eastwood, directed by Eastwood.* Effective dialogue is not always the result of literate scripts and richly expressive language. Talk is usually kept to a stark minimum in Eastwood's films. He's at his best when we must infer what he's thinking: His face is far more expressive than the way he talks, for his words are few, delivered in a matter-of-fact monotone. In Eastwood's case, less is usually more. Even in this untypical genre—a brief love affair between middle-aged characters—Eastwood's dialogue was pared down. The entire movie is a terse, almost austere adaptation of a novel that many critics regarded as floridly overwritten. Eastwood's version is subtler, tougher, and ultimately more emotionally powerful because the sentiment is held in check by the lean writing and restrained acting. *(Warner Bros.)*

Japanese. On the other hand, dubbed movies permit the spectator to concentrate on the visuals rather than the subtitles, which are distracting and can absorb much of a viewer's energy. Nobody likes to "read" a movie.

Most experienced filmgoers still prefer subtitles, however, despite their cumbersomeness. In the first place, some spectators are sufficiently conversant in foreign languages to understand most of the dialogue (especially in Europe, where virtually all educated people speak a second language, and in some cases, three or four). An actor's tone of voice is often more important than the dialogue per se, and subtitled movies allow us to hear these vocal nuances. In short, subtitles permit us to hear what the original artists said, not what some disinterested technician—however clever—decided we would settle for.

The advantages of sound, then, make it indispensable to the film artist. As René Clair foresaw many years ago, sound permits a director more visual freedom, not less. Because speech can reveal a person's class, region, occupation, prejudices, etc., the director doesn't need to waste time establishing these facts visually. A few lines of dialogue can convey all that's necessary, thus freeing

5-34. *Belle Epoque* **(Spain, 1993),** *with Jorge Sanz and Penelope Cruz, directed by Fernando Trueba.*

In most countries except the English-speaking world, foreign movies are usually dubbed into the language of the viewing audience. Generally, the sound quality of the dubbing is terrible—a crude approximation, usually by different actors with less talent than the originals. On the other hand, written subtitles can be just as exasperating, forcing us to "read" the movie instead of exploring its mise en scène. *(Sony Pictures)*

5–35. *Reservoir Dogs* **(U.S.A., 1992),** *with Steve Buscemi and Harvey Keitel, written and directed by Quentin Tarantino.*

This stylized gangster film features an almost steady torrent of foul language, as violent as the lives of the characters. In fact, eventually the swearing becomes grotesquely comical, adding to the movie's bizarre tone, which blends violence, cruelty, and pathos with black comedy. In cases like this, sanitized dialogue would be a form of aesthetic dishonesty, totally at odds with the movie's nasty edge of realism. *(Miramax Films)*

the camera to go on to other matters. There are many instances where sound is the most economical and precise way of conveying information in film.

In analyzing a movie's sound, we should ask ourselves how sound is orchestrated in each scene. Is the sound distorted? Why? Is the sound edited down and simplified or dense and complex? Is there any symbolism in the use of sound? Does the film employ repeated motifs? How is silence used? What type of musical score does the film feature? Is the score original or derived from outside sources? What type of instruments are used? How many? A full orchestra? A small combo? A solo instrument? Is music used to underline speech or is it employed only for action scenes? Or not at all? How is language used? Is the dialogue spare and functional? Or "literary" and richly textured? Does everyone speak the standard dialect or are there regional accents? How does dialogue correlate with class? What about the subtext, the emotional implications *beneath* the dialogue? How do we know what the characters want if they don't talk about it? What about language choice? Any fancy words? Swears and coarse expressions? Is there a voice-over narrator? Why was he or she chosen to narrate the story? Why not another character?

FURTHER READING

ALTMAN, RICK, ed. *Sound Theory/Sound Practice* (London and New York: Routledge, 1992). A collection of scholarly essays.

BROWN, ROYAL S., *Overtones and Undertones: Reading Film Music* (Berkeley: University of California Press, 1994). Scholarly study of the aesthetics of film music.

EYMAN, SCOTT, *The Speed of Sound: Hollywood and the Talkie Revolution 1926–1930* (New York: Simon & Schuster, 1997). A lively account of the changeover to sound.

KALINAK, KATHRYN, *Settling the Score* (Madison: University of Wisconsin Press, 1992). Music and the classical Hollywood cinema.

LOBRUTTO, VINCENT, ed., *Sound-on-Film* (New York: Praeger, 1994). Interviews with creators of film sound.

MORDDEN, ETHAN, *The Hollywood Musical* (New York: St. Martin's Press, 1982). Eccentric, astute, well written.

PRENDERGAST, ROY M., *Film Music* (New York: Norton, 1977). Excellent analysis.

SMITH, JEFF. *The Sounds of Commerce* (New York: Columbia University Press, 1999). Marketing popular film music.

WALKER, ALEXANDER, *The Shattered Silents* (New York: William Morrow, 1979). A well-written history.

WEIS, ELISABETH, and JOHN BELTON, eds., *Film Sound: Theory and Practice* (New York: Columbia University Press, 1985). A collection of scholarly articles.

6

Acting

Twentieth Century-Fox

*In the cinema the actor must think
and let his thoughts work upon his face.
The objective nature of the medium will do the rest.
A theatrical performance requires magnification,
a cinema performance requires an inner life.*
                                                    —CHARLES DULLIN

Overview

Acting classifications: nonprofessionals, extras, pros, stars. Stage and screen: amplification versus inner truth. Film acting as a directorial language system. Beauty, charm, and sex appeal. The physical requirements of acting: face, voice, body. Expressiveness in film acting. Performances constructed on the editing bench. The star system. The Golden Age of the Hollywood studios. The mythology of the stars. Stars and American popular culture. The downside of stardom. Personality stars versus actor stars. Iconography: the accretion of meaning in a star's persona. Styles of acting: realism and expressionism. National styles. Genre and its requirements. Silent film acting. Star acting: Hollywood romanticism during the big-studio era. British acting traditions. Post–World War II realism. The American Method school of acting. Texts and subtexts. Improvisation. Casting as characterization. Typecasting, casting against type. How casting determines thematic and iconographic meaning.

Film acting is a complex and variable art that can be broken down into four categories:

1. *Extras.* These actors are used primarily to provide a sense of a crowd—as in "a cast of thousands." Players of this type are used as camera material, like a landscape or a set.
2. *Nonprofessional performers.* These are amateur players who are chosen not because of their acting ability, which can be negligible, but because of their authentic appearance—they *look* right for a given part.
3. *Trained professionals.* These stage and screen performers are capable of playing a variety of roles in a variety of styles. The majority of actors fall under this category.
4. *Stars.* These are famous performers who are widely recognized by the public. Their drawing power is one of the main attractions of a film or stage play. The **star system** was developed and has been dominated by the American cinema, though it's hardly unique to movies. Virtually all the performing arts—opera, dance, live theater, television, concert music—have exploited the box-office popularity of a charismatic performer.

However a film actor is classified, virtually all performers in this medium concede that their work is shaped by the person who literally and figuratively calls the shots. Even Charlie Chaplin, the most famous movie star of his era, admitted, "Film acting is unquestionably a director's medium." In short, the movie actor is ultimately a tool of the director—another "language system" through which the filmmaker communicates ideas and emotions.

6–1. *The End of the Affair* **(Great Britain, 1999),** *with Julianne Moore and Ralph Fiennes, adapted and directed by Neil Jordan.*

Love scenes on stage are usually verbal, and rarely is there much extended love play. Nudity is extremely rare. Love scenes in movies are usually the opposite: The emphasis is on physical contact, with a minimum of dialogue. Even this film, a faithful adaptation of a classic Graham Greene novel, presents the love scenes in a graphically physical manner, converting Greene's literary descriptions into steamy sexual liaisons. Most film actors dislike playing nude scenes, which are usually performed while dozens of technicians are observing from the sidelines. Despite this unromantic public arena, the performers must act as though they're behind closed doors, drunk on intimacy and passion. *(Columbia Pictures)*

Stage and Screen Acting

The differences between stage and screen acting are largely determined by the differences in space and time in each medium (see also Chapter 7, "Drama"). In general, the live theater seems to be a more satisfactory medium for the actor because, once the curtain goes up, he or she tends to dominate the proceedings. In movies, this is not usually the case. Actress Kim Stanley expressed the differences well: "No matter what you do in film, it is, after all, bits and pieces for the director, and that's marvelous for the director but it doesn't allow the actor to learn to mold a part. In films, it's the director who is the artist. An actor has much more chance to create on stage."

Even the requirements are different in each medium. The essential requisites for the stage performer are to be seen and heard clearly. Thus, the ideal theatrical actor must have a flexible, trained voice. Most obviously, his or her voice must be powerful enough to be heard even in a theater containing thousands of seats. Because language is the major source of meaning in the theater, the nuances of the dialogue must be conveyed through vocal expressive-

6–2. *Boys Don't Cry* (U.S.A., 1999), *with Peter Sarsgaard, Hilary Swank, and Brendan Sexton III; directed by Kimberly Pierce.*
Shakespeare and the dramatists of the ancient world often employed the motif of cross dressing, if for nothing else, because women were not allowed to act on stage. This movie, based on actual events, explores cross dressing in a more realistic manner. The protagonist (Swank) tries desperately to pass as a male and for a while she succeeds. But her deception is finally discovered and she pays a fearful price for her obsession. Swank's performance is subtly nuanced, a triumph of realistically observed details of how young guys walk, talk, and swagger. The charm of Shakespeare's cross-dressing heroines lies precisely in the exquisite femininity of the characters trying to act macho. The fascination of Swank's Oscar-winning performance lies in how she submerges her femininity and creates a totally credible young male. *(Fox Searchlight Pictures)*

ness. An actor's voice must be capable of much variety. It's necessary to know what words to stress and how to stress them, how to phrase properly for different types of lines, when to pause and for how long, and how quickly or slowly a line or speech ought to be delivered. Above all, the stage actor must be *believable,* even when reciting dialogue that's highly stylized and unnatural. Most of the credit for an exciting theatrical production is given to the performers, but much of the burden is also theirs, for when we're bored by a production of a play, we tend to blame the actors.

Physical requirements are less exacting in the theater than in movies. Most obviously, the stage actor must be seen—even from the back of the auditorium. Thus, it helps to be tall, for small actors tend to get lost on a large stage. It also helps to have large and regular features, although makeup can cover a multitude of deficiencies. For this reason, casting a forty-year-old actor as Romeo is not necessarily a disaster in the theater, for if the actor is in reasonably good physical shape, his age won't show beyond the first rows of seats. Because of the low visual saturation in the theater, actors can play roles twenty years beyond their actual age, provided their voices and bodies are flexible enough.

The stage actor's entire body is always in view, and for this reason, he or she must be able to control it with some degree of precision. Such obvious activities as sitting, walking, and standing are performed differently on the stage than they are in real life. An actor must usually learn how to dance, how to fence, and how to move naturally in period costumes. An actor must know what to do with his or her hands—when to let them hang and when to use them for expressive gestures. Furthermore, stage actors must know how to adjust their bodies to different characters: A seventeen-year-old girl moves differently than a woman of thirty; an aristocrat moves differently than a clerk of the same age. The body must communicate a wide variety of emotions in pantomime: A happy person even stands differently than one who is dejected or fearful or bored.

Theatrical acting preserves real time. The performer must build—scene by scene—toward the climactic scene near the end of the play. Usually, the stage actor begins at a relatively low energy level, then increases with each progressive scene until, in the climax, the energy reaches its bursting point and finally tapers off in the resolution of the play. In short, the actor generates in psychic energy the play's own structure. Within this overall structure, the stage performer "builds" within each scene, although not every scene is automatically played at a greater intensity than its predecessor, for different plays build in different ways. What's essential for the stage actor is to sustain an energy

6-3. *Waiting to Exhale* **(U.S.A., 1995),** *with Loretta Devine, Whitney Houston, Angela Bassett, and Lela Rochon; directed by Forest Whitaker.*
An ensemble cast emphasizes the interactions of a group of equally important characters, rather than a single performer or star. Ensemble casts are more common on stage, since most of the actors are viewed in the same space at the same time. In movies, especially American movies, the star system isolates the leading player from the secondary and minor characters. Hence, live theater is sometimes thought to be a more democratic art, whereas conventional movies are thought to be more hierarchical and elitist.   *(Twentieth Century-Fox)*

level for the duration of a scene. Once the curtain rises, he or she is alone on the stage. Mistakes aren't easily corrected, nor can a scene be replayed or cut out.

In general, the film player can get along quite well with a minimum of stage technique. The essential requisite for a performer in the movies is what Antonioni called "expressiveness." That is, he or she must *look* interesting (6–4). No amount of technique will compensate for an unphotogenic face. A number of stage performers have fared badly in the movies because of this deficiency. For example, Kim Stanley and Tallulah Bankhead were among the most admired stage stars in America, but their film work failed to excite much interest. Similarly, Ian Richardson is regarded as one of the most brilliant actors of the British stage—where brilliant actors are commonplace—but his few film performances are lackluster. Some of the most famous stage actors in history—including Sarah Bernhardt—look preposterous on film: Her techniques are mannered and stagey to the point of caricature. In movies, then, too much technique can actually undercut a performance, can make it seem hammy and insincere.

Acting in the cinema is almost totally dependent on the filmmaker's approach to the story materials. In general, the more **realistic** the director's techniques, the more necessary it is to rely on the abilities of the players. Such directors tend to favor **long shots,** which keep the performer's entire body within the **frame.** This is the camera distance that corresponds to the prosce-

6–4. *The Whisperers* **(Great Britain, 1966),** *with Edith Evans, directed by Bryan Forbes.*
The cinematic close-up allows the film actor to concentrate totally on the truth of the moment—without the need to worry about projecting to the back row. Gestures and facial expressions can be exquisitely nuanced. Stage actors generally must convey such nuances through words. The Hungarian theorist Béla Balázs believed that the movie close-up can isolate the human face from its surroundings and penetrate the soul: "What appears on the face and in facial expression is a spiritual experience," Balázs observed. This experience is impossible to achieve in the live theater, because the spectator is too distant from the performer. *(United Artists)*

nium arch of the live theater. The realist also tends to favor **lengthy takes**—thus permitting the actors to sustain performances for relatively long periods without interruption. From the audience's point of view, it's easier to evaluate acting in a realistic movie because we are permitted to see sustained scenes without any apparent directorial interference. The camera remains essentially a recording device.

The more **formalistic** the director, the less likely he or she is to value the actor's contribution. Some of Hitchcock's most stunning cinematic effects were achieved by minimizing the contributions of actors. During the production of *Sabotage,* Hitchcock's leading lady, Sylvia Sidney, burst into tears on the set because she wasn't permitted to act a crucial scene. The episode involved a murder in which the sympathetic heroine kills her brutish husband in revenge for his murder of her young brother. On stage, of course, the heroine's feelings and thoughts would be communicated by words and the actress's exaggerated facial expressions. But in real life, Hitchcock observed, people's faces don't necessarily reveal what they think or feel. The director preferred to convey these ideas and emotions through **edited** juxtapositions **(6–5).**

The setting for the scene is a dinner table. The heroine looks at her husband, who is eating as usual. Then a **close-up** shows a dish containing meat and vegetables with a knife and fork lying next to it; the wife's hands are seen behind the dish. Hitchcock then cuts to a **medium shot** of the wife thoughtfully slicing some meat. Next, a medium shot of the brother's empty chair. Close-up of the wife's hands with knife and fork. Close-up of a bird cage with canaries—a reminder to the heroine of her dead brother. Close-up of wife's thoughtful face. Close-up of the knife and plate. Suddenly a close-up of the husband's suspicious face: He notices the connection between the knife and her thoughtful expression, for the camera **pans,** rather than cuts, back to the knife. He gets up next to her. Hitchcock quickly cuts to a close-up of her hand reaching for the knife. Cut to an **extreme close-up** of the knife entering his body. Cut to a **two-shot** of their faces, his convulsed with pain, hers in fear. When Sylvia Sidney saw the finished product, she was delighted with the results. The entire scene, of course, required very little acting in the conventional sense of the term.

Antonioni once said that he uses his actors only as part of the composition—"like a tree, a wall, or a cloud." Many of the major themes of his films are conveyed through long shots where the juxtaposition of people and their settings is used to suggest complex psychological and spiritual states. Perhaps more than any other director, Antonioni is sensitive to how meanings change, depending on the **mise en scène.** Similarly, the French director Robert Bresson believed that a screen actor is not an interpretive artist but merely one of the "raw materials" of the mise en scène and the editing. He generally preferred to use nonprofessional actors in his movies because trained actors tend to want to convey emotions and ideas through performance, as in the live theater. For Bresson, films should be made cinematically rather than theatrically, by "bypassing the will of those who appear in them, using not what they do, but what they *are.*"

6–5. Sequence from *Sabotage* (Great Britain, 1936), *with Sylvia Sidney and Oscar Homolka, directed by Alfred Hitchcock.*

Through the art of editing, a director can construct a highly emotional "performance" by juxtaposing shots of actors with shots of objects. In scenes such as these, the actor's contribution tends to be minimal: The effect is achieved through the linking of two or more shots. This associational process is the basis of Pudovkin's theory of constructive editing.   *(Gaumont-British)*

continued ▶

d

e

f

j

k

l

p

q

r

v

w

x

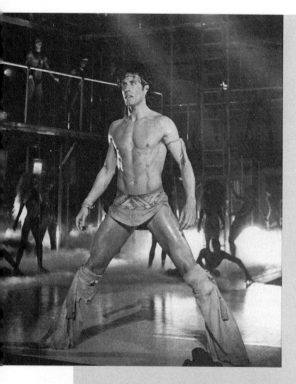

6–6a. *Staying Alive* **(U.S.A., 1983),** *with John Travolta, directed by Sylvester Stallone.* *(Paramount Pictures)*

The Naked and the Nude. A number of cultural commentators have noted the distinction between a nude figure and a naked one. A nude or semi-nude body **(6–6a)** is meant to be looked at, meant to be admired. Sexual allure is a compelling attraction in most of the performing arts, dating back to ancient times. In fact, the beauty of the human form—both male and female—has been one of the most persistent lures of the cinema almost since its inception. The appeal is both aesthetic and carnal: We're drawn to the sensual beauty of the sculpted bodies, and we want to touch, perhaps to possess. On the other hand, a naked person **(6–6b)** is usually embarrassed to be seen publicly without clothes on, a source of considerable hilarity as Cleese's would-be adulterer is caught buck naked by unexpected guests.

6-6b. *A Fish Called Wanda* **(Great Britain, 1988),** *with John Cleese, directed by Charles Crichton.* *(MGM)*

6-7. *The Gold Rush* (U.S.A., 1925), *with Charles Chaplin and Mack Swain, directed by Chaplin.*

Actors in every medium (except radio) must be conscious of body language and what it reveals about character. Silent actors were deprived of their voices, so they externalized their feelings and thoughts through gesture, movement, facial expression, and body language—all of which had to be heightened to compensate for their lack of speech. In this shot, for example, Big Jim McKay is puzzled by the scary rumbling and quaking of their cabin. The hungover Charlie explains—through pantomime—that his queasy stomach is the culprit.   *(rbc Films)*

Generalizing about acting in movies is difficult because directors don't approach every film with the same attitudes. Elia Kazan and Ingmar Bergman, distinguished stage directors as well as filmmakers, varied their techniques considerably, depending on the dramatic needs of the film. Nor is there any "correct" approach to filming a scene. A director like Chaplin might convey a specific idea through acting, whereas Bresson might approach the same idea through editing or mise en scène. Each version could be effective: Whatever *works* is right.

But whether a director is a realist or formalist, the differences between film acting and stage acting remain fundamental. For example, a player in movies is not so restricted by vocal requirements because sound volume is controlled electronically. Marilyn Monroe's small breathy voice wouldn't have projected beyond the first few rows in the theater, but on film it was perfect for conveying that childlike vulnerability that gave her performances such poetic delicacy. Some film actors are popular precisely because of the offbeat charm of their voices. Because acting in movies is not so dependent on vocal flexibility, many performers have succeeded despite their wooden, inexpressive voices: Gary Cooper, John Wayne, Clint Eastwood, Arnold Schwarzenegger.

6–8. *La Strada* (Italy, 1954), *with Richard Basehart and Giulietta Masina, directed by Federico Fellini.*
Virtually all Italian movies are dubbed after the footage has been photographed and sometimes even after it's been edited. Fellini selected his players according to their face, body type, or personality. Like many Italian filmmakers, he often used foreign actors, even in major roles. The American Richard Basehart spoke his lines in English during this film's production. Once shooting was completed, Fellini hired an Italian actor with the same vocal quality to dub in the character's voice. *(Audio-Brandon Films)*

Even the quality of a movie actor's voice can be controlled mechanically. Music and sound effects can totally change the meaning of a line of dialogue. Through electronic devices, a voice can be made to sound garbled or booming or hollow. Much of the dialogue in a movie is **dubbed,** so a director can re-record a line until it's perfect. Sometimes the director will select one or two words from one recorded take and blend them with the words of another, or even a third or fourth. This kind of synthesizing can be carried even further—by combining one actor's face with another actor's voice **(6–8).**

Similarly, the physical requirements for a film actor are different from those of a stage performer. The movie player doesn't have to be tall, even if he's a leading man type. Alan Ladd, for example, was quite short. His directors simply avoided showing his body in full unless there was no one else in frame to contrast with his height. He played love scenes standing on a box, his body cut off at the waist. **Low-angle shots** also tended to make him seem taller. A film actor's features don't have to be large, only expressive—particularly the eyes and mouth. Nor does a film actor have to be attractive. For example, Humphrey Bogart was not a good-looking man, but the camera "liked him." That is, his face was uncannily photogenic, opening up to the camera in a way that often surprised his cinematographers. Sometimes this contrast between reality and its illusion can be intimidating. Complained Jean Arthur, "It's a strenuous job every day of your life to live up to the way you look on the screen."

An actor who moves clumsily is not necessarily at a disadvantage in film. The director can work around the problem by not using many long shots and by photographing the actor *after* he or she has moved. Complicated movements can be faked by using stuntmen or stuntwomen or doubles. These shots are **intercut** with closer shots of the leading actor, and the edited juxtaposition leads the audience to assume that the main performer is involved in all the shots (see **4–16**). Even in close-up, the film performer's physical appearance can be changed through the use of special **lenses, filters,** and lights.

Because the shot is the basic building unit in film, the actor doesn't have to sustain a performance for very long—even in realistic movies in which the **takes** can run for two or three minutes. In a highly fragmented film—in which shots can last for less than a second—one can scarcely refer to the performer's contribution as acting at all: He or she simply *is.*

The shooting schedule of a movie is determined by economic considerations. Thus, the shooting of various sequences can be out of chronology. An actor may be required to perform the climactic scene first and low-keyed exposition shots later. The screen actor, then, doesn't "build" emotionally as the stage actor must. The film player must be capable of an intense degree of con-

6–9. *The Night of the Shooting Stars* (Italy, 1982), *directed by Paolo and Vittorio Taviani.* Realism in movies can be far more "real" than stage realism, for a stage actor's skill and discipline are always apparent to the audience. Film realism is often more convincing precisely because of the player's lack of technical skill. The nonprofessional players of this movie are artless and sincere, totally devoid of actorish mannerisms, and hence totally believable as ordinary peasants trying to survive during the harsh times of World War II.   *(United Artists)*

6–10. *The Ice Storm* (U.S.A., 1997), *with Christina Ricci and Tobey Maguire, directed by Ang Lee.*
Most actors agree that film is a more intimate medium than live theater. Screen actors don't have to project their voices: They can talk normally. They don't have to make their movements larger-than-life, just gesture the way they do in everyday life. They can communicate through eye contact alone: The camera magnifies their intimacy hundreds of times. Ricci and Maguire both began as child actors, and performing in front of a camera is almost second-nature to them. Maguire is a film natural, a deft underplayer who seems to be behaving rather than acting. He rarely lets the wires show, concealing his artistry behind a deceptively simple throwaway style of performance. Ricci's range is broader, extending from stylized satirical comedy (*The Opposite of Sex*) to unsentimental realism (*The Ice Storm*) to swoony romantic styles (*Sleepy Hollow*). *(Fox Searchlight Pictures)*

centration—turning emotions on and off for very short periods of time. Most of the time, the player must seem totally natural, as if he or she weren't acting at all. "You do it just like in reality," Henry Fonda explained **(6–10).** Certainly the film player is almost always at the mercy of the director, who later constructs the various shots into a coherent performance. Some directors have tricked actors into a performance, asking for one quality to get another.

Because acting in the cinema is confined to short segments of time and space, the film player doesn't need a long rehearsal period to establish a sense of ease with other actors, the set, or costumes. Many directors keep rehearsals to a minimum so as not to dissipate the spontaneity of the players, their sense of discovery and surprise. Unlike the stage player, the film actor doesn't have to create an intimate rapport with other performers: Sometimes they haven't even met until they arrive on the set or on location. Actors occasionally don't know their lines: This is remedied by having a prompter on the set or by writing the lines on a chalkboard off frame where the actor can read them.

A film actor is expected to play even the most intimate scenes with dozens of technicians on the set, working or observing **(6–1).** The actor must seem totally at ease, even though the lights are unbearably hot and his or her running makeup must be corrected between shots. Because the camera distorts, actors are required to perform some scenes unnaturally. In an embrace, for example, lovers can't really look at each other in the eyes or they will appear cross-eyed on the screen. In **point-of-view shots,** actors must direct their lines at the camera rather than at another player. Much of the time, the performer has no idea what he or she is doing, or where a shot might appear in the finished film, if indeed it appears at all, for many an actor's performance has been left on the cutting room floor. In short, the discontinuity of time and space in the cinema places the performer almost totally in the hands of the director.

The American Star System

The star system has been the backbone of the American film industry since the mid-1910s. Stars are the creation of the public, its reigning favorites. Their influence in the fields of fashion, values, and public behavior has been enormous. "The social history of a nation can be written in terms of its film stars," Raymond Durgnat has observed. Stars confer instant consequence to any film they appear in. Their fees have staggered the public. In the 1920s, Mary Pickford and Charles Chaplin were the two highest paid employees in the world. Contemporary stars such as Julia Roberts and Tom Cruise command salaries of many millions per film, so popular are these box-office giants. Some stars had careers that spanned five decades: Bette Davis and John Wayne, to name just two. Alexander Walker, among others, has pointed out that stars are the direct or indirect reflection of the needs, drives, and anxieties of their audience: They are the food of dreams, allowing us to live out our deepest fantasies and obsessions. Like the ancient gods and goddesses, stars have been adored, envied, and venerated as mythic icons.

Prior to 1910, actors' names were almost never included in movie credits because producers feared the players would then demand higher salaries. But the public named their favorites anyway. Mary Pickford, for example, was first known by her character's name, "Little Mary." From the beginning, the public often fused a star's artistic **persona** with his or her private personality. For example, Ingrid Bergman's much-publicized love affair with Italian director Roberto Rossellini created a scandalous uproar in the United States in the late 1940s. It nearly wrecked her career, not to speak of her psyche. She was a victim of her own public image, which had been carefully nurtured by her boss, producer David O. Selznick. In the public mind, Bergman was a wholesome, almost sainted woman—modest and simple, a happy wife and mother. This image was buttressed by her most popular roles: the radiantly ethereal Ilsa in *Casablanca,* the fervent political idealist in *For Whom the Bell Tolls,* the warm indomitable mother superior in *The Bells of St. Mary's,* and the noble warrior-saint of *Joan of Arc.* In reality, Bergman was an ambitious artist, anxious to play a

6–11. Metro-Goldwyn-Mayer publicity photo of Esther Williams, circa 1952.

Good looks and sex appeal have always been the conspicuous traits of most film stars, both male and female. Tall, strong, gorgeous Esther Williams was the first American female star to combine fitness with beauty. An MGM star in the 1940s and 1950s, she appeared in twenty-six light entertainment films that showcased her skill as a swimmer and diver. She was—and still is—proud that her films promoted fitness: "My movies made it clear that it's all right to be strong and feminine at the same time," Williams said. "A survey showed I received more fan mail from teenage girls than anyone in the business." After raising her family, Williams formed her own business by shrewdly exploiting her fame to establish a successful line of bathing suits. *(MGM/Turner Entertainment)*

variety of roles, including villainess parts. When she and Rossellini met, they soon fell in love, and though still married to her first husband, Bergman became pregnant with Rossellini's child. When her condition became public, the press had a field day, indulging in an orgy of lurid speculations and attacking her for "betraying" her public. She was reviled by religious groups and even denounced from the floor of the U.S. Senate, where she was described as "Hollywood's apostle of degradation" and "a free-love cultist." Bergman and Rossellini married in 1950, but their joint movies were boycotted in the United States, and she remained out of the country for several years. She was apparently "forgiven" in 1956, when she won her second Academy Award (best actress) for her performance in *Anastasia*, a big box-office success.

Unless the public is receptive to a given screen personality, audiences can be remarkably resistant to someone else's notion of a star. For example, producer Samuel Goldwyn ballyhooed his Russian import, Anna Sten, without stinting on costs. But audiences stayed away from her movies in droves. "God makes the stars," the chastened Goldwyn finally concluded. "It's up to the producers to find them."

Throughout the silent era, stars grew giddy with their wealth and power. Intoxicated by the opulence of Hollywood's royalty, the public was eager

6-12. *Taxi Driver* (U.S.A., 1976), *with Robert De Niro, directed by Martin Scorsese.*
Acting is a demanding art, requiring dedication, discipline, and Spartan endurance. De Niro is famous for his rigorous preparations prior to production, researching his roles exhaustively. Widely regarded as the greatest American actor of his generation, he prefers to bury himself in a role. He rarely exploits his personal charisma and is noticeably uncomfortable during interviews, which he rarely grants. De Niro has always insisted that life should take precedence over art. But his is an art that conceals art. "Some of the old movie stars were terrific," he explained, "but they romanticized. People chase illusions and these illusions are created by movies. I want to make things concrete and real and to break down the illusion. I don't want people years from now to say, 'Remember De Niro, he had real style.'" Many of his finest performances have been under the direction of his old friend, Martin Scorsese. *(Columbia Pictures)*

to learn more of its favorites. Fan (short for fanatic) magazines sprang up by the dozens, and the burgeoning studios churned out a steady stream of publicity—most of it imbecilic—to feed this insatiable curiosity. Paramount's rival queens, Gloria Swanson and Pola Negri, vied with each other in the extravagance of their lifestyles. Both of them married many times, and each managed to snare at least one petty nobleman among their stable of rapt admirers. "I have gone through a long apprenticeship," Swanson said. "I have gone through enough of being nobody. I have decided that when I am a star I will be every inch and every moment the star. Everyone from the studio gateman to the highest executive will know it." The mythology of stardom often incorporated this rags-to-riches motif. The humble origins of many stars encouraged the public to believe that anyone—even ordinary people—could be "discovered" and make it to Hollywood, where all their dreams would come true.

The so-called golden age of the star system—roughly the 1930s and 1940s—coincided with the supremacy of the Hollywood studio system. Most of

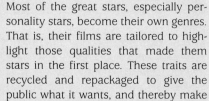

6–13a. *Jerry Maguire* (U.S.A., 1996), with Tom Cruise and Cuba Gooding, Jr.; directed by Cameron Crowe. *(TriStar Pictures)*

Most of the great stars, especially personality stars, become their own genres. That is, their films are tailored to highlight those qualities that made them stars in the first place. These traits are recycled and repackaged to give the public what it wants, and thereby make lots of money. Most of Tom Cruise's movies follow a similar generic pattern: He begins as a brash, confident youth, a bit cocky and full of himself. A great-looking guy, of course. But he's not as smart as he thinks he is, and is humbled by a conspicuous error in judgment. With the help of a supportive young woman who loves him, however, he sees the error of his ways and goes on to even greater success—only now without the swagger.

In addition to being a savvy career manager, Cruise is also an ambitious artist, eager to test his limits, unafraid of taking calculated risks by playing against type. He has expanded his range considerably in such offbeat parts as those in *The Color of Money, Born on the Fourth of July,* and *Interview With the Vampire.* In *Magnolia* he plays a strutting, woman-hating "self-empowerment" guru, so puffed up with his own irresistibility that when his pomposity is punctured, he collapses like a spent balloon. It's arguably his most brilliant performance—brazen, funny, and, finally, poignantly vulnerable.

6–13b. *Magnolia* (U.S.A., 1999), with Tom Cruise, directed by Paul Thomas Anderson. *(New Line Cinema)*

the stars during this period were under exclusive contract to the five major production companies: MGM, Warner Brothers, Paramount, Twentieth Century–Fox, and RKO—known in the trade as the Big Five, or the **majors.** Throughout this period, the majors produced approximately 90 percent of the fiction films in America. They also ruled the international market: Between the two world wars, American movies dominated 80 percent of the world's screens and were more popular with foreign audiences than all but a few natively produced movies.

    After the talkie revolution, the majors turned to the live theater for new stars. Such important newcomers as James Cagney, Bette Davis, Edward G. Robinson, Cary Grant, Mae West, and Katharine Hepburn became popular in part because of their distinctive manner of speaking—the "personality voices" as they were known in the trade. In their first years under studio contract, they were given maximum exposure. For example, Clark Gable appeared in fourteen movies in 1930, his first year at MGM. Each of his roles represented a different type, and the studio kept varying them until one clicked with the public. After a

6–14. *In the Name of the Father* (Ireland/Great Britain, 1993), *with Daniel Day-Lewis and Emma Thompson, directed by Jim Sheridan.*

Day-Lewis and Thompson are among the top British actors of their generation. Both have won American best actor Oscars, Day-Lewis for *My Left Foot* (1989), Thompson for *Howards End* (1992). Both have been weaned on Shakespeare and are equally at home on the stage or on screen, playing comedy or drama, period roles or contemporary parts, and in a variety of dialects. Like most British actors, they're extraordinarily versatile. Day-Lewis's range is awesome, from the Cockney tough in *My Beautiful Laundrette* to the fruity upper-class twit in *A Room With a View* to the New Age macho man in *The Last of the Mohicans* **(3–31b).** Thompson is equally adaptable, playing double roles in *Dead Again,* the sexy and irrepressible Beatrice in *Much Ado About Nothing,* and the drab housekeeper in *The Remains of the Day.* Thompson also wrote the much acclaimed screenplay for *Sense and Sensibility* (see **9–12).** In *In the Name of the Father,* which is based on an actual event, Day-Lewis plays an Irish hippie who is falsely imprisoned for a horrifying crime, and Thompson plays his attorney. They're both superb, as usual. *(Universal Pictures)*

6–15. *Blood & Wine* (U.S.A., 1997), *with Jennifer Lopez, directed by Bob Rafelson.*

"It's so funny that people use *ambition* like it's a bad word," Jennifer Lopez has stated. She freely admits to being fiercely ambitious. A Grammy-nominated recording artist (her album *On the 6* went double platinum), she is also a dancer as well as an actress of considerable range. "I've always chosen different kinds of roles because I didn't want to be pushed in one category," she has said. "I wanted to show that I could do anything, any type of character, any emotion—weak, strong, vulnerable, kickass, whatever." In *Selena* and *My Family/Mi Familia* she plays sweet, good-natured Latinas. In *Blood & Wine* and *U Turn* she plays dangerous *femmes fatales*. In the critically acclaimed romantic comedy *Out of Sight*, she plays a police officer who's funny, sophisticated, and very sexy. Disciplined and hard-working, Lopez doesn't drink, smoke, or do drugs. "I believe there's a certain responsibility for your actions," she insists. *(Twentieth Century–Fox)*

particularly popular performance, a star was usually locked into the same type of role—often under protest. Because the demand for stars was the most predictable economic variable in the business of filmmaking, the studios used their stars as a guarantee of box-office success. In short, stars provided some measure of stability in a traditionally volatile industry. To this day, stars are referred to as "bankable" commodities—that is, insurance for large profits to investors.

The majors viewed their stars as valuable investments, and the build-up techniques developed by the studios involved much time, money, and energy. Promising neophytes served an apprenticeship as "starlets," a term reserved for females, although male newcomers were subjected to the same treatment. They were often assigned a new name, were taught how to talk, walk, and wear costumes. Frequently their social schedules were arranged by the studio's publicity department to ensure maximum press exposure. Suitable "romances" were concocted to fuel the columns of the four hundred or more reporters and columnists who covered the Hollywood beat during the studio era. A few zealous souls even agreed to marry a studio-selected spouse if such an alliance would further their careers.

Though stars were often exploited by the studios, there were some compensations. As a player's box-office power increased, so did his or her demands. Top stars had their names above the title of the film, and they often had script approval stipulated in their contracts. Some of them also insisted on director, producer, and costar approval. Glamorous stars boasted their own camera operators, who knew how to conceal physical defects and enhance virtues. Many of them demanded their own clothes designers, hair stylists, and lavish dressing rooms **(see 6–20)..** The biggest stars had movies especially tailored for them, thus guaranteeing maximum camera exposure.

6-16. *To Die For* (U.S.A., 1995), *with Nicole Kidman, directed by Gus Van Sant.*
There are many talented and even brilliant performers who never achieve film stardom because they lack "a face that opens up to the camera," to quote from a frequent observation of cinematographers. Good bone structure helps, but it's not enough. Beautiful features and a commanding presence are also useful. But mostly, an "open" face implies a lack of self-consciousness, a willingness to let the camera capture the most intimate nuances of emotion and thought. A face like this. *(Columbia Pictures)*

And of course, they were paid enormous sums of money. In 1939, for example, there were over fifty stars who earned more than $100,000 a year. But the studios got much more. Mae West rescued Paramount from bankruptcy in the early 1930s. Later in the decade, Shirley Temple made over $20 million for Twentieth Century–Fox. Furthermore, although there were a few important exceptions, movies without stars generally failed at the box office. Serious stars used money and power to further their art, not just to gratify their vanity. Bette Davis was considered "difficult" during her stormy tenure at Warners because she insisted on better scripts, more varied roles, more sensitive directors, and stronger costars.

Top stars attracted the loyalty of both men and women, although as sociologist Leo Handel pointed out, 65 percent of the fans preferred stars of their own sex. The studios received up to 32 million fan letters per year, 85 percent of them from young females. Major stars received about three thousand letters per week, and the volume of their mail was regarded as an accurate barometer of their popularity. The studios spent as much as $2 million a year processing these letters, most of which asked for autographed photos. Box-office appeal was also gauged by the number of fan clubs devoted to a star. The stars with the greatest number of fan clubs were Gable, Jean Harlow, and Joan Crawford—all of them under contract to MGM, "The Home of the Stars." Gable alone had seventy clubs, which partly accounted for his supremacy as the top male star of the 1930s.

The mythology of stardom usually emphasizes the glamour of movie stars, lifting them above the mundane concerns of ordinary mortals. Critic Parker Tyler observed that stars fulfill an ancient need, almost religious in nature: "Somehow their wealth, fame, and beauty, their apparently unlimited field of worldly pleasure—these conditions tinge them with the supernatural, render them immune to the bitterness of ordinary frustrations." Of course, this mythology also involves the tragic victims of stardom, like Marilyn Monroe, who

6-17. *Philadelphia* (U.S.A., 1993), *with Tom Hanks, directed by Jonathan Demme.*
Some stars are so beloved by the public that they can play virtually any role and still command the audience's loyalty. In this movie, Hanks plays a gay attorney who is dying of AIDS and is being shafted by his homophobic law firm. The movie was a huge hit, thanks largely to Hanks's brilliant performance, which won him a best actor Academy Award. His popularity has been augmented by his talk show appearances, in which he is invariably witty and charming. *(Tri-Star Pictures)*

has become a symbol of the personal tragedy that can befall a star. She was born (illegitimate) to an emotionally unstable mother who spent most of her life in mental asylums. As a child, Norma Jean Baker was raised in a series of orphanages and foster homes. Even then—especially then—she dreamed of becoming a famous Hollywood star. She was raped at the age of eight, married to her first husband at sixteen. She used sex (like many before her) as a means to an end—stardom. In the late 1940s, she had a few bit roles, mostly as sexy dumb blondes. Not until John Huston's *The Asphalt Jungle* (1950) did she create much of a stir. In that same year, Joseph Mankiewicz cast her in *All About Eve,* as "a graduate of the Copacabana School of Dramatic Art," as George Sanders dryly deadpans in the film. (Sanders claimed he knew Marilyn would one day become a star "because she desperately needed to be one.") After Twentieth Century–Fox signed her to a contract, the studio didn't know what to do with her. She appeared in a series of third-rate studio projects, but despite their mediocrity, the public clamored for more Marilyn. She rightly blamed Fox for mismanaging her career: "Only the public can make a star. It's the studios who try to make a system of it," she bitterly complained.

At the peak of her popularity, she left Hollywood in disgust to study at the Actors Studio. When she returned, she demanded more money and better roles—and got both. Joshua Logan, who directed her in *Bus Stop* (1956), said she was "as near genius as any actress I ever knew." Supremely photogenic, she gave herself entirely to the camera, allowing it to probe her deepest vulnerabilities. Laurence Olivier, her costar and director in *The Prince and the Showgirl* (1957), marveled at her cunning way of fusing guilelessness with carnality—the mind and soul of a little girl wrapped in the body of a whore. Throughout her years as a top star, her private life was a shambles. "She was an unfortunate doped-up woman most of the time," biographer Maurice Zolotow observed. Her failed marriages and love affairs were constantly in the headlines, and increasingly she turned to drugs and alcohol for solace. She was notorious for her irresponsibility, often not even bothering to show up on the set for days at a time, thus incurring enormous cost overruns. Because of her addiction to drugs and alcohol, even when she did show up, she scarcely knew who—much less where—she was. She was found dead in 1962: an overdose of barbiturates and alcohol.

The realities behind the mythology of the stars is not very romantic. For every actor who manages to scale the peaks of stardom, there are hundreds of thousands who fail, their hard work wasted, their sacrifices scoffed at, their dreams shattered. Maureen Stapleton has won important acting awards for her distinguished work in films, television, and the stage, but she has spoken eloquently of the hardships actors must endure in a world that often regards them as fortunate simpletons:

> I believe in the toughness of actors. I have a feeling of genuine pride in actors as my people. . . . We're called egomaniacs; we're thought of as children. Actors are supposed to be irresponsible, stupid, unaware, and a kind of joke. They're accused of having big egos. Well, the actor's ego is no different in size because he's an *actor.* A writer or a painter or a musician can go off into a corner and lick his wounds, but an actor stands out in front of the crowd and takes it. . . . Actors spend years and years being treated like dirt. They're constantly in a state of debasement, making the rounds of casting directors and having to look happy and great. I made the rounds for years, but I wasn't good at it. But then *nobody* is. You need a very strong stomach. You need a sense of the business as a whole, so that you don't get lacerated every time somebody tells you you're lousy. You need strength, and no matter how strong you get, you always need to get stronger. (Quoted in *The Player: A Profile of an Art*)

The tabloids in supermarket racks are filled with lurid stories of how film stars have screwed up their lives or have made fools of themselves in public or behaved like selfish brats. These types of stories sell newspapers, for they appeal to the public's envy and malice.

What is far less frequently written about is how stars are hounded out of their privacy by unscrupulous reporters and paparazzi. Nor do we often read about how stars like Bob Hope and Elizabeth Taylor devoted thousands of hours to public service. Or about the patriotic activities of stars like John Wayne or Marlene Dietrich. Or the successful political careers of stars like Shirley Temple and Ronald Reagan. Or the political activism of hundreds of stars like Marlon Brando and Jane Fonda. Or the fantastic generosity of stars like Barbra Streisand and Paul Newman. Newman alone has donated over $85 million to various charities.

Stars must pay a high price for their wealth and fame. They must get used to being treated like commodities with a price tag. Even at the beginning of the star system, they were reduced to simplified types: virgins, vamps, swashbucklers, flappers, and so on. Over the years, a vast repertory of types evolved: the Latin lover, the he-man, the heiress, the good–bad girl, the cynical reporter, the career girl, and many others. Of course, all great stars are unique even though they might fall under a well-known category. For example, the cheap blonde has long been one of America's favorite types, but such important stars as Mae West, Jean Harlow, and Marilyn Monroe are highly distinctive as individuals. A successful type was always imitated. In the mid-1920s, for example, the Swedish import Greta Garbo created a sophisticated and complex type, the *femme fatale.* Garbo inspired many imitations, including such important stars as Marlene Dietrich and Carole Lombard, who were first touted as "Garbo types," only with a sense of humor. In the 1950s, Sidney Poitier became the first African American star to attract a wide following outside of his own race. In later years, a number of other black performers attained stardom in part because Poitier had established the precedent. He was one of the great originals and hence worthy of imitation.

At about the turn of the nineteenth century, George Bernard Shaw wrote a famous essay comparing the two foremost stage stars of the day—Eleonora Duse and Sarah Bernhardt. Shaw's comparison is a useful springboard for a discussion of the different kinds of film stars. Bernhardt, Shaw wrote, was a bravura personality, and she managed to tailor each different role to fit this personality. This is what her fans both expected and desired. Her personal charm was larger than life, yet undeniably captivating. Her performances were filled with brilliant effects that had come to be associated with her personality over the years. Duse, on the other hand, possessed a more quiet talent, less dazzling in its initial impact. She was totally different with each role, and her own personality never seemed to intrude on the playwright's character. Hers was an invisible art: Her impersonations were so totally believable that the viewer was likely to forget it *was* an impersonation. In effect, Shaw was pointing out the major distinctions between a **personality star** and an **actor star.**

Personality stars commonly refuse all parts that go against their type, especially if they're leading men or leading ladies. Performers like Tom Hanks would never play cruel or psychopathic roles, for example, because such parts would conflict with their sympathetic image. If a star is locked into his or her type, any significant departure can result in box-office disaster. For example, when Pickford tried to abandon her little girl roles in the 1920s, her public stayed at home: They wanted to see Little Mary or nothing. She retired in disgust at the age of forty, just when most players are at the peak of their powers.

On the other hand, many stars prefer to remain in the same mold, playing variations on the same character type. John Wayne was the most popular star in film history. From 1949 to 1976, he was absent from the top ten only three times. "I play John Wayne in every part regardless of the character, and I've been doing okay, haven't I?" he once asked. In the public mind, he was a man of action—and violence—rather than words. His **iconography** is steeped

6–18. *The Silence of the Lambs* **(U.S.A., 1991),** *with Anthony Hopkins, directed by Jonathan Demme.* Like most British-trained actors, Anthony Hopkins is extraordinarily versatile, equally at home playing Shakespeare, romantic contemporary roles, offbeat character parts, and in a variety of styles and dialects. He did not attract much popular attention until his electrifying performance as the twisted genius, Dr. Hannibal "The Cannibal" Lecter, in this film. *(Orion Pictures)*

in a distrust of sophistication and intellectuality. His name is virtually synonymous with masculinity—though his persona suggests more of the warrior than the lover. As he grew older, he also grew more human, developing his considerable talents as a comedian by mocking his own macho image. Wayne was fully aware of the enormous influence a star can wield in transmitting values, and in many of his films, he embodied a right-wing ideology that made him a hero to conservative Americans, including Ronald Reagan, Newt Gringrich, Oliver North, and Pat Buchanan.

Ironically, as Garry Wills points out in his cultural study, *John Wayne's America: The Politics of Celebrity* (Simon & Schuster, 1997), Wayne actually disliked horses, though in the popular imagination, he was the archetypal Westerner on a horse **(10–3).** He also consciously evaded the military draft during World War II, yet his roles in such popular films as *The Sands of Iwo Jima* **(7–15)** firmly established him as a military exemplar. "From now on," Wills points out, "the man who evaded service in World War II would be the symbolic man who *won* World War II." In short, a star's iconographical status can actually contradict historical truth. In a 1995 poll, John Wayne (who had been dead for over sixteen years) was named America's all-time favorite movie star.

Film theorist Richard Dyer has pointed out that stars are signifying entities. Any sensitive analysis of a film with a star in its cast must take into account that star's iconographical significance. Stars like Jane Fonda embodied complex political associations simply by demonstrating the lifestyle of their politics and displaying those political beliefs as an aspect of their personality/characterization. Like John Wayne—and most other stars—Fonda's films convey an ideology, implying ideal ways of behaving. As such, stars can have tremendous impact in transmitting values. Dyer also demonstrates how a star's iconography is always developing, incorporating elements from the star's actual life as well as previous roles. For example, Fonda's career can be divided into six phases:

1. *The father.* Her entry into the film industry in 1960 was facilitated by Henry Fonda's prestige. Physically, she clearly resembled him, and he too was a well-known liberal, with an all-American iconography. Jane's roles during this period emphasized a rambunctious sexiness, with more of the tomboy than the siren. This phase culminated in *Cat Ballou* (1965).

6–19.   *Seven* (U.S.A., 1995), *with Morgan Freeman, directed by David Fincher.*
Character actors are the unsung heroes of the profession. What they lack in glamour they usually make up in versatility and longevity. Since character actors don't trade in on their slick looks, they can continue acting well into old age. Morgan Freeman, a performer that critic Pauline Kael called "the best actor in America," didn't even break through until the age of 50. The average-looking Freeman barely eked out a living as an actor for many years. His first steady job was on television's kid's show, *The Electric Company,* hardly a great challenge to an artist as gifted as Freeman. In the mid-1980s, he burst on the scene with two radically dissimilar roles: the ferocious street pimp in *Street Smart* and the gentle, soft-spoken southern chauffeur in *Driving Miss Daisy* **(7–11b)**, a role he originally created on the New York stage. Both performances gained him Oscar nominations. Since then, Freeman has dignified every movie he's appeared in—some good, others just routine except for his performance.   *(New Line Cinema.)*

2. *Sex.* This period is dominated by Fonda's French film director husband, Roger Vadim, who exploited her good looks and sensational figure in a series of erotic films, most notably *Barbarella.* Although the marriage ended in divorce, Fonda claimed that Vadim liberated her from her sexual hangups and all-American innocence.

3. *Acting.* She returned to America, where she studied with Lee Strasberg at the Actors Studio in New York. Her depth and range as an artist expanded considerably during this period, and she was nominated for an Academy Award for her work in *They Shoot Horses, Don't They?* (1969). She won one for her performance as a prostitute in *Klute* (1971).

4. *Politics.* Fonda was radicalized by Vietnam and the women's movement. She spoke out frequently against the war, racism, and sexism. She also politicized her work, starring in movies that were frankly ideological, like *Tout va bien* (France, 1972), *A Doll's House* (Great Britain, 1973), and *Julia* (1977). Her **left-wing** political activities adversely affected her box-office popularity for a period, but she continued to speak out on important public issues, refusing to be intimidated.

5. *Independence.* Fonda's own production company produced *Coming Home* (1978). She enjoyed outstanding success as a producer. She also wrote several books and was a leader in the physical fitness movement.

6. *Middle age and retirement.* After she married media mogul Ted Turner, Fonda retired from acting in 1992. They are now separated.

The top box-office attractions tend to be personality stars. They stay on top by being themselves, by not trying to impersonate anyone. Gable insisted that all he did in front of the camera was to "act natural." Similarly, Marilyn Monroe was always at her best when she played roles that exploited her indecisiveness, her vulnerability, and her pathetic eagerness to please.

On the other hand, there have been many stars who refuse to be typecast and attempt the widest array of roles possible. Such actor stars as Davis, Barbara Stanwyck, Brando, and De Niro have sometimes undertaken unpleasant character roles rather than conventional leads to expand their range, for variety and breadth have traditionally been the yardsticks by which great acting is measured.

Many stars fall somewhere between the two extremes, veering toward personality in some films, toward impersonation in others. Such gifted performers as James Stewart, Cary Grant, and Audrey Hepburn played wider variations of certain types of roles. Nonetheless, we couldn't imagine a star like Hepburn playing a woman of weak character or a coarse or stupid woman, so firmly entrenched was her image as an elegant and rather aristocratic female. Similarly, most people know what's meant by "the Clint Eastwood type."

The distinction between a professional actor and a star is not based on technical skill, but on mass popularity. By definition, a star must have enormous personal magnetism, a riveting quality that commands our attention. Few

 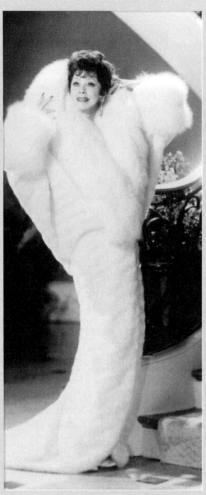 

a   b   c

6–20a, b, c, d, e, f.   *Mame* (U.S.A., 1974), *with Lucille Ball, directed by Gene Saks.*
One of the perks of the star system is a lavish wardrobe. Lucille Ball produced this musical
with her own money, and she commissioned costume designer Theadora Van Runkel to create a $300,000 wardrobe that carries Mame from 1928 to 1948. Even today, big name Holly-

continued ▶

d   e   f

wood stars can command salaries of $20 million per film, plus a wide assortment of expensive extras like an "entourage fee," which covers anyone from publicists to $500,000 managers to chefs. Other perks can include luxurious trailers on location, limos and drivers, hair stylists and makeup artists, gym equipment, and hotel suites for spouses, children, nannies, and personal trainers.   *(Warner Bros.)*

public personalities have inspired such deep and widespread affection as the great movie stars. Some are loved because they embody such traditional American values as plain speaking, integrity, and idealism: Gary Cooper and Tom Hanks are examples of this type. Others are identified with antiestablishment images and include such celebrated loners as Bogie, Clint Eastwood, and Jack Nicholson. Players such as Cary Grant and Carole Lombard are so captivating in their charm that they're fun to watch in almost anything. And of course, many of them are spectacularly good-looking: Names like Michelle Pfeiffer and Tom Cruise are virtually synonymous with godlike beauty.

Sophisticated filmmakers exploit the public's affection for its stars by creating ambiguous tensions between a role as written, as acted, and as directed. "Whenever the hero isn't portrayed by a star the whole picture suffers," Hitchcock observed. "Audiences are far less concerned about the predicament of a character who's played by someone they don't know." When a star rather than a conventional actor plays a role, much of the characterization is automatically fixed by the casting; but what the director and star then choose

6–21.   *Die Hard With a Vengeance* (U.S.A., 1995), *with Samuel L. Jackson and Bruce Willis, directed by John McTiernan.*
Actor Jack Lemmon once recounted a visit he paid to Edmund Gwenn, an elderly character actor who was dying of cancer in a hospital. "Is it hard to die?" Lemmon asked respectfully. "Yes," Gwenn replied, "but not as hard as comedy." Comic performers almost never receive as much respect or prestige as straight dramatic actors. (Ever notice how few comic performers receive the big acting awards?) Nonetheless, virtually every actor will admit that comic roles tend to be tougher to perform than most dramatic parts. Bruce Willis's comic style is so understated that he seems to be saying his lines mostly to himself. Easily the most talented artist of the action stars of his generation, Willis is also an accomplished dramatic player, capable of considerable emotional power. But audiences overwhelmingly prefer Willis as the wisecracking smartass. He is one of the few action stars who can hold his own opposite such superb coactors as Samuel L. Jackson.   *(Twentieth Century–Fox)*

to add to the written role is what constitutes its *full* dramatic meaning. Some directors have capitalized on the star system with great artistic effectiveness, particularly studio-era filmmakers **(6–22)**.

Perhaps the ultimate glory for a star is to become an icon in American popular mythology. Like the gods and goddesses of ancient times, some stars are so universally known that one name alone is enough to evoke an entire complex of symbolic associations—"Marilyn," for example. Unlike the conventional actor (however gifted), the star automatically suggests ideas and emotions that are deeply embedded in his or her persona. These undertones are determined not only by the star's previous roles, but often by his or her actual personality as well. Naturally, over the course of many years, this symbolic information can begin to drain from public consciousness, but the iconography of a great star like Gary Cooper becomes part of a shared experience. As the French critic Edgar Morin has pointed out, when Cooper played a character, he automatically "gary-cooperized" it, infusing himself into the role and the role into himself. Because audiences felt a deep sense of identification with Coop and

6–22. *Vertigo* **(U.S.A., 1958)**, *with James Stewart and Kim Novak, directed by Alfred Hitchcock.*

Perhaps Hitchcock's greatest genius was how he managed to outwit the system while still succeeding brilliantly at the box office. For example, Hitchcock knew that a star in the leading role virtually guaranteed the commercial success of his pictures. But he liked to push his stars to the dark side—to explore neurotic, even psychotic undercurrents that often subverted the star's established **iconography**. Everyone loved Jimmy Stewart as the stammering, decent, all-American idealist, best typified by *It's a Wonderful Life*. In this movie, Stewart's character is obsessed with a romantic idealization of a mysterious woman (Novak). He's convinced himself that he's desperately in love—ironically, with a woman who doesn't exist. Within the generic format of a detective thriller, Hitchcock is able to explore the obsessions, self-delusions, and desperate need that many people call love. *(Universal Pictures)*

the values he symbolized, in a sense they were celebrating themselves—or at least their spiritual selves. The great originals are cultural **archetypes,** and their box-office popularity is an index of their success in synthesizing the aspirations of an era. As a number of cultural studies have shown, the iconography of a star can involve communal myths and symbols of considerable complexity and emotional richness.

Styles of Acting

Acting styles differ radically, depending on period, **genre,** tone, national origins, and directorial emphasis. Such considerations are the principal means by which acting styles are classified. Even within a given category, however, generalizations are, at best, a loose set of expectations, not Holy Writ. For example, the realist–formalist dialectic that has been used as a classification aid throughout this book can also be applied to the art of acting, but there

6-23. *Aguirre, the Wrath of God* **(West Germany, 1972),** *with Klaus Kinski, directed by Werner Herzog.*
Expressionistic acting is generally associated with the German cinema— a cinema of directors, rarely actors. Stripped of individualizing details, this style of acting stresses a symbolic concept rather than a believable three-dimensional character. It is presentational rather than representational, a style of extremes rather than norms. Psychological complexity is replaced by a stylized thematic essence. For example, Kinski's portrayal of a Spanish conquistador is conceived in terms of a treacherous serpent. His Dantean features a frozen mask of ferocity, Aguirre can suddenly twist and coil like a cobra poised for a strike. *(New Yorker Films)*

are many variations and subdivisions. These terms are also subject to different interpretations from period to period. Lillian Gish was regarded as a great realistic actress in the silent era, but by today's standards, her performances look rather ethereal. In a parallel vein, the playing style of Klaus Kinski in such movies as *Aguirre, the Wrath of God* is stylized, but compared to an extreme form of **expressionistic** acting, such as that of Conrad Veidt in *The Cabinet of Dr. Caligari,* Kinski is relatively realistic **(6–23).** It's a matter of degree.

Classifying acting styles according to national origins is also likely to be misleading, at least for those countries that have evolved a wide spectrum of styles, such as Japan, the United States, and Italy. For example, the Italians (and other Mediterranean peoples) are said to be theatrical by national temperament, acting out their feelings with animation, as opposed to the reserved deportment of the Swedes and other Northern Europeans. But within the Italian cinema alone, these generalizations are subject to considerable modification. Southern Italian characters tend to be acted in a manner that conforms to the volatile Latin stereotype, as can be seen in the movies of Lina Wertmüller **(6–24).** Northern Italians, on the other hand, are usually played with more restraint and far less spontaneity, as the works of Antonioni demonstrate.

Genre and directorial emphasis also influence acting styles significantly. For example, in such stylized genres as the samurai film, Toshiro Mifune is bold, strutting, and larger than life, as in Kurosawa's *Yojimbo.* In a realistic contemporary story like *High and Low* (also directed by Kurosawa), Mifune's performance is all nuance and sobriety.

6–24. *The Seduction of Mimi* (Italy, 1972), *with Giancarlo Giannini and Elena Fiore, directed by Lina Wertmüller.*

Farcical acting is one of the most difficult and misunderstood styles of performance. It requires an intense comic exaggeration and can easily become tiresome and mechanical if the farceur is not able to preserve the humanity of the character. Here, Giannini plays a typical ethnic stereotype—a sleazy, heavy-lidded Lothario who, in an act of sexual revenge, embarks on a campaign to seduce the unlovely wife of the man who has cuckolded him. Giannini was Wertmüller's favorite actor, and he appeared in many of her movies. Other famous actor–director teams include Dietrich and Sternberg, Wayne and Ford, Ullmann and Bergman, Bogart and Huston, Mifune and Kurosawa, Léaud and Truffaut, De Niro and Scorsese, and many more. *(New Line Cinema)*

The *art* of silent acting encompasses a period of only some fifteen years or so, for though movies were being produced as early as 1895, most historians regard Griffith's *The Birth of a Nation* (1915) as the first indisputable masterpiece of the silent cinema. The changeover to sound was virtually universal by 1930. Within this brief span, however, a wide variety of playing styles evolved, ranging from the detailed, underplayed realism of Gibson Gowland in *Greed,* to the grand, ponderous style of such tragedians as Emil Jannings in *The Last Command.* The great silent clowns like Chaplin, Keaton, Harold Lloyd, Harry Langdon, and Laurel and Hardy also developed highly personal styles that bear only a superficial resemblance to each other.

A popular misconception about the silent cinema is that all movies were photographed and projected at "silent speed"—sixteen frames per second (fps). In fact, silent speed was highly variable, subject to easy manipulation because cameras were hand cranked. Even within a single film, not every scene was necessarily photographed at the same speed. Generally speaking, comic scenes were undercranked to emphasize speed, whereas dramatic scenes were overcranked to slow down the action, usually twenty or twenty-two fps. Because most present-day projectors feature only two speeds—sixteen silent and twenty-four sound—the original rhythms of the performances are violated. This is why actors in silent dramas can appear jerky and slightly ludicrous. In comedies, this distortion can enhance the humor, which is why the performances of the silent clowns have retained much of their original charm. Outside the comic repertory, however, due allowances must be made for the distortions of technology.

The most popular and critically admired player of the silent cinema was Chaplin. The wide variety of comic skills he developed in his early years of vaudeville made him the most versatile of the clowns. In the area of pantomime, no one approached his inventiveness. Critics waxed eloquently on his balletic grace, and even the brilliant dancer Vaslav Nijinsky proclaimed Chaplin his equal. His ability to blend comedy with pathos was unique. George Bernard Shaw, the greatest living playwright of this era, described Chaplin as "the only genius developed in motion pictures." After viewing Chaplin's powerful—and very funny—performance in *City Lights,* the fastidious critic Alexander Woolcott, who otherwise loathed movies, said, "I would be prepared to defend the proposition that this darling of the mob is the foremost living artist."

Greta Garbo perfected a romantic style of acting that had its roots in the silent cinema and held sway throughout the 1930s. Critics have sometimes referred to this mode of performance as star acting. "What, when drunk, one sees in other women, one sees in Garbo sober," said the British critic Kenneth Tynan. Almost invariably, MGM cast her as a woman with a mysterious past: mistress, courtesan, the "other woman"—the essence of the Eternal Female. Her face, in addition to being stunningly beautiful, could unite conflicting emotions, withholding and yielding simultaneously, like a succession of waves rippling across her features. Tall and slender, she moved gracefully, her collapsed shoulders suggesting the exhaustion of a wounded butterfly. She could also project a provocative bisexuality, as in *Queen Christina,* where her resolute strides and masculine attire provide a foil to her exquisite femininity.

The love goddess par excellence, Garbo was most famous for her love scenes, which epitomized her romantic style. She is often self-absorbed in these scenes, musing on a private irony that can even exclude the lover. Frequently she looks away from him, allowing the camera—and us—to savor the poignancy of her conflict. She rarely expresses her feelings in words, for her art thrives on silence, on the unspeakable. Her love scenes are sometimes played in literal solitude, with objects serving as erotic fetishes. The way she touches a bouquet of flowers, a bedpost, a telephone—these allude to the missing lover, recalling a multitude of painful pleasures. She is often enraptured by her surroundings, "like Eve on the morning of creation," to use Tynan's memorable phrase. But she is also oppressed by the knowledge that such ecstasy cannot last; she arms herself against her fate with irony and stoicism. Garbo's performances are striking examples of how great acting can salvage bad scripts, and even bad direction. "Subtract Garbo from most of her movies and you are left with nothing," one critic noted.

The most important British film actors are also the most prominent in the live theater. The British repertory system is the envy of the civilized world.

6-25. *The Rocky Horror Picture Show* **(Great Britain, 1975),** *with Tim Curry and Richard O'Brien, directed by Jim Sharman.*
A film's tone dictates its acting style. Tone is determined primarily by genre, dialogue, and the director's attitude toward the dramatic materials. The original audiences of *The Rocky Horror Picture Show* were put off by its perversely campy wit and its spirit of mockery. The straight world and its values are mercilessly assaulted by the movie's garish theatricality. The film has long been a cult favorite, grossing over $75 million on the midnight movie circuit of college towns and large cities. Most cult movies appeal to our subversive instincts, our desire to see conventional morality trashed. *(Twentieth Century-Fox)*

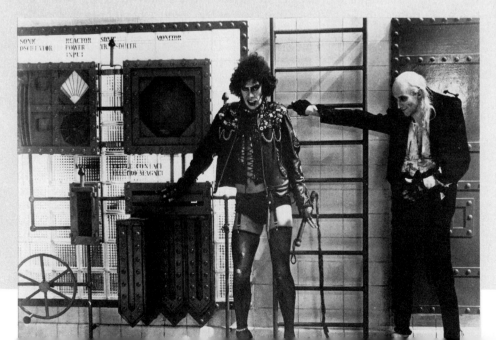

Virtually every medium-sized city has a resident drama company, where actors can learn their craft by playing a variety of roles from the classic repertory, especially the works of Shakespeare. As players improve, they rise through the ranks, attempting more complex roles. The best of them migrate to the larger cities, where the most prestigious theater companies are found. The discipline that most British actors have acquired in this repertory system has made them the most versatile of players. The finest of them are regularly employed in the theaters of London, which is also adjacent to the centers of film production in Great Britain. This centralization allows them to move from the live theater to film to TV with a minimum of inconvenience.

In the acting profession, playing Shakespeare is considered the artistic summit. If you can act in Shakespeare convincingly, the argument goes, you can act in anything, because Shakespeare requires the broadest range of an actor's technical skills and artistic insight. Shakespeare's language is 400 years old and so archaic that even highly literate people are likely to miss as much as a fourth of the dialogue. To recite the language clearly (which itself is no easy feat) is absolutely mandatory. But that's not enough: The dialogue must be spoken with feeling by flesh-and-blood human beings. That's a lot tougher. Take Hamlet's final speech at the end of Act II, when he gives vent to his self-contempt for not avenging his father's murder:

> Why, what an ass am I! This is most brave
> That I, the son of a dear murthered,
> Prompted to my revenge by heaven and hell,
> Must like a whore unpack my heart with words,
> And fall a-cursing like a very drab,
> A scullion! Fie upon it, foh!

Because the dialogue is in verse, the actor must avoid the temptation of a singsong monotony on the one hand, or at the other extreme, to deliver the musical lines with a prosey inflection in an effort to make the speech sound more "realistic." The language must be pronounced crisply or the audience will never be able to make out such odd words as "murthered," "drab," and "scullion." The actor must be skilled enough to convey the emotional content of these words even though most modern audiences are not likely to know their precise meaning. "Fie" and "foh" were common interjections to express disapproval in Shakespeare's day, but of course no one uses these expressions today. In short, it takes more than technique, intelligence, and chutzpa to successfully play a role as tough as Hamlet. It takes a kind of genius **(6–26).**

British acting traditions tend to favor a mastery of externals, based on close observation. Virtually all players are trained in diction, movement, makeup, dialects, fencing, dancing, body control, and ensemble acting. For example, Laurence Olivier always built his characters from the outside in. He molded his features like a sculptor or painter. "I do not search the character for parts that are already in me," he explained, "but go out and find the personality I feel the author created." Like most British actors of his generation, Olivier had a keen memory for details: "I hear remarks in the street or in a shop and I retain them. You must constantly observe: a walk, a limp, a run; how a head inclines to one side when listening; the twitch of an eyebrow; the hand that picks the nose when it thinks no one is looking; the mustache puller; the eyes that never look at you; the nose that sniffs long after the cold has gone."

Makeup for Olivier was magical. He loved hiding his real features behind beards, false complexions, fake noses, and wigs. "If you're wise," he warned, "you always take off the part with your makeup." He also prided himself on his ability to mimic dialects: "I always go to endless trouble to learn American accents, even for small television parts. If it's north Michigan, it's bloody well got to be north Michigan."

Olivier kept his body in peak condition. Even as an old man, he continued running and lifting weights. When illness curbed these forms of exercises, he took to swimming. At the age of 78, he was still swimming a half a mile almost every morning. "To be fit should be one of the actor's first priorities," he insisted. "To exercise daily is of utmost importance. The body is an instrument which must be finely tuned and played as often as possible. The actor should be able to control it from the tip of his head to his little toe" (quotes are from *Laurence Olivier on Acting*). Contemporary British acting has moved beyond this classical style **(6–27)**.

The post–World War II era tended to emphasize realistic styles of acting. In the early 1950s, a new interior style of acting, known as "the Method," or "the System," was introduced to American movie audiences. It was commonly associated with director Elia Kazan. Kazan's *On the Waterfront* was a huge success and a virtual showcase for this style of performance. It has since become the

6–26. *Hamlet* **(Great Britain, 1996),** *with Kenneth Branagh, directed by Branagh.*
Above all, British actors have perfected the art of reciting highly stylized dialogue—the language of Shakespeare, Wilde, and Shaw—without violating the believability of their characters. Because of their great literary heritage, British performers are almost universally considered unsurpassed masters of period styles of acting. Kenneth Branagh is widely regarded as the leading Shakespearean actor of his generation. In the grand tradition of Laurence Olivier and Orson Welles, he is also a gifted stage and film director. This ambitious uncut version of *Hamlet*, though too long, is filled with bravura flashes of brilliance, such as this scene, near the end of Act II, when Hamlet is totally disgusted by the decadence of the court and seethes at his own lack of resolution to do something—anything—to avenge his father's murder. *(Castle Rock Entertainment/Columbia Pictures)*

6–27. *Secrets & Lies* (Great Britain, 1996), *with Brenda Blethyn (extreme right), written and directed by Mike Leigh.*
Mike Leigh prefers to work with many of the same actors from film to film, much like a cinematic repertory company. They rehearse extensively, improvising much of their dialogue and reshaping the script with their insights and discoveries. The result of this artistic collaboration is a performance style of extraordinary intimacy, spontaneity, and humanity. They just don't look or sound like actors—they seem to be real people with real hang-ups. In *Secrets & Lies,* the protagonist (Blethyn) always manages to find the worst possible moment to embarrass or shock her family. Weepy, self-pitying, grotesquely funny, and desperately needy, she manages to repel us even while enlisting our compassion. It is only one of several great performances in the movie. The acting is also a far cry from the pear-shaped tones and precise diction of traditional British acting techniques. With Leigh's actors, you don't notice the technique: just the raw emotions. *(October Films)*

dominant style of acting in the American cinema as well as the live theater. The Method was an offshoot of a system of training actors and rehearsing that had been developed by Constantin Stanislavsky at the Moscow Art Theater. Stanislavsky's ideas were widely adopted in New York theater circles, especially by the Actors Studio in New York, which received much publicity during the 1950s because it had developed such well-known graduates as Marlon Brando, James Dean, Julie Harris, Paul Newman, and many others.

Kazan cofounded and taught at the Actors Studio until 1954, when he asked his former mentor, Lee Strasberg, to take over the organization. Within a short period, Strasberg became the most celebrated acting teacher in America, and his former students were—and still are—among the most famous performers in the world.

The central credo of Stanislavsky's system was, "You must live the part every moment you are playing it." He rejected the tradition of acting that emphasized externals. He believed that truth in acting can only be achieved by exploring a character's inner spirit, which must be fused with the actor's own emotions. One of the most important techniques he developed is *emotional recall,* in which an actor delves into his or her own past to discover feelings that are analogous to those of the character. "In every part you do," Julie Harris explained, "there is some connection you can make with your own background or with some feeling you've had at one time or another." Stanislavsky's techniques were strongly psychoanalytical: By exploring their own subconscious, actors could trigger *real* emotions, which are recalled in every performance and transferred to the characters they are playing. He also devised techniques for helping actors focus their concentration on the "world" of the play—its concrete details and textures. In some form or another, these techniques are probably as old as the acting profession itself, but Stanislavsky was the first to systematize them with exercises and methods of analysis (hence the terms *the System* and *the Method*). He didn't think that inner truth and emotional sincerity are sufficient. He insisted that actors need to master the externals as well, particularly for classic plays, which require a somewhat stylized manner of speaking, moving, and wearing costumes.

Stanislavsky was famous for his lengthy rehearsal periods, in which players were encouraged to improvise with their roles to discover the resonances of the text—the **subtext,** which is analogous to Freud's concept of the subcon-

6-28. *The Nun's Story* **(U.S.A., 1959),** *with Peter Finch and Audrey Hepburn, directed by Fred Zinnemann.*

Zinnemann was a master of subtexts, most subtly in this film, which deals with the life of a missionary nursing nun, Sister Luke (Hepburn). While on assignment in Africa, she meets a dedicated surgeon, Dr. Fortunati (Finch). He's a nonbeliever, but a man she respects and admires. Gradually he begins to fall in love with her, growing more frustrated with her religious vows, with her life that he feels is "against nature." But his is a love that's doomed never to be spoken of, for he knows she has committed herself to a life of service to God. We must read between the lines to understand their complex feelings: They're found not in the text, but in the subtext, in the realm of the unspeakable. See also Arthur Nolletti, Jr., "Spirituality and Style in *The Nun's Story*," *The Films of Fred Zinnemann*, edited by Nolletti (Albany: State University of New York Press, 1999). *(Warner Bros.)*

6–29a. *Yankee Doodle Dandy* (U.S.A., 1942), *with James Cagney, directed by Michael Curtiz.*
Acting styles are determined in part by a player's energy level. High-voltage performers like Cagney usually project out to the audience, commanding our attention with a bravura style. Much of our pleasure in a Cagney performance is watching him "struttin' his stuff." He was a highly kinetic performer, expressing his character's emotions through movement. His dancing is exhilarating—cocky, sexy, and funny. Even in dramatic roles, he is seldom at rest—edgy, punctuating the air with his hand gestures, prancing on the balls of his feet. "Never settle back on your heels," was his credo. "Never relax. If you relax, the audience relaxes." Other high-energy performers include Harold Lloyd, Katharine Hepburn, Bette Davis, Gene Kelly, George C. Scott, Barbra Streisand, James Woods, Joe Pesci, and Jim Carrey.   *(Warner Bros.)*

6–29b. *The Last Metro* (France, 1980), *with Gerard Depardieu and Catherine Deneuve, directed by François Truffaut.*
Low-keyed performers like Deneuve are sometimes said to work "small" or "close to the lens." Rather than projecting out to the audience, these performers allow the camera to tune *in* on their behavior, which is seldom exaggerated for dramatic effect. Eyewitness accounts of Deneuve's acting usually stress how little she seems to be working. The subtleties are apparent only at very close range. Other players in this mode include Harry Langdon, Spencer Tracy, Henry Fonda, Marilyn Monroe, Montgomery Clift, Kevin Costner, Jack Nicholson, Winona Ryder, and Tobey Maguire. Of course, dramatic context is all important in determining an actor's energy level.
(United Artists)

6–30. *On the Waterfront* (U.S.A., 1954), *with Marlon Brando and Eva Marie Saint, directed by Elia Kazan.*
Kazan considers Brando as close to a genius as he has ever encountered among actors—a view that's widely shared by others, especially other actors. Many regard his performance in this movie as his best—emotionally powerful, tender, poetic. It won him his first Academy Award (best actor) as well as the New York Film Critics' Award and the British Oscar as best foreign actor—his third year in a row. Kazan was often surprised by his gifted protégé because he came up with ideas so fresh and arrived at in so underground a fashion that they seemed virtually discovered on the spot. *(Columbia Pictures)*

scious. Kazan and other Method-oriented directors used this concept in directing movies: "The film director knows that beneath the surface of his screenplay there is a subtext, a calendar of intentions and feelings and inner events. What appears to be happening, he soon learns, is rarely what is happening. The subtext is one of the film director's most valuable tools. It is what he directs." Spoken dialogue is secondary for Method players. To capture a character's "inner events," actors sometimes "throw away" their lines, choke on them, or even mumble. Throughout the 1950s, Method actors like Brando and Dean were ridiculed by some critics for mumbling their lines.

Stanislavsky disapproved of the star system and individual virtuosity. In his own productions, he insisted on ensemble playing, with genuine interactions among the actor/characters. Players were encouraged to analyze all the

6–31. *The End of Summer* (Japan, 1961), *directed by Yasujiro Ozu.*
A master of psychological nuances, Ozu believed that in the art of acting, less is more. He detested melodramatic excesses and demanded the utmost realism from his players, who frequently chafed at his criticism that they were "acting" too much. He avoided using stars and often cast against type so audiences would view the characters with no preconceptions. He usually chose his players according to their personality rather than their acting ability. Above all, Ozu explored the conflict between individual wishes and social necessity. His scenes are often staged in public settings, where politeness and social decorum require the stifling of personal disappointment. Ozu often instructed his players not to move, to express their feelings only with their eyes. Note how the two characters on the left are privately miles away, while still conforming superficially to the decorum of the occasion. *(New Yorker Films)*

specifics of a scene: What does the character really *want?* What is his or her history, or "backstory"? What has happened prior to the immediate moment? What time of day is it? And so on. When presented with a role utterly foreign to their experience, actors were urged to research the part so it would be understood in their guts as well as their minds. Method actors are famous for their ability to bring out the emotional intensity of their characters. Method-oriented directors generally believe that a player must have a character's experience within him or her, and they go to considerable lengths to learn about the personal lives of their players in order to use such details for characterization.

In the 1960s, the French New Wave directors—especially Godard and Truffaut—popularized the technique of improvisation while their players were on camera. The resultant increase in realism was highly praised by critics. Of course, there was nothing new in the technique itself. Actors often improvised in the silent cinema, and it was the foundation of silent comedy. For example, Chaplin, Keaton, and Laurel and Hardy needed to know only the premise of a given scene. The comic details were improvised and later refined in the editing stage. The cumbersome technology of sound put an end to most of these practices. Method-trained actors use improvisation primarily as an exploratory rehearsal technique, but their performances are usually set when the camera begins to roll.

6–32. *Gigi* (U.S.A., 1958), *with Maurice Chevalier, Leslie Caron, and Louis Jourdan; directed by Vincente Minnelli.*

A traditional distinction in acting styles is presentational versus representational. A *presentational style* openly acknowledges the audience. A character sometimes even addresses us directly, establishing an intimate rapport that excludes the other characters. The Chevalier character in this famous Lerner and Loewe musical is presentational. Note how he seems to act as an intermediary between the world of the movie (Paris, 1900) and the world of the audience. A *representational style*, on the other hand, is generally more realistic and self-contained. The characters inhabit their own separate world and never acknowledge the presence of an audience or a camera. We are allowed to act as voyeurs and eavesdrop on their conversations, but actors always perform as though no one is watching or listening. The implicit ideal is an acting style so understated and natural that it seems like real life. *(MGM)*

Godard and Truffaut, to capture a greater sense of discovery and surprise, would occasionally instruct their players to make up their dialogue while a scene was actually being photographed. The flexible technology introduced by **cinéma vérité** allowed these directors to capture an unprecedented degree of spontaneity. In Truffaut's *The 400 Blows,* for example, the youthful protagonist (Jean-Pierre Léaud) is interviewed by a prison psychologist about his family life and sexual habits. Drawing heavily on his own experience, Léaud (who wasn't informed of the questions in advance) answers them with disarming frankness. Truffaut's camera is able to capture the boy's hesitations, his embarrassment, and his charming macho bravado. In one form or another, improvisation has become a valuable technique in the contemporary cinema. Such filmmakers as Robert Altman, Rainer Werner Fassbinder, and Martin Scorsese have used it with brilliant results.

Casting

Casting a movie is almost an art in itself. It requires an acute sensitivity to a player's type, a **convention** inherited from the live theater. Most stage and screen performers are classified according to role categories: leading men, leading ladies, character actors, juveniles, villains, light comedians, tragedians, ingenues, singing actors, dancing actors, and so on. Typing conventions are rarely violated. For example, even though homely people obviously fall in love, romantic roles are almost always performed by attractive players. Similarly, audiences are not likely to be persuaded by a player with an all-American iconography (like Tom Hanks) cast in European roles. Nor is one likely to accept a performer like Klaus Kinski as the boy next door, unless one lives in a very weird neighborhood. Of course, a player's range is all-important in determining his or her type. Some, like Glenn Close, have extremely broad ranges, whereas others, like Arnold Swartzenegger, are confined to variations of the same type.

Typecasting was almost invariable in the silent cinema. In part, this was because characters tended toward allegorical types rather than unique individuals and often were even identified with a label: "The Man," "The Wife," "The Mother," "The Vamp," and so on. Blonde players were usually cast in parts emphasizing purity, earthy brunettes in erotic roles. Eisenstein insisted that players ought to be cast strictly to type and was inclined to favor nonprofessionals because of their greater authenticity. Why use an actor to impersonate a factory worker, he asked, when a filmmaker can use a *real* factory worker instead?

But trained actors tend to resent being typed and often attempt to broaden their range. Sometimes it works, sometimes it doesn't. Humphrey Bogart is a good example. For years, he was stereotyped as a tough, cynical gangster, until he joined forces with director John Huston, who cast him as the hard-boiled detective Sam Spade in *The Maltese Falcon*. Huston weaned him even further from his type in *The Treasure of the Sierra Madre*, in which Bogart played a crafty paranoid, the prospector Fred C. Dobbs. The actor totally reversed his image in *The African Queen*, in which he played Charlie Allnut, a lovable and funny drunk whose vulnerability endeared him to audiences and won Bogart an Academy Award for best actor. But in *Beat the Devil*, Huston's celebrated casting instincts deserted him when he used Bogart in a role beyond his powers—as a sophisticated adventurer stranded with a shabby assortment of rogues and loons. The witty tongue-in-cheek dialogue fell flat in Bogart's self-conscious performance. A polished player like Cary Grant could have acted the part with much greater believability and grace.

"Casting is characterization," Hitchcock pointed out. Once a role has been cast, especially with a personality star, the essence of the fictional character is already established. In a sense, stars are more "real" than other characters, which is why many people refer to a character by the actor's name, rather than by the name of the person in the story. After working with Hitchcock on the script of *Strangers on a Train*, the novelist Raymond Chandler ridiculed the director's method of characterization: "His idea of character is rather primitive," Chandler complained: "Nice Young Man," "Society Girl," "Frightened Woman," and so on. Like many literary types, Chandler believed that characterization must be created through language. He was insensitive to the other

6-33. *Bicycle Thief* (Italy, 1948), *with Enzo Staiola and Lamberto Maggiorani, directed by Vittorio De Sica.*

One of the most famous casting coups in film history is De Sica's selection of Maggiorani and Staiola as an impoverished laborer and his idolizing son. Both were nonprofessionals. Maggiorani actually was a laborer and had difficulty finding a factory job after this movie. When De Sica was trying to finance the film, one producer agreed to put up the money provided that the leading role was played by Cary Grant! De Sica couldn't imagine an elegant and graceful actor like Grant in the role, and the director wisely went elsewhere for his financing.

(Audio-Brandon Films)

options available to a filmmaker. For example, Hitchcock was a cunning exploiter of the star system—a technique that has nothing to do with language. For his leading ladies, for instance, he favored elegant blondes with an understated sexuality and rather aristocratic, ladylike manners—in short, the Society Girl type. But there are great individual differences between such heroines as Joan Fontaine, Ingrid Bergman, and Grace Kelly, to mention only three of Hitchcock's famous blondes.

Hitchcock's casting is often meant to deceive. His villains were usually actors of enormous personal charm—like James Mason in *North by Northwest*. Hitchcock counted on the audience's goodwill toward an established star, permitting his "heroes" to behave in ways that can only be described as morally dubious. In *Rear Window*, for example, James Stewart is literally a voyeur, yet we can't bring ourselves to condemn such a wholesome type as Jimmy Stewart, the all-American boy (see **4–20**). Audiences also assume that a star will remain in the movie until the final reel, at which point it's permissible—though seldom

6–34a. *Romeo and Juliet* (U.S.A., 1936), *with Leslie Howard and Norma Shearer, directed by George Cukor.*
Cukor's version of Shakespeare's play is an example of the disasters that can befall a movie when a director casts against type. The lovers are a far cry from the youngsters called for in the original. Shearer was thirty-seven when she played the thirteen-year-old Juliet; Howard as Romeo was forty-four. At fifty-five, John Barrymore was preposterous as Mercutio, Romeo's firebrand friend. The spectacle of middle-aged adults behaving so childishly makes the whole dramatic action seem ludicrous. *(MGM)*

6–34b. *Romeo and Juliet* (Great Britain/ Italy, 1968), *with Olivia Hussey and Leonard Whiting, directed by Franco Zeffirelli.*
Zeffirelli's version of the play is much more successful because he cast to type and awarded the roles to two teenagers. To be sure, Cukor's actors speak the lines better, but Zeffirelli's look truer. The differences between the ages of an actor and character are far more important on screen than on stage, for the cinematic close shot can be merciless in revealing age. *(Paramount Pictures)*

advisable—to kill him or her off. But in *Psycho,* the Janet Leigh character is brutally murdered in the first third of the film—a shocking violation of convention that jolts audiences out of their complacency. Sometimes Hitchcock cast awkward, self-conscious actors in roles requiring a note of evasive anxiety, like Farley Granger in *Rope* and *Strangers on a Train.* In cases such as these, bad acting is precisely what is called for—it's part of the characterization.

    Many filmmakers believe that casting is so integral to character, they don't even begin work on a script until they know who's playing the major

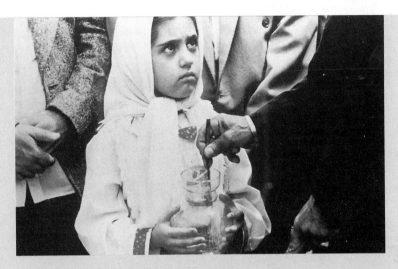

6-35. *The White Balloon* (Islamic Republic of Iran, 1995), *with Aida Mohammadkhani, directed by Jafar Panahi.*
Iranian filmmakers have received considerable international acclaim for their sensitive portrayal of children. Their movies about grownups—especially women—are so crippled by censorship that it's virtually impossible for these artists to explore mature themes without appearing downright silly. According to Iranian Islamic codes, a woman can be intimate only with the immediate members of her family. Therefore, strict dress codes require women to cover their hair in public, and wear loose-fitting outer garments to cloak their body curves. Needless to say, realistic portrayals of women have suffered. Actors playing husband and wife cannot have any physical contact on the screen unless they're married in real life. Even in the privacy of their home, female characters' hair must remain covered, since the audience would not be intimate with the actress playing the part. That's why scenes of female characters sleeping with their head scarves on or family dining scenes showing women with covered hair are commonplace in the postrevolutionary cinema. Even when the movie's plots are set before the 1979 revolution, female characters' heads still must be covered. The restrictions have made contemporary American or European films, with their more permissive themes and enticing looks, virtually impossible to import, for movie imports are entirely controlled by the government.   *(October Films)*

roles. Yasujiro Ozu confessed, "I could no more write, not knowing who the actor was going to be, than an artist could paint, not knowing what color he was using." Billy Wilder always tailored his dialogue to fit the personality of his players. When Montgomery Clift backed out of playing the lead in *Sunset Boulevard,* Wilder rewrote the part to fit William Holden, who brought totally different character nuances to the role.

Like photography, mise en scène, movement, editing, and sound, acting is a kind of language system. The filmmaker uses actors as a medium for

6-36. *The Crying Game* (Ireland/Great Britain, 1992), *with Jaye Davidson and Stephen Rea, written and directed by Neil Jordan.*

Unfamiliar performers enjoy an obvious superiority over stars—the public has no way of guessing what kind of people they're playing. Nonprofessional players and little-known actors can surprise us with astonishing revelations. In this movie, the character surprises send the story spinning into totally new directions. If the main characters had been played by personality stars, the audience would have guessed in advance what makes the characters tick, for the star system is a form of precharacterization. With actors like Davidson and Rea, we must judge the characters only as their bizarre tale unfolds. *(Miramax Films)*

communicating ideas and emotions. Merely by casting a performer like Lamberto Maggiorani rather than Cary Grant, Vittorio De Sica radically altered the artistic impact of *Bicycle Thief.* Not that Maggiorani is a better actor than Grant. Quite the reverse is true, but their artistic skills are not in question here. What is involved is the utter authenticity of Maggiorani as opposed to the complex iconography of Grant, an iconography rich in glamour, wit, and sophistication—and hence totally inappropriate for the role. As we have seen, strongly iconographic stars such as Gary Cooper and Marilyn Monroe embody a complex network of emotional and ideological values, and these values are part of the filmmaker's artistic statement.

In analyzing the acting in a movie, we should consider what type of actors are featured and why—amateurs, professionals, or popular stars? How are the actors treated by the director—as camera material or as artistic collaborators? How manipulative is the editing? Or are the actors allowed to recite their dialogue without a lot of cuts? Does the film highlight the stars or does the director encourage ensemble playing? What about the star's iconography?

6-37. *Erin Brockovich* **(U.S.A., 2000),** *with Julia Roberts, directed by Steven Soderbergh.*
"Show me an actor with no personality, and I'll show you someone who isn't a star," Katharine Hepburn once observed. In the contemporary cinema, Julia Roberts radiates personality. She is the only female star who consistently places among the top ten box office attractions in America. Beloved by the public for her spectacular good looks and captivating smile, she is an accomplished performer in straight dramatic roles. But she really shines in comedies, where her acting style is so spontaneous it hardly looks like she's working. *(Universal Studios)*

Does he or she embody certain cultural values or does the star change radically from film to film, thus preventing any iconographic buildup? If the star is highly iconographic, what values does he or she embody? How does this cultural information function within the world of the movie? What style of acting predominates? How realistic or stylized is the acting style? Why were these actors cast? What do they bring with them to enhance their characters?

FURTHER READING

BLUM, RICHARD A., *American Film Acting: The Stanislavski Heritage* (Ann Arbor, Mich.: UMI Research Press, 1984). History of Method Acting in America.

CARDULLO, BERT, et al. eds. *Playing to the Camera* (New Haven, CT: Yale University Press, 1998). A collection of articles and interviews.

DMYTRYK, EDWARD, and JEAN PORTER, *On Screen Acting* (London: Focal Press, 1984). Practical emphasis.

DYER, RICHARD, *Stars* (London: British Film Institute, 1979). A systematic analysis, well-written.

NAREMORE, JAMES, *Acting in the Cinema* (Berkeley: University of California Press, 1988). Comprehensive.

OLIVIER, LAURENCE, *Laurence Olivier on Acting* (New York: Simon & Schuster, 1986).

ROSS, LILLIAN, and HELEN ROSS, *The Player: A Profile of an Art* (New York: Simon & Schuster, 1962). A collection of interviews with actors from stage, screen, and TV.

SCHICKEL, RICHARD, *The Stars* (New York: Dial Press, 1962). See also Richard Griffith, *The Movie Stars* (Garden City, N.Y.: Doubleday, 1970). Studies by two of America's best film critics.

SHIPMAN, DAVID, *The Great Movie Stars,* Vol. I, *The Golden Years* (New York: Bonanza Books, 1970); Vol. II, *The International Years* (New York: St. Martin's Press, 1972). Encyclopedic coverage, with sane, well-written evaluations.

ZUCKER, CAROLE, ed., *Making Visible the Invisible* (Metuchen, N.J.: Scarecrow Press, 1990). A collection of essays on film acting.

7

Drama

DC Comics and Warner Bros.

*The function of the cinema is to reveal, to bring to light
certain details that the stage would have left untreated.*
—André Bazin

Overview

Live theater and movies: a comparison. How time, space, and language are used in each medium. Scene versus shot. Acting in each medium. Nudity. Stage adaptations in cinema: problems and challenges. The role of the director in film and live theater. The *auteur* theory. The role of the spectator in each medium: active versus passive. The movable camera's variable points of view and shifting perspectives. Settings and decor: dressing the story. Actual locations versus the studio. Process shots, miniatures, and special effects. The key influence of German expressionism. Realisms. The glory days of the Hollywood studios: MGM, Warner Brothers, Twentieth Century–Fox, Paramount Pictures. Studio wizardry of Fellini and company. Costumes and makeup. The ideology of clothing.

Many people cling to the naive belief that drama and film are two aspects of the same art, only drama is "live," whereas movies are "recorded." Certainly, there are undeniable similarities between the two arts. Most obviously, both use action as a principal means of communication: What people *do* is a major source of meaning. Live theater and movies are also collaborative enterprises, involving the coordination of writers, directors, actors, and technicians. Drama and film are both social arts, exhibited before groups of people, and experienced publicly as well as individually. But films are not mere recordings of plays. The language systems of each are fundamentally different. For the most part, movies have a far broader range of techniques at their disposal.

Time, Space, and Language

In the live theater, time is less flexible than in movies. The basic unit of construction in the theater is the scene, and the amount of dramatic time that elapses during a scene is roughly equal to the length of time it takes to perform. True, some plays traverse many years, but usually these years transpire "between curtains." We're informed that it is "seven years later" either by a stage direction or by the dialogue. The basic unit of construction in movies is the **shot.** Because the average shot lasts only ten or fifteen seconds (and can be as brief as a fraction of a second), the cinematic shot can lengthen or shorten time more subtly. Drama has to chop out huge blocks of time between the relatively few scenes and acts; films can expand or contract time between the many hundreds of shots. Theatrical time is usually continuous. It moves forward. Temporal dislocations like the **flashback** are rare in the live theater, but commonplace in movies.

Space in the live theater is also dependent on the basic unit of the scene. The action takes place in a unified area that has specific limits, usually defined by the proscenium arch. Drama, then, almost always deals with **closed forms:** We don't imagine that the action is being continued in the wings or the

7-1a. *The Relic* (U.S.A., 1996), *with Penelope Ann Miller, directed by Peter Hyams.*
Microspace. On stage, this shot would not be very effective: The audience would be too far away to assimilate a mere few inches of visual drama. On film, the shot is powerfully suspenseful because its mise en scène is defined (temporarily) by the frame, which foregrounds the subject matter in an intense close-up. The stage director's space is much more restricted, and uniform from scene to scene. Movie directors can get very close or very far away with equal ease. *(Paramount Pictures)*

7-1b. *Fantastic Voyage* (U.S.A., 1966), *art direction by Jack Martin Smith and Dale Hennesy, special effects by Art Cruickshank, directed by Richard Fleischer.*
Screen space can explore even microscopic areas: literally, through microcinematography, or figuratively, through special effects. The principal setting of this film—the interior of a human body—couldn't possibly be duplicated on stage. To perform a delicate brain operation, several scientists are reduced to the size of bacteria. They travel through the patient's bloodstream in a miniaturized submarine. This photo shows the crew's only survivors floating in the area of the optic nerve as they frantically search for the patient's eye so they can escape from his body before they return to normal size. *(Twentieth Century-Fox)*

7-2. *Richard III (Great Britain, 1995), with Ian McKellen, directed by Richard Loncraine.* Epic stories can be treated on the stage, but they are always stylized. Theatrical space is too constricted for a realistic presentation. On stage, when the depraved Richard III screams in the thick of battle, "A horse! A horse! My kingdom for a horse!" we don't really expect to see one, or even many soldiers. In the movie version, not only do we get horses, we also see thousands of soldiers (updated to the fascist 1930s) clashing to the death. *(United Artists)*

dressing rooms of the theater. The "proscenium arch" in film is the **frame**—a masking device that isolates objects and people only temporarily. Movies deal with a series of space fragments. Beyond the frame of a given shot, another aspect of the action waits to be photographed. A **close-up** of an object, for example, is generally a detail of a subsequent **long shot,** which will give us the context of the close-up. In the theater, it's more difficult to withhold information in this manner.

In the live theater, the viewer remains in a stationary position. The distance between the audience and the stage is constant. Of course, an actor can move closer to an audience, but compared to the fluid space in the cinema, distance variation in the live theater is negligible. The film viewer, on the other hand, identifies with the camera's lens, which is not immobilized in a chair. This identification permits the viewer to "move" in any direction and from any distance. An **extreme close-up** allows us to count the lashes of an eyelid; the **extreme long shot** permits us to see miles in each direction. In short, the cinema allows the spectator to feel mobile.

These spatial differences don't necessarily favor one medium over the other. In the live theater, space is three dimensional, is occupied by tangible people and objects, and is therefore more realistic. That is, our perception of space is essentially the same as in real life. The living presence of actors, with their subtle interactions—both with other actors and the audience—is impossible to duplicate in film. Movies provide us with a two-dimensional *image* of space and objects, and no interaction exists between the screen actors and the audience. For this reason, nudity is not so controversial an issue on the screen

7-3. *Dona Flor and Her Two Husbands* (Brazil, 1977), *with José Wilker, Sonia Braga, and Mauro Mendonca; directed by Bruno Baretto.*

Nudity is common in movies, rare in the live theater. A naked actor on stage usually triggers off a public outcry, but because movies are "only pictures," nudity seldom provokes much controversy except in puritanical communities. As a result, cinema has been able to exploit nakedness as a symbolic comment, a way of exploring universal impulses. For example, this "naughty" sex farce deals with a woman who loves two men, one a ghost. Her first husband (Wilker) was charming, exciting, and totally irresponsible. He died during one of his many sexual escapades, but his ghost—visible only to us and his former wife—returns to enjoy his conjugal prerogatives. Dona Flor's second husband is decent and reliable, a good provider, a rock of stability. He's also stupifyingly dull. To be totally happy, Dona Flor must satisfy both needs—for a dynamo in the bedroom and a pillar of society in the outside world. She accordingly manages to arrange an amiable, if somewhat ghostly, ménage à trois.

(Carnaval/New Yorker Films)

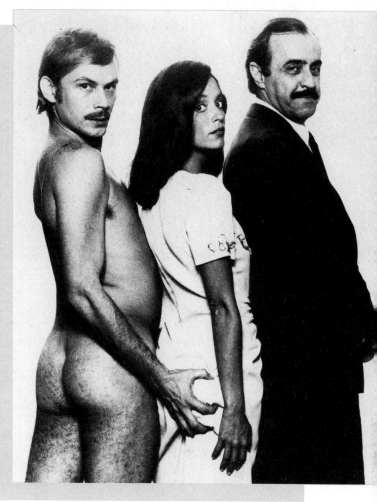

as in the live theater. On stage the naked people are real, whereas in movies they're "only pictures" **(7–3).**

The stage player interacts with viewers, establishing a delicate rapport with each different audience. The screen player, on the other hand, is inexorably fixed on celluloid: He or she can't readjust to each audience, for the worlds of the screen and the viewer aren't connected and continuous as they are in the live theater. Movies often seem dated because acting styles can't be adjusted to newer audiences. Stage actors, on the other hand, can make even a two-thousand-year-old play seem fresh and relevant, for while the words remain the same, their interpretation and delivery can always be changed to conform with contemporary acting styles.

Because of the spatial differences, the viewer's participation is different in each medium. In the theater, the audience generally must be more active. All the visual elements are provided within a given space, so the viewer must sort out what's essential from what's incidental. Disregarding for the moment the importance of language in the theater, drama is a medium of low visual sat-

7-4. *Pickpocket* (France, 1959), *directed by Robert Bresson.*
In the live drama, if a small prop (like a wallet) is important, it must be highlighted conspicuously or the audience will fail to notice its existence, much less its importance. In the cinema, small articles can be isolated from their context. In this photo, Bresson captures a pickpocket's swift stroke as he lifts a wallet from a pedestrian on a busy walkway. This snapshot quality is difficult to produce on stage: The conventions of the medium are at odds with the essence of the subject matter. *(New Yorker Films)*

uration. That is, the audience must fill in certain meanings in the absence of visual detail. A movie audience, on the other hand, is generally more passive. All the necessary details are provided by close-ups and by **edited** juxtapositions. Film, then, is a medium of high visual saturation—that is, the pictures are densely detailed with information, requiring little or no filling in.

Although both drama and film are eclectic arts, the theater is a narrower medium, one specializing in spoken language. Most of the meanings in the theater are found in words, which are densely saturated with information. For this reason, drama is generally considered a writer's medium. The primacy of the text makes it a special branch of literature. In the live theater, we tend to hear before we see. The film director René Clair once noted that a blind person could still grasp the essentials of most stage plays. Movies, on the other hand, are generally regarded as a visual art and a director's medium, for it is the director who creates the images. Clair observed that a deaf person could still grasp most of the essentials of a film. But these generalizations are relative, for some movies—many of the works of Welles, for example—are densely saturated, both visually and aurally.

Because plays stress the primacy of language, one of the major problems in adapting them to the screen is determining how much of the language is necessary in a predominantly visual art like movies. George Cukor's version of Shakespeare's *Romeo and Juliet* (**6–34a**) was a conservative film adaptation. Virtually all the dialogue was retained, even the exposition and purely functional speeches of no particular poetic merit. The result is a respectful but often tedious film in which the visuals merely illustrate the language. Often, images and dialogue contain the same information, producing an overblown, static quality that actually contradicts the swift sense of action in the stage play.

Zeffirelli's film version of this play is much more successful. Verbal exposition was cut almost completely and replaced (just as effectively) by visual exposition. Single lines were pruned meticulously from some of the speeches where the same information could be conveyed by images. Most of the great

7–5. *All About Eve* **(U.S.A., 1950),** *with Bette Davis, Marilyn Monroe, and George Sanders; written and directed by Joseph L. Mankiewicz.*

All About Eve is about the New York live theater and its fascinatingly neurotic denizens. It's one of the few movies that could probably be converted into an effective stage play, for its action consists mostly of talk—glorious talk. Mankiewicz, who was fondly described by one critic as "Old Joe, the Talk Man," is above all a *verbal* stylist, a master of sophisticated dialogue and bitchy repartee. *(Twentieth Century–Fox)*

poetry was preserved but often with **nonsynchronous** visuals to expand—not duplicate—the language. The essence of Shakespeare's play is found in the impulsive haste of its youthful protagonists, the dominolike swiftness of the chain of events, and the violence of much of the action. Zeffirelli heightened these characteristics by kineticizing many of the scenes. The fight sequences are often photographed with a hand-held camera that lurches and swirls with the combatants as they spill onto the streets of Verona. Zeffirelli's movie, though technically less faithful to the stage script, is actually more Shakespearean in spirit than the scrupulously literal version of Cukor. On the other hand, sometimes an adaptation can be *too* cinematic, like the Luhrmann version of this play **(7–13).**

Both theater and cinema are audiovisual mediums, then, but they differ in their stress of certain **conventions.** The two major sources of information in the live theater are action and dialogue. We observe what people do and what they say. Theatrical action is restricted primarily to objective long shots, to use a cinematic metaphor. Only fairly large actions are effective: the duel between Hamlet and Laertes, Amanda helping Laura to dress in *The Glass*

Menagerie, and so on. Extreme long-shot ranges—to continue the cinematic metaphor—must be stylized in the live theater. The **epic** battles of Shakespeare's plays would look ridiculous if staged realistically. Likewise, close-up actions would be missed by all but those in the front rows unless the actions were exaggerated and stylized by the actors. Except for the most intimate theaters, close-up actions in the live drama have to be verbalized. That is, the most

7–6. Publicity photo for *Magnum Force* **(U.S.A., 1973),** *with Clint Eastwood and Adele Yoshioka, directed by Ted Post.*

In the live theater, actors are selected not only on the basis of their looks and talent, but also on how well they match up with the other actors on stage. Theatrical directors must always conceive of their productions in terms of an ensemble effect. In the cinema, these considerations are secondary. In this movie, Eastwood, who stands 6′ 4″, is romantically paired with Adele Yoshioka, who is 5′ 4″. On stage, this height discrepancy would be a sight gag, but on the screen (or more accurately, off screen), the problem was easily resolved through the art of exclusion. *(Warner Bros.)*

7-7. *Twister* **(U.S.A., 1996),** *with Bill Paxton, directed by Jan De Bont.*
The cinema is well suited to dealing with the relationship between people and nature—a rare theme in the live theater, which tends to favor interior settings. Thanks to special effects, movies can even go beyond nature—by creating an approaching tornado that in no way endangers the actor who seems to be standing in harm's way. *(Warner Bros. and Universal City Studio)*

subtle actions and reactions of stage characters are usually conveyed by language rather than by visual means. We know of Hamlet's attitude toward Claudius primarily through Hamlet's soliloquies and dialogue. On the close-up level of action, then, what we see on stage is often not what people do, but what they *talk* about doing, or what's been done.

Because of these visual problems, most plays avoid actions requiring vast or minute spaces. Theatrical action is usually confined to the long- and **full-shot** range. If vast or tiny spaces are required, the theater tends to resort to unrealistic conventions: to ballets and stylized tableaux for extreme long-shot actions, and to the convention of verbal articulation for close-up actions. Movies, on the other hand, can move easily among all these ranges. For this reason, the cinema often dramatizes the action that takes place on stage only "between the curtains."

The human being is central to the aesthetic of the theater: Words must be recited by people; conflicts must be embodied by actors. The cinema is not so dependent on humans. The aesthetic of film is based on photography, and anything that can be photographed can be the subject matter of a movie. For this reason, adapting a play to the screen, although difficult, is hardly impossible, for much of what can be done on the stage can be duplicated on the screen. To adapt most movies to the stage, however, would be much tougher. Movies with exterior locations would be almost automatically ruled out, of course: How would one go about adapting John Ford's epic westerns like *Stage-*

coach? But even films with interior locations would probably be impossible to translate into theatrical terms. True, the words would present no problem, and some actions would be transferable. But how would you deal with the time and space dislocations of Richard Lester's Beatles film, *A Hard Day's Night?* Theme and characterization in Joseph Losey's *The Servant* are communicated primarily through the use of camera angles—impossible to duplicate in the theater **(11–9).** The theme of Bergman's *The Silence* is conveyed primarily through images of empty corridors, doors, and windows. How could you transfer this technique to the stage?

We shouldn't assume from this that the best method of adapting a play for the screen is to "open it up"—to substitute exterior locations for interiors. Cinema doesn't always mean extreme long shots, sweeping **pans,** and flashy editing. Hitchcock once observed that many filmed versions of plays fail precisely because the tight, compact structure of the original is lost when the film director "loosens it up" with inappropriate cinematic techniques **(7–11).** Particularly when a play emphasizes a sense of confinement, either physical or psychological—and a great many of them do—the best adaptors respect the spirit of the original by finding filmic equivalents.

7–8. ***The Dead*** **(U.S.A., 1987),** *with Donal McCann and Anjelica Huston, directed by John Huston.*
The cinema can be a medium of subtle nuances as well as epic events. This faithful adaptation of James Joyce's famous short story is comprised almost exclusively of "little things"—a touch of the hand, a wistful sidelong glance, a private moment of bitterness. On stage, such fragile materials would be considered hopelessly undramatic. But because the camera can move into the intimate ranges, such details can be woven into a poetic fabric of sheerest delicacy. *(Vestron Pictures)*

7–9. *Tootsie* (U.S.A., 1982), *with Dustin Hoffman, directed by Sydney Pollack.*

In the live theater, actors can't make elaborate costume changes unless they have enough time—usually between act breaks. In movies, costume and makeup changes can take as long as necessary, since lengthy preparations can be edited out. Much of the comedy of *Tootsie* revolves around a difficult and obsessively perfectionist actor named Michael Dorsey (Hoffman). Eventually no one wants to hire him because he's "such a pain in the ass to work with." Undaunted, he disguises himself as a middle-aged actress named Dorothy Michaels and lands him/herself a juicy role on a daytime soap opera. Dorothy turns out to be a hugely popular TV personality, much beloved by the public and by her associates at work. Some of the funniest episodes in the movie deal with the quick changes Michael must make whenever someone unexpectedly shows up at his door while he's out of character. In actuality, Hoffman was required to sit for hours as makeup specialists and costumers helped him to become Dorothy. In addition to being one of the greatest films to explore the world of actors, *Tootsie* is also a classic of the feminist cinema. In the process of playing Dorothy, Michael discovers his best self, as he grudgingly admits late in the film: "I was a much better man when I was a woman than when I was a man." Michael Dorsey/Dorothy Michaels is one of Hoffman's most brilliant creations. Sydney Pollack claims he hated directing the movie because Hoffman "was such a pain in the ass to work with." *(Columbia Pictures)*

The Director

In the mid-1950s, the French periodical *Cahiers du Cinéma* popularized the *auteur* **theory,** a view that stressed the dominance of the director in film art (see Chapter 11, "Theory"). According to this view, whoever controls the **mise en scène**—the medium of the story—is the true "author" of a movie. The other collaborators (writers, cinematographer, actors, editor, etc.) are merely the director's technical assistants. No doubt the auteur critics exaggerated the primacy of the director, particularly in America, where many film directors were at the mercy of the Hollywood studio system, which tended to emphasize group work rather than individual expression and publicized **stars** rather than directors. Nevertheless, the auteur critics were essentially correct about the most artistically significant films.

Even today, the most admired movies—from whatever country—tend to be director's films. To refer to a movie as "good except for its direction" is as contradictory as referring to a play as "good except for its script." Of course, we can enjoy a poorly directed movie or a badly written play, but what we enjoy are usually the secondary aspects of the art—a touching performance, a striking set. Good acting and stylish camerawork have often redeemed rubbish material. Such enjoyable elements generally represent the individual triumph of a gifted interpretive artist (actor, set designer, cinematographer, etc.) over the mediocrity of the dominant artist—the director in film, the writer in the live theater.

On the stage, then, the director is essentially an interpretive artist. If we see a rotten production of *King Lear*, we don't dismiss Shakespeare's play, but only a specific interpretation of the play. True, the stage director creates certain patterns of movement, appropriate gestures for actors, and spatial relationships, but all of these visual elements take second place to the language of the script, which is created by the playwright. The theatrical director's relation to the text is

7–10.   *The Little Foxes* (U.S.A., 1941), *with Dan Duryea and Carl Benton Reid, directed by William Wyler.*
André Bazin believed that in adapting a play a filmmaker's greatest challenge is translating the artificial space of the theater into the realistic space of the cinema without losing the essence of the original. For example, in Lillian Hellman's stage play, this scene between a devious father and his creepy son takes place in the same living room set as most of the other scenes. Wyler's presentation is at once more effective and realistic. The two characters are shaving in the family bathroom while they haltingly probe the possibility of swindling a relative. Neither wants to reveal himself; neither looks at the other directly. Instead, they address each other by looking in their respective mirrors, their backs turned. "There is a hundred times more cinema, and of a better kind, in a shot in *The Little Foxes*," Bazin claimed, "than in all the outdoor dolly shots, natural locations, exotic geography, and flipsides of sets with which the screen so far has tried to make up for stagey origins."   *(RKO)*

similar to the stage actor's relation to a role: He or she can add much to what's written down, but what is contributed is usually secondary to the text itself.

The stage director is a kind of go-between for the author and the production staff. That is, the director is responsible for the general interpretation of the script and usually defines the limits for the other interpretive artists: actors, designers, technicians. The director must see to it that all the production elements are harmonized and subordinated to an overall interpretation. His or her influence is stronger during rehearsals than in the actual performance. Once the curtain opens before an audience, the director is powerless to control what then takes place.

On the other hand, screen directors have a good deal more control over the final product. They too dominate the preproduction activities, but unlike the stage director, the filmmaker controls virtually every aspect of the finished work as well. The degree of precision a film director can achieve is impossible on the stage, for movie directors can rephotograph people and objects until they get exactly what they want. As we have seen, films communicate *primarily* through moving images, and it's the director who determines most of the visual elements: the choice of shots, angles, lighting effects, filters, optical effects, framing, composition, camera movements, and editing. Furthermore, the director usually authorizes the costume and set designs and the choice of locales.

The differences in control and precision can best be illustrated perhaps by examining their handling of the mise en scène. Stage directors are much more restricted: They must work within one stationary set per scene. All patterns of movement take place within this given area. Because this is a three-dimensional space, they have the advantage of depth as well as breadth to work with. Through the use of platforms, they can also exploit height on the stage. The theatrical director must use certain space conventions to assure maximum clarity. Thus, with a proscenium stage, the audience pretends it's peeping into a room where one wall has been removed. Naturally, no furniture is placed against this "wall," nor do players turn their backs against it for very long periods or their dialogue wouldn't be audible. If a thrust stage is used, the audience surrounds the acting area on three sides, forcing the performers to rotate their movements and speeches so that no side is neglected. This convention is necessary to ensure maximum clarity.

In the cinema, the director converts three-dimensional space into a two-dimensional image of space. Even with deep-focus photography, "depth" is not literal (7–12). But the flat image has certain advantages. A camera can be placed virtually anywhere, so the film director is not confined to a stationary set with a given number of "walls." The eye-level long shot more or less corresponds to the theatrical proscenium arch. But in movies, the close-up also constitutes a given space—in effect a cinematic "roomlet" with its own "walls" (the frame). Each shot, then, represents a new given space with different (and temporary) confines. Furthermore, the movable camera permits the director to rearrange the "walls" many times for maximum expressiveness with no sacrifice of clarity. Thus, in film, a character can enter the frame from below, from

7–11a. *A Streetcar Named Desire* **(U.S.A., 1951),** *with Vivien Leigh and Marlon Brando, directed by Elia Kazan.* (Twentieth Century–Fox)

There are no hard and fast rules about "opening up" a stage play when adapting it as a movie. Sometimes it's better not to expand the original, as Elia Kazan discovered when he tried to convert this famous Tennessee Williams drama into a screenplay. Originally Kazan intended to dramatize the events leading up to the introduction of the protagonist, the fragile Blanche Dubois (Leigh). On stage, these sordid events are merely discussed, not shown. But Kazan's experiment didn't work. More was lost than gained, as he admitted: "The force of the play had come precisely from its compression, from the fact that Blanche was trapped in these two small rooms where she couldn't escape if she wanted to." Kazan decided to shoot the story almost exclusively in those two cramped rooms. The movie was a huge success, winning many awards.

On the other hand, *Driving Miss Daisy* was a success in part because the play *was* opened up. On stage, Alfred Uhry's period drama was a simple three-character sketch, with virtually no sets, and the actors pantomiming their props. The screenplay (also written by Uhry) opened up the action, adding new characters and providing realistic sets for the scenes. Critics almost universally preferred the movie to the stage play because the screen version is more richly textured, more rooted in a particular time and place. The movie won a Best Picture Oscar, as well as an Academy Award for Uhry's screenplay.

7–11b. *Driving Miss Daisy* **(U.S.A., 1989),** *with Dan Aykroyd, Jessica Tandy, and Morgan Freeman; directed by Bruce Beresford.* (Warner Bros.)

7–12. *Ikiru,* **also known as** *To Live* **(Japan, 1952),** *directed by Akira Kurosawa.*
On the stage, the size of objects is constant; in movies, it's relative. In this deep-focus shot, for example, the materials of three depth planes are precisely aligned to produce an ironic contrast. The protagonist (Takashi Shimura, whose picture adorns the Buddhist altar) was a lowly bureaucrat who did something really significant with his existence only in the final months of his life, when he realized he was dying of cancer. In the flashback portions of the movie, his battered hat is a symbol of his humility and dogged perseverance. His funeral wake (pictured) is a rigid, dismal affair, attended primarily by the deceased's fellow bureaucrats. The placement of the camera in this photo implicitly contrasts the unpretentious hat with the chagrined faces of the office workers with the formal photograph and altar. Because each viewer in the live theater has a unique perspective on the stage, spatial techniques like this are rare. In movies, they are common, for the camera determines one perspective for all.
(Brandon Films)

above, from any side, and from any angle. By **dollying** or **craning,** a camera can also take us "into" a set, permitting objects to pass by us.

Because the stage director's mise en scène is confined to the unit of the scene, a certain amount of compromise is inevitable. He or she must combine a maximum of expressiveness with a maximum of clarity—not always an easy task. Film directors have to make fewer compromises of this sort, for they have a greater number of "scene-lets" at their disposal: Most movies average well over a thousand shots. The film director can give us a half dozen shots of the same object—some emphasizing clarity, others emphasizing expressiveness. Some shots can show a character with his or her back to the camera: The soundtrack guarantees the clarity of the character's speech **(2–13b).** A character can be photographed through an obstruction of some kind—a pane of glass or the dense foliage of a forest. Because the cinematic shot need not be lengthy, clarity can be suspended temporarily in favor of expressiveness.

These generalizations are postulated on the assumption that the stage is essentially **realistic** in its handling of time and space, whereas the cinema is basically **formalistic.** But the differences are relative, of course. In fact, an argument could be made that Strindberg's expressionistic plays—*The Dream Play,* for example—are more fragmented and subjective than a realistic movie like Keaton's *Steamboat Bill, Jr.,* which emphasizes the continuity of time and space.

In adapting a stage play, the filmmaker is confronted with thousands of choices, petty and monumental. These can alter the original in ways never dreamed of by the original dramatist. Even with classic texts, a filmmaker can emphasize the psychological, the social, or the epic, because these are determined in large measure by the way space is used in movies. A filmmaker can stage the action on studio sets or in a natural setting, but the choice will significantly alter the meaning of the work.

7–13.   *William Shakespeare's Romeo and Juliet* (U.S.A., 1996), *with Leonardo DiCaprio, directed by Baz Lurhmann.*

Sometimes a movie can be *too* cinematic—blasting away in six directions at once. Director Lurhmann wanted to make a truly youthful film—passionate, fast, and impulsive, like the teenage protagonists of Shakespeare's play. Speech after speech was slashed away to make room for violent displays like this. The setting was switched to a contemporary Latin Americanesque city. Two of America's most gifted young actors were brought on to play the leads, DiCaprio and the elegant Claire Danes. But their speeches are reduced to bare bones, and often the actors are leaping, running, or climbing so strenuously that even what's left is an indistinguishable vocal blur. It's like Shakespeare on steroids. Sometimes it's better to just let Shakespeare's language command the spotlight.   *(Twentieth Century–Fox)*

Settings and Décor

In the best movies and stage productions, settings are not merely back-drops for the action, but symbolic extensions of the theme and characterization. Settings can convey an immense amount of information, especially in the cinema. Stage sets are generally less detailed than film sets, for the audience is too distant from the stage to perceive many small details. The director in this medium must generally work with fewer sets, usually one per act. Inevitably, the stage director must settle for less precision and variety than screen directors, who have virtually no limits of this kind, especially when shooting on location.

Spatial considerations force stage directors to make constant compromises with their sets. If they use too much of the upstage (rear) area, the audience won't be able to see or hear well. If they use high platforms to give an actor dominance, they then have the problem of getting the actor back on the main level quickly and plausibly. Stage directors must also use a constant-sized space: Settings are usually confined to "long shots." If they want to suggest a vast field, for example, they must resort to certain conventions. They can stage an action in such a way as to suggest that the playing area is only a small corner of the field. Or they can stylize the set with the aid of a cyclorama, which gives the illusion of a vast sky in the background. If they want to suggest a confined area, they can do so only for short periods, for an audience grows restless when actors are restricted to a small playing area for long periods. Stage directors can use vertical, horizontal, and oblique lines in a set to suggest psychological states; but these lines (or colors or objects) cannot be cut out from scenes where they are inappropriate, as they could be in a movie.

The film director has far more freedom in the use of settings. Most important, of course, the cinema permits a director to shoot outdoors—an enormous advantage. The major works of a number of great directors would have been impossible without this freedom: Griffith, Eisenstein, Keaton, Kurosawa, Antonioni, Ford, De Sica, Renoir. Epic films would be virtually impossible without the extreme long shots of vast expanses of land. Other **genres,** particularly those requiring a degree of stylization or deliberate unreality, have been associated with the studio: musicals, horror films, and many period films. Such genres often stress a kind of magical, sealed-off universe, and images taken from real life tend to clash with these essentially claustrophobic qualities.

However, these are merely generalizations. There are some westerns that have been shot mostly indoors and some musicals that have been photographed in actual locations. If a location is extravagantly beautiful, there's no reason why a romantic musical can't exploit such a setting. The Paris locations of Minnelli's *Gigi* are a good example of how actual locations can enhance a stylized genre **(6–32).** In short, it all depends on how it's done. As the French historian Georges Sadoul pointed out, "The dichotomy between the studio and the street, the antithesis between Lumière and Méliès, are false oppositions when one attempts to find in them the solution to the problems of realism and

7-14a. Publicity photo of *Just Another Girl on the I.R.T.* (U.S.A., 1993), *directed by Leslie Harris (standing left, with clipboard).*

The appeal of actual locations, of course, is that they're a lot cheaper than sets that have to be constructed. Location shooting also gives a movie an irrefutable authenticity: It's the real thing. For low-budget neophyte filmmakers like Harris, these twin virtues make actual locations irresistible. *(Miramax Films)*

7-14b. *The Keep* (U.S.A., 1983), *with Scott Glenn, directed by Michael Mann.*

The main appeal of studio sets is usually their lack of reality, best illustrated by such fantasy films as *The Keep*. Studio sets like these allow the filmmaker to create a magical, ethereal world, one where even the drifting fog does what the director tells it to do. In short, the studio is a control freak's paradise, where nothing is left to chance. *(Paramount Pictures)*

art. Films completely outside time have been shot out of doors; completely realistic films have been shot in the studio."

In set design, as in other aspects of movies, the terms *realism* and *formalism* are simply convenient critical labels. Most sets *tend* toward one style or the other, but few are pure examples. For instance, in *The Birth of a Nation*, Griffith proudly proclaims that a number of his scenes are historical facsimiles of real places and events—like Ford's Theater where Lincoln was assassinated, or the signing of the Emancipation Proclamation. These scenes were modeled on actual photographs of the period. Yet Griffith's facsimiles were created in a studio. On the other hand, real locations can be exploited to create a somewhat artificial—formalistic—effect. For example, in shooting *Ten Days That Shook the World,* Eisenstein had the Winter Palace at his disposal for several months. Yet the images in the movie are baroque: richly textured and formally complex. Although Eisenstein chose actual locations for their authenticity, they are never just picturesque backgrounds to the action. Each shot is carefully designed. Each exploits the inherent *form* of the setting, contributing significantly to the aesthetic impact of the sequence. Realistic or formalistic?

Realism is never a simple term. In movies, it's used to describe a variety of styles. Some critics use modifiers like "poetic realism," "documentary realism," and "studio realism" to make finer distinctions. The nature of beauty in realism is also a complex issue. Beauty of form is an important component of poetic realism. The early works of Fellini, such as *The Nights of Cabiria*, are handsomely mounted and slightly stylized to appeal to our visual sense. Similarly, John Ford shot nine of his westerns in Monument Valley, Utah, because of its spectacular beauty. Among other things, Ford was a great landscape artist. Many realistic films shot in the studio are also slightly stylized to exploit this "incidental" visual beauty.

In other realistic films, beauty—in this conventional sense—plays a lesser role. A major criterion of aesthetic value in a movie like Pontecorvo's *Battle of Algiers* is its deliberate roughness. The story deals with the struggle for liberation of the Algerian people from their French colonial masters. It was shot entirely in the streets and houses of Algiers. The setting is rarely exploited for its aesthetic beauty. In fact, Pontecorvo's lack of formal organization, his refusal to yield an inch in matters of "style," is his principal virtue as an artist. The moral power of the materials takes precedence over formal considerations. The setting's beauty is in its truth. In films such as these, style (that is, distortion) is regarded as prettification, a form of insincerity, and therefore ugly. Even outright ugliness can be a criterion of aesthetic beauty. The gaudy sets and décor in *Touch of Evil* are organic to the nature of the materials.

To the unsympathetic, the cult of realism verges on madness. But there's a method to it. For example, John Huston shot *The African Queen* in the tropics because he knew he wouldn't have to worry about a thousand little details, such as how to get the actors to sweat a lot or how to get their clothes to stick to their bodies. Perhaps the most famous, if not infamous, example of this passion for authenticity is Erich von Stroheim, who detested studio sets. In *Greed,* he insisted that his actors actually live in a seedy boarding house to get

a

b

7–15. Production photo of *The Sands of Iwo Jima* (U.S.A., 1949), *with John Wayne (front and center), directed by Allan Dwan.* Because a studio allows a director more control and precision than an actual location, some filmmakers use the so-called **process shot** in scenes requiring exterior locations. This technique involves the rear projection of a moving image on a translucent screen. Live actors and a portion of a set are placed in front of this screen, and the entire action and background are then photographed by a camera that is synchronized with the rear projector. The finished product **(b)** looks reasonably authentic, although backgrounds tend to look suspiciously washed out and flat in comparison to foreground elements. *(Republic Pictures)*

7–16. *The Cabinet of Dr. Caligari* (Germany, 1919), *with Conrad Veidt and Werner Krauss (wearing hat); production design by Hermann Warm, Walter Röhrig, and Walter Reimann; directed by Robert Wiene.*

The German Expressionist movement of the post–World War I era emphasized visual design above all. The movement's main contributions were in the live theater, the graphic arts, and the cinema. It is a style steeped in anxiety and terror. The sets are deliberately artificial: flat, obviously painted, with no attempt to preserve the conventions of perspective and scale. They are meant to represent a state of mind, not a place. The lighting and set designs are carefully coordinated, with one shading off into the other. Horizontal and vertical lines are avoided in favor of diagonals, which produce a sense of instability and visual anguish. The jerky, machinelike acting is meant to convey the essence of depersonalization. *(Museum of Modern Art)*

the "feel" of the film's low-life setting. He forced them to wear shabby clothing and deprived them of all the amenities that their characters would lack in actuality. Perhaps because of the severe hardships his cast and crew suffered, the movie's authenticity is incontestable.

Spectacle films usually require the most elaborate sets. Historical reconstructions of ancient Rome or Egypt are enormously expensive to build, and they can make or break a film in this genre because spectacle is the major attraction. Perhaps the most famous sets of this type are found in the Babylonian story of Griffith's *Intolerance*. The unprecedented monumentality of these sets is what skyrocketed Griffith's budget to an all-time high of $1.9 million—an astronomical figure by 1916 standards, hefty even by today's. The banquet scene for Belshazzar's feast alone cost a reputed $250,000 and employed over 4,000 extras. The story required the construction of a walled city so vast that for years it remained a standing monument—called "Griffith's Folly" by cynics in

7–17a. *Siegfried* **(Germany, 1924),** *with Paul Richter, directed by Fritz Lang.* *(UFA)*

The heyday of the German Expressionist movement was the 1920s, but its influence has been enormous, especially in the United States, as can be seen in these two photos. The great stage director Max Reinhardt was a seminal influence. In his theory of design, Reinhardt advocated an ideal of "landscapes imbued with soul." The declared aim of most German Expressionists was to eliminate nature for a state of absolute abstraction. Fritz Lang's stylized set was created in a studio, whereas Burton's is out of doors, but both emphasize twisted tree trunks, tortured branches shorn of greenery, drifting fog, desiccated leaves, and a hallucinatory atmosphere of dread and angst.See Lotte Eisner, *The Haunted Screen: Expressionism in the German Cinema and the Influence of Max Reinhardt* (Berkeley: University of California Press, 1973), a copiously illustrated analysis.

7–17b. *Sleepy Hollow* **(U.S.A., 1999),** *with Johnny Depp, Christina Ricci, and Marc Pickering; directed by Tim Burton.* *(Paramount pictures and Mandalay Pictures)*

7–18. *Barton Fink* (U.S.A., 1991), *with John Turturro and Jon Polito, written and directed by Joel and Ethan Coen.*

Among the many pleasures of this period picture are the stunning Art Deco sets and furnishings. Art Deco is a style that dominated the Americas and Europe from about 1925 to roughly 1945. Streamlined, spare of adornment, elegantly curved, or playfully zig-zagging, Art Deco was considered the cutting edge of modern design. In fact, in the United States, the style was often referred to as "Moderne" in the 1930s, the heyday of Art Deco. It was sleek and sophisticated, often making use of such modern industrial materials as plastic (sometimes called Bakelite or Lucite in the 1930s), aluminum, chrome, and glass-block. Lighting sources were frequently indirect, emanating from wall sconces or streaming dramatically through translucent walls of glass that curved exuberantly in defiance of right-angled sobriety. Stylized statuary, usually slender female nudes or powerfully muscled seminude males, epitomized the glamour of being very avant-garde and incredibly cool. *(Twentieth Century–Fox)*

the trade. The set extended nearly three-quarters of a mile in length. The court was flanked by enormous colonnades supporting pillars fifty feet high, each one supporting a huge statue of an erect elephant god. Behind the court were towers and ramparts, their tops planted with cascading flowers and exotic trees representing Belshazzar's famous hanging gardens. The outer walls of the city were 200 feet high, yet were wide enough for two chariots to roar past each other on the road that perched on top. Astonishingly, this and other sets in the film were built without architectural plans. As Griffith kept making additional suggestions, his **art director,** Frank "Huck" Wortman, and his crew kept expanding the set from day to day.

Expressionistic sets are usually created in the studio, where the contaminations of reality cannot penetrate. Magic, not realism, is the aim. Méliès is the prototypical example. He was called "the Jules Verne of films" because his feats of prestidigitation astonished the public. The first in a long line of special effects wizards, Méliès usually painted his sets, often with *trompe-l'oeil* perspectives to

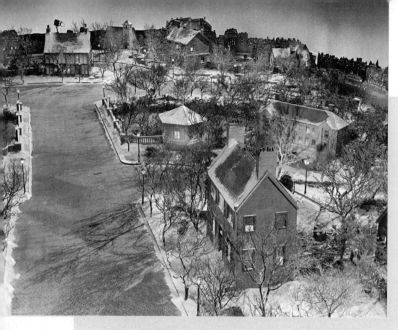

7–19.   Miniature set for *Letter From an Unknown Woman* (U.S.A., 1948), *directed by Max Ophüls.*
Period films often benefit from the slight sense of unreality of studio sets. If a set is needed only for establishing purposes, miniatures are often constructed. These scaled-down sets can be as tall as six or eight feet, depending on the amount of detail and realism needed. Note the two studio floodlights behind the houses of this miniature and the flat, two-dimensional apartment dwellings on the horizon in the upper right.   *(Universal Pictures)*

suggest depth. He combined live actors with fanciful settings to produce a dreamlike atmosphere. He used **animation, miniatures,** and a wide range of optical tricks, charming his audiences with vistas of imaginary realms (**4–4**).

Expressionistic sets appeal to our sense of the marvelous. The work of Danilo Donati, Italy's best known designer, is a good example. The extravagant artificiality of the sets and costumes in such movies as Fellini's *Satyricon, Amarcord,* and *Casanova* are pure products of the imagination—Fellini's as well as Donati's. The director often provided the designer with preliminary sketches, and the two artists worked closely in determining the visual design of each film. Their conjurations can be moving, as well as witty and beautiful. For example, *Amarcord* is a stylized reminiscence of Fellini's youth in his hometown of Rimini. (The title, from the Romagnan dialect, means "I remember.") But Fellini shot the movie in a studio, not on location. He wanted to capture feelings, not facts. Throughout the film, the townspeople feel stifled by the provincial isolation of their community. They are filled with loneliness and long for something extraordinary to transform their lives. When they hear that a mammoth luxury liner, the *Rex,* will pass through the ocean waters a few miles beyond the town's shore, many of these wistful souls decide to row out to sea to greet the ship. Hundreds of them crowd into every available boat and stream away from the beach like fervent pilgrims on a quest. Then they wait. Evening settles, bringing with it a thick fog. Still they wait. In one boat, Gradisca, the charming town sexpot, confides to some sympathetic friends her dissatisfaction with her life. At thirty, she is still single, childless, and unfulfilled. Her "heart overflows with love," yet she has never found a "truly dedicated man." In the dark silence, she weeps softly over the prospect of a barren future. Midnight passes, and still the townspeople wait faithfully. Then, when most of the characters are sleeping in their fragile boats, they're awakened by a boy's shout: "It's here!" Like a grace-

7-20a. *Grand Hotel* (U.S.A., 1932), *with Greta Garbo, art direction by Cedric Gibbons, gowns by Adrian, directed by Edmund Goulding.*
MGM, "the Tiffany of studios," prided itself on its opulent and glossy production values. It was the most prosperous studio in Hollywood in the 1930s, boasting twenty-three sound stages and 117 acres of standing backlots, which included a small lake, a harbor, a park, a jungle, and many streets of houses in different periods and styles. The "Metro look" was largely determined by Gibbons, who was the studio's art director from 1924 to 1956. *(MGM)*

7-20b. *Little Caesar* (U.S.A., 1930), *with Edward G. Robinson (standing), art direction by Anton Grot, directed by Mervyn LeRoy.*
Grot was art director at Warner Brothers from 1927 to 1948. Unlike his counterparts Gibbons, Dreier, and Polglase, however, Grot often took an active hand in designing the studio's major films. His earliest work is somewhat in the German expressionist tradition, but he soon became one of the most versatile of artists. He designed films like the gritty and realistic *Little Caesar*, as well as the Busby Berkeley musical *Gold Diggers of 1933*, with its **surrealistic**, dream-like sets. *(Warner Bros.)*

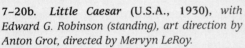

7-20c. *How Green Was My Valley* (U.S.A., 1941), *art direction by Nathan Juran and Richard Day, directed by John Ford.*
The art directors at Twentieth Century–Fox specialized in realistic sets, like this turn-of-the-century Welsh mining village, which covered eighty-six acres and was built in a California valley. Elaborate sets like these were not dismantled after production, for with suitable alterations they could be converted into other locations. For example, two years after Ford's film, this set was transformed into a Nazi-occupied Norwegian village for *The Moon Is Down*. *(Twentieth Century–Fox)*

ful apparition, the light-bedecked *Rex* glides past in all its regal grandeur **(7–21)**. Nino Rota's rapturous music swells to a crescendo as the townspeople wave and shout joyously. Gradisca's eyes stream with tears of exhilaration and yearning while a blind accordionist asks excitedly, "Tell me what it looks like!" Then, as mysteriously as it appeared, the phantom ship is swallowed by the fog and slips silently off into the night.

During the golden age of the Hollywood studio system, each of the **majors** had a characteristic visual style, determined in large part by the designers at each studio. Some were called production designers, others art directors, a few simply set designers. Their job was to determine the "look" of each film, and they worked closely with producers and directors to ensure that the sets, décor, costumes, and photographic style were coordinated to produce a unified effect. For example, MGM specialized in glamour, luxury, and opulent production values, and their art director, Cedric Gibbons, virtually stamped each film with "the Metro look" **(7–20a)**. Because all the studios attempted to diversify their products as much as possible, however, their art directors had to be versatile. For instance, RKO's Van Nest Polglase supervised the design of such diverse movies as *King Kong, Top Hat, The Informer,* and *Citizen Kane.* Paramount's Hans Dreier began his career at Germany's famous UFA studio. He was usually at his best creating a sense of mystery and romantic fantasy, as in the

7–21. *Amarcord* (Italy, 1974), *art direction and costumes by Danilo Donati, cinematography by Giuseppe Rotunno, directed by Federico Fellini.*
For Fellini, who began his career as a realist, the studio became a place to create magic—along with his fellow magicians Donati and Rotunno. "To me and other directors like me," Fellini said, "the cinema is a way of interpreting and remaking reality through fantasy and imagination. The use of the studio is an indispensable part of what we are doing." *(New World Pictures)*

films of Josef von Sternberg. Dreier also designed the superb Art Deco sets for Lubitsch's *Trouble in Paradise.* Warner Brothers' art director, Anton Grot, was a specialist in grubby, realistic locales **(7–20b).** The studio claimed that its films were "Torn from Today's Headlines!" to quote from its publicity blurbs. Warner Brothers favored topical genres with an emphasis on working-class life: gangster films, urban melodramas, and proletarian musicals. Like his counterparts at other studios, however, Grot could work in a variety of styles and genres. For example, he designed the enchanting sets for *A Midsummer Night's Dream.* Unfortunately, there's not much else in this movie that's enchanting.

Certain types of locales were in such constant demand that the studios constructed permanent **back-lot sets,** which were used in film after film: a turn-of-the-century street, a European square, an urban slum, and so on. Of course, these were suitably altered with new furnishings to make them look different each time they were used. The studio with the largest number of back lots was MGM, although Warner, Paramount, and Twentieth Century–Fox also boasted a considerable number of them. Not all standing sets were located close to the studio. It was cheaper to construct some outside the environs of Los Angeles where real estate values weren't at a premium. If a movie called for a huge real-

7-22.   *The Thirteenth Floor* (U.S.A., **1999),** *special effects coordinator John S. Baker, visual effects supervisor Joe Bauer, directed by Josef Rusnak.*
Stage sets owe relatively little to the computer, but in the cinema, and especially in sci-fi films, computer-generated sets are becoming more and more common. This movie explores the ominous possibility of computer-simulated universes, where people only believe they are real. *(Columbia Pictures)*

istic set—like the Welsh mining village for *How Green Was My Valley*—it was often built miles away from the studio **(7–20c).** Similarly, most of the studios owned western frontier towns, ranches, and midwestern type farms, which were located outside the Los Angeles area.

What matters most in a setting is how it embodies the essence of the story material. As the British designer Robert Mallet-Stevens noted, "A film set, in order to be a good set, must act. Whether realistic or expressionistic, modern or ancient, it must play its part. The set must present the character before he has even appeared. It must indicate his social position, his tastes, his habits, his lifestyle, his personality. The sets must be intimately linked with the action."

Settings can also be used to suggest a sense of progression in the characters. For example, in Fellini's *La Strada,* one of his most realistic movies, the protagonist and his simpleminded assistant are shown as reasonably happy, traveling together from town to town with their tacky theatrical act. After he abandons her, he heads for the mountains. Gradually, the landscape changes: Trees are stripped of their foliage, snow and dirty slush cover the ground, the sky is a murky gray. The changing setting is a gauge of the protagonist's spiritual condition: Nature itself seems to grieve after the helpless assistant is left alone to die.

On the stage, a setting is generally admired with the opening of the curtain, and then forgotten as the actors take over the center of interest. In the movies, a director can keep cutting back to the setting to remind the audience of its significance. A film can fragment a set into a series of shots, now emphasizing one aspect of a room, later another, depending on the needs of the director in finding appropriate visual analogues for thematic and psychological ideas. In Losey's *The Servant,* a stairway is used as a major thematic symbol. The film deals with a servant's gradual control over his master **(11–9).** Losey uses the stairway as a kind of psychological battlefield where the relative positions of

7–23. *Dodes'ka-den* **(Japan, 1970),** *art direction by Yoshiro and Shinobu Muraki, directed by Akira Kurosawa.*

As critic Donald Richie has noted, American filmmakers are supreme storytellers; Europeans excel in the treatment of theme and character; and the Japanese are unsurpassed in the creation of atmosphere. Most of the action of this movie takes place in a junkyard, an appropriate analogue for the human refuse and outcasts who inhabit it. The junkyard is sometimes matter-of-factly realistic, as in this scene. At other times, depending on what character Kurosawa focuses on, the same setting can be sinister and terrifying, or strikingly beautiful, like an enchanted landscape. *(Janus Films)*

the two men on the stairs give the audience a sense of who's winning the battle. Losey also uses the rails on the stairway to suggest prison bars: The master of the house is often photographed from behind these bars.

Even the furniture of a room can be exploited for psychological and thematic reasons. In one of his classes, Eisenstein once discussed at length the significance of a table for a set. The class exercise centered on an adaptation of Balzac's novel *Père Goriot*. The scene is set at a dinner table that Balzac described as circular. But Eisenstein convincingly argued that a round table is wrong cinematically, for it implies equality, with each person linked in a circle. To convey the stratified class structure of the boarding house, Eisenstein suggested the use of a long rectangular table, with the haughty mistress of the house at the head, the favored tenants close to her sides, and the lowly Goriot alone, near the base of the table.

Such attention to detail often distinguishes a master of film from a mere technician, who settles for only a general effect. The setting of a movie— far more than any play—can even take over as the central interest (7–24). In

7-24. *Blade Runner* **(U.S.A., 1982),** *with Harrison Ford, directed by Ridley Scott.*
A hybrid of science fiction, **film noir,** detective thriller, bounty-hunter western, and love story, *Blade Runner* is also eclectic in its visual style, a collaborative effort that includes the contributions of art director David Snyder, production designer Lawrence G. Paul, special visual effects designer Douglas Trumbull, and cinematographer Jordan Cronenweth. The story is set in Los Angeles in the year 2019. Nature has gone berserk, deluging the teeming city with an almost constant downpour. Smoke, fog, and steam add to the fumigated congestion. It is a city of dreadful night, punctuated by neon signs in Day-Glo colors, cheap Orientalized billboards, and a profusion of advertising come-ons. Hunks of long-discarded machinery litter the landscape. The soundtrack throbs with eerie sounds, echoes, pounding pistons, and the noises of flying vehicles shuttling through the poisonous atmosphere. It is a city choking on its own technology.   *(Warner Bros.)*

Kubrick's *2001*, the director spends most of his time lovingly photographing the instruments of a spaceship, various space stations, and the enormous expanses of outer space itself. The few people in the movie seem almost incidental and certainly far less interesting than the real center of concern—the setting. It would be impossible to produce *2001* on stage: The materials of the film are not theatrically convertible. Kubrick's movie is a vivid illustration of Bazin's observation that the function of the cinema is "to bring to light certain details that the stage would have left untreated."

A systematic analysis of a set involves a consideration of the following characteristics:

1. *Exterior* or *interior.* If the set is an exterior, how does nature function as a symbolic analogue to the mood, theme, or characterization?

2. *Style.* Is the set realistic and lifelike or stylized and deliberately distorted? Is it in a particular style, such as colonial American, Art Deco, Victorian, sleek contemporary, etc?

3. *Studio* or *location.* If the set is an actual location, why was it chosen? What does it say about the characters?

4. *Period.* What era does the set represent?

5. *Class.* What is the apparent income level of the owners?

6. *Size.* How large is the set? Rich people tend to take up more space than the poor, who are usually crowded in their living area.

7. *Decoration.* How is the set furnished? Are there any status symbols, oddities of taste, etc.? Is it crowded or sparsely furnished?

8. *Symbolic function.* What kind of overall image does the set and its furnishings project?

Costumes and Makeup

In the most sensitive films and plays, costumes and makeup aren't merely frills added to enhance an illusion, but aspects of character and theme. Their style can reveal class, self-image, even psychological states. Depending on their cut, texture, and bulk, certain costumes can suggest agitation, fastidiousness, delicacy, dignity, and so on. A costume, then, is a medium, especially in the cinema, where a close-up of a fabric can suggest information that's independent even of the wearer.

Color symbolism is used by Zeffirelli in *Romeo and Juliet.* Juliet's family, the Capulets, are characterized as aggressive parvenues: Their colors are appropriately "hot" reds, yellows, and oranges. Romeo's family, on the other hand, is older and perhaps more established, but in obvious decline. They are costumed in blues, deep greens, and purples. These two color schemes are echoed in the liveries of the servants of each house, which helps the audience identify the combatants in the brawling scenes. The color of the costumes can also be

7-25. *The Leopard* (Italy, 1963), *art direction by Mario Garbuglia, costumes by Piero Tosi, directed by Luchino Visconti.*
Visconti had the unusual distinction of being both a Marxist and an aristocrat (he was the Duke of Modrone). A master of the period film, he was exceptionally sensitive to the symbolic significance of costumes and décor. They are part of Visconti's political statement. For example, the clutter, texture, and florid patterns of the Victorian furnishings in this movie suggest a stifling hothouse artificiality, sealed off from nature. The costumes, impeccably accurate to period, are elegant, constricting, and totally without utility. They were meant to be. Idle people of independent income—that is, income derived from the labor of others—rarely concern themselves with utility in clothing. *(Twentieth Century-Fox)*

used to suggest change and transition. The first view of Juliet, for example, shows her in a vibrant red dress. After she marries Romeo, her colors are in the cool blue spectrum. Line as well as color can be used to suggest psychological qualities. Verticals, for example, tend to emphasize stateliness and dignity (Lady Montague); horizontal lines tend to emphasize earthiness and comicality (Juliet's nurse).

Perhaps the most famous costume in film history is Charlie Chaplin's tramp outfit. The costume is an indication of both class and character, conveying the complex mixture of vanity and dash that makes Charlie so appealing. The moustache, derby hat, and cane all suggest the fastidious dandy. The cane is used to give the impression of self-importance as Charlie swaggers confidently before a hostile world. But the baggy trousers several sizes too large, the oversized shoes, the too-tight coat—all these suggest Charlie's insignificance

7–26. Publicity photo for *Batman Forever* (U.S.A., 1995), *with Val Kilmer and Chris O'Donnell, directed by Joel Schumacher.*

A costume's silhouette refers to its outline, how much of the body is revealed or obscured by the outer form of the garment. The more formfitting the silhouette, the more erotic the costume—assuming, of course, that the wearer is in good shape. In these costumes, the male musculature is stylized and embossed into the rubberized suits. They weighed over forty pounds each and were intensely uncomfortable and hot under the studio lights. The actual bodies of Kilmer and O'Donnell, though perfectly respectable, are not quite so Michelangeloesque: The suits were designed to add muscles here and there and to flatten a few inconvenient protuberances. But there's no question that the costumes make the boys look good—powerful, sexy, pumped up for action. *(DC Comics and Warner Bros.)*

and poverty. Chaplin's view of humanity is symbolized by that costume: vain, absurd, and—finally—poignantly vulnerable.

In most cases, especially period films, costumes are designed for the performers who will be wearing them. The costumer must always be conscious of the actor's body type—whether he or she is thin, overweight, tall, short, etc.—to compensate for any deficiency. If a performer is famous for a given trait—Dietrich's legs, Marilyn's bosom, Schwarzenegger's chest—the costumer will often design the actor's clothes to highlight these attractions. Even in period films, the costumer has a wide array of styles to choose from, and his or her choice will often be determined by what the actor looks best in within the parameters defined by the milieu of the story.

During the Hollywood studio era, powerful stars often insisted on costumes and makeup that heightened their natural endowments, regardless of period accuracy. This was a practice that was encouraged by the studio bosses, who wanted their stars to look as glamourous as possible by suggesting a "contemporary look." The results are usually jarring and incongruous. Even prestigious directors like John Ford gave in to this tradition of vanity. In Ford's otherwise superb western, *My Darling Clementine* (1946), which is set in a rough frontier community, actress Linda Darnell wore glamourous star makeup and a 1940s-style hairdo, even though the character she was playing was a cheap Mexican "saloon girl"—a coy period euphemism for a prostitute. She looks as

7–27. *Il Postino,* also known as *The Postman* (Italy, 1995), *with Massimo Troisi and Philippe Noiret, directed by Michael Radford.*
Although Troisi is a better looking man than Noiret, their body language says the opposite. The Troisi character has loser written all over him. His clothes are filthy, and the way he wears them accentuates his dorky appearance: His posture is slumped, with drooping shoulders, knees and toes pointed inwardly, and the general air of a man who's been beaten down by life. Noiret, who plays a South American writer in exile on an Italian island, is wearing a crisp white suit, loose and baggy but impeccably clean. His body attitude exudes confidence: Tall and straight, with his hands casually in his pockets, he walks with a jaunty air. He's a man who knows who he is. *(Miramax Films)*

though she just stepped out of a Max Factor salon after receiving the Deluxe Treatment.

In realistic contemporary stories, costumes are often bought off the rack rather than individually designed. This is especially true in stories dealing with ordinary people, people who buy their clothes in department stores. When the characters are lower class or poor, costumers often purchase used clothing. For example, in *On the Waterfront,* which deals with dockworkers and other working-class characters, the costumes are frayed and torn. Costumer Anna Hill Johnstone bought them in used clothing stores in the neighborhood adjoining the waterfront area.

Costumes, then, represent another language system in movies, a symbolic form of communication that can be as complex and revealing as the other language systems filmmakers use. A systematic analysis of a costume includes a consideration of the following characteristics:

1. *Period.* What era does the costume fall into? Is it an accurate reconstruction? If not, why?
2. *Class.* What is the apparent income level of the person wearing the costume?

7-28. *The Breakfast Club* (U.S.A., 1984), *with Judd Nelson, Ally Sheedy, Emilio Estevez, Molly Ringwald, and Anthony Michael Hall; written and directed by John Hughes.*

"Clothing is a wonderful doorway that most easily leads you to the heart of an individual," author Tom Wolfe has noted. "It's how characters reveal themselves." Costumer Ellen Mirojnick concurs, adding that you can read 95 percent of a character entirely from visuals and body language. In many American high schools, the symbolism of clothing is intensely important in preserving one's status and public image. The main characters in this film (pictured) all conform to well-known high school stereotypes: "the criminal," "the basket case" (down below, in hiding), "the jock," "the princess," and "the brain." As the characters gradually strip off layers of psychic protection, they also begin to shed some of their outer garments, which are, after all, just coverings. *(Universal City Studios)*

3. *Sex.* Does a woman's costume emphasize her femininity or is it neutral or masculine? Does a man's costume emphasize his virility or is it fussy or effeminate?

4. *Age.* Is the costume appropriate to the character's age or is it deliberately too youthful, dowdy, or old-fashioned?

5. *Silhouette.* Is the costume formfitting or loose and baggy?

6. *Fabric.* Is the material coarse, sturdy, and plain or sheer and delicate?

7. *Accessories.* Does the costume include jewelry, hats, canes, and other accessories? What kind of shoes?

8. *Color.* What are the symbolic implications of the colors? Are they "hot" or "cool"? Subdued or bright? Solids or patterns?

9. *Body exposure.* How much of the body is revealed or concealed? The more body revealed, the more erotic the costume.

10. *Function.* Is the costume meant for leisure or for work? Is it meant to impress by its beauty and splendor, or is it merely utilitarian?

11. *Body attitude.* What about the wearer's posture? Proud and tall? Or caved in and embarrassed?

12. *Image.* What is the overall impression that the costume creates—sexy, constricting, boring, gaudy, conventional, eccentric, prim, cheap-looking, elegant?

7-29. Publicity photo of Marilyn Monroe in *The Seven Year Itch* (U.S.A., 1955), *directed by Billy Wilder.*

Variations of this image have become **iconographic** in American culture, replicated millions of times, and recognized by virtually everyone on the planet. Why did this image in particular capture the imagination of so many people? Perhaps it was the costume. (1) The *period* of the garment is 1955, but so classic in its lines that variations of the dress can still be found in stores. (2) The *class* of the dress is middle to upper-middle: It's an elegant, well-made party dress. (3) The *sex* is feminine in the extreme, emphasizing such erotic details as a plunging neckline and bare arms and back. (4) The *age* level would be suitable to any mature young woman (from the late teens to the mid-thirties) in good physical shape. (5) The *silhouette* is formfitting from the waist up, emphasizing Marilyn's famous breasts. The accordion-pleated flare skirt ordinarily would obscure her shape below the waist, but the updraft from the subway below swooshes the skirt toward her face. Her gesture of holding the skirt down near the crotch suggests a childish innocence and spontaneity. (6) The *fabric* is lightweight, suitable for a summer evening, probably a silk/cotton blend. (7) The *accessories* include only the circular earrings (hard to see in this photo) and the high-heeled strap sandals. The shoes are sexy and delicate, but not very practical. They make her look pampered and vulnerable and easy to catch. (8) The dress's *color* is white—pure, clean, untouched by the city's dirt. (9) There is quite a bit of *body exposure*—the arms, shoulders, back, cleavage, and—at least here—much of the upper thighs. (10) The *function* of the dress is recreational, not work-related. It's meant to attract attention. It's a dress to have fun in. (11) Marilyn's *body attitude* is childish exuberance—she's not in the least ashamed or embarrassed by her body and wears the outfit with confidence. (12) The general *image* suggests innocence, femininity, spontaneity, and a riveting sexual allure.   (Twentieth Century–Fox)

7-30. *Greystoke: The Legend of Tarzan, Lord of the Apes* (Great Britain, 1984), *directed by Hugh Hudson.*

Viewers are astonished by the extraordinary expressiveness of the apes in this movie, so uncanny in their ability to mimic human emotions that they almost seem human. Even more astonishing is the fact that the ape characters *are* human—they were played by actors wearing the brilliant makeup and costumes designed by Rick Baker and Paul Engelsen.   *(Warner Bros.)*

Makeup in the cinema is generally subtler than on stage. The theatrical actor uses makeup primarily to enlarge his or her features so they'll be visible from long distances. On the screen, makeup tends to be more understated, although Chaplin used stage makeup for the tramp character because he was generally photographed in long shot. Even the most delicate changes in makeup can be perceived in the cinema. Mia Farrow's pale green face in *Rosemary's Baby,* for example, was used to suggest the progressive corruption of her body while she is pregnant with the devil's child. Similarly, the ghoulish makeup of the actors in Fellini's *Satyricon* suggests the degeneracy and death-in-life aspect of the Roman population of the period. In *The Graduate,* Anne Bancroft is almost chalk white in the scene where she is betrayed by her lover.

In *Tom Jones,* Richardson used elaborate, artificial makeup on the city characters like Lady Bellaston to suggest their deceitfulness and decadence. (In the eighteenth-century comedy of manners, cosmetics are a favorite source of imagery to suggest falseness and hypocrisy.) The country characters, on the other hand, especially Sophy Western, are made up more naturally, with no wigs, powder, and patches.

330

7–31. *Aladdin* (U.S.A., 1992), *directed by John Musker and Ron Clements.*
Animation offers unlimited possibilities in terms of costumes, settings, and special effects precisely because they are all drawn into the image. It's just as easy (and just as cheap) to draw a magic carpet flying over Arabia as it is to draw two people talking in an ordinary room. Animation is able to whisk us off to fantastic worlds with the whirl of a paintbrush and a sprinkling swirl of sparkles. Not to speak of the witty transformations of a fast-talking genie, voiced by Robin Williams in his most manic motormouth mode.

Cinematic makeup is closely associated with the type of performer wearing it. In general, stars prefer makeup that tends to glamorize them. Monroe, Garbo, and Harlow usually had an ethereal quality. Marlene Dietrich probably knew more about makeup than any star of her generation—glamour makeup, that is. Straight actors and actor stars are less concerned with glamour unless the characters they're playing are in fact glamorous. In an effort to submerge their own personalities, such performers often use makeup to disfigure the familiarity of their features. Brando and Olivier were particularly likely to wear false noses, wigs, and distorting cosmetics. Because Orson Welles was known primarily for playing strong domineering roles, he resorted to such tricks in makeup to maximize the differences between his roles. Nonprofessional players probably wear the least amount of makeup, since they're chosen precisely because of their interesting and authentic physical appearance.

In exploring the dramatic aspects of a movie, we ought to ask ourselves how time, space, and language are exploited. If the film is a theatrical adaptation, was the play opened up or did the director confine the action to a limited playing area? Why? Could the movie be adapted for the stage? How prominent is the director's hand in the film? What kind of sets are used and why? What do the costumes tell us about their wearers? Is the makeup slight and realistic or are the actors' faces totally altered cosmetically?

FURTHER READING

BARSACQ, LEON, *Caligari's Cabinets and Other Grand Illusions: A History of Film Design* (New York: New American Library, 1978). Copiously illustrated, written by a distinguished French designer.

CHIERICHETTI, DAVID, *Hollywood Costume Design* (New York: Harmony Books, 1976). Lavishly illustrated.

GAINES, JANE M., and CHARLOTTE HERZOG, *Fabrications: Costume and the Female Body* (New York: Routledge, 1990). Feminist emphasis.

GARNETT, TAY. *Directing* (Lanham, Md.: Scarecrow Press, 1996). A filmmaker queries fellow directors about their art.

HEISNER, BEVERLY, *Hollywood Art* (Jefferson, N.C. and London: McFarland, 1990). Art direction during the big-studio era.

LOBRUTTO, VINCENT, ed. *By Design* (New York: Praeger, 1992). Interviews with movie production designers.

McCONATHY, DALE, and DIANA VREELAND, *Hollywood Costume* (Englewood Cliffs, N.J.: Prentice-Hall, 1977). Lavishly illustrated, authoritative.

MORDDEN, ETHAN, *The Hollywood Studios* (New York: Alfred A. Knopf, 1988). A well-written account of the "house style" of the major studios of the golden age—the 1930s and 1940s.

NEUMANN, DIETRICH, ed. *Film Architecture: Set Designs from* Metropolis *to* Blade Runner (Munich, London, New York: Prestel, 1999). Generously illustrated.

ROACH, MARY ELLEN, and JOANNE BUBOLZ EICHER, *Dress, Adornment and the Social Order* (New York: John Wiley, 1965). A collection of useful articles.

Story

8

Paramount Pictures

*Narratives are composed in order to reward, modify,
frustrate, or defeat the perceiver's search for coherence.*
—DAVID BORDWELL

Overview

Stories: showing and telling. Narratology. Who's telling the story? Voice-over narrators: characters as storytellers. Realistic, classical, and formalist narratives. Story versus plot. The role of the spectator: co-creator in making meaning. Meaning from outside: star iconography, genre expectations, the symbolic implications of titles, credit sequences, the musical score. The seductive lure of what happens next? Classical narrative structure: shaping the conflict, motivating the action. The narrative elegance of Buster Keaton's *The General*. Realistic narratives. Realism as a style: the illusion of being "lifelike." Slice-of-life, open-ended stories. The pretense of authorial neutrality. Realism's tradition of "shocking" exposés. Formalistic narratives: the importance of pattern and design as values in themselves. Intrusive narrators: brazen manipulation of the storytelling apparatus. Nonfictional narratives: documentaries and avant-garde films. New technologies, new truths: *cinéma vérité*. Neutrality versus propaganda. Genre and myth. Screwball comedies, coming-of-age films, musicals, science fiction. The need to repeat: genre cycles. Primitive, classical, revisionist, and parodic phases of a genre's evolution. Jung and Freud. The social need for myths.

Since ancient times, people have been intrigued by the seductive powers of storytelling. In *The Poetics,* Aristotle distinguished between two types of fictional narratives: *mimesis* (showing) and *diegesis* (telling). *Mimesis* is the province of the live theater, where the events "tell themselves." *Diegesis,* the province of the literary epic and the novel, is a story told by a narrator who is sometimes reliable, sometimes not. Cinema combines both forms of storytelling and hence is a more complex medium, with a wider range of narrative techniques at its disposal **(8–1).**

8–1. *Angela's Ashes* **(U.S.A., 1999),** *with Joe Breen (front center), directed by Alan Parker.*
Though the book and movie versions of *Angela's Ashes* tell the same story, the emotional effect of each is different, reflecting the strengths and weaknesses of *diegesis* (telling) versus *mimesis* (showing). Frank McCourt's literary memoir of his impoverished Irish childhood was considered "relentlessly bleak" by many critics. Nonetheless, it was a huge success, winning a Pulitzer Prize for nonfiction. The book was also translated into 25 languages and sold over 6 million copies in 30 countries. Critical commentators noted how the memoir's portrayal of appalling poverty is balanced by McCourt's frequent use of humor. In adapting the book into a screenplay, Alan Parker and Laura Jones tried to preserve this balance, but the movie version seems much harsher and more depressing because the grim visuals totally overpower the voice-over narrator's occasional humorous observations. The book's delicate balance between pathos and comedy was lost, and the movie was not a commercial success, even though McCourt expressed strong admiration for Parker's work. *(Paramount Pictures and Polygram Holding, Inc.)*

8–2a. *Speed* (U.S.A., 1994), *with Keanu Reeves and Sandra Bullock, directed by Jan De Bont.* *(Twentieth Century–Fox)*

8–2b. *The Home and the World* (India, 1984), *with Victor Bannerjee and Soumitra Chatterjee, directed by Satyajit Ray.* *(European Classic)*

Ever since the silent era, commentators have remarked on how "fast" American films move compared to the "slow" Europeans and the "very slow" movies of Asia. Even today, American films feature narratives that jump-start almost immediately and drive relentlessly toward a climactic explosion of action. *Speed,* for example, is about a psychopath who plants a bomb on a bus, which must be driven above 50 mph or it'll explode, killing all its passengers. The task of driving the vehicle through city traffic falls on the Bullock character, who is totally out of her element, though she is guided in her heroic efforts by a resourceful police officer (Reeves). Everything in the story is geared toward a fast-moving narrative: the very premise of the film, the time limit, the speed limit, the volatile urban environment, and the tense cross-cutting between the heroes and the villains. *The Home and the World* is an adaptation of a novel by the Indian Nobel laureate, Rabindranath Tagore. Set in the early twentieth century, the movie is a subtle psychological study of a triangle involving a rich, liberal, and high-caste Hindu who urges his wife (Chatterjee) to emerge from the traditional *purdah* (seclusion) to meet his best friend, a charismatic revolutionary (Bannerjee). Ironically, she eventually falls in love with the friend. The story moves slowly, emphasizing the heroine's insecure, tentative steps toward intellectual independence. There are very few big dramatic scenes, for she rarely ventures outside her home. The action is mostly interior—psychological and spiritual rather than physical. Realist film artists like the great Satyajit Ray are usually at their best when the action is slowed down to correspond to the rhythms of nature. Such stories require more patience than the lapel-grabbing urgency of a movie like *Speed.* Each movie provides its own kind of pleasure, each at its own natural pace.

Narratology

Scholars in modern times have also studied narrative forms, with most of the focus devoted to literature, film, and drama. Narratology, as this new interdisciplinary field was called in the 1980s, is a study of how stories work, how we make sense of the raw materials of a narrative, how we fit them together to form a coherent whole. It is also the study of different narrative structures, storytelling strategies, aesthetic conventions, types of stories (**genres**), and their symbolic implications.

In traditional terms, narratologists are interested in the "rhetoric" of storytelling; that is, the *forms* that "message senders" use to communicate with "message receivers." In cinema, a problem with this triadic communications model is determining who the sender is. The implied author is the filmmaker. However, many stories are not created by a single storyteller. Multiple authorship of scripts is common, especially in the United States, where the story is often pieced together by producers, directors, writers, and **stars**—a truly joint enterprise. Even prestigious filmmakers like Fellini, Kurosawa, and Truffaut preferred collaborating with others in creating the events of a story.

The problem of the elusive film author is complicated when a movie has a **voice-over** narration **(8–5).** Usually this off-screen narrator is also a character

8–3.   *Boogie Nights* (U.S.A., 1997), *with Mark Wahlberg and Burt Reynolds, written and directed by Paul Thomas Anderson.*
Some film artists are more concerned with exploring their characters than with creating a strong storyline. Anderson's fascinating portrayal of a young porn star (Wahlberg) and his "family" of work associates in the 1970s and early 1980s captures an era of radically changing sexual values in America. The narrative structure is loose and rambling, accommodating a wide variety of off-beat characters and events. Anderson's emphasis is on the damaged—and often surprisingly sympathetic—people in the pornography industry of the period.   *(New Line Cinema)*

8–4. *Masculine–Feminine* **(France, 1966),** *with Chantal Goya and Jean-Pierre Léaud, directed by Jean-Luc Godard.*

"I consider myself an essayist," Godard said, "producing essays in novel form or novels in essay form: only instead of writing, I film them." Godard's cinematic essays are a frontal attack on the dominance of classical cinema. "The Americans are good at storytelling," he noted, "the French are not. Flaubert and Proust can't tell stories. They do something else. So does the cinema. I prefer to use a kind of tapestry, a background on which I can embroider on my own ideas." Instead of scripts, Godard set up dramatic situations, then asked his actors to improvise their dialogue, as in this interview scene—a technique he derived from the documentary movement called *cinéma vérité*. He intersperses these scenes with digressions, opinions, and jokes. Above all, he wanted to capture the spontaneity of the moment, which he believed was more authentic when he and his actors had to fend for themselves, without the security of a script. "If you know in advance everything you are going to do, it isn't worth doing," Godard insisted. "If a show is all written down, what is the point of filming it? What use is cinema if it trails after literature?" See also Louis D. Giannetti, "Godard's *Masculine–Feminine*: The Cinematic Essay," in *Godard and Others: Essays in Film Form* (Cranbury, N.J.: Fairleigh Dickinson University Press, 1975). *(Columbia Pictures)*

in the story and hence has a vested interest in "helping" us interpret the events. A film's narrator is not necessarily neutral. Nor is he or she necessarily the film-maker's mouthpiece. Sometimes the narrator—as in the **first-person** novel—is the main character of a movie. (For a fuller discussion of these ideas, see the "Spoken Language" section of Chapter 5 and "Point of View" in Chapter 9.)

Narration also differs according to a movie's style. In **realistic** films, the implied author is virtually invisible. The events "speak for themselves," as they do in most stage plays. The story seems to unfold automatically, usually in chronological sequence.

In **classical** narrative structures, we are generally aware of a shaping hand in the storyline. Boring gaps in the narrative are edited out by a discreet storyteller, who keeps a low profile yet still keeps the action on track, moving toward a specific destination—the resolution of the story's central conflict.

In **formalistic** narratives, the author is overtly manipulative, sometimes scrambling the chronology of the story or heightening or restructuring events

8–5. *The Shawshank Redemption* (U.S.A., 1994), *with Morgan Freeman and Tim Robbins, directed by Frank Darabont.*

Who tells the story and why? These are two questions every spectator should ask of a story. This movie centers primarily on the character of Andy (Robbins), a man who is imprisoned for killing his wife and her lover. Inside prison he meets Red (Freeman), who becomes his closest friend. The story is narrated by Red in a voice-over. But why him? We never get inside Andy's mind the way we do with Red, who is a more ordinary person, more like us. He never fully understands what's going on in his friend's head, so we (like Red) are limited in our knowledge. We are kept in suspense about Andy until the very end—with its surprise twists. If Andy had told his own story in the first person, there would have been no suspense and no surprises because Andy would have told us in advance what he was going to do. And that's why Red tells the story. See also Sarah Kozloff, *Invisible Storytellers* (Berkeley: University of California Press, 1988), which analyzes voice-over narration in American fiction films. *(Castle Rock Entertainment)*

to maximize a thematic idea. The story is told from a subjective perspective, as in Oliver Stone's polemic *JFK* (**8–20**).

Narratology is often arcane, and occasionally incomprehensible, because of its abstract language and jargon. Exotic terms are often used to describe traditional concepts. For example, the differences between a story and its plot structure (that is, between a narrative's content and its form) can be expressed in a bewildering assortment of terms. *Story* versus *discourse* are favored by many American scholars. Others prefer *histoire* versus *discours, mythos* versus *logos*, or *fabula* versus *syuzhet*.

What are the differences between story and plot? The story can be defined as the general subject matter, the raw materials of a dramatic action in chronological sequence. The plot, on the other hand, involves the storyteller's method of superimposing a structural pattern over the story.

The implied author motivates the characters and provides a cause–effect logic to the sequence of events. Peter Brooks defines plot as "the design and intention of narrative, what shapes a story and gives it a certain direction or intention of meaning." In short, plot involves the implied author's point of view as well as the structuring of the scenes into an aesthetic pattern.

The Spectator

It's impossible to understand a movie without being actively engaged in a dynamic interplay with its narrative logic. Most of us have been watching movies and television for so long that we're hardly aware of our instantaneous adjustments to an unfolding plot. We absorb auditory and visual stimuli at an incredibly rapid rate. Like a complex computer, our brain click-clicks away in many language systems simultaneously: photographic, spatial, kinetic, vocal, histrionic, musical, sartorial, and so on.

But in the American cinema especially, the story reigns supreme. All the other language systems are subordinated to the plot, the structural spine of virtually all American fiction films, and most foreign movies as well.

David Bordwell and others have explored how the spectator is constantly interacting with a movie's narrative. We attempt to superimpose our sense of order and coherence on the film's world. In most cases, we bring a set of expectations to a movie even before we've seen it. Our knowledge of a given era or genre leads us to expect a predictable set of variables. For example, most westerns take place in the late nineteenth century and are set in the American western frontier. From books, TV, and other westerns, we have a rough knowledge of how frontier people were supposed to dress and behave.

When narratives fail to act according to tradition, **convention,** or our sense of history, as in Mel Brooks's *Blazing Saddles,* we are forced to reassess our cognitive methods and our attitude toward the narrative. Either we adjust to the author's presentation, or we reject the offending innovation as inappropriate, crude, or self-indulgent.

Narrational strategies are often determined by genre. For example, in those types of movies that thrive on suspense (thrillers, police stories, mysteries), the narrative will deliberately withhold information, forcing us to guess, to fill in the gaps. In romantic comedies, on the other hand, we generally know the outcome in advance. The emphasis is on *how* boy wins girl (or vice versa), not if he or she wins.

Our prior knowledge of a film's star also defines its narrative parameters. We wouldn't expect to see Clint Eastwood in a Shakesperean adaptation. Eastwood's expertise is in action genres, especially westerns and contemporary urban crime stories. With personality stars especially, we can guess the essential nature of a film's narrative in advance. With actor stars like Jennifer Lopez, however, we are less certain about what to expect, for Lopez's range is extraordinarily broad.

Audiences also judge a film in advance by the connotations of its title. A movie with a moronic title like *Attack of the Killer Bimbos* is not likely to be shown at the prestigious New York Film Festival. On the other hand, *Lady Windermere's*

8–6a. *Kolya* **(Czech Republic, 1997),** *with Zdenek Sverak and Andrej Chalimon, directed by Jan Sverak.* *(Miramax Films)*

Action and character might almost be viewed as natural enemies in a film's narrative. To get to know a character in depth, it's generally necessary to slow down the story's forward thrust. European filmmakers like Jan Sverak are widely regarded as masters of characterization, in part because the narrative is not forced—it's allowed to move at a realistic pace, as in *Kolya*. American movies are often criticized for piling on too much action, thus shortchanging the audience of any depth or richness or complexity in the characterization.

Movies like *Ronin* are so packed with nonstop action that critic Richard Schickel compared them to pop versions of action paintings, a kind of cinematic abstract expressionism. Watching such films is like entering a two-dimensional world where the main interest is how the director slapped, slathered, or slashed his colors onto the surface of a canvas. Though he described *Ronin* as a "sly masterpiece," Schickel believes that "the only message this film wants to convey is that in action movies it's not what you say but how smashingly you say it that counts."

8–6b. *Ronin* **(U.S.A., 1998),** *with Jean Reno, directed by John Frankenheimer.* *(United Artists)*

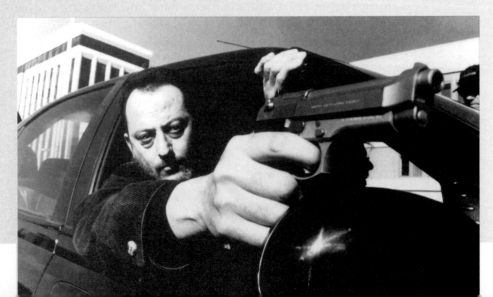

Fan would probably not play at the local mall theater because of its somewhat effete, aristocratic-sounding title. Of course, there are always exceptions. *Sammy and Rosie Get Laid* sounds like a porno film, but it's actually a respected (and sexy) British social comedy. Its title is deliberately aggressive, a bit crude. It's meant to be.

Once a movie begins, we begin to define its narrative limits. The style of the credits and the accompanying score help us to determine the tone of the picture. In the early exposition scenes, the filmmaker sets up the story variables and mood, establishing the premise that will drive the narrative forward. The beginning scenes imply how the narrative will be developed and where it's likely to end up.

The opening expository scenes also establish the internal "world" of the story—what's possible, what's probable, what's not very likely, and so on. In retrospect, there should be no loose threads in a story if the implied author has done a careful job of foreshadowing. In *E.T.: The Extra-Terrestrial*, for example, Spielberg prepares us for the supernatural events that occur in the middle and later portions of the movie because the opening scene (showing us how E.T. got left behind by his spaceship) establishes supernaturalism as a narrative variable.

When a critic asked the radical innovator Jean-Luc Godard if he believed that a movie should have a beginning, middle, and end, the iconoclastic filmmaker replied: "Yes—but not necessarily in that order." The opening exposition scenes of most movies establish the time frame of the story—whether it will unfold in **flashbacks,** in the present, or in some combination. The exposition also establishes the ground rules about fantasy scenes, dreams, and the stylistic variables associated with these levels of the story (**8–8**).

8–7. *Longtime Companion* **(U.S.A., 1990),** *with Bruce Davison and Campbell Scott, directed by Norman René.*
Many movies are structured around the Grand Hotel formula, so called after the 1932 film that features an assortment of characters who are thrown together in a single location or are unified by a common concern or a shared lifestyle. This anthology formula is ideal for exploring multiple narratives, with no single storyline predominating. *Longtime Companion* centers on a group of (mostly gay) friends and how they cope with a strange new disease—AIDS. The story begins in the early 1980s, with the discovery of the fatal illness, and ends ten years later, after many of the characters have died from it. *(The Samuel Goldwyn Company)*

8–8   *8½ (Italy, 1963), with Sandra Milo and Marcello Mastroianni, directed by Federico Fellini.* Although it is one of the most admired movies in the history of the cinema, Fellini's masterpiece features a plot that's diabolically baroque. Most viewers are unable to comprehend it all on first viewing because it's constantly shifting levels of consciousness without warning. Fantasies spill over onto reality, which splashes over memories, which fuse with dreams, which turn into nightmares, which . . .   *(Embassy Pictures)*

An elaborate game is played out between a cinematic narrative and the spectator. While watching a movie, we must sort out irrelevant details, hypothesize, test our hypotheses, retreat if necessary, adapt, formulate explanations, and so on. The spectator is constantly subjecting the narrative to questions. Why does the heroine do that? Why does her boyfriend respond that way? What will the mother do now? And so on.

The more complex the plot, the more cunning we must be—sorting, sifting, weighing new evidence, inferring motives and explanations, ever suspicious of being taken off guard. We constantly monitor the narrative for unexpected reversals, especially in deceptive genres, such as thrillers, detective movies, and police films.

In short, we are never really passive in the face of a film's plot. Even when the story is boring, mechanical, and utterly derivative, we still can get sucked into its plot machinations. We want to know where the action is leading: We can find out only if we go along.

8–9a. *My Life As a Dog* **(Sweden, 1985),** *with Anton Glanzelius (center), directed by Lasse Hallström.* (Skouras Pictures)

8–9b. *The Insider* **(U.S.A., 1999),** *with Russell Crowe, directed by Michael Mann.* (© Touchstone Pictures. All Rights Reserved.)

Some movies are so unusual that it's virtually impossible to predict where the plot will lead. In *My Life As a Dog*, for example, the young hero is separated from his parents and moves in with an eccentric uncle and aunt in a remote village. His escapades in the country are bizarre, funny, and totally unpredictable. On the other hand, creating suspense is very difficult when audiences already know the outcome of a story. For example, *The Insider* focuses on Dr. Jeffrey Wigand (Crowe), whose life was almost ruined when he blew the whistle on the tobacco industry by exposing its lies and hypocrisy on the television news magazine, *60 Minutes*. Despite its artistic excellence, the film failed to excite much interest with the public, and it was a box-office disappointment.

The Classical Paradigm

The classical paradigm is a term invented by scholars to describe a certain kind of narrative structure that has dominated fiction film production ever since the 1910s. It's by far the most popular type of story organization, especially in the United States, where it reigns virtually unchallenged. The model is called "classical" because it's a norm of actual practice, not necessarily because of a high degree of artistic excellence. In other words, bad movies as well as good ones use this narrative formula.

Derived from the live theater, the classical paradigm is a set of conventions, not rules. This narrative model is based on a conflict between a protagonist, who initiates the action, and an antagonist, who resists it. Most films in this form begin with an implied dramatic question. We want to know how the protagonist will get what he or she wants in the face of considerable opposition. The following scenes intensify this conflict in a rising pattern of action. This escalation is treated in terms of cause–effect, with each scene implying a link to the next.

The conflict builds to its maximum tension in the climax. Here, the protagonist and antagonist clash overtly. One wins, the other loses. After their confrontation, the dramatic intensity subsides in the resolution. The story ends with

8–10. The classical paradigm.

Aristotle implicitly suggested the structure of classical drama in *The Poetics,* but it was not until the nineteenth century that the inverted V structure was diagrammed by the German scholar Gustav Freytag. This type of narrative structure begins with an overt conflict, which is increasingly intensified with the rising action of the following scenes. Details that don't relate to this conflict are eliminated or kept incidental. The battle between the main character and his or her antagonists reaches its highest pitch in the climax. In the resolution, the strands of the story are tied up and life returns to normal with a closing off of the action.

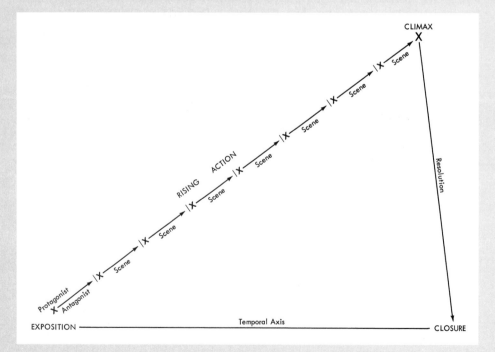

some kind of formal closure—traditionally a wedding or a dance in comedies, a death in tragedies, a reunion or return to normal in dramas. The final **shot**—because of its privileged position—is often meant to be a philosophical overview of some kind, a summing up of the significance of the previous material.

The classical paradigm emphasizes dramatic unity, plausible motivations, and coherence of its constituent parts. Each shot is seamlessly elided to the next in an effort to produce a smooth flow of action, and often a sense of inevitability. To add urgency to the conflict, filmmakers sometimes include some kind of deadline, thus intensifying the emotion. During the Hollywood studio era especially, classical structures often featured double plot lines, in which a romantic love story was developed to parallel the main line of action. In love stories, a comic second couple often paralleled the main lovers.

Classical plot structures are linear and often take the form of a journey, a chase, or a search. Even the characters are defined primarily in terms of what they do. "Action is character" insists Syd Field, the author of several handbooks on screenwriting. "What a person does is what he is, not what he says." Field and other advocates of the classical paradigm are not very interested in passive characters—people to whom things are done. (These types of characters are more typical in foreign films.) Classicists favor characters who are goal oriented so that we can take a rooting interest in their plans of action.

Field's conceptual model is expressed in traditional theatrical terms **(8–11).** A screenplay is composed of three acts. Act I, "Setup," occupies the first quarter of the script. It establishes the dramatic premise: What is the main character's goal and what obstacles are likely to get in the way of its attainment? Act II, "Confrontation," consists of the middle two quarters of the story, with a major reversal of fortune at the midpoint. This portion of the screenplay complicates the conflict with plot twists and an increasing sense of urgency, showing the main character fighting against obstacles. Act III, "Resolution," constitutes

8–11. According to Syd Field, the narrative structure of a movie can be broken down into three acts. The story should contain about ten to twenty "plot points," major twists or key events in the action. At the midpoint of the second act, there is usually a big reversal of expectations, sending the action spinning in a new direction. Although the diagram might not be helpful in analyzing most realistic or formalistic narratives, it is surprisingly apt in movies using a classical structure.

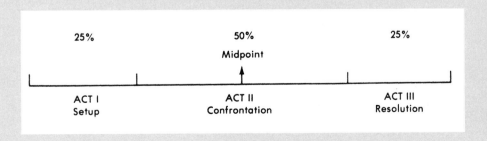

the final quarter of the story. This section dramatizes what happens as a result of the climactic confrontation.

One of the greatest plots in the history of cinema is found in Buster Keaton's *The General,* a textbook example of the classical paradigm. It fits Freytag's inverted V structure as well as Field's three-act play approach. As Daniel Moews has pointed out, all of Keaton's feature-length comedies use the same basic comic formula. Buster begins as a sincere but clumsy greenhorn who bungles every attempt to ingratiate himself with a person he holds in awe—usually a pretty girl. At the conclusion of the day, he falls asleep, lonely, depressed, and dispirited. When he awakens, he's a new man. He goes on to succeed, usually at the same or parallel activities of the earlier portions of the movie.

A Civil War comedy loosely based on an actual event, *The General* is laid out with the narrative elegance of a play by Congreve. The first act establishes the two loves in the hero's life: his train, *The General,* and Annabelle Lee, his somewhat flaky girlfriend. His only friends, apparently, are two prepubescent boys. (Among other things, the movie is a coming-of-age story.) When war is

8–12.   An outline of the plot structure of *The General*.
The plot moves forward with such smoothness and poise that we're hardly aware of its dazzling symmetry until the second chase, when most of the earlier gag clusters are triumphantly reprised.

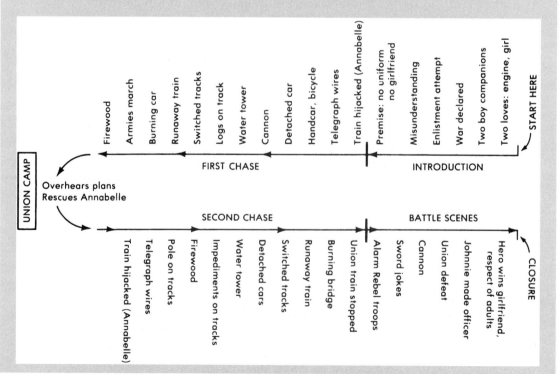

declared, our hero, Johnnie Gray, trying to impress his girl, attempts to enlist. But he's rejected by the authorities: He's more valuable to the South as an engineer. Through a misunderstanding, Annabelle thinks Johnnie is a coward. "I don't want you to speak to me again until you are in uniform," she haughtily informs him. End of Act I.

A full year is edited out of the story as we begin Act II. (The rest of the movie covers only about twenty-four hours.) We see the plans of the Union officers to hijack a Confederate train, thereby cutting off the supply lines of the Southern army. The Yankee leader's map shows the major stops and rivers along the railroad route. In fact, this map is a geographical outline of Act II.

On the day that the hijacking is to take place, Annabelle Lee boards Johnnie's train to visit her wounded father. She snubs her former suitor. The hijacking of the train sets off the rising action. The second quarter of the movie is a chase sequence: Johnnie pursues the stolen *General* (with Annabelle on board) as it flees northward. There are a series of gag clusters, each involving different props, such as telegraph wires, switched tracks, a water tower, a cannon **(8–13)**, and so on. Johnnie is usually the butt of the jokes.

At the midpoint of the film, our hero sneaks into the enemy's camp, alone and exhausted. Nonetheless, he manages to rescue Annabelle. They fall asleep in the woods in a downpour, discouraged, almost wiped out.

8-13. *The General* (U.S.A., 1927), *with Buster Keaton, directed by Keaton and Clyde Bruckman.* Silent film comedians were masters of improvisation, capable of spinning off a profusion of gags with a single prop. For example, the gag cluster involving this cannon is a miniature drama, complete with exposition, variations on a theme that constitute the rising action, and a thrilling climax that serves as a topper to the sequence. Even more extraordinary, Keaton and his regular crew never used written scripts or shooting schedules. They knew only the premise of the film and its conclusion. The rest was improvised. They shot for about eight weeks, making due allowances for baseball games between scenes. Later, Keaton viewed all the footage, edited out the dull stuff, and created the narrative structure.   *(United Artists)*

The next day, a second chase begins, reversing the pattern of the previous day, and taking up the third quarter of the plot. Now the jokes are inflicted on the pursuing Yankees as Johnnie and Annabelle speed southward in the recaptured *General*. The gag clusters are also reversed. Most of them are parallels to those of the first chase: telegraph wires, logs on the tracks, a water tower, a burning bridge, and so on. Just in time, Johnnie and Annabelle arrive at the Confederate camp and warn the troops of an impending Union attack.

Act III is a battle sequence between the two great armies. Johnnie shows himself to be a doggedly perseverant soldier, though not always a successful one. He is rewarded for his heroism with a commission in the army. He also wins back the love of his girl. All ends happily.

Keaton's narrative structure follows an elaborately counterbalanced pattern, in which the earlier humiliations are triumphantly canceled out on the second day. Described thus schematically, Keaton's plots sound rather mechanical. But as his French admirers have pointed out, his architectural rigor can be likened to the works of the great neoclassical artists of the eighteenth century, with their intricately worked out parallels and neatly balanced symmetries.

Ordinarily, one would consider such an artificial plot structure as an example of a formalist narrative. However, the execution of each section is rigorously realistic. Keaton performed all his own gags (many of them dangerous), usually on the first **take.** He also insisted on absolute accuracy in the costuming, the sets, and even the trains, which are historically true to the period. This combination of realistic execution with a formally patterned narrative is typical of classical cinema. Classicism is an intermediate style that blends conventions from both stylistic extremes.

Realistic Narratives

Traditionally, critics have linked realism to "life," formalism with "pattern." Realism is defined as an absence of style, whereas style is a preeminent concern among formalists. Realists reject artifice to portray the material world "transparently," without distortion or even mediation. Conversely, formalists are concerned with fantasy materials or throwaway subject matter to emphasize the world of the imagination, of beauty for its own sake.

Today, these views are considered naive, at least so far as realism is concerned. Contemporary critics and scholars regard realism as a *style,* with an elaborate set of conventions that are less obvious perhaps, but just as artificial as those used by expressionists.

Both realistic and formalistic narratives are patterned and manipulated, but the realistic storyteller attempts to submerge the pattern, to bury it beneath the surface "clutter" and apparent randomness of the dramatic events. In other words, the pretense that a realistic narrative is "unmanipulated" or "like life" is precisely that—a pretense, an aesthetic deception.

8–14a. *Chinatown* (U.S.A., 1974), *with Faye Dunaway and Jack Nicholson, directed by Roman Polanski.* (Paramount Pictures)

8–14b. *A Simple Plan* (U.S.A., 1998), *with Bill Paxton and Billy Bob Thornton, directed by Sam Raimi.* (Paramount Pictures)

In genres that depend on mystery and suspense for their effects, the narrative often withholds information, forcing us to fill in the gaps, teasing and tantalizing us with possible solutions to mysteries that aren't totally resolved until the end of the movie. On the other hand, some thrillers provide the viewer with all the necessary information as it's needed. In *A Simple Plan*, for example, the emphasis is as much on character development as it is on action. Scott Smith wrote both the screenplay and the best-selling novel it was based on: "I wanted to portray a group of people who begin digging a deeper and deeper hole for themselves trying to hide something they've done," Smith explained. "They become driven, and then panicked, by the fear of getting caught. Desperate people have now turned into dangerous people."

8–15a. *Late Spring* **(Japan, 1949),** *with Chishu Ryu (seated) and Setsuko Hara (center),* *directed by Yasujiro Ozu.* (New Yorker Films)

Love and Marriage from a realist perspective. One of the most common genres in Japan is the home drama. It was the only genre Ozu worked in, and he was one of its most popular practitioners. This type of film deals with the day-to-day routines of domestic life. Although Ozu was a profoundly philosophical artist, his movies consist almost entirely of "little things"—the bitter pills of self-denial that ultimately render life disappointing. Many of Ozu's films have seasonal titles that symbolically evoke appropriate human analogues. *Late Spring,* for example, deals with the attempts of a decent widower (Ryu) to marry off his only daughter (Hara) before she wilts into spinsterhood.

   True Love is a wry exploration of male–female tensions in an Italian-American working-class community shortly before the marriage of the two main characters. Like most realistic movies, the plot line is loose. The scenes are arranged in apparently random order, and the everyday events are presented matter-of-factly, with no "heightening" for dramatic effect. The dialogue is raw, the language of the streets rather than the genteel living rooms of middle America. The conclusion of the film is ambivalent and ambiguous, with no neat solutions to the complex problems that the movie addresses.

8–15b. *True Love* **(U.S.A., 1989),** *with Kelly Cinnante and Annabella Sciorra, directed by* *Nancy Savoca.* (United Artists)

Realists prefer loose, discursive plots, with no clearly defined beginning, middle, or end. We dip into the story at an arbitrary point. Usually we aren't presented with a clear-cut conflict, as in classical narratives. Rather, the conflict emerges unobtrusively from the unforced events of the exposition. The story itself is presented as a "slice of life," as a poetic fragment, not a neatly structured tale. Rarely is reality neatly structured; realistic art must follow suit. Life goes on, even after the final reel.

Realists often borrow their structures from the cycles of nature. For example, many of the movies of Ozu are given seasonal titles that symbolize an appropriate human counterpart—*Early Summer, Late Autumn, Early Spring, The End of Summer, Late Spring* (8–15a). Other realistic films are structured around a limited period of time, like summer vacation or a school semester. Such movies sometimes center on **rites of passage,** such as birth, puberty, first love, first job, marriage, painful separations, death.

Often, we can't guess the principle of narrative coherence until the end of the movie, especially if it has a circular or cyclical structure, as many realistic films do. For example, Robert Altman's *M*A*S*H* opens with the fresh arrival of two soldier-surgeons, Hawkeye Pierce and Duke Forrest. The movie ends when their tour of duty is over. Yet the M*A*S*H unit will continue saving lives, even after these two excellent surgeons have left. (This same structural principle is used in a later military comedy, Barry Levinson's *Good Morning, Vietnam.*)

The episodic structure of *M*A*S*H* is what appealed to those who adapted it as a television series. Realistic film narratives frequently seem episodic, the sequence of events almost interchangeable. The plot doesn't "build" inexorably, but seems to drift into surprising scenes that don't necessarily propel the story forward. These are offered for their own sake, as examples of "real-life" oddities.

Spectators who like fast-moving stories are often impatient with realistic films, which frequently move slowly. This is especially true in the earlier scenes, while we wait for the main narrative strand to emerge. "Digressions" often turn out to be parallels to the central plotline. But this parallelism must be inferred; it's rarely pointed out explicitly. Other traits of realistic narratives include the following:

1. A nonintrusive implied author who "reports" objectively and avoids making judgments.
2. A rejection of clichés, stale conventions, stock situations and characters in favor of the unique, the concrete, the specific.
3. A fondness for exposé, with "shocking" or "low" subject matter that is often criticized for its grittiness and "bad taste."
4. An antisentimental point of view that rejects glib happy endings, wishful thinking, miraculous cures, and other forms of phony optimism.
5. An avoidance of melodrama and exaggeration in favor of understatement and dedramatization.

8-16. *Hate (La Haine)*, **(France, 1996),** *with Vincent Cassel, Said Taghmaoui, and Hubert Kounde; directed by Mathieu Kassovitz.*
Ever since the late nineteenth century, when it became a dominant international style in the arts, realism has provoked controversy for its "sordid" or "shocking" subject matter, its pre-occupation with details that the conventional majority finds repulsive but fascinating. *La Haine* caused an uproar in France when it was released. Its uncompromising portrayal of three lower-class thugs (pictured) makes it hard to sympathize with their plight. They are vicious and violent, their language a steady torrent of filth, and their values cynically corrupt. The movie offers very little hope for this doomed underclass. Viewers are likely to ask themselves: How did the world get this way?   *(Gramercy Pictures)*

6. A scientific view of causality and motivation, with a corresponding rejection of such romantic concepts as Destiny and Fate.

7. An avoidance of the **lyrical** impulse in favor of a plain, straightforward presentation.

Formalistic Narratives

Formalistic narratives revel in their artificiality. Time is often scrambled and rearranged to hammer home a thematic point more forcefully. The design of the plot is not concealed but heightened. It's part of the show. Formalistic plots come in a wide assortment, but usually they are structured according to the filmmaker's theme. For example, Alfred Hitchcock was obsessed by themes dealing with "doubles" and "the wrong man"—a technically innocent man who is accused of a crime committed by an undetected counterpart.

8–17a. ***The Lion King*** **(U.S.A., 1994),** *directed by Roger Allers and Rob Minkoff.*
Movie plots often derive from the weirdest sources. This is a coming-of-age story of a lion cub named Simba, who is next in line to succeed his father, a benevolent and wise leader. But the king's evil brother brings about the monarch's death, and Simba's destiny is to avenge his father's death and return legitimate rule to the jungle. Sound familiar? The story is a shameless steal from *Hamlet*, with touches of *Oedipus Rex*, the story of Moses, *Bambi*, and *The Jungle Book*. Pretty classy stuff.   *(© The Walt Disney Company. All Rights Reserved.)*

8–17b. ***Face/Off*** **(U.S.A., 1997),** *with Nicolas Cage and John Travolta, directed by John Woo.*
The narrative structure of this sci-fi thriller is a riff on the symbolic implications of the title. Traditionally, a face-off is a ritualistic dual of some sort (pictured). But in this movie, the two main characters literally exchange facial features—a plot device every bit as artificial as Shakespeare's delight in doubles: twin protagonists, gender switches, and mistaken identities. By assuming each other's identities, the two central characters of *Face/Off* are able to explore their other selves, their secret selves. Could these men be mirror images? *(Paramount Pictures)*

Hitchcock's *The Wrong Man* is his most explicit treatment of these narrative motifs. The entire plot is doubled, structured in twos. There are two imprisonments, two handwriting tests, two conversations in the kitchen, two legal hearings, two visits to a clinic, two visits to the lawyer. The hero is arrested twice by two policemen. He is identified (wrongly) by two witnesses at two different shops. There are two transfers of guilt: The main character (Henry Fonda) is accused of a crime he didn't commit, and midway through the movie, his emotionally disturbed wife (Vera Miles) takes on the guilt, requiring her to be committed to an asylum. "People say that Hitchcock lets the wires show too often," Jean-Luc Godard noted. "But because he shows them, they are no longer wires. They are the pillars of a marvelous architectural design made to withstand our scrutiny."

Many formalistic narratives are intruded on by the author, whose personality is part of the show. For example, it's virtually impossible to ignore the personality of Buñuel in his films. He slyly interjects his sardonic black humor into his narratives. He loves to undermine his characters—their pomposity, their self-deception, their mean little souls **(8–18).** Godard's personality is also highly intrusive, especially in his nontraditional narratives, which he called "cinematic essays."

8–18.   *The Discreet Charm of the Bourgeoisie* (France, 1972), *directed by Luis Buñuel.*
Most of Buñuel's movies feature bizarre scenes that are left unexplained, as though they were the most normal thing in the world. He delighted in satirizing middle-class hypocrisies, treating them with a kind of affectionate bemusement mingled with contempt. In this film, he presents us with a series of loosely connected episodes dealing with the inane rituals of a group of well-heeled semizombies. Interspersing these episodes are shots of the main characters walking on an empty road (pictured). No one questions why they are there. No one seems to know where they are going. Buñuel doesn't say.   *(Twentieth Century–Fox)*

8–19. *Mon Oncle d'Amerique* **(France, 1980),** *with Gerard Depardieu, directed by Alain Resnais.*

Depardieu portrays a hardworking idealist whose conservative values and faith in God are severely tested. The significance of the title? It's taken from European pop mythology—the proverbial adventurous uncle who left for America, made a fortune, and will someday return loaded with money to solve all their problems. Resnais was also thinking of Samuel Beckett's bitter stage comedy, *Waiting for Godot*, which revolves around an obscure figure (God?) who's constantly waited for, but never shows up. *(New World Pictures)*

Formalistic narratives are often interrupted by lyrical interludes, exercises in pure style—like the enchanting dance numbers in the Fred Astaire–Ginger Rogers RKO musicals of the 1930s. In fact, stylized genre films like musicals, science fiction, and fantasies offer the richest potential for displays of stylistic rapture and bravura effects. These lyrical interludes interrupt the forward momentum of the plot, which is often a mere pretext anyway.

An excellent example of a formalistic narrative is *Mon Oncle d'Amerique* (My Uncle in America), directed by Alain Resnais, with a script by Resnais and Jean Gruault **(8–19).** The film's structure is indebted to Godard's essay form, which can combine elements from the documentary and avant-garde film with fiction. The ideas in the movie are the stuff of Psychology 101. Resnais frames and intersperses his fictional episodes with footage of an actual medical doctor and behavioral scientist, Dr. Henri Laborit, who indulges in the French mania for dissection, analysis, and classification. He wittily discusses the relationship of human behavior to the makeup of the brain, the conscious and subconscious environment, social conditioning, the nervous system, zoology, and biology. He alludes to the behavior-modification theories of B. F. Skinner and other theories of human development.

The fictional episodes in the movie are concrete demonstrations of these theories. The characters are autonomous, not mechanized zombies. Nonetheless, they are victims of forces they hardly understand. Resnais focuses on three appealing characters. Each is the product of a unique biological makeup and cultural environment. Their paths intersect by chance. "These people have everything to make them happy," Resnais observed, "yet they're not happy at all. Why?"

Resnais then shows us why through his dazzling editing and multiple narratives. In a kaleidoscope of shifting perspectives, Resnais juxtaposes snippets of the characters' lives, dreams, and memories with Dr. Laborit's abstract formulations, statistics, and wry observations. The three main characters are movie freaks, and at various points during the story, Resnais intercuts brief clips from the films of their childhood idols—Jean Marais, Danielle Darrieux, and Jean Gabin. Some of these movie clips bear a not-so-coincidental resemblance to the dramatic situations of the characters. Resnais is also paying homage to three great stars of the French cinema.

Nonfictional Narratives

There are three broad classifications of motion pictures: fiction, documentary, and **avant-garde.** Documentaries and avant-garde films usually don't tell stories, at least not in the conventional (that is, fictional) sense. Of course, documentaries and avant-garde movies are structured, but neither uses a plot. Rather, the story—if any—is structured according to a theme or an argument, especially in documentaries. In the avant-garde cinema, the structure is often a matter of the filmmaker's subjective instincts.

First, documentaries. Unlike most fiction films, documentaries deal with facts—real people, places, and events rather than invented ones. Documentarists believe that they're not creating a world so much as reporting on the one that already exists. They are not just recorders of external reality, however, for like fiction filmmakers they shape their raw materials through their selection of details. These details are organized into a coherent artistic pattern. Many documentaries deliberately keep the structure of their films simple and unobtrusive. They want their version of the facts to suggest the same apparent randomness of life itself.

Sound familiar? In fact, the concepts of realism and formalism are almost as useful in discussing documentaries as fiction films. However, the overwhelming majority of documentarists would insist that their main interest is with subject matter rather than style.

The realistic documentary is best illustrated by the **cinéma vérité** or "direct cinema" movement of the 1960s. Because of the need to be able to capture news stories quickly, efficiently, and with a minimal crew, television journalism was responsible for the development of a new technology, which in turn eventually led to a new philosophy of truth in documentary cinema. The technology included the following:

1. A lightweight 16-mm hand-held camera, allowing the cinematographer to roam virtually anywhere with ease.

8–20. *JFK* (U.S.A., 1991), *with Kevin Costner (center), written and directed by Oliver Stone.* History as narrative. As a number of historians have pointed out, "history" is actually a jumble of fragments, unsifted facts, random events, and details that no one thought were important enough to explain. This chaos is sorted out by a historian who superimposes a narrative over the sprawling materials. The historian excludes some data, heightens others. Effects are provided with causes; isolated events are connected with other superficially remote events. In short, many modern historians would insist that the past contains various histories, not just one. Each history is the product of a person who assembles, interprets, and shapes the facts into a narrative. Oliver Stone's controversial depiction of the assassination of President Kennedy is told from the point of view of New Orleans D.A. Jim Garrison (Costner). The movie does what a historian does: It offers a possible explanation for a traumatic national tragedy that was never adequately resolved in the minds of much of the American public. *JFK* is a dazzling display of bravura editing, encompassing dozens of characters, many years, thousands of miles, and hundreds of thousands of historical facts. *(Warner Bros.)*

2. Flexible **zoom lenses,** allowing the cinematographer to go from 12-mm **wide-angle** positions to 120-mm **telephoto** positions in one adjusting bar.

3. New **fast film stocks,** permitting scenes to be photographed without the necessity of setting up lights. So sensitive were these stocks to available lighting that even nighttime scenes with minimal illumination could be recorded with acceptable clarity.

4. A portable tape recorder, allowing a technician to record sound directly in automatic **synchronization** with the visuals. This equipment was so easy to use that only two people—one at the camera, the other with the sound system—were required to bring in a news story.

8-21. *Law and Order* **(U.S.A., 1969),** *directed by Frederick Wiseman.*
Cinéma vérité, or direct cinema, prided itself on its objectivity and straightforward presentation. Certainly, these documentarists realized that total neutrality is an impossible goal to achieve. Even Wiseman, among the most objective of documentarists, insists that his movies are a subjective *interpretation* of actual events, people, and places. He tries to be as "fair" as possible in presenting his materials. For example, he refuses to use off-frame narrators. The subjects of the film are allowed to speak for themselves, and the burden of interpretation is placed on the spectators, who must analyze the significance of the material on their own. Of course, most participants are aware of being photographed, and this surely influences their behavior. No one wants to look like a fool on camera. *(Zipporah Films)*

The flexibility of this hardware permitted documentarists to redefine the concept of authenticity. This new aesthetic amounted to a rejection of preplanning and carefully detailed scripts. A script involves preconceptions about reality and tends to cancel out any sense of spontaneity or ambiguity. Direct cinema rejected such preconceptions as fictional: Reality is not being observed but is being arranged to conform to what the script says it is. The documentarist is superimposing a *plot* over the materials. Re-creations of any kind were no longer necessary because, if the crew members are present while an event is actually taking place, they can capture it while it's happening.

The concept of minimal interference with reality became the dominating preoccupation of the American and Canadian schools of cinéma vérité. The filmmaker must not control events in any way. Re-creations—even with the people and places actually involved—were unacceptable. Editing was kept to a minimum, for otherwise it could lead to a false impression of the sequence of

8–22. *Harlan County, U.S.A.* **(U.S.A., 1977),** *directed by Barbara Kopple.*
Direct cinema is most effective with materials that are intrinsically dramatic, like crisis situations in which a conflict is about to reach its climax. For example, during the production of this documentary, which deals with a bitter coal-miners' strike for decent working conditions, Kopple and her crew were repeatedly plunged in the middle of violence. In one sequence, they are actually fired on by a trigger-happy yahoo. The camera recorded it all. Implicit in the concept of documentary is the verb *to document*—to verify, to provide an irrefutable record of an event. In a nonfiction film, these privileged moments of truth generally take precedence over considerations of narrative. *(Museum of Modern Art)*

events. Actual time and space were preserved whenever possible by using **lengthy takes.**

Cinéma vérité also uses sound minimally. These filmmakers were—and still are—hostile to the "voice of God" commentaries that accompanied traditional documentaries. Off-screen narration tends to interpret images for the spectator, thus relieving us of the necessity of analyzing for ourselves. Some direct cinema advocates dispense with voice-over narration entirely **(8–21).**

The tradition of the formalistic or subjective documentary can be traced back to the Soviet filmmaker Dziga-Vertov. Like most Soviet artists of the 1920s, Vertov was a propagandist. He believed that the cinema should be a tool of the Revolution, a way of instructing workers about how to view events from an ideological perspective. "Art," he once wrote, "is not a *mirror* which reflects the historical struggle, but a *weapon* of that struggle."

Documentarists in this formalistic tradition tend to build their movies thematically, arranging and structuring the story materials to demonstrate a thesis, like the news stories on television's prestigious *60 Minutes.* In many cases, the sequence of shots and even entire scenes can be switched around with relatively

8–23. *Point of Order!* **(U.S.A., 1964),** *directed by Emile De Antonio.*
Materials that might seem politically neutral can acquire ideological significance when the footage is reedited expressively. Many documentaries in the Vertov mold—like this exposé of the political sleazebag Senator Joe McCarthy—were originally photographed by relatively impartial newsreel camera operators. The ideology is conveyed by the way in which this neutral material is restructured on the editing bench, a striking instance of how "plot" (or narrative structure) can radically alter "story." All montage films making use of newsreels descend from Vertov's theories. See also Jay Leyda, *Films Beget Films* (New York: Hill & Wang, 1964). *(Continental Distributing)*

little loss of sense or logic. The structure of the film is not based on chronology or narrative coherence, but on the documentarist's argument **(8–23).**

Avant-garde films are so variable that it's hard to generalize about their narrative structures. Most of these movies don't even try to tell a story. Autobiographical elements are common. Many avant-garde artists are primarily concerned with conveying their "inner impulses," their personal and subjective involvements with people, ideas, and experiences. For this reason, avant-garde movies are sometimes obscure and even incomprehensible. Many of these filmmakers create their own personal language and symbology.

With few exceptions, avant-garde films are not written out in advance. In part this is because the same artist usually shoots and edits the footage and is therefore able to control the material at these stages of the filmmaking process. Avant-garde filmmakers also value chance and spontaneity in their movies, and to exploit these elements, they avoid the inflexibility of a script.

Maya Deren, an American avant-garde filmmaker of the 1940s, differentiated her kind of movie (which she called "personal" or "poetic") from mainstream commercial films primarily in terms of structure. Like a lyric poem, personal films are "vertical" investigations of a theme or situation. The filmmaker is not concerned so much with what's happening as with what a situ-

360

ation feels like or what it means. The film artist is concerned with probing the depths and layers of meaning of a given moment.

Fiction movies, on the other hand, are like novels and plays, according to Deren. They're essentially "horizontal" in their development. Narrative filmmakers use linear structures that must progress from situation to situation, from feeling to feeling. Fiction directors don't have much time to explore the implications of a given idea or emotion, for they must keep the plot "moving along."

Other avant-garde filmmakers disdain any kind of recognizable subject matter. Hans Richter and other early avant-garde artists in Europe totally rejected narrative. Richter was a champion of the "absolute film," which consists solely of abstract shapes and designs (see **4–7**). Insisting that movies should have nothing to do with acting, stories, or literary themes, Richter believed that film—like music and abstract painting—should be concerned with pure nonrepresentational forms. Many contemporary avant-garde filmmakers share these biases (**8–24**).

8-24. *Razor Blades* (U.S.A., 1968),
directed by Paul Sharits.
Structuralism was an avant-garde movement that rejected narrative in favor of an abstract structure that owed nothing to subject matter. In the structuralist cinema, the codes of cognition are totally self-defined. They are structured according to the principles of recurrence, dialectical polarities, time and space increments, and so on. The process of deciphering these cognitive codes and their interrelationships is analogous to the film's working itself out, fulfilling its structural destiny. In Sharits's flicker film, two images (requiring separate screens and projectors) are simultaneously juxtaposed. Each filmstrip consists of irregularly recurring images—two or three frames in duration, interspersed by blank or color frames—or purely abstract designs, like colored stripes or circular shapes. The rapid flickering of images creates a mesmerizing stroboscopic effect, testing the audience's psychological and physiological tolerance. The content of the film is its structural form rather than the subject matter of the images as images.   *(Anthology Film Archives)*

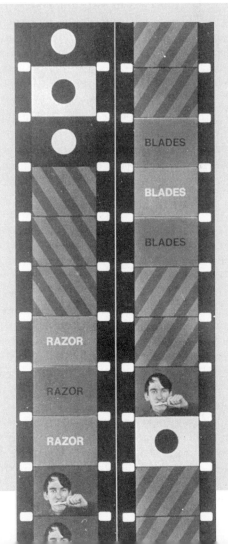

Genre and Myth

A genre film is a specific type of movie: a war picture, a gangster film, science fiction, and so on. There are literally hundreds of them, especially in the United States and Japan, where virtually all fiction movies can be classified according to genre. Genres are distinguished by a characteristic set of conventions in style, subject matter, and values. Genre is also a convenient way of focusing and organizing the story materials.

Many genre films are directed at a specific audience. Coming-of-age films are generally aimed at teenagers. Action-adventure genres tend to focus on all-male activities. Women are usually relegated to an incidental function, or they provide "romantic interest." The American **woman's picture** and Japanese mother films focus on domestic life. In these female-oriented genres, men are conventionalized in a similar manner—usually as breadwinners, sexual objects, or "the other man."

André Bazin once referred to the western as "a form in search of a content." The same could be said of all genre films. A genre is a loose set of expectations, then, not a divine injunction. That is, each example of a given story type is related to its predecessors, but not in ironclad bondage. Some genre films are good; others are terrible. It's not the genre that determines artistic excellence, but how well the artist exploits the conventions of its form.

The major shortcomings of genre pictures is that they're easy to imitate and have been debased by stale mechanical repetition. Genre conventions are mere clichés unless they're united with significant innovations in style or subject matter. But this is true of all the arts, not just movies. As Aristotle noted in *The Poetics,* genres are qualitatively neutral: The conventions of classical tragedy are basically the same whether they're used by a genius or a forgotten hack. Certain genres enjoy more cultural prestige because they have attracted the most gifted artists. Genres that haven't are widely regarded as innately inartistic, but in many cases, their déclassé status is due to neglect rather than intrinsic hopelessness. For example, the earliest film critics considered slapstick comedy an infantile genre—until such important comic artists as Chaplin and Keaton entered the field. Today, no critic would malign the genre, for it boasts a considerable number of masterpieces.

The most critically admired genre films strike a balance between the form's preestablished conventions and the artist's unique contributions. The artists of ancient Greece drew on a common body of mythology, and no one thought it strange when dramatists and poets returned to these tales again and again. Incompetent artists merely repeat. Serious artists reinterpret. By exploiting the broad outlines of a well-known tale or story type, the storyteller can play off its main features, creating provocative tensions between the genre's conventions and the artist's inventions, between the familiar and the original, the general and the particular. Myths embody the common ideals and aspirations of a civilization, and by returning to these communal tales the artist becomes, in a sense, a psychic explorer, bridging the chasm between the known and the unknown. The stylized conventions and **archetypal** story patterns of genres

8–25. *It Happened One Night* (U.S.A., 1934), *with Clark Gable and Claudette Colbert, written by Robert Riskin, directed by Frank Capra.*
Genres can be classified according to subject matter, style, period, national origin, and a variety of other criteria. In the 1930s, a new American genre was born: screwball comedy. Its heyday was roughly 1934–1945. Essentially love stories, these films feature zany but glamorous lovers, often from different social classes. More realistic than the slapstick of the silent era, screwball comedy is also more collaborative, requiring the sophisticated blending of talents of writers, actors, and directors. The snappy dialogue crackles with wit and speed. Sappy, sentimental speeches are often meant to deceive. The narrative premises are absurdly improbable, and the plots, which are intricate and filled with preposterous twists and turns, tend to snowball out of control. The movies center on a comic-romantic couple rather than a solitary protagonist. Often, they are initially hostile, with one trying to outwit or outmaneuver the other. Much of the comedy results from the utter seriousness of the characters, who are usually unaware that they're funny, even though they engage in the most loony masquerades and deceptions. Sometimes one of them is engaged to a sexless prude or a humorless bore: This lends an urgency to the attraction between the coprotagonists, who are clearly made for each other. The genre usually includes a menagerie of secondary characters who are as wacky as the lovers. *(Columbia Pictures)*

encourage viewers to participate ritualistically in the basic beliefs, fears, and anxieties of their age.

Filmmakers are attracted to genres because they automatically synthesize a vast amount of cultural information, freeing them to explore more personal concerns. A nongeneric movie must be more self-contained. The artist is forced to communicate virtually all the major ideas and emotions within the work itself—a task that preempts a lot of screen time. On the other hand, the genre artist never starts from scratch. He or she can build on the accomplish-

8-26a. *Unforgiven* (U.S.A., 1992), *with Gene Hackman and Clint Eastwood, directed by Eastwood.* (Warner Bros.)

8-26b. *The People VS. Larry Flynt* (U.S.A., 1996), *with Woody Harrelson and Courtney Love, directed by Milos Forman.* (Columbia Pictures)

8-26c. *Fargo* (U.S.A., 1996), *with Frances McDormand, written and directed by Joel and Ethan Coen.* (Gramercy Pictures)

Genres in their classical phase tend to portray a world where right and wrong are fairly clear-cut, where the moral values of the movie are widely shared by the audience, and where justice eventually triumphs over evil. Today's most respected film artists are likely to find such values out-of-touch and naive, if not out-and-out false. The contemporary cinema tends to favor genres that are revisionist—less idealistic, more ambiguous morally, and far from reassuring in their presentation of the human condition. For example, *Unforgiven* is a revisionist western whose grim protagonist, William Munny (Eastwood), is a hired killer, so lost in violence that he has doomed his soul. When a youthful crony remarks that their victim "had it coming," Munny replies, "We all got it coming, kid." *The People VS. Larry Flynt* is a biography film—not of an admirable role model or moral exemplar, but of a notorious pornographer and his zonked-out junkie wife. It's a love story. It's also a paradoxical defense of the First Amendment by a filmmaker who grew up in the communist police state of Czechoslovakia—where a Larry Flynt would never have been possible. *Fargo* is a revisionist detective film that's loosely based on an actual police case. The protagonist is Marge Gunderson (McDormand), the very pregnant police chief of Brainerd, Minnesota. The movie is often funny, interspersed with unsettling scenes of brutality and gore. Though the chief finally solves the case, the film's "happy ending" is considerably undercut by its tone of sadness and pessimism concerning our pathetic species.

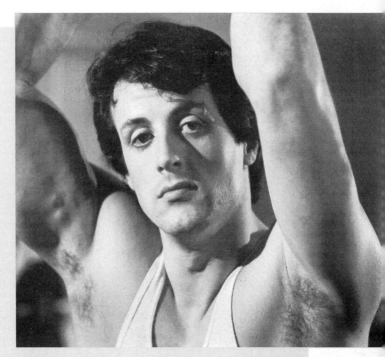

8–27a. *Rocky* (U.S.A., 1976), *with Sylvester Stallone, directed by John Avildsen.*

One of the most popular story patterns in America is the Horatio Alger myth—the inspiring tale of a social nobody who, through hard work and perseverance, and against all odds, manages to pull himself up by his bootstraps and achieve extraordinary success. *(United Artists)*

8–27b. ***Don't Be a Menace to South Central While Drinking Your Juice in the Hood*** (U.S.A., 1996), *with Marlon Wayans and Shawn Wayans, directed by Paris Barclay.*

The very title of this film suggests its parodic intent, its comic ridicule of conventional African American genres such as *Boyz N the Hood* **(10–20a)** and coming-of-age films. *Don't Be a Menace* features no less than six siblings of the talented, if slightly demented, Wayans family. *(Miramax Films)*

8–28. *Risky Business* (U.S.A., 1983), *with Tom Cruise and Rebecca De Mornay, written and directed by Paul Brickman.*

Because 75 percent of the contemporary American film audience is composed of young people, rite-of-passage comedies—also known as coming-of-age films—appeal directly to this adolescent following. The worst of them pander shamelessly to this audience's sentimental and narcissistic view of itself, but a few—like *Risky Business*—are slyly revisionist. The protagonist's transition from childhood innocence to adult experience is subtly subverted by the film's increasingly low-key lighting style and its bittersweet tone of cynicism. Cruise's character begins as a straight, hardworking high school student, naive but likable. In his impatience for worldly success and status, he betrays his parents' trust by using their home as a bordello while they are away on a short trip. With the help of an enterprising hooker (De Mornay), he pimps for his friends, supplying them with the services of several ladies of the evening, who share his entrepreneurial spirit. They reap a profit of $8000 in a single night. By the end of the movie, he is a bona fide member in good standing of the world of adults, savoring the sweet smell of success. *(Warner Bros.)*

ments of predecessors, enriching their ideas or calling them into question, depending on his or her inclinations.

The most enduring genres tend to adapt to changing social conditions. Most of them begin as naive allegories of Good versus Evil. Over the years, they become more complex in both form and thematic range. Finally, they veer into an ironic mode, mocking many of the genre's original values and conventions. Some critics claim that this evolution is inevitable and doesn't necessarily represent an aesthetic improvement.

Film critics and scholars classify genre movies into four main cycles:

1. *Primitive.* This phase is usually naive, though powerful in its emotional impact, in part because of the novelty of the form. Many of the conventions of the genre are established in this phase.
2. *Classical.* This intermediate stage embodies such classical ideals as balance, richness, and poise. The genre's values are assured and widely shared by the audience.

8–29. *On the Town (U.S.A., 1949), with (clockwise, from one o'clock) Gene Kelly, Vera-Ellen, Ann Miller, Betty Garrett, Frank Sinatra, and Jules Munshin; directed by Kelly and Stanley Donen.*
Musicals were among the most popular genres throughout the big-studio era, appealing to men as well as women, to young audiences as well as adults. Most musicals heighten the artificiality of their narrative structures. For example, in this movie, everything comes in threes—three dashing sailor heroes and three spirited working-girl heroines. *(MGM)*

3. *Revisionist.* The genre is generally more symbolic, ambiguous, less certain in its values. This phase tends to be stylistically complex, appealing more to the intellect than to the emotions. Often, the genre's preestablished conventions are exploited as ironic foils to question or undermine popular beliefs.

4. *Parodic.* This phase of a genre's development is an outright mockery of its conventions, reducing them to howling clichés and presenting them in a comic manner.

For example, the western's primitive phase is exemplified by Edwin S. Porter's *The Great Train Robbery* (1903), the first western ever made, and an enormously popular movie with the public. It was imitated and embellished on for decades. The western's classical phase could be typified by many of the works of John Ford, especially *Stagecoach* (1939), one of the few westerns of that era to win wide critical approval as well as box-office success. *High Noon* (1952) was one of the first revisionist westerns, ironically questioning many of the populist values of the genre's classical phase. Throughout the following two decades, most westerns remained in this skeptical mode, including such major works as *The Wild Bunch* (1969) and *McCabe and Mrs. Miller* (1971). Some critics pointed to Mel Brooks's parodic *Blazing Saddles* (1973) as the genre's deathblow, for many of its conventions are mercilessly lampooned. However, genres have a way of springing back to life after being allowed to rest for a few years. For example, Clint Eastwood's popular *Pale Rider* (1985) is unabashedly classical. Many cultural theorists insist that questions of individual value in a genre's evolution are largely matters of taste and fashion, not the intrinsic merit of the phase per se.

Some of the most suggestive critical studies have explored the relation-

8–30. *Invasion of the Body Snatchers* (U.S.A., 1956), *directed by Don Siegel.*
Genre films often appeal to subconscious anxieties in the audience. For example, many Japanese science-fiction films of the 1950s dealt with hideous mutations that resulted from atomic radiation. A number of cultural commentators have remarked on the "paranoid style" of most American sci-fi movies of the 1950s, when the "Red Scare" intensified the Cold War atmosphere between the United States and the Soviet Union. Siegel's low-budget classic deals with how some alien pod-people insidiously invade human bodies, reducing their owners to anonymous zombies, incapable of feelings. The movie was produced during an era when many Americans were seriously discussing the possibility of building backyard bomb shelters to "protect" themselves from an expected nuclear attack by the U.S.S.R. *(Allied Artists)*

ship of a genre to the society that nurtured it. This sociopsychic approach was pioneered by the French literary critic Hippolyte Taine in the nineteenth century. Taine claimed that the social and intellectual anxieties of a given era and nation will find expression in its art. The implicit function of an artist is to harmonize and reconcile cultural clashes of value. He believed that art must be analyzed for both its overt and covert meaning, that beneath its explicit content there exists a vast reservoir of latent social and psychic information (8–33).

This approach tends to work best with popular genres, which reflect the shared values and fears of a large audience. Such genres might be regarded as contemporary myths, lending philosophical meaning to the facts of everyday life. As social conditions change, genres often change with them, challenging some traditional customs and beliefs, reaffirming others. Gangster films, for example, are often covert critiques of American capitalism. They are often vehicles for exploring rebellion myths and are especially popular during periods of social breakdown. The protagonists—usually played by small men—are likened to ruthless businessmen, their climb to power a sardonic parody of the Horatio Alger myth. During the Jazz Age, gangster films like

8–31. ***E.T.: The Extra-Terrestrial*** (U.S.A., 1982), *with Henry Thomas and E.T., directed by Steven Spielberg.*

All narratives can be interpreted on a symbolic level. There is a principle of universality that can be inferred no matter how unique or strange a given story may be. In this scene from Spielberg's masterpiece, E.T. and his friend Eliot must say good-bye. But E.T. will live forever inside Eliot's mind. Symbolically, the boy will soon outgrow his childhood world of imaginary best friends, scary-looking creatures, and the vast Unknown. But he will never forget the beauty and innocence of that world. Nor will we. "A film is a ribbon of dreams," Orson Welles once stated. "The camera is much more than a recording apparatus; it is a medium via which messages reach us from another world that is not ours and that brings us to the heart of a great secret. Here magic begins." *(Universal Studios)*

Underworld (1927) dealt with the violence and glamour of the Prohibition era in an essentially apolitical manner. During the harshest years of the Depression in the early 1930s, the genre became subversively ideological. Movies like *Little Caesar* (1930) reflected the country's shaken confidence in authority and traditional social institutions. In the final years of the Depression, gangster films like *Dead End* (1937) were pleas for liberal reform, arguing that crime is the result of broken homes, lack of opportunity, and slum living. Gangsters of all periods tend to suffer from an inability to relate to women, but during the 1940s movies like *White Heat* (1949) featured protagonists who were outright sexual neurotics. In the 1950s, partly as a result of the highly publicized Kefauver Senate Crime Investigations, gangster movies like *The Phenix City Story* (1955) took the form of confidential exposés of syndicate crime. Francis Ford Coppola's *The Godfather* (1972) and *The Godfather, Part II* (1974) are a virtual recapitulation of the history of the genre, spanning three generations of

369

8–32. *Sweet Hours* (Spain, 1982), *with Inaki Aierra and Assumpta Serna, directed by Carlos Saura.*
Almost all civilizations have myths dealing with the rebellion of son against father, resulting in son and mother reunited in exclusive love. Sigmund Freud, the father of psychoanalysis, identified one such variant as the Oedipus complex (named for the Greek mythical hero), which he believed was the paradigm of prepubescent human sexuality. Its feminine form is known as the Electra complex, a name also derived from Greek myth. In most cases, this narrative motif is submerged beneath the surface details of a story, or sufficiently disguised to appeal primarily to the subconscious. Saura's *Sweet Hours* plays with this motif in an overt manner. The movie deals with the love affair between a filmmaker (Aierra) and an actress (Serna) who is playing his mother in an autobiographical film he is making about his childhood. *(New Yorker Films)*

characters and reflecting the weary cynicism of a nation still numbed by the hearts-and-minds hoax of Vietnam and the Watergate conspiracy. As Sergio Leone's fablelike title suggests, *Once Upon a Time in America* (1984) is frankly mythical, treating the traditional rise-and-fall structure of the genre in an almost ritualistic manner. Quentin Tarantino's *Pulp Fiction* (1994) is a witty send-up of the genre, parodying many of its conventions.

The ideas of Sigmund Freud and Carl Jung have also influenced many genre theorists. Like Taine, both psychiatrists believed that art is a reflection of underlying structures of meaning, that it satisfies certain subconscious needs in both the artist and audience. For Freud, art was a form of daydreaming and wish fulfillment, vicariously resolving urgent impulses and desires that can't be satisfied in reality. Pornographic films are perhaps the most obvious example of how anxieties can be assuaged in this surrogate manner, and in fact, Freud believed that most neuroses were sexually based. He thought that art was a by-product of neurosis, although essentially a socially beneficial one. Like neurosis, art is characterized by a repetition compulsion, the need to go over the same stories and rituals to reenact and temporarily resolve certain psychic conflicts **(8–32).**

Jung began his career as a disciple of Freud but eventually broke away, believing that Freud's theories lacked a communal dimension. Jung was fascinated by myths, fairy tales, and folklore, which he believed contained symbols and story patterns that were universal to all individuals in all cultures and periods. According to Jung, unconscious complexes consist of archetypal symbols that are as deeply rooted and as inexplicable as instincts. He called this submerged reservoir of symbols the *collective unconscious,* which he thought had a primordial foundation, traceable to primitive times. Many of these archetypal patterns are bipolar and embody the basic concepts of religion, art, and society: god–devil, active–passive, male–female, static–dynamic, and so on. Jung believed that the artist consciously or unconsciously draws on these archetypes as raw material, which must then be rendered into the generic forms favored by a given culture. For Jung, every work of art (and especially generic art) is an infinitesimal exploration of a universal experience—an instinctive groping toward an ancient wisdom. He also believed that popular culture offers the most unobstructed view of archetypes and myths, whereas elite culture tends to submerge them beneath a complex surface detail.

8–33.   *Pinocchio* (U.S.A., 1940), *by Walt Disney.*

The French cultural anthropologist Claude Lévi-Strauss noted that myths have no author, no origin, no core axis—they allow "free play" in a variety of artistic forms. Disney's work draws heavily from fairy tales, myths, and folklore, which are profuse in archetypal elements. *Pinocchio* is a good example of how these elements can be emphasized rather than submerged beneath a surface realism. Early in the film, the boy/puppet Pinocchio is told that to be a "real boy," he must show that he is "brave, truthful, and unselfish." The three principal episodes of the movie represent ritualistic trials, testing the youth's moral fortitude. He dismally fails the first two, but redeems himself in the concluding whale episode, where he does indeed demonstrate courage, honesty, and unselfishness (pictured). Other archetypal elements include a monster (Monstro, the whale), magical transformations, a father's search for his lost son, supernatural creatures like a talking cricket (Jiminy Cricket, Pinocchio's "conscience"), a son's search for his imprisoned father, an anthropomorphized portrayal of nature, and a fairy godmother who rescues the improvident young hero when he fails to act responsibly. Like most of Disney's works of this era, the values in *Pinocchio* are traditional and conservative, an affirmation of the sanctity of the family unit, the importance of a Higher Power in guiding our destinies, and the need to play by society's rules.   *(Walt Disney Productions)*

A story can be many things. To a producer it's a property that has a box-office value. To a writer it's a screenplay. To a film star it's a vehicle. To a director it's an artistic medium. To a genre critic it's a classifiable narrative form. To a sociologist it's an index of public sentiment. To a psychiatrist it's an instinctive exploration of hidden fears or communal ideals. To a moviegoer it can be all of these, and more.

In analyzing a film's narrative structure, we ought to ask ourselves some basic questions. Who's telling the story? A voice-over narrator? Why him or her? Or does the story "tell itself," like most stage plays? Who is the implied narrator of such stories, the guiding hand in the arrangement of the narrative's constituent parts? What do we as spectators supply to the story? What information do we provide in order to fill in the narrative's gaps? How is time presented—chronologically or subjectively rearranged through flashbacks and other narrative disjunctions? Is the narrative realistic, classical, or formalistic? What genre, if any? What phase of the genre's evolution? What does the movie say about the social context and period that it was made in? How does the narrative embody mythical concepts or universal human traits?

FURTHER READING

ALTMAN, RICK. *Film/Genre* (Bloomington: Indiana University Press, 1999). The evolution of film genres.

BORDWELL, DAVID, *Narration in the Fiction Film* (Madison: University of Wisconsin Press, 1985). The fullest discussion of the role of the spectator.

BROOKS, PETER, *Reading for the Plot: Design and Intention in Narrative* (New York: Knopf, 1984). Primarily about literature.

CHATMAN, SEYMOUR, *Story and Discourse* (Ithaca, N.Y.: Cornell University Press, 1978). Well written, clear, and useful, covering literature as well as film.

FIELD, SYD, *The Screenwriter's Workbook* (New York: Dell, 1984). A practical handbook, emphasizing the classical paradigm.

MARTIN, WALLACE, *Recent Theories of Narrative* (Ithaca, N.Y.: Cornell University Press, 1986). Lucid and helpful, primarily about literature.

MITCHELL, W. J. T., ed., *On Narrative* (Chicago and London: University of Chicago Press, 1981). Collection of scholarly articles, mostly on literature.

MOEWS, DANIEL, *Keaton: The Silent Features Close Up* (Berkeley: University of California Press, 1977). An excellent critical study, especially strong on Keaton's plots.

NASH, CHRISTOPHER, ed., *Narrative in Culture* (London and New York: Routledge, 1990). Multidisciplinary essays.

THOMPSON, KRISTIN. *Storytelling in the New Hollywood* (Cambridge: Harvard University Press, 1999). Narrative strategies in mainstream American films.

Writing

Writing is like prostitution. First, you do it for the love of it, then you do it for a few friends, and finally you do it for the money.

—MOLIÈRE, FRENCH PLAYWRIGHT

Overview

The written word. Screenwriters: artists, craftspeople, or hired hands? Multiple authorship and the Hollywood studios. Evaluating the writer's contribution. Writer–directors: total control. Written script versus mise en scène: two different language systems. The screenplay. How people talk: levels of usage. Ideology and language. Period dialogue: How did people talk in olden days? *North by Northwest:* the reading version by Ernest Lehman. Figurative comparisons: motifs, symbols, metaphors, allegories, and allusions. Point of view: Who's telling the story? Why? First-person narrators. The omniscient voice. The third person. The objective point of view. Literary adaptations: How close to the original? Loose, faithful, and literal adaptations.

The Screenwriter

Perhaps more than any of the director's other collaborators, the screenwriter has been brought forward from time to time as the main "author" of a film. After all, writers are generally responsible for the dialogue. They outline most of the action (sometimes in detail). And they often set forth the main theme of a movie. But generalizing about the writer's contribution in the movie-making process is an exercise in futility because the writer's role varies immensely from film to film and from director to director **(9–1).** In the first place, some filmmakers have hardly bothered with scripts. Especially in the silent era, improvisation was the rule rather than the exception. Others used only the barest outlines.

Many of the greatest directors have written their own scripts: Cocteau, Eisenstein, Bergman, and Herzog, to name only a few. In the American cinema, there are also many writer–directors: Griffith, Chaplin, Stroheim, Huston, Welles, Mankiewicz, Wilder, Sturges, Woody Allen, and Coppola are among the most famous. The majority of important directors have taken a major hand in writing their scripts, but they bring in other writers to expand on their ideas. Fellini, Truffaut, and Kurosawa all worked in this manner. Surprisingly few major directors depend totally on others for their scripts.

The American studio system tended to encourage multiple authorship of scripts. Often, writers had a certain specialty such as dialogue, comedy, construction, atmosphere, and so on. Some writers were best at doctoring weak scripts. Others were good idea people but lacked the skill to execute their ideas. In such collaborative enterprises, the screen credits are not always an accurate reflection of who contributed what to a movie. Furthermore, although many directors such as Hitchcock, Capra, and Lubitsch contributed a great deal to the final shape of their scripts, they rarely included their names in the credits, allowing the official writer to take it all.

For many years, American critics were inclined to believe that art must be solemn—if not actually dull—to be respectable. Even in the heyday of the

9-1a. *The Thin Red Line* (U.S.A., 1998), *with Nick Nolte, written and directed by Terrence Malick.*

Successful novelists rarely make good screenwriters because they tend to want the language to carry most of the meaning. But movies communicate primarily through images, and too many words can clutter the eloquence of the visuals. James Jones's famous World War II novel, *The Thin Red Line*, serves almost as an inspiration—rather than a literal source—for Terrence Malick's elliptical, poetic screenplay. The novel emphasizes soldiers in battle and among comrades, but the film is more concerned with philosophical ideas, a melancholy meditation on nature's exquisite beauty and how man defiles it. Like Malick's other movies, this film also explores the mythic idea of a lost paradise and man's corrupt nature, his original sin. *(Twentieth Century–Fox)*

9-1b. *What's Eating Gilbert Grape* (U.S.A., 1993), *with Leonardo DiCaprio and Johnny Depp, directed by Lasse Hallström.*

On the other hand, some novelists slip into the screenwriter's role with ease. Peter Hedges wrote the novel this movie is based on. He also wrote the screenplay, which is a model of intelligent adaptation, allowing its excellent actors considerable creativity in fleshing out their roles. The Swedish-born Hallström has won critical praise for three first-rate adaptations by novelists, all centering on children: *My Life as a Dog, Gilbert Grape,* and *The Cider House Rules.* See also John Irving, *My Movie Business* (New York: Random House, 1999), an account of Irving's adaptation of his novel, *The Cider House Rules,* into an Academy-Award winning screenplay. *(Paramount Pictures)*

9-2. *Howards End* (Great Britain, 1992), *with Sam West and Helena Bonham-Carter, directed by James Ivory.*
The team of director James Ivory, producer Ismail Merchant, and writer Ruth Prawer Jhabvala has been making movies together for over thirty years. The best of them are classy adaptations of prestigious literary masterpieces, like E. M. Forster's *A Room With a View* and Henry James's difficult *The Europeans* and *The Bostonians*. Jhabvala is a respected author in her own right, but her literate screenplays are her main claim to fame, and deservedly so. Nowhere is her artistry more apparent than in this sensitive adaptation of Forster's great novel, *Howards End*. The problem with filming literary masterpieces is that they tend to come off as pompous and dead from the neck down. Jhabvala's screenplay is beautifully written, in addition to being faithful to the original, funny, and emotionally involving. *(Sony Pictures)*

Hollywood studio system, a handful of intellectual writers enjoyed tremendous prestige because their scripts were filled with fine speeches dealing with Justice, Brotherhood, and Democracy. Not that these values aren't important. But to be effective artistically, ideas must be dramatized with tact and honesty, not parceled out to the characters like high-sounding speeches on a patriotic holiday. For example, in the novel *The Grapes of Wrath*, John Steinbeck frequently praises the toughness of the Joad family. They have been thrown off their farm during the Great Depression and are forced to seek a new life in California, where conditions are even worse for them.

In John Ford's movie version, there is no narrator, so the characters must speak for themselves. Nunnally Johnson's screenplay is not devoid of ideas, but the ideas are expressed in the words of the *characters*. A good example is Ma Joad's comments to her husband in the final scene of the movie. They

9–3. *Shoeshine* (Italy, 1946), *with Rinaldo Smordoni and Franco Interlenghi, written by Cesare Zavattini, directed by Vittorio De Sica.*

Zavattini is the most famous screenwriter of the Italian cinema, and one of its most important theorists. (See the section on **neorealism** in Chapter 11.) His best work was done in collaboration with De Sica, including such important works as *The Children Are Watching Us, Shoeshine, Bicycle Thief, Miracle in Milan, Umberto D, Two Women,* and *The Garden of the Finzi-Continis.* Both Zavattini and De Sica were strongly humanistic, Zavattini from a Marxist perspective, De Sica from a Christian orientation. Like François Truffaut, De Sica was a great director of children, but his sympathies extended to all people on the fringes: "My films are a struggle against the absence of human solidarity," he explained, "against the indifference of society towards suffering. They are a word in favor of the poor and the unhappy."

(Museum of Modern Art)

are in their shabby truck, driving to a new job—twenty days as fruit pickers. Pa Joad (Russell Simpson) admits to his wife (Jane Darwell) that for a while he thought the family was finished. She answers, "I know. That's what makes us tough. Rich fellas come up an' they die, an' their kids ain't no good, an' they die out. But we keep a-comin'. We're the people that live. They can't wipe us out. They can't lick us. We'll go on forever Pa, 'cause we're the people." (Quoted from Johnson's script in *Twenty Best Film Plays,* Vol. I, eds. John Gassner and Dudley Nichols; New York: Garland Publishing, 1977.) The final image of the film follows: a thrilling extreme long shot, in which the fragile Joad vehicle merges imperceptibly with a procession of other dilapidated trucks and autos, forming an unbroken river of traffic—Ford's visual tribute to the courage and resilience of the human spirit.

Generally speaking, students, artists, and intellectuals are the individuals most likely to discuss ideas and abstractions without a sense of self-consciousness. To be convincing, eloquent language must be dramatically probable. We must believe that the words aren't just the writer's preachments dressed up as dialogue.

But there are always exceptions. *Casablanca,* for example, features a traditional love triangle, in which Ilsa (Ingrid Bergman) is torn between two men—her husband, Victor Laszlo (Paul Henried), a Resistance leader whom

9–4a. *Barcelona* **(U.S.A., 1994),** *with Taylor Nichols, Tushka Bergen, Chris Eigeman, and Mira Sorvino, written and directed by Whit Stillman.* *(Castle Rock Entertainment)*

9–4b. ***There's Something About Mary*** **(U.S.A., 1998),** *with Cameron Diaz, written and directed by Peter and Bobby Farrelly.* *(Twentieth Century–Fox)*

If a comedy makes us laugh, then it has succeeded, at least in its primary aim. But there are different ways to make us laugh, some subtle and sophisticated, like Stillman's wry, understated comedy of manners, *Barcelona*; others are crude and raunchy, like the gross-out comedies of the Farrelly brothers. Stillman's sensibility is rooted in character, and most of the comedy results from the social situations his characters find themselves in and the ways they try to weasel out of them. The Farrelly boys are more joke-oriented, the grosser the better. Examples: racist gags, anti-jock jokes, fart jokes, yelping dog gags, anything involving genitals, especially male genitals that are attacked, whacked, or otherwise abused, cruel gags about deformities, jokes about old or fat people, and anything involving bodily fluids. In short, their style of comedy revels in all subjects that are likely to shock or disgust respectable citizens. Their comedy is also laugh-out-loud funny, usually. Gross and funny. Sometimes *really* gross.

she deeply respects and admires, and Rick Blaine (Humphrey Bogart), the man she loves and will always love. Throughout the movie, Rick's comments are generally terse, sardonic, and hard-boiled. He's not a man given to making pretty speeches. But in the airport scene at the end of the film **(9–5b),** his remarks to the woman he loves—and must give up—are overtly ideological:

> Inside of us we both know you belong to Victor. You're part of his work, the thing that keeps him going. If that plane leaves the ground and you're not with him, you'll regret it. . . . Maybe not today, maybe not tomorrow, but soon, and for the rest of your life. . . . Ilsa, I'm no good at being noble, but it doesn't take much to see that the problems of three little people don't amount to a hill of beans in this crazy world. Someday you'll understand that. Here's looking at you, kid. (Quoted from *Casablanca Script and Legend,* script by Julius and Philip Epstein and Howard Koch; Woodstock, N.Y.: The Overlook Press, 1973)

Some filmmakers are at their best with talky scripts—provided it's scintillating talk, as in the best movies of Wertmüller, Bergman, and Woody Allen **(9–6).** The French, Swedish, and British cinemas are also exceptionally literate. Among the important writers who have written for the screen in Great Britain are George Bernard Shaw, Graham Greene, Alan Sillitoe, John Osborne, Harold Pinter, David Storey, and Hanif Kureishi.

Despite the enormous importance that the script can play in a sound film, some directors scoff at the notion that a writer could be the dominant artist in the cinema. Antonioni once remarked that Dostoyevsky's *Crime and Punishment* was a rather ordinary crime thriller—the genius of the novel lies in *how* it's told, not in the subject matter per se. Certainly, the large number of excellent movies based on routine or even mediocre books seems to bear out such a view.

Movie scripts seldom make for interesting reading, precisely because they are like blueprints of the finished product. Unlike a play, which usually can be read with pleasure, too much is missing in a screenplay. Even highly detailed scripts seldom offer us a sense of a film's **mise en scène,** one of the principal methods of expression at the director's disposal. With characteristic wit, Andrew Sarris has pointed out how the director's choice of shot—or the way in which the action is photographed—is the crucial element in most films:

> The choice between a close-up and a long-shot, for example, may quite often transcend the plot. If the story of Little Red Riding Hood is told with the Wolf in close-up and Little Red Riding Hood in long-shot, the director is concerned primarily with the emotional problems of a wolf with a compulsion to eat little girls. If Little Red Riding Hood is in close-up and the Wolf in long-shot, the emphasis is shifted to the

9–5a. *Twentieth Century* (U.S.A., 1934), *with John Barrymore and Carole Lombard, directed by Howard Hawks.* *(Columbia Pictures)*

During the big studio era in Hollywood, most film scripts were written by committees rather than a single author. For the most part, these collaborative scripts were like patchwork quilts—some romance for the ladies, some action for the guys, a touch of comedy for the kids. Nonetheless, in some cases, collaborative writing produced excellent results, like *Twentieth Century* and *Casablanca*.

The legendary wit and ex-newspaperman Ben Hecht was perhaps the most admired screenwriter of his era. His specialty was comedy—the more outrageous, the better. *Twentieth Century* was adapted from his stage play (co-written by Charles MacArthur), with additional touches by director Hawks. Hecht delighted in satirizing American hick values and conventional morality, which he thought was as hypocritical as it was boring.

Casablanca was written by Philip and Julius Epstein and Howard Koch, three of Warner Brothers' ace writers. They agonized about how to end the movie until the final moment, when they decided that the Bogart character had to give up the woman he loves. Unwittingly, the writers struck a responsive public nerve: *Casablanca* was released during the darkest days of World War II, when Americans and their allies were being called on to make personal sacrifices for a higher cause. One critic has suggested that the movie is not a portrait of the way we were, but of the way we wanted to be.

9–5b. *Casablanca* (U.S.A., 1942), *with Humphrey Bogart and Ingrid Bergman, directed by Michael Curtiz.* *(Warner Bros.)*

9–6. *Small Time Crooks* (U.S.A., 2000), *with Tracy Ullman and Hugh Grant, written and directed by Woody Allen.*
Woody Allen is widely regarded as the most gifted writer–director of his generation, combining wit with romantic whimsy, poignancy with thought. Almost all of his movies are comedies, of virtually every type—satires, parodies, romantic comedies, fantasies, comedies of manners, and farces. He averages about one film per year. Because of his enormous cultural prestige, he can cast virtually any actor of his choice in his pictures, and most of them work for very modest pay. Allen has also written a number of stage plays and several volumes of humorous essays. Most of his essays originally appeared in the prestigious *New Yorker* magazine, which has published the writings of the finest authors in America.   *(DreamWorks Pictures)*

emotional problems of vestigial virginity in a wicked world. Thus, two different stories are being told with the same basic anecdotal material. What is at stake in the two versions of Little Red Riding Hood are two contrasting directorial attitudes toward life. One director identifies more with the Wolf—the male, the compulsive, the corrupted, even evil itself. The second director identifies with the little girl—the innocence, the illusion, the ideal and hope of the race. Needless to say, few critics bother to make any distinction, proving perhaps that direction as creation is still only dimly understood. (Quoted from "The Fall and Rise of the Film Director," in *Interviews with Film Directors;* New York: Avon Books, 1967)

9–7a. *Little Women* (U.S.A., 1994), *with (clockwise from left) Winona Ryder, Trini Alvarado, Susan Sarandon, Claire Danes, and Kirsten Dunst; directed by Gillian Armstrong.* (Columbia Pictures)

9–7b. *Chasing Amy* (U.S.A., 1997), *with Ben Affleck and Joey Lauren Adams, written and directed by Kevin Smith.* (Miramax Films)

Apples and oranges. Judging the merits of these two excellent screenplays requires a certain literary flexibility. Each is skillful, but in its own way. Robin Swicord's adaptation of Louisa May Alcott's nineteenth-century classic, *Little Women*, preserves much of the novel's flowery prose style. To modern ears, the dialogue sounds rather formal, the word choice a tad elevated in proper Victorian style, yet gently undercut by occasional touches of irony. The problem with this kind of dialogue is that it's hard to make it sound like real talk. Stylized period dialogue requires first-rate performers such as these. The screenplay of *Chasing Amy* is profuse with slang, jive, and four-letter words galore. These people love to talk and talk and talk. The dialogue is funny, sexy, filled with surprises. A revisionist romantic comedy, the story centers on two comic book artists (pictured) and their odd relationship. She's a lesbian. He falls in love with her anyway. But surprise: She also falls in love with him. Until he screws up. . . .Critic Stephen Farber noted: "The scene in which Alyssa explains to Holden that she fell in love with him not because she was programmed by society but because she chose him as an individual is one of the most stirring testaments to the mystery of love that the movies have ever offered." Both screenplays are strongly "literary" in the sense that there is a genuine sense of pleasure in demonstrating the intellectual precision, wit, and emotional richness of the English language. One is stylistically complex, feminine, and imbued with idealism; the other is raunchy, quicksilver funny, and emotionally powerful.

The Screenplay

A film script is rarely an autonomous literary product, otherwise they would be published with greater frequency. The screenplays of a few prestigious filmmakers, like Woody Allen, Ingmar Bergman, and Federico Fellini, have reached print. But even these are merely linguistic approximations of the films themselves. Perhaps the worst kind of literary by-products of movies are "novelizations"—commissioned novel versions of popular films that are usually written by hired hacks to cash in on a movie's box-office popularity.

Screenplays are often modified by the actors who play the characters. This is especially true in scripts written for personality **stars.** Naturally, their roles will usually include the qualities that make the star popular. For example, screenwriters who wrote for Gary Cooper knew that he was at his best when he said the least. In our own time, Clint Eastwood is famous for his terse one-liners: "Go ahead—make my day." Eastwood's characters, like Cooper's, are usually suspicious of people who are smooth-talkers.

On the other hand, a good talker is a joy to hear. Joseph L. Mankiewicz was one of the most admired writer–directors of the Hollywood big-studio era. His finest work, *All About Eve* (**7–5**), features several brilliantly written roles. One of the best is the acid-tongued theater critic, Addison Dewitt, played with bitchy sang-froid by George Sanders. Late in the movie, Eve Harrington (Anne Baxter), a young actress who has lied, cheated, and slept her way to the top, tries to brush off Dewitt, her current companion, because he's no longer useful to her. Dewitt sees right through her and has no intention of playing her fool. She huffily walks to the door and opens it. "You're too short for that gesture," he dryly observes. "Besides, it went out with Mrs. Fisk." He then proceeds to destroy her pretentions by exposing all of her lies. "Your name is not Eve Harrington. It is Gertrude Slecynski," he begins. "It is true that your parents were poor. They still are. And they would like to know how you are—and where. They haven't heard from you for three years."

Eve finally collapses as he finishes his withering diatribe: "That I should want you at all suddenly strikes me as the height of improbability. That, in itself, is probably the reason. You're an improbable person, Eve, and so am I. We have that in common. Also a contempt for humanity, an inability to love or be loved, insatiable ambition—and talent. We deserve each other." (Quoted from *More About All About Eve;* New York: Bantam, 1974; which contains Mankiewicz's script and a lengthy interview.)

Most of the characters in *All About Eve* are well educated and literate. Those in *On the Waterfront,* which was written by Budd Schulberg, are working-class longshoremen. Such characters usually attempt to conceal their emotions behind a macho façade. But in scenes of intense emotions, the words, though simple, are powerful. The famous taxi scene between the Malloy brothers, Charley (Rod Steiger) and Terry (Marlon Brando), is a good example. Charley, the older and shrewder of the two, once convinced his brother to throw an important boxing match. Terry is no longer a boxer, but a stooge for the same

union racketeer that Charley works for, Johnny Friendly. Charley tries to blame
Terry's manager for what happened. Angry, Terry answers:

> It wasn't him! It was you, Charley. You and Johnny. Like the night the
> two of youse come in the dressing room and says, 'Kid, this ain't your
> night—we're going for the price on Wilson.' *It ain't my night.* I'd of
> taken Wilson apart that night! I was ready—remember the early rounds
> throwing them combinations. So what happens—This bum Wilson he
> gets the title shot—outdoors in the ball park!—and what do I get—a
> couple of bucks and a one-way ticket to Palookaville. It was you,
> Charley. You was my brother. You should of looked out for me. Instead

9–8. *My Beautiful Laundrette* **(Great Britain, 1985),** *with Gordon Warnecke and Daniel Day-Lewis, written by Hanif Kureishi, directed by Stephen Frears.*
One of Britain's most outspoken young writers (plays, fiction, and autobiography as well as screenplays), Hanif Kureishi enjoys shocking the staid literary establishment. His themes characteristically revolve around conflicts between cultures, races, classes, and sexes. Most of his characters are funny as well as bright. Despite being from different classes and ethnic backgrounds, the two leading characters in this film (pictured) are business partners and lovers. They're totally unapologetic about their sexuality, which is not treated as a big deal. Kureishi, who is half English and half Pakistani, is especially interested in minorities, people outside the English mainstream, which is male, white, and heterosexual. "Gay men and black men have been excluded from history," Kureishi has said. "They're trying to understand themselves. Like women, black people and gay people have been marginalized in society, lacking in power, ridiculed." *(Orion Pictures)*

of making me take them dives for the short-end money. . . . I could've been a contender. I could've had class and been somebody. Real class. Instead of a bum, let's face it, which is what I am. It was you, Charley. (Quoted from *On the Waterfront: A Screenplay;* Carbondale: Southern Illinois University Press, 1980)

Good dialogue is often the result of having a good ear—for catching the correct rhythms of speech, the right choice of words, the length of people's sentences, the jargon, slang, or swears people use. The foulmouthed characters in Quentin Tarantino's *Reservoir Dogs* (5–35) speak in torrents of four-letter words, the linguistic equivalent of the violence of their lives. In contexts such as these, polite or laundered prose would constitute bad writing.

One of the pleasures of Nicholas Meyer's screenplay (adapted from his own novel) of *The Seven Per-Cent Solution* is the way he captures the elegantly literary nineteenth-century prose style of his protagonist, Sherlock Holmes. Here's Holmes when he's first tricked into meeting a foreign doctor at the physician's home in Vienna:

9–9. *The Gospel According to St. Matthew* (Italy/France, 1964), *with Enrique Irazoqui, directed by Pier Paolo Pasolini.*
This story of the life and teachings of Jesus is based on the New Testament writings of the Apostle Matthew. Pasolini, a Marxist and atheist, told the story sincerely and simply, blending mythology with documentary. His eclectic techniques combined a nonprofessional cast with a musical score that includes Bach, Mozart, Billie Holiday, Prokofiev, a Creole Mass, and Negro spirituals. The movie is widely regarded as a masterpiece of the Christian cinema—mysterious, poetic, and emotionally powerful. *(Continental)*

Beyond the fact that you are a brilliant Jewish physician who was born in Hungary and studied for a time in Paris, and that some radical theories of yours have alienated the respectable medical community so that you have severed your connections with various hospitals and branches of the medical fraternity—beyond this, I can deduce little. You are married, with a child of five; you enjoy Shakespeare and possess a sense of honor. (Quoted from *Film Scenes for Actors,* ed. Joshua Karton; New York: Bantam Books, 1983)

The doctor turns out to be none other than Sigmund Freud. Naturally, he's astonished that Holmes can deduce so much upon merely entering a room.

Most screenplays are businesslike and practical. Because they are not meant for publication, the action sequences are usually described simply, with no literary flourishes. There are a few exceptions to this rule, however. One of them is John Osborne's polished screenplay of *Tom Jones,* based on the eighteenth-century English novel by Henry Fielding. The fox hunting scene in the movie is magnificently effective, thanks to Tony Richardson's skillful direction. But Richardson obviously got his inspiration from Osborne's screenplay:

The hunt is no pretty Christmas calendar affair but a thumping dangerous vicious business, in which everyone takes part so wholeheartedly

9-10. *Some Like It Hot* (U.S.A., 1959), *with Jack Lemmon and Tony Curtis, screenplay by Billy Wilder and I. A. L. Diamond, directed by Wilder.*
Billy Wilder was one of the most respected writer–directors of the post–World War II era. He was regarded as a master of the well-made scenario: Each detail has a precise interlocking function. "In a good script, *everything* is necessary or it ain't good," he insisted. "And if you take out one piece, you better replace it with a different piece, or you got trouble." He was able to mine comedy from the unlikeliest sources, like transvestism. Forced to disguise themselves as women while on the lam from the mob, the musician heroes of this film join an all-girl band to escape detection. Most of the gags revolve around the incongruity of two virile men trying to cope with the agony of womanhood. Lemmon, for example, keeps losing one of his chests. *(United Artists)*

that it seems to express all in the raw, wild vitality that is so near to the surface of their lives. It is passionate and violent. Squire Western howls dementedly as he flogs his horse over the muddy earth. The curate kicks his beefy heels in the air, bellowing with blood and pleasure. Big, ugly, unlovable dogs tear at the earth. Tom reels and roars on his horse, his face ruddy and damp, almost insensible with the lust and the cry and the gallop, with the hot quarry of flesh in the crisp air, the blood and flesh of men, the blood and fur of animals. Everyone is caught up in the bloody fever. (Quoted from *Tom Jones, A Film Script,* by John Osborne; New York: Grove Press, 1964)

North by Northwest: Reading Version

Ernest Lehman's screenplay for Hitchcock's *North by Northwest* has considerable fluidity as a piece of writing. Its excellence consists not of its literary distinction so much as its clearly defined actions, providing the director with the raw materials for the **shots** of the movie. The following is a lengthy excerpt from the screenplay. How Hitchcock translated this literary description into the individual sequence of shots in the movie can be seen in Chapter 4, "Editing."

Like many of Hitchcock's movies, *North by Northwest* revolves around the wrong-man theme. The protagonist is an innocent man accused of and persecuted for a crime he didn't commit. In this film, Roger Thornhill (Cary Grant), a glib but charming advertising executive, is accidentally mistaken for a government agent named Kaplan. Thornhill is abducted by enemy agents, almost murdered by them, then fatefully implicated in the murder of a U.N. diplomat. Pursued by both the police and the enemy agents, he flees to Chicago in desperation, hoping to discover the real Kaplan, who presumably will establish Thornhill's innocence. When he arrives in Chicago, he is told that Kaplan will meet him alone at a designated location. The following excerpt relates what then takes place.

Helicopter Shot—Exterior, Highway 41—Afternoon

WE START CLOSE on a Greyhound bus, SHOOTING DOWN on it and TRAVELING ALONG with it as it speeds in an easterly direction at seventy m.p.h. Gradually, CAMERA DRAWS AWAY from the bus, going higher but never losing sight of the vehicle, which recedes into the distance below and becomes a toylike object on an endless ribbon of deserted highway that stretches across miles of flat prairie. Now the bus is slowing down. It is nearing a junction where a small dirt road coming from nowhere crosses the highway and continues on to nowhere. The bus stops. A man gets out. It is THORNHILL. But to us he is only a tiny figure. The bus starts away, moves on out of sight. And now THORNHILL stands alone beside the road—a tiny figure in the middle of nowhere.

On the Ground—with Thornhill—(Master Scene)

He glances about, studying his surroundings. The terrain is flat and tree-less, even more desolate from this vantage point than it seemed from the air. Here and there patches of low-growing farm crops add some contour to the land. A hot sun beats down. UTTER SILENCE hangs heavily in the air, THORNHILL glances at his wristwatch. It is three twenty-five.

In the distance, the FAINT HUM of a MOTOR VEHICLE is HEARD. THORN-HILL looks off to the west. The HUM GROWS LOUDER as the car draws nearer. THORNHILL steps closer to the edge of the highway. A black sedan looms up, traveling at high speed. For a moment we are not sure it is not hurtling right at THORNHILL. And then it zooms past him, recedes into the distance, becoming a FAINT HUM, a tiny speck, and then SILENCE again.

THORNHILL takes out a handkerchief, mops his face. He is beginning to sweat now. It could be from nervousness, as well as the heat. Another FAINT HUM, coming from the east, GROWING LOUDER as he glances off and sees another distant speck becoming a speeding car, this one a closed convertible. Again, anticipation on THORNHILL's face. Again, the vague uneasiness of indefinable danger approaching at high speed. And again, ZOOM—a cloud of dust—a car receding into the distance—A FAINT HUM—and SILENCE.

His lips tighten. He glances at his watch again. He steps out into the middle of the highway, looks first in one direction, then the other. Nothing in sight. He loosens his tie, opens his shirt collar, looks up at the sun. Behind him, in the distance, another vehicle is HEARD approaching. He turns, looks off to the west. This one is a huge transcontinental moving van, ROARING TOWARD HIM at high speed. With quick apprehension he moves off the highway to the dusty side of the road as the van thunders past and disappears. Its FADING SOUND is replaced with a NEW SOUND, the CHUGGING of an OLD FLIVVER.

THORNHILL looks off in the direction of the approaching SOUND, sees a flivver nearing the highway from the intersecting dirt road. When the car reaches the highway, it comes to a stop. A middle-aged woman is behind the wheel. Her passenger is a nondescript MAN of about fifty. He could certainly be a farmer. He gets out of the car. It makes a U-turn and drives off in the direction from which it came. THORNHILL watches the MAN and takes up a position across the highway from him. The MAN glances at THORNHILL without visible interest, then looks off up the highway toward the east as though waiting for something to come along.

THORNHILL stares at the MAN, wondering if this is George Kaplan.

The MAN looks idly across the highway at THORNHILL, his face expres-sionless.

THORNHILL wipes his face with his handkerchief, never taking his eyes off the MAN across the highway. The FAINT SOUND of an APPROACHING

PLANE has gradually come up over the scene. As the SOUND GROWS LOUDER, THORNHILL looks up to his left and sees a low-flying biplane approach from the northwest. He watches it with mounting interest as it heads straight for the spot where he and the stranger face each other across the highway. Suddenly it is upon them, only a hundred feet above the ground, and then, like a giant bird, as THORNHILL turns with the plane's passage, it flies over them, and continues on. THORNHILL stares after the plane, his back to the highway. When the plane has gone several hundred yards beyond the highway, it loses altitude, levels off only a few feet above the ground and begins to fly back and forth in straight lines parallel to the highway, letting loose a trail of powdered dust from beneath the fuselage as it goes. Any farmer would recognize the operation as simple crop-dusting.

THORNHILL looks across the highway, sees that the stranger is watching the plane with idle interest. THORNHILL's lips set with determination. He crosses over and goes up to the MAN.

THORNHILL: Hot day.

MAN: Seen worse.

THORNHILL: Are you . . . uh . . . by any chance supposed to be meeting someone here?

MAN (still watching the plane): Waitin' for the bus. Due any minute.

THORNHILL: Oh . . .

MAN (idly): Some of them crop-duster pilots get rich, if they live long enough . . .

THORNHILL: Then your name isn't . . . Kaplan.

MAN (glances at him): Can't say it is, 'cause it ain't. (He looks off up the highway). Well—here she comes, right on time.

THORNHILL looks off to the east, sees a Greyhound bus approaching.

The MAN peers off at the plane again, and frowns.

MAN: That's funny.

THORNHILL: What?

MAN: That plane's dustin' crops where there ain't no crops.

THORNHILL looks across at the droning plane with growing suspicion as the stranger steps out onto the highway and flags the bus to a stop. THORNHILL turns toward the stranger as though to say something to him. But it is too late. The man has boarded the bus, its doors are closing, and it is pulling away. THORNHILL is alone again.

Almost immediately, he HEARS THE PLANE ENGINE BEING GUNNED TO A HIGHER SPEED. He glances off sharply, sees the plane veering off its parallel course and heading toward him. He stands there wide-eyed, rooted to the spot. The plane roars on, a few feet off the ground. There are two men in the twin cockpits, goggled, unrecognizable, menacing. He yells out to them, but his voice is lost in the NOISE OF THE PLANE. In a moment it will be upon him and decapitate him. Desperately he drops to the ground and presses himself flat as the plane zooms over him with a great noise, almost combing his hair with a landing wheel.

THORNHILL scrambles to his feet, sees the plane banking and turning. He looks about wildly, sees a telephone pole and dashes for it as the plane comes at him again. He ducks behind the pole. The plane heads straight for him, veers to the right at the last moment. We HEAR two sharp CRACKS of GUNFIRE mixed with the SOUND of the ENGINE, as two bullets slam into the pole just above THORNHILL's head.

THORNHILL reacts to this new peril, sees the plane banking for another run at him. A car is speeding along the highway from the west. THORNHILL dashes out onto the road, tries to flag the car down but the driver ignores him. He dives into a ditch and rolls away as another series of SHOTS are HEARD and bullets rake the ground that he has just occupied.

He gets to his feet, looks about, sees a cornfield about fifty yards from the highway, glances up at the plane making its turn, and decides to make a dash for the cover of the tall-growing corn.

SHOOTING DOWN FROM A HELICOPTER about one hundred feet above the ground, WE SEE THORNHILL running toward the cornfield and the plane in pursuit.

SHOOTING FROM WITHIN THE CORNFIELD, WE SEE THORNHILL come crashing in, scuttling to the right and lying flat and motionless as WE HEAR THE PLANE ZOOM OVER HIM WITH A BURST OF GUNFIRE and bullets rip into the corn, but at a safe distance from THORNHILL. He raises his head cautiously, gasping for breath, as he HEARS THE PLANE MOVE OFF AND INTO ITS TURN.

SHOOTING DOWN FROM THE HELICOPTER, we see the plane leveling off and starting a run over the cornfield, which betrays no sign of the hidden THORNHILL. Skimming over the top of the cornstalks, the plane gives forth no burst of gunfire now. Instead, it lets loose thick clouds of poisonous dust which settle down into the corn.

WITHIN THE CORNFIELD, THORNHILL, still lying flat, begins to gasp and choke as the poisonous dust envelops him. Tears stream from his eyes but he does not dare move as he HEARS THE PLANE COMING OVER THE FIELD AGAIN. When the plane zooms by and another cloud of dust hits him, he jumps to his feet and crashes out into the open, half blinded and gasping for breath. Far off down the highway to the right, he SEES a huge Diesel gasoline-tanker approaching. He starts running toward the highway to intercept it.

SHOOTING FROM THE HELICOPTER, WE SEE THORNHILL dashing for the highway, the plane leveling off for another run at him, and the Diesel tanker speeding closer.

SHOOTING ACROSS THE HIGHWAY, WE SEE THORNHILL running and stumbling TOWARD CAMERA, the plane closing in between him, and the Diesel

9–11. *North by Northwest (U.S.A., 1959), with Cary Grant, screenplay by Ernest Lehman, directed by Alfred Hitchcock.*

Much of the success of this movie is due to Grant's engaging performance as Roger O. Thornhill (the "O" stands for nothing), who's a little too slick for his own good. Only an actor of Grant's great skill could handle the comedy of his role without sacrificing credibility as a person who is being put through a living hell. *(MGM)*

tanker approaching from the left. He dashes out into the middle of the highway and waves his arms wildly.

The Diesel tanker THUNDERS down the highway toward THORNHILL, KLAXON BLASTING impatiently.

The plane speeds relentlessly toward THORNHILL from the field bordering the highway.

THORNHILL stands alone and helpless in the middle of the highway, waving his arms. The plane draws closer. The tanker is almost upon him. It isn't going to stop. He can HEAR THE KLAXON BLASTING him out of the way. There is nothing he can do. The plane has caught up with him. The tanker won't stop. It's GOT to stop. He hurls himself to the pavement directly in its path. There is A SCREAM OF BRAKES and SKIDDING TIRES, THE ROAR OF THE PLANE ENGINE and then a tremendous BOOM as the Diesel truck grinds to a stop inches from Thornhill's body just as the plane, hopelessly committed and caught unprepared by the sudden stop, slams into the traveling gasoline tanker and plane and gasoline explode into a great sheet of flame.

In the next few moments, all is confusion. THORNHILL, unhurt, rolls out from under the wheels of the Diesel truck. The drivers clamber out of the front seat and drop to the highway. Black clouds of smoke billow up from the funeral pyre of the plane and its cremated occupants. We recognize the flaming body of one of the men in the plane. It is LIGHT, one of THORNHILL's original abductors. An elderly open pickup truck with a second-hand refrigerator standing in it, which has been approaching from the east, pulls up at the side of the road. Its driver, a FARMER, jumps out and hurries toward the wreckage.

FARMER: What happened? What happened?

The Diesel truck drivers are too dazed to answer. Flames and smoke drive them all back. THORNHILL, unnoticed, heads toward the unoccupied pickup truck. Another car comes up from the west, stops, and its driver runs toward the other men. They stare, transfixed, at the holocaust. Suddenly, from behind them, they HEAR THE PICKUP TRUCK's motor starting. The FARMER who owns the truck turns, and is startled to see his truck being driven away by an utter stranger.

FARMER: Hey!

He runs after the truck. But the stranger—who is THORNHILL—steps harder on the accelerator and speeds off in the direction of Chicago.

9-12. *Sense and Sensibility* (Great Britain, 1995), *with Emma Thompson, directed by Ang Lee.*

In the 1990s, virtually all of Jane Austen's six major novels were made into movies and television series, most of them quite fine. *Sense and Sensibility* is perhaps the finest, thanks in part to Emma Thompson's superlative screenplay, which won an Academy Award. It was her first screenplay. Thompson wrote several drafts over a period of four years. "The novel is so complex and there are so many stories in it that bashing out a structure was the biggest labor," she admitted. As an actress, she knew that some of the dialogue in the novel would not translate well to film, so she turned to Austen's letters (Miss Jane was a prodigious letter writer), which contained simpler language. "Some of the sentences in the book go on forever," Thompson says, but in the letters, "Austen's personal style was very clear and elegant. And very funny." In addition to writing the screenplay, Thompson also played one of the leading roles, brilliantly. *(Columbia Pictures)*

Figurative Comparisons

In his essay "La Caméra-Stylo," Alexandre Astruc observed that one of the traditional problems of film has been its difficulty in expressing thought and ideas. The invention of sound, of course, was an enormous advantage to filmmakers, for with spoken language they could express virtually any kind of abstract thought. But film directors also wanted to explore the possibilities of the image as a conveyor of abstract ideas. Even before the sound era, filmmakers had devised a number of nonverbal figurative techniques.

A figurative technique can be defined as an artistic device that suggests abstract ideas through comparison, either implied or overt. There are a number of these techniques in both literature and cinema. The most common are **motifs, symbols,** and **metaphors.** In actual practice, there's a considerable amount of overlapping between these terms. All of them are "symbolic" in the sense that an object or event means something beyond its literal significance. Perhaps the most pragmatic method of differentiating these

9–13. *Day for Night* **(France, 1973),** *with François Truffaut (leather jacket), directed by Truffaut.*

Film titles are chosen with great deliberation because they are meant to embody the central concept behind a movie. Film titles, in short, are symbolic. The original-language title of this film is *La Nuit Américaine,* "The American Night." It reflects Truffaut's great love for American culture, especially its cinema, and deals with the making of an "old-fashioned" kind of movie—the kind they made in Hollywood in the 1940s. (Truffaut even includes a tender homage to *Citizen Kane.*) "La nuit américaine" is also what the French call the day-for-night filter, which converts sunlit scenes into nighttime scenes. The filter transforms reality—makes it magical. For Truffaut, cinema is magic.   *(Warner Bros.)*

techniques is their degree of obtrusiveness. Instead of locking each term into an airtight compartment, however, we ought to view them as general demarcations, with motifs representing the least obtrusive extreme, metaphors representing the most conspicuous, and each category overlapping somewhat with its neighbor.

Motifs are so totally integrated within the realistic texture of a film that we can almost refer to them as submerged or invisible symbols. A motif can be a technique, an object, or anything that's systematically repeated in a movie yet doesn't call attention to itself. Even after repeated viewings, a motif is not always apparent, for its symbolic significance is never permitted to emerge or detach itself from its context **(9–14)**.

Symbols can also be palpable things, but they imply additional meanings that are relatively apparent to the sensitive observer. Furthermore, the symbolic meanings of these things can shift with the dramatic context. A good example of the shifting implications of a symbol can be seen in the uncut version of Kurosawa's *The Seven Samurai* **(9–15)**. In this movie, a young samurai and a peasant girl are attracted to each other, but their class differences present insurmountable barriers. In a scene that takes place late at night, the two accidentally meet. Kurosawa emphasizes their separation by keeping them in sepa-

9-14. *Cries and Whispers* (Sweden, 1972), *with Liv Ullmann (a) and Kari Sylwan (b), written and directed by Ingmar Bergman.*
A recurrent motif in this movie is the human face split in two, suggesting self-division, the hidden self, the public versus the private self.   *(New World Pictures)*

a   b

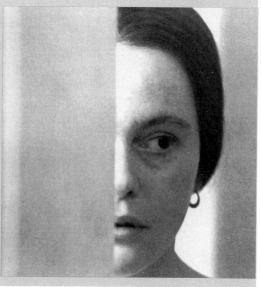

rate **frames,** a raging outdoor fire acting as a kind of barrier **(a and b).** But their attraction is too strong, and they then appear in the same shot, the fire between them now suggesting the only obstacle, yet paradoxically also suggesting the sexual passion they both feel **(c).** They draw toward each other, and the fire is now to one side, its sexual symbolism dominating **(d).** They go inside a hut, and the light from the fire outside emphasizes the eroticism of the scene **(e).** As they begin to make love in a dark corner of the hut, the shadows cast by the fire's light on the reeds of the hut seem to streak across their bodies **(f).** Suddenly, the girl's father discovers the lovers, and the billowing flames of the fire suggest his moral outrage **(g).** He is so incensed that he must be restrained by the samurai chief, both of them almost washed out visually by the intensity of the fire's light **(h).** It begins to rain, and the sorrowing young samurai walks away despondently **(i).** At the end of the sequence, Kurosawa offers a close-up of the fire as the rain extinguishes its flames **(j).**

A *metaphor* is usually defined as a comparison of some kind that cannot be literally true. Two terms not ordinarily associated are yoked together, producing a sense of literal incongruity. "Poisonous time," "torn with grief," "devoured by love" are all verbal metaphors involving symbolic rather than literal descriptions. Editing is a frequent source of metaphors in film, for two shots can be linked together to produce a third, and symbolic, idea. In *2001: A Space Odyssey,* director Stanley Kubrick joined two shots that are separated by millions of years to create a startling metaphor of human intelligence. In one sequence depicting "the dawn of man," we see a tribe of apes attacking another tribe. One ape picks up a thigh bone and uses it to kill his enemy. It is, in effect, a primitive weapon, a kind of machine. The victorious ape triumphantly hurls the bleached out thigh bone in the air. As it falls back to earth in slow motion, Kubrick cuts to a shot of a white spaceship, shaped like the bone, floating effortlessly through space, in the year 2001. The bone-cudgel and the spaceship are being compared: Both are machines, and both represent giant leaps in human intelligence.

There is usually a sense of shock in metaphorical comparisons. Two traits are violently joined together, often in violation of common sense. For example, in *Trainspotting* **(5–29),** which explores the desperate lifestyle of several Scottish heroin addicts, the protagonist (Ewan McGregor) is forced to satisfy his drug habit anally, with a heroin suppository. While sitting on "the filthiest toilet in the world," he accidentally expels the suppository. In desperation, he literally dives into the toilet and swims frantically through a quagmire of urine and feces, while he retrieves his suppository. Obviously, the sequence—which is shocking, disgusting, and funny at the same time—is not meant to be taken literally. His swimming through his own fetid waste is a metaphor to dramatize how all-consuming his addiction is. This is also a good illustration of the *power* of metaphors: We are not likely to want to try using heroin after seeing this stomach-churning scene, which is more effective than ten sermons on the dangers of drugs. Another striking use of metaphor is found in *American*

9-15. ***The Seven Samurai*** **(Japan, 1954),** *directed by Akira Kurosawa.*
Realistic films tend to use symbols less densely than formalist movies, and the symbolism is almost always contextually probable. For example, in addition to being a symbol, the fire in this scene is also a fire.   *(Toho International)*

continued ▶

Beauty, where the hero's sexual fantasies are associated with red rose petals (see **C.P.3**).

There are two other kinds of figurative techniques in film and literature: **allegory** and **allusions.** The first is seldom used in movies because it tends toward simplemindedness. What's usually involved in this technique is an avoidance of realism. A correspondence exists between a character or situation and a symbolic idea or complex of ideas **(9–17).** One of the most famous examples of

e

f

g

h

i

j

9-16.   *Psycho* **(U.S.A., 1960),** *directed by Alfred Hitchcock.*
Cinematic metaphors can be created through the use of **special effects,** as in this **dissolve**
which yields the final shot of the film—the dredging up of a car from a swamp. Three images
are dissolved: **(1)** a shot of a catatonic youth (Anthony Perkins) looking directly at us; **(2)** a
duplicate shot of his mother's skeleton, whose skull flickers briefly beneath her son's features
and whose personality he has now assumed; and **(3)** a heavy chain which seems anchored to
his/her heart, hauling up the murder victim's car which contains her corpse.   *(Paramount Pictures)*

allegory is the character of Death in Bergman's *The Seventh Seal.* There's not
much ambiguity involved in what the character is supposed to symbolize. Allegorical narratives are especially popular in the German cinema. For example,
virtually all the works of Werner Herzog deal with the idea of life in general, the
nature of the human condition in broadly symbolic terms.

An *allusion* is a common type of literary analogy. It's an implied reference, usually to a well-known event, person, or work of art. The protagonist of
Hawks's *Scarface* was modeled on the gangster Al Capone (who had a well-
publicized scar in the shape of a cross on his cheek), an allusion that wasn't lost
on audiences of the time. Filmmakers often draw on religious mythology for
their allusions. For example, the Judeo-Christian myth of the Garden of Eden is
used in such disparate works as *The Garden of the Finzi-Continis, Days of Heaven,
How Green Was My Valley, The Tree of the Wooden Clogs,* and *The Thin Red Line.*

9–17. *Strawberry and Chocolate* (Cuba, 1994), *with Jorge Perugorria and Vladimir Cruz, directed by Tomás Gutiérrez Alea (with Juan Carlos Tabío).*

Not all allegories are self-consciously symbolic: Some are slyly so. *Strawberry and Chocolate* seems to be a realistic study of life in contemporary Havana, but the movie is also a thinly veiled political allegory—sadly, an honorable genre in communist and ex-communist countries. The film explores an unlikely friendship between Diego (Perugorría) and David (Cruz). Diego is gay, artistic, and a "freethinker"—all dangerous traits in Castro's Cuba. David is straight, sober, and a committed communist zealot. Alea, one of Cuba's most respected filmmakers, pointed out that the movie is really about living under the rule of a repressive government: "As a society we are becoming aware of the mistakes we have made over the years, and it's time for a change," Alea has said. "*Strawberry and Chocolate* points out a basic problem within Cuban society—our inability to accept others who are different from ourselves." *(Miramax Films)*

In the cinema, an overt reference or allusion to another movie, director, or memorable shot is sometimes called a **homage.** The cinematic homage is a kind of quote, the director's graceful tribute to a colleague or established master **(9–18b).** Homages were popularized by Godard and Truffaut, whose movies are profuse in such tributes. In Godard's *A Woman Is a Woman,* for example, two decidedly nonmusical characters burst out in spontaneous song and dance while expressing their desire to appear in an MGM musical by Gene Kelly, choreographed by Bob Fosse. Fosse's *All That Jazz* contains many homages to his idol Fellini, and especially to *8½.* Steven Spielberg often pays tribute to his two idols, Walt Disney and Alfred Hitchcock.

9–18a. *Hot Shots! Part Deux* **(U.S.A., 1993),** *with Charlie Sheen and Valeria Golino, directed by Jim Abrahams.*
An allusion is an indirect reference, sometimes respectful, other times scornful, to an artist or work of art. This movie is filled with comical film allusions, some of which are recognizable only to the cognoscenti, hard-core film fans. For example, this shot is a playful allusion to a scene from the Disney animated romance, *The Lady and the Tramp,* in which two moonstruck canines share a platter of spaghetti.   *(Twentieth Century-Fox)*

9–18b. *Pennies From Heaven* **(U.S.A., 1981),** *directed by Herbert Ross.*
This movie, a brilliantly innovative musical, includes many popular songs of the Depression era of the 1930s. It also includes a number of visual homages to the great American painter, Edward Hopper. This shot, a striking recreation of Hopper's famous painting, "Nighthawks," emphasizes the loneliness and alienation of the Era. *Pennies From Heaven* might well be the darkest musical ever made—both technically and thematically. It was photographed by Hollywood's prince of darkness, Gordon Willis.   *(MGM)*

Point of View

Point of view in literary fiction generally concerns the narrator, through whose eyes the events of a story are viewed. The ideas and incidents are sifted through the consciousness and language of the storyteller. He or she may or may not be a participant in the action, and may or may not be a reliable guide for the reader to follow. There are four basic types of point of view in literary fiction: (1) the first person, (2) the omniscient, (3) the third person, and (4) the objective. In movies, point of view tends to be less rigorous than in novels, for although there are cinematic equivalents of the four basic types of narration, fiction films tend to fall naturally into the omniscient form.

The **first-person narrator** tells his or her own story. In some cases, he or she is an objective observer who can be relied on to relate the events accurately. Nick Carraway in Fitzgerald's *The Great Gatsby* is a good example of this kind of narrator. Other first-person narrators are subjectively involved in the main action and can't be totally relied on. In *Huckleberry Finn*, the immature Huck relates all the events as he experienced them. Huck obviously can't supply his readers with all the necessary information when he himself does not possess it. In using this type of first-person narrator, the novelist must somehow permit the reader to see the truth without violating the plausibility of the narrator. Generally, a novelist solves this problem by providing the reader with clues that permit us to see more clearly than the narrator. For example, when Huck enthusiastically recounts the glamour of a circus and the "amazing feats" of its

9–19. *The Lady from Shanghai* (U.S.A., 1948), *with Rita Hayworth, Orson Welles, and Everett Sloane; directed by Welles.*
Voice-over commentaries are commonplace in the genre known as *film noir.* Movies of this type often feature flashback images of the past accompanied by a present-tense off-screen narrator who tells us how he managed to get himself in such a desperate crisis. This film is narrated by Orson Welles, who plays an innocent and not-very-bright sailor who lives to tell his tale—just barely. *(Columbia Pictures)*

performers, the more sophisticated reader sees beyond Huck's words and infers that the performers are in fact a rather shabby crew and their theatrical acts merely cheap deceptions.

Many films use first-person narrative techniques, but only sporadically. The cinematic equivalent to the "voice" of the literary narrator is the "eye" of the camera, and this difference is an important one. In literature, the distinction between the narrator and the reader is clear: It's as if we were listening to a friend tell a story. In film, however, the viewer identifies with the lens, and thus tends to *fuse* with the narrator. To produce first-person narration in film, the camera would have to record all the action through the eyes of the character, which, in effect, would also make the viewer the protagonist.

In *The Lady of the Lake,* Robert Montgomery attempted to use the first-person camera throughout the film. It was an interesting experiment, but a failure, for several reasons. In the first place, the director was forced into a number of absurdities. Having the characters address the camera was not too much of a problem, for **point-of-view shots** are common in most movies. However, there were several actions where the device simply broke down. When a woman walked up to the hero and kissed him, for example, she had to slink toward the camera and begin to embrace it while her face came closer to the lens. Similarly, when the hero was involved in a fistfight, the antagonist literally had to attack the camera, which jarred appropriately whenever the "narrator" was dealt a blow. The problem with the exclusive use of the first-person camera, then, is its literalness. Furthermore, it tends to create a sense of frustration in the viewer: we want to *see* the hero. In fiction, we get to know people through their words, through their judgments and values, which are reflected in their language. But in movies, we get to know a character by seeing how he or she reacts to people and events. Unless the director breaks the first-person camera convention, we can never see the hero, we can only see what he sees.

The **omniscient point of view** is often associated with the nineteenth-century novel. Generally, such narrators are not participants in a story but are all-knowing observers who supply the reader with all the facts we need to know to appreciate the story. Such narrators can span many locations and time periods and can enter the consciousness of a number of different characters, telling us what they think and feel. Omniscient narrators can be relatively detached from the story, as in *War and Peace.* Or they can take on a distinct personality of their own, as in *Tom Jones,* where the amiable storyteller amuses us with his wry observations and judgments.

Omniscient narration is almost inevitable in film. Each time the director moves the camera—either within a shot or between shots—we are offered a new point of view from which to evaluate the scene. The filmmaker can cut easily from a subjective point-of-view shot (first person) to a variety of objective shots. He or she can concentrate on a single reaction (close-up) or the simultaneous reactions of several characters **(long shot).** Within a matter of seconds, film directors can show us a cause and an effect, an action and a reaction. They can connect various time periods and locations almost

9–20. *Nashville* **(U.S.A., 1975),** *with Lily Tomlin and Robert Doqui, directed by Robert Altman.*

Throughout the 1970s, Altman revolutionized filmmaking with his improvisational techniques. Though the screenplay to *Nashville* is credited to Joan Tewkesbury, in fact she never wrote a conventional script. As she explained, "What you have to do for a director like Bob is to provide an environment in which he can work." For example, *Nashville* is structured mosaically, tracing the activities of twenty-four eccentric characters over a five-day period in the city of Nashville, the heart of the country music industry. One wag referred to the film as "twenty-four characters in search of a movie." Tewkesbury created many of the characters in sketch form, then mapped out what each major character would be doing at any given time. Most of the dialogue and details for the actions were created by the actors. They even composed their own songs. "It's like jazz," Altman explained. "You're not planning any of this that you film. You're capturing." *(Paramount Pictures)*

instantaneously (parallel editing), or literally superimpose different time periods (dissolve or **multiple exposure).** The omniscient camera can be a dispassionate observer, as it is in many of Chaplin's films, or it can be a witty commentator—an evaluater of events—as it often is in Hitchcock's films or those of Lubitsch.

In the third person, a nonparticipating narrator tells a story from the consciousness of a single character. In some novels, this narrator completely penetrates the mind of a character; in others, there is virtually no penetration. In Jane Austen's *Pride and Prejudice,* for example, we learn what Elizabeth Bennet thinks and feels about events, but we're never permitted to enter the consciousness of the other characters. We can only guess what they feel through Elizabeth's interpretations—which are often inaccurate. Her interpretations are not offered directly to the reader as in the first person, but through the intermediacy of the narrator, who tells us her responses.

9–21. *They Shoot Horses, Don't They?* **(U.S.A., 1969),** *with Bonnie Bedelia, Bruce Dern, Jane Fonda, and Red Buttons; directed by Sydney Pollack.*

Much is usually eliminated from a novel as complex as Horace McCoy's grim masterpiece about a 1930s marathon dance contest. The novelist can focus on only a few details at a time in a linear sequence. Movies can bombard us with hundreds of details simultaneously, as Leo Braudy has pointed out: "The muted emphasis on gesture, makeup, intonation, and bodily movement possible in film can enrich a character with details that would intrude blatantly if they were separately verbalized in a novel." For example, in the novel, McCoy can tell us what was going on in the grueling race pictured, but only selectively, with a few telling details. The movie version, shot partly in slow motion, shows us all the agonized faces and twisted bodies of the contestants, who are exhausted to stupefaction, as they doggedly trudge forward, supporting and even hauling their collapsed partners, while the cheering spectators urge on their favorites. It is a choreographed vision of Hell.   *(Palomar/ABC Cinerama)*

In movies, there is a rough equivalent to the third person, but it's not so rigorous as in literature. Usually, third-person narration is found in documentaries where an anonymous commentator tells us about the background of a central character. In Sidney Meyer's *The Quiet One,* for example, the visuals dramatize certain traumatic events in the life of an impoverished youngster, Donald. On the soundtrack, James Agee's commentary tells us some of the reasons why Donald behaves as he does, how he feels about his parents, his peers, and his teachers.

The *objective point of view* is also a variation of the omniscient. Objective narration is the most detached of all: It doesn't enter the consciousness of any character, but merely reports events from the outside. In fact, this voice has been likened to a camera in that it records events impartially. It presents facts and allows readers to interpret for themselves. The objective voice is more congenial to film than to literature, for movies literally do use a camera. The cinematic objective point of view is generally used by realistic directors who keep their camera at long shot and avoid all distortions or "commentary" such as **angles, lenses,** and **filters.**

Literary Adaptations

A great many movies are adaptations of literary sources. In some respects, adapting a novel or play requires more skill and originality than working with an original screenplay. Furthermore, the better the literary work, the more difficult the adaptation. For this reason, many film adaptations are based on mediocre sources, for few people will get upset at the modifications required in film if the source itself isn't of the highest caliber. There are many adaptations that are superior to their originals: *The Birth of a Nation,* for instance, was based on Thomas Dixon's trashy novel *The Klansman,* which is more blatantly racist than the film. Some commentators believe that if a work of art has reached its fullest artistic expression in one form, an adaptation will inevitably be inferior. According to this argument, no film adaptation of *Pride and Prejudice* could equal the original, nor could any novel hope to capture the richness of *Persona,* or even *Citizen Kane,* which is a rather literary movie.

9-22. *The Talented Mr. Ripley* (U.S.A., 1999), *with Cate Blanchett and Matt Damon, adapted and directed by Anthony Minghella.*

This movie is a good example of the oversimplification of critical terms. Most people would probably identify the film as a faithful adaptation of Patricia Highsmith's novel, since the film follows the main lines of the book fairly closely. However, Minghella made two major changes. He invented the Blanchett character, a flighty rich American, probably to add some comic relief to this downbeat tale of deception and murder. Even more of a departure from the novel is the Damon character. In the book, Tom Ripley is an envious, calculating opportunist. When he murders the object of his envy, he does so with total premeditation, relishing how he will destroy his enemy. In the movie, Ripley kills him spontaneously, furious that the object of his admiration (and repressed lust) is rejecting him. As played by the all-American Matt Damon, Ripley is more sympathetic in the film, more normal, more like us. The movie probably falls somewhere between a loose and a faithful adaptation. *(Paramount Pictures and Miramax Films)*

There's a good deal of sense in this view, for we've seen how literature and film tend to solve problems differently, how the true content of each medium is organically governed by its forms.

The real problem of the adapter is not how to reproduce the *content* of a literary work (an impossibility), but how close he or she should remain to the raw data of the *subject matter.* This degree of fidelity is what determines the three types of adaptations: the **loose,** the **faithful,** and the **literal.** Of course, these classifications are for convenience only, for in actual practice most movies fall somewhere in between **(9–22).**

The *loose adaptation* is barely that. Generally, only an idea, a situation, or a character is taken from a literary source, then developed independently. Loose film adaptations can be likened to Shakespeare's treatment of a story from Plutarch or Bandello, or to the plays of ancient Greek dramatists, who often drew on a common mythology. A film that falls into this class is Kurosawa's *Ran,* which transforms Shakespeare's *King Lear* into a quite different tale set in

9–23.   *Throne of Blood* (Japan, 1957), *based on Shakespeare's* **Macbeth,** *directed by Akira Kurosawa.*
The loose adaptation takes a few general ideas from an original source, then develops them independently. Many commentators consider Kurosawa's film the greatest of all Shakespearean adaptations precisely because the filmmaker doesn't attempt to compete with *Macbeth.* Kurosawa's samurai movie is a *cinematic* masterpiece, these commentators claim, owing relatively little to language for its power. Its similarities to Shakespeare's literary masterpiece are superficial, just as the play's similarities to Holingshed's *Chronicles* (Shakespeare's primary source) are of no great artistic significance.   *(Audio-Brandon Films)*

9–24. *The Man Who Would Be King* (U.S.A., 1975), *with (right to left) Sean Connery and Michael Caine, written by John Huston and Gladys Hill, based on a story by Rudyard Kipling, directed by Huston.*
Virtually all of Huston's works are based on novels, plays, and short stories. Critic James Agee noted that the better the original material, the better Huston functions as an artist. His adaptations have encompassed such disparate authors as Dashiell Hammett, B. Traven, Stephen Crane, Herman Melville, Arthur Miller, Tennessee Williams, Carson McCullers, Flannery O'Connor, James Joyce, and the writers of the Book of Genesis. "I don't seek to interpret, to put my own stamp on the material," Huston pointed out. "I try to be as faithful to the original material as I can." *(Allied Artists)*

medieval Japan, though the filmmaker retains several plot elements from Shakespeare's original (see also **9–23**).

Faithful adaptations, as the phrase implies, attempt to re-create the literary source in filmic terms, keeping as close to the spirit of the original as possible **(9–24)**. André Bazin likened the faithful adapter to a translator who tries to find equivalents to the original. Of course, Bazin realized that fundamental differences exist between the two mediums: The translator's problem in convert-

9–25. *The Member of the Wedding* (U.S.A., 1952), *with Julie Harris and Ethel Waters, directed by Fred Zinnemann.*
Literal film adaptations are pretty much restricted to stage plays. Both the language and the actions transfer easily to the movie screen. One of the problems facing the film director who wishes to adapt a play is whether to "open it up." That is, whether to dramatize off-stage actions on the screen. Doing so would run the risk of releasing the spatial tensions of the original. Zinnemann's adaptation of Carson McCullers's play (itself based on her novel) confines most of the action to a single location. The young protagonist's longing to "bust loose" is conveyed primarily by close, tightly framed shots that seem to restrict her movements. *(Columbia Pictures)*

ing the word *road* to *strada* or *strasse* is not so acute as a filmmaker's problem in transforming the word into a picture. An example of a faithful adaptation is Richardson's *Tom Jones.* John Osborne's screenplay preserves much of the novel's plot structure, its major events, and most of the important characters. Even the witty omniscient narrator is retained. But the film is not merely an illustration of the novel. In the first place, Fielding's book is too packed with incidents for a film adaptation. The many inn scenes, for example, are reduced to a central episode: the Upton Inn sequence.

Literal adaptations are usually restricted to plays **(9–25)**. As we have seen, the two basic modes of drama—action and dialogue—are also found in films. The major problem with stage adaptations is in the handling of space and time rather than language. If the film adapter were to leave the camera at long shot and restrict the editing to scene shifts only, the result would be similar to the original. But we've seen that few filmmakers would be willing merely to record a play, for in doing so they would lose much of the excitement of the original and contribute none of the advantages of the adapting medium, particularly its greater freedom in treating space and time.

Movies can add many dimensions to a play, especially through the use of close-ups and edited juxtapositions. Because these techniques aren't found in the theater, even "literal" adaptations are not strictly literal; they're simply more subtle in their modifications. Stage dialogue is often retained in film adaptations, but its effect is different on the audience. In the live theater, the meaning of the language is determined by the fact that the characters are on the same stage at the same time, reacting to the same words. In a movie, time and space are fragmented by the individual shots. Furthermore, because even a literary film is primarily visual and only secondarily verbal, nearly all the dialogue is modified by the images.

A systematic analysis of the writing in a movie would explore the following questions. How "literary" is the film? Is there an emphasis on lengthy speeches, verbal wit or adroitness, talky scenes? How articulate are the characters? If not very, how do we get to know what's bothering them? Who contributed what to the screenplay? (This is not easily determined information, except for the most critically admired movies, which have been researched more exhaustively than routine pictures.) Is the dialogue stylized or does it aim to sound like realistic speech? Does the movie contain any figurative tropes: motifs, symbols, metaphors? How do these deepen and enrich the movie? Whose point of view is the film told from? Is there a voice-over narrator? What kind of rapport does the narrator establish with us? If the movie is a literary adaptation, is it loose, faithful, or literal?

FURTHER READING

BLUESTONE, GEORGE, *Novels into Film* (Baltimore, Md.: Johns Hopkins University Press, 1957). Classic study, with a valuable introductory essay.

BLUM, RICH, *Television and Screen Writing: From Concept to Contract*, 3rd ed. (New York: Focal Press, 1995). Practical manual.

BOYUM, JOY GOULD, *Double Exposure: Fiction into Film* (New York: New American Library, 1985). Analyses of eighteen literary adaptations by an intelligent critic.

BRADY, JOHN, *The Craft of the Screenwriter* (New York: Touchstone, 1982). Interviews with six American screenwriters, including Chayefsky, Goldman, Lehman, and others.

CORLISS, RICHARD, *The Hollywood Screenwriters* (New York: Avon Books, 1972). Encyclopedic coverage of many of the best screenwriters of the Hollywood studio era.

Creative Screenwriting is the leading American journal devoted to television and movie writing. It features critical articles, script excerpts, and interviews with writers.

GOLDMAN, WILLIAM, *Adventures in the Screen Trade* (New York: Warner Books, 1983). Personal account by a respected Hollywood screenwriter.

GRANT, BARRY KEITH, *Film Genre Reader* (Austin: University of Texas Press, 1986). A collection of scholarly essays.

HORTON, ANDREW, *Writing the Character-Centered Screenplay* (Berkeley: University of California Press, 1994). Practical advice on building characters.

SEGER, LINDA, *The Art of Adaptation* (New York: Henry Holt, 1992). Subtitled *Turning Fact and Fiction Into Film*. Practical emphasis.

Ideology

*The history of all human society, past and present,
has been the history of class struggle.*
—KARL MARX, PHILOSOPHER AND POLITICAL SCIENTIST

Overview

Ideology: a set of values and priorities. Pleasure versus instruction. Degree of explicitness: neutral, implicit, and explicit. Hidden values: the star system, sympathetic characters, genre. The left-center-right model. Key comparisons: democratic–hierarchical, environment–heredity, relative–absolute, secular–religious, future–past, cooperation–competition, outsiders–insiders, international–nationalistic, sexual freedom–monogamy. Culture, religion, and ethnicity. National film traits. Religious values left and right. Ethnic tensions. Sexual politics: feminism and gay liberation. The Third World and Japan: the oppression of women. The camp sensibility. Tone: What's the movie *really* saying? Ideological subtexts: the role of acting, genre, narration, and music in establishing tone.

Ideology is usually defined as a body of ideas reflecting the social needs and aspirations of an individual, group, class, or culture. The term is generally associated with politics and party platforms, but it can also mean a given set of values that are implicit in any human enterprise—including filmmaking. Virtually every movie presents us with role models, ideal ways of behaving, negative traits, and an implied morality based on the filmmaker's sense of right and wrong. In short, every film has a slant, a given ideological perspective that privileges certain characters, institutions, behaviors, and motives as attractive, and downgrades an opposing set as repellent.

Since ancient times, critics have discussed art as having a double function: to teach and to provide pleasure. Some movies emphasize the didactic, the teaching function. How? The most obvious method is simply to preach at the audience. Such movies try to sell us a bill of goods, like TV commercials or propaganda films such as *October* **(10–6)** or *Triumph of the Will* **(10–12).** At the opposite extreme, the abstract wing of the **avant-garde** cinema, the pictures seem totally devoid of moral values, because in effect they have no subject matter other than "pure" forms. Their purpose? To provide pleasure.

The tradition of **classical cinema** avoids the extremes of didacticism and pure abstraction, but even light entertainment movies are steeped in value judgments. "Classical cinema is the ventriloquist of ideology," states critic Daniel Dayan. "Who is ordering these images and to what purpose? are questions classical filmmakers wish to avoid, for they want the movie 'to speak for itself.'" Viewers can absorb the ideological values without being aware of it, as in *Pretty Woman* **(10–1).**

In actual practice, movies are highly variable in their degree of ideological explicitness. For purposes of convenience, we can classify them under three broad categories:

Neutral. Escapist films and light entertainment movies often bland out the social environment in favor of a vaguely benevolent setting that allows the story to take place smoothly. The emphasis is on action,

10–1. *Pretty Woman* (U.S.A., 1990), *with Julia Roberts and Richard Gere, directed by Garry Marshall.*
A film's narrative can be profoundly ideological, even when the movie purports to be light entertainment. Loosely based on the Pygmalion myth, *Pretty Woman* is about a love affair that develops between a ditsy hooker with the proverbial heart of gold (Roberts) and a rather cold and wealthy businessman (Gere) who hires her as a paid companion. Feminists were appalled by the film because it implicitly reinforces the notion of male supremacy and reduces the heroine to a sex object needing to be "rescued" by a Prince Charming who will make her life meaningful—a narrative pattern that feminists refer to as "the Cinderella syndrome." *(Touchstone Pictures)*

pleasure, and entertainment values for their own sake. Issues of right and wrong are treated superficially, with little or no analysis, as in *Bringing Up Baby* **(10–33).** The most extreme examples of this category are nonrepresentational avant-garde films like *Allures* **(1–7)** and *Rhythmus 21* **(4–7),** which are virtually devoid of ideology; their values are mainly aesthetic—a color, a shape, a kinetic swirl.

Implicit. The protagonists and antagonists represent conflicting value systems, but these are not dwelled on. We must infer what the characters stand for as their tale unfolds. Nobody spells out "the moral of the story." The materials are slanted in a particular direction, but transparently, without obvious manipulation, as in *Splash* **(11–10a),** *L'Avventura* **(3–7),** and *Pretty Woman* **(10–1).**

Explicit. Thematically oriented movies aim to teach or persuade as much as to entertain. Patriotic films, many documentaries, political films like Oliver Stone's *JFK* **(8–20),** and movies with a sociological emphasis such as John Singleton's *Boyz N the Hood* **(10–20a)** fall under this category. Usually an admirable character articulates the values that are really important, like Bogart's famous speech at the end of *Casablanca* **(9–5b).** The most extreme examples of this category include propaganda films, which repeatedly advocate a partisan point of view with an overt appeal to our sympathy and support. Serious film critics often zap hard-sell movies like these, but a few—like *Roger & Me* (10–2)—are admired for their wit or their stylistic panache.

The overwhelming majority of fiction films fall into the implicit category. In other words, because the characters don't talk at length about what they believe in, we've got to dig beneath the surface and construct their value systems on the basis of what their goals are, what they take for granted, how they behave with others, how they react to a crisis, and so on. Filmmakers create sympathetic characters by dramatizing such traits as idealism, courage, generosity, fair play, kindness, and loyalty.

In the American cinema especially, the star system is often a clue to values, especially when the protagonist is played by a **personality star** like John Wayne (10–3). **Actor stars** are less likely to be ideologically weighted. For example, Glenn Close has played villainous characters as well as admirable heroines.

Good looks and sex appeal are compelling traits, predisposing us in favor of a given character. Sometimes an actor's appeal is so strong that he or

10–2.   *Roger & Me* (U.S.A., 1989), *with Michael Moore (center); written, directed, and produced by Moore.*
The premise of this controversial documentary is that if only Moore could get to talk to Roger Smith, the then-president of General Motors, perhaps Smith could explain G.M.'s closing of its Flint, Michigan, plants in favor of cheap foreign labor abroad. The premise is a pretext for showing us the harsh economic consequences of the closedown on the residents of Flint—a sad tale of desperation, resourcefulness, and despair. The movie is frankly one-sided and manipulative—a hard sell. But it's also compassionate, shrewd, and very funny.   *(Warner Bros.)*

10-3. *The Searchers* (U.S.A., 1956), *with John Wayne, directed by John Ford.*
Personality stars frequently convey a ready-made ideology—a set of values that are associated with a given star because of his or her previous film roles. Their **personas** often incorporate elements from their actual lives as well. For example, John Wayne was associated in the public mind with a **right-wing** ideology. Most of his roles were military commanders, western heroes, law-and-order advocates, and authoritarian patriarchs. In private life, he was an outspoken conservative, an America-first patriot who championed respect for authority, family values, and military supremacy. *(Warner Bros.)*

she can win over an audience even in ideologically opposite roles, like Tom Cruise in the **right**-leaning *Top Gun* or the **left-wing** *Born on the Fourth of July.* Similarly, Julia Roberts's performance in *Pretty Woman* is so spontaneous and charismatic that she can almost make us forget that her character as written is little more than a compendium of sexist clichés.

There are a variety of other methods to enlist our sympathies. Underdogs almost automatically win us over to their side. Emotionally vulnerable characters appeal to our protective instincts. People who are funny, charming, and/or intelligent are similarly winning. In fact, these traits can do much to soften our dislike of an otherwise negative character. In *The Silence of the Lambs,* the character of Hannibal the Cannibal (Anthony Hopkins) is a psychotic killer, but because he's also witty and imaginative, we are oddly attracted to him—at least from a distance **(6–18).**

Negatively drawn characters incorporate such traits as selfishness, meanspiritedness, greed, cruelty, tyrannical behavior, disloyalty, and so on. Villains and other repellent characters are often played by actors who are made to look unattractive. The more explicit the ideology, the more such traits are portrayed without mitigation. However, except for melodramas, in which good and evil are usually treated in black-and-white terms, most film characters combine positive and negative traits. This is especially so in movies that purport to be lifelike and realistic, like *Story of Women* **(10–4).**

Analyzing a character's ideological values is often a difficult task precisely because many characters are a fusion of contradictory sentiments. To further complicate the issue, a character's ideological values are not necessarily those of the filmmaker. For example, the movies of the French director Jean-Luc Godard often feature characters of various ideologies, and we can never be entirely certain whether Godard agrees with them or to what extent.

Some filmmakers are so technically skillful that we can be swept up by a character's values even when we don't hold them in actuality. For example, many of the positive values of D. W. Griffith's *The Birth of a Nation* are embodied

10–4.   *Story of Women* (France, 1988), *with Isabelle Huppert, directed by Claude Chabrol.* In realistic films especially, characterization is generally complex and ambiguous, filled with the contradictions of life. Based on an actual series of events that took place in France during the Nazi occupation, *Story of Women* deals with a working-class housewife (Huppert) who comes to the aid of a desperate girlfriend who feels trapped by an unwanted pregnancy. The Huppert character helps her by performing an illegal abortion. Later she helps another despairing woman who has had six offspring in seven years and is wracked with guilt because she no longer loves her children. Soon the protagonist is running a profitable abortion business, becoming coarser with each transaction. Eventually, she is arrested, tried, and executed for her crimes by an all-male system of justice. Our sympathies are torn both ways. On the one hand, the protagonist is strong and independent, a loyal friend and a shrewd critic of the old-boy network that forces women to be baby machines for the state. On the other hand, as a result of her greed, she wrecks her marriage and destroys the lives of her own children, not to speak of her sleazy association with a Nazi collaborator who becomes her lover.   *(An MK2/New Yorker Films Release)*

in the character of "the little colonel"—one of the founders of the Ku Klux Klan. Few of us would applaud the racist values of the Klan in real life, but while watching the movie, it's necessary to suspend our personal beliefs in order to enter the worldview of the protagonist and the filmmaker. For those who cannot, the film must remain a moral failure, notwithstanding its stylistic brilliance.

In short, ideology is another language system in film, albeit an often disguised language that usually speaks in codes. We have seen how dialects can be ideological, as in *All Screwed Up* (**5–28**) and *Trainspotting* (**5–29**). Editing styles—especially a manipulative style like Soviet montage—can be profoundly ideological, like the Odessa Steps sequence from *Potemkin* (**4–21**). Costumes and décor can suggest ideological ideas, as can be seen in movies like *The Leopard* (**7–25**). Even space is ideologically charged in such films as *The Grifters* (**2–20**), *Henry V,* and *Dances with Wolves* (**10–13a** & **b**). In other words, political ideas can be found in form as well as content.

A lot of people claim that they're not interested in politics, but virtually everything is ultimately ideological. Our attitudes toward sex, work, power sharing, authority, the family, religion—all of these involve ideological assumptions, whether we are conscious of the fact or not. In movies, too, characters rarely articulate their political credos, but in most cases, we can piece together their ideological values and assumptions on the basis of their casual remarks about these topics.

A word of caution. Ideological labels are just that—labels. Seldom do they approach the complexity of human beliefs. After all, most of us are liberal about some matters, conservative about others. The same can be said about movies and the characters in them. The following value systems are merely roadmaps that can be helpful in determining a movie's ideology, but unless they're applied with sensitivity and common sense, these labels can be crudely simplistic.

The Left–Center–Right Model

Traditionally, journalists and political scientists have used the tripartite left–center–right model in differentiating political ideologies. In actual practice, these orientations can be broken down even further, as in Figure **10–5**. An example of the extreme leftist position would be communism under Stalin (**10–6**); at the extreme right, the Nazi empire under Hitler (**10–12**). Both extremes are totalitarian systems, of course.

We can differentiate a film's ideology by focusing on some key institutions and values and analyzing how the characters relate to them. Some of these key elements are presented next in bipolar categories. Neither the left nor the right is necessarily better or worse than the other. There have been eloquent proponents for each side. However, the totalitarian extremes have produced few rational enthusiasts.

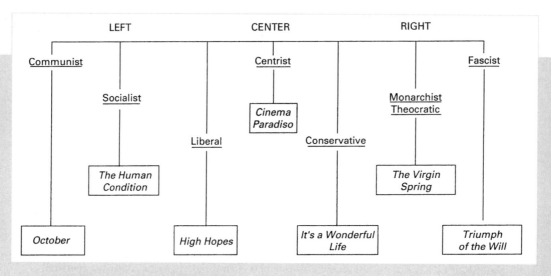

```
        LEFT              CENTER              RIGHT
```

Communist _____ Centrist _____ Fascist

    Socialist   Monarchist / Theocratic

Cinema Paradiso

    Liberal   Conservative

The Human Condition

The Virgin Spring

October   *High Hopes*   *It's a Wonderful Life*   *Triumph of the Will*

10–5. Ideology spectrum.

Democratic Versus Hierarchical

Leftists tend to emphasize the similarities among people. We all eat about the same amount of food, breathe the same amount of air. Likewise, leftists believe that a society's resources should be distributed in roughly equal portions, as is implied in *The Human Condition* (**10–7**) and *Pixote* (**10–14**). Authority figures are merely skilled managers and not intrinsically superior to the people they are responsible to. Important institutions should be publicly owned. In some societies, all basic industries such as banking, utilities, health, and education are operated for the equal benefit of all citizens. The emphasis is on the collective, the communal.

Rightists emphasize the differences among people, insisting that the best and the brightest are entitled to a larger share of power and the economic pie than less productive workers, as is implied in *Henry V* (**10–13a**). Authority should be respected. Social institutions are guided by strong leaders, not the rank-and-file or even average citizens. Most institutions should be privately owned, with profit as the main incentive to productivity. The emphasis is on the individual and an elite managerial class.

Environment Versus Heredity

Leftists believe that human behavior is learned and can be changed by proper environmental incentives. Antisocial behavior is largely the result of poverty, prejudice, lack of education, and low social status rather than human nature or lack of character, as in *The Chant of Jimmie Blacksmith* (**10–19**).

Rightists believe that character is largely inborn and genetically inherited. Hence the emphasis of many right-wingers on lineage and the advantage of

418

10–6. *October* (U.S.S.R., 1928), *directed by Sergei Eisenstein.*
Also known as *Ten Days That Shook the World,* Eisenstein's movie is a celebration of the 1917 Russian Revolution. Frankly propagandistic, the film is filled with hope for the future as well as contempt for the Czarist past, which is portrayed as a Dark Age. An **epic** requires an epic hero—in this case, Lenin (pictured), the Father of the Soviet Revolution. He is seen here dramatically highlighted by smoke and lightbeams, like a god rising from the ashes of battle. Though the movie is crudely explicit ideologically, it contains images of striking beauty, boldly juxtaposed in Eisenstein's **dialectical** style of editing.
(Sovkino)

coming from "a good family," as in *Late Spring* (**8–15**) and *Late Autumn* (**10–16**). In some Asian societies especially, ancestor worship is common.

Relative Versus Absolute

People on the left believe that we ought to be flexible in our judgments, capable of adjusting to the specifics of each case. Children are characteristically raised in a permissive environment and encouraged in self-expression, as in *My Life as a Dog* (**8–9a**). Moral values are merely social conventions, not eternal verities. Issues of right and wrong must be placed in a social context, including any mitigating circumstances, before we can judge them fairly.

Rightists are more absolute in judging human behavior. Children are expected to be disciplined, respectful, and obedient to their elders. Right and

10–7. *The Human Condition—No Greater Love* **(Japan, 1959),** *with Tatsuya Nakadai (left), directed by Masaki Kobayashi.*
Kobayashi's *The Human Condition* trilogy (1959–1961) is a scathing indictment of the atrocities committed by the Japanese Imperial Army during World War II. The trilogy stirred up a fierce controversy with its depictions of torture, persecution, and kidnapped Chinese civilians forced to become slave laborers in a Japanese prisoner-of-war camp. The other two installments are entitled *A Soldier's Prayer* and *The Road to Eternity.* Each film of the trilogy is over three hours long and is told from the point of view of its idealistic hero (Nakadai), a socialist who romanticizes the Soviet Union as a Promised Land of human fellowship. Ironically, in the final installment of the trilogy, he is captured by the Soviets, interred in a brutal prisoner-of-war camp, and killed by his Russian captors. As critic Joan Mellen has noted, the hero comes to realize that political tyranny—whether fascist or communist—has the same face: cruel authoritarian rule, hierarchies elevating a privileged few, contempt for foreigners, and a deep hostility toward the individual. *(Museum of Modern Art)*

wrong are fairly clear-cut and ought to be evaluated according to a strict code of conduct, as in *Pinocchio* **(8–33).** Violations of moral principles ought to be punished to maintain law and order and to set an example for others.

Secular Versus Religious

Leftists believe that religion, like sex, is a private matter and should not be the concern of governments. Some left-wingers are atheists or agnostics, although some of the most famous have been members of the clergy, like the leaders of the American Civil Rights movement in the 1960s. Most leftists are humanists. Religious skeptics frequently invoke the authority of science to refute traditional religious beliefs. Others are openly critical of organized religion, which they view as simply another social institution with a set of economic interests to protect, as in *Aguirre, the Wrath of God* **(6–23).** Leftists who are religious tend to be attracted to "progressive" denominations, like those of *The Preacher's Wife* **(10–17a)**. These denominations are more democratically organized than authoritarian or hierarchical religions.

Rightists accord religion a privileged status, as in *The Virgin Spring* **(10–11)**. Some authoritarian societies decree an official faith for all their citizens, and nonbelievers are sometimes treated as second-class citizens, if they are tolerated at all. The clergy enjoy a prestigious status and are respected as moral arbiters. Piety is regarded as a sign of superior virtue and spirituality.

Future Versus Past

In general, leftists view the past with disdain because it was dominated by ignorance, class conflict, and exploitation of the weak. The future, on the other hand, is filled with hope, with infinite promise of improvement, as can be seen in *High Hopes* **(10–8)**. The optimism that typifies many left-wingers is based on the idea of progress and evolution toward a more just and equitable society.

10-8. *High Hopes* **(Great Britain, 1988),** *with Ruth Sheen, Edna Dore, and Philip Davis, directed by Mike Leigh.*
British society has always been class conscious, especially during the 1980s under Prime Minister Margaret Thatcher. She dominated this decade in the United Kingdom just as her friend and fellow conservative Ronald Reagan dominated the political climate in America. Like many liberal English artists of his generation, Mike Leigh was sickened by the materialism of British society during this era. His satirical targets range over a wide spectrum and are richly deserving of their skewering. Only an eccentric hippie couple (Sheen and Davis) provide an island of decency in this sea of greed, pretentiousness, and conspicuous consumption.   *(Skouras Pictures)*

People on the right have a deep veneration for the past, for ancient rituals, and especially for tradition. Virtually all of the films of Yasujiro Ozu typify these traits. Rightists tend to disdain the present as a corruption of a lost golden age, like John Ford's *The Man Who Shot Liberty Valance.* They view the future with skepticism, for it holds only more change—and change is what trashed the glories of the past. Consequently, rightists tend to be pessimistic about the human condition, citing the laxness of standards and crumbling morality of modern life. Many of the films of Ingmar Bergman reflect this pessimistic view.

Cooperation Versus Competition

People on the left believe that social progress is best achieved by a cooperative effort on the part of all citizens toward a common goal, as in *October* **(10–6).** The role of government is to guarantee the basic needs of life—work, health, education, etc.—and this can be most efficiently accomplished if everyone feels he or she is contributing to the common good.

10–9.   *Cinema Paradiso* (Italy, 1988), *with Philippe Noiret (top) and Salvatore Cascio, directed by Giuseppe Tornatore.*

This movie is told in **flashbacks,** from the point of view of a successful middle-aged film director who recalls his childhood and adolescence in a Sicilian village. The flashback strategy provides an ironic double perspective, contrasting *Then* with *Now.* When he is a boy (pictured), his mentor and surrogate father (Noiret) hires him as an assistant movie theater projectionist. The child's life as a result is emotionally rich and communal, for the theater is the social center for the townspeople. But life in this conservative village is class-bound and provincial, and his mentor advises the youth to leave if he wishes to have a better life. The filmmaker's present-day lifestyle in Rome is artistically satisfying and financially secure, but perhaps a bit lonely, notwithstanding the succession of pretty women who have shared his bed. The movie is quintessentially **centrist.** Tornatore is saying that we need to strike a balance between the past and the present, emotion and thought, nurturance and independence. *(Miramax Films)*

Rightists emphasize open market principles and the need for competition to bring out the best in everyone, as in *Safety Last* (**4–26**), a classic film text of the American "go-getter" philosophy of the 1920s. Social progress is fueled by ambition and a strong desire to win, to dominate, as in *Mildred Pierce* (**11–13a**) and *Without Limits* (**3–31a**). The role of government is to protect private property, provide security through a strong military, and guarantee maximum freedom, at least in the economic realm.

Outsiders Versus Insiders

Leftists identify with the poor, the disenfranchised. They often romanticize rebels and outsiders, like *Bonnie and Clyde* (**1–12**) and *Robin Hood: Prince of Thieves*. Leftists are pluralistic in the sense that they respect and value ethnic diversity and are sensitive to the needs of women and minorities. Left-leaning

10–10.   *It's a Wonderful Life* (U.S.A., 1946), *with James Stewart and Donna Reed (left), directed by Frank Capra.*
Capra was the foremost American film spokesman for a conservative ethic, stressing such traditions of Americana as good neighborliness, faith in God, committed leadership, and family values. He championed such middle-class ideals as hard work, frugality, and healthy competition, but also generosity and wit. A character's wealth is measured not by income, but in terms of his or her family and friends. Capra's ideal was a romantic past of small towns, Christian values, close-knit families, and supportive neighbors.   *(RKO)*

movies often feature protagonists who are ordinary people, especially working-class characters, peasants, and laborers, such as those in *Bicycle Thief* **(6–33)** and *Open City* **(11–2).**

Rightists tend to identify with the Establishment—the people in power, the people who run things. They emphasize the importance of leadership in determining the main course of history, as in the *Rambo* films and *Henry V* **(10–13a).** Right-leaning movies tend to feature protagonists who are authority figures, patriarchs, military commanders, and entrepreneurs, as in *The Searchers* **(10–3),** *Patton,* and *Bugsy.*

International Versus Nationalistic

Leftists are global in their perspective, emphasizing the universality of human needs irrespective of country, race, or culture, as in *Hearts and Minds* **(1–3).** They often refer to "the family of man" as a more appropriate perspective than the narrow limits of the nuclear family.

10–11. *The Virgin Spring* **(Sweden, 1959),** *with Max von Sydow (center), directed by Ingmar Bergman.*

Bergman's movie, set in the medieval period, validates the Christian faith of the characters with a miracle which concludes the story. But faith does not come easily, for Bergman's God is inscrutable, beyond reason, as critic Lloyd Rose pointed out: "Bergman is the son of a severe, distant, often wrathful Lutheran minister, a real Old Testament God of a father, and he absorbed his chill upbringing into his marrow. There's never been a director more Protestant. . . . Carried to its (theo)logical extreme, Protestantism is as absurd as something out of Beckett. It completely jettisons cause and effect. God may save you or He may damn you, but your actions have nothing to do with it; you depend on His grace. You're born stained with sin but there's nothing you can do to erase it and if God—by an act of divine judgment totally beyond your comprehension—decides to let you burn, tough luck."   *(Janus Films)*

Right-wingers tend to be strongly patriotic, often regarding people from other countries as vaguely inferior. "Family, Country, and God" is a popular slogan in many right-wing societies. It might well represent the credo of the great American director John Ford, whose epic westerns are fervently nationalistic—*Wagon Master, My Darling Clementine,* and *Fort Apache,* to name just three. Unlike leftists, who believe that criticism makes a country stronger and more flexible, right-wingers believe that criticism weakens a nation, making it more vulnerable to outside attack.

Sexual Freedom Versus Marital Monogamy

Leftists believe that who you have sex with is nobody else's business. They often accept homosexuality as a valid lifestyle, as in *Gods and Monsters* **(10–28),** and they reject attempts to regulate sexual behavior among consenting adults, as in *Seven Beauties* **(10–21).** In the area of reproduction, too, leftists emphasize privacy, personal choice, and noninterference. Birth control—including abortion as well as contraception—is regarded as a basic right.

10-12. *Triumph of the Will* **(Germany, 1935),** *directed by Leni Riefenstahl.*
Hitler (pictured) himself commissioned Riefenstahl to direct this three-hour-long documentary celebrating the Nazi's first party convention at Nuremberg in 1934. Thirty **cinematographers** were assigned to photograph the event, which was staged especially for the cameras. Not surprisingly, she presents Hitler as a virtual deity, the charismatic master of a master race. Riefenstahl's stylistic virtuosity is dazzling, so aesthetically compelling that the Allies banned the film from circulation for several years after the Nazi defeat. After the war, Riefenstahl served four years in prison for her participation in the Nazi propaganda machine.   *(Museum of Modern Art)*

10–13a. *Henry V* **(Great Britain, 1989),** *with Kenneth Branagh (center), directed by Branagh.* Form is the embodiment of content. In these two photos, we can see how **mise en scène** embodies ideology. *Henry V,* based on Shakespeare's play, is monarchist in its values, like the original source. The story deals with a **rite of passage**—how the former hell-raiser, Prince "Harry," proves himself as a great leader in battle and a worthy king. His army, although not anonymous, is kept in the background. Henry is in the foreground, centered in the composition at the full front position, charging toward the camera, his sword held high. He is flanked by two lieutenants, the Dukes of Gloucester and Bedford, his brothers. Shakespeare would have approved. *(The Samuel Goldwyn Company)*

10–13b. *Dances With Wolves* **(U.S.A., 1990),** *with Kevin Costner (left), directed by Costner.* *Dances With Wolves* is liberal in its values. The story deals with the gradual assimilation of a U.S. Army officer (Costner) into the Sioux Indian tribe during the Civil War era. In this photo, he is placed at the edge of the composition, an invited guest who is respectful of his hosts, whom he comes to admire more and more as he realizes that the Sioux have a morally superior culture to his own. *(Orion Pictures)*

Rightists regard the family as a sanctified institution, and anything that threatens the family is viewed with hostility, as in Ford's *The Grapes of Wrath* (**10–15**). Premarital sex, homosexuality, and extramarital sex are condemned. Similarly, right-wingers tend to oppose abortion, which they consider a form of infanticide. In some societies, sex is justified only as a means of procreation, and contraception is forbidden. Heterosexual monogamy within the institution of marriage is the only acceptable expression of sexuality, as can be illustrated by most American mainstream movies before the 1960s.

Even ideologically explicit movies don't hit on all of these value structures, but virtually every fiction film deals with some of them.

Culture, Religion, and Ethnicity

A social culture encompasses the traditions, institutions, arts, myths, and beliefs that are characteristic of a given community or population. In heterogeneous societies such as Israel and the United States, many cultural groups coexist within one national boundary. In homogeneous nations such as Japan or Saudi Arabia—which are ethnically uniform—a single cultural hegemony tends to be the rule.

Cultural generalizations—like most generalizations—are true *most* of the time. But there are many exceptions, especially in the arts, which often go against the grain in terms of generally accepted cultural norms. Without a knowledge of these norms, however, it's hard to relate to some movies—especially foreign films—because their cultures are radically different from our own.

Cultural generalizations can easily degenerate into stereotypes unless they're applied judiciously, with respect for nuances. For example, Japanese movies, like Japanese society in general, tend to be ideologically conservative, stressing such values as social conformity, the supremacy of the family system, patriarchy, and the wisdom of consensus. The movies of the Japanese master Ozu typify these values best, most notably *Late Spring* (**8–15a**) and *An Autumn Afternoon* (**11–21**). Most Japanese people view nonconformity and individualism with abhorrence, a ridiculous form of egotism and arrogance. Yet the works of Kobayashi (**10–7**) and Naruse (**10–24**) side with protagonists who are oppressed by their cultures.

For people who haven't been exposed to alternative cultures, their own norms might seem universal. Their knowledge of other cultures is often derived from movies. For example, American films typically sympathize with the individual versus society. Most movies romanticize underdogs, rebels, outlaws, and mavericks, especially in such **genres** as gangster films, westerns, and action movies, which stress violence and extremes of individuality. American films are also strongly sexual and fast paced compared with most foreign movies. Typically, many people outside our borders stereotype Americans as lawless, sex-obsessed, and "fast."

Likewise, American audiences are often puzzled by foreign movies

10–14. *Pixote* (Brazil, 1981), *with Fernando Ramos da Silva and Marilia Pera, directed by Hector Babenco.*

Third World filmmakers are often left-wing in their orientation, championing the cause of the poor, the forgotten, and the despised. Babenco's film explores the culture of poverty by focusing on the violent life of Pixote (Peewee), a lonely youth who is typical of millions of abandoned street urchins. In a country of 168 million, over 95 percent live in desperate poverty, forced to scratch out a meager survival by whatever means they can. Fernando Ramos da Silva, who plays Pixote, was one of ten children who grew up in the dog-eat-dog barrios of São Paulo. Seven years after this movie was made, he was shot and killed in an attempted armed robbery. He was seventeen. *(A Unifilm/Embrafilme Release)*

because they're looking for familiar (that is, American) cultural signposts. Failing to find them, they dismiss the movie rather than their irrelevant cultural assumptions. For example, characters in Japanese movies seldom disagree publicly. This would be considered rude. Consequently, we must read between the lines to discover what they're really thinking. Similarly, Japanese characters rarely look each other steadily in the eyes when conversing, unless they are interacting with intimates or social equals. In America, maintaining eye contact is considered sincere, forthright, and honest. In Japan, it's considered impertinent and disrespectful.

Every nation has a characteristic way of looking at life, a set of values that is typical of a given culture. The same can be said of their movies. For example, because of England's glorious literary heritage and international preeminence in the live theater, British movies tend to be strongly literary, with an emphasis on polished scripts, literate dialogue, urbane acting, and lavish costumes and décor. Many of the best English movies are literary and theatrical adaptations—most notably, the works of Shakespeare **(10–13a).**

10–15. *The Grapes of Wrath* (U.S.A., 1940), *with Jane Darwell (center) and Henry Fonda, directed by John Ford.*

Charting a movie's ideological values can be a labyrinthine exercise. Widely regarded as the greatest film dealing with the Depression of the 1930s, *The Grapes of Wrath* centers on a dispossessed family of "Okies" and their odyssey from the drought-stricken plains of Oklahoma to the Promised Land of California. In adapting John Steinbeck's famous book, Ford transformed the **Marxist** outrage of the novel into a masterpiece of Christian humanism, emphasizing the indomitability of the Joad family, which is held together by the powerful matriarch, Ma Joad (Darwell). Like many conservatives, Ford believed that the role of women in society is a noble one—to uphold the values of home and hearth, to preserve the institution of the family above all others. *(Twentieth Century-Fox)*

But there is always The Other—a countertradition that's dialectically opposed to what might be considered the dominant strain in a culture. In the British cinema, this counterculture is represented by a left-wing school of filmmaking that emphasizes working-class life, contemporary settings, regional dialects, loose scripting, a more emotional **Method**-oriented style of acting, and a strong antiestablishment ideology. Movies like *High Hopes* (**10–8**) are typical of this countertradition.

Similarly, the cinema of Sweden is dominated by the austere Lutheranism that underlies the psychology of many Swedish movies, especially those of their greatest filmmaker, Ingmar Bergman (**10–11**). Third World films tend to be preoccupied with issues such as neocolonialism, underdevelopment, the oppression of women, and especially poverty (**10–14**).

In culturally diverse countries like the United States, there are many subcultures—pockets of cultural values that coexist within the dominant ideology. Movies that explore subcultures generally emphasize the fragile balance between conflicting cultural values, like the Okies of *The Grapes of Wrath*

10–16. *Late Autumn* **(Japan, 1960),** *with Yoko Tsukasa and Setsuko Hara, directed by Yasu-jiro Ozu.*

Sometimes religious values are presented so subtly that they don't seem apparent to outsiders. In the films of Ozu, the style is spare, understated. The camerawork is spartan in its austerity, the editing clean and functional. "Less Is More" might well serve as his artistic credo. Critic Donald Richie has pointed out that Ozu's style embodies the Buddhist ideals of simplicity, restraint, and serenity. His movies have been compared to *haiku* poems, which consist of only a few lines encapsulating a striking image, or to a *sumi-e* ink drawing, which evokes its subject through a few strokes of the pen or brush. The fragment symbolizes the whole; the microcosm evokes the macrocosm. See *Ozu,* by Donald Richie (Berkeley: University of California Press, 1974). *(New Yorker Films)*

(10–15) and the hostility they encounter when they try to integrate with established communities in California. Other American movies emphasize lifestyle subcultures, like the military personnel of *Rambo,* the hippies of *Easy Rider,* the junkies of *Drugstore Cowboy,* and the gay friends of *Longtime Companion* **(8–7).**

An added complication of any ideological analysis involves period and historical context. For example, American films made during the Depression in the 1930s reflect many of the left-wing values of Roosevelt's New Deal. During the turbulent Vietnam–Watergate era (roughly from 1965 to 1975), the American cinema became increasingly violent, confrontational, antiauthoritarian. During the Reagan era of the 1980s, American movies turned to the right, like American society in general. Many movies made during that period emphasize military supremacy, competition, power, and wealth.

Religious values involve many of the same complexities. Even religions that purport to be universal, like Roman Catholicism, are radically different from country to country. These differences are reflected in their movies. For example, in Europe the Church is regarded as a pillar of conservatism. French Catholicism is strongly influenced by Jansenism, an austere, quasi-deterministic

10-17a. ***The Preacher's Wife***
(U.S.A., 1996), *with Courtney B.*
Vance and Whitney Houston, directed
by Penny Marshall.

Most religions can be divided into liberal and conservative wings, each
with its own agenda of priorities. Fundamentalist sects are right-wing in
their values, emphasizing strict conformity to a body of religious and
moral beliefs, usually based on a traditional holy book. Protestant fundamentalists can further be differentiated by race. White fundamentalists
are deeply conservative on virtually
all matters. But African-American religious groups tend to be liberal politically. They were in the forefront of the
Civil Rights movement of the 1960s,
and its leader of course was a clergy-
man, the Reverend Martin Luther
King, Jr. However, black fundamentalists tend to be staunchly conservative in matters of faith
and morals, as *The Preacher's Wife* demonstrates. *(Touchstone Pictures/Samuel Goldwyn)*

10-17b. ***Dead Man Walking***
(U.S.A., 1995), *with Sean Penn and*
Susan Sarandon, directed by Tim
Robbins.

In Europe and the United States, the
Roman Catholic Church tends to be a
conservative institution in which
women play only a minor role in
determining church policies. However, this old boy club has been chal-
lenged in recent years by such unconventional nuns as Sister Helen
Prejean (Sarandon), whose book
formed the basis of *Dead Man Walking*. In offering spiritual comfort to a
vicious convicted killer (Penn), she
went against the wishes of several of her (male) superiors, who considered her behavior
unseemly and inappropriate. She didn't pay much attention to them and followed her conscience instead. *(Gramercy Pictures)*

10–18.   Ethnic Variations.   A cliché of American culture is the metaphor of the melting pot—a tendency for the children of foreign-born American citizens to bland out, to intermarry with other ethnicities, producing a kind of natural-selection hybrid. In actuality, many ethnic subcultures have retained their separate identities, and the result has been a patchwork quilt of diversity, a source of considerable cultural richness in the United States.

10-18a.   *He Got Game* (U.S.A., 1998), *with Denzel Washington and Ray Allen, written and directed by Spike Lee.*
Spike Lee might almost be viewed as the godfather of the ethnics, a pioneer in bringing African-American stories to the screen. He opened the door of opportunity to a floodgate of talent, especially among artists of color. Working out of New York rather than Hollywood, Lee's style has a distinctly hard-edged, gritty Brooklyn flavor. He is especially strong in highlighting three traditional strongholds of black American culture—sports, music, and politics.
(© Touchstone Pictures)

10-18b.   *Smoke Signals* (U.S.A., 1998), *with Irene Bedard and Adam Beach, written by Sherman Alexie, directed by Chris Eyre.*
Although they constitute America's oldest minority, Native Americans have rarely had access to the mainstream media. Consequently, their culture has been represented primarily by out-

siders, some of them sympathetic, most of them racist and ignorant. This movie is the first full-length feature film written, directed, and coproduced by American Indians. A Spokane Coeur d'Alene Indian, writer Sherman Alexie is one of the most famous Native American authors in history. He has written two novels, two short story collections, nine books of poetry, and the screenplay to this movie.   *(Miramax Films)*

continued   ▶

10–18c. *Mi Vida Loca/My Crazy Life* (U.S.A., 1993), *with Julian Reyes and Marlo Marron, written and directed by Allison Anders.*

Hispanics are the largest ethnic minority in the United States, but their culture is rarely represented in American movies, and then usually negatively. This powerful study of Latina gangs in Los Angeles is a sympathetic portrayal of the frustrations many Hispanic women face, especially with the violence and machismo of poor, inner-city communities. *(Sony Pictures Classics)*

10–18d. *Fiddler on the Roof* (U.S.A., 1971), *with Topol, directed by Norman Jewison.*
Jews are probably the most successful assimilators of all the ethnic groups that came to America. Their contributions to the arts and entertainment fields have been enormous. The Broadway stage musical is overwhelmingly a Jewish stronghold. Cole Porter was the only Gentile among the top ranks of American musical composers and lyricists, which include such famous names as Rodgers and Hammerstein, Stephen Sondheim, Leonard Bernstein, Lerner and Loewe, Kurt Weill, Lorenz Hart, and George Gershwin, to mention only a few. This movie, a first-rate adaptation of the smash Broadway hit, is based on the short stories of Sholem Aleichem, the Yiddish chronicler of life in the villages of Tsarist Russia in the late 19th and early 20th centuries. The musical was the creation of playwright and librettist Joseph Stein, lyricist Sheldon Harnick, and composer Jerry Bock. *(United Artists)*

10–19. *The Chant of Jimmie Blacksmith* (Australia, 1978), *with Angela Punch and Tommy Lewis, directed by Fred Schepisi.*

This film is based on an actual series of events that took place around 1900. Jimmie Blacksmith (Lewis), half white and half aborigine, is rescued from a life of misery by a Caucasian missionary couple. They raise him to be docile and respectful, to admire all that is white, despise all that is black. The Reverend Mrs. even advises the youth to marry a white farm girl, produce children, who in turn will produce children who would be "scarcely black at all." The roots of racism, Schepisi demonstrates, are both economic and sexual. Whites exploit Jimmie and other aborigines as cheap labor and fear them as sexual threats. *(New Yorker Films)*

sect that somewhat resembles Calvinism or Scandinavian Lutheranism. Many of the films of Robert Bresson reflect these Jansenist values.

In Italy, on the other hand, Catholicism takes on a more theatrical, aesthetic flavor—as in the movies of Federico Fellini. Italy's rich heritage in the decorative and fine arts was largely Church-sponsored during the medieval period and the Renaissance. In much of Catholic Latin America, the Liberation Theology movement is strongly left-wing and even revolutionary in its orientation.

Protestantism too is a virtual smorgasbord of religious diversity. There are vast differences between the joyous black fundamentalism of *The Preacher's Wife* (**10–17a**) and the stern, born-again faith of the protagonist of *Tender Mercies* (**11–20**)**,** who is white, southern, working class, and "country." Similarly, to non-Islamic peoples the differences between moderate Sunni and fundamentalist Shiite Muslims might seem minor, but they have prompted many passionate conflicts in the Middle East.

Sometimes one religious sect strongly objects to the portrayal of a revered figure in the arts. For example, Martin Scorsese's *The Last Temptation of Christ,* based on the Greek novel by Nikos Kazantzakis, portrays Jesus from a humanist perspective. All Christians believe in the divinity of Jesus, but most

10–20a. *Boyz N the Hood* (U.S.A., 1991), *with Cuba Gooding Jr., Larry Fishburne, and Ice Cube; written and directed by John Singleton.*

Films with an ethnic slant are generally mounted in a realistic style to depict the authentic textures of everyday life. *Boyz N the Hood* is a powerful coming-of-age drama set in the mean streets of the black ghettos of Los Angeles. Director John Singleton made this debut film on a small budget when he was only twenty-two years old. He was the youngest director in history to be nominated for an Academy Award in directing. *(Columbia Pictures)*

10–20b. *Breaking Away* (U.S.A., 1979), *with Dennis Christopher (lower right), directed by Peter Yates.*

"America is another word for opportunity," Ralph Waldo Emerson observed. No other country has been so hospitable to foreign talent. Since 1927, the first year that the Academy Awards were given, a staggering 41 percent of the Best Picture Oscars have been won by foreign-born directors, including such major figures of the American cinema as Frank Capra, Alfred Hitchcock, William Wyler, Michael Curtiz, Billy Wilder, Elia Kazan, Fred Zinnemann, and Milos Forman, among others. *Breaking Away,* a coming-of-age story set in Bloomington, Indiana, is a slice of pure Americana. Interestingly, it was written by a Yugoslavian immigrant, Steve Tesich, and directed by an Englishman. Charles Chaplin, the most famous immigrant of his era, said of his adoptive country: "I felt at home in the States—a foreigner among foreigners." *(Twentieth Century–Fox)*

denominations emphasize the god rather than the man. Hence the fierce outcry from Christian fundamentalists about Scorsese's movie, which portrays Jesus as flawed, tormented with doubt. Critic Scott Eyman responded to these attacks:

> In daring to give us a Christ of flesh and blood, Scorsese has violated what protesters, in their mad, delusive certainty, believe to be their copyright on Jesus. But simply because their minds are most comfortable with, and are probably only capable of encompassing a dashboard Jesus, is no reason for those terms to define the limits of public discussion.

Ethnic groups are distinct social communities within a larger cultural system that claim or are accorded special status (usually inferior) on the basis of such considerations as religion, language, ancestry, and race—in short, what we call minority groups. In the United States, such groups include African Americans, Hispanics, Native Americans, and of course the many waves of immigration from abroad, especially those who have not been fully integrated into the American mainstream, like the Chinese Americans of *The Joy Luck Club*.

Movies with an ethnic slant usually dramatize the tensions between the dominant culture and the beleaguered values of a minority community. For example, in the Australian cinema, a number of movies have dealt with the clash between the predominantly white, Anglo-Saxon power structure and the dark-skinned aboriginal peoples, who have a long heritage of oppression and exploitation, as in *The Chant of Jimmie Blacksmith* **(10–19).** Similarly, *Come See the Paradise* deals with the forced evacuation of Japanese Americans into "relocation camps" during World War II. America was also at war with Germany and Italy during this era, but no one suggested that people of German and Italian descent might constitute a security risk. Germans and Italians are Caucasians.

African-American film historians have chronicled the sad, shameful treatment of blacks in American movies—a mean-spirited reflection of their treatment in American society as a whole. For the first fifty years of the American cinema, black characters were usually relegated to demeaning stereotypes. The title of Donald Bogle's history of blacks in American films says it all: *Toms, Coons, Mulattoes, Mammies & Bucks*. The most positive images of African Americans during this half century were generally faithful servants, like the roles played by Hattie McDaniel, the first black performer ever to win an Academy Award (for *Gone With the Wind* in 1939). Singers like Lena Horne and Ethel Waters, and dancers like the brilliant Nicholas Brothers, were also exceptions to the rule.

In the 1950s, actor Sidney Poitier rose to the top ten not as a singer, dancer, or comedian, but as a straight leading man. Poitier's wholesome good looks and all-American sense of decency were admired by white and black audiences alike. Poitier's enormous popularity was an opening wedge in the treatment of African-American characters in movies: Images of blacks improved steadily (but slowly) after the 1950s. However, even today racist stereotypes are hardly unusual in American films and television.

In the contemporary cinema, no African-American filmmaker has provoked more controversy than Spike Lee **(10–18a).** Much of this criticism has been directed at people of his own race. In *Do the Right Thing,* Lee explores the smoldering tensions between black ghetto dwellers and an Italian-American family that owns a pizzeria in an inner-city neighborhood **(5–14).** In *Jungle Fever,* Lee dramatizes the problems of an interracial couple. The story ends with the lovers calling it quits—defeated by the prejudices of their own communities as well as their personal failings.

Ethnic filmmakers tend to favor **realism** as a style **(10–20a).** In the first place, realism is cheaper. Scenes can be shot in the streets, without the need for expensive studio sets. Such filmmakers often must work with small budgets, and consequently they rarely include costly special effects or elaborate equipment. Realism also excels in portraying the actual textures and sociological details of authentic locations. This preference for realism is by no means universal, however. For example, Spike Lee's movies are often stylized—with vibrant Day-Glo colors, audacious editing techniques, and virtuosic camera movements.

Feminism

The late 1960s was an era of intense political turmoil, not only in America but also much of western Europe. Feminism—also known as the Women's Liberation Movement, or simply the Women's Movement—was one of several militant ideologies that emerged during this period. In the field of cinema, the achievement of the Women's Movement has been considerable, though most present-day feminists would insist that there is still much to be accomplished in the battle against patriarchal values **(10–21).**

During the heyday of the big Hollywood studios—and especially the 1930s through the 1950s—the status of women within the industry was dismal. There were no women in the upper echelons of management. Out of the thousands of movies produced by the studios, only a handful were directed by women, and virtually none were produced by them. The unions also discriminated against females, allowing very few of them to enter their ranks.

True, there were some women in the areas of screenwriting, editing, and costuming, but only in the field of acting did women enjoy a degree of prominence. After all, it was simply not economically feasible to exclude women from in front of the camera. To this day, most of the powerful women in Hollywood have come from the acting ranks.

Even female stars were treated like second-class citizens during the big-studio era. Rarely did the leading lady get top billing over the male lead. Females usually received smaller salaries than males—a pattern that still persists. Females usually had shorter careers because they were thought to be too old for leading roles once they were past forty. Male stars like Cary Grant, Gary Cooper, and John Wayne were still playing leads in their sixties. They were often paired with women twenty or thirty years younger than themselves, a pattern rarely permitted for those few female stars who somehow managed to hold on past forty. For example, actresses like Joan Crawford and Bette Davis spent

the final twenty years of their long careers playing mostly grotesque carica-
tures—it was the only work they could get.

Within the movies themselves, women were usually socially constructed
as "the other" or "the outsider" in a male-dominated world, as feminist critic
Annette Kuhn has pointed out. Women didn't get to tell their own stories
because the images were controlled by men. Generally, women were treated as
sex objects—valued primarily for their good looks and sex appeal. Their main
function was to support their men, seldom to lead a fulfilling life of their own.
Marriage and a family were their most frequent goals, rarely a meaningful
career.

In the majority of studio-produced films, female characters were marginalized, seldom at the center of the action. The heroine's function was to
cheer from the sidelines, to wait passively until the hero claimed her for his
reward. Certain characteristics were regarded as intrinsically "masculine": intel-

**10-21.   *Seven Beauties* (Italy, 1976), *with Giancarlo Giannini and Elena Fiore, directed by
Lina Wertmüller.***

Arguably the greatest of all women directors, Lina Wertmüller was criticized by some feminist film critics for featuring vulgar, garrulous female characters who look like Rubens and
Titian nudes—put together. Indeed, one critic headlined her review: "Is Lina Wertmüller
Really Just One of the Boys?" Wertmüller delights in irony, in paradoxes. She has been a con-
sistent champion of the cause of women, but she's not a propagandist. However funny her
women characters are (and the men are just as funny), Wertmüller's females are usually
strong, with a surer sense of personal identity than the males. In this, perhaps her greatest
film, she satirizes the macho "code of honor" by equating a bullying older brother (pictured)
with the institutions of patriarchy, the Mafia, and fascism itself.   *(Warner Bros.)*

lect, ambition, sexual confidence, independence, professionalism—all of these traits were generally presented as inappropriate and unseemly in women.

Certain Hollywood genres were more hospitable to women—love stories, domestic family dramas, **screwball** and romantic comedies, musicals, and **women's pictures**—usually domestic melodramas emphasizing a female star and focusing on "typical" female concerns such as getting (or holding on to) a man, raising children, or balancing a career with marriage. Marriage was almost invariably presented as the wiser choice when a woman was confronted with a conflict between her career and her man. Women who chose otherwise usually suffered for their folly—like the heroine of *Mildred Pierce* **(11–13a).** It was in such genres as these that some of the studio era's greatest actresses flourished—Bette Davis, Katharine Hepburn, Claudette Colbert, Barbara Stanwyck, Carole Lombard, Marlene Dietrich, and Greta Garbo, to name a few.

Today there are about two dozen women directors working in the mainstream Hollywood film industry, and their presence has made a difference: The range of female roles has broadened considerably since the 1960s.

10–22. *Octopussy* **(Great Britain, 1983),** *with Roger Moore, directed by John Glen.*
Feminists rarely object to portraying women as sexually attractive; they merely insist that other aspects of their humanity also be dramatized. Perhaps nothing angers them so much as reducing women to sex objects. In this photo, for example, five young women are reduced to buxom bimbos who encircle the James Bond character like matching baubles around his neck. The title of the film drips with condescension and sexist innuendo. Feminists argue that popular entertainments such as the James Bond series validate for millions of impressionable young males that it's okay to view women merely as pleasure machines. *(MGM/United Artists Entertainment)*

Outside of North America and Europe, however, sexism is as dominant as ever, especially in the Third World, where the oppression of women is harshest, both in films and in the larger society. Women in the Third World are often denied equal nutrition and healthcare because they are valued less than men. In southern Asia and sub-Saharan Africa, females lag behind males at all levels of achievement, power, and status, as can be seen in movies like *Tilai* (**10–32**).

Female infanticide is common in many parts of China and India, especially in rural areas. Traditional rituals, including female circumcision, are practiced throughout much of Africa and parts of the Middle East, contributing to poor reproductive health. In Africa alone, 80 million women undergo circumcision, which involves removing a female's clitoris, thus depriving her of one of the main sources of sexual pleasure. Many African cultures regard this as a "purifying" practice, deadening a woman's interest in sex. Sexual pleasure is regarded as appropriate only in males. Women are their sexual objects, a view not entirely foreign in the West (**10–22**).

According to the Worldwatch Institute, reproductive problems are the leading killer of women of childbearing age throughout the Third World. At least 1 million females die each year and more than 100 million suffer disabling illnesses from circumcision, unsafe abortions, pregnancy complications, and childbirth. AIDS claims 100,000 women's lives annually, mostly in Africa.

10–23. *Raise the Red Lantern* (China/Hong Kong, 1991), *with Gong Li (center), written and directed by Zhang Yimou.*
Zhang Yimou is China's foremost film artist, and all of his works to date have dealt with the problems of women in Chinese society, both past and present. The beautiful Gong Li has played the leading roles in most of his movies.   *(Orion Classics)*

The revolutionary filmmaker Yilmaz Güney was a powerful champion of women's rights. In *Yol* he dramatized how women are sometimes treated worse than livestock in his native Turkey. Even fundamentally decent men, themselves victims of oppression, victimize the women they love, rarely questioning the sexist values of their culture. "Can a man's mind be his own enemy?" the protagonist asks, when he is expected to kill his wife in retribution for her adultery. Everyone expects nothing less—even the members of her own family, who have kept her chained in the cellar for eight months, giving her only bread and water, not even allowing her to wash. The man still loves his wife, yet he is torn between pity and hatred, between the demands of social convention and his private anguish. He decides instead to "let God kill her." In an agonizing trek across a vast snow-covered pass, he and their son, followed by the flimsily attired, exhausted wife, trudge through the freezing terrain.

10-24. *Late Chrysanthemums* **(Japan, 1954),** *with Haruko Sugimura and Ken Uehara, directed by Mikio Naruse.*

The Japanese cinema abounds in female genres. Two great film artists excelled at women's pictures—Kenji Mizoguchi and Naruse. "The Naruse heroine can be seen as a symbol for everyone who has ever been caught between ideals and reality," critic Audie Bock has noted. "Women alone: widows, geisha, bar hostesses, young women from poor families with poor marriage prospects—all those who are not favored by the traditional family system form the essential material of the Naruse film." Feminism has had relatively little impact in Japan, and Naruse's heroines—like Japanese women in general—rarely organize to protest their lot. As Bock has pointed out, Naruse's protagonists "are outsiders, and they feel their exile keenly. But they do not blame society, or the system, or men in general for their deprivations. Naruse's heroines accept exploitation by men as part of what life brings." In this scene, an old lover of a retired geisha returns for a visit. She tries to remain calm, even though he may be her last chance for a respectable life. As it turns out, he has come to borrow money. *(East-West Classics)*

In Japan there has been a long tradition of women's pictures that characteristically center on the injustices of the ubiquitous family system. Filmmakers such as Kenji Mizoguchi and Mikio Naruse **(10–24),** both males, specialized in women's genres. There is an old Confucian adage that a female should obey her father when she is a girl, her husband when she is mature, and her son when she is old. This has been the prevailing view in Japan throughout most of its history.

Japanese girls are brought up to believe that marriage and motherhood are the most rewarding achievements in life; a career and economic independence are poor substitutes. Women constitute only about 20 percent of the university population, and they are still discriminated against in the job market, where they aren't taken seriously. Women almost never hold upper management positions.

The divorce rate in Japan is still only about one-eighteenth of that in America, in part because older women find it virtually impossible to make a decent living wage. In present-day Japan, the lot of women is improving, but they are still an oppressed group compared with their Western counterparts.

10–25.   *Thelma & Louise* (U.S.A., 1991), *with Susan Sarandon and Geena Davis, directed by Ridley Scott.*
Feminism was one of many liberation movements that rose to prominence in America and Europe during the 1960s. Virtually every powerful woman in the Hollywood film industry today has been influenced by the movement—not to speak of many male allies. *Thelma & Louise* explores the intimate bond between two best friends (pictured) whose weekend getaway unexpectedly takes them on an adventure across America. The movie explores such themes as marriage, work, independence, female bonding, and male chauvinism, often from a humorous perspective. Interestingly, the movie's structure is indebted to two traditionally male genres—the buddy film and the road picture. See also *Chick Flicks*, by B. Ruby Rich (Durham, NC: Duke University Press, 1999).   *(MGM)*

The sympathy of filmmakers like Mizoguchi and Naruse was based not on sentimentality, but on hard social realities.

Despite attempts by the unsympathetic to reduce the Women's Movement to trivialities like bra burning, contemporary feminists have concentrated on such fundamentals as equal pay for equal work, adequate prenatal care for pregnant women, domestic violence, abortion rights, child care, sexual harassment on the job, date rape, and female solidarity (**10–25**).

Not all women filmmakers are feminists (and not all feminists are women). Lina Wertmüller's movies usually feature male protagonists (**10–21**). The films of Randa Haines *(Children of a Lesser God, The Doctor)* and those of Penny Marshall, like *Big* (**2–22**) and *Awakenings,* are gender neutral. However, most women directors tend to favor female protagonists.

Feminist filmmakers—both male and female—are attempting to overcome prejudice through their movies by providing fresh perspectives (**10–26**). "What do women *want?*" Freud once asked in exasperation. Film critic Molly Haskell has answered succinctly: "We want nothing less, on or off the screen, than the wide variety and dazzling diversity of male options."

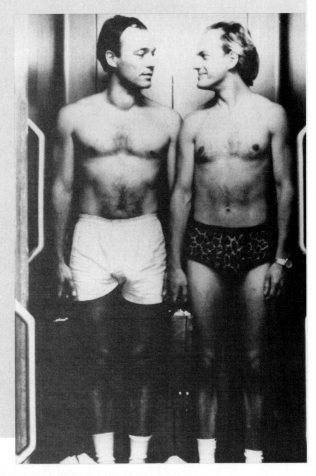

10–26. *Men* (West Germany, 1985), *with Heiner Lauterbach and Uwe Ochsenknecht, directed by Doris Dörrie.*

A number of feminist film critics have written about "the male gaze," sometimes known simply as "the gaze." The term refers to the voyeuristic aspects of cinema—sneaking furtive glances at the forbidden, the erotic. But because most filmmakers are males, so too is the point of view of the camera: Everyone looks at the action through male eyes. The gaze fixes women in postures that cater to male needs and fantasies rather than allowing women to express their own desires and the full range of their humanity. When the director is a woman, the gaze is often eroticized from a female point of view, offering us fresh perspectives on the battle between the sexes, as well as among the same sex, as in Dörrie's good-natured social satire, *Men. (New Yorker Films)*

Gay Liberation

The Gay Liberation Movement drew much of its inspiration from other revolutionary groups of the 1960s, especially feminism and the Black Liberation Movement. There was a difference, however. Whereas women and people of color could not pretend to be "the other," most homosexuals could pass for straight. They often did—and still do—because of the social prejudice against them. Hence the phrase "in the closet"—when a gay person conceals his or her sexual identity from the outside world and passes for straight.

Sexual researchers are by no means in agreement on what causes homosexuality. Following the lead of Freud, such researchers as Kinsey and Masters and Johnson regard all sexual behavior as learned, not innate. Freud believed that the libido—sexual energy—is nondiscriminatory, amoral, and channeled by social conventions. In short, we have to learn what's "normal" sexually. Other researchers believe that homosexuality is inborn, like other genetic characteristics. Recent medical findings on the structure of the brain tend to support a physiological basis for homosexuality.

Both groups agree that gender identity is formed before puberty, before a person has any conscious sense of his or her sexuality. Hard-core heterosexuals who view lesbians and gays as "not natural" are missing the point, these researchers insist. A person's same-gender orientation is not something he or she chooses. Rather, it chooses them. Their sexuality is as natural to them as that of heterosexuals.

The Kinsey Institute for Sex Research has found that homosexuality is more widespread than is generally believed. In a variety of scientific surveys, researchers have estimated that roughly 10 percent of the American population is homosexual. A much larger percentage—as high as 33 percent—have had at least one homosexual experience. Many commentators believe that sexual labels are convenient fictions, that all of us have our masculine and feminine sides.

"The big lie about lesbians and gay men is that we do not exist," noted film historian Vito Russo. Because of their long history of persecution, homosexuals until the 1960s kept a low profile. A hundred years ago, homosexuality was punishable by death in Great Britain. In many societies, it is still a prisonable offense, even between consenting adults. The Nazis incarcerated in concentration camps hundreds of thousands of homosexuals along with Jews, gypsies, Slavs, and other "undesirables."

Homosexuality is commonplace in the arts and entertainment fields, where it's not regarded as relevant to talent. Bisexuality is even more common. In the larger society, however, the hostility toward gays has been so strong that most artists—especially actors—have gone to considerable lengths to conceal their sexual identity. Bisexual film stars like Marlene Dietrich, Cary Grant, Errol Flynn, and James Dean were regarded as straight in their own day. Very few people outside of show business knew that Montgomery Clift and Rock Hudson (10–27b) were gay. Such public knowledge would undermine their credibility as romantic leading men, they believed.

10–27a. *A Foreign Affair* (U.S.A., 1948), *with Marlene Dietrich, directed by Billy Wilder.*
Dietrich came of age during the heady 1920s in Berlin, which was considered the sexiest, most tolerant city in Europe. Her open bisexuality created something of a scandal when she first arrived in Hollywood, but filmmakers often exploited her ambiguous sexuality with great success. Her career spanned an amazing six decades. She was 48 when she made this movie, and as this photo irrefutably documents, the famous Dietrich gams still looked sensational. *(Paramount Pictures)*

10–27b. *Pillow Talk* (U.S.A., 1959), *with Rock Hudson and Doris Day, directed by Michael Gordon.*
Throughout most of his lengthy career, Rock Hudson was an action/adventure hero, a romantic leading man, and a deft light comedian (pictured). His striking good looks and masculine manner made him a favorite with both women and men. Within the film industry, it was common knowledge that Hudson was gay, but he was well liked in Hollywood, and the public for the most part was unaware of his sexual identity—until he contracted AIDS. When he finally went public with his illness shortly before his death in 1985, he created a new sympathetic climate of opinion in the United States, and Americans finally began to take the AIDS epidemic seriously. *(Universal Pictures)*

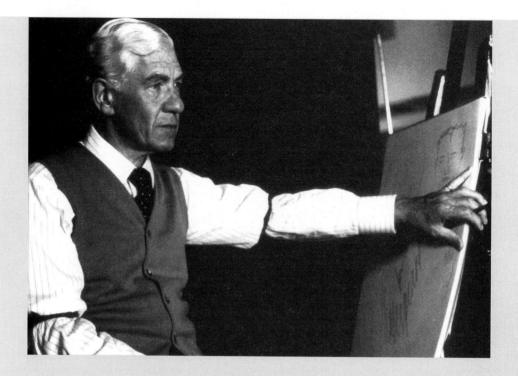

10–28.   *Gods and Monsters* (Great Britain, 1998), *with Ian McKellen, directed by Bill Condon.*
In more recent times, a number of actors have publicly come out of the closet, most notably the celebrated Shakespearean performer Sir Ian McKellen. He usually plays heterosexuals, usually with great distinction. *Gods and Monsters* is a touching account of the last days of the British director, James Whale, who was openly homosexual, and directed such excellent movies as *Frankenstein, The Invisible Man, The Bride of Frankenstein,* and the great musical, *Showboat*.   *(Lions Gate Films)*

Of course, this secrecy also made them easy prey to blackmail—one of the main reasons militant gays insist on the need to acknowledge their sexuality publicly. Interestingly, androgynous traits in such female stars as Dietrich, Garbo, and Mae West seemed to make them popular, but seldom were male stars allowed any sexual ambiguity on the screen.

Homophobia, like racism and sexism, was widespread in the cinema until recently. Gay men were characteristically stereotyped as "sissies" and "pansies." Lesbians were portrayed as mannish "bull dykes." There were some exceptions, however, most notably in the avant-garde cinema and the pre-Nazi German cinema of the 1920s. In more recent times, the films of François Truffaut feature characters who happen to be gay but don't make a big deal out of it.

10–29. *Carrington* (Great Britain, 1995), *with Jonathan Pryce and Emma Thompson, directed by Christopher Hampton.*
A recent development in critical theory is the field of Gay Studies, sometimes wittily self-described as Queer Theory. Specialists in this field are concerned with how homosexuality impinges on heterosexual society, especially in the arts, where gays have traditionally been prominent. For example, the British cultural movement known as the Bloomsbury Group around the turn of the last century was heavily gay and bisexual, including such important figures as Oscar Wilde, Virginia Woolf, E. M. Forster, and the cultural historian, Lytton Strachey. This movie explores the bizarre love affair (platonic) between the homosexual Strachey (Pryce) and his adoring (heterosexual) protégée, Dora Carrington (Thompson). *(Gramercy Pictures)*

The bisexual writer Gore Vidal, who has written several Hollywood screenplays, has stated, "As for overt homosexuality in pre-1960 films, it was not attempted and not possible . . . but subtexts did occasionally insert themselves." Vidal is referring to movies that seem heterosexual on the surface, but homosexual undertones are implied. No one *says* outright that the characters played by Elisha Cook, Jr., and Peter Lorre in *The Maltese Falcon* are gay, but the film is strewn with hints to that effect. Other movies with gay **subtexts** include *Queen Christina, Ben-Hur* (both versions), *Gilda, The Outlaw, Rope, Rebel Without a Cause, Strangers on a Train, Spartacus, Mean Streets,* and most **buddy films.**

After the 1960s, movies dealing overtly with gay themes became more common, especially in America and Europe. In part this was because the old Production Code, the Hollywood film industry's censorship arm, was scrapped in favor of the present-day rating system. Many of these movies portrayed gays as deeply neurotic, sex-obsessed, and self-loathing. Often they ended with the

10–30. *The Adventures of Priscilla, Queen of the Desert* (Australia, 1994), *with Guy Pearce and Hugo Weaving, written and directed by Stephan Elliott.*
This cheerfully outrageous comedy about three lip-synch performers (two drag queens and a trans-sexual) is a quintessential example of campy humor, demonstrating the eternal adage that yes, "good taste is timeless." See also *The Politics and Poetics of Camp,* by Morris Meyer (London: Routledge, 1994).
(Gramercy Pictures)

gay character committing suicide. Nonetheless, such important movies as *Dog Day Afternoon, Cabaret, Another Country, Sunday Bloody Sunday, My Beautiful Laundrette, Working Girls, Performance, La Cage aux Folles, Mona Lisa, Longtime Companion, Philadelphia,* and many of the works of Germany's Rainer Werner Fassbinder and Spain's Pedro Almodóvar are multidimensional in their treatment of gay characters.

The **camp sensibility** is especially associated with the culture of male homosexuals, though it's not their exclusive province. Female heterosexuals like Mae West, Carol Burnett, and Bette Midler are strongly campy in their work. Nor is it necessarily typical of all male gays. For example, Eisenstein, Murnau, Jean Vigo, and George Cukor were all homosexuals, but there's nothing campy about their movies. (Well, perhaps Cukor's *The Women.*) Pedro Almodóvar is the supreme master of the camp sensibility in such contemporary social comedies as *Matador, Women on the Verge of a Nervous Breakdown,* and *All About My Mother.*

10–31a. *Big Night* (U.S.A., 1996), *with Stanley Tucci and Tony Shalhoub, directed by Tucci and Campbell Scott.* (Rysher Entertainment)

Analyzing a film's portrayal of key social institutions like the family is a useful entry into the movie's ideological underpinnings. *Big Night* is about two Italian-American brothers (pictured) whose priorities in running their restaurant are radically at odds. The Tucci character is the business manager of the partnership. He's bottom-line oriented, insisting that profit should take precedence over gastronomical pedantry. His brother, the chef, is equally insistent that authentic food properly prepared should be their main concern. Despite their differences, their loyalty is unwavering, and the movie solidly endorses the family as a source of strengh, love, and comfort. *The Ref* portrays the family as a totalitarian institution—dysfunctional, crippling, and steeped in hostility. The marriage between Davis and Spacey is crumbling, and their son is becoming a juvenile delinquent. The family members are constantly bickering and slashing away at one another. Both movies employ a comic tone—gentle and ironic in *Big Night,* bitterly neurotic and satirical in *The Ref.* Both are very good movies.

10–31b. *The Ref* (U.S.A., 1994), *with Judy Davis, Denis Leary, and Kevin Spacey; directed by Ted Demme.* (Buena Vista Pictures Distribution, Inc.)

Comic mockery is a pervasive trait in camp movies, especially when it involves anything bizarre and outrageous, like the characters in the cult classic *The Rocky Horror Picture Show* **(6–25).** Camp delights in artistic excess, anything artificial, kitschy, and florid—like Carmen Miranda's garish banana dance in *The Gang's All Here,* choreographed by a grand master of camp, Busby Berkeley.

Camp frequently uses theatrical metaphors: role-playing, hammy performances, and life-as-theater comparisons, like Sonia Braga's "tormented heroine" in *Kiss of the Spider Woman.* Lavishly gaudy costumes and sets—anything in *really* bad taste—are also campy **(10–30).** Camp favors certain female stars as cult idols, especially plastic performers like Joan Crawford and Lana Turner, whose glossy women's pictures were originally intended to be taken seriously. These martyrs love not wisely but too well. They suffer. They survive. But mostly they suffer. And they do it all in glitzy designer clothes and sumptuously appointed dwellings.

Tone

A movie's tone refers to its manner of presentation, the general atmosphere that a filmmaker creates through his or her attitude toward the dramatic materials. Tone can strongly affect our responses to a given set of values. Tone can also be elusive in movies, especially in those works in which it deliberately shifts from scene to scene.

In movies like David Lynch's *Blue Velvet,* for example, we can never be sure of what to make of the events, because Lynch's tone is sometimes mocking, other times bizarre, and occasionally terrifying. In one scene, an innocent high school girl (Laura Dern) recounts to her boyfriend (Kyle MacLachlan) a dream she had about a perfect world. With her blonde hair radiating with halo lighting, she seems almost angelic. In the background, we hear organ music emanating from a church. The music and lighting subtly mock her naiveté as a form of stupidity.

A film's tone can be orchestrated in a number of ways. Acting styles strongly affect our response to a given scene. In Ouedraogo's *Tilai* **(10–32),** for example, the tone is objective, matter-of-fact. The acting style by the largely nonprofessional cast is scrupulously realistic. They don't exaggerate the desperation of their situation with heightened emotional fervor.

Genre also helps determine a film's tone. **Epic** films are generally presented with a dignified, larger-than-life importance, as in *The Searchers* **(10–3)** or *October* **(10–6).** The best thrillers are usually tough, mean, and hard-boiled, like *Double Indemnity* **(1–17)** and *The Grifters* **(2–20).** In comedies, the tone is generally flip, playful, and even silly.

A **voice-over** narrator can be useful for setting a tone that's different from an objective presentation of a scene, creating a double perspective on the events. Voice-overs can be ironic, as in *Sunset Boulevard* **(5–30),** sympathetic, as in *Dances With Wolves* (10–13b), paranoid, as in *Taxi Driver,* or cynical as in *A Clockwork Orange,* which is narrated by a thug.

Music is a common way to establish a movie's tone. A music track consisting primarily of rock 'n' roll will be very different in tone from a picture that's accompanied by Mozart or Ray Charles. In Spike Lee's *Jungle Fever,* the Italian-American scenes are accompanied by the ballads of Frank Sinatra; the African-American scenes are underscored by gospel and soul music.

Without taking a film's tone into account, a mechanistic analysis of its ideological values can be misleading. For example, Howard Hawks's *Bringing Up Baby* (10–33) might be interpreted as a leftist critique of a decadent society. Set in the final years of the Great Depression, the movie deals with the desperate schemes of an idle society woman (Katharine Hepburn) in luring a dedicated scientist (Cary Grant) away from his work—to join her in amorous frolic. This is hardly a goal that would be applauded by most leftists, who tend to disapprove of frivolous play.

But the movie's tone says otherwise. In the first place, the Grant character is engaged to be married to a prim, sexless associate who is utterly devoid of humor. She regards their work as all important—even to the exclusion of taking a honeymoon or eventually having children. She is the Work Ethic incarnate. Enter the Hepburn character—flighty, beautiful, and rich. Once she discovers that Grant is about to be married, she determines that only she must

10-32. *Tilai* **(Burkino Faso, 1990),** *with Rasmane Ouedraogo (with water jug) and Ina Cisse (collapsed), directed by Idrissa Ouedraogo.*
Winner of the Special Jury Prize at the Cannes Film Festival, *Tilai* is the story of a love triangle that tears a family apart in a remote African village. The tone is dedramatized, simple, and ultimately tragic. The film is complemented by a spare and poignant score by the great jazz musician, Abdullah Ibrahim.   *(New Yorker Films)*

10-33.   *Bringing Up Baby* (U.S.A., 1938), *with Cary Grant and Katharine Hepburn, directed by Howard Hawks.*
The tone of this movie—like that of most screwball comedies—is zany, silly, and fun. Grant plays an absent-minded professor type whose absorption in his work is so obsessive that he neglects other important facets of his life—especially excitement and romance. These are provided by a high-spirited, flighty heroine (Hepburn) who reduces her swain to a state of thralldom. No one was funnier than Grant in conveying the impotent exasperation of the polite male who does *try* to be understanding. His scenes are profuse in rituals of masculine humiliation, in which he's virtually (and sometimes literally) stripped of his stodgy identity.   *(RKO)*

have him and she contrives a series of ruses to lure him away from his fiancée. Hepburn's character is exciting and exasperating—but fun. Grant is forced to shed his stodgy demeanor merely to keep up with her desperate antics. She proves to be his salvation, and they are united at the film's conclusion. Clearly, they are made for each other.

In short, the charm of Hawks's screwball comedy lies precisely in what critic Robin Wood described as "the lure of irresponsibility." The middle-class work ethic is portrayed as joyless—as dry as the fossil bones that Grant and his fiancée have devoted their lives to.

Is the film devoid of ideology? Certainly not. During the 1930s, there were many American movies that dealt with the style and glamour of the rich, who were often portrayed as eccentric and good-hearted. Hawks's film is very much in this tradition. The hardships of the Depression are not even alluded to in the movie, and the film's settings—expensive nightclubs, swanky apartments, gracious country homes—are precisely what audiences of that era craved in order to forget about the Depression.

But the movie is not overtly political. The emphasis is on the charisma of the leading players and the madcap adventures they pursue. The luxurious lifestyle of the heroine enhances her appeal, and the fact that she doesn't have a job (nor seem to want one) is simply not relevant. *Bringing Up Baby* is a comedy and a love story, not a social critique.

The ideologies outlined in this chapter are conceptual models that can be helpful in understanding what a given movie seems to be saying (consciously or unconsciously) in terms of values. But they are merely formulas and clichés unless they seem relevant to our emotional *experience* of a movie.

In analyzing a film's ideology, we need to determine its degree of explicitness. If the values are implicit, how do we differentiate the good guys from the bad? Do the stars embody ideological values or were the actors cast precisely because they don't convey a ready-made set of moral assumptions? Are the cinematic techniques ideologically weighted—the mise en scène, the editing, costumes, décor, dialects? Is the protagonist a spokesperson for the filmmaker? How do you know? Is the protagonist primarily a leftist, centrist, or rightist? What cultural values are embodied in the film? What role—if any—does religion play? Are there any ethnic values present? What about sexual politics? How are women portrayed? Any gay characters? Does the movie adhere to the genre's usual conventions or are they subverted? What is the film's tone? Does the tone reinforce or mock the values of the characters?

FURTHER READING

BRONSKI, MICHAEL, *Culture Clash: The Making of Gay Sensibility* (Boston: South End Press, 1984). Covers film, theater, and publishing, with historical survey.

Cineaste, edited by Gary Crowdus, is America's leading magazine on the art and politics of movies, featuring well-written articles on a wide variety of ideologies, mostly from a leftist perspective.

DE LAURENTIS, TERESA, *Alice Doesn't* (Bloomington: Indiana University Press, 1984). Feminist essays, with a strong theoretical emphasis.

DOWNING, JOHN D. H., ed., *Film and Politics in the Third World* (New York: Praeger, 1988). Collection of scholarly essays.

HASKELL, MOLLY, *From Reverence to Rape,* 2nd ed. (Chicago: University of Chicago Press, 1987). The treatment of women in movies—a historical survey. A well-written feminist history.

NICHOLS, BILL, *Ideology and the Image* (Bloomington: Indiana University Press, 1981). Social representation in movies and other media. Perceptive and copiously illustrated.

POLAN, DANA B., *The Political Language of Film and the Avant-Garde* (Ann Arbor, Mich.: UMI Research Press, 1985). Volume in the *Studies in Cinema* series (no. 30).

QUART, BARBARA KOENIG, *Women Directors: The Emergence of a New Cinema* (New York: Praeger, 1988). Covers women directors in the Americas, Europe, and the Third World.

RUSSO, VITO, *The Celluloid Closet* (New York: Harper & Row, 1981). Homosexuality in the movies; a well-written survey.

RYAN, MICHAEL, and DOUGLAS KELLNER, *Camera Politica: The Politics and Ideology of Contemporary Hollywood Film* (Bloomington: Indiana University Press, 1988).

Theory

*Surely there are no hard and fast rules: It all depends on
how it's done.*

—PAULINE KAEL, FILM CRITIC

Overview

Theoretical question: What is the essential nature of cinema? The three focus points: the work of art, the artist, the audience. Theories of realism: a mirror of the real world. The self-effacing artist. The values of discovery, intimacy, and emotional richness. The avoidance of artifice. Italian neorealism. Formalist film theories: imaginary worlds. A place of magic. The pleasure principle. The film artist: the auteur theory. The French *nouvelle vague*. Eclectic and synthetic theories. The American tradition of practical criticism. Eclecticism: Whatever works is right. Structuralism and semiotic theories. The complexity of film: codified data in a deep structure. Quantifying the ineffable. Thematic polarities and the nonlinear methodology of structuralism. Historiography: the assumptions and biases of writing histories. Aesthetic approaches. Technological approaches. Economic histories. Social histories.

Most theories of film are concerned with the wider context of the medium—its social, political, and philosophical implications. Theorists have also explored the essential nature of cinema—what differentiates it from other art forms,

11–1.   *The Maltese Falcon* (U.S.A., 1941), *with Humphrey Bogart, Peter Lorre, Mary Astor, and Sydney Greenstreet; directed by John Huston.*
Theory is the handmaiden of art, not vice versa. Movies can be explored from a variety of theoretical perspectives, each with its own set of values and parameters of inquiry. Your theoretical orientation will depend in large part on what you're looking for. For example, *The Maltese Falcon* can be placed in at least seven theoretical contexts: **(1)** An auteur critic would regard it as a typical Huston film. **(2)** It could also be analyzed as a Bogart vehicle, exploiting and expanding the **star's iconography. (3)** An industry historian would place the picture within its commercial context—as a superior example of the Warner Brothers product of this era. **(4)** A **genre** theorist would be interested in it as a classic example of the detective thriller, and one of the first of the so-called deadly female pictures that were so popular in the United States during World War II. **(5)** A theorist interested in the relationship of movies to literature might focus on Huston's script, based on Dashiell Hammet's celebrated novel of the same title. **(6)** A stylistic critic would analyze the picture within the context of **film noir,** an important style in the American cinema of the 1940s. **(7)** A **Marxist** might interpret the movie as a parable on greed, an implicit condemnation of the vices of capitalism. Each theoretical grid charts a different cinematic topography. *(Warner Bros.)*

what its basic properties are. For the most part, film theory has been domi-nated by Europeans, especially the French and British. The tradition of criti-cism in the United States has been less theoretical and more pragmatic in its thrust. In recent times, however, American movie critics have shown a greater interest in the theoretical implications of the medium, though the bias in favor of practical criticism remains strong. A theory is an intellectual grid, a set of aesthetic generalizations, not eternal verities. Some theories are more useful than others in understanding specific movies. No single theory can explain them all. For this reason, recent developments in the field have stressed an eclectic approach, synthesizing a variety of theoretical strategies (11–1).

Traditionally, theorists have focused their attention on three areas of inquiry: **(1)** the work of art, **(2)** the artist, and **(3)** the audience. Those who have stressed the work of art have explored the inner dynamics of movies—how they communicate, the language systems they use. Film theorists can be divided into **realists** and **formalists,** just as filmmakers tend to favor one style or the other. The most important artist-oriented approach is the **auteur theory,** the belief that a movie is best understood by focusing on its artistic creator, pre-sumably the director. Structuralism and semiology were the dominant theories after 1970, and both tend to emphasize a synthetic approach, combining such concerns as genre, authorship, style, **iconography,** social context, and ideology. In the area of historiography—the theoretical assumptions underlying film his-tory—recent trends have also emphasized an integrated approach.

Theories of Realism

Most theories of realism emphasize the documentary aspects of film art. Movies are evaluated primarily in terms of how accurately they reflect exter-nal reality. The camera is regarded as essentially a recording mechanism rather than an expressive medium in its own right. The subject matter is paramount in the cinema of realism, technique its discreetly transparent handmaiden. As we have seen in the case of André Bazin (Chapter 4), most theories of realism have a moral and ethical bias and are often rooted in the values of Islamic, Christian, and Marxist humanism.

Realist theorists like Cesare Zavattini and Siegfried Kracauer believe that cinema is essentially an extension of photography and shares with it a pro-nounced affinity for recording the visible world around us. Unlike other art forms, photography and cinema tend to leave the raw materials of reality more or less intact. There is a minimum of interference and manipulation on the artist's part, for film is not an art of invention so much as an art of "being there."

Roberto Rossellini's *Open City* (11–2) inaugurated the Italian **neorealist** movement, one of the triumphs of the cinema of realism. The movie deals with the collaboration of Catholics and Communists in fighting the Nazi occupation of Rome shortly before the American army liberated the city. Technically, the film is rather crude. Good quality film stock was impossible to obtain, so Rossellini had to use inferior newsreel stock. Nevertheless, the technical flaws and the resultant grainy images convey a sense of journalistic immediacy and authenticity. (Many neorealists began their careers as journalists, and Rossellini himself began as a documentarist.) Virtually all the movie was shot at actual locations, and there are many exterior shots in which no additional lights were used. With the exception of the principal players, the actors were nonprofessionals. The structure of the movie is episodic—a series of vignettes showing the reactions of Roman citizens to the German occupation.

11–2. *Open City* **(Italy, 1945),** *with Marcello Pagliero, directed by Roberto Rossellini.*
The torture scenes of this famous Resistance film were so realistic that they were cut out of some prints. In this episode, a Nazi S.S. officer applies a blowtorch to the body of a Communist partisan in an effort to force him to reveal the names of his comrades in the underground. The crucifixion allusion is deliberate, even though the character is a nonbeliever. It parallels the death of another partisan, a Catholic priest, who is executed by a military firing squad. The French critic André Bazin was a champion of Italian neorealism, applauding its moral fervor even more than its technical restraint. "Is not neorealism primarily a kind of humanism, and only secondarily a style of filmmaking?" he asked.   *(Pathé Contemporary Films)*

Open City is saturated with a sense of unrelenting honesty. "This is the way things are," Rossellini is said to have declared after the film premiered. The statement became the motto of the neorealist movement. The film provided a rallying point for an entire generation of Italian filmmakers whose creative talents had been stifled by the repressive Fascist regime of the prewar era. Within the next few years, there followed an astonishing series of movies that catapulted the Italians into the front ranks of the international cinema. The major filmmakers of the movement were Rossellini, Luchino Visconti, and Vittorio De Sica and his frequent scriptwriter Cesare Zavattini.

There are considerable differences between these men and even between their early and later works. Furthermore, neorealism implied a style as well as an ideology. Rossellini emphasized the ethical dimension: "For me, Neorealism is above all a moral position from which to look at the world. It then became an aesthetic position, but at the beginning it was moral." De Sica, Zavattini, and Visconti also stressed morality as the touchstone of neorealism.

The main ideological characteristics of the movement can be summarized as follows: **(1)** a new democratic spirit, with emphasis on the value of ordinary people such as laborers, peasants, and factory workers; **(2)** a compassionate point of view and a refusal to make facile moral judgments; **(3)** a preoccupation with Italy's Fascist past and its aftermath of wartime devastation, poverty, unemployment, prostitution, and the black market; **(4)** a blending of Christian and Marxist humanism; and **(5)** an emphasis on emotions rather than abstract ideas.

The stylistic features of neorealism include **(1)** an avoidance of neatly plotted stories in favor of loose, episodic structures that evolve organically from the situations of the characters; **(2)** a documentary visual style; **(3)** the use of actual locations—usually exteriors—rather than studio sets; **(4)** the use of non-professional actors, sometimes even for principal roles; **(5)** an avoidance of literary dialogue in favor of conversational speech, including dialects; and **(6)** an avoidance of artifice in the **editing,** camerawork, and lighting in favor of a simple "styleless" style.

Realists have shown a persistent hostility toward plot and neatly structured stories. For example, Cesare Zavattini defined the ordinary and the everyday as the main business of the cinema. Spectacular events and extraordinary characters should be avoided at all costs, he believed. He claimed that his ideal movie would consist of ninety consecutive minutes from a person's actual life. There should be no barriers between reality and the spectator, no directorial virtuosity to "deform" the integrity of life as it is. The artistry should be invisible, the materials "found" rather than shaped or manipulated.

Suspicious of conventional plot structures, Zavattini dismissed them as dead formulas. He insisted on the dramatic superiority of life as it is experienced by ordinary people. Filmmakers should be concerned with the "excavation" of reality. Instead of plots, they should emphasize facts and all their "echoes and reverberations." According to Zavattini, filmmaking is not a mat-

11-3. De Sica, Renoir, and Ray were world-class cinematic realists, and these three movies are among their most celebrated masterpieces.

11-3a. *Umberto D* (Italy, 1952), with Carlo Battisti (right), directed by Vittorio De Sica.
Scripted by Cesare Zavattini, *Umberto D* concentrates on "small subjects," ordinary people, and the details of everyday life. The story explores the drab existence of a retired pensioner who's being forced out of his modest apartment because he can't afford the rent hike. His only comfort is his adoring pet dog who accompanies him in his desperate attempts to come up with the necessary cash. *(Museum of Modern Art)*

continued ▶

11-3b. *The Rules of the Game* (France, 1939), *directed by Jean Renoir.*
"Everyone has his reasons," Jean Renoir once observed of his characters. In this wise and profound comedy of manners, Renoir refuses to divide people glibly into good guys and bad, insisting that most people have logical reasons for behaving as they do. Sometimes good people commit horrible deeds—like this enraged working-class husband who blasts away with a shotgun at the man he thinks has seduced his wife. Incongruously, he does so in the middle of a luxurious salon filled with (mostly) innocent bystanders.   *(Janus Films)*

11–3c. *Pather Panchali (The Song of the Road,* India, 1955), *with Kanu Bannerjee, directed by Satyajit Ray.*

Like his idols De Sica and Renoir, Ray was a humanist, exploring a wide range of emotions. *Pather Panchali* is a study of grinding poverty in a remote Indian village. It packs a powerful emotional punch. Terrible catastrophes seem to strike out of nowhere, almost crushing their victims and plunging them into unspeakable grief. Surviving this squalor and desperation is human hope, flickering like a candle against the wind, refusing to be extinguished.   *(Audio-Brandon Film)*

Why should we watch such depressing stories? Hedonists might well complain that movies like these bring you down, that they're painful to watch, a kind of cinema for masochists. The answer is complex. Such movies often *are* painful to watch. But they're also insightful, dramatizing what it's like to be up against the wall, to be really desperate. They show us the toughness and resilience of our brothers and sisters. At their best, movies like these can be profoundly spiritual—offering us privileged glimpses into the nobility of the human spirit.

ter of "inventing fables" that are superimposed over the factual materials of life, but of searching unrelentingly to uncover the dramatic implications of these facts. The purpose of the cinema is to explore the "dailiness" of events, to reveal certain details that had always been there but had never been noticed.

In his book *Theory of Film: The Redemption of Physical Reality,* the German-trained theorist Siegfried Kracauer also attacks plot as a natural enemy of realism. According to Kracauer, the cinema is characterized by a number of natural affinities. First of all, it tends to favor "unstaged reality"—that is, the most appropriate subject matter gives the illusion of having been found rather than arranged. Second, film tends to stress the random, the fortuitous. Kracauer is fond of the phrase "nature caught in the act," meaning that film is best suited to recording events and objects that might be overlooked in life. The realistic cinema is a cinema of "found moments" and poignant revelations of humanity. A third affinity that Kracauer notes is indeterminacy. The best movies suggest endlessness. They imply a slice of life, a fragment of a larger reality rather than a self-contained whole. By refusing to tie up all the loose ends at the conclusion of the movie, the filmmaker can suggest the limitlessness of reality.

Kracauer is hostile toward movies that demonstrate a "formative tendency." Historical films and fantasies he regards as tending to move away from the basic concerns of the medium. He also dismisses most literary and dramatic adaptations because he believes that literature is ultimately concerned with "interior realities," what people are thinking and feeling, whereas movies explore surfaces, exterior reality. He regards all stylistic self-consciousness as "uncinematic," because instead of emphasizing the subject matter, the filmmaker calls attention to *how* it is presented.

Theories of film realism are not very helpful in understanding the complexities of formalist movies—the works of a Sergei Eisenstein or a Steven Spielberg. On the other hand, they do help to explain the raw emotional power of such masterpieces of realism as *Bicycle Thief,* which was directed by Vittorio De Sica and scripted primarily by Zavattini **(6–33).**

Bicycle Thief was acted entirely by nonprofessionals and consists of simple events in the life of a laborer (played by Lamberto Maggiorani, who was an actual factory worker). In 1948, when the film was released, nearly a quarter of the work force in Italy was unemployed. At the opening of the movie, we are introduced to the protagonist, a family man with a wife and two children to support. He has been out of work for two years. Finally, a billboard-posting job opens up, but to accept it, he must have a bicycle. To get his bike out of hock, he and his wife pawn their sheets and bedding. On his first day on the job, the bicycle is stolen. The rest of the movie deals with his attempts to recover the bike. The man's search grows increasingly more frantic as he crisscrosses the city with his idolizing son, Bruno. After a series of false leads, the two finally

11–4.   *The Tree of the Wooden Clogs* (Italy, 1978), *directed by Ermanno Olmi.*
As a movement, Italian neorealism was pretty much over by the mid-1950s, but as a style and an attitude toward reality, its influence spread to many other countries. A number of present-day Italian filmmakers have continued in the tradition of neorealism. For example, Olmi's movies are steeped in the values of Christian humanism. In this film, which was shot on authentic locations with nonprofessional players, he celebrates the everyday lives of several peasant families around 1900. For them, God is a living presence—a source of guidance, hope, and solace. Their faith is childlike, trusting, like that of St. Francis of Assisi. In a series of documentarylike vignettes, Olmi unfolds their gentle drama, extolling their patience, their tough stoicism, their dignity. Above all, he exalts the sacredness of the human spirit. For Olmi, they are the salt of the earth.   *(New Yorker Films)*

track down one of the thieves, but the protagonist is outwitted by him and humiliated in front of his boy. Realizing that he will lose his livelihood without a bike, the desperate man—after sending his son away—sneaks off and attempts to steal one himself. But the boy observes from a distance as his father peddles frantically to escape a pursuing mob. He is caught and again humiliated in front of a crowd—which includes his incredulous son. With the bitterness of betrayed innocence, the youngster suddenly realizes that his dad is not the heroic figure he had formerly thought, but an ordinary man who in desperation yielded to a degrading temptation. Like most neorealist films,

11–5.   *Closely Watched Trains* (Czechoslovakia, 1966), *with Václav Neckar and Jitka Bendová, directed by Jiri Menzel.*
One of the hallmarks of realism is intimacy—a sense of discovering a small private moment that might easily have been overlooked because it's not a big deal. These little nothings—a stolen kiss, a quick sidelong glance, an incongruous detail—are what make realism a celebration of the poetry of everyday life.   *(Museum of Modern Art)*

Bicycle Thief doesn't offer a slick solution. There are no miraculous interventions in the final reel. The concluding scene shows the boy walking alongside his father in an anonymous crowd, both of them choking with shame and weeping silently. Almost imperceptibly, the boy's hand gropes for his father's as they walk homeward, their only comfort a mutual compassion.

Formalist Film Theories

Formalist film theorists believe that the art of cinema is possible precisely because a movie is unlike everyday reality. The filmmaker exploits the limitations of the medium—its two-dimensionality, its confining **frame,** its frag-

11–6. *Ugetsu* **(Japan, 1953),** *with Masayuki Mori and Machiko Kyo, directed by Kenji Mizoguchi.*

Realistic critics and theorists tend to underestimate the flexibility of an audience's response to nonrealistic movies. Of course, it's easier for a filmmaker to create the illusion of reality if the story deals with everyday events, for the world of the movie and the actual world are essentially the same. On the other hand, a gifted artist can make even fantasy materials "realistic." A movie like *Ugetsu*, which is set in the remote past and features spirits and demons, presents us with a self-contained magical universe which we are able to enter by temporarily forgetting the outside world of reality. In short, audiences are highly sophisticated in their responses to nonrealistic films. We can almost totally suspend our disbelief, partially suspend it, or alternate between extremes according to the aesthetic demands of the world of the movie.   *(Janus Films)*

mented time–space continuum—to produce a world that resembles the real world only in a superficial sense. The real world is merely a repository of raw material that needs to be shaped and heightened to be effective as art. Film art doesn't consist of a reproduction of reality, but a translation of observed characteristics into the *forms* of the medium.

Rudolf Arnheim, a gestalt psychologist, put forth an important theory of cinematic formalism in his book *Film As Art*, which was originally published in German in 1933. Arnheim's book is primarily concerned with the perception of experience. His theory is based on the different modes of perception of

11–7a.   Publicity photo for *The Wizard of Oz* (U.S.A., 1939), *with Jack Haley, Ray Bolger, Judy Garland, Frank Morgan, and Bert Lahr; directed by Victor Fleming.*

Formalism luxuriates in the artificial. "I don't think we're in Kansas anymore, Toto," Dorothy observes to her dog when they are whisked into an enchanted place where nothing looks real. The wondrous world of the MGM musical was a triumph of artifice: lions that talked (and cried), flying creatures in the sky, scarecrows that danced (beautifully), swaying fields that sparkled like diamonds, and a superb musical score by E. Y. Harburg and the great Harold Arlen.   *(MGM)*

11–7b.   *Muppets From Space* (U.S.A., 1999), *with Pepe, Animal, Gonzo, Rizzo, Miss Piggy, Fozzie Bear, and Kermit the Frog, directed by Tim Hill.*

Gifted filmmakers can create a believable world even without using human beings. The Muppet characters from the Jim Henson organization all have unique personalities—familiar to millions of children all over the world. You don't have to be a child to appreciate the oddball denizens of Muppetland, who are more credible than a lot of so-called "live" characters. In this movie, our stalwart astronauts embark on an extraterrestrial adventure in the hopes of finding Gonzo's long-lost family from a distant planet.   *(Jim Henson Pictures)*

11–8a. *Robocop* **(U.S.A., 1987),** *with Peter Weller, directed by Paul Verhoeven.*
If realism tends to favor the didactic, the teaching function of art, then formalism tends to favor the pleasure principle. Implicit in the concept of formalism is the supremacy of pattern over life, of aesthetic richness over literal truth. Even in movies that attempt a superficial realism, the subject matter itself is often fantastic, with an emphasis on special effects and the visual appeal of the shapes, lines, textures, and colors of the images. *(Orion Pictures)*

11–8b. *Being John Malkovich* **(U.S.A., 1999),** *with Catherine Keener and John Cusack, directed by Spike Jonze.*
Independent filmmaker Spike Jonze believes that modern movies have become slaves to boring reality. Even fanciful genres like science fiction contain recognizable character types and situations from other movies. This Pirandellian film dares to reintroduce the inexplicable and the surrealistic into movies. The main character (Cusack), an alienated puppeteer, discovers that he can situate himself in the brain of actor John Malkovich, who's one of the main performers of the film, presumably playing himself. Cusack can accomplish this amazing feat by working in an office with very low ceilings. When his 15 minutes of alternate reality are over, he's unceremoniously dropped on the side of the New Jersey Turnpike. But you're allowed to repeat. *(Gramercy Pictures)*

11-9. *The Servant* (Great Britain, 1963), *with Dirk Bogarde (foreground), directed by Joseph Losey.*

A scene can be photographed in literally hundreds of different ways, but the formalist selects the camera **setup** that best captures its symbolic or psychological implications. In this shot, for example, a young woman (Wendy Craig) suddenly realizes the enormous power a valet (Bogarde) wields over her weak fiancé (James Fox). She is isolated on the left, half-plunged in darkness. A curtained doorway separates her from her lover, who is so stupefied with drugs he scarcely knows where he is, much less what's really going on. The servant cooly turns his back on them, the camera's low angle further emphasizing his effortless control over his "master." *(Landau Distributing)*

the camera on the one hand and the human eye on the other. Anticipating some of the theories of the communications specialist Marshall McLuhan, Arnheim insists that the camera's image of a bowl of fruit, for instance, is fundamentally different from our perception of the fruit bowl in actual life. Or, in McLuhan's terms, the information we receive in each instance is determined by the form of its content. Formalist theorists celebrate these differences, believing that what makes photography fall short of perfect reproduction is also what makes cinema an art, not just a species of xerography.

Formalists have pointed out many instances where divergences exist between the camera's image of reality and what the human eye sees. For example, film directors must choose which viewpoint to photograph a scene from. They don't necessarily choose the clearest view, for often this does not emphasize the major characteristics of the scene, its expressive essence. In life, we perceive objects in depth and can penetrate the space that surrounds most things. In movies, space is an illusion, for the screen has only two dimensions, permitting the director to manipulate objects and perspectives in the **mise en scène.** For example, important objects can be placed where they are most likely to be noticed first. Unimportant objects can be relegated to inferior positions, at the edges or "rear" of the image.

In real life, space and time are experienced as continuous. Through editing, filmmakers can chop up space and time and rearrange them in a more meaningful manner. Like other artists, the film director selects certain expressive details from the chaotic plenitude of physical reality. By juxtaposing these

11–10a. *Splash* (U.S.A., 1984), *with Daryl Hannah and Tom Hanks, directed by Ron Howard.*

A common misconception about formalistic films is that they are merely light entertainment, far removed from serious concerns. For example, this movie deals with a young man who falls in love with a strange young woman, who turns out to be a mermaid. The film is a symbolic fantasy, and it's certainly entertaining, but it also explores fundamental values—about loyalty, family, work, and commitment.   *(Buena Vista Pictures)*

11–10b. *The Legend of Bagger Vance* (U.S.A., 2000), *with Will Smith, J. Michael Moncrief, and Matt Damon, directed by Robert Redford.*

Will Smith plays a mysterious golf caddy named Bagger Vance—a character who turns out to be supernatural, not "real." Yet the style of the film is an accurate recreation of the 1930s milieu. Is the movie formalistic or realistic?   *(DreamWorks Pictures)*

space and time fragments, the filmmaker creates a continuity that doesn't exist in raw nature. This, of course, was the basic position of the Soviet montage theorists (Chapter 4).

Formalists are always concerned with patterns, methods of restructuring reality into aesthetically appealing designs. Patterns can be expressed visually, through the photography and mise en scène; or aurally, in stylized dialogue, symbolic sound effects, and musical **motifs.** Camera movements are often **kinetic** patterns superimposed on the visual materials, commenting on them in some heightened manner.

The problems with most formalist theories are the same as with realists: There are too many exceptions. They are certainly useful in an appreciation of Hitchcock's works, for example, or Tim Burton's. But how helpful is the theory in explaining the films of Spike Lee or De Sica? We respond to their movies because of their similarities with physical reality, not their divergences from it. Ultimately, of course, these are matters of emphasis, for films are too pluralistic to be pigeonholed into one tidy theory **(11–10b).**

The Auteur Theory

In the mid-1950s, the French journal *Cahiers du Cinéma* revolutionized film criticism with its concept of *la politique des auteurs.* This committed policy of authors was put forth by the pugnacious young critic François Truffaut. The auteur theory became the focal point of a critical controversy that eventually spread to England and America. Before long, the theory became a militant rallying cry, particularly among younger critics, dominating such lively journals as *Movie* in Great Britain, *Film Culture* in America, and both French- and English-language editions of *Cahiers du Cinéma.* Although a number of writers rejected the theory as simplistic, auteurism dominated film criticism throughout the 1960s.

Actually, the main lines of the theory aren't particularly outrageous, at least not in retrospect. Truffaut, Godard, and their critical colleagues proposed that the greatest movies are dominated by the personal vision of the director. A filmmaker's "signature" can be perceived through an examination of his or her total output, which is characterized by a unity of theme and style. The writer's contribution is less important than the director's because subject matter is artistically neutral. It can be treated with brilliance or bare competence. Movies ought to be judged on the basis of *how,* not *what.* Like other formalists, the auteur critics claimed that what makes a good film is not the subject matter as such, but its stylistic treatment. The director dominates the treatment, provided he or she is a strong director, an *auteur.*

Drawing primarily from the cinematic traditions of the United States, the *Cahiers* critics also developed a sophisticated theory of film genre. In fact, André Bazin, the editor of the journal, believed that the genius of the American cinema was its repository of ready-made forms: westerns, thrillers, musicals, action films,

11–11. Photo montage of Jean-Pierre Léaud as Antoine Doinel in (left to right) *Love on the Run* (1979), *Stolen Kisses* (1968), "Antoine et Colette" (an episode in the anthology film, *Love at Twenty,* 1962), and the drawing from *The 400 Blows* (1959). Missing from the Doinel series is *Bed and Board* (1970).

Above all, the auteurists emphasized the personality of the artist as the main criterion of value. François Truffaut, who originally formulated *la politique des auteurs,* went on to create some of the most distinctively personal movies of the New Wave. His Doinel series is one of the crowning achievements of the *nouvelle vague*. These semiautobiographical movies trace the adventures (mostly amorous) of its likable but slightly neurotic hero, Antoine Doinel. Truffaut's protégé Léaud was the best known actor of the French New Wave. *(New World Pictures)*

comedies, and so on. "The tradition of genres is a base of operations for creative freedom," Bazin pointed out. Genre is an enriching, not a constricting, tradition. The auteurists argued that the best movies are **dialectical,** in which the conventions of a genre are held in aesthetic tension with the personality of the artist.

The American auteurs that these critics praised had worked within the studio system, which had broken the artistic pretensions of many lesser filmmakers. What the auteurists especially admired was how gifted directors could circumvent studio interference and even hackneyed scripts through their technical expertise. The subject matter of Hitchcock's thrillers or Ford's westerns was not significantly different from others working in these genres. Yet both auteurs managed to create great films, precisely because the real content was conveyed through the mise en scène, the editing, and all the other formal devices at the director's disposal.

The sheer breadth of their knowledge of film history permitted these critics to reevaluate the major works of a wide variety of directors. In many instances, they completely reversed previous critical judgments. Before long, personality cults developed around the most popular directors. On the whole, these were filmmakers who had been virtually ignored by the critical establishment of the previous generation: Hitchcock, Ford, Hawks, Lang, and many others. The auteur critics were often dogmatic in their dislikes as well as their likes. Bazin expressed alarm at their negativism. To praise a bad movie, he felt, was unfortunate; but to condemn a good one was a serious failing. He especially disliked their tendency to hero worship, which led to superficial a priori judgments. Movies by cult directors were indiscriminately praised, whereas those by directors out of fashion were automatically condemned. Auteurists were fond of ranking directors, and their listings could be bizarre. Perfectly routine commercial directors like Nicholas Ray were elevated above such important masters as John Huston and Billy Wilder.

The principal spokesman for the auteur theory in the United States was Andrew Sarris, the influential critic of the *Village Voice*. More knowledgeable about the complexities of the star and studio system than his French counterparts, Sarris nonetheless defended their basic argument, especially the princi-

11–12. *Fanny and Alexander* **(Sweden, 1983),** *with Bertil Guve and Pernilla Allwin, written and directed by Ingmar Bergman.*
A towering giant of the cinema, Ingmar Bergman has written all of his movies by himself. His films are often semiautobiographical, like *Fanny and Alexander,* one of his many masterpieces. In addition, Bergman worked with the same cast and crew for years, a virtual repertory company. In short, his movies are indisputably those of an auteur. *(Svenska Filminstitutet and Embassy Pictures)*

ple of tension between an artist's personal vision and the genre assignments that these directors were given by their Hollywood bosses.

Quite correctly, these critics insisted that total artistic freedom isn't always a virtue. After all, Michelangelo, Dickens, and Shakespeare, among others, accepted commissioned subjects. Though this principle of dialectical tension is a sound one—in the other arts as well as cinema—some auteurists carried it to ridiculous extremes. In the first place, there is the problem of degree. It's doubtful that even a genius like Bergman or Kubrick could do much with the script and stars of *Abbott and Costello Meet the Mummy*. In other words, a director's got to have a fighting chance with the material. When the subject matter sinks beneath a certain potential, the result is not tension but artistic annihilation.

The most gifted American directors of the studio era were **producer–directors** who worked independently within the major studios. These tended to be the same artists the auteur critics admired most. But the lion's share of American fiction movies produced during this era were studio films. That is, the director functioned as a member of a team and usually had little to say about the scripting, casting, or editing. Many of these directors were skillful technicians, but they were essentially craftsmen rather than artists.

Michael Curtiz is a good example. For most of his career, he was a contract director at Warner Brothers. Known for his speed and efficiency, Curtiz directed dozens of movies in a variety of styles and genres. He often took on several projects at the same time. Curtiz had no "personal vision" in the sense that the auteur theory defines it: He was just getting a job done. He often did it very well. Even so, movies like *Yankee Doodle Dandy, Casablanca,* and *Mildred Pierce* **(11–13a)** can be discussed more profitably as Warner Brothers movies rather than Michael Curtiz movies. The same principle applies to most of the other Hollywood studios. In our day, it applies to films that are dominated by producers and financiers rather than artists.

Other films have been dominated by stars. Few people would think of referring to a Mae West movie as anything else, and the same holds true for the W. C. Fields comedies and the works of Laurel and Hardy. The ultimate in the star as auteur is the so-called star vehicle, a film specifically tailored to showcase the talents of a performer **(11–14).**

The auteur theory suffers from a number of other weaknesses. There are some excellent films that have been made by directors who are otherwise mediocre. For example, Joseph H. Lewis's *Gun Crazy* is a superb movie, but it's atypical of his output. Conversely, great directors sometimes produce bombs. The works of such major filmmakers as Ford, Godard, Renoir, and Buñuel are radically inconsistent in terms of quality, and some of their movies are outright awful. The auteur theory emphasizes history and a director's total output, which tends to favor older directors at the expense of newcomers. Some artists have explored a variety of themes in many different styles and genres: Carol Reed, Sidney Lumet, and John Frankenheimer are good examples. There are also some great filmmakers who are crude directorial technicians. For example, Chaplin and

11–13a. *Mildred Pierce (U.S.A., 1945), with Joan Crawford, directed by Michael Curtiz.*
Particularly during the golden age of the big-studio era (roughly from 1925 to 1955), most American mainstream movies were dominated by the imprimatur of the studio rather than the director, who was regarded more as an executor of a collaborative enterprise rather than a creative artist in his own right. *Mildred Pierce* has "Warner Brothers" written all over it. Typically tough and proletarian in emphasis, the movie features Joan Crawford as a self-made woman who kills a man. It was regarded as her comeback performance after many years as a glamourous star at Metro-Goldwyn-Mayer. The movie, based on James M. Cain's hard-boiled novel, was adapted by Ranald MacDougall, a studio scribe. It was directed by Michael Curtiz, Warners' ace director, who was known for his speed, efficiency, and versatility. He was also able to control Warners' feisty stars, who were known to be difficult and rebellious. Even Bette Davis, the gutsiest of them all, was cowed by Curtiz. When she complained that he hadn't allowed her any break for lunch, he replied majesterially, "When you work for me, you don't need lunch. You just take an aspirin." *(Warner Bros.)*

11-13b. *Primary Colors (U.S.A., 1998), with John Travolta, directed by Mike Nichols.*
In the contemporary American cinema, most mainstream movies are still collaborative enterprises, with the director—even one as brilliant as Mike Nichols—serving as a coordinator of talent. The film is based on a political novel by "Anonymous"—actually journalist Joe Klein. The book is a thinly disguised account of the first presidential primary of Bill Clinton, his wife Hillary, and their political organization. The smart and wickedly funny screenplay was written by Elaine May. A first-rate cast is headed by Travolta, who does an uncanny impersonation of the gregarious and charismatic Clinton, who is at once a genuine democrat, a dedicated public servant, and a womanizing opportunist. The miracle of the movie is that it's so seamless, with its multiple individual contributions blended into a unified artistic whole. *That* was Mike Nichols's contribution. *(Universal Studios)*

11-14. *Terminator 2: Judgment Day* (U.S.A., 1991), *with Arnold Schwarzenegger and Edward Furlong, directed by James Cameron.*
Many movies are dominated by stars rather than directors, studios, or genres. *Terminator 2* is a star vehicle for Schwarzenegger, one of the top box-office attractions of the contemporary American cinema. The film is specifically tailored to showcase his comic abilities as well as his popularity as an action/adventure star. He is rarely off camera, and the plot is pretty much a pretext to allow him maximum creative freedom. The movie is skillfully directed, but the dominant artistic personality is clearly in front of the camera, not behind it.   *(Tri-Star Pictures)*

Herzog in no way approach the stylistic fluency of Michael Curtiz, or a dozen other contract directors of his era. Yet there are very few artists who have created such distinctively personal movies as Chaplin and Herzog.

Despite its shortcomings and excesses, the auteur theory had a liberating effect on film criticism, establishing the director as the key figure at least in the art of cinema, if not always the industry. By the 1970s, the major battle had been won. Virtually all serious discussions of movies were at least partly couched in terms of the director's personal vision. To this day, the concept of directorial dominance remains firmly established, at least with films of high artistic merit (**11–15**).

11–15.   Today, the term "auteur" is commonly used to designate a film artist, an individual whose personality is indelibly stamped onto his or her work. An auteur controls the major modes of expression—script, performance, execution—whether working within the commercial industry, like a Spielberg, a Scorsese, or a Spike Lee, or working outside the studio system, in what has been called the independent cinema.

11–15a.   *Sling Blade* (U.S.A., 1996), *with Billy Bob Thornton, written and directed by Thornton.*
Independent filmmakers have much more control over their product than most mainstream directors, in part because independent movies are usually made on low budgets. Most of the people involved are working for free, or very little, compared to Hollywood studio personnel. These alternative artists can also explore unusual or unfashionable subjects. For example, though more than 40 percent of Americans attend religious services weekly, this fact is rarely acknowledged in mainstream movies. But an important element of *Sling Blade* is its strong Southern Baptist flavor, lending the bizarre tale a spiritual richness.   *(Miramax Films)*

11–15b.   *The Opposite of Sex* (U.S.A., 1997), *with Martin Donovan and Lisa Kudrow, written and directed by Don Roos.*
The protagonists of mainstream movies are almost exclusively heterosexual, and rarely do they suffer from any sexual problems. Independent films can be more real. This film's gay protagonist (Donovan) has just had his lover stolen from him by his manipulative sixteen-

year-old half sister (Christina Ricci at her most evil). His best friend (Kudrow) is sexually repressed and hopelessly in love with him. That's just *part* of their problems. Mainstream movies are rarely as witty and bitchy and shrewd about the subject of sex. Nor do they usually offer such juicy roles for women, who are every bit as neurotic as the men.   (TriStar Pictures)

continued   ▶

11–15c. *Go* (U.S.A., 1999), *with Jay Mohr and Scott Wolf, directed by Doug Liman.*
Mainstream movies tend to reaffirm conventional morality. They also tend to be highly predictable. Within the first ten minutes of watching a typical genre film, we can usually guess how it'll end. The good guys will triumph, decency will be restored, blah blah blah. Independent movies can be more perverse. Like this black comedy, written by John August. The two main characters (pictured) are selfish, nasty, and egregiously narcissistic. They're also fun to watch and surprisingly unpredictable. These movies also tend to attract ambitious young rising actors like Mohr and Wolf, or established stars like Holly Hunter, Harvey Keitel, Cameron Diaz, or Sean Penn, who are more interested in their art than in making a lot of money playing unchallenging roles. *(Columbia Pictures)*

Eclectic and Synthetic Theories

Eclecticism isn't really a theory so much as a method of practical criticism. This is the favored approach of many film critics in the United States, such as the former critic of *The New Yorker,* Pauline Kael, who once wrote, "I believe that we respond most and best to work in any art form (and to other experience as well) if we are pluralistic, flexible, relative in our judgments, if we are eclectic." Such critics place a movie in whatever context seems most appropriate, drawing from diverse sources, systems, and styles. Actually, almost all critics are eclectic to some degree. For example, although Andrew Sarris has been identified with the auteur theory, he is equally at home approaching a movie in terms of its star, its period, its national origin, or its ideological context.

Eclecticism is sometimes called the tradition of sensibility because a high value is placed on the aesthetic discriminations of a person of taste and discernment. Such critics are often urbane, well educated, and conversant in the other arts. The cultural cross-references in the writings of such critics as Roger Ebert and Frank Rich range over a wide spectrum, including literature, drama, politics, and the visual arts. They frequently allude to the ideas of such seminal thinkers as Freud, Marx, Darwin, and Jung. Sometimes critics combine an ideological perspective—such as feminism—with practical criticism, sociology, and history, as in the criticism of Molly Haskell and Julia Lesage (**11–16**). The best eclectic critics are gifted writers, including such distinguished prose

11–16. *Clueless* (U.S.A., 1995), *with Justin Walker and Alicia Silverstone, written and directed by Amy Heckerling.*
Eclectic critics often combine movie criticism with social movements such as feminism, exploring not only the sexual values within a film but also the ideological context of its production. Traditionally, women have been excluded from positions of power within the American film industry. (The situation is even worse in most other countries.) Some, like Amy Heckerling, circumvented this legacy of discrimination by producing their low-budget films independently. Her success as an independent filmmaker eventually opened doors to the mainstream industry. *(Paramount Pictures)*

stylists as James Agee and Pauline Kael. Polished writing is valued *as* writing, in addition to the ideas it conveys.

Eclectic critics reject the notion that a single theory can explain all movies. They regard this as a cookie-cutter approach to criticism. Most of them insist that an individual's reaction to a film is deeply personal. For this reason, the best a critic can do is explain his or her personal responses as forcefully as possible. But it's just an opinion, however well founded or gracefully argued. The best criticism of this type is informative even if we disagree with its conclusions. Because personal taste is the main determinant of value in eclectic criticism, these commentators often admit to their blind spots—and *all* critics have blind spots. Everyone has had the experience of being left totally cold by a movie that's widely hailed as a masterpiece. We can't help the way we *feel*, however much our feelings go against popular sentiment. Eclectic critics usually begin with their feelings about a movie, then work outward, trying to objectify these instincts with concrete arguments. To guard against personal eccentricity, they implicitly place a film within the context of a great tradition of masterpieces—that is, those works that have stood the test of time and are still considered milestones in the evolution of the cinema. This great tradition is constantly under reevaluation. It's a loose critical consensus rather than an ironclad body of privileged works.

11–17. *Independence Day* (U.S.A., 1996), *directed by Roland Emmerich.*
This movie was a huge commercial hit, gobbling up over $300 million domestically and close to $490 million in foreign markets. It also generated $500 million in so-called ancillary revenues, including video and television rights. Twentieth Century–Fox spent $30 million for advertising alone—an investment that obviously paid off. The film's special effects constituted its main box-office appeal. In this sequence, for example, the U.S. White House is attacked by an alien force of incredible magnitude. Serious film critics either ignored the movie or dismissed it as drivel. So who's right, the public or the "experts"? It depends on how you look at it. The mass audience tends to seek escapist entertainment: Movies are a way of forgetting their troubles. Film critics must endure a constant barrage of such pictures in their daily line of work. Hence, they tend to get bored with anything that treads the tried (and tired) and true. What they seek in movies is something unusual, challenging, and daring. *Independence Day* did not meet these expectations. *(Twentieth Century–Fox)*

Eclecticism has been faulted on a number of counts. Because of its extreme subjectivity, this approach has been criticized as mere impressionism by more rigorously systematic theorists. They insist that aesthetic evaluations ought to be governed by a body of theoretical principles rather than a critic's unique sensibility, however refined. Eclectic critics are rarely in agreement because each of them is reacting to a movie according to his or her own tastes rather than a larger theoretical framework, with its built-in system of checks and balances. For all their vaunted expertise and cultural prestige, eclectic critics have track records that don't always bear close scrutiny. For example, when Fellini's *8½* was released in 1963, many critics in America and Europe dismissed the movie as self-indulgent, formless, and even incoherent. Yet in a 1972 survey of international critics, *8½* placed fourth in their list of the ten greatest films of all time. Conversely, even good critics have pronounced a film an instant masterpiece—only to regret their impetuosity in the cool distance of time, after the movie has been long forgotten.

Eclectic critics tend to be stoical about these matters, accepting them as perils of the trade. Perhaps Pauline Kael has expressed their attitude best:

The role of the critic is to help people see what is in the work, what is in it that shouldn't be, what is not in it that could be. He is a good critic if he helps people understand more about the work than they could see for themselves; he is a great critic, if by his understanding and feeling for the work, by his passion, he can excite people so that they want to experience more of the art that is there, waiting to be seized. He is not necessarily a bad critic if he makes errors in judgment. (Infallible taste is inconceivable; what could it be measured against?) He is a bad critic if he does not awaken the curiosity, enlarge the interests and understanding of his audience. The art of the critic is to transmit his knowledge of and enthusiasm for art to others. (Quoted from *I Lost It at the Movies;* New York: Bantam, 1966)

Structuralism and Semiology

Kael and her fellow eclectics celebrate the subjective, individual element in film criticism. Others have lamented it. In the early 1970s, two interrelated cinematic theories developed, partly in response to the inadequacies of the criticism of personal sensibility. *Structuralism* and *semiology* were attempts to introduce a new scientific rigor to film criticism, to allow for more systematic and detailed analyses of movies. Borrowing their methodology from such diverse disciplines as linguistics, anthropology, psychology, and philosophy, these two theories first concentrated on the development of a more precise analytical terminology.

Structuralism and semiology have also focused intently on the American cinema as the principal area of inquiry, for a number of reasons. In the first place, these theories have been dominated by the British and French, traditionally the most enthusiastic foreign admirers of the cinema of the United States. American movies also provided these critics with a stylistic norm—the **classical paradigm.** Marxists among this group have explored the implications of the capitalistic mode of production of American films. Cultural commentators have concentrated on characteristically American myths and genres.

Semiology (or *semiotics,* as it's also called) is a study of *how* movies signify. The manner in which information is signified is indissolubly linked with *what's* being signified. The French theorist Christian Metz was in the forefront in developing semiotics as a technique of film analysis. Using many of the concepts and much of the terminology of structural linguistics, Metz and others developed a theory of cinematic communication founded on the concept of signs or codes. The language of cinema, like all types of discourse, verbal and nonverbal, is primarily symbolic: It consists of a complex network of signs we instinctively decipher while experiencing a movie **(11–18).**

In most discussions of film, the **shot** was generally accepted as the basic unit of construction. Semiotic theorists rejected this unit as too vague and inclusive. They insisted on a more precise concept. Accordingly, they suggested

11–18. *Blonde Venus* **(U.S.A., 1932),** *with Marlene Dietrich, directed by Josef von Sternberg.*

Semiologists believe that the shot—the traditional unit of construction in film—is too general and inclusive to be of much use in a systematic analysis of a movie. The symbolic sign, they argue, is a more precise unit of signification. Every cinematic shot consists of dozens of signifying codes that are hierarchically structured. Using what they call the "principle of pertinence," semiologists decode cinematic discourse by first establishing what the dominant signs are, then analyzing the subsidiary codes. This methodology is similar to a detailed analysis of mise en scène, only in addition to spatial, textural, and photographic codes, semiologists would also explore other relevant signs—kinetic, linguistic, musical, rhythmic, etc. In this shot, a semiologist would explore the symbolic significance of such major signs as Dietrich's white suit. Why a masculine suit? Why white? What does the papier-mâché dragon signify? The distorted perspective lines of the set? The "shady ladies" behind the archways? The symbolism of stage and audience? The tight framing and closed form of the image? The protagonist's worldly song? Within the dramatic context, semiologists would also explore the rhythms of the editing and camera movements, the symbolism of the kinetic motions of the performer, and so on. Traditionally, critics likened the cinematic shot to a word, and a series of edited shots to a sequence of words in a sentence. A semiologist would dismiss such analogies as patently simpleminded. Perhaps an individual *sign* might be likened to a word, but the equivalent to a shot—even a lousy one—would require many paragraphs if not pages of words. A complex shot can contain a hundred separate signs, each with its own precise symbolic significance.   *(Paramount Pictures)*

that the sign be adopted as the minimal unit of signification. A single shot from a movie generally contains dozens of signs, forming an intricate hierarchy of counterpoised meanings. In a sense, this book, and especially the earlier chapters, can be viewed as a classification of signs, although necessarily more limited in scope than the type of identification and classification envisioned by Metz and other semiologists.

For example, each of these chapters is concerned with a kind of master code, which can be broken down into code subdivisions, which themselves can be reduced to even more minimal signs. Thus, Chapter 1 might be called a photography master code. This master could be broken down into subdivisions: shots, **angles,** lighting keys, colors, lenses, filters, optical effects, and so on. Each of these, in turn, could be subdivided again. The shots, for example, could be broken down to **extreme long, long, medium, close-up, extreme close-up, deep focus.** This same principle could be applied to other master codes: spatial codes (mise en scène), kinetic codes (movement), and so on. Codes of language would be as complex as the entire discipline of linguistics; acting codes would involve a precise breakdown of the various techniques of signification used by players.

Semiotic techniques can be valuable in aiding film critics and scholars to analyze movies with more precision. But the theory suffers some defects. For one thing, these are descriptive classifications only, not normative. In other words, semiotics will permit a critic to discern a sign, but it's still up to the critic to evaluate how effective artistically any given sign is within an aesthetic context. Formalist movies seem to lend themselves to easier classification than realistic movies. For example, it's much simpler to describe the complex mise en scène of *What Dreams May Come* than to explicate the meanings of Chaplin's expression in *The Bank* (**11–19a & b).** These signs aren't really comparable. They exist on incompatible levels, like different language systems of a computer. Because formalist signs are easier to quantify, some critics tend to value films with a greater number of signs (or at least a greater number of classifiable signs) as more complex than, and hence aesthetically superior to, a film with a lower density of signs.

Another serious problem with this theory is its awful jargon, which sometimes verges on self-parody. All specialized disciplines—including cinema—have a certain number of necessary technical terms, but semiotics often chokes on its own "scientific" wordiness. Even within the field, one commentator pointed out that referring to a perfectly ordinary phenomenon as "signifier" or "signified," "syntagm" or "paradigm" doesn't in itself advance social knowledge to any particular degree.

As Metz pointed out, semiology is concerned with the systematic classification of types of codes used in the cinema; structuralism is the study of how various codes function within a single structure, within one movie. Structuralism is strongly eclectic and often combines the techniques of semiotics with other theoretical perspectives, such as auteurism, genre studies, ideology, stylistic analyses, and so on. For example, Colin MacArthur's *Underworld USA* is a

11–19a. *What Dreams May Come* (U.S.A., 1999), *with Robin Williams and Annabella Sciorra, directed by Vincent Ward.* (Polygram Films)

Semiotics can help critics to isolate and identify signs in a movie, but not to show how skillfully they function within the film. Because the theory stresses quantification, it tends to be more effective in analyzing formalist films, which contain more classifiable signs. But different types of signs or codes are not compatible, and hence qualitative judgments are difficult to make on strictly quantitative data. For example, the shot from *What Dreams May Come* contains many different signs, which are structured into an image of great visual complexity. Special effects give the classicized landscape a magical luminosity. Chaplin's shot, on the other hand, is relatively simple and contains very few signs other than the expression on the tramp's face. Vincent Ward is an artist of considerable skill, but he's not in Chaplin's class. Yet a semiotic analysis of these two works might lead to the conclusion that Ward is the superior filmmaker, because he used more signs in his movie.

11–19b. *The Bank* (U.S.A., 1915), *with Charles Chaplin, directed by Chaplin.* (Museum of Modern Art)

11–20. *Tender Mercies* (U.S.A., 1983), *with Robert Duvall and Allan Hubbard, directed by Bruce Beresford.*
A crucial shortcoming of semiotic methodology is its failure to deal with nonmaterialist *values* in cinema. For example, this movie explores how a drunken country music star (Duvall) finds spiritual redemption in the born-again Christian faith of the woman he loves. A strictly semiotic analysis of the film would prove inadequate in exploring these spiritual values. *(Universal Pictures)*

structuralist analysis of gangster and crime films and the style known as **film noir.** MacArthur uses semiotic classifications in exploring the iconography of the genre films of such artists as Billy Wilder (**1–17**) and others.

Structuralists and semiologists have been fascinated by the concept of a *deep structure*—an underlying network of symbolic meaning that is related to a movie's surface structure but is also somewhat independent of it. This deep structure can be analyzed from a number of perspectives, including Freudian psychoanalysis, Marxist economics, Jungian concepts of the collective unconscious, and the theory of structural anthropology popularized by the Frenchman Claude Lévi-Strauss.

The methods of Lévi-Strauss are based on an examination of regional myths, which he believed express certain underlying structures of thought in codified form. These myths exist in variant forms and usually contain the same or similar binary structures—pairs of opposites. By collapsing the surface (narrative) structure of myths, their symbolic motifs can be analyzed in a more systematic and meaningful manner. These polarities are usually found in dialectical conflict: Depending on the culture analyzed, they can be agricultural (for example, water vs. drought), sexual (male vs. female), conceptual (cooked vs. raw), generational (youth vs. age), and so on. Because these myths are expressed in symbolic codes, often their full meanings are hidden even from

484

their creators. Lévi-Strauss believed that once the full implications of a myth are understood, it's discarded as a cliché.

These structural techniques can be used to analyze a national cinema, a genre, or a specific movie. For example, the conflict between "traditional" and "modern" values can be seen in virtually all Japanese movies, and in Japanese society in general **(11–21)**. The roots of this conflict extend back to the later nineteenth century, when Japan transformed itself from a feudal country to a modern technological society patterned after the Western industrial states,

11-21. *An Autumn Afternoon* **(Japan, 1962),** *with Chishu Ryu (right), directed by Yasujiro Ozu.*

The films of Ozu were not widely seen in the West until the 1970s. Prior to this time, his movies were regarded as "too Japanese" to be appreciated by foreign audiences because he was a champion of traditional values, particularly that quintessential Japanese institution, the family. If Kurosawa is the artistic spokesman for modern values and the anguished individual, then Ozu speaks for the conservative majority, especially parents. But his movies are not mindless endorsements of family life, for Ozu was also an ironist, well aware of the gap between reality and the ideal—the principal source of his irony. In this film, for example, the protagonist (Ryu) is a gentle, aging widower who lives with his unmarried daughter in mutual devotion. His loneliness is assuaged by a few drinking buddies who spend much of their free time at the local bar. After hearing of the marriage of a friend's daughter, the widower decides that it's time for his daughter to move on as well. He arranges a marriage with a decent young man recommended by his friends. The movie ends on a bittersweet note of irony as the father muses contentedly on the success of his arrangements. He also realizes that he's getting on in years. And that he is alone.   *(New Yorker Films)*

especially Great Britain and the United States. The Japanese are simultaneously repelled and attracted by both sets of polarities:

Traditional	Modern
Japanese	Western
Feudal	Democratic
Past	Future
Society	Individual
Hierarchy	Equality
Nature	Technology
Duty	Inclination
Self-sacrifice	Self-expression
Consensus	Diversity
Age	Youth
Authority	Autonomy
Conservative	Liberal
Fatalism	Optimism
Obedience	Independence
Form	Substance
Security	Anxiety

A number of structuralists have explored genre films in a similar manner. For example, Jim Kitses, Peter Wollen, and others have pointed out how westerns are often vehicles for exploring clashes of value between East and West in American culture. By clustering the thematic motifs around a "master antimony" (a controlling or dominant code), a western can be analyzed according to its deep structure rather than its plot, which is often conventionalized (and less meaningful) in genre films. Such critics have demonstrated how each cultural polarity symbolizes a complex of positive and negative traits:

West	East
Wilderness	Civilization
Individualism	Community
Self-interest	Social welfare
Freedom	Restriction
Anarchy	Law and order
Savagery	Refinement
Private honor	Institutional justice
Paganism	Christianity
Nature	Culture
Masculine	Feminine

West	East
Pragmatism	*Idealism*
Agrarian	Industrial
Purity	Corruption
Dynamic	Static
Future	Past
Experience	Knowledge
American	European

Semiotics and structuralism expanded the parameters of film theory considerably. Their pluralistic approach allows for much more flexibility, complexity, and depth in the critical enterprise. But these theories are merely tools of analysis. By themselves, they can tell us nothing of the *value* of signs and codes within a film. Like every other theory, then, these are only as good as their practitioners. The writer's intelligence, taste, passion, knowledge, and sensitivity are what produce good criticism, not necessarily the theoretical methodology used.

Historiography

Historiography deals with the theory of history—the assumptions, principles, and methodologies of historical study. Film history is a relatively recent area of inquiry—a hundred years is not a very lengthy period of study compared to that of the traditional arts. As in other areas of film theory, much of the best work in film historiography has taken place during the past two decades.

Film historians scoff at the naive notion that there is *a* film history. Rather, they insist that there are many film histories, and each is defined by the historian's particular interests, biases, and prejudices. Theorists have charted four different types of film history, each with its own set of philosophical assumptions, methods, and sources of evidence: (1) aesthetic film histories—film as art; (2) technological film histories—motion pictures as inventions and machines; (3) economic histories—film as industry; and (4) social histories—movies as a reflection of the audience's values, desires, and fears.

Most film historians regard cinema as too sprawling and complex to be covered by any single history. They view the field as a vast, infinite mass of data that needs to be sifted through and organized to be made coherent. Each historian concentrates on a given type of evidence, highlighting its significance while deemphasizing or ignoring "irrelevant" data. Critics sometimes refer to this process of selection and emphasis as **foregrounding**—isolating fragments of evidence for the purpose of closer study. Foregrounding is always an implicit value judgment. Each type of film historian necessarily wrenches these fragments from their ecological context, thus presenting us with a somewhat skewed view of the whole. Each type of historian will also choose to focus on different movies, personalities, and events.

Aesthetic film historians concern themselves with a tradition of masterpieces and great filmmakers. Constantly subject to reevaluation, this tradition encompasses a broad consensus of critics, historians, and scholars. This is an elite form of history, ignoring the vast majority of motion pictures to concentrate on a relative handful of important works of art that have endured the test of time—that is, movies that are still great despite our viewing them in a totally different context. Aesthetic historians value a work primarily for its artistic richness, irrespective of whether the film was commercially successful. Thus, in most aesthetic histories, a huge popular success like *Independence Day* receives much less discussion than *Citizen Kane,* which failed at the box office.

Most college textbook histories—such as Gerald Mast's *A Short History of the Movies,* David A. Cook's *A History of Narrative Film,* and Louis Giannetti and Scott Eyman's *Flashback*—attempt to integrate as much as possible from

11–22.   *Short Cuts* (U.S.A., 1993), *with Lily Tomlin and Tom Waits, directed by Robert Altman.*

Aesthetic film historians and elitist critics tend to concentrate on such movies as *Short Cuts* because of their cultural prestige. Robert Altman is regarded as one of the great artists of the contemporary cinema, creator of such movies as *M*A*S*H, McCabe and Mrs. Miller, Nashville,* and *The Player.* Based on the short stories of Raymond Carver, *Short Cuts* is faithful to its source, including its tone of cynicism and bitterness. The film features an embarrassment of richness in the cast, many of them important stars who would have worked for Altman for nothing because of his enormous prestige within the world film community. Though widely praised by critics and nominated for a number of awards, the movie failed to arouse much interest with the general public, and its box-office revenues were small.   *(Fine Line Features)*

technological, economic, and social film histories, but their main emphasis is on film as art. Opponents of this type of history have scoffed at its "Great Man" assumptions—that is, film history is largely the study of a few gifted individuals, not the dynamic matrix of social, industrial, and technological influences that inevitably affect all filmmakers, gifted or not.

The American scholar Raymond Fielding has put forth the philosophy of technological historians succinctly: "The history of motion pictures—as an art form, as a medium of communication, and as an industry—has been determined principally by technological innovations." Historians of this type are also concerned with "Great Men," such as W. K. L. Dickson, Thomas Edison, George Eastman, and Lee Deforest—inventors and scientists rather than artists or industry moguls. Technological historians are concerned with the implications—artistic, commercial, and ideological—of such innovations as portable cameras, **synchronous sound,** color, improved film stocks, 3-D, stereophonic sound, steadycams, and so on **(11–23).**

11-23. *Medium Cool* (U.S.A., 1969), *with Robert Forster (at camera) and Peter Bonerz (sound), directed by Haskell Wexler.*
Technological film histories stress the importance of mechanical innovations in the evolution of the cinema. New technologies create new aesthetics. For example, in the late 1950s, television journalists needed simple, lightweight equipment to capture news stories quickly, while they were actually happening. The development of the so-called hand-held camera (actually, usually mounted on a shoulder harness or tripod), portable sound equipment, **zoom lenses,** and more light-sensitive **fast film stocks** was in response to this need. In the 1960s, this new technology was appropriated by fiction filmmakers, allowing them to shoot movies more spontaneously and in actual locations, thus creating a more authentic style of realism.   *(Paramount Pictures)*

Cinema is the most expensive artistic medium in history, and its development has been largely determined by its financial sponsors—this is the thesis of most economic film histories, such as Benjamin B. Hampton's *History of the American Film Industry from Its Beginnings to 1931* and Thomas H. Guback's *The International Film Industry: Western Europe and America Since 1945*. In most European countries, the cinema in its early stages of development fell into the hands of artists who shared most of the values and tastes of the educated elite. In the former Soviet Union and other ex-communist countries, film production was carefully regulated by the government, and the movies produced in those countries reflected most of the values of the political elite.

In America, the film industry developed within a capitalistic system of production. The Hollywood studio system was an attempt on the part of a handful of large corporations—MGM, Paramount, Warner Brothers, etc.—to monopolize the production of fiction films, and hence maximize their profits. For about three decades—roughly from 1925 to 1955—the major studios succeeded, producing about 90 percent of the fiction films in America, largely because the companies were **vertically integrated.** That is, they controlled all three phases of the industry: **(1)** production—the Hollywood studios; **(2)** distribution—financial headquarters in New York; and **(3)** exhibition—the large chains of big-city first-run theaters owned by the company.

During the era of studio dominance, virtually every filmmaker had to come to grips with this economic reality. The studio system was the only ballgame in town, and the **majors** were in business to make profits, the bigger the

11–24. *City of Hope* (U.S.A., 1991), *with John Sayles, written, edited, and directed by Sayles.*

Economic film histories concentrate on who pays the bills, who sponsors the making of a movie, and why. Like many European filmmakers, Sayles finances his movies independently, guaranteeing him total artistic control. His goal is not the amassing of huge profits, but creative freedom. Most of his movies have been made on small budgets, with the same loyal crew of actors and technicians. This communal spirit has allowed them to produce nearly one movie a year. Though Sayles's films have not been huge hits, most of them were sufficiently profitable to maintain a constant cash flow. Sayles usually plays small roles in his own films, generally sleazoids, jerks, or villains. He is an artist of exceptional integrity. *(The Samuel Goldwyn Company)*

better. In short, the profit motive has been the main driving force in the evolution of the American film industry, and movies tend to reaffirm the ideological values of their sponsors. However, even economic historians would concede that other motives have also figured in the production of American movies—the desire for prestige, artistic integrity, and so on. Likewise, movies made in communist countries were occasionally critical of the social system that produced them. History—of any kind—is filled with contradictions.

Social histories are mainly concerned with the audience. They emphasize film as a collective experience, as a reflection of mass sentiments during any given era. These sentiments can be overtly articulated or subliminally insinuated by appealing to our subconscious desires. Social historians often turn to statistics and sociological data for supporting evidence. Books like Robert Sklar's *Movie-Made America* and Garth Jowett's *Film: The Democratic Art* are filled with revealing statistics about audience likes and dislikes.

Social historians have also devoted a great deal of attention to the American star system, arguing that popular stars are usually a reflection of audience values and anxieties. Unfortunately, these concerns do not lend themselves to quantitative analysis, and social historians are sometimes criticized for their intuitive leaps in logic. Historians of this sort are also interested in social stereotypes—how a movie portrays blacks, women, authority figures, and so on.

In *Film History: Theory and Practice*, Robert C. Allen and Douglas Gomery set forth the principal advantages and shortcomings of the various types of film history, arguing that a more integrated approach would minimize the dangers of distortion. As in other areas of film theory, film history is increasingly being viewed as a monolithic ecological system that must be studied from various perspectives to be comprehensively understood.

Different theorists ask different types of questions. Those interested in the essential nature of the film medium would probably focus on such traditional concerns as the realism–formalism dichotomy. The auteur theory is helpful if you want to ask questions about how a particular movie typifies the filmmaker's thematic and stylistic traits. Obviously, this approach is not a very fruitful technique for exploring movies like *Mildred Pierce* or *Independence Day*, pictures that were constructed by committee for the purpose of maximizing profits. Eclectic critics ask whatever questions they think will help people understand and appreciate the movie better. Why is this film good (or bad, or mediocre)? How could it be better? What brings it down? And so on. Structuralists ask questions about a movie's underlying infrastructure: What thematic motifs are explored in the film's narrative? What are its mythic elements? What kind of codes—both thematic and stylistic—does the movie favor? How does the film's genre influence the particulars of this specific movie? Does it invent, reinforce, subvert, or ridicule the genre's conventions?

Depending on their orientation, historians also ask different types of questions. The arty ones are concerned with a movie's aesthetic worth and why attention should be paid. The techies are more likely to ask questions about the film's special effects, any outstanding technical achievements, such as the huge, near-scale proportions of the doomed ship in James Cameron's *Titanic.* Industry historians tend to ask questions concerning a movie's production expenditures and practices, how it was promoted, and what kind of tie-in products it generated. Social historians mostly ask questions about the audience. Why did the public love one movie and hate another? How does a film appeal to the public's subconscious fears and yearnings? What does a given movie say about its era? About its icons?

In short, there are literally thousands of questions that could be asked concerning a movie's theoretical context. What you are looking for will determine most of your questions and how to focus them.

FURTHER READING

ALLEN, ROBERT C., ed., *Channels of Discourse* (Chapel Hill and London: University of North Carolina Press, 1987). An illuminating collection of scholarly essays, primarily about television.

ALLEN, ROBERT C., and DOUGLAS GOMERY, *Film History: Theory and Practice* (New York: Alfred A. Knopf, 1985). A provocative study of the problems of writing film history.

ANDREW, DUDLEY, *Concepts in Film Theory* (New York: Oxford University Press, 1984). A lucid exploration of the major areas of debate within the field.

——, *The Major Film Theories* (New York: Oxford University Press, 1976). A helpful and clearly written exposition of the theories of such figures as Arnheim, Eisenstein, Kracauer, Bazin, Metz, and others.

CARROLL, NOEL, *Mystifying Movies: Fads and Fallacies in Contemporary Film Theory* (New York: Columbia University Press, 1988). A skeptical critique of modern film theory.

CARSON, DIANE, LINDA DITTMAR, and JANICE R. WELSCH, eds., *Multiple Voices in Feminist Film Criticism* (Minneapolis: University of Minnesota Press, 1994). An assortment of scholarly essays.

HOLLOWS, JOANNE, and MARK JANCOVICH, eds., *Approaches to Popular Film* (Manchester and New York: Manchester University Press, 1995). An excellent collection of articles by British critics.

MAST, GERALD, and MARSHALL COHEN, eds., *Film Theory and Criticism*, 3rd ed. (New York: Oxford University Press, 1985). An excellent collection of articles, from a variety of perspectives.

SARRIS, ANDREW, *The American Cinema* (New York: Dutton, 1968). A basic document of the auteur theory.

TUDOR, ANDREW, *Theories of Film* (New York: Viking, 1974). Includes essays on Eisenstein, Grierson, Bazin, Kracauer, auteurism, and genre theory.

WILLIAMS, CHRISTOPHER, ed., *Realism and the Cinema: A Reader* (London: Routledge & Kegan Paul, 1980). A collection of scholarly articles, primarily by British writers.

Synthsis

Citizen Kane

RKO

*The motion-picture medium has an extraordinary range
of expression. It has in common with the plastic arts
the fact that it is a visual composition projected on a
two-dimensional surface; with dance, that it can deal in the
arrangement of movement; with theatre, that it can create
a dramatic intensity of events; with music, that it can
compose in the rhythms and phrases of time and can be
attended by song and instrument; with poetry, that it
can juxtapose images; with literature generally, that it can
encompass in its sound track the abstractions available
only to language.*

—MAYA DEREN, FILMMAKER AND THEORIST

493

As Maya Deren's observation suggests, analyzing a movie is no easy task. The previous chapters of this book isolate the various language systems of movies, exploring each system's range of expression. Film is a more complex medium than the traditional arts because movies synthesize many language systems simultaneously, bombarding the spectator with literally hundreds of symbolic ideas and emotions at the same time, some of them overt, others subliminal. Of course, filmmakers rarely use each language system at full tilt. In every scene—indeed, in every shot—there is a principle of hierarchical subordination. The combinations are constantly in flux, like the couplings, divergencies, and recouplings of a group of dancers.

The French critic André Bazin described *Citizen Kane* as "a discourse on method" because of its encyclopedic technical range. The film, directed by Orson Welles (1915–1985), is an ideal choice to demonstrate how these various language systems interact dynamically within a single text. The following pages can only touch on the high points of this famous movie, but the analysis can serve as a guide for a systematic explication of any film.

Citizen Kane is the life story of a powerful newspaper magnate, Charles Foster Kane, who is as contradictory as he is controversial. The film is a fictionalized biography of the ruthless publishing baron William Randolph Hearst (1863–1951). Actually, the characters in the movie are composites, drawn from the lives of several famous American tycoons, but Hearst was the most obvious. Herman Mankiewicz, the coauthor of the screenplay, knew Hearst personally and was a friend of the old yellow journalist's mistress, screen **star** Marion Davies. Davies was among the best-liked personalities in the film industry, and except for her fondness for alcohol and jigsaw puzzles, was quite unlike the Susan Alexander character in *Citizen Kane.*

The movie recounts the major events of the protagonist's lengthy life. Born in comparative obscurity, the eight-year-old Charles is sent away to boarding school after his mother inherits a huge fortune through a fluke. Kane's guardian throughout his youth is the banker Walter P. Thatcher, a pompous blowhard and political reactionary. After living a life of frivolous self-indulgence, Kane decides in his midtwenties to become a newspaper publisher. Along with his close associates, the doggedly loyal Bernstein and the suave Jed Leland, he dedicates himself to championing the cause of the underprivileged and attacking corrupt institutions of power. At the height of his career, Kane marries the refined Emily Norton, niece of the President of the United States. But the marriage eventually turns stale, then rancid. In middle age, Kane consoles himself by secretly taking a mistress, Susan Alexander, a pretty but rather empty-headed shopgirl with vague aspirations of becoming a singer.

Buoyed by his fame and popularity, Kane runs for governor of New York. His opponent, Boss Jim Gettys, attempts to blackmail him into withdrawing from the race by threatening to go public with the hypocrisy of Kane's marriage and to expose his cozy arrangement with Susan. Outraged, Kane refuses to capitulate, even though he knows that the scandal will publicly humiliate his wife, his son, and Susan. Kane loses the election and the respect of his best friend, Jed Leland. Emily divorces Kane, taking their young son with her.

Kane redirects his energies toward the career of a proxy, his new young wife, Susan Alexander Kane. He is determined to make her into a great opera star, despite the inconvenient fact that she has no discernible talent. Ignoring her objections, indifferent to her public mortification, Kane pushes the talentless Susan to the brink of suicide. Thwarted again, he finally agrees to give up on his scheme to make her an opera star. Instead, he builds an enormous isolated palace, Xanadu, where he and Susan retire into semiseclusion. After years of being bullied into submission by Kane, Susan rebels and walks out on him. Finally, alone and embittered, the old man dies amidst the empty opulence of Xanadu.

Photography

Cinematographer Gregg Toland considered *Citizen Kane* the high point of his career. The veteran cinematographer thought he might be able to learn something from the "boy genius," whose accomplishments were mostly in radio and the Broadway theater. Welles, used to setting up his own lights in the live theater, thought that movie directors were also responsible for the lighting. Intrigued, Toland let him go ahead, allowing Welles to determine the design of most of the lights but quietly instructing the camera crew to make the necessary technical adjustments.

12-1. Publicity photo of Orson Welles and cinematographer Gregg Toland during the production of *Citizen Kane* **(U.S.A., 1941).**
Toland, the most admired cinematographer of his generation, asked Welles if he could photograph the young director's first feature film. He was fascinated by Welles's bold theatricality, and he often suggested more effective ways of shooting scenes. They discussed each shot in the movie, which is eclectic in its visual style, integrating a variety of influences. Welles was strongly drawn to the lighting theories of such theatrical designers as Gordon Craig and Adolphe Appia and to many of the techniques of the German expressionist movement. Welles was also influenced by the moody low-key photography of John Ford's *Stagecoach*. Welles was so grateful for the help of the veteran cinematographer that he gave Toland a conspicuous credit title—unusual in this era. *(RKO)*

Everyone saw at once that *Citizen Kane* didn't look like most American movies of its era. There is not an indifferently photographed image in the film. Even the exposition scenes—normally dispatched with efficient **medium two-shots**—are startlingly photographed **(12–2).** Not that the techniques were new. **Deep-focus, low-key lighting,** rich textures, audacious compositions, dynamic contrasts between foregrounds and backgrounds, **backlighting,** sets with ceilings, side lighting, steep **angles, epic long shots** juxtaposed with **extreme close-ups,** dizzying **crane shots,** special effects galore—none of these was new. But no one had previously used them in such a "seven layer-cake profusion," to quote critic James Naremore.

Photographically, *Kane* ushered in a revolution, implicitly challenging the **classical** ideal of a transparent style that doesn't call attention to itself. In *Citizen Kane,* the stylistic virtuosity is part of the show. The lighting in the movie is generally in moderate **high key** in those scenes depicting Kane's youth and those dealing with his years as a crusading young publisher. As he grows older and more cynical, the lighting grows darker, more harshly contrasting. Kane's home, the palatial Xanadu, seems steeped in perpetual night. Only spotlight patches of light penetrate the oppressive gloom, revealing the contours of a chair, a sofa, yet another piece of heroic sculpture. But the pervasive atmosphere is dank, impenetrable. The darkness shrouds an unspeakable evil.

12–2.   *Citizen Kane.*
Kane ushered in an era of flamboyant visual effects in the American cinema, and as such represented an assault on the classical ideal of an invisible style. Lights are often from below or other unexpected sources, creating startling clashes and abstract patterns and infusing the photographed materials with a sense of visual exuberance. There's nothing invisible about the lighting of this shot, for example. As written, the scene is merely exposition, setting up the movie's narrative premise. Some reporters are talking in a screening room, and while they talk, the light from the projection booth splashes into the darkened auditorium, flooding the silhouetted figures in a sea of undulating luminescence.   *(RKO)*

Spotlights are also used in closer shots for symbolic effects. The mixture of decency and corruption in Kane is suggested by the contrasting lights: Sometimes his face seems split in half, with one side brightly illuminated, the other hidden in darkness. What is concealed is often more important than what's revealed. In an early scene between the idealistic Kane and his two associates, for example, the protagonist tells Bernstein and Leland of his intention to publish a "Declaration of Principles" on the front page of his newspaper, promising his readers that he will be an honest and tireless champion of their rights as citizens and human beings. When Kane bends down to sign the document, however, his face is suddenly plunged in darkness—an ominous foreshadowing of Kane's later character.

Gregg Toland had often experimented with deep-focus photography during the 1930s, mostly while working with director William Wyler **(see 1–18b).** But the deep focus in *Kane* is more flamboyant than Wyler's use of this technique **(12–3).** Deep-focus photography involves the use of **wide-angle lenses,** which tend to exaggerate the distances between people—an appropriate symbolic analogue for a story dealing with separation, alienation, and loneliness.

12–3. *Citizen Kane, with Orson Welles and (at far end of the table) Joseph Cotten and Everett Sloane.*
Welles's deep-focus photography is meant to be admired for its virtuosity as well as its functionalism. André Bazin, an enthusiastic champion of deep-focus techniques, believed that it reduces the importance of editing and preserves the cohesiveness of real space and time. Many spatial planes can be captured simultaneously in a single **take,** maintaining the objectivity of a scene. Bazin felt that audiences were thus encouraged to be more creative—less passive—in understanding the relationships between people and things. In this photo, for example, we are free to look at the faces of over two dozen characters. "The public may choose, with its eyes, what it wants to see of a shot," Welles said. "I don't like to force it." *(RKO)*

Deep focus also tends to encourage the audience to actively mine a shot for its information. In a scene involving Susan Alexander's suicide attempt, for example, a cause–effect relationship is suggested in the opening shot. Susan has taken a lethal dose of medication and lies comatose on her bed in a semidarkened room. At the bottom of the screen, in **close-up** range, stands an empty glass and a bottle of medication; in the middle of the screen, in medium range, lies Susan, wheezing softly; in the upper portion of the screen, in long-shot range, Kane bangs outside the door, then forces it open and enters the room. The layering of the **mise en scène** is a visual accusation: **(1)** the lethal dose was taken by **(2)** Susan Alexander Kane because of **(3)** Kane's inhumanity.

Special effects are used throughout the movie for a variety of reasons. In some settings—such as the exterior shots of Xanadu—the special effects lend the locale a slightly phantasmagorical quality. In other scenes, such as the political rally, special effects provide a realistic facsimile of large crowds and a huge auditorium **(12–4).**

12–4.   *Citizen Kane,* with Ray Collins.
RKO's highly respected special effects department consisted of thirty-five people, most of whom worked on *Kane.* Vernon L. Walker was in charge. Over 80 percent of the movie required some kind of special effects work, such as miniatures, **matte shots, double** and **multiple exposures.** Many scenes required reprinting—that is, combining two or more separate images onto one through the use of the **optical printer.** For example, this shot combines three separately photographed images—Boss Jim Gettys (Collins) standing on a balcony overlooking Madison Square Garden, with Kane down below delivering a campaign speech to a huge audience. The frame of the balcony masks the dividing line between the two areas. The auditorium area combines live action (stage) with a matte painting (audience); the balcony set consists of two walls. Welles was thus able to give the movie an **epic** scope, while keeping production costs relatively low. Total cost of the picture: just under $700,000—not lavish by the standards of 1941.   *(RKO)*

The American cinema of the 1940s was to grow progressively darker, both thematically and photographically, thanks in part to the enormous influence of *Citizen Kane*. The most important style of the decade was **film noir**—literally, "black cinema." It was a style suited to the times. Welles's style continued in a noir vein, especially in such movies as *The Lady from Shanghai* and *Touch of Evil*. Toland's death in 1948 at the age of forty-four was an irreparable loss to the American cinema.

Mise en Scène

Coming from the world of live theater, Welles was an expert at staging action dynamically. Long shots are a more effective—and more theatrical—medium for the art of mise en scène, and hence the movie contains relatively few close shots. Most of the images are tightly framed and in **closed form.** Most of them are also composed in depth, with important information in the foreground, midground, and background. The **proxemic ranges** between the characters are choreographed balletically, to suggest their shifting power relationships. For example, an early scene in the movie shows Kane, Bernstein, and Leland taking over the staid offices of *The Inquirer,* the conservative newspaper young Kane has just bought because he thinks it might be fun to run a newspaper. While workers and assistants stream in and out of the frame, carrying equipment, furniture, and personal belongings, Kane carries on a whimsical conversation with the stuffy, soon-to-be ex-editor, Mr. Carter, a Dickensian study in spluttering comic exasperation.

Perhaps the best way of understanding the complexity of Welles's mise en scène is to analyze a single shot. The dramatic context of **12–5** is offered in the caption.

1. *Dominant.* Because of his central position within the frame and the high contrast between his dark clothes and the glaring snow, Charles tends to attract our eye first. He is also the subject of controversy in the foreground.

2. *Lighting key.* The interior is photographed in moderate high key. The exterior—consisting mostly of blinding white snow—is in extreme high key.

3. *Shot and camera proxemics.* This is a deep-focus shot, extending from a medium range in the foreground to an extreme long-shot range in the background. The camera is at a personal distance from Thatcher and Mrs. Kane, a social distance from Kane senior, and a public distance from Charles. The boy is playing happily, shouting disconnected phrases like "The Union forever!" Kane senior is stubbornly resisting their plans, while Thatcher and Mrs. Kane, more frigid than the outside weather, listen wearily.

4. *Angle.* The camera is at a slightly high angle, because more of the floor can be seen than the ceiling. The angle suggests a slight air of fatality.

12–5. *Citizen Kane, with Harry Shannon, Buddy Swan (in window), George Coulouris, and Agnes Moorehead.*
Almost all of the compositions in *Kane* are intricate and richly textured, at times baroquely ornate. But the visual complexity is not mere rhetorical ornamentation. The images are designed to reveal a maximum of information, often in an ironic manner. In this scene, for example, eight-year-old Charles plays with his sled outside in the snow while his future is being determined indoors by his mother and Thatcher. The boy's father watches impotently, sputtering a few feeble protests. The mise en scène is compartmentalized into twos, with the wall serving as the vertical dividing line. Kane senior and young Charles are grouped to the left in the upper portion of the frame; Thatcher and the severe Mrs. Kane dominate the right lower half, their pens poised to sign the contract that will soon separate Charles from his parents. Ironically, Mrs. Kane is motivated by love and self-sacrifice. She is sending Charles away to protect him from his father, a swaggering lout whose treatment of his son veers from forced jocularity to unpredictable outbursts of anger. *(RKO)*

5. *Color values.* Not applicable: The film is in black and white.
6. *Lens/filter/stock.* Though it is difficult to discern in this photo, a wide-angle lens is used to capture its depth of field. The lens exaggerates the distances between the characters. No apparent filters. Probably slow stock requiring lots of lights.
7. *Subsidiary contrasts.* Our eye travels from Charles (the dominant) to Kane senior to Thatcher, Mrs. Kane, and the spotlighted document

they are preparing to sign. On the small TV screen, Charles would probably be lost and Kane senior would then constitute the dominant.

8. *Density.* The image is densely packed with information, thanks to the high-key lighting and the richly textured details of the sets and costumes.

9. *Composition.* The image is split vertically in half, a tug of war, with two figures on the left, two on the right. The foreground table balances off the background table and rear wall. The composition segments and isolates the characters.

10. *Form.* The image is in closed form, its carefully coordinated components suggesting the self-containment of a stage setting enclosed by a proscenium arch.

11. *Framing.* The shot is tightly framed, with little latitude for movement. Each character seems confined to his or her own space cubicle. The excluded Charles is imprisoned within the frame of the window—an enclosure within an enclosure. His freedom is illusionary.

12. *Depth.* The image is photographed in four depth planes: **(a)** the foreground table and its occupants; **(b)** Kane senior; **(c)** the rear portions of the parlor; and **(d)** Charles playing outside in the distance.

13. *Character placement.* Charles and Kane senior occupy the upper portions of the image, Thatcher and Mrs. Kane the lower—an ironic placement, because those in the "inferior" positions actually control the situation. Husband and wife are maximally separated at the opposite edges of the composition, forcing Charles to be coupled in the center with Thatcher—an intimacy both come to regret.

14. *Staging positions.* Kane senior is in the quarter-turn position, relatively intimate vis-à-vis the spectator. Thatcher is at full front, but his eyes are lowered, avoiding our gaze. Mrs. Kane is in the profile position, preoccupied with her spouse.

15. *Character proxemics.* Thatcher and Mrs. Kane are in intimate proximity. They are at an aloof social distance from Kane senior, and a remote public distance from Charles.

Movement

From the very beginning of his film career, Welles was a master of the mobile camera. In *Citizen Kane,* camera movements are generally equated with the vitality and energy of youth. A static camera, on the other hand, tends to be associated with illness, old age, and death. These same **kinetic** principles apply to Kane's movements. As a young man, he is a whirlwind of energy, playfully gliding through life with scarcely enough breath to finish his sentences before his attention is distracted and he sweeps to another location. As an old man, however, he almost groans with each calculated step. Often he is photographed

12–6. *Citizen Kane, with Dorothy Comingore (at lower left base of fireplace) and Orson Welles.*

In scenes depicting Kane as an old man, the camera is often far away, making him seem remote, inaccessible. Even when he is closer to the lens, as in this shot, the deep-focus photography keeps the rest of the world at a distance, with vast empty spaces between him and other people. We are often forced to search the mise en scène to locate the characters. In this photo, for example, Susan is dwarfed into insignificance by the enormous fireplace and the heroic sculpture behind her. She is a mere **subsidiary contrast,** not even so important as the statuary and much less important than the **dominant,** Kane. These static shots are so totally drained of intimacy and spontaneity that they're almost funny, if they weren't so sad. *(RKO)*

in stationary positions or sitting down. He seems bored and exhausted, especially in the Xanadu scenes with Susan (see **12–6).**

No one has used crane shots so spectacularly as Welles. But once again, the virtuosity is rarely indulged in for its own sake. The bravura crane shots embody important symbolic ideas. For example, after learning of Kane's death, a reporter attempts to interview Susan Alexander. The sequence begins in a torrential rainstorm. We see a poster and picture of Susan, advertising her engagement as a singer in a nightclub. As the soundtrack shudders with a rumble of thunder, the camera cranes up, up through the rain, up to the roof of the building, then plunges through a garish neon sign, "El Rancho," descends to the skylight where a blinding flash of lightning masks the camera's passage through the window itself, sweeps down to the deserted night-club, where Susan is hunched at a table in a drunken stupor, prostrate with grief. (She is the only character in the film who is devastated by the news of Kane's death.) Both the camera and the reporter encounter numerous obstacles—the rain, the sign, the very walls of the building must be penetrated before we can even see Susan, much less hear her speak. The crane shot embodies a brutal invasion of privacy, a disregard for the barriers Susan has placed around her in her misery.

In Susan's opera debut, a traveling shot is used for comic effect, its payoff a virtual punch line. As she begins her first aria, the camera begins to rise, as if to ascend to the heavens. While she continues singing, her thin, watery voice grows progressively more feeble as the camera continues its upward journey, past sandbags, ropes, and platforms, until it finally comes to rest on two stage-hands on the catwalk, looking down at the performance. They listen for a moment longer, then turn to face each other. One stagehand waggishly pinches his nose, as if to say, "She really stinks."

Like all movies—like every human enterprise—*Citizen Kane* is flawed. A number of scenes in the film are merely adequate, nothing more. One such scene, singled out by several critics, appears late in the movie, when Susan finally walks out on Kane forever. Enraged, the old man tears up Susan's bed-

12–7. *Citizen Kane.*
In many respects, *Kane* is structured like a mystery story, a search to penetrate a great enigma. Welles is able to suggest this idea in the very opening sequence, through a series of dissolves and traveling shots. The movie begins with a sign: NO TRESPASSING. Ignoring it, the camera cranes up over the sign and over a wire fence. We dissolve from an ornate grillwork to an iron gate showing the letter "K." Xanadu is in the background, suffocating in mist, a solitary window light its only sign of habitation. Here lies the mystery. Here the search begins. *(RKO)*

12-8. *Citizen Kane, with Everett Sloane, Orson Welles, and Joseph Cotten.*
As a young man, Kane is a dynamo of energy, and his youthful high spirits are often conveyed kinetically—with brisk traveling shots that parallel the protagonist's movements. In this scene, for example, he nervously lurches forward and backwards, then forward again, the camera retreating and lunging back with him. *(RKO)*

12-9. *Citizen Kane, with George Coulouris, Orson Welles, and Everett Sloane.*
Welles frequently used lengthy takes in his staging, choreographing the movements of the camera and the characters rather than cutting to a series of separate shots. Even in relatively static scenes such as this, these lengthy takes provide the mise en scène with a sense of fluidity and dynamic change, while still entrapping the three characters within the same space. The setting is a large office in 1929. The Great Depression has dealt Kane a severe setback, forcing him to relinquish control over his publishing empire. The sequence begins with a close shot of a legal document, while Bernstein recites its contents. He lowers the document, thus revealing Thatcher, now an old man, presiding over the dissolution. The camera adjusts slightly, and we then see Kane, listening grimly. *(RKO)*

room, scattering its contents and demolishing its furnishings. Welles obviously wanted to convey Kane's fury through the sheer kinetic energy of the old man destroying the room. But the shots tend to be too lengthy and the camera too distant from the action. The violence of Kane's rage would be more effectively communicated if Welles had kept the camera closer in, so that the movements would dominate more. He also should have **edited** more, to convey the idea of fragmentation and confusion. As played, the scene works well enough, but for many viewers it seems somewhat anticlimactic. Kinetic energy must parallel its subject matter or the motion can seem too much—or too little.

Editing

The editing in *Citizen Kane* is a calculated display of virtuosity, leaping over days, months, even years with casual nonchalance. John Spalding has pointed out that Welles often used several editing styles in the same sequence. When Susan recalls her opera career, for example, the singing lesson with her exasperated voice teacher is photographed in a lengthy take. The backstage chaos prior to the curtain going up is edited in short bursts of fragmentary shots to emphasize the utter confusion of her opera debut. Welles used parallel editing to contrast Susan's terror on stage with Leland's contemptuous boredom in the auditorium. Kane's argument with Susan over her disastrous reviews is cut according to classical conventions. Thematic montage is used to condense her national tour on the road **(12–13).** The final scene of the sequence, Susan's suicide attempt, opens with a deep-focus lengthy take, as Kane crashes into Susan's hotel room and discovers her comatose in bed.

12–10. *Citizen Kane, with Orson Welles and Ruth Warrick.*
Welles often combined editing with another technique, which he used as a payoff. In the famous breakfast montage sequence portraying the disintegration of Kane's marriage to Emily, for example, he concluded with this final shot. The distance between the two says it all: They have nothing to say to each other. *(RKO)*

It's difficult to isolate the editing in this film because it often works in concert with the sound techniques, not to speak of the fragmentation of the story. Often Welles used editing to condense a great deal of time, using sound as a continuity device. For example, to demonstrate Kane's gradual estrangement from his first wife, Emily, Welles features a series of breakfast scenes, using only a few lines of dialogue with each brief episode. Beginning with some honeymoon sweet-talk, the mood quickly shifts to slight irritation, then strained annoyance, bitter resentment, and finally silence and alienation. The sequence begins with the lovers sharing the intimacy of the same medium shot. As the marriage deteriorates, Welles cross-cuts to separate shots of each, even though they are sitting at the same table. The one-minute sequence ends with a long shot of the two at opposite ends of a lengthy table, each reading a different newspaper **(12–10).**

12–11.   *Citizen Kane, with Orson Welles.*
Budgetary considerations often determined the cunning editing strategies of the film, which was edited by Robert Wise. In the political campaign sequence, for example, Welles cut from long shots of Kane delivering his speech to closer shots of his family and associates listening in the audience. These isolated fragments are intercut with **reestablishing shots** of the entire auditorium (see **12–4**). The huge hall and its thousands of inhabitants weren't real: The cutting makes them *seem* real—by association.   *(RKO)*

Welles used a similar technique in showing how Susan Alexander eventually becomes Kane's mistress. The first time he meets her, he is splashed with mud on the street. She offers him some hot water, if he wants to come up to her small apartment for it. While there, they become friends. She admits that she sings a little and he asks her to perform for him. While she begins to sing her song at an old piano, the image **dissolves** to a parallel shot, only now she is in a large, handsomely decorated apartment, where she finishes the song at a grander piano, dressed in an elegant gown. We don't need to be shown what happened "between" these two shots. We can infer what happened by Susan's much improved circumstances.

Sound

Coming from the world of live radio drama, Welles was often credited with inventing many film sound techniques when in fact he was primarily a consolidator, synthesizing and expanding the piecemeal accomplishments of his predecessors. In radio, sounds have to evoke images. An actor speaking through an echo chamber suggests a visual context—a huge auditorium, for example. A distant train whistle suggests a panoramic landscape, and so on. Welles applied this aural principle to his movie soundtrack. With the help of his sound technician, James G. Stewart, Welles discovered that almost every visual technique has its sound equivalent. Each of the shots, for example, has an appropriate sound quality involving volume, degree of definition, and texture. Long and extreme long-shot sounds are fuzzy and remote; close-up sounds are crisp, clear, and generally loud. High-angle shots are often accompanied by high-pitched music and sound effects; low-angle shots by brooding and low-pitched sounds. Sounds can be dissolved and overlapped like a **montage** sequence.

Welles frequently leaped from one time period or location to another with a shocking sound transition. For example, the film's opening prologue concludes with Kane's death, which is accompanied by the gradual snuffing out of the sound. Suddenly, we are almost assaulted with a Voice-of-God narrator booming out "News on the March!"—the beginning of the newsreel sequence. In another sequence, Jed Leland is delivering a campaign speech, in which he describes Kane as "the fighting liberal, the friend of the working-man, the next governor of this state, who entered upon this campaign . . ." Cut to Kane in Madison Square Garden, continuing ". . . with one purpose only . . ."

Welles frequently overlapped his dialogue, especially in the comical sequences where several people are trying to speak at the same time. In Xanadu, the rooms are so huge that Kane and Susan must shout at each other to be heard, producing an incongruous effect that's both sad and funny **(12–6)**. The Madison Square Garden facsimile is convincing in part because we *hear* the shouts and cheers of the enormous crowds and hence imagine that we see them as well.

12–12. Publicity photo of Orson Welles and composer–conductor Bernard Herrmann during a recording session for *Citizen Kane*.
Herrmann was the composer for Welles's Mercury Theatre of the Air, and when Welles went to Hollywood, he took Herrmann with him. *Citizen Kane* was his first movie score. The two worked closely together, Welles often cutting his film to accommodate the musical numbers, rather than vice versa, which was usually the case in Hollywood. Herrmann was present throughout the production, taking twelve weeks to compose the score, an unusually lengthy period of time. Difficult, intensely egotistical, an uncompromising perfectionist, Herrmann did most of his best work for Welles and Alfred Hitchcock, including the scores for *The Magnificent Ambersons, Vertigo, North by Northwest, Psycho,* and many others. *(RKO)*

Bernard Herrmann's musical score is similarly sophisticated. Musical motifs are assigned to several of the major characters and events. Many of these motifs are introduced in the newsreel sequence, then picked up later in the film, often in a minor key, or played at a different tempo, depending on the mood of the scene. For example, the poignant Rosebud motif is introduced in the opening sequence, and when Rosebud is brought up during the course of the investigation, a variation of the musical motif often underlines the dialogue. When Welles finally reveals to us—but not to the characters—the mystery of Rosebud, the musical motif swells powerfully into prominence, producing one of the most thrilling revelations in all of cinema.

Herrmann's score often parallels Welles's visuals. For instance, in the montage of breakfast scenes between Kane and his first wife, the disintegration of the marriage is paralleled by the variations in the music. The sequence opens with a soft romantic waltz, tenderly underscoring the fascination each feels for the other. This is followed by a slightly comical musical variation. As the relationship becomes more strained, the orchestration becomes harsher, more dissonant. In the final scene, neither one bothers to speak anymore. Their silence is accompanied by a brooding, neurotic variation on the opening musical theme.

In many scenes, Welles used sound for symbolic purposes. For example, he used a dissolve and montage sequence to show Susan on her disastrous

508

12–13. *Citizen Kane, with Dorothy Comingore.*
Kane demonstrates that virtually every kind of visual has its aural counterpart. This montage sequence is reinforced by an aural montage of Susan Alexander's shrieking arias, orchestral music, popping flashbulbs, and the sounds of newspaper presses rolling. The pounding sounds are machinelike and inexorable, battering their sacrificial victim until she is stupefied by terror and exhaustion. *(RKO)*

operatic tour **(12–13).** On the soundtrack, her aria can be heard, distorted into a screeching, dismal wail. The sequence ends with the gradual dimming of the light, to symbolize Susan's increasing despair. On the accompanying soundtrack, we hear her voice winding down to a wounded moan, as though someone pulled the plug on a record player in the middle of a song.

Acting

Welles had his own stable of writers, assistants, and actors, who worked with him in both radio and the New York live theater. When he went to Hollywood, he took many of them with him, including fifteen actors. Except for Welles, none of these players was well known, and even Welles was known primarily as a radio performer. (He captured the imagination of the mass audience when his notorious *War of the Worlds* broadcast of 1938 panicked thousands of Americans, who believed that we were actually being invaded by creatures from Mars. Welles was delighted, of course. As a result of this cause célèbre, he got his picture on the cover of *Time* when he was only twenty-two years old.)

Citizen Kane boasts a first-rate cast. There are a few so-so performances, but none that is weak, and several that are outstanding, most notably those of Welles, Dorothy Comingore, Joseph Cotten, Everett Sloane, and Agnes Moorehead. Like most performers who are used to acting repertory-style, members of the cast work as an ensemble; the total effect is one of dramatic scenes that mesh seamlessly. The Mercury players look like seasoned film performers, not the young neophytes they actually were. For most of them, this was their first movie, yet they are always natural, sincere, and believable.

Even some of the cameo roles are performed with distinction. Because these parts are limited to only a few lines of dialogue, the actors must be able to convey the complexity of their characters—who are often contradictory—without appearing inconsistent. For example, Ray Collins performs Boss Jim Gettys as a cunning survivor. Streetwise and cynical, he is a man who has seen it all. Or at least he thought he had seen it all until he came up against Kane. Gettys seems quietly shocked that Kane, a supposedly high-class opponent, would be so low-class as to publish a doctored photo of Gettys "in a convict suit with stripes, so his children could see the picture in the paper, or his mother." We can't help but sympathize with Gettys's outrage, notwithstanding the fact that otherwise he is a creep.

Although she appears in only one scene, Agnes Moorehead as Kane's mother leaves an indelible impression. (Moorehead was to go on to an even more brilliant performance in Welles's next movie, *The Magnificent Ambersons*.)

12–14.   *Citizen Kane, with Dorothy Comingore.*
Comingore's brilliant performance as Susan provides considerable warmth to an otherwise cold and intellectual film. The few close-ups in the movie are reserved primarily for her, forcing us to become more involved with Susan's feelings. Like most of the major characters, she is a study in contradiction, screechy and pitiful at the same time. She can also be very funny. "A person can go crazy in this dump," she complains in her typical whining monotone. "Nobody to talk to, nobody to have any fun with. Forty-nine thousand acres of nothing but scenery and statues." *(RKO)*

Moorehead's Mary Kane might almost have stepped out of a tale by Hawthorne: stern, puritanical, joyless. She is a woman who found out too late that she has married a fool. Trapped, she will endure the humiliation of her marriage, but she will not subject her son to the same fate. In her mind, he is meant for better things, even if that means she must part with the only person she loves. Mrs. Kane is a woman of few words, but her determination is communicated by her steely stoicism, her decisive movements, her ramrod-straight back. This is not a lady to mess with.

Everett Sloane and Joseph Cotten are flawless as Bernstein and Leland. Bernstein's uncritical hero-worship of Kane establishes him as the less intelligent of the two, a man who—unlike Leland—puts friendship above principle. But the endearing Bernstein is something of a comic innocent, so blinded by loyalty that he is incapable of seeing Kane's flaws, much less his vices. As an old man, Bernstein is still funny, a successful businessman, but no shallow materialist. "It's no trick to make a lot of money," he scoffs, "if all you want is to make a lot of money." He recognizes that Kane's motives ran deeper than the crassly entrepreneurial. He is still awed by the mysterious depths of Kane's inner spirit. And perhaps a bit saddened by the contrast with his own ordinary soul.

Welles's performance as Kane was lavishly praised. John O'Hara, reviewing the movie for *Newsweek*, said, "There has never been a better actor than Orson Welles." D. W. Griffith described it as the greatest film performance he had ever seen. Tall and imposing, with a deep, flexible voice capable of a wide spectrum of nuances, Welles was an astonishing technician, equally convincing as a brash young man, a rigid autocrat in middle years, and a burned-out, hulking septuagenarian. At twenty-five, Kane is charming and charismatic, with an insolent skepticism toward all forms of authority. In fact, he is so charming that we hardly notice some of his questionable methods, his insistence on having everything his way. As a middle-aged man, Kane is more somber. The element of threat is more brazenly paraded. He no longer argues that the end justifies the means—he automatically assumes it, expecting others to acquiesce to his views. As an old man, Kane is among the walking wounded, a man who has repeatedly fought and lost.

Drama

The live theater was Welles's first love. As a youth, he attended a progressive prep school, where he directed and acted in over thirty plays. Shakespeare was his favorite dramatist. In 1930, at the age of fifteen, Welles left school permanently. With money left from an inheritance, he traveled to Europe, where he bluffed his way into the Gate Theatre in Dublin, claiming to be a well-known Broadway star. The managers didn't believe him but were impressed nonetheless, and they hired him. For about a year, Welles directed and acted in many stage classics, mostly of the Elizabethan period.

When he returned to America in 1933, he finagled an acting job touring with Katherine Cornell, one of the major stage stars of that era. They performed mostly Shakespeare and Shaw. In 1935 in New York, Welles joined forces with the aspiring theatrical producer (and later actor and director) John Houseman.

In 1937, Welles and Houseman formed their own company, The Mercury Theatre. Several of their productions were hailed for their brilliance, most notably a modern-dress, antifascist production of *Julius Caesar.* Welles not only starred and directed but also designed the sets, costumes, and lighting. The influential theater critic John Mason Brown pronounced it "a production of genius." Critic Elliot Norton described it as "the most compelling Shakespeare of this generation."

Welles financed his theater with his earnings as a radio star. During his halcyon years in the late 1930s, he was earning $3000 per week in radio, two-thirds of which was plowed back into the Mercury Theatre. The company was a shoestring operation, constantly on the brink of collapsing. In 1939, after its first flop, the Mercury Theatre folded. Welles originally went to Hollywood with

12–15.   Artist's rendering of the interior set of Xanadu for *Citizen Kane.*
In the area of set design and décor, Welles was fortunate in his choice of studio, for RKO's art director, Van Nest Polglase, was among the best in the industry. Perry Ferguson, who actually designed the sets under Polglase's general supervision, shared his boss's preference for monumental sets with unusual sources of lighting and richly textured details.   *(RKO)*

the intention of earning some quick cash so he could return to New York and revive the Mercury.

Welles's experience in the live theater proved invaluable when he turned to making movies. He regarded film as essentially a dramatic rather than literary medium. As we have seen, the lighting style of *Citizen Kane* is more indebted to the stage than the screen, and Welles's use of **lengthy takes** is similarly derived from the need in the live theater to stage the action in a unified space.

In the area of art direction too, Welles was able to save hundreds of thousands of dollars by showing only parts of sets rather than entire rooms. For example, the office set consists only of a desk and two walls, yet we seem to be in a huge luxurious office **(12–9)**. Similarly, in the Xanadu scenes, Welles spotlit an oversized piece of furniture, a sculpture, or a fireplace, leaving the rest of the room in darkness—as though it were too enormous to be adequately illuminated. (The rooms are actually sparsely furnished.) When these techniques were insufficient, Welles was able to count on the RKO special effects department to create an epic canvas through such techniques as **animation,** matte shots, and **miniatures.**

Edward Stevenson's costumes adhere closely to the actual styles of each period. Because the movie traverses nearly seventy years and the events are not chronologically presented, the costumes had to be instantly recognizable for

12–16.   Exterior set of Xanadu for *Citizen Kane.*
The mist-shrouded tropic setting groans under the weight of the sprawling, towering Xanadu, unfinished and already beginning to decay, like a rotting mausoleum from the pages of Edgar Allan Poe. Although the palm trees sway as the wisps of fog drift past dreamily, the set was actually a matte painting, only a few feet high.   *(RKO)*

a   b   c

12–17. Three photos of Orson Welles as Charles Foster Kane at various periods in his life. Welles was required to age about fifty years during the course of the story. Thanks in part to the makeup artistry of Maurice Seiderman, Welles is completely convincing, whether playing Kane at twenty-five **(a)**, forty-five **(b)**, or seventy-five **(c)**. As Kane grows older, his hair grays and recedes, his jowls sag, his cheeks grow puffier, and the bags beneath his eyes grow more pouchy. Seiderman created a synthetic rubber body suit to suggest the increasingly flabby torso of an older man. *(RKO)*

the audience to know the period of each scene. Kane's childhood has a nineteenth-century flavor—a cross between Charles Dickens and Mark Twain. The former can be seen in Thatcher's stiff collar and stovepipe hat; the latter in the plain frontier simplicity of the clothes of Mary and Jim Kane.

Costumes are symbolic as well as functional. As a crusading young publisher, Kane favors whites. He often removes his jacket and tie while working. Later in life, he is almost always in black business suits and ties. Emily's clothes look expensive, but with an understated elegance. She always looks like a well-bred young matron—fashionable, modest, and feminine. Susan favors simple clothes before meeting Kane. After meeting him, she is generally dressed in ritzy patterned dresses, sometimes sprinkled with sequins—like an aging showgirl parading her loot.

The following is an analysis of Susan's opera costume **(12–18)**, a triumph of irony and wit:

1. *Period.* Ostensibly nineteenth century, though in fact an amusing pastiche of various periods and "Oriental" influences.
2. *Class.* Royalty. The costume is profusely festooned with pearls, precious jewels, and other queenly niceties.
3. *Sex.* Female, with an emphasis on curved, swaying lines and peekaboo slits in the skirt. Only the turban provides a masculine touch, though it is whimsically inflected with fluffy white feathers.

514

12–18. Publicity photo of Dorothy Comingore in opera costume for *Citizen Kane*.
Bernard Herrmann composed the film's opera, *Salommbô*, in the style of nineteenth-century French "Oriental" operas. Edward Stevenson's costumes are in this same **campy** style of mockery. For example, Susan's outlandish regalia is a send-up of what the well-dressed French-Oriental opera queen might wear while suffering the agonies of unrequited love, torment, and despair. *(RKO)*

4. *Age.* The costume is designed for a woman in her twenties, at the peak of her physical attractiveness.

5. *Silhouette.* Formfitting, unabashedly highlighting the wearer's curvacious contours.

6. *Fabric.* Silks, beaded ornamentation encrusted with jewels.

7. *Accessories.* Turban, pearl strands, incongruous Joan Crawford-style ankle-strap shoes.

8. *Color.* The film is in black and white, but most of the fabric has a metallic sheen, suggesting gold and ebony.

9. *Body exposure.* The costume reveals and highlights such erotic areas as the breasts, midriff, and legs.

10. *Function.* The costume is totally without utility, difficult even to walk in. It is intended for a person who does not work, but is displayed.

11. *Body attitude.* Tall and proud, with head and breasts held high, like a Vegas showgirl flashing her gaudy plunder.

12. *Image.* Every inch the opera queen.

Story

The differences between story and plot can be best illustrated by comparing the narrative in chronological order with the restructured sequence of the plot. When Herman Mankiewicz approached Welles with the idea of the story, Welles was concerned that the materials would be too sprawling, too unfocused. To sharpen the story line and infuse it with more dramatic urgency, he suggested scrambling the chronology of events through a series of **flashbacks,** each narrated from the point of view of the person telling the story. Welles had used this multiple flashback technique in a number of his radio dramas.

He and Mankiewicz also introduced a note of suspense. In his final moments of life, Kane mumbles the word *Rosebud* **(12–19).** No one seems to know what it means, and its significance piques the curiosity of a newspaper reporter, Thompson, who spends the remainder of the movie questioning Kane's former associates about this mystery, which he hopes contains the key to Kane's conflicting character.

Welles claimed that the Rosebud **motif** was merely a plot gimmick, intended to hook the audience on a dramatic question that's really a wild goose chase. But the gimmick works. Like the hopeful reporter, we too think that Rosebud will unlock Kane's ambiguous personality. Without this gimmick, the story would have remained rambling and unfocused. The search for the meaning of Rosebud shapes the narrative, providing it with a forward thrust, with a dramatic question we all want answered. This is what foreign critics mean by the American genius for storytelling.

12–19. *Citizen Kane.*
Like a number of Welles's other movies, *Kane* begins with the end—the death of its protagonist when he is about seventy-five. In his final moments of life, the old man holds a small crystal ball containing a miniature scene that flurries with artificial snow when shaken. With his last dying breath, he utters the word "Rosebud." Then the glass ball crashes to the floor, splintering into a thousand fragments. The plot of the movie is structured like a search—for the meaning of this final utterance. *(RKO)*

The flashback structure of *Citizen Kane* allows Welles to leap through time and space, cutting to various periods of Kane's life without having to adhere to a strict chronology. To provide the audience with an overview, Welles introduced most of the major events and people of Kane's life in a brief newsreel shown early in the film. These events and people are explored in more depth in the individual flashbacks that follow.

Many critics have marveled at the intricate, jigsaw-puzzle structure of the movie, with its interlocking pieces that don't click together until the final scene. The following plot outline sets forth the main structural units of the film and the principal characters and events of each:

1. *Prologue.* Xanadu. Kane's death. "Rosebud."

2. *Newsreel.* Death of Kane. Enormous wealth and decadent lifestyle. Contradictory political image. Marriage to Emily Norton. Exposé of "love nest." Divorce. Marriage to Susan Alexander, "singer." Political campaign. Opera career. The Great Depression and Kane's financial decline. Lonely, secluded old age in Xanadu.

3. *Premise.* Thompson is instructed by his editor **(12–2)** to discover the mystery of Rosebud by questioning Kane's former associates. "It will probably be a very simple thing." False step: Susan refuses to speak to Thompson.

4. *Flashback: The Memoirs of Walter P. Thatcher.* Kane's childhood. Thatcher becomes guardian. Kane's first newspaper: *The Inquirer.* Introduction of

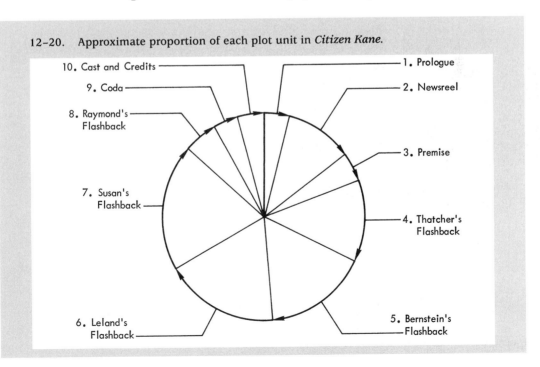

12–20. Approximate proportion of each plot unit in *Citizen Kane.*

10. Cast and Credits
9. Coda
8. Raymond's Flashback
7. Susan's Flashback
6. Leland's Flashback
1. Prologue
2. Newsreel
3. Premise
4. Thatcher's Flashback
5. Bernstein's Flashback

Bernstein and Leland. Newspaper crusading years. Kane's financial decline in the 1930s.

5. *Flashback: Bernstein.* Early days at *The Inquirer.* "Declaration of Principles." Building a publishing empire. Engagement to Emily Norton.

6. *Flashback: Jed Leland.* Disintegration of marriage to Emily. Kane meets Susan. Political campaign in 1918. Exposé, divorce, remarriage. Susan's opera career. Final break between Kane and Jed.

7. *Flashback: Susan Alexander Kane.* Opera debut and career. Suicide attempt. Years of semiseclusion with Kane at Xanadu. Susan leaves Kane.

8. *Flashback: Raymond, butler at Xanadu.* Kane's final days. "Rosebud."

9. *Coda.* Revelation of Rosebud. Reverse of opening Prologue, producing closure.

10. *Cast and credits.*

The ten sections of the film vary in length. A diagram charting the approximate proportion of each section is shown in Figure **12–20**.

Writing

Citizen Kane is often singled out for the excellence of its screenplay—its wit, its taut construction, its thematic complexity. The script's authorship provoked considerable controversy, both at the time of the movie's release and again in the 1970s, when critic Pauline Kael contended that Welles merely added a few polishing touches to Herman Mankiewicz's finished product. Mankiewicz was a Hollywood regular, a notorious drunk—charming, witty, and almost totally unreliable. When he approached Welles with the original idea for *American* (it was later called *John Citizen, U.S.A.,* and finally *Citizen Kane*), Welles asked his former partner, John Houseman, to help Mankiewicz write the screenplay, preferably in an isolated place, far removed from temptation.

Welles made extensive revisions on the first few drafts of the screenplay—so extensive that Mankiewicz denounced the movie because it departed radically from his scenario. Nor did he want Welles's name to appear on the screenplay credit, and he took his case to the Writers Guild. At this time, a director was not allowed any writing credit unless he or she contributed 50 percent or more of the screenplay. In a compromise gesture, the guild allowed both of them credit, only with Mankiewicz receiving top billing.

When the controversy resurfaced in the 1970s, the American scholar Robert L. Carringer settled the case once and for all. He examined the seven principal drafts of the screenplay, plus many last-minute revision memoranda and additional sources. Carringer's conclusion: The early Mankiewicz drafts contain "dozens of pages of dull, plodding material that will eventually be discarded or replaced altogether. And most tellingly, there is virtually nothing in them of that stylistic wit and fluidity that is the most engaging trait of the film itself." In short, Mankiewicz provided the raw material; Welles provided the genius.

The script sparkles with surprises. The main characters are a far cry from the tired stereotypes of most movies of this era. Only Thatcher seems conventional, a variation of the 1930s tycoon. The writing is often tersely funny. During Kane's noisy marriage to Susan, for example, the couple is surrounded by pushy reporters. When asked what he's going to do now, Kane replies, "We're going to be a great opera star." Susan chimes in: "Charlie said if I didn't, he'd build me an opera house." The gallant Kane demurs: "That won't be necessary." Cut to a newspaper headline: KANE BUILDS OPERA HOUSE.

There are also moments of pure poetry, like Bernstein's surprising reply to Thompson after the reporter scoffs at Bernstein's suggestion that Rosebud might be a long-lost love. "You take me," the old retainer explains. "One day, back in 1896, I was crossing over to Jersey on the ferry, and as we pulled out, there was another ferry pulling in, and on it there was a girl waiting to get off. A white dress she had on. She was carrying a white parasol. I only saw her for one second. She didn't see me at all, but I'll bet a month hasn't gone by since, that I haven't thought of that girl." Welles always loved that speech—and wished that he had written it.

Thematically, *Kane* is so complex that only a brief itemizing of some of its themes is possible within these few pages. Like most of Welles's other movies, *Citizen Kane* might well be entitled *The Arrogance of Power.* He was attracted to themes traditionally associated with classical tragedy and the epic: the downfall of a public figure because of arrogance and pride. Power and wealth are corrupting, and the corrupt devour themselves. The innocent usually survive, but they are severely scarred. "All of the characters I've played are various forms of Faust," Welles stated. All have bartered their souls and lost.

Welles's sense of evil is mature and complex, seldom conventionalized. He was one of the few American filmmakers of his generation to explore the darker side of the human condition without resorting to a simplified psychology or to moralistic clichés. Though his universe is essentially doomed, it's shot through with ambiguities, contradictions, and moments of transient beauty. Welles considered himself a moralist, but his movies are never priggish or sanctimonious. Instead of facile condemnations, *Kane* laments the loss of innocence: "Almost all serious stories in the world are stories of a failure with a death in it," Welles stated. "But there is more lost paradise in them than defeat. To me that's the central theme in Western culture, the lost paradise."

When a story isn't told in a straightforward, chronological manner, something is lost and something is gained. What's lost is the suspense of any conventionally told tale, which usually asks, What does the protagonist want and how is he or she going to get it? In *Citizen Kane,* the protagonist is dead almost from the start. We are forced to piece together his life from the points of view of others. This technique of multiple narration forces us to gauge the biases and prejudices of each narrator. *Citizen Kane* is their story, too.

There are five different storytellers, and each tells us a different story. Even when the events overlap, we view them from a different perspective. For example, Leland's account of Susan's operatic debut is colored by his condescending attitude toward her. Her performance is viewed primarily from the audience, where Leland is sitting. When Susan recounts the same event, the camera is primarily on stage, and the tone of the sequence is no longer comic but agonized.

Welles's narrative strategy is something like a prism: The newsreel and the five interviewees each offer a unique view of the same man. The newsreel offers us a quick tour of the highlights of Kane's public life. Thatcher's account is tainted by his absolute confidence in the moral superiority of the rich and powerful. Bernstein's story is steeped in the gratitude and loyalty he felt for Kane when they were young. Leland offers a more rigorous perspective: He judges Kane by what he actually does, rather than what he says. Susan is the most victimized of the storytellers. Yet she is also the most compassionate and sensitive. Raymond, the butler, pretends to know a lot more than he does. His brief flashback merely concludes Thompson's investigation.

12–21. Production photo of Orson Welles (in middle-aged makeup) and Gregg Toland lining up a shot for the postelection scene between Kane and Jed Leland.

Welles used low-angle shots as a motif throughout the picture, especially to emphasize the awesome power of the protagonist. In this scene, the angle is so low that the floorboards of the set had to be torn away to allow for the camera's placement. Combined with the perspective-distorting wide-angle lens, such low-angle shots portray Kane as a towering colossus, capable of crushing anything that gets in his way. *(RKO)*

There are literally dozens of symbolic motifs in the movie. Some of them are technical, such as the film's predominantly low camera angles **(12–21)**. Others are more content oriented, such as the series of fences the camera must penetrate before we are able to see Kane. There are also persistent motifs of stillness, decay, old age, and death. The two most important motifs in the movie are Rosebud and the fragmentation motif.

Rosebud turns out to be a favorite childhood possession. Scholars and critics have argued about Rosebud for decades. Welles himself described it as "dollar-book Freud"—that is, a convenient symbol of childhood innocence. The ideas of Freud gained wide currency in the American cinema of the 1940s, especially the centrality of a child's prepubescent life in determining his or her later character.

But Rosebud is also a more generalized symbol of loss. Consider: Kane is a man who lost his parents when he was a child. He was brought up by a bank. He lost his youthful idealism as a publisher. He lost in his bid to be governor. He lost his first wife and son. He lost in his efforts to make Susan an opera star. He lost Susan. Because it's much more than a mere object, more even than a symbol of Edenic innocence, the revelation of Rosebud to the audience delivers a powerful emotional impact.

12-22. *Citizen Kane, with William Alland and Paul Stewart.*
Near the end of the movie, Thompson (Alland) admits defeat. He never does find out what Rosebud means, and he describes his investigation as "playing with a jigsaw puzzle," while the camera cranes back and up, revealing thousands of crates of artwork, memorabilia, and personal effects—the fragmented artifacts of a person's life. "I don't think any word can explain a man's life," Thompson continues. "No, I guess Rosebud is just a piece in a jigsaw puzzle, a missing piece." *(RKO)*

The fragmentation motif acts as a foil to the simpleminded notion that any single word could "explain" a complex personality. Throughout the movie, we are presented with images that suggest multiplicity, repetition, and fragments of a larger whole. Examples of this motif are the jigsaw puzzles, the profusion of crates, boxes, and artwork. The very structure of the movie is fragmented, with each narrator providing us with only a partial picture. In Raymond's flashback at the end of the film, the elderly Kane mutters "Rosebud" when he discovers a glass globe. Dazed, he walks down a corridor, the globe in his hand. As he passes a set of facing mirrors, we see his image multiplied into infinity. All of them are Kane.

Ideology

Welles was a lifelong liberal, firmly committed to the values of the moderate left. The New York theater scene of the 1930s was intensely political and **left-wing** in its leanings. Like most intellectuals of that era, Welles was a Roosevelt enthusiast, strongly pro-New Deal in his sympathies. In fact, he helped write several of President Roosevelt's famous radio speeches.

Not surprisingly, *Citizen Kane* can be classified as liberal in its ideological slant. However, the movie is definitely in the implicit range in terms of its bias. It refuses to be the purveyor of glib certainties about its values: The characters are too complex, often paradoxical. The film is filled with the messy contradictions of life.

The protagonist is a "fighting liberal" as a young editor. Jed Leland is his comrade in arms, his conscience figure **(12–23).** But as he grows older, Kane moves further to the **right,** ending finally as an authoritarian bully. Kane also believes that environment is a stronger force than heredity. In one scene,

12–23. *Citizen Kane, with Joseph Cotten.* Jed Leland (Cotten) represents the moral conscience of the film, Kane's idealistic alter ego. Roles like this are difficult to play well, because they can easily degenerate into sentimental clichés of piety. Cotten toughens up the role by refusing to make Leland too likable. Although sensitive and intelligent, Leland is also a bit of a prig, "a New England schoolmarm," to use his own phrase. Like Bernstein, he loves Kane and is loyal to him when they are all young and committed to social reform. But when he finally recognizes Kane's ego for the destructive force it is, Jed pulls back, disillusioned. *(RKO)*

he says that he might have become a really great man if he hadn't grown up rich.

Kane is a relativist in terms of his morality. When he no longer loves his wife Emily, he forms an adulterous liaison with Susan. To him, his marriage certificate is merely a document, something that bears no relation to his feelings. Nowhere in the film does Kane express an interest in religion. He is a thorough secularist.

As a young man, Kane displays nothing but contempt for tradition, the past, and authority figures. Well into middle age, he is oriented more toward the future—building up his newspaper, courting Emily, expanding his empire, running for governor, guiding Susan's career. Only as an old man does he withdraw from the arena of life, shutting himself off from the outside world, "lording it over the monkeys" in Xanadu.

Similarly, as a young man, Kane emphasizes the communal. His newspaper is a collaborative effort, with him at the helm, flanked by his two faithful lieutenants, Bernstein and Leland. As he grows older, he no longer consults his colleagues. He issues them orders, brooking no disagreements. As a young editor, he identifies with common workingpeople, promising to become their spokesman. As an older man, he seeks out the company of important world leaders, shakers, and movers. He surrounds himself with yes-men.

12-24. *Citizen Kane, with Joseph Cotten and Everett Sloane.*
Kane's rampant consumerism is best illustrated by his mania for collecting European art treasures. Not because he enjoys art—indeed, he scarcely ever mentions it—but because of its value as a status symbol. His conspicuous consumption becomes a habit rather than a passionate interest. After a while, no one even bothers to uncrate his purchases—they're simply stored away with all his other possessions. *(RKO)*

Citizen Kane is also strongly feminist in its sympathies. The three main female characters are all victimized. Mary Kane is trapped in a loveless marriage and feels she must sacrifice raising her son to get him away from his bullying father.

Emily Norton Kane is a decent if somewhat conventional young woman. She has been raised by the book and obviously takes seriously her duties as a wife and mother. She is propriety incarnate. Kane betrays her faith and love through no apparent fault of her own. He got bored with her.

Susan Alexander Kane is the most sympathetic of the three and the most ill-used. She endures great suffering and spiritual anguish, all in the name of love. She doesn't care much about money or social position, which merely complicate her life. She is one of the few characters capable of forgiveness. After the reporter Thompson listens to her sad tale of humiliation and loneliness, he says, "All the same, I feel kind of sorry for Mr. Kane." Blinking back her tears, Susan replies, "Don't you think I do?"

Theory

Citizen Kane is a masterpiece of formalism. True, there are some realistic elements in the film—its basis in fact, the newsreel sequence, the deep-focus photography that was so highly praised by realist critics like André Bazin. For the most part, however, it's the bravura sequences that are most memorable in the movie. Welles was one of the great **lyricists** of the cinema, and his stylistic rapture is best illustrated by the ornate visuals, the dazzling traveling shots, the richly textured soundtrack, the kaleidoscopic editing style, the highly fragmented narrative, and the profusion of symbolic motifs. The movie is brazen in its technical audacity.

Kane is the work of an indisputable *auteur.* Welles not only produced the film, he also coauthored its script, selected the cast and crew, starred in its leading role, and directed the entire production without interference. The movie is also typical in that it explores a complex of characteristic Wellesian themes and is executed in a showy style that became a virtual signature of its author. Welles was always generous in his praise of his coworkers, especially actors and cinematographers, but there is no question that he was totally in command during the production of this film.

The commercial and critical history of *Citizen Kane* is a fascinating story in its own right. Shortly after the collapse of the Mercury Theatre, RKO offered the twenty-four-year-old Welles an unheard-of contract: He was to be paid $150,000 per picture, plus 25 percent of the gross receipts. He could produce, direct, write, or star in any of his films, or function in all four capacities if he wished. He was granted total artistic control, answerable only to George Schaefer, the enlightened head of the studio.

RKO was in financial distress, as it had been throughout most of its brief span. The studio was founded in 1928 by the financier Joseph P. Kennedy

12–25. Promotional poster for *Citizen Kane*.
Then as now, a studio's advertising emphasized a picture's commercial appeal. Then as now, sex and violence were the most common ploys to lure the mass audience. The promotional campaign for *Citizen Kane* was somewhat classier. It stressed Welles's box-office appeal as the film's star and the controversy surrounding the picture's release. Posters and lobby displays also exaggerated the love angle, presumably to appeal to women patrons: "I hate him!" Susan proclaims. "I love him!" Emily counters. (Neither statement is in the movie, of course.) Interestingly, this poster crudely parallels the multiple points of view found in the film itself. *(RKO)*

(the father of the later president) and by David Sarnoff, the head of RCA and later NBC. Sarnoff hoped that the studio would become an "NBC with pictures." Kennedy soon withdrew, with a profit of some $5 million. After a promising start, RKO fell on hard times, primarily because of the constant reshuffling of management, which gave it no continuity. Unlike the other majors, RKO had no consistent identity or characteristic style.

Sarnoff and his new partner, Nelson Rockefeller, wanted RKO to produce sophisticated and progressive films, but they discovered that artistic worth and box-office success were not easily united. Rockefeller and Sarnoff were pleased with Schaefer's idea to hire Welles, for they reasoned that if anyone could produce quality movies that also made profits, surely it was the boy genius, fresh from his Broadway and radio triumphs.

When Welles arrived in Hollywood in 1939, the resentment against him was immense. Most directors considered themselves lucky if they were permitted to direct an **A-film** before they were thirty-five, yet here was a mere stripling, an outsider at that, who was given total autonomy on his first time out. "This is the biggest electric train a boy ever had," he quipped when he saw the production facilities at RKO. The flamboyant Welles was regarded as arty, supercilious, and arrogant by most industry regulars. He didn't help matters by openly sneering at the film community: "Hollywood is a golden suburb, perfect for golfers, gardeners, mediocre men, and complacent starlets," he announced with obvious amusement. He was an incorrigible smartass. He paid dearly for the flippant wit of his youth.

Almost from the start, the production of *Citizen Kane* was sparked by controversy. A master publicist, Welles had the film colony buzzing with speculation. The movie was shot in "absolute secrecy." Rumors were rife about the identity of the leading character, and when the syndicated Hearst gossip columnist, Louella Parsons, heard that the picture was to deal with her boss's private life, a campaign against the movie was launched by La Parsons, with Hearst's blessings and full cooperation.

As the film neared completion, Hearst's campaign got ferocious. He threatened the industry with a series of scandals and exposés unless the picture was destroyed before release. His stooge, MGM's Louis B. Mayer, the most powerful man in the industry, offered to reimburse RKO's costs, plus a tidy profit, if the studio would destroy the negative. Hearst pressured the other studios to refuse to book the film in their theaters. His newspapers attacked Welles as a Communist and suggested he was a draft dodger. (Welles was rejected for military service for medical reasons.) RKO stalled, paralyzed with indecision. Welles threatened to sue unless the movie was released. Finally, the studio decided to take the risk.

With only a few exceptions, *Citizen Kane* received rave reviews. Bosley Crowther of *The New York Times* called it "one of the greatest (if not the greatest) films in history." It won the New York Film Critics Award as best picture of 1941, which was a very good year for American movies. It received nine Academy Award nominations, but at the ceremonies, Welles was booed whenever his name was mentioned. Significantly, the only Oscar that the movie won was for its screenplay. Pauline Kael suggested that this was intended as a gesture of sup-

12–26. *The Magnificent Ambersons* **(U.S.A., 1942),** *with Dolores Costello, Agnes Moore-head, Joseph Cotten, and Ray Collins; directed by Orson Welles.*
Like most of Welles's movies, this, his favorite work, deals with the theme of a lost paradise. Unlike *Kane*, however, the tone is warm and nostalgic, the images more softly lyrical. Welles does not appear in the film, though he does narrate the story off screen. He concludes with a shot of a microphone on a swinging boom, accompanied by his spoken credit: "I wrote the picture and directed it. My name is Orson Welles." *(RKO)*

port for Mankiewicz, the Hollywood regular, and as a rebuke to Welles, the upstart, who lost out on the acting, directing, and best picture awards.

Incredibly, *Citizen Kane* failed at the box office. It was the beginning of the end for Welles in Hollywood. When it failed to please several sneak-preview audiences, his next masterpiece, *The Magnificent Ambersons* (1942), was cut by RKO from its 131-minute length to 88 minutes, and a happy ending was tacked on. It too failed at the box office. Shortly afterwards, there was a management shuffle at RKO and both Welles and Schaefer were ousted.

Welles was always a favorite with critics, especially in France. As early as the 1950s, excerpts from his scripts appeared in such journals as *Image et Son* and *Cinéma d'Aujourd'hui.* Welles was an idolized source of inspiration for the critics at *Cahiers du Cinéma,* who spearheaded the French **New Wave.** "All of us will always owe him everything," gushed Jean-Luc Godard. Truffaut claimed that *Citizen Kane* inspired the largest number of French filmmakers to begin

12–27. *Othello* **(Morocco, 1952),** *with Orson Welles and Suzanne Cloutier, directed by Welles.* In 1948, Welles, discouraged by a string of box-office failures, left for Europe and Africa, where he hoped to work as an independent **producer–director.** His first movie was this adaptation of Shakespeare. The project was a nightmare. It was over three years in the shooting, and Welles had to interrupt production many times to seek additional funding. He lost several players in the process. There were three Desdemonas, four Iagos. Sequences had to be reshot time and again. But finally the movie was finished. On the Continent, it was enthusiastically praised and swept the Grand Prix at the Cannes Film Festival. But British and American critics complained of its crude soundtrack. This was to be the pattern of virtually all his subsequent work outside America. *(United Artists)*

their own careers, and he included a tender tribute to this famous movie in *La Nuit Américaine* (literally, "The American Night," but released in the United States as *Day for Night*).

Welles's critical reputation continued to rise. In the year of his death, 1985, three books were published about him. In a poll of international film critics, conducted every ten years by the prestigious British journal *Sight and Sound, Citizen Kane* has consistently topped the list of the ten greatest films of all time. The filmmaker who consistently receives the most votes as the greatest director in the history of the cinema: Orson Welles.

FURTHER READING

BAZIN, ANDRÉ, *Orson Welles: A Critical View* (New York: Harper & Row, 1978). Critical study by France's greatest film critic.

CALLOW, SIMON, *Orson Welles: The Road to Xanadu* (New York: Penguin, 1996). First volume of a projected two, covering Welles's life up to his *War of the Worlds* broadcast, written by a distinguished British actor.

CARRINGER, ROBERT L., *The Making of Citizen Kane* (Berkeley: University of California Press, 1985). Definitive.

GOTTESMAN, RONALD, ed., *Focus on Orson Welles* (Englewood Cliffs, N.J.: Prentice-Hall, 1976). A collection of critical essays, filmography, and bibliography. See also Gottesman's *Focus on Citizen Kane* (Englewood Cliffs, N.J.: Prentice-Hall, 1971). Two excellent anthologies.

HIGHAM, CHARLES, *The Films of Orson Welles* (Berkeley: University of California Press, 1970). Critical study and psychobiography. Very well illustrated. See also Higham's *Orson Welles: The Rise and Fall of an American Genius* (New York: St. Martin's Press, 1985).

KAEL, PAULINE, *The Citizen Kane Book* (Boston: Little, Brown, 1971). Reading version and a cutting continuity of *Kane,* prefaced by Kael's controversial essay on the authorship of the script.

LEAMING, BARBARA, *Orson Welles: A Biography* (New York: Viking, 1985). Extensive interviews with Welles; somewhat idolatrous.

MCBRIDE, JOSEPH, *Orson Welles* (New York: Viking, 1972). A perceptive critical study. Filmography. Stage, radio, television, acting credits.

NAREMORE, JAMES, *The Magic World of Orson Welles* (New York: Oxford University Press, 1978). Critical study.

THOMPSON, DAVID, *Rosebud* (New York: Knopf, 1996). A well-written biography, with sixty-nine photos.

Glossary

A

actor star. See *star.*

aerial shot (T). Essentially a variation of the *crane shot,* though restricted to exterior locations. Usually taken from a helicopter.

aesthetic distance (C). Viewers' ability to distinguish between an artistic reality and external reality—their realization that the events of a fiction film are simulated.

A-film (I). An American studio era term signifying a major production, usually with important stars and a generous budget. Shown as the main feature on double bills.

aleatory techniques (C). Techniques of filmmaking that depend on the element of chance. Images are not planned out in advance but must be composed on the spot by the camera operator. Usually used in documentary situations.

allegory (C). A symbolic technique in which stylized characters and situations represent rather obvious ideas, such as Justice, Death, Religion, Society, and so on.

allusion (C). A reference to an event, person, or work of art, usually well known.

angle (G). The camera's angle of view relative to the subject being photographed. A high-angle shot is photographed from above, a low angle from below the subject.

animation (G). A form of filmmaking characterized by photographing inanimate objects or individual drawings *frame* by frame, with each frame differing minutely from its predecessor. When such images are projected at the standard speed of twenty-four frames per second, the result is that the objects or drawings appear to move, and hence seem "animated."

anticipatory camera, anticipatory setup (C). The placement of the camera in such a manner as to anticipate the movement of an action before it occurs. Such setups often suggest predestination.

archetype (C). An original model or type after which similar things are patterned. Archetypes can be well-known story patterns, universal experiences, or personality types.

Myths, fairy tales, *genres,* and cultural heroes are generally archetypal, as are the basic cycles of life and nature.

art director (G). The individual responsible for designing and overseeing the construction of sets for a movie, and sometimes its interior decoration and overall visual style.

aspect ratio (T). The ratio between the horizontal and vertical dimensions of the screen.

auteur theory (C). A theory of film popularized by the critics of the French journal *Cahiers du Cinéma* in the 1950s. The theory emphasizes the director as the major creator of film art, stamping the material with his or her own personal vision, style, and thematic obsessions.

available lighting (G). The use of only that light which actually exists on location, either natural (the sun) or artificial (house lamps). When available lighting is used in interior locations, generally a sensitive *fast film stock* must also be used.

avant-garde (C). From the French, meaning "in the front ranks." Those minority artists whose works are characterized by an unconventional daring and by obscure, controversial, or highly personal ideas.

B

backlighting (G). When the lights for a shot derive from the rear of the set, thus throwing the foreground figures into semidarkness or silhouette.

back lot (I). During the studio era, standing exterior sets of such common locales as a turn-of-the-century city block, a frontier town, a European village, and so on.

B-film (G). A low-budget movie usually shown as the second feature during the big-studio era in America. B-films rarely included important stars and took the form of popular *genres,* such as thrillers, westerns, or horror films. The major studios used them as testing grounds for the raw talent under contract.

bird's-eye view (G). A shot in which the camera photographs a scene from directly overhead.

blimp (T). A soundproof camera housing that muffles the noise of the camera's motor so sound can be clearly recorded on the set.

blocking (T). The movements of the actors within a given playing area.

boom, mike boom (T). An overhead telescoping pole that carries a microphone, permitting the *synchronous* recording of sound without restricting the movement of the actors.

buddy film (G). A male-oriented action genre, especially popular in the 1970s, dealing with the adventures of two or more men, usually excluding any significant female roles.

C

camp, campy (C). An artistic sensibility typified by comic mockery, especially of the straight world and conventional morality. Campy movies are often ludicrously theatrical, stylistically gaudy, and gleefully subversive.

cels, also **cells (T).** Transparent plastic sheets that are superimposed in layers by *animators* to give the illusion of depth and volume to their drawings.

centrist (C). A political term signifying a moderate ideology, midway between the extremes of the *left* and *right* wings.

cinematographer, also **director of photography** or **D.P. (G).** The artist or technician responsible for the lighting of a shot and the quality of the photography.

cinéma vérité, also **direct cinema (C).** A method of documentary filming using *aleatory* methods that don't interfere with the way events take place in reality. Such movies are made with a minimum of equipment, usually a hand-held camera and portable sound apparatus.

classical cinema, classical paradigm (C). A vague but convenient term used to designate the style of mainstream fiction films produced in America, roughly from the midteens until the late 1960s. The classical paradigm is a movie strong in *story, star,* and *production values,* with a high level of technical achievement, and edited according to conventions of *classical cutting.* The visual style is functional and rarely distracts from the characters in action. Movies in this form are structured narratively, with a clearly defined conflict, complications that intensify to a rising climax, and a resolution that emphasizes formal closure.

classical cutting (C). A style of editing developed by D. W. Griffith, in which a sequence of shots is determined by a scene's dramatic and emotional emphasis rather than by physical action alone. The sequence of shots represents the breakdown of the event into its psychological as well as logical components.

closed forms (C). A visual style that inclines toward self-conscious designs and carefully harmonized compositions. The *frame* is exploited to suggest a self-sufficient universe that encloses all the necessary visual information, usually in an aesthetically appealing manner.

close-up, close shot (G). A detailed view of a person or object. A close-up of an actor usually includes only his or her head.

continuity (T). The kind of logic implied between edited shots, their principle of coherence. *Cutting to continuity* emphasizes smooth transitions between shots, in which time and space are unobtrusively condensed. More complex *classical cutting* is the linking of shots according to an event's psychological as well as logical breakdown. In *thematic montage,* the continuity is determined by the symbolic association of ideas between shots, rather than any literal connections in time and space.

convention (C). An implied agreement between the viewer and artist to accept certain artificialities as real in a work of art. In movies, editing (or the juxtaposition of shots) is accepted as "logical" even though a viewer's perception of reality is continuous and unfragmented.

coverage, covering shots, cover shots (T). Extra shots of a scene that can be used to bridge transitions in case the planned footage fails to edit as planned. Usually *long shots* that preserve the overall continuity of a scene.

crane shot (T). A shot taken from a special device called a crane, which resembles a huge mechanical arm. The crane carries the camera and the *cinematographer* and can move in virtually any direction.

creative producer (I). A producer who supervises the making of a movie in such detail that he or she is virtually its artistic director. During the studio era in America, the most famous creative producers were David O. Selznick and Walt Disney.

cross-cutting (G). The alternating of shots from two sequences, often in different locales, suggesting that they are taking place at the same time.

cutting to continuity (T). A type of *editing* in which the shots are arranged to preserve the fluidity of an action without showing all of it. An unobtrusive condensation of a continuous action.

D

day-for-night shooting (T). Scenes that are filmed in daytime with special *filters* to suggest nighttime settings in the movie image.

deep-focus shot (T). A technique of photography that permits all distance planes to remain clearly in focus, from close-up ranges to infinity.

dialectical, dialectics (C). An analytical methodology, derived from Hegel and Marx, that juxtaposes pairs of opposites—a thesis and antithesis—to arrive at a synthesis of ideas.

dissolve, lap dissolve (T). The slow fading out of one shot and the gradual fading in of its successor, with a superimposition of images, usually at the midpoint.

distributor (I). Those individuals who serve as go-betweens in the film industry, who arrange to book the product in theaters.

dolly shot, tracking shot, trucking shot (T). A shot taken from a moving vehicle. Originally, tracks were laid on the set to permit a smoother movement of the camera.

dominant contrast, dominant (C). That area of the film image that compels the viewer's most immediate attention, usually because of a prominent visual contrast.

double exposure (T). The superimposition of two literally unrelated images on film. See also *multiple exposure.*

dubbing (T). The addition of sound after the visuals have been photographed. Dubbing can be either *synchronous* with an image or *nonsynchronous.* Foreign language movies are often dubbed in English for release in this country.

E

editing (G). The joining of one shot (strip of film) with another. The shots can picture events and objects in different places at different times. In Europe, editing is called *montage.*

epic (C). A film *genre* characterized by bold and sweeping themes, usually in heroic proportions. The protagonist is an ideal representative of a culture—national, religious, or regional. The tone of most epics is dignified, the treatment larger than life. The western is the most popular epic genre in the United States.

establishing shot (T). Usually an *extreme long* or *long shot* offered at the beginning of a scene, providing the viewer with the context of the subsequent closer shots.

expressionism (C). A style of filmmaking emphasizing extreme distortion, *lyricism,* and artistic self-expression at the expense of objectivity.

extreme close-up (G). A minutely detailed view of an object or person. An extreme close-up of an actor generally includes only his or her eyes or mouth.

extreme long shot (G). A panoramic view of an exterior location, photographed from a great distance, often as far as a quarter-mile away.

eye-level shot (T). The placement of the camera approximately five to six feet from the ground, corresponding to the height of an observer on the scene.

F

fade (T). The fade-out is the snuffing of an image from normal brightness to a black screen. A fade-in is the opposite.

faithful adaptation (C). A film based on a literary original which captures the essence of the original, often by using cinematic equivalents for specific literary techniques.

fast motion (T). Shots of a subject photographed at a rate slower than twenty-four fps, which, when projected at the standard rate, convey motion that is jerky and slightly comical, seemingly out of control.

fast stock, fast film (T). Film stock that's highly sensitive to light and generally produces a grainy image. Often used by documentarists who wish to shoot only with *available lighting.*

fill light (T). Secondary lights that are used to augment the *key light*—the main source of illumination for a shot. Fill lights soften the harshness of the key light, revealing details that would otherwise be obscured in shadow.

film noir (C). A French term—literally, black cinema—referring to a kind of urban American *genre* that sprang up after World War II, emphasizing a fatalistic, despairing universe where there is no escape from mean city streets, loneliness, and death. Stylistically, *noir* emphasizes *low-key* and *high-contrast* lighting, complex compositions, and a strong atmosphere of dread and paranoia.

filters (T). Pieces of glass or plastic placed in front of the camera lens that distort the quality of light entering the camera and hence the movie image.

final cut, also **release print (I).** The sequence of shots in a movie as it will be released to the public.

first cut, also **rough cut (I).** The initial sequence of shots in a movie, often constructed by the director.

first-person point of view. See *point-of-view shot.*

flashback (G). An editing technique that suggests the interruption of the present by a shot or series of shots representing the past.

flash-forward (G). An editing technique that suggests the interruption of the present by a shot or series of shots representing the future.

focus (T). The degree of acceptable sharpness in a film image. "Out of focus" means the images are blurred and lack acceptable linear definition.

footage (T). Exposed film *stock.*

foregrounding (C). When a critic isolates and heightens one aspect of a work of art from its context to analyze that characteristic in greater depth.

formalist, formalism (C). A style of filmmaking in which aesthetic forms take precedence over the subject matter as content. Time and space as ordinarily perceived are often distorted. Emphasis is on the essential, symbolic characteristics of objects and people, not necessarily on their superficial appearance. Formalists are often *lyrical,* self-consciously heightening their style to call attention to it as a value for its own sake.

frame (T). The dividing line between the edges of the screen image and the enclosing darkness of the theater. Can also refer to a single photograph from the filmstrip.

freeze frame, freeze shot (T). A shot composed of a single *frame* that is reprinted a number of times on the filmstrip; when projected, it gives the illusion of a still photograph.

f-stop (T). The measurement of the size of the lens opening in the camera, indicating the amount of light that's admitted.

full shot (T). A type of *long shot* that includes the human body in full, with the head near the top of the *frame* and the feet near the bottom.

G

gauge (T). The width of the filmstrip, expressed in millimeters (mm). The wider the gauge, the better the quality of the image. The standard theatrical gauge is 35 mm.

genre (C). A recognizable type of movie, characterized by certain preestablished conventions. Some common American genres are westerns, thrillers, sci-fi movies, etc. A ready-made narrative form.

H

hand-held shot (G). A shot taken with a moving camera that is often deliberately shaky to suggest documentary footage in a uncontrolled setting.

high-angle shot (T). A shot in which the subject is photographed from above.

high contrast (T). A style of lighting emphasizing harsh shafts and dramatic streaks of lights and darks. Often used in thrillers and melodramas.

high key (T). A style of lighting emphasizing bright and even illumination, with few conspicuous shadows. Used mostly in comedies, musicals, and light entertainment films.

homage (C). A direct or indirect reference within a movie to another movie, filmmaker, or cinematic style. A respectful and affectionate tribute.

I

iconography (C). The use of a well-known cultural symbol or complex of symbols in an artistic representation. In movies, iconography can involve a star's *persona,* the preestablished conventions of a *genre* (like the shootout in a western), the use of *archetypal* characters and situations, and such stylistic features as lighting, settings, constuming, props, and so on.

independent producer (G). A producer not affiliated with a studio or large commercial firm. Many stars and directors have been independent producers to ensure their artistic control.

intercut (T). See *cross-cutting.*

intrinsic interest (C). An unobtrusive area of the film image that nonetheless compels our most immediate attention because of its dramatic or contextual importance.

iris (T). A *masking* device that blacks out portions of the screen, permitting only a part of the image to be seen. Usually, the iris is circular or oval in shape and can be expanded or contracted.

J

jump cut (T). An abrupt transition between shots, sometimes deliberate, which is disorienting in terms of the continuity of space and time.

K

key light (T). The main source of illumination for a *shot.*

kinetic (C). Pertaining to motion and movement.

L

leftist, left-wing (G). A set of ideological values, typically liberal in emphasis, stressing such traits as equality, the importance of environment in determining human behavior, relativism in moral matters, emphasis on the secular rather than religion, an optimistic view of the future and human nature, a belief in technology as the main propellant of progress, cooperation rather than competition, an identification with the poor and the oppressed, internationalism, and sexual and reproductive freedom.

lengthy take, long take (C). A shot of lengthy duration.

lens (T). A ground or molded piece of glass, plastic, or other transparent material through which light rays are refracted so they converge or diverge to form the photographic image within the camera.

linear (C). A visual style emphasizing sharply defined lines rather than colors or textures. *Deep-focus* lenses are generally used to produce this hard-edged style, which tends to be objective, matter-of-fact, and antiromantic.

literal adaptation (C). A movie based on a stage play, in which the dialogue and actions are preserved more or less intact.

long shot (G). A shot that includes an area within the image that roughly corresponds to the audience's view of the area within the proscenium arch in the live theater.

loose adaptation (C). A movie based on another medium in which only a superficial resemblance exists between the two versions.

loose framing (C). Usually in longer shots. The *mise en scène* is so spaciously distributed within the confines of the framed image that the people photographed have considerable freedom of movement.

low-angle shot (T). A shot in which the subject is photographed from below.

low key (T). A style of lighting that emphasizes diffused shadows and atmospheric pools of light. Often used in mysteries and thrillers.

lyrical (C). A stylistic exuberance and subjectivity, emphasizing the sensuous beauty of the medium and producing an intense outpouring of emotion.

M

majors (I). The principal production studios of a given era. In the golden age of the Hollywood studio system—roughly the 1930s and 1940s—the majors consisted of MGM, Warner Brothers, RKO, Paramount Pictures, and Twentieth Century–Fox.

Marxist (G). An ideological term used to describe any person or film that is biased in favor of *left-wing* values, particularly in their more extreme form.

masking (T). A technique whereby a portion of the movie image is blocked out, thus temporarily altering the dimensions of the screen's *aspect ratio*.

master shot (T). An uninterrupted shot, usually taken from a *long-* or *full-shot* range, that contains an entire scene. The closer shots are photographed later, and an *edited* sequence, composed of a variety of shots, is constructed on the editor's bench.

matte shot (T). A process of combining two separate shots on one print, resulting in an image that looks as though it had been photographed normally. Used mostly for special effects, such as combining a human figure with giant dinosaurs, etc.

medium shot (G). A relatively close shot, revealing the human figure from the knees or waist up.

metaphor (C). An implied comparison between two otherwise unlike elements, meaningful in a figurative rather than literal sense.

Method acting (C). A style of performance derived from the Russian stage director Stanislavsky, which has been the dominant acting style in America since the 1950s. Method actors emphasize psychological intensity, extensive rehearsals to explore a character, emotional believability rather than technical mastery, and "living" a role internally rather than merely imitating the external behavior of a character.

metteur en scène (C). The artist or technician who creates the *mise en scène*—that is, the director.

mickeymousing (T). A type of film music that is purely descriptive and attempts to mimic the visual action with musical equivalents. Often used in cartoons.

miniatures, also model or miniature shots (T). Small-scale models photographed to give the illusion that they are full-scale objects. For example, ships sinking at sea, giant dinosaurs, airplanes colliding, etc.

minimalism (C). A style of filmmaking characterized by austerity and restraint, in which cinematic elements are reduced to the barest minimum of information.

mise en scène (C). The arrangement of visual weights and movements within a given space. In the live theater, the space is usually defined by the proscenium arch; in movies, it is defined by the *frame* that encloses the images. Cinematic mise en scène encompasses both the staging of the action and the way that it's photographed.

mix (T). The process of combining separately recorded sounds from individual soundtracks onto a master track.

montage (T). Transitional sequences of rapidly edited images, used to suggest the lapse of time or the passing of events. Often uses *dissolves* and *multiple exposures*. In Europe, montage means the art of editing.

motif (C). Any unobtrusive technique, object, or thematic idea that's systematically repeated throughout a film.

multiple exposures (T). A special effect produced by the *optical printer,* which permits the superimposition of many images simultaneously.

N

negative image (T). The reversal of lights and darks of the subject photographed: blacks are white, whites are black.

negative space (C). Emply or unfilled space in the *mise en scène,* often acting as a foil to the more detailed elements in a shot.

neorealism (C). An Italian film movement that produced its best works between 1945 and 1955. Strongly *realistic* in its techniques, neorealism emphasized documentary aspects of film art, stressing loose episodic plots, unextraordinary events and characters, natural lighting, actual location settings, nonprofessional actors, a preoccupation with poverty and social problems, and an emphasis on humanistic and democratic ideals. The term has also been used to describe other films that reflect the technical and stylistic biases of Italian neorealism.

New Wave, nouvelle vague (C). A group of young French directors who came to prominence during the late 1950s. The most widely known are François Truffaut, Jean-Luc Godard, and Alain Resnais.

nonsynchronous sound (T). Sound and image that are not recorded simultaneously, or sound that is detached from its source in the film image. Music is usually nonsynchronous in a movie, providing background atmosphere.

O

oblique angle, tilt shot (T). A shot photographed by a tilted camera. When the image is projected on the screen, the subject itself seems to be tilted on a diagonal.

oeuvre (C). From the French, "work." The complete works of an artist, viewed as a whole.

omniscient point of view (C). An all-knowing narrator who provides the spectator with all the necessary information.

open forms (C). Used primarily by *realist* filmmakers, these techniques are likely to be unobtrusive, with an emphasis on informal compositions and apparently haphazard designs. The *frame* is exploited to suggest a temporary *masking*, a window that arbitrarily cuts off part of the action.

optical printer (T). An elaborate machine used to create special effects in movies. For example, *fades, dissolves, multiple exposures,* etc.

outtakes (I). Shots or pieces of shots that are not used in the final cut of a film. Leftover footage.

overexposure (T). Too much light enters the aperture of a camera lens, bleaching out the image. Useful for fantasy and nightmare scenes.

P

painterly (C). A visual style emphasizing soft edges, lush colors, and a radiantly illuminated environment, all producing a romantic lyricism.

pan, panning shot (T). Short for panorama, this is a revolving horizontal movement of the camera from left to right or vice versa.

parallel editing. See *cross-cutting.*

persona (C). From the Latin, "mask." An actor's public image, based on his or her previous roles, and often incorporating elements from their actual personalities as well.

personality star. See *star.*

pixillation, also **stop-motion photography (T).** An *animation* technique involving the photographing of live actors *frame* by frame. When the sequence is projected at the standard speed of twenty-four fps, the actors move abruptly and jerkily, like cartoon figures.

point-of-view shot, also **pov shot, first-person camera, subjective camera (T).** Any shot that is taken from the vantage point of a character in the film, showing what the character sees.

process shot, also **rear projection (T).** A technique in which a background scene is projected onto a translucent screen behind the actors so it appears that the actors are on location in the final image.

producer (G). An ambiguous term referring to the individual or company that controls the financing of a film, and often the way it's made. The producer can concern himself or herself solely with business matters, or with putting together a package deal (such as script, stars, and director), or the producer can function as an expeditor, smoothing over problems during production.

producer–director (I). A filmmaker who finances his or her projects independently, to allow maximum creative freedom.

production values (I). The box-office appeal of the physical mounting of a film, such as sets, costumes, props, etc.

prop (T). Any movable item that is included in a movie: tables, guns, books, etc.

property (I). Anything with a profit-making potential in movies, though generally used to describe a story of some kind: a screenplay, novel, short story, etc.

proxemic patterns (C). The spatial relationships among characters within the *mise en scène,* and the apparent distance of the camera from the subject photographed.

pull-back dolly (T). Withdrawing the camera from a scene to reveal an object or character that was previously out of *frame.*

R

rack focusing, selective focusing (T). The blurring of focal planes in sequence, forcing the viewer's eyes to travel with those areas of an image that remain in sharp focus.

reaction shot (T). A cut to a shot of a character's reaction to the contents of the preceding shot.

realism (G). A style of filmmaking that attempts to duplicate the look of objective reality as it's commonly perceived, with emphasis on authentic locations and details, *long shots, lengthy takes,* and a minimum of distorting techniques.

reestablishing shot (T). A return to an initial *establishing shot* within a scene, acting as a reminder of the physical context of the closer shots.

reprinting (T). A special effects technique in which two or more separately photographed images are rephotographed onto one strip of film.

reverse angle shot (T). A shot taken from an angle 180° opposed to the previous shot. That is, the camera is placed opposite its previous position.

reverse motion (T). A series of images are photographed with the film reversed. When projected normally, the effect is to suggest backward movement—an egg "returning" to its shell, for example.

rightist, right-wing (G). A set of ideological values, typically conservative in emphasis, stressing such traits as family values, patriarchy, heredity and caste, absolute moral and ethical standards, religion, veneration for tradition and the past, a tendency to be pessimistic about the future and human nature, the need for competition, an identification with leaders and elite classes, nationalism, open market economic principals, and marital monogamy.

rite of passage (C). Narratives that focus on key phases of a person's life, when an individual passes from one stage of development to another, such as adolescence to adulthood, innocence to experience, middle age to old age, and so on.

rough cut (T). The crudely edited footage of a movie before the editor has tightened up the slackness between shots. A kind of rough draft.

rushes, dailies (I). The selected footage of the previous day's shooting, which is usually evaluated by the director and *cinematographer* before the start of the next day's shooting.

S

scene (G). An imprecise unit of film, composed of a number of interrelated *shots,* unified usually by a central concern—a location, an incident, or a minor dramatic climax.

screwball comedy (C). A film *genre,* introduced in the 1930s in America and popular up to the 1950s, characterized by zany lovers, often from different social classes. The plots are often absurdly improbable and have a tendency to veer out of control. These movies usually feature slapstick comedy scenes, aggressive and charming heroines, and an assortment of outlandish secondary characters.

script, screenplay, scenario (G). A written description of a movie's dialogue and action, which occasionally includes camera directions.

selective focus. See *rack focusing.*

sequence shot, also *plan-séquence* **(C).** A single lengthy shot, usually involving complex staging and camera movements.

setup (T). The positioning of the camera and lights for a specific shot.

shooting ratio (I). The amount of film stock used in photographing a movie in relation to what's finally included in the finished product. A shooting ratio of 20:1 means that twenty feet of film were shot for every one used in the *final cut.*

shooting script (I). A written breakdown of a movie story into its individual shots, often containing technical instructions. Used by the director and his or her staff during the production.

short lens. See *wide-angle lens.*

shot (G). Those images that are recorded continuously from the time the camera starts to the time it stops. That is, an unedited strip of film.

slow motion (T). Shots of a subject photographed at a faster rate than twenty-four fps, which when projected at the standard rate produce a dreamy, dancelike slowness of action.

slow stock, slow film (T). Film stocks that are relatively insensitive to light and produce crisp images and a sharpness of detail. When used in interior settings, these stocks generally require considerable artificial illumination.

soft focus (T). The blurring out of focus of all except one desired distance range. Can also refer to a glamorizing technique that softens the sharpness of definition so facial wrinkles can be smoothed over and even eliminated.

star (G). A film actor or actress of great popularity. A *personality star* tends to play only those roles that fit a preconceived public image, which constitutes his or her *persona.* An *actor star* can play roles of greater range and variety. Barbra Streisand is a personality star; Robert De Niro is an actor star.

star system (G). The technique of exploiting the charisma of popular performers to enhance the box-office appeal of films. The star system was developed in America and has been the backbone of the American film industry since the mid-1910s.

star vehicle (G). A movie especially designed to showcase the talents and charms of a specific star.

stock (T). Unexposed film. There are many types of movie stocks, including those highly sensitive to light *(fast stocks)* and those relatively insensitive to light *(slow stocks).*

storyboard, storyboarding (T). A previsualization technique in which shots are sketched in advance and in sequence, like a comic strip, thus allowing the filmmaker to outline the *mise en scène* and construct the *editing* continuity before production begins.

story values (I). The narrative appeal of a movie, which can reside in the popularity of an adapted *property,* the high craftsmanship of a script, or both.

studio (G). A large corporation specializing in the production of movies, such as Paramount, Warner Brothers, and so on; any physical facility equipped for the production of films.

subjective camera. See *point-of-view shot.*

subsidiary contrast (C). A subordinated element of the film image, complementing or contrasting with the *dominant contrast.*

subtext (C). A term used in drama and film to signify the dramatic implications beneath the language of a play or movie. Often, the subtext concerns ideas and emotions that are totally independent of the language of a text.

surrealism (C). An *avant-garde* movement in the arts stressing Freudian and Marxist ideas, unconscious elements, irrationalism, and the symbolic association of ideas. Surrealist movies were produced roughly from 1924 to 1931, primarily in France, though there are surrealistic elements in the works of many directors, and especially in music videos.

swish pan, also **flash** or **zip pan (T).** A horizontal movement of the camera at such a rapid rate that the subject photographed blurs on the screen.

symbol, symbolic (C). A figurative device in which an object, event, or cinematic technique has significance beyond its literal meaning. Symbolism is always determined by the dramatic context.

synchronous sound (T). The agreement or correspondence between image and sound, which are recorded simultaneously, or seem so in the finished print. Synchronous sounds appear to derive from an obvious source in the visuals.

T

take (T). A variation of a specific shot. The final shot is often selected from a number of possible takes.

telephoto lens, long lens (T). A lens that acts as a telescope, magnifying the size of objects at a great distance. A side effect is its tendency to flatten perspective.

thematic montage (C). A type of *editing* propounded by the Soviet filmmaker Eisenstein, in which separate shots are linked together not by their literal continuity in reality but by symbolic association. A shot of a preening braggart might be linked to a shot of a toy peacock, for example. Most commonly used in documentaries, in which shots are connected in accordance to the filmmaker's thesis.

three-point lighting (T). A common technique of lighting a scene from three sources. The *key light* is the main source of illumination, usually creating the *dominant contrast,* where we look first in a shot. *Fill lights* are less intense and are generally placed opposite the key, illuminating areas that would otherwise be obscured by shadow. *Backlights* are used to separate the foreground elements from the setting, emphasizing a sense of depth in the image.

three-shot (T). A *medium shot,* featuring three actors.

tight framing (C). Usually in close shots. The *mise en scène* is so carefully balanced and harmonized that the people photographed have little or no freedom of movement.

tilt, tilt shot (T). See *oblique angle.*

tracking shot, trucking shot. See *dolly shot.*

two-shot (T). A *medium shot* featuring two actors.

V

vertical integration (I). A system in which the production, distribution, and exhibition of movies are all controlled by the same corporation. In America, the practice was declared illegal in the late 1940s.

viewfinder (T). An eyepiece on the camera that defines the playing area and the *framing* of the action to be photographed.

voice-over (T). A *nonsynchronous* spoken commentary in a movie, often used to convey a character's thoughts or memories.

W

wide-angle lens, short lens (T). A lens that permits the camera to photograph a wider area than a normal lens. A side effect is its tendency to exaggerate perspective. Also used for *deep-focus* photography.

widescreen, also **CinemaScope, scope (G).** A movie image that has an *aspect ratio* of approximately 5:3, though some widescreens possess horizontal dimensions that extend as wide as 2.5 times the vertical dimension of the screen.

wipe (T). An *editing* device, usually a line that travels across the screen, "pushing off" one image and revealing another.

women's pictures (G). A film *genre* that focuses on the problems of women, such as career versus family conflicts. Often, such films feature a popular female *star* as protagonist.

Z

zoom lens, zoom shot (T). A lens of variable focal length that permits the cinematographer to change from *wide-angle* to *telephoto shots* (and vice versa) in one continuous movement, often plunging the viewer in or out of a scene rapidly.

Index

H

I